NORWAY   FINLAND
SWEDEN ESTONIA   RUSSIA
ETH.   DEN.   LATVIA
                   LITHUANIA
         POLAND BELARUS
GERMANY
BEL. CZ.   UKRAINE MOLDOVA
LUX. SLK.   KAZAKHSTAN   MONGOLIA
FRANCE HUNG. ROM.
SLN.   BULG.   GEORGIA   UZBEKISTAN
WITZ. ITALY YU.
       CR.   MAC.   TURKMENISTAN   KYRGYZSTAN
       B.H.   TAJIKISTAN
ALBANIA TURKEY ARMENIA
GREECE CYPRUS   AZERBAIJAN   N. KOREA
TUNISIA MALTA SYRIA   AFGHANISTAN   PEOPLE'S REPUBLIC OF CHINA   S. KOREA JAPAN   PACIFIC OCEAN
         LEBANON IRAQ   IRAN
LGERIA LIBYA ISRAEL   TAIWAN
              EGYPT JORDAN KUWAIT BAHRAIN PAKISTAN   BHUTAN
                              QATAR   NEPAL
              SAUDI   OMAN   BANGLADESH
NIGER CHAD   ARABIA UNITED   MYANMAR LAOS   Mariana   Wake I.
              ARAB   INDIA (BURMA)   Islands
       SUDAN EMIRATES YEMEN   THAILAND VIETNAM   Guam   Marshall
BENIN   ERITREA   Islands
NIGERIA   DJIBOUTI   CAMBODIA PHILIPPINES
       CENTRAL ETHIOPIA   (KAMPUCHEA)   Belau   Caroline Islands
       AFRICAN REP.   SRI LANKA   KIRIBATI
O CAMEROON   BRUNEI
EQ.   UGANDA KENYA   MALDIVES   MALAYSIA
GUINEA GABON RWANDA   SINGAPORE   NAURU
O TOME   ZAIRE BURUNDI   INDIAN OCEAN   TUVALU
AND   CONGO TANZANIA   INDONESIA PAPUA
PRINCIPE   NEW
              MALAWI SEYCHELLES   GUINEA
ANGOLA   ZAMBIA   VANUATU
       COMOROS   FIJI
NAMIBIA ZIMBABWE MADAGASCAR
BOTSWANA   MAURITIUS   New Caledonia
       MOZAMBIQUE   AUSTRALIA
SOUTH SWAZILAND
AFRICA LESOTHO   NEW
                                                                   ZEALAND

ABBREVIATIONS	
AUS.	AUSTRIA
BEL.	BELGIUM
B. H.	BOSNIA AND HERZEGOVINA
BULG.	BULGARIA
CR.	CROATIA
CZ.	CZECH REPUBLIC
DEN.	DENMARK
HUNG.	HUNGARY
LUX.	LUXEMBOURG
MAC.	FORMER YUGOSLAV REPUBLIC ÉOF MACEDONIA
NETH.	NETHERLANDS
ROM.	ROMANIA
SLK.	SLOVAKIA
SLN.	SLOVENIA
SWITZ.	SWITZERLAND
YU.	YUGOSLAVIA

20¡E   40¡E   60¡E   80¡E   100¡E   120¡E   140¡E   160¡E

Politics and
Government
in Europe
Today

Politics and Government in Europe Today

SECOND EDITION

Colin Campbell
Georgetown University

Harvey Feigenbaum
George Washington University

Ronald Linden
University of Pittsburgh

Helmut Norpoth
State University of New York—Stony Brook

HOUGHTON MIFFLIN COMPANY   Boston   Toronto
Geneva, Illinois   Palo Alto   Princeton, New Jersey

SENIOR SPONSORING EDITOR: Jean L. Woy
SENIOR ASSOCIATE EDITOR: Frances Gay
SENIOR PROJECT EDITOR: Susan Westendorf
PRODUCTION/DESIGN COORDINATOR: Carol Merrigan
SENIOR MANUFACTURING COORDINATOR: Marie Barnes

Cover design: Catherine Hawkes

Cover image: Satellite image of Europe/Worldsat Productions/NRSC/Science Photo Library/Photo Researchers

Credits:

Copyright page continues on page 631.

Printed in the U.S.A.

Library of Congress Catalogue Card Number: 94-76494

ISBN: 0-395-66128-5

123456789-DH-98 97 96 95 94

he authors wish to dedicate this book to:
Moya Langtry
The Feigenbaum family
Edna and Chet Linden
Werner Zimmerman

List of Figures

Contents

PART **II** The United Kingdom 40

PART **III** rance 200

PART **IV**  ermany 300

Preface

This edition of *Politics and Government in Europe Today* covers five years full of change. In the complete span of European history that equals a mere moment. From our perspective, however, it encompasses changes of epochal proportions.

Just as the first edition of this text was going to press, revolutions signaled the beginning of the end for communist rule in Eastern and Central Europe. Americans have felt these events as the end of the Cold War. For Europeans they have meant many new day-to-day challenges.

Eastern and Central Europeans now struggle to adapt their societies and political systems to a market economy and to democracy. The past five years have demonstrated that this is no mean task. Many thought that the easy part was the market economy. Adverse economic conditions and haste in introducing markets, however, have already led to relapses of popular support for the tried, if not so true, way of socialism. Only Poland, Hungary, and the Czech and Slovak Republics have made any measurable and sustained progress toward democracy. The rest have badly floundered. And the collapse of the Soviet Union and Yugoslavia has added to the number of both republics and headaches in the world.

Those in more established European democracies have struggled to incorporate their neighbors to the east politically and economically into what had become a postwar success story. Western Europe had since 1945 overcome tendencies toward authoritarianism and totalitarianism. Most nations in this part of Europe, in fact, ran vigorous democracies. Many had also taken their highly protected economies and placed them in the European Community. The EC had become a dynamo of the world economy by 1990.

All eyes looked toward 1992 when the Community would become the Union—politically integrated and economically open.

Yet, just as such great hopes reached new heights, it became clear that parts of the European Union clung to narrower national aspirations. As well, welcoming Eastern and Central Europe into the continental mainstream became much more onerous than anticipated. West Germany was by far the most adventurous in this effort, but absorbing East Germany proved to be a much larger task than anyone anticipated.

"Tired" probably best describes Western Europe these days. The regimes of Britain, France, and Germany all seem to have run out of steam. The voters seem as unsure as their leaders of which way to turn. Nonetheless, we should not assume that the transitions to the next generation of leaders will run as smoothly as they once did in these tired democracies.

THE APPROACH OF THIS BOOK

We have found that any course on European politics and government inevitably involves a juggling act between materials. Books covering a large number of European countries and even some from other continents may not give students enough detail for them to make a reasoned evaluation of political events. Some faculty members choose individual books for each country. This allows for greater depth, but single volumes normally emphasize significantly different core themes.

We have chosen to give in-depth coverage to those four countries that virtually every course on European politics and government would include. Britain, France, Germany, and Russia clearly fall within this group. We also provide individual chapters on Latin Europe, Scandinavia, and Eastern Europe. This allows instructors to acquaint students with systems other than the countries examined in detail.

We believe that thematic continuity serves as the key to any successful comparative politics and government course. While we have organized this book on a country-by-country basis, we have taken pains to develop the same core issues throughout the book. For each of the major countries, we provide chapters on the current situation, historical antecedents, political culture, parties and elections, government structures, and public policy issues. This structure gives students a firm grasp of the basic system of each country.

Students also need a consistent theoretical outlook. We have selected five propositions that appear to us to pervade European politics and government today. They are: first, that voters have become disillusioned about politics; second, that their views of the role of the state have become constricted; third, that their institutions have become ossified; fourth, that their national aspirations have become more pronounced; and finally, that their efforts to redefine the outward boundaries of market-oriented and democratic Europe have, ironically, raised self-doubts not present in the body politic since the late 1950s.

We see our task as alerting students to what they should be watching as events unfold in Europe over the next few years. We also hope that they will be able to set what they observe within the wider frame of continental economic and political integration and, more broadly, globalization.

WHAT IS NEW IN THE SECOND EDITION?

This edition begins with an expanded overview section. It now comprises three separate chapters that offer a more comprehensive orientation to comparative political theory, a detailed discussion of the five propositions that serve as the focus of our analysis, and an overview of the history, structure, operation, and prospects of the European Union.

In the section on the United Kingdom, we have made every effort to relate our materials to the factors that led to the decline and fall of Margaret Thatcher and the subsequent difficulties encountered by John Major. We have added considerable material on issues such as Britain's economic performance, changes in political culture, recent indications of weakness in the judicial system, and tensions concerning integration with Europe. We have a detailed analysis of the 1992 election, and we offer new perspectives on the future of the Labour Party as a potential alternate government.

The chapters on France have also received considerable updating and augmentation. Chapter 11 is entirely new. Every chapter has been revised so as to include all significant events since the publication of the first edition. These include the results of the March 1993 French legislative elections and the new economic policies that ensued; participation in the Gulf War; France's role in the transformation of the European Community into the European Union; and new trade issues such as the role of audiovisual industries in the GATT.

The German section of this revised edition treats the Federal Republic created as a result of the recent unification of Germany. An additional chapter (19) traces the fashioning of the new Germany, a process that included both the high politics of the world powers and the street politics of mass protest in the communist former East Germany. Another new chapter (26) probes the major consequences of political unification in the context of economic policymaking. The other chapters were adapted to take account of differences and similarities between Westerners and Easterners.

The revised version also replaced the in-depth coverage of the 1987 Bundestag election with that of the 1990 election, the first one of the unified Germany. The judiciary receives more attention in the new edition, as does, regrettably, the threat posed by right-wing extremist groups.

The new section on Russia draws relatively little from the first edition or from the older scholarship. Chapters devoted to Russia deal not only with a new government but a new form of government, a new political landscape, and a dramatically changed economic and international environment. Despite the difficulty of describing a rapidly changing scene, we identify and analyze several key benchmarks. These include national parliamentary elections and the adoption of a new constitution, the emergence of market economic forces, the making and remaking of a political culture in flux, and that most central question in political science, the struggle for power in the new Russia.

Turning to the regional chapters, that on Latin Europe has been expanded to include the dramatic transformation of Italian politics that took place after the change in election laws in 1993 and the subsequent rise of Silvio Berlusconi and the participation of neofascists in the Italian government after the 1994 election. Moreover the entire chapter has been revised to include the latest scholarship on Spain and southern Europe.

Regarding Scandinavia, measured adaptation remains a trademark of politics in this area. However, our revised chapter does take note of the mounting problems faced by the Social Democratic model, especially in Sweden. A center-right government under a conservative prime minister took office in Sweden in 1991, following the footsteps of Denmark where such a government ruled for most of the 1980s. Social Democracy remains most strongly entrenched in Norway, under Gro Harlem Bundtland, now in her third term.

The chapter on East Europe assesses the current condition of this region, five years after the revolutionary year of 1989. With this focus, it reviews what recent elections in several of the states tell us about the dissatisfaction with the pace and pain of change. Finally, the chapter assesses why it is that only in the former Yugoslavia have frustrated political aspirations resulted in open warfare.

NEW INSTRUCTOR'S RESOURCE MANUAL

Marianne Stewart of the University of Texas at Dallas contributed the excellent Instructor's Resource Manual. This manual is designed to assist the instructor in using the text in class lectures and engaging students in class discussions, and to help the students in preparing for tests and writing papers.

The manual has four sections. The first offers two sample syllabi reflecting the organization of the text. One employs a country-by-country approach beginning with an overview and proceeding with the United Kingdom, France, Germany, Russia, and Latin Europe, Scandinavia, and East Europe. The other uses a topic-by-topic approach that also starts with an overview and then takes up the basic topics of the text: current developments, past developments, political culture, representative institutions, government structures, and public policymaking.

The second section features instructional applications of the text. In this section, each general part is summarized with useful lists of learning objectives and further readings, while each specific chapter also is summarized with helpful lists of learning objectives, key terms, and classroom activities.

The third section supplies essay and multiple-choice questions for each general part and each specific chapter, and the fourth section supplies answers to the multiple-choice questions.

ACKNOWLEDGMENTS

One would think that with four people writing this book, there would not be other chefs. However, each of us is only one person, and a great deal was taking place in our countries during the past five years.

Colin Campbell had three very fine research assistants helping him on the first three chapters and the section on Britain. They were Jonathan Ball, Marcello Cabrol, and Gary Sloan. His administrative assistant, Nancy Farley, did an excellent job of keeping track of work-in-progress and supervising her putative boss, as always. Keeping close contact with astute observers of British politics such as Richard Chapman at the University of Durham, Peter Hennessy at the University of London, Gillian Peele at Oxford University, and Graham Wilson at the University of Wisconsin has helped immeasurably well. Nuffield College at Oxford served as gracious host to Campbell in Winter 1993.

Harvey Feigenbaum is grateful to Timothy Piro, who served as research assistant for the French and Latin Europe parts of this book. His colleague, Lee Sigelman, was extremely helpful in regarding the organization and representation of statistical data in Chapter 11.

Ronald Linden—who assumed responsibility for Russia and Eastern Europe—is pleased to recognize the tireless work of several research assistants including Pat Altdorfer, Ben DeDominicus, Carolyn Dudek, and Emil Nagengast. He would like to express special thanks to his colleague Jonathan Jarris whose own struggles to comprehend the new Russian reality allowed him to be both an active sounding board and an informative guide to that new reality.

Helmut Norpoth wishes to thank Wolfgang Gibowski, Dieter Roth, and the Forschungsgruppe Wahlen, Mannheim, for providing material and advice on German public opinion and elections. Norpoth is also grateful to the German Information Center in New York City for its services. Inter Nationes was kind enough to invite Norpoth on an election tour in 1990; a special note of thanks goes to Frau Simons, the official in charge. That election tour featured personal meetings with Helmut Kohl, Oskar Lafontaine, Count Lambsdorff, and Herr Lippelt. For a great many tips on German politics that elude someone not living there all the time, Norpoth is indebted to his brother Albert-Leo.

The authors also wish to thank the academic reviewers who read drafts of the manuscript and made numerous helpful suggestions:

Nack Young An, Georgia State University
Steve E. Boilard, Western Kentucky University
Robert Farlow, University of St. Thomas
Gary Freeman, University of Texas, Austin
Richard Lane, San Jose State University
Mark J. Miller, University of Delaware
Donald Pienkos, University of Wisconsin, Milwaukee
Curtis Reithel, University of Wisconsin, La Crosse
John D. Robertson, Texas A & M University
Christian Soe, California State University, Long Branch

All of the authors greatly appreciate the support and help of those at Houghton Mifflin who worked on various phases of this book—namely, Margaret Seawell, Jean Woy, Frances Gay, and Susan Westendorf. We believe that the final product has benefited immensely from their professionalism. While we did not always welcome their tight deadlines, we share their delight that the book has indeed come out on schedule!

On the dedication page of this book, the authors have identified the people whom they want to remember in a special way in the publication of this work. Colin Campbell's dedication is to his wife, Moya Langtry; Harvey Feigenbaum's to his family, Ron Linden to his parents, Edna and Chet Linden; Helmut Norpoth to his German teacher in the last two years of high school, Dr. Werner Zimmerman.

Politics and
Government
in Europe
Today

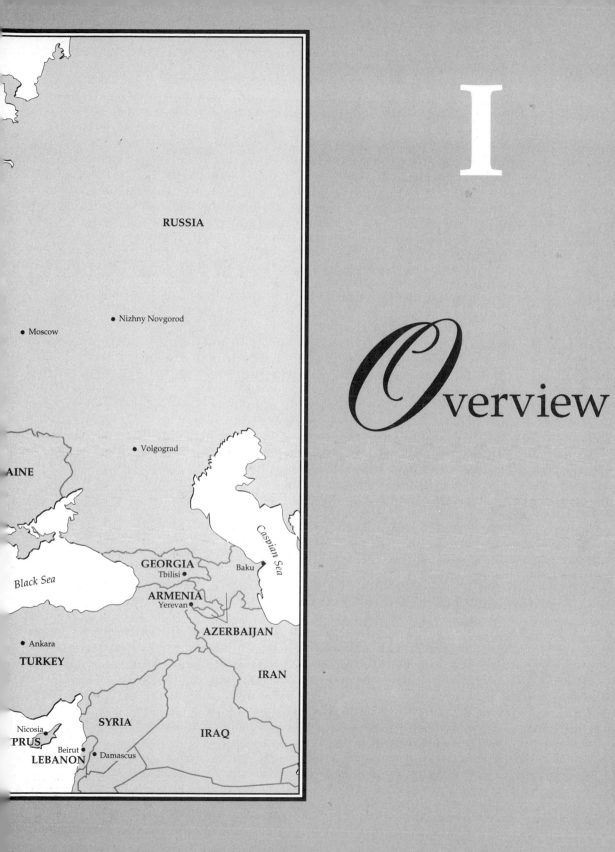

I

*O*verview

1

Introduction

Professors teaching courses covering one or another aspect of politics and government in Europe do not have to tell their students that this is an important topic. Maybe things will change in the next few years. However, at this writing Americans find so much coverage about what is happening on the other side of the Atlantic that they might understandably conclude that Europe has crowded the United States out of the news! Central and Eastern Europe have not settled entirely into the post-Communist era. Indeed, the autumn of 1993 witnessed a major struggle between the Russian president, Boris Yeltsin, and the Parliament. At first, the latter appeared to have lost. But then parliamentary elections seemed to produce opposite results from what Boris Yeltsin would want.

Almost daily one reads stories of unrest in various former Soviet republics such as Georgia and Ukraine. And, of course, the seemingly insoluble crisis in Bosnia—part of the former Yugoslavia—continues completely to befuddle political leaders elsewhere in the West.

On a less sensational level, Western European nations—especially the countries that belong to the European Union (EU)—have identified efforts to achieve a greater degree of economic integration. In the European Union, this process passed a milestone in 1992 when members lifted all barriers to trade within the Union. In the buildup, some member nations sought to mark this important event by extracting from fellow members firmer commitments to increased political integration. The result, the Maastricht Treaty, faced bitter opposition in some corners of the Union. This proved especially the case in Denmark and the United Kingdom. In each instance, only concessions that diluted the impact of the treaty made ultimate ratification possible. The boldest dreams of the framers of the treaty—movement toward a federal state and a unified currency and monetary policy—will have to await further negotiations.

You have probably already concluded for yourself that this is a thick book. But Europe is a huge topic. We have sought to put in one volume a manageable proportion of the fundamental material that students should command if they wish to make sense of European politics and government. This chapter highlights the importance of starting with a realistic understanding of the type of knowledge we seek to obtain by studying Europe. It will then point up themes that help make the study of Europe so compelling for anyone concerned about the future of democracy on this continent to which so many of us owe our origins.

WHAT DO WE SEEK TO KNOW BY A COMPARATIVE STUDY OF POLITICS AND GOVERNMENT?

Breaking ground in a new course is not easy. However, some subjects lend themselves more than others to students' making sense of all of the confusing facts. For students good at memorizing and in possession of strong logical powers, languages can be a snap. Those with facility at storing away what to many would appear to be unrelated details can readily master the declension of nouns and the conjugation of verbs. They can even go far in learning precise usage by memorizing entire expressions. Calculus is bewildering to the uninitiated; however, the adroit reasoner can quickly gain command of equations and their derivation.

Chemistry and physics likewise rely heavily upon the student's ability to handle equations; to score well in exams, students of these subjects must also learn how to calculate accurately when rushed.

Political science, on the other hand, lacks the degree of exactness that characterizes many other disciplines. Normally, it proves very difficult to discover nifty boxes for every fact. And there are lots of problems that go unsolved. This often appears especially the case with comparative politics. There one constantly runs into the "apples and oranges" problem—the meaning of a point of comparison of very high relevance in one country might be of little salience in another. For instance, the Nazi and fascist experiences of Germany and Italy in the middle part of this century make one substantially more concerned about the far Right in these nations than in other European democracies. Does this mean that comparative politics takes the line of least resistance—that it calls itself a *science* but lacks rigor? There is a science to comparative politics. However, it builds on some very subtle skills that most students' education left pretty much untutored.

American high schools give students a fairly good base in civics. That is, they provide young people with serviceable knowledge about how the American political system should work—at least, according to the Constitution and the laws of the land. High schools do less well at imparting an understanding of how things actually operate. Further, they generally do very poorly at conveying an appreciation of how political systems other than the American one operate.

This does not mean that American students know absolutely nothing about the world around them. Readers should not despair because their high school provided no formal training on the topic of this book. Most of you will find, as you read on, that you already know more about politics and government in Europe than you thought. Much of this you will have picked up in the newspaper, on TV, or even in conversations with people who know something about Europe. Some of you will even know a great deal and take to this book as a duck takes to water. Others will find it an uphill struggle at first. However, things that you already knew will eventually come back to you and you will develop a capacity to digest with increasing facility all the new facts.

Whatever your starting point, you will find yourself developing images that will help you absorb all of the details. Most of you will use the American system as your reference point, and learn to compare and contrast in your minds.

As you develop your skills, you will begin to discover more generalized points of reference. You will start getting a notion of how some European systems have common traits; you will begin, for instance, to think of France in relation to Britain and Germany rather than simply to the United States. The comparative examination of many aspects of politics in Russia might appear more formidable. But as we will see, things have changed very rapidly there. Even your authors have had to work overtime to develop new ways of thinking of the Russian enigma!

COMPARATIVE POLITICS AND THE USE OF IMAGES

Comparative politics is a very old discipline, going back at least as far as Plato, the Greek philosopher who lived from 428 to 348 B.C. In one of his most important works, *The Republic*, Plato focused his attention on the circumstances under which the "just" state likely would emerge and prosper. He employed a wealth of illustrations drawn from his knowledge of the ways in which various Greek city-states functioned as—to use our current expression—political systems. However, he left his real mark through the brilliance of the images he employed to convey his message.

Among such images were those Plato used for his classifications of the different types of people within society. Relatedly, he categorized political systems according to the levels of society that exerted the greatest influence on the actual form that governance took in a given state. Philosopher kings, imbued with wisdom, ruled the ideal or just state. Ambitious men in search of honor—that is, the spirited part of society—dominated in a timocracy. Those for whom wealth served as the driving force established oligarchy. More than a little disdainfully, Plato noted that when the rich degenerate, the poor will take the opportunity to take control. And the state will soon reflect the tendency of base individuals to yield to the pleasure of the moment.

Importantly for the history of western civilization, the debate did not end on this pessimistic note. Aristotle (384–322 B.C.) took Plato to task. To be sure, Plato's rich images and adroit marshaling of detail elevated the comparison of political systems to a lofty plane. But Aristotle searched for less rigid approaches to the fundamentals of politics. His tack originated in his view of science. For instance, he had said in *Physics*: "Now what is to us plain and obvious at first is rather confused masses the elements and principles of which become known to us later by analysis." In a word, our images of reality come only gradually, after much observation. They should not be forced. In addition, Aristotle cautioned in his *Ethics* that we cannot achieve the same level of certitude in matters dealing with human behavior and institutions as we might attain in natural sciences:

> Our discussion will be adequate if it has as much clearness as the subject matter admits of, for precision is not to be sought for alike in all discussions, any more than in all the products of the crafts.

Among Aristotle's many insights, three from his *Politics* worked an especially profound effect on the way we in the West view governance as related to various types of societies. First,

Aristotle did not believe that political systems must adhere to rigid principles to achieve justice. Rather he conceived of political systems as building upon the natural desire to seek moral perfection. The state thus emerged as a natural social organism—like, but infinitely more complex than, a biological organism.

This perception led to Aristotle's second contribution, the assertion that a healthy constitution is one in which all the elements of society have given their assent to and strive for the state's development and survival. And third, Aristotle concluded, after probing the strengths and weaknesses of various forms of government, that the most practicable political system is one in which the middle class holds the balance of power. That is, people in the middle rungs of society must exceed in strength—both qualitative and quantitative—the very rich and the very poor. For instance they must control more aggregate wealth than the very rich and outnumber the poor.

We cannot overstate the importance of Aristotle's image of the state as a social organism to the development of the western view of politics. Above all, the Judeo-Christian understanding of political community dovetailed very nicely with Aristotelianism. The Jewish tradition portrays God as having chosen Israel as his very own domain. Obviously, this sense of purpose would affect immensely the way in which the Jewish people would view governance. Under Christianity, Jesus presented himself as sent by God to establish his kingdom here on earth. Jesus used especially powerful imagery in portraying the development of his reign in terms of the growth of his kingdom from utter insignificance—for instance, a small flock or a tiny mustard seed—into a spiritual force that would encompass all nations.

At the time in which Jesus lived, the Roman Empire did dominate all of the western world. When the empire began to crumble, Christianity filled the vacuum. For much of the Dark Ages (A.D. 476 to 1000), the Church provided the only coherence that Europe enjoyed. The strong, centralized nation-state did not begin to assert itself fully until well into this millennium. At first, it coexisted with the Church. Indeed, temporal rulers found that the strong kingdom imagery of the gospels provided fertile soil for earthly monarchies. The magnificent Gothic cathedrals, which dominated Church architecture from the twelfth through the fifteenth century, unhesitatingly affirm that the temporal kingdom reflects divine rule. However, the more that kings struggled to consolidate their power, the more they began to steep their appeals in the imagery of the divine rule. For example, James I of England (1603–1625) considered himself a vicar of Christ with absolute authority over his realm.

Coincident with the absolutist phase of the British crown, in the seventeenth century Thomas Hobbes wrote his *Leviathan*. This work, more than any other, ushered in the modern era of thought about politics. Here starts the gradual process whereby political philosophers began to cast aside organic views of the state. Hobbes himself stood Aristotle on his head by stating that individuals' desire for self-preservation, not moral perfection, served as the natural end of the "commonwealth." Much taken by modern physics, Hobbes saw the study of politics as the science whereby the appetite for personal liberty along with dominion over others might be controlled.

Sir Isaac Newton, writing in the latter part of the seventeenth century, confirmed for the natural sciences—especially physics—the dominance that they would enjoy through the next century. Just as human reason had proven itself capable of penetrating to startling new truths about physical reality, it was then thought that reason could decode the essence of politics. In the mid-eighteenth century, Montesquieu, a French political philosopher filled with the new scientific spirit, set about comparing European political systems. He believed that liberty might well derive from proper institutional arrangements more than from some special disposition on the part of a citizenry. His conclusion—in favor of the separation of pow-ers between the executive, the legislature, and the judiciary—worked a seminal influence on the thinking behind the U.S. Constitution.

Ironically, Montesquieu became an advocate of the separation of powers after examining the British political system. Even as Montesquieu wrote, however, Britain had started on the road toward a system characterized by relative unity among the three branches of government. Montesquieu favored the continuation of the monarchical system in France. He believed, however, that an autonomous legislature and judiciary would counter the tendency of French monarchs toward absolutism.

The history of political philosophy hardly ends with Montesquieu. In fact, he remains a lesser light beside the likes of Locke (a prede-cessor), Rousseau, Hegel, and Marx. All of these—and several others—influenced Euro-pean views of political systems much more than did Montesquieu. Yet Montesquieu shaped American images of politics in Europe more than any other writer. Indeed, until the 1960s, American textbooks on European poli-tics still tended to limit themselves to detailed inventories of the relative power positions of different elements of the political system. The almost mechanistic preoccupation with achiev-ing the optimal balance between countervail-ing structures served as the main concern of American students of European politics.

THE BLOSSOMING OF COMPARATIVE POLITICS IN AMERICA

Until the 1960s, American comparative politics was the last field one would expect to set off sparks. Deeply imbued with a mechanistic view of the political system, its practitioners did not stray far from cataloging the various institutional arrangements for the perform-ance of governmental and political functions. Scholars pursued their research in a legalistic and formalistic way. That is, they dwelt on the prescriptive dimensions to constitutions and institutional arrangements. They did not exam-ine rigorously whether structures actually car-ried out the specific functions they were designed to perform.

Several developments made the decline of this approach to comparative politics inevita-ble. Most decisive were the rise of communism in Russia, the emergence of Nazism in Ger-many, and the development of fascism in Italy. It became clear that no amount of constitutional engineering could prevent despotism if social, economic, and cultural factors favored its emergence. In the immediate postwar period, the new comparative politics became riveted on the problem of Europe. What fanned the flames of totalitarianism and authoritarianism? Now that the war was won, how might democ-racy be reestablished? What might be done to stem the expansion of communism outside of the Soviet Union?

As if what had happened in Europe in the middle part of the century did not provide enough food for thought, a great deal had taken place in political science as a discipline. Scholars in the field began to consider them-selves as *social* scientists. Increasingly, they drew upon the theories and methods of psy-chology and sociology in framing their hy-potheses and conducting their research. Here too we find a European link. Many students of politics who first introduced these approaches to the United States came from Europe or had studied under Europeans who had immigrated to the United States.

The reorientation of the discipline to social science—beginning in the 1930s and deepen-ing during the 1940s and the 1950s—laid the groundwork for a rush of comparative re-search in the 1960s. In large part this was due to a generational transition: the young schol-ars who had delved into psychology and soci-ology as graduate students in the 1930s and the 1940s had come into their own as mature researchers.

From the standpoint of images of the political system, nothing short of a revolution had occurred. Once again, the concept of the political system as a living organism began to take hold. Social sciences had developed around biological models rather than those taken from physics. Applied to politics, this meant that purpose or direction takes root in fundamental systemic principles. These amount to more than simply the sum of all the parts. The study of systems entails the search for cyclical processes and inherent goals that govern the shape of political structures and how they perform various functions. Like biological organisms, political systems change according to the phases through which they pass.

David Easton provided the first full-fledged systems theory for political science.[1] With a starting point similar to that taken by Aristotle, Easton cautioned that we had first to look at political phenomena through a "weak telescope" so that we would see the whole system.[2] This is why students of politics have over the ages turned to natural sciences for analogues. In this regard, the utility of viewing politics as involving a system of processes and relationships becomes clear. It highlights the distinction between each "political system" and the environment in which it functions. It therefore defines political life as human behavior that operates within and responds to a system's environment. This enables us to examine political structures and functions in relation to external factors such as social, economic, and cultural conditions.

Each system bases its existence on interactions. In politics, these center on what Easton termed "the authoritative allocation of values."[3] In other words, the system takes certain decisions and actions, and individuals accept these as legitimate. The allocative process tends to focus on the persistence of the political system. It tries, in other words, to cope with internal and external stress. Because it is a complex of human relationships, however, the political system exceeds its biological analogue in one crucial respect: it has an innate capacity for self-transformation of its goals, its practices, and the very structure of its internal organization. Political systems more than simply adapt to internal and external circumstances; they also consciously partake of the creative act of innovation.[4]

Despite its widespread use, Easton's framework drew serious challenges from some students of comparative politics. Many believed that—disclaimers notwithstanding—Easton betrayed a conservative bias. He focused on the persistence of the system to an extent that led some to conclude that he took a regime's desire to survive as a common denominator of all political systems. By seemingly lowering its sights, the model did not invite fundamental questions about the character of a regime.

Gabriel Almond did much to plant systems theory more firmly within a context more open to the prospect of fundamental change. For the concept *persistence*, he substituted that of "levels of development." He noted, for instance, that democracy had proved integral to political systems' responsiveness to human needs and, ultimately, sensitivity to general welfare.

Almond believed that rational norms must permeate every level of the political system before true development emerges.[5] Structures must differentiate roles more clearly, subsystems within political systems must achieve a higher degree of autonomy from one another, and society itself must shed traditional cultures in favor of modern ways of doing things. Indeed, political scientists must facilitate modernizers as they go through the process of discovering in science, technology, education, bureaucracy, and open political association means for fulfilling human capacities more effectively than did traditional ways of operating.[6]

Karl W. Deutsch, while not denying the superiority of Easton's approach to legalistic and formalistic comparative studies, also objected to systems theory's focus on regime persistence. He suggested that political scientists should canvass other analogues to see if these might serve inquiry better than biological models. Citing the paleontologist and philosopher Pierre Tielhard de Chardin, Deutsch called for a comparative political science that would allow for "genuine evolution." Such a stance would constantly leave analysis open to the emergence of sudden change and true novelty. Importantly, Deutsch saw the political system "as an open-ended process containing the possibility of *self-disruption* or *self-destruction,* as well as a change of goals."[7] Unlike Almond's critique of systems theory, Deutsch's seemed to accept that students of comparative politics must equip themselves to examine regress as well as progress.

Along similar lines, Harold D. Lasswell, a student of American politics who had centered his previous research largely on political psychology, entered the debate. Like Deutsch, Lasswell attempted to place political processes in the context of evolution. Drawing upon the work of the philosopher Alfred North Whitehead, he set the unfolding of political reality within the frame of the "creative advance of nature" toward "events" that never took place before.[8] The models we employ in analyzing the significance and direction of political events cannot help but take sides.[9] They must show a preference toward the accumulation and distribution within the state of core human values. These include power, enlightenment, wealth, well-being, skill, affection, respect, and rectitude.[10]

Notwithstanding the correctives of Almond, Deutsch, Lasswell, and many others, systems theory never really completed the task of settling on an analogue that would exceed the explanatory power of Easton's biological model. People who employed the approach seemed to agree that persistence hardly captured the potential richness of development. However, they could not come to a viable consensus on the other criteria by which they should evaluate the performance of political systems.

Two blind spots seemed to have impaired the systems movement. First, some adherents to the approach placed far too much trust in technology and "rational" procedures. Almond's estimation of the inherent capacity of modernization and democratization to trigger and sustain development serves as the clearest illustration of this defect. He did not seem to entertain the prospect that the developments in participatory democracy, bureaucratization of the state, and the secularization of society might reach plateaus—even recede monumentally—in times during which political systems undergo especially intense stress.[11]

Europe became a laboratory for democracy by the 1960s—with the most creative changes bursting forward in the latter part of that decade. However, since the late 1970s, many European states have rolled back a substantial number of reforms designed to enhance the direct involvement of the people in the policy process. Many planning-oriented bureaucracies that placed immense trust in their ability to make decisions on the basis of rational criteria proved woefully inadequate at addressing the severe economic decline in many European countries during the 1980s. On the right side of the political spectrum, radical politics has begun again to assert itself in Europe to the point where—as is clear in France, Italy, and Germany—neo-fascism has appealed to a significant portion of the population (largely disaffected youths). On the Left, the rise and continued appeal of movements like the Greens (radical environmentalists) in Germany. The strength of anti-Europeanists in Britain suggests that not everyone in Europe has locked arms and marched in unison toward "modernization" and "integration."

Second, theoreticians like Deutsch and Lasswell, who pleaded for more comprehensive criteria for systemic analysis than simply persistence or modernization, left us with an overwhelmingly difficult task. These authors tried to focus our attention on the inexhaustible potential of political development. They seemed, however, too ready to stretch our horizons beyond the capacity of political science. A fully inclusive view of the political system might take us from political analysis to "metaphysical pathos."[12] That is, we might reach the point where we abandon the rigor of science in favor of appeals to individuals' beliefs about what human institutions should strive to achieve.

Our own view is that the comparative study of politics and government finds its most salient analogues in the psychology of the human being and the sociology of groups. If adopted, analogies from neither of these realms would allow for anywhere near the specificity that Easton found in the parallels between biological and political systems. We have eschewed, thus, the temptation to limit ourselves to one analogue. Further, we recognize that political science has not covered as much new ground since Aristotle as many people appear to believe. We will not claim greater exactitude in the comparative study of European politics and government than it is capable of producing.

THE AGE OF DECLINE AND THE EMERGENCE OF OPEN-ENDED THEORORIZING

When comparative politics was blossoming in the 1960s, scholars were still wondering just how secure European democracies were. The rise of fascism in the 1930s had shaken the confidence of even the firmest believers in the feasibility of structural checks on despotic rule. Further, the Soviet Union demonstrated that unchecked state power can arise from the Left as well as the Right. The Spain and Portugal of the 1960s served as reminders that not even Western Europe had rid itself entirely of dictatorships. In addition, two of the region's democracies—France and Italy—did not appear very stable. Finally, deep doubts persisted about the suitability of the German national character for democracy. Scholars found it hard to forget the horrors of Nazism.

Notwithstanding all of these doubts, the comparative politics of the 1960s had not anticipated what would prove to be the overwhelming preoccupation of the discipline beginning in the late 1970s and continuing on into our present decade. The focus of comparative politics shifted dramatically from questions about the viability of democracy to profound worries about economic *decline*. Two developments associated with the world economy initially provoked this anxiety. First, the two energy crises—in 1973 and 1979—had abruptly impressed upon Europeans a sense of their dependence on reliable and cheap sources of petroleum. Second, European economies, like the American economy, were discovering the difficulty of competing with Japan and other Asian countries for their share of overseas markets. In the 1990s, Western Europeans continue to wrestle with clear signs of economic failure—especially slow economic growth and intractable rates of unemployment. At the point when Europe seemed at the cusp of economic explosion, even the prosperous part has slumped badly. The immense optimism of the late 1980s in anticipation of the elimination of trade barriers between European Union countries in 1992 has given way to pessimism about how far European integration will go.

Within the context of decline, a long menu of theoretical approaches has emerged in the last two decades. Each has attempted to respond to flux in European politics and government while addressing especially issues of comparative interests. Here the most prominent items fit broadly under the heading *political economy*—an approach adopted from macroeconomics. Analysts working under this category focus mainly on the consequences of governmental policies on the countries' economic performance.

The fiscal pressures afflicting industrialized countries, beginning in the 1970s and still present in the 1990s, have provided the impetus for the rise of political economy. Mounting gloom over the possibility of ever returning to the salad days of the 1950s and 1960s has accentuated even more the emphasis on economic and political "decline." This has signaled the demise of the previous developmental view, advanced in the early 1950s by Seymour M. Lipset and other intellectuals. In a seminal article published in 1953, Lipset predicted that constant political stability was possible given ever-growing economies. Lipset argued that continuous economic growth would bring western-style democracies to countries with different political systems, and democracy would in turn guarantee political stability.[13] The impressive growth of the global economy in the 1950s and early 1960s seemed to ensure continuous economic growth. One decade later, the successive economic crises affecting Europe and the rest of the industrialized world made it clear that the expectation of continuous economic growth was overly optimistic. A new paradigm linking politics and economics was urgently needed.

Many new issues emerged as scholars searched for alternate paradigms. Mancur Olson, Robert Bates, and other scholars linked the economic decline to the expanded role of the public sector during the boom years.[14] Others—known as neo-corporatists—analyzed the narrower issue of the relationship between social groups, especially business and labor, and the state.[15] Such scholars sought to ascertain the continued salience of research in the 1950s and 1960s that revealed the degree to which private accommodations by elites define the contours of politics and government in many European states. Neocorporatism places its distinctive focus on the state and its relationships with groups that have garnered a high degree of legitimacy. This recognition gives groups near-monopolistic power to speak for specified categories of people.

In the 1960s, scholars believed that corporatist approaches worked democratically only in European countries with relatively contained and routinized approaches to reconciliation of social and political differences. They obviously had not worked in larger systems—like pre-Nazi Germany and prefascist Italy—where the scale of the systems and the depth of divisions meant that corporatism would have to be imposed through authoritarian means.

In this regard, Philippe Schmitter convincingly introduced the distinction between state and societal corporatism, the former being associated with authoritarian regimes where the state dominates the groups completely—now common in the developing world—and the societal form, which is still common in parts of Europe, where social groups act on equal footing with the state. In stark contrast with Olson's position, the societal variety of corporatism was presented as a mature, democratic and internationally open form of governance where groups had a positive role in governance and economic growth. However helpful this distinction might prove in delineating which states might lend themselves to corporatism, recent events in Italy suggest that the darker side of corporatism still holds sway. In such settings, private accommodations seem only to invite conniving and profound popular alienation from the political elite.

A third group of political scientists has studied the growing internationalization of politics and economics.[16] In this group, Peter Gourevitch argued that the nation-state as a political unit had lost its capacity successfully to implement policies in isolation from the rest of its neighbors and trade partners. Policy-making at the national level was thus being constrained by the growing internationalization of economics. Countries were no longer able to sustain policies that were in contradiction with those of their commercial partners.[17] This approach is particularly relevant in the context of the efforts toward integration in Europe discussed in Chapter 3 of this book. William Wallace, for example, has maintained that in the internationalization of politics and economics resides the main justification for the European Union.[18]

In addition to the political economy approach, "islands of theory" have arisen for specific subject areas that are not contained in a single paradigm.[19] One of the areas that has grown in sophistication is voting behavior analysis. For example, in 1979 Hans-Dieter Klingemann found that Italian voters are more than twice as likely as Americans to be classified as ideologues, and that Dutch and German electorates display higher levels of political awareness.[20] More recent studies demonstrate the connection between the European political environment and European publics' ideological views of policies and government.[21]

Other specific subject areas have been explored such as political parties systems, bureaucratic behavior, and value change.[22] The role of the state and state-society relations merits a special mention because extensive research has signaled the importance of a strong, independent state influencing policy outcomes. Scholars such as Theda Skocpol and Peter Katzenstein have asserted that state elites are, to a significant degree, autonomous from society and that growth-stimulating policies can only be achieved by strong, autonomous, "smart" states.[23]

Although the variety of approaches and the development of subject areas have provided great diversity and depth to the discipline, many scholars have complained that these features have also introduced an element of anarchy into the comparative study of European politics and government. In spite of these difficulties, it has become increasingly clear that efforts aimed at generating a single and overarching "grand theory" have failed and that "middle-range" theories are better tools to analyze culture-area levels. Middle-range theory focuses on propositions that are significant and useful for comparing regions or similar countries rather than the entire universe of nations.

The growing importance of both islands of theory and middle-range theories for political analysis is reflected in this book. For example, individual countries are examined in terms of their party systems, bureaucratic structures, and other particularized features contributing to their political, social, and economic environments. In addition, the versatility of middle-range theory allows us to probe a set of propositions broadly emerging from dynamic processes currently taking place in Europe. These concern voter disillusionment with conventional political alternatives, declining support for government intervention in the social and economic spheres, ossification of political and governmental institutions, conflicting paradigms regarding economic integration and national sovereignty, and the danger of overload as Central and Eastern Europe attempt to catch up with a continent that has left them far behind both in democratic development and economic integration.

THE PLAN FOR THIS BOOK

This book has six parts. Four of these examine the politics and government of, respectively, the United Kingdom, France, Germany, and Russia. Before launching into that discussion, however, we provide two chapters giving an overview of Europe today. One of these outlines our five propositions about politics and government within European states and the process of European integration; the other examines the structure of the European Union and briefly assesses how it actually operates. The final part of the book will look at European politics and government outside our four core countries. It consists of three chapters focusing on Latin Europe (Italy, Spain, and Portugal), Scandinavia (Sweden, Norway, and Denmark), and Eastern Europe (the seven countries in Europe, besides Russia and other former Soviet republics and the nations of the former Yugoslavia in which communists previously ruled).

Not all of the parts dedicated to specific countries nor the chapters focusing on regions will cover every topic in precisely the same order. However, we have taken care to examine the same issues in each of our considerations. These include:

1. an overview of the current condition of each core nation or region with regard to social, political, economic, and international circumstances;

2. the historical antecedents to the current situation;

3. the constraints and strengths of the societal culture upon which the political system builds;

4. the ways in which individuals are socialized into their roles as citizens and the degree to which they participate in the political process;

5. the ways in which political parties and electoral processes operate;

6. the functioning of the formal governmental process as embodied in the executive, the bureaucracy, the legislature, and the judiciary; and

7. intergovernmental dynamics within the political system (for example, between the national and local governments) and with other nations (for example, between a member nation and the European Union).

In addition, each of the four country parts will examine two policy cases—one domestic and the other involving foreign affairs—that illustrate the ways in which key issues facing each political system reach resolution or remain intractable.

NOTES

1. David Easton, *The Political System* (New York: Knopf, 1953); and *A Framework for Political Analysis* (Englewood Cliffs, N.J.: Prentice Hall, 1965).
2. Easton, *Framework*, p. 2.
3. Easton, *Framework*, pp. 49–50.
4. Easton, *Framework*, p. 100.
5. Gabriel A. Almond and G. Bingham Powell, *Comparative Politics: A Developmental Approach* (Boston: Little, Brown, 1966), p. 300.
6. Gabriel A. Almond, "Political Development: Analytical and Normative Perspectives," *Comparative Political Studies,* 1 (1969), 456–463.
7. Karl W. Deutsch, *The Nerves of Government: Models of Political Communication and Control* (New York: Free Press, 1966), p. 37.
8. Heinz Eulau, "The Maddening Methods of Harold D. Lasswell: Some Philosophical Underpinnings," *Journal of Politics,* 30 (1968), 3–24.
9. Harold D. Lasswell, "The Policy Sciences of Development," *World Politics,* 17 (1965), 290.
10. Harold D. Lasswell and A. R. Holmberg, "Toward a General Theory of Directed Value Accommodation and Institutional Development," in *Political and Administrative Development,* ed. Ralph Braibanti (Durham, N.C.: Duke University Press, 1969), pp. 356–357.
11. Colin Campbell, "Current Models of the Political System: An Intellectual-Purposive View," *Comparative Political Studies,* 4 (1971), 29.
12. Martin Landau, "Political and Administrative Development," in *Political and Administrative Development,* ed. Braibanti, pp. 334, 346.
13. Seymour M. Lipset, "Some Social Requisites of Democracy," *American Political Science Review,* 53 (March 1959); and Phillips Cutright, "National Political Development: Its Measurement and Social Correlates," in Nelson Polsby et al., eds., *Politics and Social Life* (Boston: Houghton Mifflin, 1963).
14. Mancur Olson, *The Rise and Decline of Nations: Economic Growth, Stagflation and Social Rigidities* (New Haven: Yale University Press, 1982); and Robert Bates, *Markets and State in Tropical Africa: The Political Basis of Agricultural Policies* (Berkeley: University of California Press, 1981).
15. Suzanne Berger, *Organizing Interests in Western Europe: Pluralism, Corporativism, and the Transformation of Politics* (Cambridge: Cambridge University Press, 1981); and Philippe Schmitter, "Interest Intermediation and Regime Governability in Contemporary Western Europe and North America," in Suzanne Berger, ed., *Organizing Interests.*
16. Peter Gourevitch, "The Second Image Reversed: The International Sources of Domestic Policies," *International Organization,* 32 (1979); and Jeffrey Frieden, "Invested Interests: The Politics of National Economic Policies in a World of Global Finance," *International Organization,* 45 (1991).
17. Peter Gourevitch, *Politics in Hard Times: Comparative Responses to International Economic Crisis* (Ithaca: Cornell University Press, 1986).

18. William Wallace, *The Dynamics of European Integration* (London: Pinter Publishers, 1990).

19. The concept *island of theory* was coined by Stanley Hoffman. He argued that comparativists should accept the fact that there is not a single paradigm on which all or even most of the students in the field can agree. Quoted by Howard Wiarda, *New Directions in Comparative Politics* (Boulder, Colo.: Westview Press, 1985).

20. Hans-Dieter Klingemann, "Measuring Ideological Conceptualization," in Samuel Barnes, ed., *Political Action* (Beverly Hills: Sage Publications, 1979).

21. Dieter Fuchs and Hans-Dieter Klingemann, "The Left-Right Schema," in Kent Jennings, ed., *Continuities in Political Action* (Berlin: DeGruyter, 1989).

22. Giovanni Sartori, *Parties and Party System* (Cambridge and New York: Cambridge University Press, 1976); Francis Rourke, *Bureaucracy, Politics and Public Policy* (Boston: Little, Brown, 1984); Jack Knott and Gary Miller, *Reforming Bureaucracy: The Politics of Institutional Choice* (Englewood Cliffs, N.J.: Prentice Hall, 1987); and Howard Wiarda, "The Ethnocentrism of the Social Sciences: Implications for Research and Policy," in *Review of Politics*, 42 (April 1981), 163–197.

23. Theda Skocpol, "Bringing the State Back In: Strategies of Analysis in Current Research," in Peter Evans, ed., *Bringing the State Back In* (Cambridge: Cambridge University Press, 1985); and Peter Katzenstein, *Small States in World Markets* (New York: Cornell University Press, 1985).

REFERENCES AND SUGGESTED READINGS

DeFelice, E. Gene. 1980. "Comparison Misconceived: Common Nonsense in Comparative Politics." *Comparative Politics* 13:119–26.

Heckscher, Gunnar. 1957. *The Study of Comparative Government and Politics.* London: George Allen and Unwin.

Mayer, Lawrence C. 1989. *Redefining Comparative Politics: Promise Versus Performance.* Newbury Park: Sage Publications.

Merrit, Richard. 1970. *Systematic Approaches to Comparative Politics.* Chicago: Rand McNally.

Ragin, Charles C. 1987. *The Comparative Method: Moving Beyond Qualitative and Quantitative Strategies.* Berkeley: University of California Press.

Rogowski, Ronald. 1993. "Comparative Politics," in Ada W. Finifter, ed. *The State of the Discipline II.* Washington, D.C.: American Political Science Association.

Smelser, Neil. 1976. *Comparative Methods in the Social Sciences.* Englewood Cliffs, N.J.: Prentice Hall.

2

Europe Today:
Five Propositions

Your authors have come to the conclusion that all Europe has entered into an encounter with decline. When we published the previous edition of this book (1990), this had only become apparent in the United Kingdom. And plenty of reasons suggested themselves as to why Britain was running behind the pack during the European economic explosion of the late 1980s. Many Britons remained "in" but not "of" the European Community—that is, psychologically distant from the continent. Too much of Britain's infrastructure remained relatively obsolete and many of its institutions had become hidebound.

Now even the parts of Europe that appeared to work phenomenally well in the late 1980s are encountering serious difficulties. We can see in bold relief a large piece of the experience of advanced liberal democracies in the current era. We can no longer argue so strenuously the case for British exceptionalism within Europe. And we must accept as well more commonality between the challenges faced by advanced democracies in Europe and those experienced by the United States. We see economies that no longer generate new wealth with ease. We see signs that the very fabric of democratic politics and governance has begun to fray around the edges.

Meanwhile, the former communist states have found it considerably more difficult than anticipated to develop market economies and establish themselves as democracies. Indeed, many in these nations have come to the conclusion that the two objectives are irreconcilable. The diehards would like to return to communism whereas the disillusioned have begun to flirt with authoritarian rule.

We have identified five pressure points associated with the condition of democracy in Europe. *First,* voters have become disillusioned with the pattern whereby parties or coalitions in power would alternate. *Second,* they and the elites who dominate their political systems have adopted relatively constricted views of what the state should do. The economic decline of the past few years has exacerbated citizens' disenchantment with government involvement in their lives. *Third,* ossification of institutions—a malady most clearly apparent in the United Kingdom—has begun to manifest its effects elsewhere in Europe. Of course, one of the great struggles of revitalization in former communist countries focuses on entirely scrapping virtually every institution previously dominated by old regimes—whether governmental, industrial, or social. *Fourth,* Europe needs the benefits of economic integration to adapt to the new circumstances of world trade. Yet the political harmonization required to achieve economic integration comes at the costs of sacrifices in sovereignty that some nations hesitate to make.

Finally, the *fifth* point relates to the collapse of communism in Eastern and Central Europe as this phenomenon has redefined the potential parameters of integration. The absorption of East Germany by West Germany so far has revealed to all concerned a greater sense of the costs than benefits of absorption of former communist nations into the European mainstream. These problems exacerbate the difficulties that have arisen surrounding the capacity for the former communist states to pursue capitalism and democracy simultaneously. A review of these five pressure points gives rise to five propositions about where Europe is and where it might be headed.

Proposition 1. The concept that tax-and-spend politics led to economic decline has become firmly established in voters' minds. This has meant that they remain extremely skeptical of the parties that governed during the expansionary period of their respective states.

The economic pressures building in the 1970s began to work dramatic effects on the political climate during the latter part of the decade and the early 1980s. In Britain, the Labour government faced a bitter defeat at the hands of the Conservatives. The government had failed in subduing labor unions' demands for the wage increases necessary to keep up with inflation, which had risen well above 10 percent. The resulting strikes during the 1978–1979 "Winter of Discontent" had left the voters with the impression that Labour had lost its capacity to govern. Changes in France and West Germany lagged behind those in Great Britain. In 1981, François Mitterrand led the socialists to power. He had pitched his appeal to voters on the argument that the French government had to intervene more concertedly and vigorously to reverse the tide of rising inflation and unemployment (see Figures 2.1 and 2.2). West Germany had withstood the economic pressures of the 1970s better than either Britain or France. However, inflation and unemployment began to worry voters in the early 1980s. In 1982, the Social Democrats—who had controlled the government since 1969—fell to a vote of no confidence that the electorate endorsed by returning a Christian Democratic government in March 1983.

In each of these cases, the parties that had held governments during the worst of the economic crises of the later 1970s and early 1980s have not been able to rehabilitate their images. This is even the case with the French. The division of executive power in the Fifth Republic allows the French electorate to split their allegiance, giving the presidency to one party and the prime ministership to the other. Twice in this current era of electoral skepticism, the

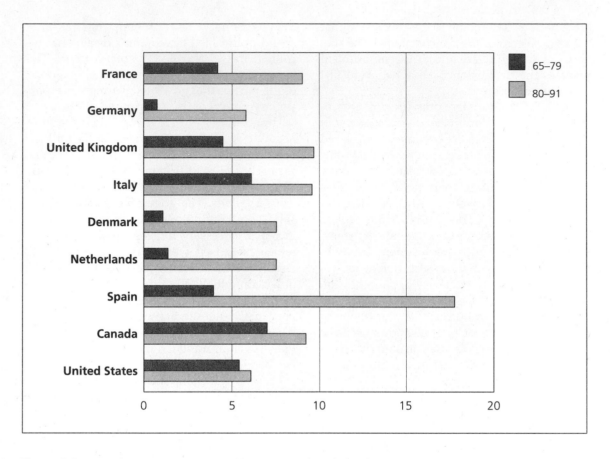

Figure 2.1 Unemployment rates compared (Percentage of total labor force). Source: OECD, Country Surveys (various issues).

French have returned the prime ministership to the conservatives. However, the mounting grievances against the present beneficiaries of this tack—the government of Edward Balladur—fail to suggest a full reinstatement of the hegemony the conservatives enjoyed before the decline.

In the United Kingdom, not even the unceremonious removal of Margaret Thatcher from power in 1990 and the always bland and frequently inept leadership of her successor John Major have prompted voters to return Labour to power. By the most recent election, 1992, Labour had done much to adjust its platform to the strictures of the age of constraint. Most observers agree that they ran a superlative campaign. Still, voters scurried back to the Conservatives in the final days of the election. The government party had simply to reignite fears of a return to the chaos of the late 1970s and the battle was theirs, handily.

In Germany, the Christian Democrats under Helmut Kohl have found the merging of East and West Germany a considerably more costly and difficult task than they had anticipated. Voters' exasperation with the process has become intense. It even includes very distressing signs that marginal and alienated members of

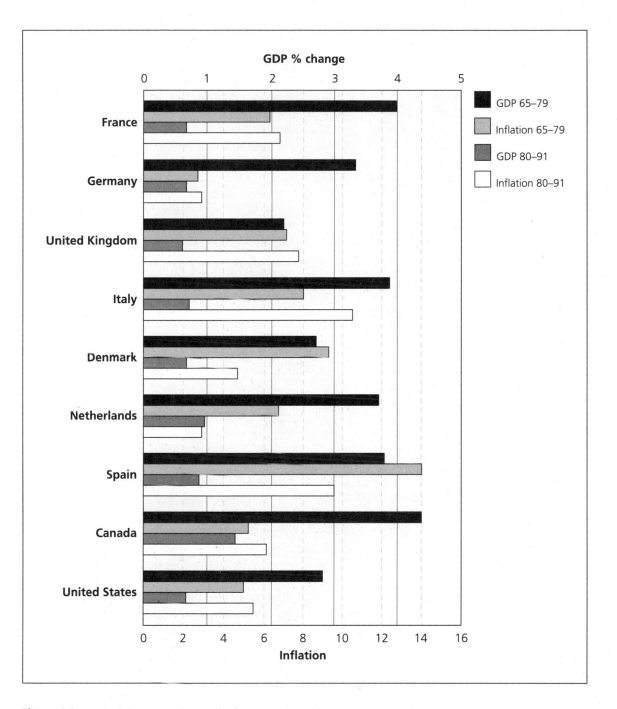

Figure 2.2 Gross domestic product and inflation compared (1965–1979 and 1980–1991 averages). Source: OECD, Country Surveys (various issues).

the public—especially youths—have turned to neofascism as a panacea. However, the existing evidence gives little indication that all of this will pave the road for the Social Democratic Party to return to power.

Significantly, we find similar patterns outside Europe. In the 1980s, American voters passed up two opportunities to forgive the Democrats for the economic debacle that occurred under Jimmy Carter's presidency. They now have restored Democrats to the White House. However, the continued appeal of Ross Perot indicates a deep discontent with both the Democrats and the Republicans. Further, President Bill Clinton's shaky approval ratings might serve notice that a second term could elude him just as it did Carter.

Canadians renewed the Progressive Conservatives' mandate in the autumn of 1988, even though the government of Brian Mulroney had made innumerable political blunders. It was only the profoundly inept 1993 campaign of the Conservatives under Mulroney's successor, Kim Campbell, that drove enough voters back to the Liberals for them to resume power. Still, the people most deeply disaffected by the Liberals in the late 1970s and early 1980s— western Canadians who believed the Liberals had encroached upon their rights over energy resources and Québecois who believed that the Liberals had betrayed Quebec in the 1982 Constitutional Accord—refused to shift their votes from Conservatives to Liberals. Thus they gave their support to, respectively, the Reform Party and the Bloc Québecois.

In the process, the same voters who served as the building blocks for the two large Conservative majority governments handed the party such a crushing defeat that it lost its status as an official party in House of Commons. This collapse of support—certainly the most precipitous fall of a mainline party in the national government of any advanced liberal democracy—should alert all to a very foul mood among many electorates. Voters have es-

chewed the parties in power in the late 1970s and early 1980s because they stand in their minds as the purveyors of the old-style politics that put western economies on the road to decline. When they see leadership in successor parties that evokes memories of that approach, they will abandon them.

In Australia, the Labor Party—first under Bob Hawke and then under Paul Keating—has won no fewer than five elections against the conservative coalition parties since 1983. It has done this by coopting many key neoliberal themes that are central to the Right's appeal. They have also proven successful, especially in the heat of election campaigns, at painting the coalition as that same ragtag group that presided over the collapse of Australia's competitive position in the world market.

In the minds of voters in established democracies, economic decline is due to the expansion of government in the 1960s and 1970s. By the late 1970s, Richard Rose and B. Guy Peters anticipated a backlash over the size of government in their book, *Can Government Go Bankrupt?*[1] They maintained that electorates had supported the rapid expansion of government programs in the postwar years because their net impact was to increase the average voters' disposable—that is, after-tax—income. In the 1970s, governments were approaching the threshold beyond which the funding of additional programs would actually bite into disposable income. Simultaneously, sluggish economies—laboring under high unemployment and inflation—meant that nations were generating less of the new wealth essential to the gradual enhancement of wage earners' take-home pay.

Rose and Peters thus focus our attention on a deeply transactional perception on the part of electorates about government spending: namely, governments must offset the added costs of increased spending with economic performances that give voters more disposable income. Rose and Peters did not dwell, however, on the possibility that parties can go into *political* bankruptcy too. That is, voters might indefinitely suspend their affective allegiance from parties until they return to the business of selecting policies which will improve the lot of the average citizen. Voters' first targets here have been parties whose administrations got the more-government-spending/increased-disposable-income transaction wrong in the late 1970s. However, they have been increasingly standoffish even about the parties that they actually put into power.

Studies of the motivations behind voters' electoral preferences have increasingly centered on economic conditions. For example, scholars of U.S. politics have even rejected the view that Ronald Reagan's winning personality and style secured him his second term in 1984. They point up that in fact changes in his approval ratings had followed relatively auspicious decreases in unemployment levels and inflation along with increases in disposable income.[2] It appears that George Bush benefited from a similar effect in 1988. When the economy turned sour in 1991, voters began to judge Bush more by his lack of attention to domestic concerns than his triumph in the Persian Gulf. The result was his expulsion from office.

Parties that have presided over the economic recovery of the 1980s have been quick to remind voters of how poorly their predecessors did. Certainly, Ronald Reagan and George Bush both adeptly reminded Americans of how bad things became during the "Carter recession." People forget that the worst stages of the economic downturn took place during the first half of Reagan's first term. Evidence suggests that politicians can whip up paranoia among voters by laying all of the blame for economic decline on their opponents.

This clearly occurred in Britain. The economic downturn deepened considerably in Margaret Thatcher's first two years, beginning in May 1979. In fact, voters began to blame her for the nation's worsening predicament.[3] How-ever, the economy started to pull out of its dive by 1981. We must also take into consideration Thatcher's handling of the Argentinean invasion of the Falkland Islands in 1982. For those attributing the 1978–1979 Winter of Discontent to Labour's pandering to unions, Thatcher's steely resolve regarding the Falklands War suggested that she would give equally short shrift to disruptive strikes.

Even data from the 1987 and 1992 British elections still point up the halo effect around the Conservatives that contrasted with Labour's disrepute. Polls before the 1987 and 1992 elections found British voters still extremely skittish about Labour's ability to manage the economy.[4] In one 1987 survey, 46 percent of respondents believed that Labour's campaign promises would cost too much. Only 18 percent considered the Conservative's commitments as extravagant. Fully 56 percent of respondents feared an economic crisis if Labour assumed power. Before the 1992 election, two Gallup polls revealed that voters overwhelmingly believed that taxes would increase under Labour. Private Labour polls indicated that many voters simply did not trust the party to run the economy.

Such skepticism about a former governing party raises a serious question about the political systems of well-established democracies. A very large literature has developed over the years about critical elections in which it appeared that voters fundamentally realigned their allegiances from one party to the other.[5] However, we have tended to associate such occurrences with cathartic experiences. The 1930s Depression clearly ranked as an epochal event of this kind.

During the late 1970s and the early 1980s, voters throughout Western Europe encountered a prolonged period of *stagflation*—that is, simultaneously high inflation and unemployment. The economic decline fell considerably short of a depression. Nonetheless, the electorates in many Western European countries seem no longer to view the responsible parties as capable of managing the economy. Further, they become extremely disillusioned when current governments appear to have adopted approaches similar to those of the ousted parties.

It is now clear that Proposition 1 emerges from voters' long memories over who presided during the period of stagflation. Voters will not countenance current governments that attempt to point up ways in which the public must sacrifice to help make ends meet. This poses two difficulties. First, parties must skirt the issue of deficit reduction rather than confronting it head on. Second, they find virtually every course of action proscribed as they attempt to address new public interest concerns. These may or may not fit within what the public is now prepared to support. Whichever, proposals that address the problems must profess to offer solutions that come at no additional cost to taxpayers.

Proposition 2. Perceptions of the role of the state and sectors within it change according to the values that dominate a political system at a given point in history.

When we speak of the welfare state, we note that the conventional concept of governance within a nation includes a high value on the promotion and maintenance of social goals like income support, housing, and health care. No modern state can withdraw completely from providing social services. However, the economic crisis of the late 1970s—along with the public backlash to ever-growing public expenditure—has led to virtually every European government rolling back the level of social services provision to which it commits itself. Relatedly, many European nations have curtailed their involvement in the production of goods and operation of services, such as petroleum products or airlines, through state-owned corporations. We term the withdrawal of governments from state enterprise "privatization."

Major shifts in what governments do—either through providing social services or engaging in commercial enterprise—tip us to transformations in the very nature of the state. Focusing on Norway but adducing many points that can be applied to other systems, Johan Olsen traces the contours of these types of changes. Olsen starts by making the point that we should be paying a great deal more attention to the relationship between economic conditions and political leaders' views of what the state should do. In Norway, he maintains, the interval of conservative-center government in the early 1980s reversed the inclination for the government to relate essentially to special interests as embodied in organized groups. Norwegian governments therefore had tended to adapt their policies according to the power constellations that formed around various issues.[6]

In large part the approach to government in Norway prior to the conservative-center coalition stemmed from the explosive growth of the welfare state after World War II. The sheer proportions of the expansion of the state required the devolution of a substantial amount of political discretion to the bureaucracy. In turn, this led to the widespread use of consultative mechanisms granting organized interests direct access to governmental decisions. Only these devices could lend political legitimacy to decisions that elected political leaders had delegated to civil servants.

The conservative-center government started the process of privatization and deregulation, which was aimed essentially at reestablishing the boundaries of the state. The approach went beyond simply making the state smaller. It also tried to reaffirm the traditional view that elected politicians make policy, whereas bureaucrats simply administer the law. For instance, the former would now give more political direction to economists rather than simply deferring to their judgment.[7] Further, they would impose monetarist and free-market views of economics on the grounds that more conventional approaches had not adapted to the times.

Proposition 2 is explicitly inspired by Olsen's observations and it will guide the comparative analyses contained in this book. The period of economic crisis induced deep fears about financial security at the expense of other societal goals throughout Western Europe. In order to adapt, tremendous pressures built up that reoriented governmental structures from providing social benefits and producing goods and services to promoting the growth of the economy. The politicians who took over governments in this period had come to believe that economic recovery would prove elusive unless government shrank and deregulation freed up markets. In short, they sought to reverse the course of governance. Inevitably, this tack has introduced immense changes in the roles of governmental and political institutions.

Proposition 3. Though much more complex than the individual exercise of willpower, political systems can reach the point where groups and alliances recognize that they must radically alter their forms of association.

It has become an old saw of economics that Germany and Japan lost the battle—World War II—but won the real war: the struggle to capture more than their shares of world markets. As the theory goes, the destruction suffered by both nations' industrial bases during World War II forced both economic systems into modernizing themselves through redesign and reconstruction. On the other hand, Britain and the United States muddled through with piecemeal revamping of their industrial capacities. Especially in manufacturing, the two "victor" nations ultimately found that their plants had fallen so far behind the state-of-the-art facilities in Germany and Japan that the only way out was to shut down. Thus the emergence of the "rust belt" in the American Midwest and "de-

industrialization" in the British North point up what happens when nations' manufacturing capacities age and ossify.

Mancur Olson in his book, *The Rise and Decline of Nations,* asserts that the aging process in advanced industrial nations does not stop with closed and rusting plants. It permeates social and political institutions so that government loses its capacity to respond in a timely and effective fashion to economic threats.[8] Olson employs a powerful analogue in making his case. He asserts that political systems can develop institutional sclerosis. That is, so many strong organizations and alliances can make their will felt in any given issue that the countervailing pressures can clog the policy-making process. Just as with excessive cholesterol in the human body, the surfeit of powerful special pleaders leads ultimately to the ossification of the main decisional arteries of the political system.

Olson's book dwells on the relative success of West Germany and Japan at avoiding the stagflation that robbed the United States and Britain of economic growth during the late 1970s and early 1980s. He also notes that even France, though less than a paragon of economic performance, weathered the crisis better than either the United States or Britain.

The logic supporting Olson's argument is convincing. Both formal organizations and secret arrangements dedicated to collective action in an economic sector develop slowly when societies first democratize. In time they take root more readily. And existing organizations and arrangements tend to persist, even if through inertia rather than vitality. This bias toward survival hinges largely on the stake that group and alliance leaders have in the status quo.

Eventually, the proliferation of organizations and arrangements induces fragmentation of sectors of the economy. For instance, the members of several different unions might work in a single plant. This would contrast with a situation whereby all employees in a factory belong to a single, industrywide union. With this fragmentation, groups and alliances lose sight of the overall profitability of the sector. Instead, they concentrate their attention on maximizing their share of income and other benefits. The cumulative effect of such strategies makes it increasingly difficult for the sector to obtain optimal economies and output.

In assessing the political and economic systems of Britain, France, West Germany, and Japan, Olson concluded that the British case presents a classic instance of institutional sclerosis. Throughout this century, Britain has experienced a lower rate of economic growth than any of the other developed democracies. The country's long experience with stable democracy secure from foreign invasion has provided a perfect breeding ground for the proliferation of collective organizations and secret commercial alliances. Britain experienced, by far, higher inflation *and* unemployment during the period of stagflation than did France or West Germany. It did this, Olson maintains, because both industry and labor continued to seek large enhancements of income—even though the economy was straining to achieve any growth at all.[9]

In Olson's view, the experiences of West Germany and Japan contrasted sharply with Britain's. World War II had done more than level the industrial plant of the two countries. It—along with the totalitarian regimes that had provoked hostilities in the first place—had essentially uprooted the organizational and associational life of both nations. After the war, interest groups and commercial alliances in both countries reemerged from scratch. Neither society, in the thirty years leading up to the economic crisis, experienced the proliferation of special pleaders with narrow appeals necessary for ossification to occur. As a result, both political systems kept in check extravagant demands for shares of income and benefits from

production. This becomes manifest in their relative avoidance of inflation, which in turn fostered an economic climate in which high employment could be maintained.

Olson suggests that France, though spared much of the war's devastation, mimicked some of the traits of West Germany and Japan. That is, its lack of constitutional stability and immunity from invasion through the entire period of industrialization and democratization retarded the growth of organizations and alliances. While it did not come through the economic crisis as well as did West Germany and Japan, France's performance exceeded stereotypical views that suggested that the French economy is relatively inefficient.

Do Olson's findings tell us that war must devastate and uproot aging political systems like those of Britain and the United States before these societies can overcome ossification? Olson himself envisions the prospect that a gradual process might lead societies suffering from institutional sclerosis to change their ways. Such a process would depend on the extent to which other researchers corroborate his findings. It also would require the dissemination of this consensus through the educational system and mass media. That is, the electorates of these nations would have to come to the realization that institutional sclerosis made governments incapable of responding effectively to economic challenges.

It is here that we can find further guidance on treatment of institutional sclerosis in Olson's implicit analogue—the human cardiovascular system. In the case of arterial sclerosis in the human being, we know that individuals can follow diets that dramatically reduce their levels of cholesterol. They might also engage in exercise regimens that help the cardiovascular system avoid occlusion through inefficient processing of cholesterol. They might even adopt very stringent dietary practices in lieu of medications. That is, they might choose to lower their cholesterol levels through willpower rather than through artificial means that carry undesirable side effects.

Proposition 3, which derives from this human analogue for institutional sclerosis, will be examined at length in this book. The chapters related to the United Kingdom will analyze the many ways in which the British political system has ossified. Successive chapters will also note how other European systems have developed less institutional sclerosis or have dealt with it more effectively than has Britain. However, we will not cast our assessments in stone. We might find in the next ten years that in Britain the lesson has finally sunk in and that the political system began to transform itself. On the other hand, nations that did better than Britain during the economic crisis might be approaching the phase of their development in which ossification becomes a real danger.

In this regard, Germany has taken a huge dose of anti-ossification medication by assuming the gargantuan challenge of merging West and East Germany. On the other hand, we see ominous signs of nonadaptability in France. This has proven especially the case in instances such as the 1992 *blocage* by truckers—most of whom are not unionized—that paralysed the French highway system for two weeks, or the 1993 attempt by farmers to tie the government in knots as it attempted to negotiate the French position in the latest round of negotiations on General Agreement on Tariffs and Trade.

Proposition 4. Europe will gradually advance toward a federal form of union. However, the road toward integration will prove considerably more tortuous than previously thought.

Paul Kennedy has studied ebbs and flows in the strength of great powers since 1500.[10] He observes that the standing of nations shifts according to dynamics originating in economic and technological developments. Human beings' "innate drive" to improve their lot depends upon innovation. And the ways in which societies induce and adapt to change vary greatly according to how they are positioned and how they exploit their advantages.

Nations develop different images of what they want to be. Kennedy calls these "models for emulation." "Trading states" have tried to keep military expenditure to a minimum in order to free their resources for domestic consumption and industrial development. On the other hand, "militarized" economies tolerate levels of defense expenditure that weigh onerously on domestic consumption and industrial development. They view this as essential to maintaining national security. The classic trading state is Japan since World War II. European countries that fall into the category include Switzerland, Sweden, and Austria. The Soviet Union was one European system that operated a militarized state.

Kennedy argues that we can no longer construe the leading Western European countries—Britain, Germany, and France—as powers *per se*. Rather their standing in the world has become inextricably linked with the fate of the rest of Europe—especially as embodied in the European Union (EU). The United Kingdom and Germany have to a degree cast their lot for military power with the North Atlantic Treaty Organization (NATO). France and Germany have entered into an agreement for forward deployment in Germany of French troops. They also have taken the first steps toward Franco-German army units. All three countries operate militarily within Pax Americana. Neither in terms of conventional forces nor nuclear power could the combined strength of Britain, Germany, and France withstand determined aggression from the East. Of course, with the collapse of the Soviet Union this has become an increasingly unlikely prospect.

During the Cold War period, the dependence of Britain, Germany, and France on one another's forces—backed by the military power of the United States—worked a subtle influence on these nations' "models of emulation." Increasingly, their world standing hinged at least as much on their ability to succeed as trading states as to maintain their credentials as military powers. This realization, much more than military integration, has led the three countries and the entire European Union to operate more as a single political system. The effects of Union membership now pervade both the economic and political life of Britain, Germany, and France. In 1992, integration took a giant leap forward with the abolition of all remaining barriers to trade among members of the Union.

Since the autumn of 1991, European integration has begun to run into snags. Many of the difficulties centered on negotiation of the Maastricht Treaty and its eventual ratification by the governments of the Union. Issues like the move toward a unified currency, the establishment of a "social charter"—focusing especially on the rights of workers, and whether federalism should become the official objective of the Union proved especially divisive. The first Danish referendum on Maastricht failed. One in France just barely passed. Judicial review of the implications of Maastricht for relations between the federal and state governments in Germany greatly delayed that country's ratification. In Britain, John Major never won parliamentary approval of the treaty— having ultimately to base Britain's ratification on royal assent. Meanwhile, Britain's abandonment of the European Monetary System in September 1992 has led to a virtual implosion of mechanisms for coordinating the values of European currencies. This has introduced a great deal of uncertainty to trade in the Union. Layered over these problems have been the general downturn in the world economy.

The recent difficulties suggest several caveats about the speed of European integration. First, differences in the national characters of nation-states will continue to bring about serious variability in support of specific steps toward integration. Second, structural differences— like the use of referenda and the roles of courts—will work their effects on the timing of various steps of the process. Observers have only in the past two years focused on a third caution that applies to projections of the rate of European integration. In auspicious economic times, member states will encounter less resistance at home when advocating the next steps in the process. When the economy turns sour, however, they will inevitably find themselves coping with the belief that further integration will come at too great a cost.

These various factors prompt us to revise the view that prevailed in the late 1980s that the European Union would lead ultimately to full integration as a federal state. As Proposition 4 suggests, we now foresee a more gradual and difficult road toward the goal of integration.

Proposition 5. We have entered an era of particularistic expression that might rival the explosion of nationalism in the nineteenth century. This inevitably will add greatly to the burden of "The Other Europe"—the former communist nations—seeking European integration.

Can the four propositions derived from the Western European experience be applied to former communist nations? To varying degrees, these nations will undoubtedly become forces to contend with in the wider context of European power. However, through their experiences with communism, each has developed political histories and cultures that differ profoundly from the experience in Western Europe.

We have discovered, for instance, that an assessment of the bankruptcy of parties in the East means focusing our attention on the very nature and viability of the political system. This is because the party in former communist states essentially became associated as one and the same thing with the various organs of government. Thus fundamental institutions such as the bureaucracy and the legislature lack almost entirely a legacy of autonomy from the party.

For instance, when Boris Yeltsin dissolved the Russian Parliament, he acted extra-constitutionally. He got away with this because Parliament enjoyed little or no institutional legitimacy. To make matters worse, people resisting the president's actions appeared to have involved themselves in a rear guard action for the former regime.

A wild card presents itself here. Some reformers in the East have pushed very hard for "shock treatments"—efforts to make the people stop cold turkey their dependence upon state support and enterprises. The painfulness of such rapid adjustments toward market economies has produced serious backlashes. In the circumstances, reformist leaders have begun to run the risk of going bankrupt even before ever gaining solvency. In this regard, the successes of communists in the 1993 Polish elections appear somewhat ominous.

Ossification is a big problem in the East. We noted above Mancur Olson's argument that states undergoing wholesale change often stand the best chance to adapt to the challenges of the future. He cites Japan and West Germany as cases in point. But the former communist states face considerably different circumstances. To date, the West's assistance to the East has been sporadic, uneven, and parsimonious. We have seen nothing akin to the aid provided West Germany and Japan by the United States after World War II. Even if the physical dimension of production had been greatly damaged by the war, enough of it remained as the base for a viable economy. In the case of Germany, democracy even found some fairly strong roots in the generation educated before the Nazi era.

The East presents an entirely different picture. Far too much inefficient industry there simply lacks viability under true market circumstances. As well, none of the elites have even the slightest experience with leadership within private corporations and democratic institutions. Overcoming ossification will be no simple matter.

Finally, the collapse of communism in the East has made integration hugely complicated.

Even West Germany's absorption of East Germany has become immensely burdensome to the former—in both financial and psychic terms. A pecking order of states has emerged. Poland, Hungary, and the Czech Republic reveal the best prospects. The Slovak Republic and the southern central states of Romania, Bulgaria, and Albania hold much less prospect for economic and democratic viability. Yugoslavia, of course, is a nightmare. If the European Union looks to the East to expand, one finds it difficult to see where it would go without taking inordinate risks. In the former Soviet Union—now the Commonwealth of Independent States (CIS), one sees enough regional and ethnic division to keep the new republics busy for years. Even the most optimistic analyst would recognize that the CIS is a commonwealth in name only.

The collapse of communism has brought The Other Europe into Europe. However, the myriad regions and groups that make up this addition to capitalist Europe must work through very deep antagonisms associated with repression during communist rule and Soviet hegemony.

CONCLUSION

This chapter has provided an overview of the issues that make the study of politics and government in Europe so fascinating. We have developed five propositions to guide work in the rest of the book. These are: conventional parties have lost their appeal with increasingly skeptical voters; economic constraints have altered perceptions of what the state can do; ossification has greatly hampered some European societies in adapting to the current circumstances; economic and political integration have become more, not less, elusive; and the entrance of the East into the Westrn European mainstream has become much more difficult than anticipated and places an added obstacle to rapid European integration. Before proceeding to our analyses of individual countries and regions, we will next look at the integrated structures already in place for collective governance and action in Europe. We, of course, will focus our attention on the European Union.

NOTES

1. Richard Rose and B. Guy Peters, *Can Government Go Bankrupt?* (New York: Free Press, 1978), pp. 33–34.
2. D. Roderick Kiewiet and Douglas Rivers, "The Economic Basis of Reagan's Appeal," in *The New Direction in American Politics*, John E. Chubb and Paul E. Peterson, eds. (Washington: Brookings Institution, 1985), pp. 79–81.
3. Helmut Norpoth, "Guns and Butter and Government Popularity in Britain," *American Political Science Review,* 81 (1987), 949–959.
4. David Butler and Dennis Kavanagh, *The British General Election of 1987* (Houndmills: Macmillan, 1988), pp. 134, 248, 258, 273–274; and *The British General Election of 1992* (Houndmills: Macmillan, 1992), pp. 56, 96.
5. V. O. Key, "A Theory of Critical Elections," *Journal of Politics,* 17 (1955), pp. 3–18; James L. Sundquist, *Dynamics of the Party System: Alignment and Realignment of Political Parties in the United States,* rev. ed. (Washington: Brookings Institution, 1983).
6. Johan P. Olsen, "Administrative Reform and Theories of Organization," in *Organizing Governance: Governing Organizations,* Colin Campbell and B. Guy Peters, eds. (Pittsburgh: University of Pittsburgh, 1988), pp. 233–254.
7. Johan P. Olsen, *Organized Democracy: Political Institutions in a Welfare State: The Case of Norway* (Oslo: Universitetsforlaget, 1983), p. 100.
8. Mancur Olson, *The Rise and Decline of Nations: Economic Growth, Stagflation and Social Rigidities* (New Haven: Yale University Press, 1982), pp. 75–79.
9. Olson, pp. 217–218.
10. Paul Kennedy, *The Rise and Fall of the Great Powers: Economic Change and Military Conflict from 1500 to 2000* (London: Unwin Hyman, 1988). See especially pp. 439, 445–446, 488, 513–514.

REFERENCES AND SUGGESTED READINGS

Kennedy, Paul. 1988. *The Rise and Fall of the Great Powers: Economic Change and Military Conflict From 1500 to 2000.* London: Unwin Hyman.

Olsen, Johan P. 1983. *Organized Democracy: Political Institutions in a Welfare State: The Case of Norway.* Olso: Universitetsforlaget.

Olson, Mancur. 1982. *The Rise and Decline of Nations: Economic Growth, Stagflation and Social Rigidities.* New Haven: Yale University Press.

3

The European Union

he European Union (EU) was born from two important ideas, one political and one economic. The political impetus for the Union grew out of the shock of the Second World War. The leaders of Western Europe were convinced that the succession of wars that Europe had known since earliest historical times could no longer be tolerated. Weapons had become too devastating and the human costs of any conflict among industrial states were no longer acceptable. Moreover, the rise of fascism, closely associated with nationalism and xenophobia, was viewed as the proximate cause of the 1939–1945 conflagration. Nationalist loyalties needed to be moderated and cooperation among the peoples of Europe needed to be encouraged.

This political reasoning dovetailed with an economic argument. The countries of the Old World were simply too small to achieve the maximum benefits of a market economy. Trade barriers needed to be broken down to increase the size of markets for European producers. With larger markets, European companies could grow larger and achieve economies of scale. Moreover, along the lines of the theory of comparative advantage,[1] countries could devote their resources to the production of goods in which they were especially efficient, and trade for goods in which they were less efficient. Economists reasoned that turning Europe into one big market, without distorting tariffs, would be to everyone's benefit. For evidence they pointed to the United States, which had no trade barriers between its member states, and consequently had the largest and most efficient firms of any industrial nation. It was no accident, the economists argued, that the United States was the wealthiest country in the world.

These two sets of reasons gave impetus to the movement for European integration. Not everyone, like its foremost exponents, Jean Monnet and Ernst Haas,[2] favored pushing European integration to its logical conclusion, a United States of Europe, but most European politicians favored mechanisms that would reduce tariff barriers and increase cooperation. Moreover, the United States used its influence to encourage this movement. A more united and prosperous Europe, American officials reasoned during the Cold War, would be more likely to reduce the influence of communist parties in domestic politics, and strengthen the West against the Soviet Union in international politics.

HISTORY

The first effort at integration, the European Coal and Steel Community, was especially influenced by the politics of the early postwar period. This organization in 1951 created a joint management of coal and steel resources by the original six members of what would become the European Community: France, Germany, Belgium, the Netherlands, Luxembourg, and Italy. Economically it had the effect of pooling the resources of this basic commodity, while politically it was especially appealing to France, because it gave the French a say in the disposition of German raw materials that were crucial to the defense industry. Since the European Coal and Steel Community was founded at a time of tremendous demand for coal and steel, as Europe reconstructed itself from the ashes of the war, the organization was closely associated with economic success, and the result encouraged the six member states to experiment further.

In 1957 these six European governments signed the Treaty of Rome, which established Euratom (the European Atomic Energy Community) and the European Economic Community. The latter organization went much further than any other trade zone in the world. Not only was the new organization a customs union—that is, an area that gradually reduced trade barriers between its members and established a single tariff schedule for all members vis à vis nonmembers, it went much further. The EEC, or Common Market, established a mechanism to allow its members to coordinate their domestic economic policies, established joint funds for severe economic problems such as regional disparities, and created a truly supranational policy to manage agriculture.

At the heart of the Common Market were France and Germany, the prime movers of the new organization. Great Britain was originally a part of the negotiations, but ultimately declined to join, fearing that the supranational institutions would eclipse Parliament, and that it would be forced to abandon its special trading relationships with the British Commonwealth of Nations. The Germans, anxious to find a new role for themselves in a democratic Europe, were willing to accept the common agriculture policy that mainly helped France (and, to a lesser extent, Italy). In exchange, they got a large market for German industrial products and recognition as a leader of the most important democratic club in Europe.

The economies of the Common Market grew like Topsy, although some economists argued that the economies of the member states would have grown as fast without the organization. Britain reconsidered its position in the 1960s and petitioned to be admitted. By this time General de Gaulle had become president of France, and fearing that the United Kingdom would be a Trojan horse for American interests, vetoed the British request. It was not until 1973, four years after de Gaulle's death, that Great Britain (along with Ireland and Denmark) were allowed to join. The EC expanded again in the 1980s, admitting the newly democratic Greece, Spain, and Portugal. By this time the European Economic Community and the European Atomic Energy Community had merged with the European Coal and Steel Community to form the European Community.

Historically, not all political and economic groups in Europe have favored joining the European Union. Parties of both the Right and Left have criticized it. On the Right, the supranationality of the European Union institutions offended nationalist sensibilities. In Britain especially, much of the Conservative Party saw it as a threat to parliamentary sovereignty. Parties on the Left, the communists in France and Italy, saw the Union as essentially procapitalist. This was because it was much easier for capital to circulate in the Community than it was for labor. Rich people could move their factories to wherever labor was cheapest, while it was much harder for labor unions to form alliances across national borders. This was especially true because labor unions were organized along craft lines in some countries, and along industry lines in others. Some union federations were religiously based, while others were not. Small shopkeepers also opposed the Union, fearing it would favor mass retailing outlets, drowning out mom-and-pop shops in a tidal wave of chain stores.

Whatever the economic value of the European Union, it could not stem the effects of stagnation during the 1970s and early 1980s. Many considered the organization to be moribund. However, this changed when the moderate French socialist Jacques Delors assumed the presidency of the European Commission, the executive branch of the Community. The energetic Delors urged a new phase of integration and was the principal force behind the Single European Act, which went into effect in 1987. The idea was to reduce the remaining trade barriers among the twelve member states, thus accelerating economic integration. It was under Delors's leadership that a new treaty was signed in Maastricht, the Netherlands, in 1992. The treaty integrated its signatories even further than the Single European Act. Most importantly, it set up a timetable for development of a single European Central Bank.

Most national parliaments were willing to ratify the Maastricht Treaty on European Union. However, Ireland, Denmark, and France held referenda on the issue in 1992. It was endorsed overwhelmingly in Ireland, halfheartedly in France, and was rejected in Denmark. Times had changed, and the idea of a gradual progression toward a greater political union was no longer as popular as it once was. The Union was no longer seen as supranational phoenix rising from the ashes of a Europe devastated by centuries of nation-state hostilities. Rather, the rising bureaucracy of Brussels, home of the Community institutions, was seen as a threat to the pleasures and peculiarities of national ways of life. As Europe experienced its worst recession since 1982, the voters on Maastricht were more fearful of the downside to integration than they were optimistic about its potential. Eventually, in the spring of 1993, there was a second referendum in Denmark, with the most objectionable aspects of Maastricht amended. The voters agreed, but the momentum was gone. Dutifully, in the autumn of 1993, obeying the instructions of the treaty, the European Community changed its name to *European Union,* but most viewed the name change as premature. European integration was put on "hold."

INSTITUTIONAL FRAMEWORK

This section intends to provide a brief overview of the major institutions of the European Union, their functions and powers, and their roles in the legislative processes. The Commission of the European Communities and the Council of the European Union are the Union's core institutions, backed up by the European Parliament and the European Court of Justice.

The Commission of the European Communities

The European Commission, as it is usually called, is a body composed of seventeen members appointed for a renewable term of five years. The "big five"—Britain, France, Germany, Italy, and Spain—send two representatives apiece, while the remaining countries send one each. Commissioners are appointed by their own governments but they are not nominated to defend their countries' interests; they are selected to serve Europe's interests impartially. After being nominated, all the commissioners, including the president and the vice-president, should be approved by the European Parliament, and the Parliament can, at any time, force the Commission's resignation. Individual members, however, can only be dismissed after the Court of Justice, by application of the Council or the Commission, retires them.

The commissioners meet weekly and take their decisions by the method they have agreed upon such as vote, consensus, unanimity, and so on. Each commissioner heads one or two policy areas of the Commission called Directorates General, and they are organized along functional lines resembling national ministries and civil service departments—for example, external relations, agriculture, competition (antitrust), and so on. Decisions, however, are taken in a collegial manner and all commissioners try to be informed of the whole of the work of the Commission.

Article 155 of the Rome treaty describes the functions of the Commission as the following:

1. It shall ensure that the provisions of the treaty are applied;

2. It shall formulate recommendations or deliver opinions on matters dealt with in the treaties, either if the treaty provides for such actions or if the Commission considers it necessary;

3. It shall have its own power of decision and participate in the shaping of the legislation by Council and Parliament;

4. It shall exercise the powers conferred by the Council, for the implementation of the rules laid down by Council.

Experts in the field agree that the treaty has given the Commission functions that are not easy to fulfill. Enforcing the provisions of the treaty is a mixture of bureaucratic, administrative, and judicial responsibilities and the broad nature of the role has proven problematic. An episode that occurred in 1991 illustrates this fact. In 1991, the commissioner for competition policy blocked the proposed takeover of the Canadian aircraft firm De Havilland by an Italian-French consortium, causing protests in both countries, especially France. After the French government protested the Commission's action, Jacques Delors, the Commission's president, threatened to resign. Delors stressed the collegial and independent nature of the Commission's decision, as opposed to its being a champion of national interests.

The Commission also acts as the motor of the European integration by exercising its executive functions. These functions include the responsibility to initiate new legislation, to oversee the implementation of the already-existing legislation, and to implement the European Union's budget and administer its funds. The Commission is also the external representative for the Union in the economic and diplomatic fields.

The Council of the European Union

Known formerly as the Council of Ministers, this group is composed of representatives of the member countries, usually ministers whose portfolios correspond to the policy areas of the Council. The Council's presidency rotates every six months among the country members. This position is, by far, the most relevant in the Council's composition because the president has the function of coordinating the majority of the activities, actively participating in agenda-setting and acting as mediator if disputes among members arise.

Article 145 of the treaty establishing the ECC gives the Council the function of coordinating the countries' economic policies. Consequently, the Council can take decisions on the Commission's proposed legislation and give rules to the Commission regarding the implementation of these decisions. These functions are similar to those performed by a national legislature.

Like the Commission, the Council is divided along functional lines. Consequently, it is possible to talk about councils composed of different individual specialists in particular areas. For example, a draft dealing with monetary issues would be discussed by representatives from the central banks or ministries of finance of the countries. Each council meets within a regular schedule according to the importance of the issue—for example, the Council of Foreign Affairs meets monthly, but Tourism meets once or twice a year.

Drafts have to be approved by the Council's Committee of Permanent Representatives (COREPER) before they are discussed by the specific councils. COREPER is staffed by senior and junior country representatives in charge of screening or "sifting" drafts before they are actually discussed by the ministers. This function gives COREPER great power in the decision-making process and it is important in molding politically feasible proposals for all the countries, before they receive full consideration. On the other hand, COREPER powers of gatekeeper can be judged as excessive and as a serious limitation to the democratic process of decision-making.

The European Council

The European Council is composed of the heads of states or government and meets twice a year, normally for no more than a day. Emergency meetings are scheduled from time to time. Foreign ministers are the only national officials allowed to participate in these meetings in addition to heads of state. Agendas are normally set up before meetings, based on suggestions made by participants.

The European Council's original function was to be a forum where the nations' leaders could meet in a quasi-informal setting and develop recommendations for the Union. Over the years, however, this original conception of the Council's role has deteriorated.

Nowadays, the Council is both an initiating and a decision-making body that sets the pace for the EU's policy-making process. This is explained by the crisis situations that have triggered changes in policy such as the unification of Germany, the Persian Gulf War, and more recently, civil war in the former Yugoslavia.

Decisions are reached by political agreement and, according to the specific area to which these decisions are related, details are left to be worked out by the specific councils within the Council of the European Union. The appropriate Council is then in charge of proceeding with adoption by the Union any instrument that the European Council agreement has unblocked.

The European Parliament

Article 137 of the Rome treaty declared that "The Assembly, which shall consist of representatives of the peoples of the states brought together in the Community, shall exercise the advisory and supervisory powers which are conferred upon by this Treaty." In the 1960s the Assembly was renamed the European Parliament and since then, the institution has been fighting to gain more legitimacy and power.

Until 1979, the European Parliament was composed of country representatives indirectly elected by the governments, rather than directly by their populations. This procedure violated the spirit of Article 138 of the treaty establishing that all representatives were to be elected by popular suffrage conducted by the same electoral procedure. In 1979, the first parliamentary elections by direct popular vote were carried out, bringing more legitimacy to the institution. The issue of choosing a homogenous procedure still remains unresolved and each country uses its own system to elect delegates. An additional unresolved problem is the location of the institution that meets in Strasbourg, when most of the committee work is done in Brussels or Luxembourg. Although it is widely believed that the Parliament's location conspires against its coherence and effectiveness, any solution for its relocation has proved elusive so far.

The Parliament is composed of 567 members (MEPs) who are elected every five years to represent some 340 million citizens of the twelve member countries. Seats are divided according to population, giving Germany, France, Italy, and the United Kingdom all over 80 members each. Next is Spain with 64 seats. Seats for the smaller states—the Netherlands, Belgium, Greece, Portugal, Denmark, and Ireland range between the middle teens to the lower thirties. Luxembourg, the smallest member of the European Union, has six seats.

The Parliament is organized into eighteen committees assigned to diverse functional areas like: agriculture, budgetary control, environment, and health and consumer affairs. Members of the European Parliament are assigned to these committees according to their preferences, and all the proposals are discussed and drafted in committee before they are submitted to a plenary session of the Parliament.

After being elected, members are grouped in accordance with their political parties—disregarding their nationalities. This does not mean that nationalities are not important. The European Parliament political parties—also called groups or groupings—are basically organized according to national political parties with more or less homogenous ideologies. Since their formation, however, these groups have not lived up to the expectation that they would link the national electorates with their members, advancing the democratic process in Europe. The groups remain weak and the members' influence in the national parties is still small. In spite of this, a very positive development has stemmed from the electoral process: the process of negotiating common manifestoes for the European elections has created more communication among national parties. These parties have now a more or less well developed European policy in their own manifestoes.[3]

Table 3.1 shows the composition of each party and the votes that each of them obtained in the last two elections:

A comparison between 1984 and 1989 shows that there has been a general movement of voters from the parties holding national power to the fringe parties. "Protest" votes, especially in France and Britain, favored non-traditional parties reflecting the growing distrust of the traditional leaders in the countries' populations. The Center-Right coalition that traditionally dominated the European Parliament was replaced in 1989 by a Center-Left coalition. The Communist Party disappeared and two groups from the Left emerged.

At this writing, the available analysis of the 1994 election is preliminary. However, a general swing to the right took a substantial proportion of traditional Christian Democratic support over to more ideological fringe groups. British voters' disenchantment with their Conservative government accounted for nearly all of the gains made by the Socialists. While the results pointed to continuation of the Center-Left coalition, Christian Democrats have been working intensely with small groups on the right with a view to thwarting such a government.

Table 3.1

Political party or group	1984	1989	1994*
Socialist Group	166	180	221
European People's Party (Christian Democratic Group)	112	122	204
Liberal and Democratic Reformists	45	49	28
European Democratic Group (British and Danish Conservatives)	66	34	—
The Green Group	—	29	33
Communists	48	—	—
European Unitarian Left	—	28	—
European Democratic Alliance (Gaullist, Fianna Fail, Scottish Nationalist)	30	22	7
Technical Group of the European Right	16	17	12
Left Unity	—	14	28
Rainbow Group	20	14	8
Independent and Others	15	9	34
Total	518	518	565

*Preliminary results, with two seats unassigned.

Source: European Parliament, List of members, Luxembourgh (February 12, 1990) and *The Guardian*, (June 14, 1994).

The level of turnout for the European Parliament elections is low (for European standards); usually only about 60 percent of the eligible voters participate in these elections and this figure has been decreasing in past elections. Opinion polls, however, show a paradoxical picture. They demonstrate the willingness of the majority of the European Union citizens to support a more powerful institutional position for the Parliament.[4]

It is clear from the treaty's description of Parliament's functions that its original role was far from one resembling a national legislature. The supervisory and advisory functions are less far-reaching than most legislatures in Europe now. In spite of this, Union experts agree that the Parliament has evolved considerably—both by acquiring more *de facto* and *de jure* power.

A major supervisory power is Parliament's ability to dismiss the Commission. Although never used by Parliament, a potential vote of censure has an important capacity to put pressure on the Commission and, ultimately, over the Council to compromise on an issue over which the Parliament disagrees.

Maybe the most visible and effective of Parliament's supervisory powers is its capacity to control, in conjunction with the Council, the budgetary process. Parliament can adopt or reject the budget discussed in December of each year. In the discussions, Parliament normally exposes its own priorities in the financial spheres. In the past years, these priorities have been mainly related to unemployment, social and regional policy, energy, and development.

In discussing Parliament's advisory powers, it should be noted that the original treaties did not endow the institution with a meaningful role in the legislative process. The Council was only required to receive Parliament's view on the issues, but it was not bound by this view. In 1987, the Single European Act (SEA) gave Parliament a limited but effective role when the issues at hand are related to internal markets and related affairs. The act mandates a second reading by Parliament of the Council's decisions—even though Parliament submits its recommendation before the decision. In the second reading, Parliament can accept, reject, or amend the Council's policy within three months. If rejected, the Council's policy can only be approved if unanimity exists among Council members. If the proposal is amended, a complex procedure ensues whereby Parliament's amendments are normally accepted in a modified form. This development is said to have marked the beginning of a "participatory" role for the Parliament instead of a simple "advisory" one.

THE EUROPEAN COURT OF JUSTICE

Although the formal role of the European Court of Justice (ECJ) has not changed since the Treaty of Rome, this institution has been growing in importance. Article 164 of the EEC stated that it is the Court's task to ensure that the law is observed in the interpretation and application of the EEC treaty.

Since 1974, the Court has been composed of thirteen judges, all of them with outstanding judicial credentials and recruited from the best senior levels at the national judicial systems. The judges are assisted by six advocates-general whose mission is to analyze cases and, in some instances, to give opinions about them.

The Court hears cases brought by the Commission against member states or against the Council, cases brought by one member against another or against the Commission or the Council, or by natural or legal persons against a Union decision that affects them. More important, Article 173 gives the Court the power to "review the legality of the acts of the Commission and the Council" and may also rule on the Council's failure to act.

The Court may impose fines for the infringement of regulations. It also interprets treaties and related secondary legislation. What brings legitimacy to the Court is the fact that states, in the majority of the cases, respect its decisions.

In fact, Union law is said to be superior—but complementary—to the states' laws.

In recent years, the European Court of Justice has become a powerful institution behind the process of integration. It has rendered important decisions going beyond strictly legal interpretations. The *Cassis de Dijon*[5] ruling serves as an example of the growing importance of the Court.

In 1978, a West German company called Rewe Central wanted to import a French liqueur, Cassis de Dijon. The German government refused to allow it to be imported as a liqueur on the grounds that the beverage did not contain a large enough percentage of alcohol as determined by West German standards. Rewe started legal proceedings that eventually led to the European Court of Justice. The company argued that West German standards discriminated against foreign liqueurs, thus violating the Single European Act. After considering the case, the Court ruled that West Germany did not have the right to block the importation of a drink that was on sale in France, unless it could be shown that it was blocked for reasons of health, fiscal supervision, fair trading, or consumer protection.

With this decision the Court gave substance to the "principle of mutual recognition," that products lawfully produced or marketed in one member nation can have access to all member countries. This principle, and its ratification by the Court, is the bedrock for the rapid harmonization of standards and regulations within the European Union in the last decade and the ensuing improvement of the free movement of goods within the European Union.

ECONOMIC AND SOCIAL COMMITTEE

The Economic and Social Committee (ESC) represents three groups: employers, employees, and independent workers. The Committee is generally defined as a "consultative assembly" and is composed of 189 members who are appointed by the Council after having been nominated by their respective countries.

The Committee is organized into eight committees (sections) among which, by mandate of Article 197 of the EEC treaty, there must be agriculture and transport sections. The treaty also mandates that the Economic and Social Committee should be consulted, and the Council normally does so. Since the mid-1970s, the Committee role of consultation has been expanding. Today it has the right to present its own initiatives to the Council.

POLITICAL COOPERATION AND POLITICAL CULTURE

The analysis of the institutional framework seems to suggest that we are in the presence of an extremely formalized system, where each institution's functions and roles have been perfectly defined. The European Union is, in fact, perhaps the most organized and well-functioning of any multilateral institution in the history of the world, an institution that has almost equalized the power of its members in spite of the differences between politically and economically dominant countries and the rest of the Union.

Despite all these factors, political cooperation is still very much played at a bilateral level, where "preferential," *long-term* political relationships develop from common interests among countries, shared ideologies, and even the harmonious—or contrasting—personalities of countries' leaders. Philippe de Schoutheete defines these relationships as subsystems. Schoutheete asserts that "the negotiating process [in a multilateral setting] changes if a particular bilateral coalition [a subsystem] becomes a durable, predictable feature."

It is easy to recognize the existence of subsystems within the Union. These are long-term relationships that have not only proved effective for the subsystem member, but have also been politically accepted by the rest of the members. Arguably, the Franco-German subsystem is the more visible and relevant of the Union. The relationships—or lack thereof—of the United Kingdom with Germany and France are also important. This also applies to Italy's relationships with France and Germany.

By virtue of their economic and political power, France and Germany form the hard core of the European Union. It is almost surprising that these two former enemies have come to develop such a level of political cooperation, becoming the very heart of Europe. It has been demonstrated, for example, that Germany and France were the forces behind the European Monetary System (EMS). Although the adoption of the system followed a decision of the Council of Ministers in December 1978, the initiative came from Germany and France—most specifically, then Chancellor Helmut Schmidt and then President Valéry Giscard d'Estaing. The system was aimed at accelerating the process of economic integration by promoting monetary stability in Europe. Monetary stability was of special interest for both Germany and France. On one hand, currency stabilization facilitated the control of inflation—a central consideration for Germany. On the other, the system gave Europe a certain level of independence from the United States in monetary affairs—a primary concern for France.

The monetary system that emerged in 1979 was built on the Exchange Rate Mechanism (ERM). The mechanism is basically a grid that assigns to each currency an exchange parity with each of the others. The currencies' values can fluctuate only between prescribed bands. If the value of a country's currency with respect to another's goes beyond the band, the other members of the grid must intervene to right the balance. Germany and France have also strongly promoted the European Currency Unit (ECU). Many advocates of integration view the ECU as on track to replace individual national currencies as the principle vehicle of economic exchange in Europe.

Also in keeping with their roles as the engines behind the most dramatic components of integration, France and Germany have promoted an independent policy on research and technology for Europe. The two countries contribute more than 90 percent of the funding for EUREKA. EUREKA is a program designed to finance private projects related to cutting-edge technologies.[6]

Two basic arguments can help explain how such a relationship emerged. The first is rooted in the very pragmatic thinking behind the notion of European Union: Europe could not afford another conflict like World War II, and economic union—to be followed by political union—was the best means to avoid war by increasing interdependence. The second argument underscores the importance of the quality of the bonds that have existed between successive leaders of both countries since the war: in the 1960s, France's President Charles de Gaulle and Germany's Chancellor Konrad Adenauer had a majestic relationship that culminated in the signing of the Elysée Treaty of 1963; President Giscard d'Estaing and Chancellor Schmidt also had an excellent political association that was extended to our days by the relaxed relationship between President François Mitterrand and Chancellor Helmut Kohl.

The United Kingdom's relationship with Germany and France is interesting to the extent that it defies what would have been predicted, given the traditional political, diplomatic, and economic importance of the United Kingdom. Britain has been reluctant in building a close relationship with either of these countries, taking a rather watchful (even guarded) position on the political and economic developments of the continent. There is an obvious tactical reason behind this kind of attitude: Britain has tried to keep its options open and has acted accordingly with its interest focused on the issue at hand.

We have suggested when discussing the definition of subsystems that such an arrangement implies a long-term relationship that intrinsically limits the partners' choices. The United Kingdom's judgment is that it cannot afford to compromise in some areas of the integration process, and thus it abstains from participating in any subsystem. One area where the United Kingdom has used its independence has been in its successful challenge of the federative thinking expressed by the majority of the countries in Maastricht in 1991.

In the buildup to the treaty, British fears were expressed by Prime Ministers Thatcher and Major when they insisted that the British Parliament would not agree to give up any measure of sovereignty. The establishment of common social policies is another highly contested area in which the British have refused to go along with the rest of Europe. In fact, Britain was the only country that did not sign the fourteenth protocol to the Maastricht Treaty—the protocol concerned with the development of a common social policy.

In addition to any "tactical" considerations, cultural factors are brought to bear in the British case. Cultural disparity between the United Kingdom and the continent can be found in many instances. An example is the British reluctance to sacrifice its national currency, the pound sterling, for a European currency. Another excellent—and insightful—example is given by James Christoph when comparing the British and the continental administrative traditions. Christoph notes that British bureaucrats in Brussels have a very difficult time trying to adapt to the less hierarchical and mostly decentralized decision-making process and structure—the French bureaucratic model—prevalent in the Union bureaucracy. This disparity between bureaucracies reflects a cultural difference with obvious limitations for effective British integration to the rest of the European Union.

Italy, originally the least-developed economy of the European "big six," has taken a pragmatic position regarding Union issues. Often diplomatically isolated by the Franco-German relationship, Italy has made this isolation an advantage by selecting different allies according to its convenience in each situation. This issue-by-issue approach does not respond to a "principist" posture as in the United Kingdom situation, but rather reflects the country's flexibility to adapt to different political and economic developments.

Other factors, such as Italy's frequent changes of government and the lack of a Mediterranean subsystem can also partially explain the fact that Italy does not belong to a particular subsystem. On one hand, the constant rotation of prime ministers makes impossible the development of any personal relationship resembling that of the Franco-German leaders. On the other, even though Spain, Greece, and Portugal often share Italy's position on Union issues, a Mediterranean subsystem has not appeared. In fact, these countries seem to have a pragmatic posture similar to Italy's.

Unresolved Issues

If the complex political structures described in the last section are added to cultural and leadership differences, it should not be surprising, as we briefly noted in the history section of this chapter, that some issues remain unresolved or at least very generally defined, ultimately becoming obstacles in the integration process.

The area of social policy, for example, has been one of the most difficult in the process of integration. Social policy had almost no relevance until the 1960s and 1970s. The achievement of a common market, customs unions, and a common agricultural policy had, by far, more weight among the Union's objectives. The 1980s, however, came with the realization that harmonization of social policies was needed to achieve the goal of economic union. A unified social policy would achieve free movement of the labor force—a condition for

an efficient free market—but most importantly, it would dampen any possibility of "social dumping," where countries compete for investment by unilaterally lowering the standards of their social and labor legislation, thus increasing firms' bargaining power. A unified and homogenous social market would limit business dominance of the market and it would allow efficient use of labor.

The existence of regions with lower wages and less expensive social security provisions—predominantly in the south of Europe and in Ireland—was of special concern for unions in the North. The unions feared that business would move capital to these regions unless a policy of gradually equating salaries and social cost was put in place. A related objective was to ensure that all the groups within the Community would reap the benefits of a free market that, without a social policy, would be concentrated in the hands of political and business elites.

The growing concern for social policy remains a bitter point of division between the United Kingdom and the continent. In 1989, reflecting the growing concern for this issue, the Commission presented a draft of the Social Charter that was approved by the Strasbourg European Council with the exception of the British government. The Social Charter established the usual rights of social protection, freedom of association, free movement of workers, and so on but it also established what the British government considers a more proactive social policy with issues like mandatory childcare for working parents or a mandatory minimum wage. For all the states on the mainland, these requirements do not demand more than a little adjustment to their current policy and, in addition, they believe that they would gain more by discouraging any country's adoption of a weak social policy. On the other hand, the British government asserts that a more regulated social policy is contrary to its national interests.

The Social Charter problem and many others can be discussed within the more general context of Europe's efforts toward political integration. The crux of the issue is whether Europe can become more than a well-developed international organization. Jacques Delors pressed forward the concept of a federation, but this is a controversial idea. The formation of a federative entity will require a single market, economic and political union, a common external policy, shared security institutions, and control of the armed forces by the federal government. These goals are a very tall order in the 1993 political and economic contexts. Today, the Union has to deal with the dilemma of expansion—incorporating new countries, or consolidation—achieving more consensus among existing members on economic and institutional policies. Also, there is the always-present threat of economic and political dissolution of Eastern Europe and the question of providing for defense inside or outside NATO.

The Maastricht Treaty was, without doubt, a leap forward in the process of integration. However, this history of the Union demonstrates that the integration process tends to be stalled by economic problems affecting the countries. Europe is showing the signs of a stagnant and declining economy. This situation does not help the federalist aspiration to the extent that nationalist politicians can blame the European Union for the economic distress of the national economies. We can conclude that, as it stands today, Europe can better aspire to become a "confederal" state, with most of the attributes of a federation but with each sovereign member retaining veto power in key areas (defense and foreign affairs). Today's reality, however, seems to indicate that Europe can be better characterized as what Lijphart would describe as a "consociation," a group of countries more inward-looking than concerned with links among themselves. The process of integration is today fueled only by the elite's support of it and not by the European people's determination. Agreements among elites about the integration process will result only in the formation of a "weak" common interest characteristic of a consociation. The "strong" common interest that defines a federation and that Delors and the other supporters of European unity envision will not easily flourish in today's economic climate.

Notes

1. This theory was first put forth by the nineteenth-century classical economist David Ricardo. Ricardo argued that even if a country was less efficient in all areas of economic production, it should specialize in products in which it was *relatively* (or comparatively) more efficient (its "comparative advantage"), and trade for products that it produced less efficiently. Since the nineteenth century, the theory has been criticized, largely because it is "static." Most political economists argue that comparative advantage can change as a result of government policy. The French and Japanese governments are the most well-known proponents of this view. See especially John Zysman, *Governments, Markets and Growth* (Ithaca: Cornell University Press, 1983).

2. Ernst Haas's writings on political integration include *The Uniting of Europe* (Stanford, Calif.: Stanford University Press, 1958) and *Beyond the Nation State* (Stanford University Press, 1964).

3. The 1992 manifestoes of the Labour, Conservative, and Social Democrat parties in Britain all have a special section in which their "European policies" are delineated.

4. Commission of the European Communities, *Eurobarometer 2*, No. 33 (June 1990).

5. Case 120/78 (1979) ECR. 649.

6. See Peter Ludlow (1982).

References and Suggested Readings

Christoph, James. 1993. "The Effects on Britons in Brussels: The European Community and the Culture of Whitehall." *Governance*, 6, 518–537.

Clive, A., and F. Butler. 1992. *The European Community: Structure and Process*. New York. St. Martin's Press.

Commission of the EC, *Eurobarometer 2*, No. 33 (June 1990).

Corona-Viron, P. 1991. "Social Protection," in Hurwitz, L., ed., *The State of the European Community: Policies, Institutions & Debates in the Transition Years.* London: Longman.

de Schoutheete, Phillipe. 1990. "The European Community and its sub-systems," in Wallace, W., ed. *The Dynamics of European Integration.* London: Pinter Publishers.

El-Agraa, A. 1990. *The Economics of the European Community.* New York: St. Martin's Press.

Lijphart, A. 1969. "Consociational Democracy," *World Politics,* 21 (2), 205–225.

Ludlow, Peter. 1982. *The Making of the EMS.* London: Butterworths.

Nicoll, W., and T. Salmon. 1990. *Understanding the European Communities.* Savage, Barnes & Noble Books.

Schmuck, O. 1991. "The European Parliament as an Institutional Actor," in L. Hurwitz, ed. *The State of the European Community: Policies, Institutions & Debates in the Transition Years.* London: Longman.

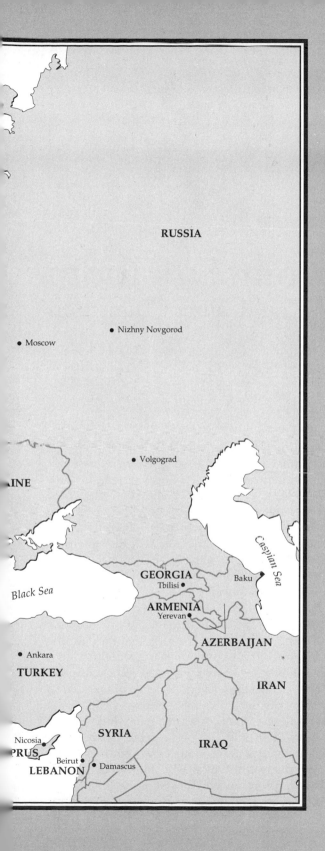

RUSSIA

• Nizhny Novgorod

• Moscow

• Volgograd

INE

Caspian Sea

GEORGIA
Tbilisi •   Baku •

Black Sea

ARMENIA
Yerevan •

AZERBAIJAN

• Ankara

TURKEY

IRAN

Nicosia

SYRIA

IRAQ

PRUS

Beirut •   • Damascus

LEBANON

II

The
United
Kingdom

4

The Current Situation:
The Realm of Transition

History presents us with many lessons. Never to assume that governments and political systems remain stable certainly ranks at the top of the list. Yet somehow we expect Britain not to change substantially. This chapter will suggest several areas in which much change has occurred. Subsequent ones will examine in greater detail developments in British political culture; socialization and participation; party and electoral behavior; executive and bureaucratic leadership; intra-, inter-, and extragovernmental relations; and policy processes. Taken together, they reveal tremendous flux.

This chapter provides a broad context for an examination of change in the United Kingdom. It takes the view that the "atmospherics" of the setting for British government and politics have meant a great deal of pitching and yawing as the ship of state plies its course. We will focus on two dimensions of these contexts. First, we will look at changes in Britain's constitutional system that suggest that the rules of the game have come increasingly under question. Second, we will review the performance of Britain's economy with special reference to its competitive standing in the world and the internal distribution of wealth and opportunities. These issues have risen to prominence for two reasons.

First, the British no longer view their constitution with the complacence that they did previously. It is not running as smoothly as it once seemed to. And the standards for constitutional rule now fit within the wider compass of the development of democracy throughout Europe. In the last century, Britain led the rest of Europe into democracy. Now it finds that it lags in some respects.

Second, the economy has provided the battleground for political struggle in the past fifteen years. The specter of decline has transfixed nearly everyone—from the wealthy who claim the state shackles them with taxes and interference to the poor who increasingly fall victim to joblessness and shrinking state benefits. Prime Minister Margaret Thatcher (and the subsequent policy doctrine she put into practice, "Thatcherism") attempted to put things right by rewarding enterprise and shrinking the state. The results proved disillusioning at best. People remain reluctant to return the Labour Party to power (the party has not formed a government since 1974). However, the failure of the Conservatives to reverse decline has introduced a note of pronounced skepticism to the British political culture.

We should make one note before launching our analysis. No one can understand Britain today without a grasp of Margaret Thatcher's influence on it. Some readers might ask, "Why do we have to know so much about Thatcher; isn't John Major prime minister?" The answer is simple. In this century only Thatcher held power for as long as eleven years. David Lloyd George and Winston Churchill led with the vigor and authority of Thatcher, but neither established a political legacy. Each of the men became prime minister because he appeared to have the qualities necessary to lead the country to victory in war—Lloyd George in World War I and Winston Churchill in World War II. Mrs. Thatcher gained power when the nation was engaged in combat with itself. She set out to right the balance between free enterprise and the role of the state in favor of the former. She became increasingly radical as she progressed. She exerted a powerful influence on the leadership in her party. When she left office, not a single member of her cabinet had served in her initial cabinet. She had eliminated every retread from the previous Conservative epoch.

Furthermore, the best and brightest of the young members of Parliament who had gained seats in the House of Commons in the 1983 and 1987 elections held a strong allegiance to Thatcherism. Indeed many of the new Conservative members elected under Major's leadership in 1992 viewed themselves as Thatcherites first. After the Conservatives won the 1987 election, Thatcher mused about her leading the United Kingdom into the twenty-first century. She will not. However, her definition of the role of the state has permeated every dimension of governance in modern Britain. It even has caused the Labour Party to transform its positions on the division between enterprise and the state. The effects of Thatcherism will be felt for decades to come.

CONSTITUTIONAL UNCERTAINTIES

The United Kingdom, unlike the United States and most other advanced democracies, lacks a *written* constitution. It does, of course, have a constitution. Every nation must have principles and rules determining the structure of government, its operations, and how its authorities—elected and appointed—assume and exercise power. However, no central document specifies the elements of these principles and rules for the United Kingdom. Instead they reside in acts of Parliament, judicial decisions that interpret these statutes within common law, and conventions that effectively enjoy the standing of law. In this context, common law encompasses the British tradition whereby judges take into consideration the legal treatises of great jurists and the successive decisions of courts before rendering a decision. It can come into play both when judges determine the applicability of specific statutes to individual cases and when they make rulings that derive their entire force from custom.

The absence of a written constitution presents especially serious difficulties in the field of human rights. The vast majority of advanced democracies have enumerated the fundamental protections of individuals in one document—for example, the U.S. Bill of Rights—and enshrined these in their formal constitutions. This practice tends to focus judicial interpretation on one central document that enjoys clear paramountcy over statutes, common law, and constitutional conventions. It also provides greater protection against arbitrary majority rule. That is, people wishing to modify the enshrined rights of individuals must, in most such systems, garner support appreciably beyond simple majorities of the legislators in the national government.

The British do not find themselves utterly devoid of individual protections against arbitrary action by the government. These simply have not been collected in a single succinct document, much less one that enjoys paramountcy over acts of Parliament. Not even the 1215 Magna Carta or the 1689 Bill of Rights satisfy these criteria. The Magna Carta states a constitutional principle that attained royal assent, the Bill of Rights is a mere act of Parliament. Both documents focus on the limits to the monarch's powers: first, in relation to the accepted customs of the realm—including what we now call "common law"—and second, with respect to Parliament.

Notwithstanding this peculiar arrangement, the British system places great stock in what is called "the rule of law." This refers to the entire complex of unwritten protections provided to individuals in Britain against arbitrary government. These include the following principles:

Individuals have a right to legal advice and to full knowledge of the provisions of the law.

The government must base its actions on the law and cite specifically what in it has been breached whenever arresting individuals.

Only an impartial tribunal can establish whether an individual has in fact violated the law.

Existing law—not the transient wishes of the government—must guide judicial judgment.

In theory, the rule-of-law concept involves a transaction between the government and citizens. On the one hand, it evokes from citizens a high degree of voluntary compliance with specific laws. On the other, it sustains an environment in which individuals feel secure that they will be prosecuted only if they violate the law.

As has become patently clear in some countries, not even an enshrined charter of individuals' rights can offer absolute protection from arbitrary rule. Thus we should not ascribe mystical power to written bills of rights. And we should acknowledge that the British constitutional system knows few rivals in the effective protection of individual rights. As we will see, however, Britons increasingly believe that their rights should be enshrined in a single document. In addition, Britain's membership in the Council of Europe gives its citizens recourse to Europe's Convention on Human Rights.

The lack of clarity in the distribution of government powers among its branches is another characteristic of Britain's unwritten constitution. In fact, the executive, legislative, and the judicial branches are all interconnected. Convention dictates that members of the cabinet belong to Parliament—in either the House of Commons or the House of Lords. This arrangement assures that members who exert executive authority either collectively (in consultation with their cabinet colleagues) or individually (as ministers responsible for the specific actions of government departments) derive their power from the support of the legislative branch.

The *lord chancellor*, a member of the cabinet and of the House of Lords, presides over the administration of the courts in the United Kingdom, thus serving as a link among all three branches. Finally, the Judicial Committee of the House of Lords, the highest appellate body in the land, overlaps the legislative and judicial branches.

Scholars have noted that the lack of demarcation of the three branches helps make government more efficient in Britain. In this context, some American observers have looked longingly at the British system. Many believe, for example, that stronger links between Congress and the president would inevitably result in more consistent policies in the United States. Yet, the framers of the U.S. Constitution clearly opted for a division of powers on the grounds that too much unity between the branches could lead to abuse of authority—especially on the part of the executive branch. They chose to err on the side of checks and balances rather than that of consistency. And experience certainly tells us that British cabinets can rigidly adhere to policies after they have lost the support of the general populace. If it has control of the majority in the House of Commons, the government party need only fear a mandatory election every five years.

No matter how firm its hold on the House of Commons, any reasonable government will partially base its decisions and initiatives on its likely impact on voters reflected in the next election. The system offers no better device for compelling responsiveness to shifts in the electorate's will. Strictly speaking, Parliament includes the monarch as well as the House of Commons and the House of Lords. For example, every piece of legislation must obtain the assent of the monarch before it becomes an act of Parliament. Queen Anne (1702–1714) was the last monarch actually to veto a piece of legislation.

Financial bills need not attain passage through the House of Lords. The House of Commons can overrule the House of Lords on other matters as long as thirteen months have elapsed and it reintroduces the measure in a new parliamentary session. When we add to these points the fact that the courts cannot rule on an act of Parliament *ultra vires* (beyond its

legal authority), we begin to see the degree to which the power to determine the law of the land resides ultimately in the House of Commons.

This arrangement leaves most observers with the conclusion that the House of Commons expresses the will of the people more authoritatively than any other organ of government. Yet one should not leap from this observation to the conclusion that sovereignty wholly emanates from the House of Commons. If that were so, this institution would achieve much more than it does in monitoring and checking the actions of ministers and the bureaucracy.

A paradox rests at the heart of this issue. The House of Commons formally plays the decisive role in deeming what will become a law. Yet the cabinet—that is, the prime minister and the secretaries of the various government departments—determines by far the bulk of what the House of Commons will consider. It also governs the implementation of legislation. At the same time, the permanent bureaucracy retains control over the day-to-day functioning of departments. Higher civil servants also use their detailed knowledge of the operation of policies to advise ministers on the most expedient means for fulfilling the political agenda.

Both the cabinet and the permanent bureaucracy function behind a veil of secrecy. On the grounds that they serve as custodians of the interests of the state, they deliberately conceal much of what they do even from parliamentary surveillance. Thus the prime minister and cabinet ministers determine what even members of Parliament should know about the actual operation of the executive branch. Party discipline, coupled with a strong tradition of deference, make it relatively easy for the executive branch to keep detailed information on sensitive matters from members of Parliament on the grounds that full disclosure would damage the state. Party discipline is the tradition whereby British members of Parliament attempt to maintain a united front by not publicly criticizing the leadership of their respective parties. This is usually strongest among members belonging to the party from which the "government of the day"—that is, the prime minister and cabinet secretaries—is drawn. Members from the party that has formed the government will think twice before questioning its performance in a way that might undermine its support.

This entire emphasis on secrecy and discipline points up a simple fact: the formal paramountcy of the House of Commons disguises a considerable confusion over sovereignty. Everyone gives due obeisance to the principle of parliamentary supremacy. Yet bureaucrats behave very much as the custodians of the secrets of the crown—from which they trace their lineage, and ministers work out the parliamentary game plan with minimum consultation— even of fellow members who belong to the government party. Thus in practice, sovereignty divides at least three ways. Permanent officials, clinging to the monarchical legacy, try to exert effective custodianship of the administrative apparatus. Cabinet ministers, invoking their retention of the confidence of the House of Commons, define the contours of the vast majority of measures that will be set before Parliament. The House of Commons technically has the last say. Any substantial shifts in public opinion do not normally manifest themselves in legislation unless the cabinet has voluntarily adapted its positions or an election results in a new government party.

A LOOK AT THE PRESSURE POINTS IN THE CONSTITUTIONAL SYSTEM

Obviously, the United Kingdom's constitutional system is a huge topic. Identifying all of the areas where it has experienced special strain goes far beyond the scope of this chapter. However, we can focus on a few areas that exemplify the ways in which new and unre-

solved constitutional issues have emerged. These include the following developments:

1. an erosion of party discipline, which has made it somewhat more difficult for recent governments to deliver their legislative programs with the "efficiency" that we normally ascribe to the British parliamentary system;

2. the decline of the creative dimensions to the adversarial dynamics between the government party and the other parties making up the "loyal opposition"; and

3. the pressures from unfavorable decisions by the European Court on Human Rights, along with growing concerns within the United Kingdom about individual protection, raise serious questions about whether Parliament should enact a British bill of rights.

The Decline of Party Discipline

Strict party discipline has become so central to the British political landscape that many observers had forgotten how recently it had entered the scene. In the middle part of the nineteenth century, prime ministers had to logroll to obtain parliamentary support. That is, they had to negotiate with factions within their and other parties to secure victory in votes of the House of Commons. With the gradual extension of the franchise, in the latter part of the last century and the early part of this, parties became the focal points of mass action and machine politics. It is only with the full blossoming of the electronic era in the past few decades that parties have lost their old touch in delivering the vote. As well, the example of more interventionist legislatures—preeminently the U.S. Congress—has put pressure on the leadership within British political parties to provide members of Parliament greater freedom.

We will examine in greater detail in another chapter the degree to which party discipline has declined in the House of Commons. However, specific cases and several important studies provide clear indications of a substantial shift in the willingness of members of Parliament to adhere to strict party discipline—that is, to temper all public criticism of their leadership and to refrain from voting at variance with their party's official stances.[1] For recent Labour governments—1964–1970 headed by Harold Wilson, and 1974–1979 led by Wilson until 1976, when James Callaghan took over—these changes in attitudes of members of Parliament actually resulted in defeat on several important pieces of legislation. For Edward Heath (prime minister from 1970 to 1974), they produced in 1972 a near failure on the European Communities Bill and forced embarrassing amendments to the Industry Bill.

Even Thatcher had to weather stiff backbench opposition from her own party. Not only was she forced to alter legislation, ultimately she was impelled to resign. In May 1980, she had to withdraw a key provision in legislation imposing trade sanctions against Iran. The provision had specified that the measure would apply retroactively. The whips found that enough Conservative members opposed the provision that the entire bill might fail to win the approval of the House of Commons. In July 1985, she saw her majority of 140 cut to a mere 17 votes in the wake of a Conservative backbench revolt against pay raises of up to 46% for the most senior civil servants. Forty-eight of her members had voted against her—even after the chief whip had cautioned dissenters that she might resign over the issue. In December 1986, her environment minister reversed himself on important elements of a new formula for deciding the size of grants from the government to local authorities. Some fifty backbenchers had threatened a revolt.

Ultimately, waning party discipline cost Thatcher her job. Frontal attacks in the House of Commons from former cabinet members Michael Heseltine and Geoffrey Howe on That-

cher's European policy began her fall. Stealth maneuvers by backbenchers in support of John Major and Douglas Hurd as potential party leaders clinched it. When Michael Heseltine and Prime Minister Thatcher faced off in the former's challenge for the Conservative Party leadership, Thatcher received fifty-two more votes than her opponent, but that fell four votes short of the majority required to secure her position. A second ballot was slated. Before it was taken, Thatcher, at the urging of several of her ministers, resigned as leader of her party and, therefore, as prime minister. She retired to the backbenchers—contributing her share to party discipline's decline until she went to the House of Lords in 1992.

John Major, after election as leader of the Conservative Party, faced revolts from the former prime minister and other backbench members of Parliament. Dissension by Conservative backbenchers caused Major to do a 180-degree turn on his initial support of a policy regarding a per capita local government levy known as the "poll tax." In Parliament, Margaret Thatcher attacked Major's dissension on the poll tax, characterizing it as "a step on the road to ruin." In addition, the former prime minister also caused a profound split in the Conservative Party with her adamant opposition to the 1992 Treaty on European Union (or the Maastricht Treaty). In an interview with a European newspaper, she dubbed the treaty a "ruinous straitjacket" for Britain's political and economic freedom.

A divided Conservative Party has reduced the government's capacity to pursue market policies. In October 1992, for example, the government's determination to shut down almost half of Britain's coal pits (31 pits with 30,000 miners' jobs) brought a widespread revolt among Conservative members. The cabinet itself forced Michael Heseltine, the powerful president of the Board of Trade, to back off from the policy that he had previously characterized as "irreversible." Conservative mem-

John Major has never totally mastered how to contend with Margaret Thatcher's opposition to his policies.

bers, threatening to break the government's majority, forced the cabinet to make a U-turn in what was seen as a central piece of its energy policy. In the summer of 1993, the principle of party discipline faced another blow at the hands of Conservatives who were unhappy with the Maastricht Treaty. A bill intended to provide parliamentary approval of the treaty failed to pass the House of Commons. This forced Major to resort to royal assent as the sole legitimizing instrument for Britain's acceptance of Maastricht.

Obviously, the ground rules have changed for the level of loyalty that parties require of their members. The exact implications of these developments will become clear in Chapter 9. However, three points have attained such overarching importance that we should keep them in focus throughout our assessment of contemporary British government and politics. First, we can no longer ascribe the degree of effi-

ciency to the British system that it formerly manifested. That is, the benefits associated with the unity between the executive and legislative branches no longer reveal themselves as unambiguously as they did immediately after World War II. Governments just cannot get what they want out of their members of Parliament as readily as they could formerly. As demonstrated by the fall of Margaret Thatcher, members may even wield an ax over a prime minister.

Second, events have not spared the opposition parties of a similar depletion of loyalty. In fact, 27 of the 28 members who had joined the newly formed Social Democratic Party, from its creation in 1981 to the dissolution of the 1979–1983 Parliament, had been elected under the Labour banner. And internal struggles between the left and right of the Labour Party continue to hobble its role as the official opposition. Before the last general election in 1992, a strong yearning for power, as well as then Labour leader Neil Kinnock's political savvy, kept the party united on the surface. And rifts persisted under his immediate successor, John Smith.

Third, over the past two decades governments have had to make concessions to members' demands for greater scrutiny of executive branch initiatives and administration. The enhancement of the committee system in the House of Commons stands as the major effort at such accommodations. The result is the emergence for the first time in the British Parliament of specialized legislative bodies modeled after U.S. congressional committees. The British variants have a long way to go before they even approximate their American counterparts. However, these committees have asserted themselves with increasing effectiveness by tirelessly challenging the traditional privileges of ministers and the secrecy of permanent officials. The number of major committees in the House of Commons has grown from only two (Public Accounts Committee and Estimates Committee) prior to the 1960s, to twenty-six in 1994. These twenty-six include sixteen Departmental Select Committees. The purpose of the select committees is to "examine the expenditure, administration and policy of the principal Government Departments." Over the years, these committees have enhanced their ability to generate public interest, attract the attention of members of Parliament, examine witnesses, and issue credible reports. Members of all political stripes have joined in the task of improving the House of Commons' surveillance of the executive branch.

It is difficult to ascertain exactly where the relaxation of party discipline and the accompanying assertiveness of the House of Commons are taking parliamentary government. The developments do suggest that Americans should exercise more caution in asserting that British governments find it vastly easier to win their way with Parliament than do U.S. administrations with Congress. Also we perhaps should

put less of a premium on "efficiency" in extolling the virtues of the British system. Over the past two decades of emergent assertiveness among members, backbench rebellions have actually diverted governments from stances that would have deeply antagonized voters.

Hard Times for Adversarial Creativity

British observers have not all agreed that party discipline of the type that prevailed through much of this century actually served democracy. Some have believed that voting unfailingly with one's party demeans a member of Parliament, impinging on the principle that legislatures derive their legitimacy from the fact that their members serve at the pleasure of the electorate in specified constituencies.

In classic terms, the argument comes down to whether elected representatives serve as *delegates* or *trustees*. If the former, then they must always vote according to the will of the constituents they represent. If the latter, they can choose to vote according to other criteria, using representational discretion. This allows them to choose what they discern to be best for their constituencies, independent of their assessment of the electorate's will. Such discretion provides the framework in which members choose to bow to strict discipline in the interests of their party and the nation.

Despite their growing self-assertiveness, British members of Parliament, unlike U.S. senators and representatives, still usually fit themselves into the trustee mold. Most justify this on the grounds that their party, in order to retain or gain power, must present a united front. And invoking the received wisdom, they argue that partisan coherence ultimately provides the type of government necessary for effective pursuit of the national interest.

Within the somewhat more rigid format than prevails in the U.S. Congress, the style of politi-

---

Your representative owes you, not his industry only, but his judgment; and he betrays, instead of serving you, if he sacrifices it to your opinion.

Source: Edmund Burke, *Letter to his Constituents in Bristol,* 1774.

---

cal discourse in the House of Commons follows relatively adversarial contours. The prime minister, members of the cabinet, and members of Parliament in the government party must defend their policies to the hilt. Only reluctantly will they acknowledge defects in the design of legislative initiatives or the execution of existing policies. By the same token, members of the opposition parties must find fault with the government, no matter how reasonable its proposals or how effective and efficient its handling of the affairs of state.

To the American visitor, the actual acting-out of these adversarial roles in the House of Commons might appear to be simply high theater. But many Britons staunchly defend these dynamics, believing that they result in a creative tension through which the government knows that its proposal and administration of policies must withstand even unreasonable criticism. Meanwhile, the opposition finds in the adversarial House of Commons a vital forum for championing the causes of regions, groups, and individuals with grievances against the government.

More important, opposition parties try to turn the confrontational dynamics to their advantage in an overarching strategic process. This involves convincing voters that the government party has done so badly that it does not deserve a renewed mandate in the next general election.

To win sufficient votes away from the government party, an opposition party must convince the electorate that it will pursue superior policy objectives and run a more effective and efficient government. That is, it must become a credible choice in the minds of the voters. Of the opposition parties, only Labour comes close to presenting itself as a viable alternative to the Conservatives. In the elections of 1983 and 1987, the Alliance—an amalgam of the Liberals and the Social Democrats, now called simply the Liberal Democrats—attained neither the unity nor the number of members of Parliament necessary to challenge the Conservatives seriously. After a formal merger and now under one banner, the party and its leader—Paddy Ashdown—presented no real threat of forming a government in 1992, either. Labour's swing toward the center has drawn down the Liberal Democrats' constituency, and the Conservatives' "kinder and gentler" approach under John Major appropriated many of the ideas behind the Liberal Democrats' promise of a "social market economy."

The case of the Labour Party poses a more serious question with very significant possible consequences for the operation of the parliamentary system in the United Kingdom. Since the late 1970s, Labour has found itself under heavy fire on both flanks. The troubles started with the growing dissent among far-left elements of the party. This contributed greatly to the defections from Labour of the twenty-seven members of Parliament previously mentioned who joined the Social Democratic Party after its formation in 1981. The fractiousness of the far left also contributed to the eventual resignation of the Labour leader, Michael Foot, who served from 1980 to 1983 as James Callaghan's immediate successor.

As suggested by the vastly superior 1987 election campaign to that of 1983, Neil Kinnock managed to restore a semblance of order to Labour. Five years later, by appealing to the center of British politics—promising unified, popular policies, and playing on Conservatives' woes—Kinnock and his brain trust moved Labour ahead of the Conservatives in the polls and to victory in several important

If people could be sure that we would never have another socialist government, increasing state control, increasing control of ownership . . . then I think the prospects for this country would be really bright . . . and if only we could get rid of socialism as a second force and have two [parties that] fundamentally believed that political freedom had to be backed by economic freedom . . . I think you could get another realignment in British politics . . . After two more victories.

Source: Margaret Thatcher in an interview with the *Financial Times*, November 19, 1986.

by-elections (interim elections that fill vacancies in the legislative branch). This did not mean, however, that he reined in the left completely; and this exposed the party to continued frontal assault from the Conservatives. The attacks went beyond the Conservatives, who incessantly incanted catch phrases like "Looney Left" to remind voters that Kinnock still had not gained complete control of his party. They extended to explicit efforts to press the view that the Labour Party did not present a viable and practical option and could no longer serve as the nation's alternative government party.

A fundamental convention of British parliamentary democracy is that the main opposition party is construed as the "loyal opposition." It derives its legitimacy from the fact that—while advocating different positions from the government party—the main opposition party strives always to base its criticism on its rendering of the national interest. During her term, Thatcher increasingly attacked Labour's exercise of this prerogative. She maintained that the advances of the welfare state after World War II must be rolled back radically if Britain is to adapt to its transformed economic circumstances. Even the threat of a government sympathetic to "state socialism" would make it impossible for Britain to realize its full potential as an economic power.

John Major has not to date attacked Labour in such strident tones. However, he has consistently characterized it as the high-tax, high-spend party—a line that proved useful to Republicans in the United States until November 1992. He has asserted that Labour's promises for increased spending in health and housing, pension benefits, education, infrastructure, and overseas aid were leftovers of a discredited socialist doctrine and would bankrupt the government or require greatly increased taxes. In any case, such government intervention would not allow efficient production in the marketplace. The post election 1992 budget of the Conservatives—issued March 16, 1993—removed one prong of this attack by greatly increasing taxes.

Unease About Life Without a Bill of Rights

The growing evidence strongly suggests the need for some sort of action toward stronger protection of human rights under the British constitution. The building pressures come both from unfavorable decisions of the European Court on Human Rights, and from recurrent episodes in which the government or the courts in Britain reveal serious insensitivity to the requirements of individual liberties.

Britain has allowed individual citizens to take their cases to the human rights court since 1966. Since then, the number of registered applications to the European Commission of Human Rights concerning the United Kingdom has risen to more than 200 by 1991.

Between the time of its first verdict—1975—and 1989, the European Court on Human Rights ruled against the British government in 23 of 37 cases. No other European government has had so many cases referred and suffered so many negative judgments.[2] The cases largely concerned the rights of detainees and prisoners—especially in Northern Ireland; other cases have involved corporal punishment of students, labor rights, homosexual rights, rights of mental health patients, women's rights, freedom of the press, and telephone tapping.

Britons who oppose the enactment of an indigenous bill of rights argue that this would undermine the sovereignty of Parliament. Judges would have to apply an omnibus provision enumerating fundamental liberties to each contentious case. This would contrast sharply with their traditional perceptions of their roles. Judges prefer now to view themselves as simply ascertaining the will of Parliament as embodied in legislation addressed to specific areas of law. An overarching bill of rights would place judges in the position of having to reconcile conflicts between an act of Parliament that itemizes fundamental constitutional guarantees and other statutes. In applying the law to specific cases, they would find themselves in a new predicament: they would probably have to overrule certain acts of Parliament on the grounds that the acts did not adhere to the bill of rights.

Notwithstanding the reluctance of many Britons to entrench individual rights in an indigenous bill, the concept of the primacy of acts of Parliament in determining legal cases has lost ground in the past decade. Unfavorable decisions by the human rights court quickened this process. If a European court takes precedence over British courts, one can logically infer that the 1950 European Convention on Human Rights enjoys primacy over any British statutes within its area of competence. However, this conclusion remained only a theoretical possibility until 1987.

In March of that year, a case heard by three Appeal Court judges brought the direct application of the European Convention on Human Rights by British courts that much closer. The case involved a woman employee's claim to equal wages for equal work. It was a bit tricky

. . . When people come to her door, not seldom accompanied by young children in desperate states and at all hours because, being in danger, they cannot go home . . . the appellant does not turn them away. . . . And what happens . . . ? She finds herself the defendant in criminal proceedings at the suit of the local authority because she has allowed the inmates of her house to exceed the permitted maximum, and to that charge, I believe, she has no defence in law. My Lords, this is not a situation that can be regarded with complacency by any member of your Lordships' House, least of all by those who are compelled to do justice according to the law as it is, and not according to the state of affairs as they would wish it to be.

Source: Lord Hailsham—a senior justice—reflecting in 1977 on the inability of the courts to assist a woman who had taken in battered women in a case in which she was charged with violating crowding restrictions in her boarding house. Cited by Budge and McKay et al., *The New British Political System*, 1985.

in that the company for whom she worked had engaged one man in a group otherwise staffed by women—to buttress its claim that the women were not being paid less than men in comparable jobs.

The British judges invoked European law—in this case, Article 119 of the 1957 Treaty of Rome—to rule that an industrial tribunal must hear the plaintiff's case. This decision stood in direct contradiction to the 1970 English Equal Pay Act that prevented such a claim. In a sense, the British judges anticipated an unfavorable ruling from the European court. Their decision paved the way for similar referrals to the European Convention on Human Rights and the decisions of the human rights court.

Parallel to their increased recourse to European law, British courts, in a series of cases, have become more wary of arbitrary actions on the part of the government. One particularly dramatic case that unfolded from 1986 to 1988 illustrates developments especially well. This involved Peter Wright, a retired member of MI5, the British intelligence and security agency that handles domestic operations. Wright attempted to publish a book in Australia detailing supposed treasonous behavior on the part of his former colleagues. Among other things, the book entailed evidence that a former head of MI5, Sir Roger Hollis, was actually a Soviet spy, and further reported an MI5 plot to overthrow Harold Wilson by creating a rumor that he was a Soviet agent.

In its effort to prevent publication of these allegations, the government faced long and unsuccessful litigation. To begin with, the Australian courts refused to accept its case that Wright had broken his obligation, as a government official, of confidentiality. They also rejected the argument that publication of his book would constitute a threat to national security. In Britain, the government had won a court injunction in 1986 against newspapers publishing the details of the contents of Wright's book.

The government's persistence in pressing the case in Britain backfired. The process followed a tortuous route that ultimately ended in failure in a succession of proceedings in several courts. For example, the head of the High Court's chancery division summarily dismissed the government's charges in June 1987. He did so because the government's arguments, if allowed, "would have subverted the basic principles of civil law and led to unacceptable restrictions on press freedom." When push comes to shove, seemingly arbitrary actions by the government have moved British judges—no matter how reluctant—into invoking broad constitutional principles, as well as the law, in arriving at their decisions.

The government's efforts to neutralize or deflect potential judicial challenges stemming from European law are better illustrated by the Patricia Hewitt and Harriet Harman case. The two women were placed under surveillance by the MI5 during the 1970s and were wrongly classified as "subversive and Communists." In 1988, the European Commission on Human Rights decided to accept applications filed by Hewitt and Harman concerning the violation of their right to privacy, citing the lack of effective remedies in the British system. Facing this and other embarrassments, the government sanctioned the 1989 Security Service Act aimed at limiting the powers given to MI5 by the Official Secret Act and providing a tribunal to hear appeals against allegedly improper or illegal acts. The effectiveness of the newly created Security Service Tribunal was, however, quite dubious since the body convened only in secret and its rulings were not subject to appeal. In December 1990, the human rights commission ruled that Hewitt and Harman's rights had been violated, but it accepted from the British authorities that the Security Service Tribunal would offer the women a remedy. Ten months later, the tribunal, citing an ambiguous clause of the 1989 Security Act, dismissed the case, ruling that it had no powers to act on files opened before 1989. The government's handling of the Hewitt-Harman case made it clear that the British authorities are less than eager to provide effective oversight of the security service and that the new legislation did not provide a "public interest" defense or an adequate substitute.

A TROUBLED ECONOMY

Political scientists talk a great deal these days about governments trying to manage the economics of decline. In other words, they are examining the process whereby mighty industrial powers such as the United Kingdom and the United States have had to cope with a diminished role for their manufacturing sectors. Americans have become familiar with the term "Rust Belt," denoting the areas of the United States in which countless factories have lost their economic viability. The decline has left entire industrial towns blighted and millions of workers out of jobs.

Britain has struggled with much more widespread abandonment of manufacturing industries than has the United States. The British postwar economy did not compete well, even when the North Atlantic enjoyed relative dominance of the world's manufacturing industries. The nation's industrial base was nearly obsolete. Neither its management nor workers excelled in comparative productivity. Thus, the United Kingdom was not adapting well to the new challenges to North Atlantic economies—especially those from Japan and other Asian countries. Further, the 1973 and 1979 energy crises struck before U.K. North Sea oil was in full flow. All of these factors added up to one seemingly unavoidable outcome. Britain ran the risk of becoming one huge rust belt.

Numerous American columnists, ranging from conservatives like George Will to liberals like David Broder, wrote stories for their U.S. readership on the 1987 British election campaign. The election itself marked Thatcher's triumphant assumption to a third term—an event unprecedented by any prime minister in this century. In unison, the American commentators extolled the success of Thatcherism in articles laced with catch phrases and statistics lifted right off Conservative Party campaign literature. Thatcher had brought Britain back, they proclaimed. British economic growth had been outstripping that of any other Western European nation. And the government's privatization of several former state enterprises—British Telecom and British Gas, for example—had stemmed the tide of socialism. That is, the acquisition of shares in former state corporations by citizens who previously owned no stocks had brought about a surge of "popular capitalism."

One does not like to dampen enthusiasm. However, Britain had a long way to go before it was "back" in 1987, and still does. In fact, current indications suggest that it has contin-

ued to lose ground. This section will examine the issue of economic decline and recovery in the United Kingdom. It will first ascertain how the English economy stacks up in comparison to other Western European powers. It will then look at how Thatcherism differed from the approaches to economic management for other postwar British governments. It will assess the effects of Thatcherism on regional and social disparities in the way in which economic goods are distributed in Britain. Finally, it will appraise John Major's inheritance from Margaret Thatcher, along with Labour's aspirations to seize power.

The Patient Was Getting Better, but then Had a Relapse

During the 1987 campaign, the Conservative Party made much of what at first blush appeared to be an astounding set of statistics. Apart from Japan's and Denmark's, Britain's economy had grown faster since 1981 than any other industrial nation's. Further, the rise in overall productivity—the average yield from one worker's labor—had outstripped that of all other industrialized nations except Japan. In manufacturing industries, productivity actually increased in the United Kingdom more than in any other developed economy in the West.

In assessing the significance of this achievement, one must keep in mind an important omission. Thatcher's government began in 1979, *not* 1981. The British economy went into a precipitous decline from the end of 1979 through 1980. Although associated with a world recession, the dive owed much of its sharpness to the policies of the new government. These included an increase of the value-added tax—a form of sales tax—to 15 percent, deep cuts in public expenditure, and stringent interest rates designed to harness the money supply. As illustrated by Figure 4.1, the cumu-

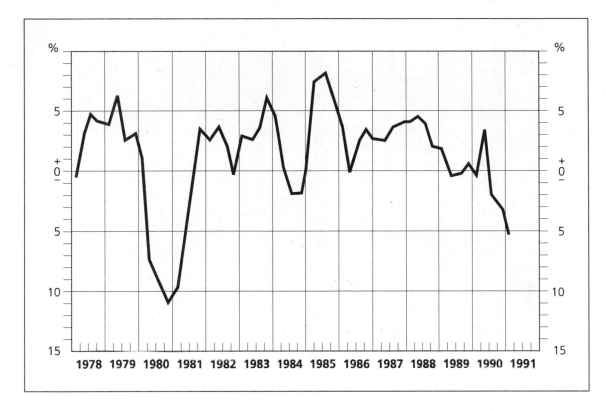

Figure 4.1 Industrial Production in the United Kingdom (percent of changes from the prior year). Based on index of output of the production and construction industries.   Source: *The Economist Diary,* 1992. © 1992 The Economist Newspaper, Ltd. Reprinted with permission.

lative impact of these economic depressants hit industrial production especially hard.

Having dug a big hole for Britain in 1979, Thatcher claimed in the 1987 Conservative campaign a full reversal of the United Kingdom's economic fortunes. However, statistics from a host of reputable sources, including Lloyds Bank, the National Institute of Economic and Social Research, and even the government's Central Statistical Office, all presented a substantially different picture. Between 1979 and 1981, manufacturing output fell in the United Kingdom by 15 percent. This decline resulted in the loss of 1.5 million jobs. Even by the spring of 1987, manufacturing re-

mained about 1.5 percent below its production level when the Conservatives took over in May 1979. And capital investment—expenditure of industry in its productive capacity—came in 17.5% below its 1979 level. In fact, the government failed to bring the number of unemployed below 3 million in time for the 1987 election. Its efforts fell short, despite several changes in its data calculations that were designed to make the task of achieving a figure below 3 million much easier than it would have been in 1979. In that year, there were 1.2 million unemployed Britons. In fact, economists agree that this problem has become a structural one for the British economy. By the end of the

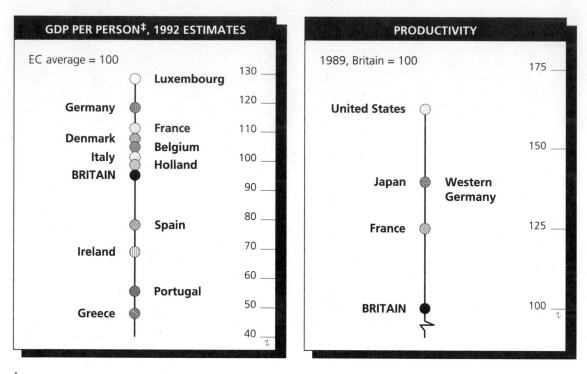

GDP PER PERSON‡, 1992 ESTIMATES

EC average = 100

Luxembourg — 130
Germany — 120
France — 110
Denmark
Italy — Belgium — 100
BRITAIN — Holland — 90
80
Spain — 80
Ireland — 70
60
Portugal — 50
Greece — 40

PRODUCTIVITY

1989, Britain = 100

175

United States — 175

150

Japan — Western Germany — 150
France — 125

BRITAIN — 100

‡Source: OCED *National Statistics*.

Figure 4.2 British gross domestic product and productivity compared. Source: *The Economist*, February 27, 1992. © 1992 The Economist Newspaper, Ltd. Reprinted with permission.

Thatcher government in 1990, unemployment had reached almost 2 million, whereas in January 1993 it had reached 2.99 million.

Thus it comes as no surprise that Britain's actual performance during Thatcher's entire tenure proved somewhat less robust, in comparative terms, than the Conservatives' analyses had suggested. Between 1979 and 1990, gross domestic product and all industrial production, which takes in manufacturing and other forms of production, grew on average 3.1% and 1.3%, respectively. In Japan, the figures were respectively 4.1% and 4.5%, and 3.5% and 3.0% in the United States. British productivity growth stayed pretty much on

its long-term, postwar average. This meant that U.S. workers were three times as efficient as their British counterparts, and Japanese, French and West German labor about 1.75 times as efficient.

Figure 4.3 puts another light on this debate. Notwithstanding the battle between the Conservatives and the opposition parties over whether Thatcherism has worked, Britons still find themselves behind many other Europeans in average income. Most of the United Kingdom maintains the same national income per person as northern Italy and the poorer parts of France. Western Germans, who trailed Britons badly in 1958, currently remain far ahead. The

Table 4.1 STATISTICS COMPARING SOME ASPECTS OF LIFE BETWEEN BRITAIN AND THE REST OF THE EUROPEAN COMMUNITY		
Latest figures available	**Britain**	**EC average**
People/square kilometer	235	146
Forest, percent of total land	9.4	23.8
Percent of people aged 60+	20.7	19.6
Average age, first marriage		
Men	25.8	27.4
Women	23.9	24.9
Doctors per 1,000 people	1.4	2.3
Enrollment in education,[1] percent	35	55
Workforce, percent in:		
Agriculture	2.2	7.1
Industry	32.6	33.2
Services	65.2	59.7
Hours worked per week[2]	43.6	40.7
Monthly earnings, two-child family[3]	1,750	1,300

[1]Immediately after completing compulsory education.
[2]One income at purchasing-power standard, net of tax.
[3]Fulltime employees, estimate excluding Italy.
Source: Europe in Figures EUROSTAT, September 22, 1992.

Italians, formerly far behind the British, have come up quickly. In fact, the Italians, claiming that their "black economy" should be taken into account, now maintain that they have surpassed Britons in per person income. (The term "black economy" refers to the portion of production that tax evaders do not report to the government.)

Compared with the rest of the countries in the 24-member Organization for Economic Cooperation and Development, Britain ranks eighteenth in per capita national output. Thus Britain is now a relatively poor European country. At the 1992 exchange rate, its per capita gross domestic product was only 94% of the European average. Estimates for 1992 show that only Spain, Ireland, Portugal, and Greece trailed Britain in gross domestic product per person.

Thatcherism as an Experiment

Whatever her success, Margaret Thatcher's management of the British economy departed radically from that of other prime ministers, whether Conservative or Labour, since World War II. This section will explore how her approach differed from previous approaches. The next section will examine what the early returns from various segments of British society tell us about who has lost and who has gained from fifteen years of unbroken Conservative rule.

The consensus that guided British governments from 1945 to 1979 took its roots in developments in the 1930s. In the early part of that decade, *classic monetarism* prevailed. This view held that only a strong currency could provide sufficient confidence in the economy to foster

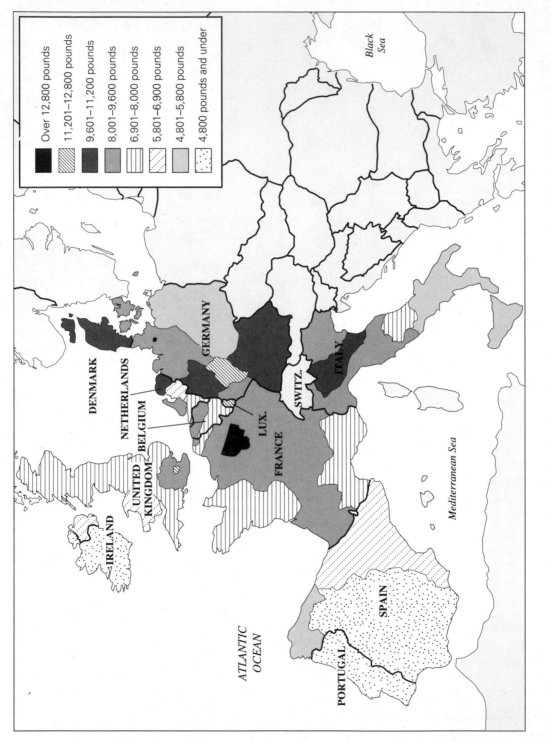

Figure 4.3 Income per person—by region (converted to pounds sterling at the average exchange rate for 1992).   © 1992 The Economist Newspaper, Ltd. Reprinted with permission.

Table 4.2 COMPARISON OF OECD NATIONAL OUTPUT PER CAPITA	
1990 GDP per capita in dollars	
United States	21,449
Switzerland	20,997
Luxembourg	19,340
Canada	19,120
West Germany	18,291
Japan	17,634
France	17,431
Sweden	16,867
Denmark	16,765
Austria	16,620
Finland	16,453
Belgium	16,405
Italy	16,021
Australia	15,951
Norway	15,921
Iceland	15,851
Netherlands	15,766
United Kingdom	15,720
New Zealand	13,258
Spain	11,792
Ireland	10,659
Portugal	8,389
Greece	7,349
Turkey	3,316

Source: Organization for Economic Cooperation and Development, *OECD 1990 Survey,* December 1990. Used by permission.

industrial development. The National Government, a broad coalition consisting of Conservative, National Labour, Liberal National, and Liberal members of Parliament, stressed economic policies that influenced the margins of industrial activity. However, the 1930s did mark a gradual acceptance among political leaders of the need to regulate certain sectors of industry and agriculture. Also the planning movement, which argued that government had to take a more active role in reconciling

industry and the needs of society, took on growing importance.

The theories of John Maynard Keynes entered the picture by the mid-1930s. Economies, Keynes maintained, could fulfill currency stability for extended periods without fully utilizing their resources. One of the resources most likely to remain untapped was labor. Such a situation spelled protracted periods of unemployment for many workers. Governments, however, could override this inertia by raising the threshold of equilibrium between prices and demand. Within limits, they could increase expenditure in order to enhance demand. The resulting stimulation of industrial production would reduce unemployment.

To varying degrees, all of the postwar governments before Margaret Thatcher's followed Keynesianism. Similarly, they also embraced both the welfare state and state ownership of key industrial sectors. The Labour government between 1945 and 1951 under Clement Attlee greatly increased social services, especially through the creation of socialized medicine under the National Health Service in 1946. Although other public-sector enterprises already existed, the same Labour government had by 1949 nationalized the central bank (the Bank of England), coal, civil aviation, electricity, railways and canals, gas, and iron and steel. Significantly, the Conservative governments that followed Labour from 1951 to 1964 made no substantial efforts to scale down the welfare state. And they maintained all of the newly acquired public-sector enterprises except trucking and iron and steel. Labour renationalized iron and steel during Harold Wilson's 1964–1970 government.

Until the mid-1970s, a consensus between the two parties prevailed on both prongs of the interventionist state: social programs and public-sector enterprises. Within a Keynesian framework, this meant that two engines drove successive governments' use of public expenditure to stimulate economic growth. The resulting thrust forced governments of both stripes to claim for the state increasing shares of the gross domestic product. For example, the Conservative government under Edward Heath contributed the lion's share of the enhancement of the state's portion of gross domestic product from 40.5% to 46.4% between 1970 and 1974. Even under Thatcher, the same figure grew from 44% to 48% in response to pressures for expenditure brought on by a precipitous drop in industrial production and the emergence of double-digit unemployment for the first time since 1938.

The state's seemingly insatiable appetite for ever-larger claims on gross domestic product spawned profound worries about the decline of private enterprise in the United Kingdom. Within the right wing of the Conservative Party, these became especially intense after Edward Heath's total failure to reverse the tide. There emerged a core group of disaffected Conservatives who were intensely dedicated to the idea of reintroducing private-sector market forces to diverse fields of British life that had come under government dominance. By 1974, the movement congealed under the leadership of Sir Keith Joseph, a secretary of state for Health and Social Security under Heath who had become utterly disillusioned with efforts simply to control the size of government.

The market-oriented Conservatives drew upon a special resource. Under Joseph's leadership, they developed a think tank called the Centre for Policy Studies. This highly partisan research organization received Margaret Thatcher's full blessing when she assumed the Conservative leadership in 1975. It also began to eclipse the Conservative Research Department as the principal source of policy proposals and analyses for the party's leadership in Parliament. By 1977—two years before the Conservatives returned to power—Joseph won a consensus document from the principal members of the shadow cabinet concerned with economic policy. The Conservative Party had

The current round of unemployment under John Major has hit the relatively wealthy South of England worse than the North. Young educated people—many of whom did extremely well during the Thatcher years—now have to cope with prolonged joblessness.

abandoned Keynesianism in favor of *monetarism* and a centrist position on the role of the state in favor of a market-oriented view.

The Thatcher and Major governments' actual follow-through with this ideological shift has proven uneven. This does not mean that the shift has failed to work momentous effects on the distribution of wealth through various segments of British society, as will become clear in the section that follows. To begin with, the Conservatives relaxed their monetarist views in 1981 when it became clear that excessively high interest rates had both greatly exacerbated the 1980 decline and made recovery much more difficult. They also secured a pre-election economic boom in 1986 by encouraging a 15% deflation in the value of the British pound. This gave British goods added competitiveness in foreign markets. The move, combined with increasing debt-financed consumer spending, eventually resulted in too much expansionary pressure, leading the economy to overheat. Chancellor of the Exchequer Nigel Lawson had masked his expansionary moves in such a way that businesses did not perceive a need for increased inventories. Thus suppliers were unprepared for the increase in demand, and upward pressure was exerted on prices and interest rates. The "Lawson Boom" started with pragmatic cuts in interest and exchange rates, but ended in a balance of payments deficit and inflation.

After the Lawson fiasco, the Thatcher government decided to fight inflation by raising interest rates—they peaked at 15.07% in the fourth quarter of 1989. The cost of this decision was a deep economic recession.

In October 1990, a month before her resignation, Thatcher reluctantly decided to incorporate Britain in the European Community's Exchange Rate Mechanism. The Conservatives now argued that added discipline in the fight against inflation would be achieved by linking the pound to currencies with a proven track record of low inflation (for example, the German mark). However, on September 16, 1992, after what was called "Black Wednesday," the British government was forced to retire the pound from the Exchange Rate Mechanism. The withdrawal of the pound amounted to an automatic devaluation, leaving the government free to cut interest rates (floating the sterling)—which it did—to spur economic growth.

This change demonstrated a lack of long-term economic strategy aimed at reaching last-ing recovery or real economic performance. John Major's short-term interest was to stimulate the economy for political purposes.

The residual effects of the 1980 decline—much more than cuts in government expenditure—have made people on the lower rungs of the socioeconomic ladder somewhat worse off than they were in 1979. This is mostly due to the large number of the less well positioned who cannot find jobs. Cuts in government programs have appreciably lowered the level of social security and services like health and education. However, the Conservatives have stopped short of full abandonment of any major social program. Instead, Margaret Thatcher and John Major have attempted to reweave Britain's social safety net. During her third term, Thatcher announced several new initiatives designed to finish the work of subsuming social provision under the "enterprise culture." These reforms sought to restructure the health care, housing, and education systems radically. In spite of his initial criticism of "economic individualism without social responsibilities," John Major has continued his predecessor's social policies. In education, Major's government has sought to further the opt-out system. Under that plan, public schools can choose to be grant-maintained without undergoing supervision by the local authorities. In health care, the government launched in April 1991 what is considered the most expansive reform since the National Health Service's inception in 1948. Fifty-seven hospitals were allowed to become "self-governing trusts," semiautonomous institutions that compete for funds given to districts and family doctors by the National Health Service. The government argued that the reform amounted to the introduction of a market mechanism at the level of health care. It would take power away from the center and give it to patients who now would be free to choose the most "attractive" hospitals and services. The reform has not, however, solved the already-chronic underfunding of the National Health

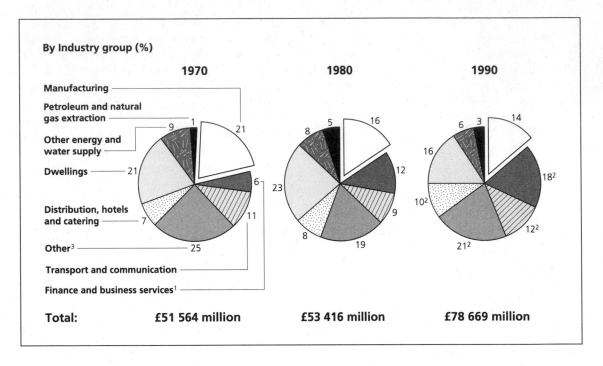

By industry group (%)

Manufacturing

Petroleum and natural gas extraction

Other energy and water supply

Dwellings

Distribution, hotels and catering

Other[3]

Transport and communication

Finance and business services[1]

1970

1980

1990

| **Total:** | **£51 564 million** | **£53 416 million** | **£78 669 million** |

Figure 4.4   Gross fixed capital investment in the United Kingdom (millions of pounds at 1985 prices).   Source: *The Economist Diary*, 1992. © 1992 The Economist Newspaper, Ltd. Reprinted with permission.

Service. With upward of 1 million people waiting for operations at any given time, the trusts—on course to account for 95 percent of hospitals and community services by 1994—have been quick to cut jobs or divert staff to create profitable enterprises. Therefore, the immediate consequence of the reform has been a *de facto* rationing of health care.

As already noted, the market-oriented dimension to the Conservative approach has also manifested itself most in the state divesting itself of corporate assets. This process has involved the selling of shares in such public-sector enterprises as British Aerospace, British Telecom, British Gas, British Airways, Rolls-Royce, and the British Airports Authority.

One field where the Thatcher and Major governments clearly have not advanced according to plan is taxation. After dramatic cuts in income tax in 1979, the first year of the current

Conservative era, the government has taken a cautious approach in this area—despite its belief that cutting down on the drag that the state places on the economy requires radical changes in taxation, in addition to simply reducing expenditure in government programs and rolling back the size of public-sector enterprise. From the beginning, strict Thatcherites held that the nature of British taxation must undergo transformation, focusing on consumption and, therefore, taking the form of sales taxes such as the value-added tax. Income taxes, it was felt, operate as disincentives to working *and* saving, whereas extension of the value-added tax—even to essential goods like food—would encourage both. This approach to fiscal policy still remains unrealized in the Major administration: even when the 1993–1994 budget reduced the basic income tax rate from 25% to 20% and introduced a value-added tax on domestic fuel and power, two-fifths of consumer spending continued to be zero-rated or exempt. In addition, the government introduced an increase in the rate of national insurance contributions (equivalent to Social Security in the United States). This adds a regressive component to direct taxation. If the national insurance rate is added to the actual income tax rate, an income of £22,000 pounds is taxed at a 34% marginal tax rate; by contrast, only a 25% marginal tax rate applies to a person earning one-third more. Potentially damaging political consequences have deterred the Conservatives from pursuing their view on consumption taxation: the British electorate has historically approved the progressiveness of high income and property taxes combined with lower general consumption taxes. As was demonstrated by the poll-tax flap, any intent to tilt the balance in taxation can be catastrophic for the government.

The Costs of Thatcherism

Insofar as the Conservatives under Thatcher sought to refurbish British manufacturing, they failed. Figure 4.4 demonstrates this point dramatically. Manufacturing attracted 21% of fixed capital investment in 1970. This figure fell to 16% and 14% in 1980 and 1990, respectively. On the other hand, the portion of fixed capital investment that is attracted has grown dramatically in the finance and business services sector. It stood in 1990 at 18%, having risen in 1980 to 12% from a 1970 figure of 6%.

This outcome stands to reason. Monetarist policies have kept British interest rates at very high levels in comparison to those of other nations. This makes dealing in pounds—through the London financial houses—an especially attractive proposition. It does not mean that foreign investors have chosen to put their money into British manufacturing. The government's withdrawal from state intervention in industry has involved the dismantling

Cuts to the National Health Service in the name of efficiency and effectiveness have taken their toll in long waiting lists and, in some cases, denial of care.

of incentive systems that might have funneled more funds into manufacturing. In this regard, the tax cuts in 1979 did little to spark investment; they simply put extra cash in upper- and middle-class pockets. Government failed to provide structures whereby a substantial part of this extra money would end up in manufacturing.

It is interesting to note here that Thatcher explicitly dismissed manufacturing growth as an indicator of economic health. And the Tories (Conservatives) until recently toed that line—arguing that today's economy depends largely on the information and service sectors. In this, they failed to recognize that a nation's manufacturing base supports other economic activity. Early in 1993, John Major disavowed this view in an interview with *The Independent*.

Notwithstanding all the excitement over "popular capitalism," tax cuts and the privatization of public-sector enterprises have worked no clear effect on the distribution of wealth in the country. According to statistics released in 1990 by the Board of Inland Revenue (the equivalent of the U.S. Internal Revenue Service), the Thatcher years have actually seen an abrupt halt and reversal of the gradual deconcentration of personal wealth that had prevailed since the war. For example, the proportion of wealth held by the richest 5% of the population stood at 56% in 1966. It dropped to 52%, 39%, and 35% in 1971, 1977, and 1984, respectively. Between 1985 and 1988, it grew again to 38%.

Perhaps more distressing is the evidence that Thatcherism has deepened social divisions within the United Kingdom. The service sector gravitates toward the Southeast of England.

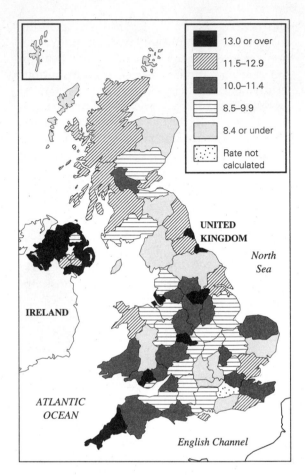

Figure 4.5   Unemployment rates in the United Kingdom (Percent, January 1991).   Source: From Department of Employment Central Statistical Office, 1992. Used by permission.

... What I want to see is the country back into growth, see us actually create new jobs ... There are areas of manufacturing where I think we can begin to re-enter, where perhaps it has fallen away in recent years. And this is not just a question of investment, it is partly a question of attitude ... We need to build a much closer relationship with industry and commerce and perhaps manufacturing industry than we have had in the past.

Source: John Major interviewed by the BBC Radio's "The World at One." Reported by Anthony Bevins of *The Independent* on January 2, 1993.

The explosive expansion of the banking and finance sector in London reflects this trend especially vividly. Meanwhile, heavy manufacturing industries have traditionally operated in the northern regions of England more than in the southern ones. As these have remained depressed, regional disparities between the North and the South have tended to take on added significance. Figure 4.5 illustrates the extent to which unemployment has taken a much greater toll in the North of England, Wales, the

Table 4.3 PER CAPITA DISPOSABLE INCOME					
	£ per capita				£ per capita index UK = 100
	1986	**1988**	**1989**	**1990**	**1990**
United Kingdom	4,644	5,537	6,140	6,703	100.0
England	4,721	5,641	6,258	6,830	101.9
North	4,235	4,962	5,448	5,920	88.3
Yorkshire and Humberside	4,402	5,123	5,691	6,373	95.1
East Midlands	4,445	5,245	5,903	6,520	97.3
East Anglia	4,570	5,524	6,166	6,793	101.3
Southeast	5,288	6,415	7,111	7,650	114.1
Greater London	5,767	6,884	7,877	—	—
Rest of Southeast	4,978	6,117	6,624	—	—
Southwest	4,732	5,468	6,703	6,779	101.1
West Midlands	4,233	5,120	5,652	6,233	93.0
Northwest	4,269	5,093	5,642	6,112	91.2
Wales	3,999	4,814	5,403	5,827	86.9
Scotland	4,473	5,209	5,710	6,290	93.8
Northern Ireland	4,407	4,790	5,325	5,795	86.5

Source: Central Statistical Office, 1992. *Regional Trends 27,* London: Her Majesty's Stationery Office.

West of Scotland, and all of Northern Ireland than it has in the South.

Table 4.3 demonstrates the relatively poor standing of every region in comparison to the Southeast in terms of personal disposable income. To cite the worst case in England proper, the North's average personal, disposable income was £1,234 pounds per head—£366 pounds less than Greater London's—in 1975. In 1988, the gap had widened to 1,922 pounds, and in 1990 reached 2,429 pounds. Put another way, disposable income in Greater London was 39% larger than that in the North in 1985, whereas the differential for the same indicator in 1988 was 44%. Disposable income in Greater London had grown from 20% to 27% above the British average between 1975 and 1985.

As the structure of the economy shifts in favor of the service sector, the relative economic positions of the North and Southeast may change. In the recession of early 1990, Britons in the Southeast fared worse than those in the North. Because of the higher concentration of service jobs in the South and the postslump sluggishness of services, the recession has hit the Southeast's economy more than it did the North's. At this point, however, Britons in the North remain worse off overall, compared to their neighbors to the south.

We will leave a more detailed examination of regional electoral behavior until chapter 5. However, we should not end our discussion of key changes in the economic context of British politics without pointing up the degree to which regional disparities have begun to reveal themselves in the deeper electoral cleavages between the North and the South. In the 1987 and 1992 elections respectively, the Southwest,

Southeast, and East Anglia gave only 6 and 16 of their 176 seats to either the Labour or the Liberal Democratic parties. As one might expect from its greater social diversity, London yielded—in 1987 and 1992, respectively—26 and 36 of its 84 seats for the opposition parties. The border areas split their tickets. West Midlands and East Midlands produced 67 of 100 seats for the Conservatives in 1987, and 53 in 1992. Further north, the Northwest and Yorkshire/Northumberland gave Labour a slight edge with 69 and 78 of their 127 seats in 1987 and 1992, respectively. Meanwhile, the North, Scotland, and Wales all gave overwhelming support to Labour. The increases in Labour's 1987 vote over the 1983 election in the Northwest, Yorkshire/Northumberland, the North, Scotland, and Wales exceeded 5% in each case.

In spite of the 1992 Conservative triumph, the comparison between the electoral results of the 1992 and 1987 elections brought good news for the Labour Party: in the south of England and the Midlands—both Conservative strongholds—the swing from Conservative to Labour voting was almost 5%, compared with 3% throughout the whole country.

John Major's Inheritance

When she resigned the leadership, Margaret Thatcher left an economy wrought with problems for her successor to manage. Unemployment, inflation, and interest rates were up; productivity, investment, and export growth were down. Her legacy was a return to stagflation—precisely the malady that her harsh policies had promised to forestall. The difficulty of balancing fiscal and monetary policy to decrease price levels and increase employment in an environment marked by interest rate coordination and budgetary constraint came home most vividly to John Major's Conservatives in September 1992, when they unceremoniously yanked the pound from the European Economic Community's Exchange Rate Mechanism.

In November of 1990, inflation in Britain stood at 9.5%. Production was down because high prices had dampened demand. The government set interest rates at 14.8% (in comparison to 13.9% a year earlier) in an attempt to stifle rising price levels. Investment, suffering from the high cost of capital reflected in financial markets, fell 18.6% in the second half of 1990. Unemployment had reached 5.8%. Indeed, it assumed a sharp trajectory that would take it beyond 10% by 1992. A worldwide recession exacerbated the difficulties of achieving a favorable trade balance through export growth.

Margaret Thatcher had fiercely opposed and then acceded to the membership in the European Monetary System. Under the Exchange Rate Mechanism, members peg the value of their currencies to one another through a managed float. This allows exchange rates to fluctuate, but only within set bands. Outside the Exchange Rate Mechanism, Britain can manipulate its interest rates to induce dramatic changes in the exchange rate for the pound. Inside the Exchange Rate Mechanism, constraints on fluctuations in the value of the pound limited the extent to which Britain could resort to adjustments in interest rates designed to induce export-driven growth.

In addition to pressures on the pound, the Major government has faced fiscal limitations. Declining economic conditions affected both the private sector and the public sector. The cost to the government of delivering social programs has increased because of two factors—increased unemployment and the added burden on entitlements due to the economic downturn. The government has needed to increase revenues, but has found it difficult to agree on a vehicle for doing so.

John Major's handling of the mixed Thatcher legacy has alternated between resolute and shaky. Major had served for a year as chancellor of the exchequer before he became prime minister. With his move from No. 11 Downing Street to No. 10, he left behind policies that comported fully with Thatcherism. As prime minister, Major—with the help of his first chancellor, Norman Lamont—struggled with the difficult task of forging an independent economic policy without appearing to abandon the broad elements of Thatcherism that had appealed so strongly to Conservative supporters.

The first Major budget (1991) would fight inflation with interest rates. As prices fell, so would the cost of capital. The economy would have to be consumer driven. The government would not increase spending. Major and Lamont gambled on stagflation ending and inflation rates falling, even at the cost of further unemployment. In a political decision, they hoped that voters would care more about the purchasing power of the pounds in their pockets than about their fellow Britons who had dropped out of the labor force.

Major also took a more conciliatory approach to the European Union. He and his advisers believed that as European markets integrated, the movement of goods and capital across country borders would bring interest rates and exchange rates in line across EU members. To handle fiscal problems, Major agreed to short-term borrowing and to a temporary increase in the value-added tax. In most other policy matters, Major was more open minded than Thatcher. He was willing to hear out his cabinet members, consult with his European partners, and take into consideration popular opinion before making his decisions.

Looking back to the 1992 election, Labour took a longer-term approach to Thatcher's departure. John Smith, from 1992 to 1994 Labour's leader but then its shadow chancellor of the exchequer, promised interest rate cuts, incentives for private investment, and retraining for displaced workers. Beyond this, Labour's policies were intentionally vague. Knowing

that the electorate viewed Labour as less competent at economics than the Conservatives, Labour forced John Major to run on his past performance while setting broad goals for future Labour government. The party pressed its promises for a more equitable Britain. A Labour government would have revitalized inner cities; set standards of pay, conditions, and equal opportunity in projects funded with public money; and spurred competitiveness by focusing on science, technology, and research. Nationally increased social spending would make everyone better off under a Labour government.

Since the 1992 election, Labour has been trying to redefine the party's ideological foundations. A young and dynamic generation of politicians has started to reestablish the party as the champion of a majority exploited by Tory-backed vested interests, such as bankers and farmers. More important, they have signaled a break with Labour's previous embrace of economic planning and public ownership of the means of production while seeking to rehabilitate the party's image in certain social areas, such as the widespread perception that Labour governments are soft on criminals. Up to his untimely death, John Smith's leadership fit this need. His successor, Tony Blair, will continue this approach.

CONCLUSION

This chapter focused on the context of British government and politics. It has dwelt on two issues. First, it has outlined the nature of the British constitution. Second, it has examined economic conditions in which the political system operates. With regard to both contexts, this chapter has highlighted ways in which relatively dramatic developments have triggered processes of change that call for adaptation within the political system.

In our treatment of its constitutional context, we saw that the British political system operates without a written document that defines structures, powers, and rights. Thus many ambiguities surround the actual legitimacy of various conventional doctrines that guide the operation of the political system.

Recently, serious questions have emerged about three elements of the constitution. First, the erosion of party discipline has threatened the ability of British government to maintain the high level of efficiency for which it became famous. However tentatively, the elements of a separation of powers between the executive and legislative branches have taken root. Access by members of Parliament to forums—notably select committees—that put government policies under closer scrutiny has strengthened this tendency.

The decline of party discipline has undermined the ability of the opposition parties to maintain the unity necessary to preserve their status as the "loyal opposition." The Conservative Party has seized upon this weakness. Along the way, it has raised questions about the future viability of the socialist Labour Party both as the "official opposition" and as the aspiring government party.

Finally, the wider European constitutional context—including the European Convention on Human Rights—has begun to impinge on the British judiciary, especially its preference for narrow legal interpretation and its deference to the sovereignty of the British Parliament. In addition, Britain has come off as less than a paragon in protection of human rights. The two developments have provoked discussion of the desirability of a written guarantee of human rights.

The examination of Britain's economic context revealed the degree to which the country has fallen behind other advanced Western systems, especially in industrial performance. This state of affairs has had serious consequences on the average Briton's standard of living.

Thatcher's revolutionary economic policies tried to redress the situation. Her policies contributed to an economic boom in the southern regions of the country. However, they also exacerbated the divide between the economic performance and well-being of the South as against the North of England, Scotland, Wales, and Northern Ireland. That Britain stood a chance of regaining lost ground in its competition with other economic powers was heartening news for people in the South during the heady days of Thatcherism. Yet the gap between their prospects and those of Britons not in the South injected a critical item for the political agenda midway through the third Thatcher term and beyond. The recession of the early 1990s brought reality crashing down, even for the South.

NOTES

1. John E. Schwarz, "Exploring a New Role in Policy Making: The British House of Commons in the 1970s," *American Political Science Review*, **74** (1980), 23–27; Leon D. Epstein, "What Happened to the British Party System?," *American Political Science Review*, 74 (1980), 9–22; Philip Norton, *The Constitution in Flux* (Oxford: Martin Robertson, 1982).

2. European Court on Human Rights, *Survey of Activities: 1959–1989*, Strasbourg, January 24, 1990.

REFERENCES AND SUGGESTED READINGS

Alderman, Geoffrey. 1989. *Britain: A One Party State?* London: Christopher Helm.

Arndt, Heinz W. 1978. *The Rise and Fall of Economic Growth*. London: Longman.

Bacon, Robert, and Walter Eltis. 1976. *Britain's Economic Problem: Too Few Producers*. London: Macmillan.

Birch, Anthony H. 1964. *Representative and Responsible Government*. London: George Allen and Unwin.

Budge, Ian, and David McKay. 1985. *The New British System: Government and Society in the 1980s*. London. Longman.

Clarke, Harold, and Paul Whiteley. 1990. "Perceptions of macro-economic performance, government support and Conservative Party strategy in Britain 1983–7." *European Journal of Political Research* 18:97–120.

Drewry, Gavin. 1975. *Law, Justice and Politics*. London: Longman.

Epstein, Leon D. 1980. "What Happened to the British Party System?" *American Political Science Review* 74:9–22.

Griffith, J.A.G. 1991. *The Politics of the Judiciary*. London: Fontana Press.

Harvey, J., and L. Bather. 1982. *The British Constitution and Politics*. London: Macmillan.

Hogwood, Brian. 1992. *Trends in British Public Policy*. Buckingham: Open University Press.

Hyman, Richard. 1992. "Trade Unions and Industrial Relations," in Catterral, P. ed. *Contemporary Britain: An Annual Review 1992*. Oxford: Blackwell.

Jowell, Jeffrey, and Oliver Dawn. 1989. *The Changing British Constitution*. Oxford: Clarendon Press.

Keegan, William, and Rupert Pennant-Rea. 1979. *Who Runs the Economy?: Control and Influence in British Economic Policy*. London: Maurice Temple Smith.

Kavanagh, Dennis. 1987. *Thatcherism and British Politics: The End of Consensus*. Oxford: Oxford University Press.

————. 1984. *Mrs. Thatcher's Economic Experiment*. Harmondsworth: Penguin.

Norton, Philip. 1982. *The Constitution in Flux*. Oxford: Martin Robertson.

————. 1985. "Behavioural Changes: Backbench Independence in the 1980s," in Catterral, P. ed. *Parliament in the 1980s*. Oxford: Blackwell.

Rush, Michael. 1990. *Parliament and Pressure Politics*. Oxford: Clarendon Press.

Schwarz, John E. 1980. "Exploring a New Role in Policy Making: The British House of Commons in the 1970s." *American Political Science Review* 74: 23–37.

Street, Harry. 1963. *Freedom, the Individual and the Law*. Harmondsworth: Penguin.

Wood, David M., and Alan R. Wood. 1992. *The Times Guide to the House of Commons*. London: Times Book.

5

Historical Background:
Likely or Unlikely Paragon

The student reading a textbook like this in the early 1960s would find a glowing report on the United Kingdom. Every other major European power had proven unequal to the task of sustaining uninterrupted democracy during this century. To be fair, France had succumbed to the Nazi conquest. Yet, the Fourth Republic—the French constitution from 1946 to 1958—had just collapsed. As for West Germany, Americans held their breath. They feared either Soviet invasion or a re-emergence of the totalitarian reflexes that had led to Nazism. Russia remained so far from democracy that one could scarcely conceive of it as a European nation.

In some respects, Britain even struck observers as surpassing the United States as a democracy. Despite sharp differences between their forms of government, Americans feel an institutional affinity with Britain. In part this is due to the many elements in the U.S. constitutional system that owe their origin to British antecedents. Although it is a constitutional monarchy, the United Kingdom pioneered the extension of representative and responsible government from the city to the nation-state. Britain lacks a written constitution—including a bill of rights. However, its common law system places strong emphasis on protection of individuals from arbitrary rule.

With this backdrop, American students in the early 1960s often heard their professors speak admiringly about numerous features of the British democracy. Students might easily have gained the impression that somehow things just worked better in Britain. The British people demonstrated better reflexes for leadership than did Americans. They seemed to manifest clearer ideas about what democracy expected from them. John F. Kennedy had to exhort Americans in his 1961 inaugural address to ask what they could do for their country rather than what their country could do for them. Britons seemed to work this out by instinct.

Britain was a lot more than simply a paragon for boosters of democracy. Notwithstanding the ravages of war, some of its industries gave competitors in other Western nations a run for their money, especially in heavy industry. Person for person, British scientists claimed more than their share of Nobel laureates. Oxford and Cambridge universities knew few rivals either elsewhere in Europe or in the United States. The compactness of the United Kingdom meant that high-quality daily newspapers— *The Times* of London, *The Manchester Guardian*—and two Sunday papers, *The Sunday Times* and *The Observer,* reached every corner of the nation. Meanwhile the majority of U.S. citizens relied on local papers whose diminishing number—which continues to this day—became painfully apparent.

Comparative studies indicated that Britons in the early 1960s did not distinguish themselves as joiners. That is, they lagged well behind Americans in active participation in community organizations, interest groups, and political parties. Yet Americans envied the tidiness of the British system. At the time the U.S. government and many of the states locked themselves in combat over social legislation and civil rights, Britain boasted a *unitary system.* That is, there was no level of government between the nation and the localities, and local

"authorities" were creatures of the national government. Further, pressures for greater self-determination in Scotland and Wales, along with the civil strife in Northern Ireland, had yet to emerge.

Along the same lines, the British party and Parliamentary systems struck many as models of what the United States had missed out on. Many states in the united States were "one-party": either the Republicans or Democrats dominated their government. Scholars described the government in Washington as a four-party system consisting of congressional Democrats and Republicans and presidential Democrats and Republicans. Many Americans had become tired of the resulting paralysis— especially those who sought a more activist federal government in economic regulation, social welfare, and civil rights. The two-party system in Britain could not have presented a more stark contrast. The two main parties— Conservatives and Labour—both had formed majority governments since World War II. Although they represented, respectively, the right and the left, each broadly supported the intervention of the state, where necessary, in the economic and the social realms.

Americans can betray an inferiority complex when dealing with Britons. Nothing would bring this out more than a comparison of how British and American bureaucracies functioned. The British one, known as Whitehall, appeared vastly more efficient. At the highest levels, it was run by career civil servants with impeccable taste and discretion. No one would think of doubting their intelligence; most of them claimed Oxford and Cambridge degrees with high honors. Whatever the abilities of American permanent public servants, the fact remained that much less predictable and reliable political appointees stood at the apexes of bureaucratic power in Washington.

In the early 1960s, Britons did a good job of concealing their decline as a world power. Americans remembered that the United Kingdom had bravely stood alone against the Nazis from the collapse of France till the United States entered World War II in 1941. Even the postwar Labour government came readily to the conclusion that Britain should stay right up there with the big boys. Thus the Labour cabinet gladly rubberstamped the decision of Clement Attlee, their prime minister, to develop an all-British nuclear deterrent. Even in the painful task of dealing with its dwindling empire, Britain showed much more grace than other fading colonial powers, seeming to recognize the writing on the wall sooner. Institutionally, Britain had left former colonies with better legacies with respect both to parliamentary institutions and to administrative machinery.

Americans also viewed Britain as the head of the Commonwealth of former colonies. This loose political alliance had a far more significant economic side: its intricate web of special trade relations preserved for Britain dependable supplies of raw materials and fixed markets for manufactured products. Observers did not grasp entirely the degree to which "commonwealth" did not equal "empire." A system of preferential tariffs fell short of the economic control that an imperial power exerts over its colonies. The empire had served as the beast of burden for Britain's domination of the world economy in the nineteenth century. In time, the United Kingdom would abandon its economic alliances with Commonwealth countries in favor of fuller integration with Europe. In a sense, it cast its imperial lot with the prospect of a European powerhouse.

The United States has not remained static since the early 1960s. Thus it should not surprise us that the Britain of today looks much different from the one just described above. However, political and historical events have occurred less convulsively than in the United States. No prime minister has been assassinated. No covert criminal activities have paralyzed a government, much less forced the resignation of a prime minister—at least, dur-

ing the past 30-odd years. No Vietnam-like, unwinnable war agonized the nation and depleted its physical and psychic resources.

Only the combination of little things tipped the balance toward change—more than appears at first blush. Even in the mid-1980s, a sense of incongruity greeted American visitors in London's Waterloo Station when they heard martial music piped over the sound system. The bowler hats, swagger-style umbrellas, and pinstripe trousers with black coats no longer appeared among the brigades of commuters; the music provided the only hint of nostalgia for a more glorious past. By the late 1980s, the streets and pedestrian underpasses even in the "posh" neighborhoods in London presented themselves as extremely dirty and littered. Today, the frequent intrusion of graffiti makes one wonder if London has headed in the same direction as New York City.

Visitors to Britain in recent years have asked themselves whether there is more psychosis in the body politic than existed in the 1960s. The verbal ramblings of taxi drivers suggests this. For example, visitors to London during the Thatcher years often heard that the prime minister is just what the doctor ordered: "We need a dictator to tell people what to do." The listener might not have thought for a moment that the prime minister had indeed become a dictator. However, such approving assertions on the part of ordinary citizens made one wonder what had happened to the paragon of civic culture. Indeed, one might even be provoked to look more carefully at the historical legacy upon which the British political system is based.

The rest of this chapter will do two things. First, it will provide a developmental history of the United Kingdom. This will highlight four central contributions of the British legacy. These are:

1. the rise of a parliament that exerted hegemony over the Crown;

2. the eventual domination of Parliament by an elected lower house;

3. the gradual—and somewhat imperfect—shift of governance from rule by nobility to rule by the monied, to rule by the people—that is, from aristocracy to oligarchy, to democracy;

4. the abandonment of laissez-faire principles in favor of the social democratic welfare state.

Second, this chapter will examine this legacy as it projects into the present. How did the glory of "what was" obscure the signs of decline? Did Britons take their democracy for granted? Has their aptitude for participation in democracy atrophied? Has the two-party system—which served the gradual adaptation of governance to new challenges so well—begun to fail? How viable are Britain's governmental institutions today? What about sovereignty in Britain—how has it been affected by the rise of nationalism in Scotland, Wales, and Northern Ireland and membership in the European Union? As the reader will be able to see, these questions will only receive detailed consideration in the chapters that follow. However, our initial discussion in this chapter will attempt to root that analysis in a sense of how Britain has come to a crossroads in its history.

A NOBLE PEDIGREE, BUT A MIXED PAST

We have an expression, "age before beauty." In some respects, American commentators have tended to ascribe to the United Kingdom's political system both qualities. Thus students might come to romanticize the legacy upon which modern British democracy stands. This section offers a brief political history of Britain. As noted above, it will look at four areas of development toward a full-fledged democracy:

Parliament's eventual hegemony over the crown,

the House of Commons's gradual ascendancy over the House of Lords,

universal suffrage's incremental triumph over oligarchy, and

the welfare state's step-by-step mollification of the social dysfunctions of classic capitalism.

The aptness of adjectives like "eventual," "gradual," "incremental," and "step-by-step" has caused many commentators to lionize Britain's political history. To be sure, many political systems—not the least of which is that of the United States—have sought to attain the same level of relatively peaceful and non-convulsive transformation that characterizes much of the United Kingdom's evolution toward democracy.

Indeed, one sometimes discerns among Americans pangs of guilt over the fact that the thirteen colonies—unlike more passive siblings like the Canadian and Australian colonies—ultimately severed their ties with Britain violently through revolution. We should not forget, however, that Britain moved too ponderously in responding to the legitimate demands of the American colonies. This fact should alert us to the possibility that British gradualism did not always function as smoothly as some would have us believe.

The Emergence of Parliament's Hegemony over the Crown

The history of parliamentary government on the British Isles takes us back to the Saxon era, which began in the fifth century A.D. Kings and subjects in this period came to accept—with breaches in observance—two conventions concerning their rule. First, kings should consult counselors on the important matters of state such as making laws or levying taxes. Second, kings alone would initiate such consultations. The counselors formed no continuous or readily identifiable body. However, they were drawn from the hierarchy of the church, the nobility, and the knights. The latter group consisted of commoners who had distinguished themselves in the service of the king—initially in military campaigns and eventually in the administration of the realm.

After the Norman conquest of England in 1066, events moved to a formalization of the consultative process. The succession of wars, including costly crusades, greatly increased the dependence of kings on taxes. Meanwhile, merchants in cities and towns began to emerge as a monied class in their own right. Kings had to devise ways of extracting funds from them. At the same time, pressures mounted among the merchants for a role in consultative processes.

In 1215, King John, under pressure from the nobility, acceded to the Magna Carta. This most revered of British constitutional documents established the Common Council of the Kingdom whose consent was now required before the monarch could levy taxes for his various "extraordinary" needs. This council ultimately became known as the House of Lords. The House of Commons emerged later in the thirteenth century as a less regularized forum for knights' and merchants' deliberations over taxes.

The power of Parliament ebbed and flowed over the next 400 years. In the long run, developments added up to a consolidation of Parliament's role. By the latter part of the fourteenth century, kings served at the pleasure of Parliament. Indeed, Parliament deposed Richard II in 1399. However, monarchs began to reassert themselves by the end of the fifteenth century. The thirty-year Wars of the Roses—civil hostilities that saw the kingdom change hands four times—had disrupted the rule of law. Henry VII, who reigned from 1485 to 1509, felt compelled to convene Parliament only seven times. The notorious Henry VIII, ruling from 1509 to 1547, saw on the other hand that Parliament could prove a strong ally in achieving his various objectives. For example, he resorted to Parliament to legitimize his campaign to achieve

This photograph of a painting by Van Dyck reflects the aggrandizement of Charles I as emperor. The king's absolutist approach to the monarchy led to his beheading.

the autonomy of the church in England from Roman Catholicism. Elizabeth I, ruling from 1558 to 1603, followed in this tradition. However, the great military expenses during her rule made her increasingly dependent on the willingness of Parliament to agree to taxes.

The Stuart period, beginning with James I in 1603, proved to be a watershed for the relationship between monarchs and Parliament. Taking a cue from their European cousins, the Stuarts attempted to aggrandize their role by invoking a divine right to rule. This included the right to override or ignore Parliament even in the imposition of taxes.

Charles I, who inherited the throne in 1625, ultimately pressed this notion too far. His contempt for Parliament led to a bitter civil war and his own beheading in 1649. An interval of extreme instability ensued. This included a regime characterized as rule by a council of state and a military dictatorship presided over by Oliver Cromwell. The period of experimentation came to an end with the restoration of the Stuarts in 1660 under Charles II. However, both Charles II and his successor, James II, took their dynasty right back into the trap that had snared their ancestors. In 1688, James II fled the country in face of what now stands in British history as the definitive repudiation of the divine right to rule.

This time Parliament left nothing to chance in filling the throne. It enacted statutes expressly to limit royal prerogatives. And it placed on the throne William III and Mary of Orange—the son-in-law and daughter of James II. Mary died in 1694. William, who ruled until 1702, eschewed the Stuarts' proclivity for divine aggrandizement.

Two statutes bore special importance in this era. The 1689 Bill of Rights enshrined the powers of Parliament in relation to the crown. Here Parliament stipulated that the crown could not enact or suspend laws, raise taxes, or maintain an army without Parliament's consent. Further, it defined the right of free speech within Parliament itself as absolute. The second measure, the 1701 Act of Settlement, set the terms for succession to the throne—including the exclusion of Roman Catholics from the monarchy. It also established that only Parliament could dismiss judges. These enactments, following as they did upon the discredited monarchical legacy left by the Stuarts, ensconced Parliament in a new position of constitutional legitimacy, enabling it, over the next 150 years, to establish unquestioned hegemony over the crown.

The Rise of the House of Commons

The House of Commons, or lower house, did not become a distinct entity within Parliament until Henry VIII's reign. Before that time, the title "House of Lords" applied to the assemblies of peers that excluded members of Parliament who belonged to neither the church hierarchy nor the nobility. As a body, the "Lords" served as the major pool from which the Tudor monarchs selected their key officeholders. When it emerged as a separate body, the House of Commons based its power on the requirement that it originate tax measures.

The turmoil of the Wars of the Roses weakened the nobility in England, and the tendency for the Tudors to look to the House of Commons for legitimization of its policies further weakened the stature of the House of Lords. On the other hand, the Stuart monarchs attempted to use the House of Lords to offset the power of the House of Commons. The former had so aligned itself with Charles I that the Council of State, which governed England immediately after the king's execution, abolished the House of Lords. The upper house reconvened (it was not formally reestablished) in 1660. However, the House of Commons soon passed legislation that sought to constrain the lords' power. A 1671 resolution denied the upper house the power to amend a tax. And a 1678 measure stipulated that only the lower house could originate bills involving expenditure of funds.

These actions did not prevent lords from resuming their previous role of providing the pool from which monarchs drew most of their ministers, including the most prominent. Even on this front, however, political expedience often forced monarchs to dip into the House of Commons to fill some key posts. In 1684, for example, William III constructed a cabinet in which four of nine ministers belonged to a powerful faction of the "Whigs." At that time, the Whig members of Parliament controlled the

House of Commons. Until early in the nineteenth century, struggles between the Whigs and the "Tories" would dominate political life in Britain. The former stood for the rights of Parliament and political reform while the latter attempted to defend royal prerogatives and the status quo.

The Tortuous Path From Aristocracy to Democracy

Even with the major advances toward entrenchment of parliamentary government during the seventeenth century, Britain remained far from a democracy. Men with significant property holdings dominated both the House of Lords and the House of Commons. Regarding the former, eighteenth-century monarchs created peerages to the point that the association of lords with "nobility" became debased. With respect to the latter, the combined efforts of monarchs and lords preordained that only those belonging to the upper ranks of the propertied or those beholden to the monied stood much of a chance of obtaining seats in the House of Commons. Even candidates for nomination required connections and resources beyond those of the average property holders and merchants. Thus the nobility still exerted immense influence over the types of people who actually put themselves forward for nomination for seats in the House of Commons. Once official nominees, candidates required the capacity to "buy" votes whenever necessary.

The Industrial Revolution in Britain intervened—beginning in the mid-eighteenth century—to alter radically the distribution of wealth among classes. Eventually industry and commerce reached levels never dreamed of by the traditional elite. A whole new breed arose of monied individuals who became restless under the yoke of aristocratic rule.

The Whigs, who had suffered a reversal of fortunes at the turn of the eighteenth and nineteenth centuries, began in the late 1820s to mobilize renewed impetus for parliamentary reform. Their attention focused on the abysmal state of representative government in Britain. A large proportion of the boroughs upon which electoral districts were based claimed fewer than a hundred voters. Two constituencies actually housed no inhabitants whatsoever. Meanwhile, communities that had flourished since the industrial revolution—especially those in the North—found themselves grossly underrepresented. Indeed, the thriving cities of Manchester, Birmingham, and Leeds sent no members to the House of Commons. The Whigs found fertile ground for the reform movement.

The Whig coalition broke through in 1832 with passage of the Reform Act. Yet, the movement to expand suffrage started modestly. To be sure, it freed up 143 seats from depopulated boroughs and shifted them to expanding centers in the North. It also liberalized the qualifications for the franchise. Tenants who rented property worth specific values would now qualify for a vote. All told, however, the measures only added just over 200,000 electors to the 400,000 or so who already enjoyed a franchise. An 1867 Reform Act further reduced qualifications for renters. An individual male householder simply had to occupy the same dwelling for a year and pay the poor tax in order to enfranchise himself. These changes extended the right to vote to virtually all working-class men who headed households in the urban areas. However, it added only about 50% to the rolls of rural voters. And the fact that secret ballots were yet to be established meant that electors in the small country areas still followed the cues of the aristocracy in casting their votes.

Parliament approved the secret ballot in 1872. The Representation of People Act of 1884 rectified the imbalances between urban and rural franchises. In the following year, the Redistribution of Seats Act set 50,000 voters as the desirable population for each electoral district and went a considerable distance toward eliminating multiple member constituencies.

The 1867 expansion of the franchise is seen as a leap into the unknown.

In absolute terms, the two most dramatic increases in the number of eligible voters came as a result of legislation early in this century. The 1918 Representation of the People Act replaced the complex array of qualifications for males with a single six-month residency requirement for the right to vote in a constituency. In keeping with the gradualist approach of the British, however, the same legislation's gesture toward extending the franchise to women stopped short of those under 30 years of age. Nonetheless, the 1918 act increased the electorate from 8 to 21 million. Ten years later, Parliament's extension of suffrage to all women 21 years old or older expanded the electorate by another 7 million. Like other advanced democracies concerned about the alienation of youth in the late 1960s, Britain enfranchised 18- to 20-year-olds in 1969.

The Inroads of Welfare Provision Against Social Ills

Today many Britons register grave doubts about the efforts of the Conservative Party under Margaret Thatcher and John Major to cut back on social programs. They believe that the state must still provide for the unemployed and sick, and see to the education of the nation's children and youths. Many fear the return of laissez-faire in which people with money and in control of enterprise give little or no consideration to the needs and rights of ordinary workers and their families.

We know that the Great Depression seared in the minds of people who grew up in America in the 1930s great anxieties about debt and a lack of financial security. Much more profoundly, the abuses of the Industrial Revolution established in the minds of working-class Britons a suspicion that unbridled capital will exploit them and then cast them on the social garbage heap. To understand these fears, we must first look at the stark reality of the nineteenth century attitude toward labor and human suffering. This will allow us to see why the shift to the socially attuned state comprised such a stunning development in the minds of many people. As well, we can access why so many Britons prize their social provision system as one of the jewels of their democracy.

A Dark Page in History.   At the time that Britain was developing parliamentary democracy, it was also receiving praise elsewhere in Europe for the liberties enjoyed by her citizens. Voltaire, for example, praised Britain to the skies for the relative security of the people from seizure of property, arbitrary arrest and conviction, and restrictions of expression through the press and speech.

Compared to continental Europeans, Britons did enjoy exceptional freedoms. However, much of the solicitousness of the state accommodated the accumulated claims of a vigorous and ever-expanding middle class. To be sure, they applied to all Britons—roughly the same rubrics of judicial process prevailed, independent of the social origins of the accused. However, the entire structure defining crimes and punishments placed extreme emphasis on retribution for violations of property. From 1660 to 1819, for example, Parliament devised 187 offenses that warranted the death penalty. The vast majority of these dealt with crimes against property. Indeed, attempted murder remained simply a "misdemeanor" until 1803.

The ensuing executions for such a wide range of capital offenses led ultimately to a backlash. Between 1779 and 1788, 531 of the 1,152 who had received death sentences actually went to the gallows. From 1799 to 1808, only 804 people received capital sentences, and of these, all but 126 won commutations. Increasingly, transportation to penal colonies began to serve as a substitute for hanging as the deterrent against violations of property. Between 1717 and 1776, Britain transported some 40,000 convicts to the American colonies and the Caribbean.

During the eighty years of Australian transportation (1788 to 1868), courts banished 150,000 convicts down under. The offenses of some on board the first fleet give us an idea of the resolve with which the state sought to discourage crimes against property: a seventy-year-old woman had stolen 20 pounds of cheese; a laborer had appropriated two hens—one live and the other dead; an unemployed woman had pilfered from a kitchen some bacon, flour, raisins, and butter—she went to Australia on commutation of her death sentence for this outrageous crime; a West Indian man raided a garden of twelve cucumbers; a nineteen-year-old man took a wooden box that contained some linen and five books; and an eleven-year-old boy lifted ten yards of ribbon and a pair of silk stockings. Only a society obsessed with the sanctity of property could expel such petty criminals from their homeland and send them in chains on a seven-month voyage to the edge of the earth.

At the heart of the immense amount of thievery and the absorption of the system with meting out punishments stood the desperate conditions to which laborers and the poor were subjected. Those who accumulated great wealth during the Industrial Revolution did so on the backs of the working class who became exceedingly vulnerable to swings in the performance of the economy. Most workers lived at a level that usually kept adequate housing, clothing, and food far out of reach. Children tended to take employment around the age of six. Not surprisingly, laborers burned out relatively early in their adult years. In addition, some occupations—like coal mining and weaving—lent themselves to chronic disabilities whose progression preordained untimely curtailment of one's productive years.

All the people who fell out of the labor force with no means of support became a great burden to society—even if they did not turn to crime. During the nineteenth century, however, Parliament and the civil service either ignored poverty or channeled their efforts toward defining it out of existence. This becomes most clear when we consider the great famine in Ireland between 1845 and 1849. During this period, more than a million people—one of every eight Irish—died of starvation and attendant diseases. Around the same number migrated to England, Scotland, Wales, or North America—many against their own will. Tens of thousands of these died either in transit or soon after their arrival, as was the case of some 37,000 of the approximately 100,000 who went to the Canadian colonies in 1847.

The famine had resulted from potato crop failures on the undesirable land where the Irish poor eked out their existence. The Irish, as a conquered people, could make no effective claims on the grain, cereal, and livestock agriculture that thrived on the estates of Ireland's landholders. The latter overwhelmingly either considered themselves as English or had become so "Anglicized" that they bore little or no sense of obligation toward their fellow countrymen.

Throughout the famine, London dithered over issues like the type of aid that would be given, where foodstuffs would be purchased, who would finance the assistance, and who would receive it. Thus virtually all of the relief that actually reached the poor proved to be too little, too late. Meanwhile, the human suffering approached holocaust proportions—albeit through displacement and starvation rather than direct genocide. In the words of Charles E. Trevelyan, the civil servant who headed the treasury and fashioned the government's response to the famine, England must leave Ireland to "the operation of natural causes."

The potato famine simply serves as the most grotesque instance of official complacence about destitution. The case also points out in bold relief legal structures that effectively hobbled the government in responding to such crises. The first of these, the Corn Laws, strictly limited the importation of agricultural products from outside the British Isles. This policy maintained robust prices for landholders but exacerbated the inability of the poor to afford even minimum sustenance. Even in years when the potato crop succeeded, one in every four Irish would remain seriously malnourished.

Sir Robert Peel, the prime minister at the outset of the potato famine, had in fact been looking for several years for an opportunity to move toward repeal of the Corn Laws. The circumstances surrounding the initial signs of serious famine in Ireland allowed him to get a bill through Parliament in June 1846. However, the political backlash immediately resulted not just in his loss of the confidence of the House of Commons, but in removal from power. The ensuing confusion and the lagged implementation of the repeal meant that the new trade regime would do virtually nothing to ameliorate conditions in Ireland. However, the repeal paved the way for improved accessibility of foodstuffs to the poor throughout the British Isles in the second half of the nineteenth century.

The second legal structure that hobbled the government's response to the potato famine similarly curtailed the capacity of the state to address destitution elsewhere in the British Isles. This was the reformed Poor Law of 1834. The legislation evolved from a debate similar to one being waged to this day about the poor. While society might willingly assist people who are "deserving" of assistance, it does not want to throw away money on those who prefer to exploit the system rather than support themselves. The parameters of this debate have changed considerably since the nineteenth century; modern political systems tend to give the benefit of the doubt to those applying for assistance. Nonetheless, certain segments of contemporary society become outraged over any instances in which the able-bodied receive benefits.

The Problem of Establishing Need and the Rise of Universal Programs.

We can understand why the politicians in the 1830s tried to differentiate between the genuinely needy and the undeserving in the provision of welfare. Their initiatives attempted to negotiate around two seemingly irreconcilable goals: addressing the problem of destitution throughout the land, and satisfying taxpayers that assistance programs did not squander their money.

The 1834 Poor Law—the first attempt by Parliament to resolve the conundrum—proved as cumbersome as it was parsimonious. It took two approaches. First, it extended the workhouse system in which recipients of food assistance would live and work only in institutions. This prevented the poor from obtaining support and working on the side. Second, it provided that the standard of living within the poorhouse (where work was not forced upon paupers) would be kept at the lowest level possible. This assured that the poor would ask for admittance only out of desperation. In the case of the potato famine, the channeling of assistance through poorhouses effectively proscribed even minimal assistance to destitute Irish laborers.

The workhouse mentality touched more than just the victims of agricultural and economic catastrophes. It meant that any members of the working class who lost their jobs or earned insufficient money to purchase necessities simply went without. Even as late as the turn of the century, officials rated thousands of working class young men who presented themselves to fight in the Boer War (1899–1902) unfit. They lacked the basic level of physical development and health necessary for military service.

Notwithstanding the gloomy status quo, reformers gradually made advances against the unvarnished capitalism that motivated draconian policies toward the poor. Parliament began in 1833 to restrict the employment of children. From the 1850s, it permitted local boards of health to impose regulations guiding sanitation and require the vaccination of entire populations against certain diseases. In the 1890s, local governments began to provide alternate housing to the unspeakably crowded and filthy tenements in which most urban workers dwelled. A series of statutes beginning in 1870 and ending in 1891 set up a system of free, universal, and compulsory elementary education. To an extent, these changes attempted to head off unrest in the increasingly enfranchised working class. However, they also responded to the growing feeling among the more sensitive in the middle and upper classes that *laissez faire* had gone too far.

The dawning of the twentieth century also marked the turning point for the emergence of the welfare state. Parliament, largely in response to the shocking evidence of working-class malnutrition found among volunteers for the Boer War, introduced school meals in 1906. Old-age pensions and limited sickness and unemployment insurance followed in 1908 and 1911, respectively. Though minimal, these programs departed radically from the workhouse mindset. Both imparted direct, but limited, entitlement that was not conditional on compulsory intutionalization.

Two factors quickened the process in which Britain embraced a limited welfare state. First, the state drew upon the young men of the working class during World War I (1914–1918) to an unprecedented degree. This elevated the working class's expectations. They had proven themselves worthy of a higher stake in society. Second, the economy had gone into a sharp decline by 1920.

As unemployment rose exponentially, the government recognized that the working class's sense of greater self-esteem was turning

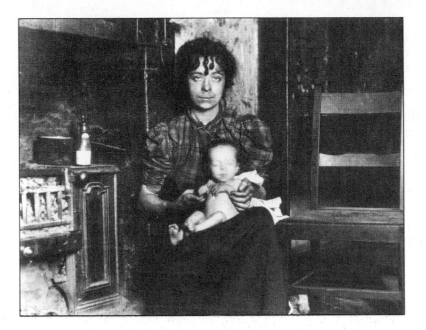

This photograph of a woman and a child in a Glasgow, Scotland tenement captures the wretched conditions of the poor in the first decade of this century.

into anger over continued hardship. Through the 1920s, state contributions to the unemployment fund were increased. This allowed provision of benefits beyond those supported by the premiums paid by the employed. It also eliminated in 1927 tests of "means" (such as whether claimants had access to the earnings of others or had assets that they could sell), and of "genuinely seeking work." Through the creation of the Unemployment Advisory Board in 1934, it extended unemployment benefits to all without work—even those who had not gained entitlements through payment of insurance premiums.

After World War II, the 1946 National Insurance Act brought all of the benefit systems for unemployment, sickness, retirement, and maternity under one statute. The 1948 National Health Service Act followed as the final iteration in the evolution of the welfare state. It guaranteed free and universal health care to all Britons.

Both post-World War II statutes took the British considerably beyond the United States in the inclusiveness of social benefits. They thus became the object of envy among people in this country who were impatient with the reluctance of the U.S. government to go all the way down the road to the welfare state. On the other hand, Americans who opposed additional programs like comprehensive health care viewed the British welfare state as an anathema. Thus they did not hesitate to point to the defects of the British system to prove that "cradle to grave" coverage stifled enterprise and individual initiative.

Both groups missed a very important point. With the exception of health care, the actual benefits and services Britons receive through these various programs fell considerably short of what people receive in the less-universal programs found in other long-standing democracies. This applies even to recent years. In 1981, when welfare reached its height in the United Kingdom, Britain's total welfare bill as a percent of gross domestic product came thirteenth out of the nineteen advanced economies that belonged to the then Organization for Economic Cooperation and Development (OECD). At that time, the United Kingdom spent a smaller proportion of its gross domestic product on pensions, child allowances, unemployment and sickness benefits than France and Germany. The U.K. social expenditure as a portion of the gross domestic product came only three percentage points above that of the United States and two points below the OECD average. With the help of Prime Minister Margaret Thatcher's stringent regime, through 1989 the United Kingdom remained behind both France and Germany in the amount of gross national product it spent on these benefits. A married man's unemployment benefit declined by 1989 to 27.5% of national average earnings. This compared most unfavorably with 68% and 75% of per capita income that, respectively, his West German and French counterparts would receive.

THE POSTWAR PERIOD— AN ANGUISHED PRESENT

Britain established herself in the latter part of the nineteenth century and the first half of the twentieth century almost as the epitome of industrialized societies. It maintained a resilient parliamentary democracy, and its vast empire ran relatively efficiently and humanely. By the early 1950s, the signs of decline were manifest to the astute observer. Ten years of engagement in global conflict through two world wars in the span of 31 years had sapped the British spirit and also weighed down domestic enterprise and colonial governance.

The Early Signs of Decline

Most fundamentally, the two world wars had changed matters too much for Britain to sustain its accustomed role in international affairs and the world economy. The United States and the Soviet Union had established themselves as superpowers in a league of their own. The postwar rebuilding of Western Europe—largely through the auspices of the U.S. Marshall Plan—had left Britain's natural economic competitors in a vastly better relative position than what had prevailed after World War I. In 1958, the European Economic Community, which initially included France, West Germany, Italy, and several smaller European states—but not Britain, emerged. Its success would ultimately convince many Britons of the value of regional economic solidarity. The economic motive for maintaining the commonwealth, let alone the empire, was increasingly coming into question.

As often happens in such circumstances, the flaws in the very fabric of British society became more visible. Some have argued that the United Kingdom would have been better off economically if, like Germany, it had suffered immense destruction of its industrial capacity during the war. Instead, Britain patched up its aging and damaged productive resources and muddled through the 1950s and the 1960s. And much the same process occurred in the social and political realms.

Certainly Britain was not the first imperial power to slide down a slippery slope. However, the very nature of British society made it difficult for the country to check what increasingly appeared as historically inevitable. By the early 1960s, Britain had chipped away class barriers less than any other major European power. The vitality of the monarchy in Britain did not spell the Camelot image that the pageantry of great events like royal weddings conjured up in American minds. Together with the persistence of nobility, the entire monarchical tradition spoke of Britons' undiminished loyalty to privilege.

Education was just one area in which the position of the most advantaged was maintained. Precious few sons and daughters of blue-collar workers aspired to attend a university. If they did, the state still did scandalously little to assure that capable children of the less advantaged received an education worthy of their abilities. Meanwhile, private schools, most of which demand very substantial fees, continued their traditional function for the children of the upper classes. Their students obtained a vastly disproportionate share of the most prized university positions, especially those at Oxford and Cambridge.

Rigidities such as those found in education showed their effects in many other corners of social life. In the workplace, these translated into the intractability of management and labor. Britain had made less progress toward worker participation in industrial decision-making than most other Western European nations. Indeed, serious antagonism characterized relations between management and various elements of the union movement.

The decline and loss of the empire, the failure to revitalize its industrial base and systems, and the persistence of antiquated social barriers and divisions combined to make Britons a defeatist society. Industrial innovators wrestled with a "show me" rather than a "can do" attitude among potential backers and collaborators. Government appeared much more concerned about pinching pennies from university budgets than fostering the research necessary for British scientists to contribute to industrial revitalization. Many gifted young people did not bother to dream of rewarding employment because of the obstacles placed before them by the educational system. In a highly patrician social system, even accents doomed talented plebeians to permanent second-class citizenship.

Are Britons Too Passive?

The visitor to the United Kingdom cannot help but note the civility of the people. One cannot even get through a restaurant meal without a succession of "pleases" (waiters delivering your order will actually say things like, "Your steak and kidney pie, Sir, please!") and thank yous that leaves Americans wondering what is wrong—are Americans too perfunctory or their hosts too servile? Around the fringes, things have changed. It is not pleasant to be on the Underground (subway) in London when drunken youths on their way to or from a football (soccer) match swamp your train. Some neighborhoods appear downright threatening. Yet reserve prevails in most public behavior. This usually borders on silence in cramped places such as the Underground. Most working-class neighborhoods simply appear frumpish—à la 1950s—rather than dangerous.

All of this pleasantness conceals a great deal of hostility. In the 1960s, political scientists believed that Britons demonstrated so much civility because they recognized the intrinsic merits of behaving respectfully and decently. The jury is out right now. Obviously, football rampages and inner-city riots suggest that the canons of behavioral restraint have been eroded; a closer look suggests that many of these were a veneer. Britons were very passive-aggressive subjects. Beneath the external calm resided deepseated resentments. Only with an understanding of these can observers grasp why trade unions became so militant in the 1970s. The broken silence of other disaffected groups—especially ethnic and racial minorities—also suggests a great deal of pent-up frustration.

The release of profound antagonisms has not confined itself to social groups that have chosen to register their disenchantment. It has become patently clear that the unitary structure of government—that is, the system whereby all political authority originates in London—inadequately accommodates regional differences even in England itself. Where ethnic factors buttress regional loyalties—that is, in Scotland, Northern Ireland, and Wales—the national fabric of the United Kingdom actually has begun to tear.

The case of Northern Ireland has brought especially acute embarrassment to the British. The use of military force and suspension of many civil liberties have left many blots on the democratic copybook of the United Kingdom. The European Court on Human Rights has found more infractions of civil liberties in Northern Ireland than anywhere else in the European Community. In English cities, persistent racial strife suggests that Britons' tolerance may have been skincolor-deep.

A Flabby Body Politic

Britons do not work very hard at what they do. London commuters still stream out of the Underground at 10:00 A.M. Most senior civil servants show up for work around 9:00—an hour and a half after their counterparts in Washington. Even in the nerve centers of government along Whitehall, virtually no lights burn as late as 8:00 P.M.

Thus it should not come as a surprise that the average citizen does not make much effort to participate politically. Yet it is disturbing to see that even activists seem somewhat lethargic. In the height of an election, always call a campaign headquarters before trying to visit it in the evening or on weekends. Chances are you will find it abandoned. And do not expect in

Britain the plethora of volunteers canvassing neighborhoods that one finds in the United States—at least reminding voters that there is an election on. Increasingly, British campaigns have become television events run from London. The legwork required to blanket a constituency and pinpoint voter support has become passé. Britons go beyond simply eschewing political involvement. They do not try too hard even when they do take on a political task. Self-starters must buck social conventions against appearing too eager; and all must observe the canons of social deference.

The dysfunctions of a relatively nonparticipatory political society, due to lack of energy and legitimacy, are disconcerting. In 1982, Margaret Thatcher's use of the territorial crisis in the Falkland Islands to reverse her sagging political support demonstrated the degree to which splendid patriotic theater can cover a multitude of deficiencies in executive leadership. Workers' perennial outrage with the government and employers masks the unions' stubborn disinclination to encourage rank-and-file participation in their own organizations. As for the press, tabloid-style alarmism about domestic and world affairs has even invaded well-regarded papers like *The Times*.

A Party System in Transition

Perhaps the widest rips in the fabric of British politics have occurred in the party system. Britain operates a parliamentary government that bases representation on single-member districts. Just as in elections to the U.S. Senate and House of Representatives, the candidates who win the most votes in their respective constituencies take their seats even if they fall short of an absolute majority.

This system operates in favor of one or two dominant parties. Unlike proportional representation, it makes no allowances for small parties, which might attain a significant amount of support across the country. The Liberal Democratic Party, for example, drew 18.3% of the vote in the 1992 election. However, such small parties might also fail to obtain the most votes in a substantial number of constituencies; the Liberal Democrats won only 20 of the 634 House of Commons seats in 1992 (3.2%).

Since World War II, in all governments but two one of the main parties—either the Conservatives or Labour—has enjoyed an absolute majority of seats in the House of Commons. The two exceptions were governments formed in 1974 in which Labour, headed by Harold Wilson, lacked the support of a clear majority of members of Parliament. In the first of these, formed in March, Labour emerged 17 seats short of an absolute majority; in the second, formed in October, it squeaked by with a one-seat edge, which it lost in a January 1975 by-election.

An electoral system such as Britain's that allows two parties to dominate has its drawbacks. First, supporters of small parties continually find that their votes do not translate into seats. They may become extremely disenchanted. Second, the solidarity necessary to maintain a united front in the House of Commons means that members of Parliament vote very reluctantly against their party on major legislation. As a result, many members frequently find themselves voting against their own convictions and/or the wishes of their constituents.

Of course, the two-party-dominant system has not produced majority governments easily; however, in Britain, it has run more smoothly since World War II than it did before. Of the eleven elections between 1900 and 1935, only six granted a single party an absolute majority of seats.

Cracks in the postwar two-party system appeared simultaneously with the fall of the Conservative government in 1974 and the difficulties of the subsequent Labour government. Many in the Labour Party believed that

unions had gone too far in asserting their claims. Besides, many radical fringe movements—dubbed the "Loony Left"—had attached themselves to the party. In 1981, widespread doubts about the direction of Labour took formal shape with the institution of the Social Democratic Party and the defection to it of several Labour members of Parliament—including former cabinet ministers.

The confrontational politics of the 1970s played heavily in the emergence of a fourth party and contributed to the suspension of the tendency among blue-collar and white-collar moderates to shift their support to the party out of office. That is, some voters who might normally have changed their allegiance to Labour have continued to support the Conservatives. This owed in no small extent to the extremism of the far-left elements of the Labour party. A prolonged hesitancy about radicalism seemed in the latter part of the 1980s to result in a realignment of potential Labour supporters permanently to the Conservative camp. Under the direction of Neil Kinnock, however, mainstream Labour factions once again began to appeal to the median voter. With a shift back to the center of the political spectrum, the Labour Party under Kinnock not only reclaimed many defectors, it also drew away marginal Conservatives. These gains, however, fell short of electoral victory for Labour in 1992.

New Questions About Old Institutions

The governmental apparatus associated with Britain's parliamentary democracy consists of Parliament—including the monarch; the cabinet; the permanent civil service; and the judiciary. The elective House of Commons and the House of Lords make up the two chambers of Parliament. The House of Lords includes members who take their places by hereditary right and those appointed for life. It retains a suspensory veto over legislation whereby it can delay bills passed by the House of Commons for up to one year.

The cabinet takes in the principal members of the ministry—mostly the heads of government departments of state. Other ministers assume executive functions in departments but do not belong to the cabinet. As most departments claim only two or three ministers, they must rely very heavily on permanent civil servants both for advice on policy options and for day-to-day management.

The British judiciary maintains a strong tradition of detachment from politics. This is partially due to the fact that lower court judges attain their positions by appointment rather than by election. The judicial community in the higher reaches of the system plays a very substantial role in determining who will assume vacancies on the most senior courts.

Many elements of this institutional framework command envy and praise outside Britain. For example, American authors have celebrated the efficient operation of the two-party system in the House of Commons, the degree of executive harmony stemming from the cohesiveness of cabinets, the "neutral competence" of the career civil service, and the high quality of judicial opinions. Over the past few decades, events suggest that foreign commentators had an idealized view of British governmental performance.

At this writing, the cracks in the two-party system have appreciably altered the dynamics of the House of Commons. Continuous infighting between "Thatcherites" and "Majorites" has illustrated the fact that party discipline has lost some of its force. John Major's leadership style includes "going public" to overcome opposition in an age when the prime minister can appeal directly to the people. The bureaucracy has begun to reveal clear signs of politicization and demoralization, and judicial decisions increasingly expose the degree to which the

courts, while stalwartly independent, habitually side with convention.

Some observers might have exaggerated the width of the fissures in the governmental apparatus; and some of the changes have had positive side effects or grappled with the inherent dysfunctions in the parliamentary system. For example, the moderation of party discipline has allowed members of Parliament to strengthen their monitoring of the executive. The emergence of "priministerial" government responds in part to the heightened emphasis of central coordination required by all advanced democracies to bring bureaucracy under control. In some respects, Britain's system remains a model for other nations—especially those within the parliamentary fold. However, it lacks the tidiness—largely putative, we now recognize—that it formerly enjoyed.

Unitary, But . . .

Britain resolutely retains its unitary form of government. The failure of 1979 referenda on the devolution of substantial central government powers to Scottish and Welsh parliaments took the issue out of the political agenda for the foreseeable future. And John Major continued a Thatcher legacy, gradually restructuring the relations between the central and local governments. The latter now enjoy much less latitude for independent action than they did in the past three decades.

It is not always that easy to keep a tight ship. The mere existence of special bureaucratic departments for Scottish and Welsh affairs points up the degree to which the effective handling of regional imperatives requires decentralization of the administrative apparatus. Of course, Northern Ireland presents a case in which administrative decentralization, coupled with a separate parliament (now defunct), collapsed under the weight of hostility between Protestants and Catholics. Even with regard to local governments, the Department of Environment—the ministry responsible for local governments—has faced defiance from Labour-dominated local councils that have bitterly resisted Conservative efforts to limit their activities through stringent fiscal constraints.

Britain's joining the European Community (now called the European Union) in 1973 further complicated the picture. Now British cabinet ministers must mesh many of their policy stances with European Union positions and initiatives. Some spend almost as much time in discussions with their opposite numbers in other European countries as they do with their own colleagues in the cabinet. Since 1979, Britons have elected representatives to the European Parliament. The European courts of Justice and Human Rights have impinged on the administration of justice in the United Kingdom. Further, 1992 saw the complete integration of European markets in a "free trade zone," forcing the United Kingdom to give up some of its economic sovereignty and therefore budgetary flexibility. There is talk of a further alignment of taxes among European Union members, and adoption of a single European currency close on the heels of the tax plan.

Compared to the United States, the European Union remains a very loose federation indeed. However, United Kingdom membership in this organization has clearly altered the parameters of unitary government in Britain. Increasingly, Britons relate to a center of political authority separate from London.

CONCLUSION

Americans have often labored under a lot of illusions in their view of Britain; it is important to clean out the cobwebs before we launch into a detailed examination of the United Kingdom. It probably remains the most important system for Americans to understand—even if they simply want to derive a comparative grip on the context of their own politics and form of government. It would be a shame for readers to find only halfway through this section of the book that their misconceptions—based on others' renderings of a more innocent epoch for Britain (the immediate post–World War II period)—prevented them from comprehending the roots as well as the changes of the past three decades and their ramifications.

REFERENCES AND SUGGESTED READINGS

Alt, James. 1979. *The Politics of Economic Decline: Economic Management and Political Behaviour in Britain Since 1964.* Cambridge: Cambridge University Press.

Dahrendorf, Ralf. 1982. *On Britain.* London: BBC.

Dearlove, John, and Peter Saunders. 1984. *Introduction to British Politics: Analyzing a Capitalist Democracy.* Cambridge: Polity.

Harvey, J., and L. Bather. 1982. *The British Constitution and Politics.* London: Macmillan.

Hennessy, Peter. 1992. *Never Again: Britain 1945–1951.* London: Jonathan Cape.

Holmes, M. 1985. *The First Thatcher Government, 1979–1983: Contemporary Conservatism and Economic Change.* Brighton: Wheatsheaf.

Hughes, Robert. 1986. *The Fatal Shore.* New York: Vintage Books.

Norton, Philip. 1984. *The British Polity.* New York: Longman.

Olson, Mancur. 1982. *The Rise and Decline of Nations.* New Haven: Yale University Press.

Parry, Geraint, George Moyser, and Weil Day. 1992. *Political Participation and Democracy in Britain.* Cambridge: Cambridge University Press.

Riddel, Peter. 1985. *The Thatcher Government.* Oxford: Blackwell.

Woodham-Smith, Cecil. 1962. *The Great Hunger: Ireland 1845–1849.* New York: Harper & Row.

Young, Hugo, and Anne Sloman. 1986. *The Thatcher Phenomenon.* London: BBC.

6

Political Culture:
The British Limits

he preceding chapter examined the context of the British political system, focusing on historical and current issues. This chapter looks at the building blocks of British politics: individual citizens. More precisely, it will assess the nature of the British citizenry.

Healthy democracies do not run on institutions alone. They require committed individuals to operate them. Most obviously, they depend on political leaders capable of maintaining balance. Leadership consists of one part exertion of authority and another part responsiveness to the public one seeks to serve. At the same time, democracies require the support and the participation of ordinary citizens. If the chemistry between the general public and the political leadership goes wrong—or never adequately develops—then the latter will find it extremely difficult to reconcile authority and responsiveness.

When we talk about the nature of a citizenry we really open three issues. One of these is overarching; the other two show how authority and responsiveness reflect the vigor of the ties between the political leaders and the public. The first we call *political culture*. The others we call *socialization* and *participation*.

If you were arrested in London, chances are that the police constables would behave in a surprisingly respectful way. They probably would not use guns—even if they were among the rare police officers who actually carry them. They would be unlikely to rough you up or use abusive language. Indeed, if they discussed you on the car radio with the local police station, they might even go out of their way to use courteous terms such as "citizen" when mentioning you. Probability does play a role here. The constable might behave differently depending on your skin color, your dress, your accent, whether you had a vehicle, and if so, whether it was a battered Volkswagen Beetle or a sleek new Jaguar. Your and the constable's behavior, however, would remain within significantly tighter parameters than those that prevail in the United States.

The above scenario illustrates an underlying concept of political culture. The hypothetical situation evokes substantially different behavioral expectations in a British setting than it does in an American one. Therefore we speak of political culture as distinctive to each nation. When a killer opens fire on innocent passersby in the United States, we are alarmed at the immense violence that exists in this country. However, we would probably not consider the occurrence surprising or attribute it to an external influence. This is not the case in the United Kingdom. Such incidents happen rarely—and when they do, they strike a much deeper horror in the public consciousness. More to the point, commentators tend almost invariably to interpret such events as inspired by and mimicking U.S.-style social pathology depicted in American television and movies.

The term *political culture* refers to a complex array of attitudes, beliefs, values, and skills that predispose citizens toward various types of political behavior. Even though we know individuals well, we can never predict with total certainty what they will actually do in various circumstances. By the same token, we cannot reliably forecast political behavior. Still, the waters of national character run deep; and anyone who professes to know about the politics of a country surely must have become acquainted

with the accumulated record on its political psyche.

The sections below focus on various dimensions of British political culture. Along the way, they will examine patterns in political socialization and participation. The former topic concerns the transmission of political attitudes and values between generations. The latter measures the ordinary citizen's attention to and direct involvement in the political process.

DEFERENTIAL POLITICS

In 1959, two American scholars, Gabriel A. Almond and Sidney Verba, headed a study of political culture in Britain. Their interviews formed part of a cross-national project including the United States, West Germany, Italy, and Mexico. When they reported their findings, the authors concluded that Britain was a *deferential* political culture. To understand what they meant, we should look briefly at their classification system.

To ascertain the nature of a political culture, you must examine the orientations of the citizenry to various dimensions of the political system. The dimensions include:

1. the system as a broad phenomenon—its history, size, location, power, constitutional characteristics, and so on;

2. the "input" elements of the system—the organizations and the elites that determine the shape of government policies;

3. the actual "outputs" of government—the substantive nature of government policies and the vagaries of delivery and enforcement; and

4. perceptions of the place of individual citizens as participants in the political process.

Orientations toward the dimensions of the political system fall under three categories:

1. cognition—how much individuals actually know about the individual dimensions;

2. affect—their favorable or unfavorable feelings toward them; and

3. evaluation—their considered judgments about them.

Three types of political culture emerge from this framework. A *parochial* culture is a primitive society in which the average person has little knowledge of any of the dimensions of the political system. A *subject* culture is a traditional political society whose citizens are benignly aware of a pervasive phenomenon identified as the political system. They are also conscious of its benefits, taxes, and regulations, but they fail to influence its policies; in short, they are politically passive—they see themselves more as subjects than as full-fledged citizens. A *participant* culture is an advanced democracy in which individuals reveal strong orientations toward all four dimensions of the political system.

When Almond and Verba designated Britain as a deferential political culture they did not mean to diminish its standing as an advanced democracy. Instead, they simply employed the concept to reconcile two potentially contradictory findings. Britons interviewed in 1959 reported reasonably robust levels of participation in their political system. Yet they maintained a very strong deference to the authority of the state. The authors argued that in some respects this situation was preferable to that in the United States. Americans, they believed, demonstrated a penchant for criticism and a level of participation bordering on meddlesome. The deferential culture hypothesis rests, of course, upon inferences about the inculcation of political orientations and individuals' attitudes toward political participation. These require closer scrutiny.

Almond and Verba interviewed more than 900 Britons as part of their research project. From these, they selected five case histories to illustrate the dominant clusters of orientations found in their sample. However, a lot has

To some extent, the British political culture represents a more effective combination of the subject and participant roles. . . . The development of the participant orientation in Britain did not challenge and replace the more deferential subject orientations, as was the tendency in the United States. Despite the spread of political competence and participant orientations, the British have maintained a strong deference to the independent authority of government.

Source: Gabriel A. Almond and Sidney Verba, *The Civic Culture*, 1963.

changed in Britain since 1959, as we learned in Chapter 4. It is doubtful that the "deferential British participant" will dominate the political horizon. Unfortunately, no subsequent studies of political culture in Britain have come anywhere near the comprehensiveness of Almond's and Verba's work. In the search for changes since then, we must rely on somewhat fragmentary lessons from polling data and anecdotal material.

To illustrate this analysis, Almond and Verba chose from their respondents an archetypal deferential participant. This man belonged to the working class but supported the Conservative government. He generally spoke favorably of government and politics. And he was inclined to believe in the efficacy of his participation in the political system. In itself, this profile fitted a long-standing tradition among certain segments of the working class and did not warrant special comment.

Several other features of the profile raise flags for the inquiring mind in light of developments since 1959. Specifically, we should ask how it stands up to the recent decline of the economy in the North and the related deepening cleavage between the northern and southern electorates that was manifested in the 1987 and 1992 general elections.

The subject, "Mr. H," worked as a unionized baker in a large industrial city in the North. He had eight grown children, all of whom worked hard and made their way—all the sons found careers in skilled trades. Mr. H. himself noted how different this was from when he started out. At that time there was no assurance that you would find security even if you had ability and worked hard. Mr. H. viewed the central government very positively. He also believed that the local government was equally effective.

If we could track down Mr. H.'s eight children, what would we find? Have they kept their jobs through the decline of the North? What are their own children doing? Have they found their ways into careers that offer the same promise of security that their parents have? What do the parents and the children think now about the central government—the political leadership, Parliament, and the bureaucracy? In the great battle waged under Margaret Thatcher between the central government and the local authorities, which side have they taken? Obviously, we cannot ask these questions of Mr. H's descendants. However, we can look at some more recent data on British political culture to identify the areas in which there might have been shifts or changes in the deferential society. For more definitive answers, we will have to await a full replication of the Almond and Verba study.

POLITICAL SOCIALIZATION

Political socialization includes the inculcation of political orientations and values. It may begin as soon as a child becomes conscious of the outside world. It certainly intensifies during the school years. And it may well continue into early adulthood.

The very nature of the deferential culture suggests that political socialization normally shapes budding British citizens into loyal "sub-

jects." This section examines the various contexts in which political socialization takes place. Along the way, it will be alert to developments since the early 1960s that suggest political socialization operates differently from the way it did when Almond and Verba studied it.

Given the span of years in which political socialization takes place, we must allow for the fact that various settings work their effects on the development of a child into a full-fledged citizen. Among these, the family, the educational system, social class, where one grows up, and one's ethnic background merit our closest attention.

Family

If political socialization takes place in childhood, then family background is one of the strongest factors determining a citizen's political views. How much of a family's table conversation centers on politics? If it's a great deal, we can expect children to absorb political ideas and learn how to express these much earlier than would children whose families do not discuss or demonstrate politics within the home. Are members of the family politically active? For example, do they involve themselves in campaign work and/or attempt to influence political decisions? If so, the children will tend to see such involvement as a natural part of citizenship. Are the parents deeply partisan? Then their children will probably adopt stronger party loyalties than children from a nonpartisan home.

All of these features are manifest in the families of most democratic societies. Britain is singularly distinguished from the United States (and other democracies) to the degree that class consciousness is passed on to the next generation. Unlike Americans, Britons do not tend to expect that their children will experience upward mobility. In fact, many working-class parents actively discourage their children from aspiring to occupations that would elevate their socioeconomic standing.

Several studies have revealed these patterns. David Butler and Donald Stokes found in a 1970 survey that only 20% of their respondents had experienced upward mobility. Less than 10% had lost socioeconomic standing. Another study that compared the inflation-adjusted earnings of residents of York in the 1970s with those of their fathers in the 1950s yielded a very high correlation.[1] More recent studies with contemporary subjects have reiterated these findings. For example, most of the respondents of a 1987 survey identified with their parents' social class, with only 2% giving a "Don't Know" response when asked to which social class they believed they belonged.[2]

Richard Rose's assessment of respondents' party identification in the 1987 British Election Survey points up two ways in which family experiences prove immensely durable. He looked at several potential influences—both formative and contemporary—on voters' preferences. He found that the fathers' class and

parents' party preference accounted for almost 50% of respondents' party preferences, whereas a political party's current performance influenced only 21%.[3]

Education

Several distinctive elements of the British educational system merit close scrutiny here. The first of these is that Britons receive their education in politics less formally than do Americans. Thus primary and secondary schools do not require that every student receive at least some explicit training in civics. Much of the material that falls under the compass of politics and government comes to students only indirectly in history classes. Indeed, even contemporary history courses sometimes cut off at the turn of the century.

In the United Kingdom, advanced secondary school students specialize as they progress toward the final years of their education. At this stage, many British students might not even list a liberal arts class among their courses, let alone a course that deals substantially with government and politics. Universities proved loath to acknowledge political science as a separate degree. In fact, most departments go by the name *politics* or *government*. Oxford still grants a catchall degree called "philosophy, politics, and economics." The program's critics claim that it offers a classic "jack of all trades, master of none" curriculum.

To say that education in politics and government occurs informally does not imply that it fails to take place entirely. Britons who seek comprehensive and reliable coverage of current affairs may choose among three national newspapers that maintain reportorial standards that exceed those of U.S. papers. In fact, only *The New York Times* even comes close to filling a comparable role in the United States. Both the government-owned British Broadcasting Corporation and the private Inde-

Table 6.1   SOCIAL CLASS BY SELF-ASCRIPTION, 1987
Question: Which social class would you say you belong to?

	Self, percent	Parents, percent
Upper-middle	1.5	2.3
Middle	26.0	17.7
Upper-working	21.3	12.1
Working	46.0	59.1
Poor	2.9	6.8
Don't know	1.4	1.2

Source: R. Jowell, S. Witherspoon, and L. Brook, *British Social Attitudes, The Fifth Report, 1988–1989*, p. 227. Used by permission of Dartmouth Publishing Co., Ltd.

pendent Television Network provide strong, in-depth coverage of the news. And their documentaries enjoy a loyal following among viewers who wish to maintain a high level of information about public affairs. Further, numerous magazines such as *The Economist, The New Statesman,* and *New Society* have a significant and loyal readership among people who watch politics closely.

These informal vehicles for imparting political knowledge, maintaining effective support of the system, and providing assessments of major issues still do not mean that the United Kingdom is not politically in a somewhat precarious situation. In the first place, children do not normally avail themselves of such resources until they have entered their teens; thus they can develop erroneous views of their political system. For example, British children frequently carry the illusion into their teens that the queen, rather than the prime minister with the support of Parliament, rules the country.

Further, too much reliance on the media as political educators can leave the children of the masses informationally far behind those of the elite. Most Britons read atrocious tabloid newspapers rather than the high-quality national papers. And with four television channels to choose from, one can find at least one light-entertainment alternative to more serious public affairs programs.

The inherent elitism of British education poses a major obstacle to the informal transmission of knowledge of, affection for, and evaluation of the political system among the lower classes. To this day, parents in the highest socioeconomic brackets tend to send their children to schools requiring tuition. Although called "public schools," these institutions remain fiercely private. They employ social as well as academic criteria for admission and charge as much as the equivalent of $15,000 for a year's tuition, room, and board.

On the other hand, state-supported secondary education has gone through turmoil over

Table 6.2   TABLOID AND "MIDDLE-BROW" PAPERS OUTSELL HIGH-QUALITY NEWSPAPERS BY FAR

Daily papers	July–Dec 1990	Percent of total
Sun	3,855,000	27
Daily Mirror	3,083,000	21
Daily Mail	1,708,000	12
Daily Express	1,585,000	11
Daily Telegraph	1,076,000	8
Daily Star	912,000	6
Today	540,000	4
Guardian*	424,000	3
Times*	420,000	3
Independent*	411,000	3
Financial Times*	290,000	2

Sunday papers		
News of the World	5,056,000	26
Sunday Mirror	2,894,000	15
The People	2,566,000	13
The Mail on Sunday	1,903,000	10
Sunday Express	1,664,000	8
Sunday Post (Glasgow)	1,227,000	6
Sunday Times*	1,165,000	6
Sunday Mail (Glasgow)	888,000	4
Sunday Telegraph	594,000	3
The Observer*	551,000	3
Sunday Sport	402,000	2
Independent on Sunday*	352,000	2
Sunday Mercury	151,000	1
Sunday Sun	117,000	1

*Denotes national, established newspaper.
Source: *The Economist Diary.* © 1992 The Economist Newspaper Group. Reprinted with permission. Further reproduction prohibited.

the past two decades. Until the 1960s, local education authorities ran two types of institutions: grammar schools, which selected only the very brightest students, and secondary moderns, which took everyone else. The "11-plus exam" separated the fliers from the plodders at the age of 11. The strategy of offering an exceptionally high caliber of education to a select few led to many grammar school graduates finding their ways to Oxford and Cambridge universities and, eventually, into the higher end of the social and political establishment.

The verdicts from the 11-plus exam did not allow for late bloomers. In fact, many educators began to worry that the nation might well be denying itself a great deal of talent by such an early and severe separation of the gifted and the average. The Labour Party introduced comprehensive secondary schools when it controlled the government from 1964 to 1970. These merged the grammar and secondary modern schools with a view to allowing students to reach their optimal levels at their own respective paces.

The governments of Margaret Thatcher and John Major have taken a dim view of the effectiveness of these institutions. They have launched a major drive to encourage superior comprehensive schools to separate themselves from local educational authorities and charge fees. In addition, they have sought to re-introduce mandatory testing of students, claiming that this is a suitable device for measuring the efficiency of schools and teachers.

These initiatives appear to be moving the educational system even further from the former idea that the state owes every child a reasonable chance to develop fully at his or her own speed. If the Tories fully implement their plans, the United Kingdom might revert to a situation in which it employs strongly nonegalitarian criteria for ascertaining which students will avail themselves of the educational opportunities that are requisite for leadership in society. Recent data, however, suggest the rather skeptical reception of these measures. By June 1992, only 200 out of 4,200 eligible schools had separated from the control of local authorities. In addition, the majority of the independent schools were not administering tests to their students.

Social Class

Class consciousness has a discernable influence on British politics. Recent studies suggest, however, that the proportion of the population identifying with a specific class has remained pretty much the same between the mid-1960s and mid-1980s, with around 50% of respondents in surveys associating themselves with a class. In the same interval, however, the proportion of manual workers who placed themselves in the working class has declined from 46% to 39%.[4]

Scholars offer several reasons for this slippage. The one most commonly invoked argues that class-based inequalities and conflicts of interest in Britain have always competed with patriotism in the consciousness of the less advantaged. The strongly deferential nature of Britons allows for a situation in which concern for the national interest—as defined by the ruling elite—serves as a strong counterweight to pursuit of class-oriented goals.

The higher standard of living in Britain since World War II constitutes another major factor in the lessening of class divisions. The broad consensus between the Conservative and Labour parties over the mixed economy and the welfare state certainly shifted the tenor of political debate in the 1950s and 1960s from fundamental issues to details. As a result, voters—especially those at the border among the classes—switched their party preferences more easily.

Developments over the past two decades have diminished the influence of class within the political system. The spate of strikes and battles over government attempts to limit wage increases during the 1970s revealed many gaping holes in the politics of consensus. Thatcher saw herself as ringing the death knell on the old order by appealing for a new politics of commitment. This approach worked electoral miracles.

Some doubts arise as to the ultimate impact of Thatcherism. Will it lead eventually to a permanent polarization of the British electorate? The 1987 and 1992 general election results suggest that the country has indeed divided sharply between the North and the South (see Table 6.3). The former, of course, has gone against the national mood and repudiated Thatcherism and the subsequent Conservative government. In this regard, some studies of the sectors of the populace that maintain deep class-based antagonisms prove instructive.[5] Strong working-class sentiments have persisted most among people with traditional manual jobs in narrow-based industrial areas. Moreover, if the ambience of a community remains "working class," the relationship between voters' occupations and their electoral preferences intensifies.[6] A comparison of the party vote distributions in the last two general elections further illustrates this point: polarization at the level of occupational class has not only persisted, but has increased between the 1987 to the 1992 elections. All of this suggests that the growing rift between the North and the South partially masks class-related antagonisms.

Regional Differences

It is perhaps too easy to think only of Scotland, Northern Ireland, and Wales when considering the significance of region in British political socialization. Each of these jurisdictions remains culturally distinctive. And the British government has partially accommodated this fact by delegating responsibility for the administration of many government programs to the Scottish Office, the Northern Ireland Civil Service, and the Welsh Office. Indeed, the administrative practices in some fields like law and order, education, and health care vary greatly in the three areas. Of course, Northern Ireland continues to comprise a special case

Table 6.3 VOTING PATTERNS BY OCCUPATIONAL CLASS IN THE 1987 AND 1992 GENERAL ELECTIONS (ROW PERCENTAGES)

	1987			1992		
	Con	Lab	Dem	Con	Lab	Dem
Professional/Managerial (AB)	52	15	31	56	20	21
Routine nonmanual (C1a)	54	21	23	49	28	20
Skilled manual (C1b/C2)	38	41	20	39	40	18
Unskilled manual (D/E)	31	47	22	30	51	14

Sources: The 1987 figures are taken from Ivor Crewe, Neil Day, and Anthony Fox, *The British Electorate, 1963–1987: A Compendium of Data from the British Election Studies* (Cambridge: Cambridge University Press, 1991). The 1992 figures are taken from the Gallup post-election survey.

due to the deep divisions between its Protestants and Catholics on whether the territory should remain in the United Kingdom or become a part of the Republic of Ireland.

In the rest of Britain, factors other than economic decline work their effects toward deepening regional differences. Even the influx of Irish migrants, beginning with the potato famine in the late 1840s, tended to center on Glasgow, Liverpool, and Cardiff as ports of entry. To this day, Irish Catholics constitute a highly significant cultural and political force in Glasgow and Liverpool and their surrounding communities.

The North of England also experienced a considerable influx of Eastern Europeans—especially after the various persecutions during this century. This has further strengthened the influence of Roman Catholicism in the area. West Indian, Pakistani, and Indian immigrants have also gravitated to industrial cities of the North and the smaller textile-producing towns of the North. With the economic decline centered in this region of the country—by April 1990, the jobless rate was two times higher than the rate in the Southeast—religious or racial barriers exacerbate the frustration caused by economic stagnation.

Ethnic Background

The British have not become as sensitive to racism as Americans have. Even in polite company, Britons frequently make Irish immigrants the butts of their humor. In fact, one periodically sees articles and books that develop the view that such diminution is healthful. As the arguments go, every nation has to have another people to whom they feel superior and many of the jokes, it is said, base themselves on the real-life quirks of the Irish.

As for blacks and East Indians, many Britons persist in using offensive terms such as "Negro" and "colored" when referring to non-whites. It is wise, if one is in a taxi driven by a nonimmigrant, not to mention any topic like crime, unemployment, or the appearance of neighborhoods, because the driver might consider the comment an open door to a discussion about immigrants. As often as not, cabbies will seize the opportunity to present a diatribe about how the immigration of nonwhites has ruined Britain. One sees even in the nationwide, respected newspapers and on television—even on the BBC, an astonishing amount of racial stereotyping; much of it is so blatant that it would arouse angry protests from whites and nonwhites in the United States.

Part of the difficulty rests in the tremendous influx of nonwhites since the 1950s. In 1951, only one-fifth of 1% of the population was nonwhite. Since then, immigration from the Commonwealth gradually led to heavy concentrations of nonwhites in urban and industrial centers. In the 1950s, any member of a Commonwealth country or colony in the empire could invoke his or her status as British subjects and settle in the United Kingdom. Even with the imposition of increasingly stringent immigration rules and procedures, non-whites residing in the United Kingdom reached, with significant variations among areas, 5.5% of the population by 1991. In inner London, more than a quarter of the population comes from visible minorities while in the North and Scotland only one person in a hundred is nonwhite. A figure like 5.5% remains insignificant by American standards. Yet it has caused alarm—in many cases, overt racism—among Britons who view their society as white.

Ethnicity raises important questions associated with political socialization in the United Kingdom. Successive governments have struggled with two related tasks. First, they have tried to control the influx of nonwhites. Here the more benevolent regimes have viewed this task as limiting the flow to a manageable

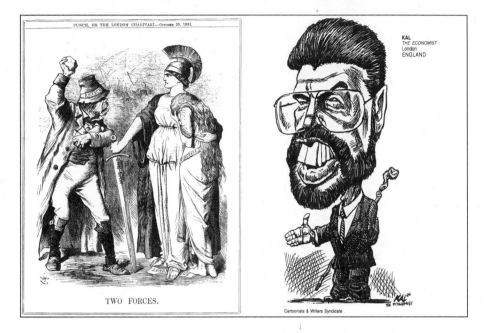

Nineteenth-century cartoonists regularly attributed to the Irish apelike features. The illustration on the left was published in *Punch* in 1881. It portrays Britannia protecting a distraught Hibernia (Ireland) from an Irish anarchist. The genre survives to this day. The illustration on the right from *The Economist* (February 12, 1994) likewise assigns apelike features to Gerry Adams, the head of Sinn Fein—a legal party in Northern Ireland that is the political wing of the Irish Republican Army.

level. This, presumably, would allow time for Britons to get used to the notion of their being a multiracial society. It would also assure that state and market machinery for socializing immigrants would not become swamped. Other governments have taken a harder line and adopted policies that simply try to stem the flow as much as possible. Detention of immigrants is one example of the hard-line approach to discourage immigration: according to a survey published in June 1993, more than 10,000 potential immigrants are detained without charge every year in the United Kingdom.

The assumption of either strategy does not necessarily follow the dividing line between Conservatives and Labour. However, the Conservatives under Thatcher and Major have tightened access the most. When in power, Labour proved somewhat more accommodating of nonwhites in its own policies and organization than have the Conservatives. The Conservatives in particular have had to contend with very strong anti-immigrant sentiment from time to time. In the late 1950s, Enoch Powell—a Conservative member of Parliament—became the leading spokesman of those seeking to exclude immigrants of "color." His arguments played on the racially oriented fears of many citizens. These feelings still receive considerable voice in some sections of the party.

A young man was killed in Newcastle-upon-Tyne while police chased him during a joy ride. The victim's father (left, wearing sun glasses) attends the funeral with other family members. Angry youths rioted in response to the death—starting fires that gutted some buildings. Stealing cars and driving them at high speed has become an outlet for poor English youths.

A new dimension has entered racial politics since the beginning of the Thatcher government. The "uncaring" image of the prime minister made her a target for blame in racial unrest. This became the case particularly in 1981 and 1985 when riots broke out in several heavily nonwhite urban areas in the country. Politicians from the right of the political spectrum blamed this unrest on the lack of assimilation of nonwhites. However, this analysis overlooked the fact that many of the rioters were white.

It is safe to assume that these and other such occurrences have flowed from a cocktail with three volatile ingredients: deep alienation among nonwhite youths, resentment among young unemployed whites, and aggressive—bordering on hostile—policing of nonwhite neighborhoods. In so far as Margaret Thatcher and John Major have failed to pursue policies that might have alleviated unfavorable economic conditions, they have shaken the cocktail and have already caused several small explosions.

Developments on the five fronts of political socialization examined here suggest reasons why we might well expect some erosion in the deferential political culture observed by Almond and Verba. Family background persists as a strong determinant both of one's social class and of one's party identification. In the expansionary period of the late 1950s, people with low incomes perhaps thought less of this. They still could earn decent livings and see tangible improvements in their living circumstances, if not in their social standing.

The less auspicious economic conditions of the present should at least alert us to the possibility that adversity might make its victims more conscious of material and other barriers to socioeconomic improvement. Disillusionment with efforts to improve the access of all classes to education has induced a backlash now embodied in policies that will usher in the return of the social stratification of opportunities. Will the British working class respond to this process with the deference they displayed in the 1950s? Probably not. The immediacy of the electronic era will confront the British leadership with the fact that voters will know when their educational system denies them equality of opportunity.

In the 1950s, its higher degree of industrialization and continued use of coal as a fuel made the North dirtier than the South. But it was prosperous. Now it struggles with a bleak economic future—even though the collapse of many manufacturing industries and the use of cleaner fuels makes it a brighter place to live. The evidence suggests that class antagonisms have deepened in the North and focused on the South. Ethnicity has reared its head in a new politics of despair. In the 1950s, whites worried about the influx of nonwhite immigrants. What effects would it have on the British pedigree? Now the sources of resentment have become more concrete. Poor white youths in particular believe that nonwhites have taken their jobs. Meanwhile, a generational shift has occurred among nonwhites. Whereas their parents readily found their place in the work force—albeit not always at levels commensurate with their education and abilities—nonwhite youths now find themselves trapped in ghettos that doom them to inadequate education and the social stigma of belonging to the underclass.

POLITICAL PARTICIPATION

As noted above, Almond and Verba distinguished between the subject and the participation-oriented citizen. The former takes in knowledge, affection for, and favorable evaluations of the political system—whose existence looms as an overarching reality— and the specific actions of the government. The participation-oriented possess the same three characteristics with the additional belief that they can contribute to the political process and avail themselves of channels for influencing their government.

In designating Britain as a deferential political culture, Almond and Verba stressed the fact that less participation exists in the United Kingdom than in the United States, but that more subject orientation exists. Britons do not place the same demands on government for participation that Americans do. As a result, British channels available for influencing government have lagged behind those in the United States. The British apparatus that connects the public will and the government lacks the multiplicity of forums and channels, the refinement of advocacy skills, and the relative democratic pluralism of the U.S. system.

Of course, Almond and Verba conducted their research in the late 1950s. The tumultuous 1960s and 1970s, followed by polarization between the North and the South, have led some scholars to expect that the deferential culture might have waned in Britain.

We should keep in mind the deep, historical roots of the deferential, political culture. Even within this century, people who could not meet the property requirement were denied the vote until, respectively, 1918 and 1928. Until 1948, university graduates and owners of businesses enjoyed the privilege of an extra vote. We cannot expect a nation—especially a gradualist one like Britain—to be rapidly transformed into a participatory culture when it held off so long the most elemental requisites of electoral equality.

Britons remain significantly deferential. In a survey published in 1984 and notwithstanding their adverse economic conditions in comparison with much of the rest of Europe, the British registered the highest level of satisfaction with their political system.[7] In one mid-1970s survey, only 20% of the respondents said that they would engage in civil disobedience.[8] The same study also discovered that citizens overwhelmingly support strong actions against protestors—including stiff jail sentences.[9] Britons also grant unusual legitimacy to most authoritative and coercive institutions of governance such as the police and armed forces. A 1988 survey of popular confidence in major institutions in the United Kingdom, United States, France, West Germany, and Spain revealed that only in the United States do the police and the armed forces enjoy more popular trust than in the United Kingdom.[10]

On the other hand, Britons thought the least of institutions through which citizens can conceivably influence public affairs. Only Spaniards gave less credence to the legislative and executive branch than did Britons. Moreover, only in Spain are the judicial branch and the educational system, commonly regarded as core governmental institutions, more poorly regarded than they are in Britain. Britons also had lower esteem for the press than did respondents in the other countries. Twenty-nine percent of Britons registered confidence in trade unions; this figure is 23 percentage points short of the comparable U.S. figure, and 7 and 14 percent below that for France and Germany, respectively.

Slippage on Several Fronts

In the late 1960s and early 1970s, Britain—as did many other Western countries—witnessed an explosion of participatory approaches to government. Key to these were efforts to involve citizens more in groups and institutions that affected the way in which they were governed. The 1980s and 1990s have seen a contraction of these avenues in Britain. Here three developments are especially notable. The great push in the 1970s to devolve some central government powers to separate parliaments in Scotland and Wales came to an abrupt halt with the failure of the 1979 devolution referendums. Of course, political unrest in Northern Ireland continues to serve as London's rationale for sharply constricted civil liberties in that province. The Conservatives under Thatcher and Major have greatly decreased the powers of local governments. And, unions—which scored an "own goal" in the bitter strikes of the winter of 1978–1979—have suffered both a loss of public support and the imposition of highly restrictive legislation by the Conservatives.

In the late 1980s, some observers saw one bright light—Thatcher's "popular capitalism" in which average citizens theoretically acquired a stake in British enterprise. However, the privatization of public corporations that served as the linchpin of this strategy indeed did little to distribute the ownership of capital.

The whole move toward devolution of some central government powers to Scotland and Wales collapsed after the failure of referendums on that issue in 1979. The proposals called for separate assemblies in Edinburgh and Cardiff, which would pass legislation fitting within the devolved powers.

The Welsh referendum lost by a huge margin. The Scottish vote carried by a slim majority, with 51.6% in favor to 48.4% opposed. However, the terms of the referendum stipulated that a majority of eligible voters must support devolution before it took effect. All of this does not spell the end of frustrated national aspirations for people in Scotland. A 1992 Independent Television News/*Scotsman* poll showed that 50% of the voters supported independence; in the same survey, devolution achieved 27%. These figures are very significant because in 1987, independence and devolution showed a support of 33% and 47%, respectively. This reverting tendency signals a growing regionalism and potential problems for the Conservative government. Scottish rejection of the Conservative electoral hegemony does not help the situation either. In the 1992 election, only 11 of Scotland's 72 seats went to the Conservatives.

A separate parliament in Belfast, called Stormont, operated in Northern Ireland from 1921 until its suspension in 1972. This body enacted legislation in a host of fields in which various Irish ministries administered the affairs of state. The line departments—those with direct responsibility for the operation of government programs—included Home Affairs, Development, Education, Agriculture, Commerce, and Health and Social Services. Of course, acts of Westminster took precedence over those of Stormont in all fields. And Stormont was prohibited from involving itself in legislative areas that remained under the direct control of Westminster.

The events of the late 1960s and early 1970s made the devolution of legislative authority to Northern Ireland unworkable. The Catholic minority simply refused to remain under the sway of the Protestant majority. The fact that the latter outnumbered the former two to one made it highly unlikely that the transition to some legislative institution with built-in safeguards of effective representation for Catholics would occur rapidly. Thus Whitehall has run the province directly since 1972.

Beneath the question of political participation in Ireland lies the economic one. Catholics find it extremely difficult to participate in the economy through meaningful and adequate employment in either the private or the public sector. In 1991, the unemployment rate for Catholics remained five percentage points above that for Protestants, bringing the total

Table 6.4 PROTESTANTS HOLD THE MAJORITY OF PUBLIC JOBS IN NORTHERN IRELAND

RELIGIOUS REPRESENTATION IN NORTHERN IRELAND PUBLIC BODIES (%)

	Protestants	Catholics
Housing Executive	54	46
Health Board	56	44
Education Boards	58	42
NI Civil Service	63	37
Local District Councils	67	33

Source: Based on research conducted by the Fair Employment Commission. From *The Independent*, December 23, 1992. Used by permission.

jobless rate in Northern Ireland to almost 14%. Recent data confirm patterns of discrimination against Catholics: a 1992 survey by the Fair Employment Commission showed that none of the twenty-six local councils in Northern Ireland has an equitably structured work force (see Table 6.4).

Increasingly, Irish-Catholics in the United States have encouraged American investors to withdraw their funds from Northern Irish subsidiaries that do not observe the McBride Principles—a series of guidelines for eliminating job discrimination against Catholics. Partially in response to the McBride movement, Whitehall tightened its own sanctions late in 1987 against Northern Irish firms that practice discrimination.

While ambiguity has always surrounded devolution of authority to the provinces, local governments in the various parts of Britain have until recently enjoyed a relatively high degree of legitimacy.[11] This is due, to a certain extent, to the association of local government with the Conservative and Liberal parties. During various Labour administrations since the war, local governments became vehicles of resistance to the socialist tendency to centralize policymaking and standardize programs.

Thatcher's approach to local government revealed that the Conservatives perhaps lacked a dedication to local government in itself. We find, in fact, that the Thatcher and Major governments have displayed a penchant for centralization that increasingly resembles the mindset of Labour in the bygone era. However, the Conservative's efforts toward centralization differ from Labour's in two important respects. First, although Labour governments have adopted expansive perspectives on the role of local governments in the furtherance of social welfare and the standardization of services, the Conservatives have taken an extremely restrictive view. Second, the Thatcher and Major governments have been much more successful at imposing their will on local authorities than any Labour government.

Thatcher laid the groundwork for the process through political maneuvers that altered the constitutional position of local authorities.[12] As a result, the viability of these institutions as outlets for political participation has diminished immensely. The steps include:

1. The Conservatives have shifted the effective locus of authority in the unitary state from Parliament to "the government," meaning the cabinet, thereby enabling it to force conformity from local authorities even in the absence of express legislation.

2. They have placed statutory limits on the discretion of local leaders, thereby reducing the local authority to the handling of administrative matters, as distinct from policy issues.

3. They have sharply curtailed the latitude for local authorities to determine their own expenditure levels.

4. They have abolished elective councils—for example, in Greater London and six metropolitan

county areas—and often shifted the residual powers to central departments or appointive boards rather than to other elective local jurisdictions.

To add to this litany, the Conservatives under Margaret Thatcher entirely abolished property taxes and replaced these with a "community charge." Known to its opponents as a poll tax, the latter was a per capita levy against all voting-age residents of a locale. It was a highly regressive measure: it placed a much greater burden on the poor than did the property tax. The Conservatives embraced this approach, however, as a means to harness Labour-dominated local authorities. As the theory went, councils that spent generously on social programs would run the risk of antagonizing the very voters whom they sought to help—the poor.

The first poll tax bills arrived in voters' mail boxes in 1990. The shock contributed to the sharp decline in Thatcher's popularity. Shortly after assuming the government, John Major tried to ameliorate the regressiveness of the poll

---

The story of the years since 1979 is of increasing centralization. Local authorities feel that their autonomy and discretion have been diminished.

. . . The new feature of Mrs. Thatcher's government is that it has jettisoned previous conservative beliefs in a balanced or mixed constitution, based on a sharing of powers between a number of institutions, in favor of a more continental, or even Marxist, notion of state as a single unified entity, whose only alternative is the market. Ideology has driven this government to an extent never seen in British Conservative government before. Its ideology of fundamental change has led to a challenge of the very foundations of local government.

Source: George W. Jones, *Governance*, p. 176.

---

tax by cutting, on average, £140 off each bill. The revenue shortfall was compensated by an increase in the value-added tax. Of course, this increase fell hardest on the very people who suffered most from the poll tax—those with low to middle incomes. Ten months after taking over the government, Major realized that replacement of the poll tax had become an unavoidable political necessity. The new tax was named the council tax. It was a mildly progressive program with tax bands based on the capital value of houses. The council tax proved to be only slightly less controversial—and no more effective as a revenue instrument—than its predecessor. The basic problem was that the people felt that the government's valuation of houses was excessive. After the artificially high real estate values of the Thatcher years, the succeeding recession pushed down real property values. This factor was not fully accounted for by governmental appraisers. Many people have appealed the tax and refused to comply with it, producing delays and collection problems for the government. In spite of the government's difficulties, the council tax deepens local governments' dependence—especially Labour-controlled councils—on the central government, a basic postulate of the Conservative government. Although the Treasury financed the transition from the poll tax to the council tax, this assistance is conditioned on the local governments' implementation of spending limitations.

One bromide that appears in the U.S. press asserts that Thatcher introduced an age of "popular capitalism" in the United Kingdom. We might infer from this nomenclature that the privatization of former public corporations has increased the involvement of the average citizen in the ownership of shares in British business. In turn, giving people "a piece of the rock" conceivably would enhance their self-reliance and sense of political efficacy.

Some of the hard data run against this inference, notwithstanding its intuitive appeal. As we saw in Chapter 4, the Thatcher years have actually heralded an abrupt halt to the wider distribution of wealth down to lower strata in society. Further, the sale of shares to rank-and-file citizens does not mean that they will retain them.[13] This was the case with several of Thatcher's major share sales. Within a few months, the original number of shareholders tended to collapse to a much more modest figure: for British Aerospace, from 158,000 to 27,000; Amersham International, from 62,000 to 10,000; Jaguar, from 125,000 to 49,000; British Telecom, from 2.2 million to 1.6 million; British Airways, from 1.2 million to 420,000.

It becomes obvious that many small shareholders quickly sell their stocks to larger shareholders. They choose, in other words, to pocket the difference quickly between the low, attractive price set by the government and the actual return that they can command on the open market. And it becomes clear that institutional investors—large pension funds, insurance companies, and trusts—quickly vacuum up the discarded shares. For example, while the ratio of equities in institutional versus private hands reached 1.7 in 1992, it stood at 1.2 in 1970. Thus, the Conservative government must go a long way before returning popular capitalism to its 1970 level.

Indeed, one major share sale pointed up the degree to which institutional buying can actually threaten national security. One week after the October 1987 stock market crash, Thatcher persisted in selling the 32% share that the United Kingdom government held in British Petroleum. The uncertainties brought on by the crash, however, had scared off most individual investors. Institutional buyers moved in at bargain-basement rates. Leading the pack was the Kuwaiti government, which ended up with over 20% ownership of British Petroleum. A year later, the U.K. Department of Trade and Industry, citing the obvious national security issue, ordered Kuwait to divest itself of over half its shares.

In assessing popular capitalism, we should also keep in mind the fact that Thatcher's—and Major's—stress of the service sector over manufacturing propelled a sharp decrease in union membership. When Thatcher came to power in 1979, 53% of workers belonged to unions; in 1993 only 38%. The United Kingdom would require a great deal more individual ownership of stocks than actually presented itself from share sales to offset the losses of leverage suffered by workers through the precipitous decline of the unions.

Limits to the Public's Right to Know

As we saw in Chapter 4, Britain has no bill of rights. Of course, this does not mean that Britons entirely lack freedoms comparable to those enjoyed by Americans. They simply cannot call upon an entrenched guarantee of their rights. This constitutional condition bears clear implications for political participation. In no small measure, democracy runs on the public's knowledge about how the government operates and how it disposes of the various matters that it treats.

The strong traditions of freedom of the press and the public's right to know that prevail in the United States greatly contribute to the participatory nature of American politics. However, many influential Britons believe that such openness is, at best, untidy and inefficient—and at worst, dangerous to the security of the state. Without a written constitution or even statutory vehicles like Freedom of Information legislation available in the United States, people who become disturbed over government secrecy find little recourse. The dominant elite's views regarding how much the public needs to know determine almost entirely the contours of what the government will expose to outside scrutiny.

Until 1989, section 2 of the 1911 Official Secrets Act, more than anything else, stood in the way of freer access to government information. This act strictly proscribed civil servants from providing information of any kind to people outside government unless specifically authorized to do so by their superiors. As a result, interactions between Whitehall bureaucrats and journalists technically operated within the confines of official briefings by departments' information staff and severely limited sessions with line civil servants. Similar strictures applied to officials' interactions with interest groups and members of Parliament.

There are ways of getting around this system. Top journalists frequently enjoy informal ties with the Whitehall elite. This permits them to take top officials to lunch and extract information off the record. Many relationships become so strong that officials will take phone calls from journalists or send them government documents through the mail in plain brown envelopes. The upper echelons of Whitehall turn a blind eye to many of these activities. In fact, it is not unusual for officials to participate in the unauthorized sharing of information—often for reasons that relate to intramural conflicts with other top mandarins or to severe differences with the political leadership. However, such tactical leaking can severely damage officials' credibility and careers if they become indiscreet.

After 1984, events placed the conventions that surround this cat-and-mouse game under severe strain. First, a case in 1984 involved Clive Ponting, a rapidly rising assistant secretary in the Ministry of Defense who had received kudos and an honor—Officer in the Order of the British Empire—from Thatcher for his work in an earlier efficiency exercise in his department. Ponting had moved to a unit responsible for determining, among other things, what type of information should be made available to Parliament.

Part of Ponting's work involved advising ministers on how much they should disclose to the House of Commons Foreign Affairs Committee, which was conducting an inquiry into Britain's war with Argentina over the Falkland Islands in 1982. In the course of this activity, Ponting became convinced that ministers would have to reveal an embarrassing fact: the Argentinean cruiser, *General Belgrano*, had actually turned away from the British exclusionary zone surrounding the Falklands before it was attacked and sunk. When it became clear that the government would not divulge this information—indeed, that it would continue to tell Parliament the opposite, Ponting took matters into his own hands and sent copies of the relevant documents to a Labour member of Parliament.

The government readily traced the leak to Ponting and chose to prosecute him. The justice who presided at the trial gave strict instructions to the jury. He even impugned Ponting's defense that he had only the interest of the state in mind by telling the jurors that there was no distinction between the interests of the current government and those of the state. Unswayed, the jury acquitted Ponting. In the process, they raised fresh questions about the future viability of section 2 of the Official Secrets Act.

We discussed in Chapter 4 the successor to this case. It involved Peter Wright's revelations in the book *Spycatcher* of the inner operations of MI5, Britain's highly secret domestic security agency. After tortuous legal proceedings that had the crown arguing its case in Australia, Hong Kong, and New Zealand—as well as in England—the juridical standing of official secrecy has eroded further. Now, even a crown prosecution that invoked an alleged "life-long duty of confidentiality" rather than the Official Secrets Act has failed. The British tradition of uneven enforcement of secrecy had not helped the crown's case; during proceedings in Australia, Wright's attorney revealed that the gov-

ernment had chosen not to halt the publication of a book appearing in 1981 that contained the essence of his client's revelations about MI5.

Signs of strain developed elsewhere in the British tradition of selective transmission of information. In the autumn of 1986, two well-respected newspapers, *The Guardian* and the newly formed *Independent*, decided to take on one of the most venerable institutions in the British system of secret government: the daily briefing given to selected journalists, called "lobby correspondents," by the prime minister's press secretary. The two papers claimed that such sessions often involve government manipulation of the news—even disinformation that deliberately misleads the public. They chose to boycott these briefings until they could at least attribute the source of the material they receive from the press secretary. Currently, lobby correspondents must employ euphemisms like "a Whitehall source" so as to obscure the fact that they have been spoonfed pablum by No. 10 Downing Street.

More alarming, very serious differences have arisen between the Thatcher and Major governments and the British Broadcasting Corporation. As a state-owned broadcasting system, it has earned a worldwide reputation for even-handed coverage of public affairs. The maintenance of this record requires, presumably, that the network render critical assessments of government positions and actions that do not stand up well under analysis. Normally, British governments grouse when they believe that the BBC has slipped into excessively negative coverage. Yet they generally eschew specific actions that might cross the line between displeasure and interference.

The Conservative governments have changed the atmosphere very substantially by in fact making it increasingly difficult for the BBC to do its job. The winter of 1986–1987 marked a low point for the BBC. In October 1986, Norman Tebbit—then a cabinet minister and chairman of the Conservative Party—issued a scathing attack on the BBC's coverage of the U.S. bombing raid on Libya that had taken place earlier that year. Several other interventions followed this one.

In the first rounds, Alasdair Milne—the BBC director general—seemed to have effectively held off Tebbit. But the government moved with full force in January 1987. In one installment of a six-part series on British freedom of information, called "Secret Society," the BBC planned to disclose details about an intelligence program whose existence, if generally known, could acutely embarrass the government. Called "Zircon," the project cost some £500 million to build a spy satellite for the United Kingdom.

Theoretically, Zircon would make Britain less reliant upon the United States for intelligence. However, two aspects of the program made it highly vulnerable to public criticism. First, the government had kept Zircon under a veil of strict secrecy—even keeping Parliament in the dark. This violated a concordat it had struck with Parliament. Specifically, it had agreed to notify the chairman of the House of Commons Public Accounts committee, in confidence, whenever it embarked on a secret project totalling more than £250 million during its life. Second, the satellite itself was judged as nearly technologically obsolete. (Indeed, the government abandoned Zircon entirely in the summer of 1987.)

When the government found that the BBC's "Secret Society" series would reveal the existence of Zircon, it put pressure on Director General Milne to ban the film. However, a reporter who had worked on the series chose to publish the essence of the Zircon story in his magazine, *The New Statesman.* In what appeared as a vindictive step, the government then raided the BBC offices in Glasgow where the series was produced, and confiscated all of the tapes of the programs and the film from which they were derived. Only a few days before,

Milne had resigned as director general in response to an invitation from the chairman of the BBC board—a Thatcher appointee who had only recently assumed his position—to leave quietly.

In the aftermath of the *Spycatcher* scandal, some reforms were introduced by the government. The 1989 Security Service Act put the secret service on a statutory basis, clarifying the grounds for nondisclosure to include defense, security, intelligence, and confidential information. Even though John Major has committed himself to strip away secrecy, progress in this area has been slow. For example, while in May 1992 the names, makeup, and terms of reference of the standing cabinet committees were published for the first time, ad hoc committees and the list of the ministers whom the prime minister meets daily are still not provided. It is clear that these measures were not the product of the government's commitment to reform. They are the result of fear of embarrassment, and they still do not provide the necessary information to improve the administrative process.

CONCLUSION

This chapter has probed the important area of governance that relates to political culture. It observed at the outset that democratic systems must seek a delicate balance between the authority of the state and its responsiveness to the public will. It also noted that Britain has erred traditionally on the side of the former. In fact, scholars have characterized it as a deferential political culture in which citizens, although reasonably well oriented to political participation, tend to give the benefit of the doubt to political authorities.

The turmoil of the 1970s and 1980s might have altered this situation. However, we lack comprehensive studies to ascertain the dimensions of changes—if, indeed, they have occurred. Suffice it to say that the fault lines of social division seem to be shifting. With respect to political socialization, immense class differences persist. However, these do not translate all that clearly into class consciousness. Regional differences and ethnicity—both of which can accentuate class consciousness—loom as the clearest threats to the politics of deference. Region plays an important role because of the degree to which the North has lagged behind the South in economic performance. Ethnicity has achieved high salience because nonwhites have become disillusioned with the struggle for integration in British society, and whites—especially working-class youths—have convinced themselves that nonwhites have robbed them of economic opportunities.

With respect to participation, Britons remain more strongly oriented to support of the current regime. However, their opportunities for involvement in groups and institutions that influence the course of political life seem to have contracted rather than expanded. Indeed, citizens seem to have lost ground in several areas in the past decade. Despite their strong national feelings, the Scots and the Welsh have little hope of devolution. The Catholics in Northern Ireland continue to bottle up their aspirations in face of the impasse between the *Protestant majority* and the U.K. government. Successive Conservative governments have beaten down assertive local authorities and substantially altered their constitutional position. Economic forces and public impatience with labor strife have led to a dramatic decline in union membership.

Some find cause for celebration in the Conservative's selling off state-owned enterprises. However, the data suggest that privatization has failed to usher in the era of popular capitalism. More alarming, the limited scope of the reforms that followed the Ponting, Wright, lobby correspondent, and BBC cases suggests that recognition of the public's need to know

runs against the intransigence of the opposition from politicians and career civil servants alike.

NOTES

1. Philip Norton, *The British Polity* (London: Longman, 1984), p. 18.
2. R. Jowell, S. Witherspoon and L. Brook, *British Social Attitudes, The Fifth Report, 1988–89.* (Aldershot: Gower, 1988), Q76, p. 227.
3. Richard Rose, *Politics in England: Persistence and Change* (London: Macmillan Press Ltd., 1989).
4. Ian Budge and David McKay et al., *The Changing British Political System: Into the 1990s,* 2nd ed. (London: Longman, 1988), p. 79.
5. Ian Budge and David McKay et al., *The New British Political System: Government and Society in the 1980s* (London: Longman, 1985), pp. 84–85.
6. W. L. Miller, "Social Class and Party Choice in England: A New Analysis," *British Journal of Political Science,* 8 (1978), 257–284, as cited by Budge and McKay et al., p. 82.
7. R. Jowell and C. Airey, eds., *British Political Attitudes: The 1984 Report* (Aldershot: Gower, 1984), p. 31.
8. Alan C. Marsh, *Protest and Political Consciousness* (London: Sage, 1978), p. 118, as cited by Dennis Kavanagh, *British Politics: Continuities and Change* (Oxford: Oxford University Press), p. 48.
9. Marsh, as cited by Rose, *Politics in England: Persistence and Change* (Boston: Little, Brown, 1986), p. 124.
10. Lawrence Parisot, *Attitudes about the Media: A Five-Country Comparison,* Public Opinion 10, 5 (1988).
11. George W. Jones, "The Crisis in British Central-Local Government Relationships," *Governance: An International Journal of Policy and Administration,* 1 (1988), 165–167.
12. Jones, 171.
13. Roger Buckland, "The Costs and Returns of Privatization of Nationalized Industries," *Public Administration,* 65 (1987), 241–258.

REFERENCES AND SUGGESTED READINGS

Almond, Gabriel A., and Sidney Verba. 1963. *The Civic Culture: Political Attitudes and Democracy in Five Nations.* Princeton: Princeton University Press.

Buckland, Roger. 1987. "The Costs and Returns of Privatization of Nationalized Industries." *Public Administration* 65:241–258.

Budge, Ian, and David McKay *et al.* 1985. *The New British Political System: Government and Society in the 1980s.* London: Longman.

Dearlove, John, and Pete Saunders. 1991. *Introduction to British Politics: Analyzing a Capitalist Democracy.* Cambridge: Blackwell Press.

Evans, G., A. Heath, and C. Payne. 1991. "Modelling Trends in the Class/Party Relationship 1964–87." *Electoral Studies.*

Gamble, A. 1989. *The Free Economy and the Strong State: The Politics of Thatcherism.* London: Macmillan.

Jones, George W. 1988. "The Crisis in British Central-Local Government Relationships." *Governance: An International Journal of Policy and Administration* 1:162–183.

Jowell, Jeffrey, and Oliver Dawn. 1989. *The Changing Constitution.* Oxford: Clarendon Press.

Jowell, Roger, and Sharon Witherspoon. 1990. *British Social Attitudes: The 7th Report.* Aldershot: Gower.

Kavanagh, Dennis. 1979. "Political Culture in Great Britain: The Decline of the Civil Culture," in Almond, G. A. and Verba, S., eds. *Civic Culture Revisited,* Gabriel A. Almond and Sidney Verba, eds. Boston: Little, Brown. *1985 British Politics: Conti-*
nuities and Change. Oxford: Oxford University Press.

Kay, J. A., and M. A. King. 1990. *The British Tax System.* Oxford: Oxford University Press.

Marsh, Alan C. 1978. *Protest and Political Consciousness.* London: Sage.

Messina, Anthony. 1989. *Race and Party Competition in Britain.* London: Clarendon Press.

Miller, W. L. 1978. "Social Class and Party Choice in England: A New Analysis." *British Journal of Political Science* 8:257–284.

Norton, Philip. 1984. *The British Polity.* London: Longman.

Parry, Geraint, George Moyser, and Neil Day. 1992. *Political Participation and Democracy in Britain.* Cambridge: Cambridge University Press.

Ponting, Clive. 1985. *The Right to Know: The Inside Story of the Belgrano Affair.* London: Sphere.

Riddell, Peter. 1989. *The Thatcher Era.* London: Blackwell.

Rose, Richard. 1978. "Ordinary People in Extraordinary Economic Circumstances." In *Challenge to Government.* London: Sage. 1986. *Politics in England: Persistence and Change.* Boston: Little, Brown.

Wright, Peter. 1987. *Spycatcher: The Candid Autobiography of a Senior Intelligence Officer.* New York: Viking.

7

Parties and Elections

n the United States, pursuit of the presidency has reached such proportions that campaigns for party nominations and the election appear to drag on interminably. The paramountcy of the presidential race over congressional elections reflects the U.S. voters' greater interest in persons than in competing political parties. With the separation of powers, a party can fail to gain control of even one house of Congress—as the Republicans have in most of the elections since World War II—and still determine the national agenda through possession of the presidency.

The visitor to Britain would be astounded during the first few weeks after an election. Discussions turn immediately to party matters. They concentrate on how the winners as a team are either gearing up to seize control of and redirect the ship of state—or, in the case of a reelected government, retooling to ensure the maximum possible thrust from their renewed mandate. There is also a surprising amount of discussion about the losers. Newspapers devote pages, and TV and radio networks dedicate hours, to analyses of how the vanquished will possibly alter their organization and appeal so as to prepare themselves better for the next election.

Of course, the victorious party—provided it has an absolute majority of seats—need not face the voters until the expiration of the five-year life of a parliament. Thus the public fascination with intramural party politics, even in the wake of an election, tells us something. An assessment of electoral politics in Britain must go beyond the party system and voting behavior. It must also examine several issues associated with the internal operation of political parties. These include the patterns of membership, relations between the leadership and the rank and file, and the effects of intramural dynamics on how a party adapts its appeal to changes in the electoral environment.

This chapter will take on two tasks. First, it will examine the various issues surrounding party organization—especially those that have assumed special importance for the Conservatives, Labour, the Liberals, and the Social Democrats in the eras of Margaret Thatcher and John Major. We will also look at the very substantial differences in party platforms, especially those between the Conservatives and Labour. Second, we will outline key elements of the operation of the electoral system in Britain—in particular, insofar as these amplify trends in voting behavior.

To this end, we will take a close look at the 1987 and 1992 elections in an effort to ascertain what they tell us about the condition and direction of party politics in Britain. The former deserves special attention because it gave legitimacy to the shift to the right in Britain that previously was lacking. The two other Conservative victories under Thatcher—1979 and 1983—fell short of this definitional significance. Critics could explain away 1979 as the culmination of voters' frustration with the alleged ineptitude of Labour in coping with unions. As well, they could dismiss 1983 as a consequence of the halo effect that enshrouded Thatcher after Britain's triumph in the Falklands War of 1982. On the other hand, 1987 proved to be a free-standing accomplishment. Voters chose decisively to stick with a free-market approach to governance, and 1992 underscored the significance of the shift. Even though Thatcher had pushed further to the right than her electoral mandate and in 1990 faced a forced resignation, her party returned to the polls espousing the core of her approach to governance—albeit sweetened

by such concepts as a "citizens' charter" for public services.

PARTIES

Origins

There are now three main parties in Britain. These are the Conservatives, who currently form the government, Labour, the largest party in the opposition, and the Liberal Democrats, a new party formed in 1988 through the amalgamation of the Liberal Party and the Social Democratic Party.

Both the Conservative and Liberal parties emerged in the nineteenth century. Their development coincided with the expansion of the voting franchise. It also marked prime ministers' heightened awareness of the need to base their governments on a relatively reliable corps of members of Parliament. A centralized party machinery helped members compete for the votes of the ever-expanding electorate. In exchange, the members of Parliament committed their support to whoever carried their party banner in the House of Commons.

The Conservatives formalized their party in the 1830s, before the Liberals. Those who embraced the Conservative Party tended to uphold the traditions of the aristocracy. Most members of the party's leadership belonged to the nobility or were large landholders. For this reason, the party inherited the label "Tories" from their eighteenth-century antecedents. It stressed the values of agricultural interests, the Church of England, and the constitutional status quo that the Tories had championed. However, the Conservative Party differed from the Tories in the degree to which it tempered its stances to attract the support of newly enfranchised segments of society.

The party experienced a period of decline with the defeat of agricultural interests when the Corn Laws passed in 1846. However, it eventually recovered and learned how to package its traditional values in ways that would appeal to the continually broadening electorate. The party consistently resisted political and social reforms, but it always seemed to know when it should make accommodations. After World War II, it embraced views of welfare programs and the role of state ownership of various industrial sectors that did not vary radically from the stances taken by the other parties.

The Liberal Party also developed only gradually into a formal organization. After the 1868 election—the first following the 1867 expansion of the franchise—the party took full shape. It consisted of members from three separate political traditions.

First, the Whigs represented people who enjoyed the franchise before the reforms that began in 1832. While the Whigs had constantly struggled with the Tories over parliamentary reform, many of their policies derived from the peculiar preoccupations of wealthy merchants and industrialists. Second, Liberals became a force in the great movements of the mid-1800s. They fought for the expansion of the franchise and the abolition of the Corn Laws. They rallied around the belief that individual—as opposed to group—concerns should govern politics. They decried the tendency for special interest groups, like landholders and people involved in commerce, to dominate elections and Parliament. Third, Radicals took the Liberal suspicion of politics based on special interests one step further. They believed that ultimately individual interests—rather than those of groups within society—should determine the great issues of state. This required a process of mobilizing mass involvement in politics and revamping parliamentary government to assure that legislation actually reflected the will of the majority.

Encompassing these three disparate traditions meant that the Liberal Party lacked the natural constituency that the Conservatives enjoyed. After taking formalized shape in 1868, it established itself as the first modern political machine in Britain, organizing itself on a representational basis throughout the country, and held a large annual conference that actually adopted policies the leadership took seriously. Further, its members in the House of Commons displayed an unprecedented degree of discipline.

In many respects, the Liberal Party became a victim of its own success. Among its many accomplishments, it enshrined the doctrine of *free trade* (which assured that the working class would benefit from increasing supplies of relatively affordable food), worked to extend the franchise to all adult males, laid the groundwork for the welfare state, and imparted legal recognition to the trade union movement. Taken together, these policies both strengthened the place of the working class in British society and legitimized its efforts toward collective action. After World War I, the Liberal Party began to yield to Labour. The latter had become the natural party of those who had benefited the most from the Liberals' policies.

The Labour Party started in 1900 as a political movement called the Labour Representation Committee. This organization consisted originally of trade union officials and socialists working to complete the expansion of the franchise. It also sought to promote working-class candidates for Parliament.

The Labour Representation Committee became the Labour Party in 1906. In the same year, twenty-nine Labour candidates won seats in the House of Commons. The party drew 22% of the vote—against 12% for the Liberals—in the first election (1918) in which the franchise extended to all adult males. In several subsequent elections, it enjoyed somewhat smaller edges over the Liberals. However, it pulled ahead decisively in 1935, with 38% of the vote compared to the Liberals' 6%. From 1918 to 1935, the non-Conservative vote split so that the Conservatives—either by themselves or in coalition—managed to stay in power. Labour, however, won a landslide victory in 1945 and formed its first government. It subsequently formed governments after the elections of 1964, 1966, and February and October 1974.

The Labour Party has struggled with ideological baggage that has limited its ability to attract voters in the middle of the political spectrum. Through the 1950s, its commitment to further the nationalization of industries and the expansion of the welfare state stood at variance with the mood of the country. Harold Wilson's ability to steer the party to more pragmatic approaches through its long-range agenda contributed greatly to the recovery in its political fortunes in the 1960s. However, the party never fully shed the literalism of its commitment to socialism. For example, it refused to rescind Clause IV of its 1929 constitution calling for "common ownership of the means of production, distribution, and exchange, and . . . popular administration and control of each industry and service."

Since the 1960s, the party has also promoted several causes that, however worthy, have tended to arouse fears among voters in the center. Among these are advocating that Britain renounce the use of nuclear weapons and bar them from the United Kingdom. The party also has significantly promoted the rights of women, ethnic and racial minorities, and gays. In the United States, the Democratic Party's commitment to the protection of similar groups has earned them the accusation that they have succumbed to special interest politics. In the United Kingdom, a blunter term—"Loony Left"—points up the degree to which average Britons remain somewhat less sensitized than Americans to the extent of discrimination.

The efforts to establish the Social Democratic Party emerged after Labour lost power in 1979. Disillusionment among moderate Labour members of Parliament and activists over the prospects of a Labour Party that was increas-

ingly under the sway of the left spawned the move. The Social Democratic Party did not formally organize itself as a separate party until 1981. Before the election of 1983, it had acquired 28 members of Parliament, all but one of whom had defected from Labour. After two relatively weak performances in the elections of 1983 and 1987, it combined with the Liberal Party in 1988.

Organization

Any American observer of British party politics will soon note one phenomenon: the Conservative and Labour parties took increasingly polar positions from the mid-1970s to the mid-1980s. This is due in no small part to their different ways of operating. In the 1960s and 1970s, Labour's membership pushed hard for a democratization of their party's internal procedures. By the early 1980s, the party had become more responsive to rank-and-file participation; but this had the negative effect of frightening many traditional party supporters. Meanwhile, the Conservative Party made virtually no advances toward democratization.

The heightened accommodation within the Labour Party to strident voices opened it to the accusation that it had sold out to the "loony" segments of society. Through a relentless process of attrition, moderate Labourites felt increasingly isolated in their own party. This goes a long way toward explaining why the Social Democratic Party emerged in 1981. It also accounts for the degree to which the Conservative Party under Margaret Thatcher departed from centrist positions. The only other party realistically capable of forming a government appeared to have slipped into doctrinal disarray.

The Conservatives functioned in a more hierarchical manner than did the Labour Party— even when the latter kept its house in relatively strict order. The Conservatives' disciplined style has combined in an especially potent way with the slippage in Labour's appeal to the center. It has allowed radical Conservatives to weigh in heavily in their party and swing the balance further to the right.

Within parties, *wards* are the building blocks of organization. Ward boundaries roughly correspond to the electoral divisions of local governments. Parliamentary constituency organizations thus brigade together several wards. At both levels, parties will hold general meetings; elect executive committees, chairpersons, and secretaries; and, in many cases, retain a paid agent.

At the national level, each party holds an annual conference in the early fall. Each constituency sends one or more delegates, depending on its size, to this meeting. The conference also includes the representatives of affiliated groups such as advocates for women's and youth issues, and trade unions. Here rests one of the acute difficulties of the Labour Party: the block of delegates either directly representing or controlled by unions used to make up approximately 90% of the annual conference—although starting in 1992 this figure went down to a still significant 70%. It is now slated to decrease to 55%. Ninety percent union legislation and its concomitant effect on the tone and actions of conferences, contributes greatly to Labour's difficulties in appealing to the center.

Labour's natural constituency has also declined. In 1974, when Labour chalked up two victories in general elections, 29% of the electors were trade-unionist; in 1992, only 19% were, and of those less than half voted Labour. The decline in union membership over the past decade, along with the militant stances of organized labor, have made the average voter skeptical about the legitimacy of Labour's system of representation. Union-dominated annual conferences tend to make them downright skittish.

Obliged to confront this problem, Labour's leadership under the late John Smith—Neil Kinnock's immediate successor—recognized the undemocratic image that the bloc vote to the party. Smith favored reforms that would establish the one-member, one-vote system in the election of party leadership and parliamentary candidates.

Each of the parties maintains central bureaucracies in London. Between elections these attend to various functions necessary for keeping the party fit for the next contest. The central offices can hold considerable sway over constituency associations—especially if the party has launched a program of reforms to improve its performance. In this regard, local party agents work at least as much to the agenda set in London as to constituency needs. The central bureaucracies also include research capabilities.

Here the Conservative Party has enjoyed an edge. It operates two policy staffs. The oldest—the Conservative Research Department—provides some 12 to 15 professionals. These people advise ministers on policy within their portfolios. Between 1974 and 1979, when the party was in opposition, the research department played an important role in supporting shadow ministers. Indeed, it helped ministers devise detailed plans that quickly came to the fore once Margaret Thatcher became prime minister. Meanwhile, the Centre for Policy Studies—created in 1974 with Thatcher's enthusiastic support—issued a plethora of papers that contributed greatly to the ideological reorientation of the party. None of the other parties' research facilities has attained the level of funding, the clarity of mission, or the effectiveness of these two units.

This brings us to the nub of the organizational issue as it affects the orderly relationship of the three main parties. Each leader—who becomes prime minister if the party forms the government—differs as to the sway that he or she might hold over the respective organizations. The Conservative leader—currently John Major—appoints the party chairperson. This

THERE'S STILL A LOONY LEFT!

YOUR FUTURE IN HIS HANDS?

Neil Kinnock made great strides during his years as leader in moderating the leftist tendencies of the Labour Party. However, the residual effects of the "Loony Left" era under Michael Foot made it easy for the Conservatives to ridicule Kinnock.

individual, in turn, presides at party conventions and directs the central office in London. Party conventions do not select the leader of the party. Instead, a meeting of the parliamentary party—all Conservative members of Parliament—elects the leader. In addition, the chairperson of the party tightly stage-manages annual conferences so that only resolutions conforming to the acceptable line reach the floor.

Theoretically, the central office, whose staff retain their positions at the pleasure of the chairperson and the leader, shares power with the National Union, an umbrella organization of constituency associations. However, the central office has over the past several years largely eclipsed the authority of the National Union. In fact, a 1987 rule change provides that central office guidelines for constituency operations—termed *model rules*—take precedence over all other procedural norms.

Notwithstanding the strength of her control over the Conservative Party through the central office, Thatcher did come in for a surprise in the autumn of 1987. Norman Tebbit—the minister we met in Chapter 6 who had fired several shots across the British Broadcasting Corporation's bow during the buildup to the election—relinquished his cabinet membership after the 1987 election. He also revealed that he wanted to resign as chairman of the party. Thatcher hoped to maneuver Lord Young into the post.

Young—though also a minister—had never run for election. He could not even serve in the cabinet had Thatcher not appointed him to the

House of Lords in 1984. Thatcher increasingly relied on him for alternate advice. At various times during the 1987 campaign he even began to vie with Tebbit for the limelight as the prime minister's principal political adviser. However, a revolt within her cabinet scotched the Young appointment. Young had just received a major cabinet promotion when Thatcher moved him from the Department of Employment to the Department of Trade and Industry. Ministers believed that entirely too much power would be concentrated in his hands. They forced Thatcher to appoint another minister to the post.

Even though the Labour Party has always given obeisance to the rhetoric of a mass party, it managed itself along hierarchical lines until the early 1980s. Ironically, the changes adopted at that time constituted a delayed reaction to the pressures for democratization that had built up beginning in the late 1960s. However, these reforms took so long to be realized that the public mood had changed by the time they received assent—often grudging—from the party leadership. This turn of events has put the party in an awkward situation. On the one hand, it continues to grapple with the manifest untidiness of implementing broader participation. On the other, democratization no longer engages the attention of the public to the degree that it did during the late 1960s and most of the 1970s. Labour has found itself in that least enviable of situations: following an agenda that has become passé—or worse, unpopular.

Until the changes in rules, the parliamentary party elected the leader—as remains the case with the Conservatives. The National Conference theoretically established party policy. In reality, the parliamentary party determined the timing and the substance of Labour's efforts to press these objectives. On the other hand, the Labour leader has not usually enjoyed the control over the party headquarters that the Conservative leader has over the central office.

Instead, the National Executive Committee maintains a strong influence over the party headquarters.

The annual conference elects the National Executive Committee members, who include backbench members of Parliament, union leaders, and other party activists, in addition to members of the parliamentary party leadership. The two main officers of the committee—the chairperson, who normally holds the post for only one year and the general secretary—both serve at its pleasure. Thus, even before democratization, these arrangements limited the usefulness of party headquarters to the leadership, even during elections.

Substantial reforms in the early 1980s followed three general lines. First, local constituency selection committees received enhanced powers with respect to the choosing and reviewing of candidates for the House of Commons. Since 1981, all approved candidates, even sitting members of Parliament, must face mandatory reselection proceedings before receiving the *nihil obstat* of their constituency association. Second, the National Executive Committee has increasingly taken to itself the writing of the party program and manifesto. Third, according to a procedure adopted in 1981, an electoral college, rather than the parliamentary party, selects and annually reviews the leader and deputy leader of the party. Within the college, affiliated trade unions claimed 40% of the members while the parliamentary party and constituency organizations each obtained 30% of the electors.

Of all the reforms, those centering on the choice and reselection of parliamentary candidates have caused the greatest embarrassment to Labour since their implementation. This became painfully apparent to the party leadership during the buildup to the 1987 election, when selection committees held captive by the far left produced candidates whose very nominations raised grave concerns about the direction of Labour. The situation stemmed largely

. . . In the final week of the [1974] campaign . . . a number of operations handled by the Labour Party organisation, then located in Transport House in Smith Square, went sadly, if hilariously, wrong. The arrangements for the party leader's meetings and of media coverage were often appalling. In the middle of the campaign Transport House completely ran out of paper and was therefore unable to print and issue enough press handouts (officials had failed to foresee that an election campaign would require extra paper). One of the better senior officials frequently broke down and wept. An early sign of his feeling stress was when he agitatedly took off his shoes in the middle of a committee or conference; a final sign was when he stormed out of the meeting in his socks. On the Friday after the election Mr. Wilson flew back from his Liverpool constituency with his team while the final results were still being declared and the outcome was as yet unclear. On landing at Heathrow Airport he telephoned Transport House to discover whether the final results would confirm that there would be a Labour Government; however, nobody at party headquarters appeared to be following the results, in which they might have been presumed to have had an interest. Sadly . . . much of the energy as existed in the then upper levels of Transport House was devoted to petty jealousies and internal squabbling, with little apparent concern for the need to unite in order to defeat the Conservatives.

Source: Bernard Donoughue—former adviser to Harold Wilson and James Callaghan—in *Prime Minister,* 1987, p. 43.

from the practice in which branches of the local organization appointed delegates to selection committees. This practice severely limited individual party members' access to the process.

Neil Kinnock, Labour's leader from 1983 to 1992, achieved an important reform that should mitigate the degree to which radical branches of the party can gain control of the selection process. In the autumn of 1987, he won the party conference over to greater accommodation of the principle of one person, one vote. From then on, any party member could attend a selection meeting. Labour did not entirely abandon special recognition of people affiliated with branches of the party. Voters without affiliation will have their ballots weighted so that their aggregate value will not exceed the proportion of nonaffiliated delegates under the old system. For example, if nonaffiliated delegates constituted three-quarters of the voters under the old system, their votes would make up only 70% of the weighted ballots under the new procedure.

These reforms were not enough to give Labour a victory in the 1992 election. It was clear that the party needed to make further advances toward the implementation of the principle of one member, one vote. After the election, the party's new leader, John Smith, worked toward the elimination of what it considered 'Labour's weakest link,' political domination by the unions. During the 1993 Party Convention, Smith maintained that the bloc vote was a symbol of political privilege in a party that preaches equality and that it needed to be eliminated. In spite of the strong protests from the unions, Smith was successful in reducing the union's share of power from 40 percent to a third in the election of the party leader and his deputy. Likewise, the unions accepted the gradual diminution of the bloc vote at the conference to 50 percent of the total. One member, one vote would tackle two out of the three elements that go toward genuine party democracy—namely, a new mechanism for electing a party leader and selecting parliamentary candidates (or deselecting sitting members of Parliament). Significantly, it has yet to tackle entirely the third and most crucial area: replacement of the union bloc vote at the policy making annual conference.

The Liberal Democratic Party was formed in 1988 by a merger of the long-established Lib-

But it was Ms. Mary Duffy from Stockton, who gave a vivid description of life in a constituency Labour Party, who roused the conference. "I don't know what kind of delegates you have on your [own local] GMC [General Management Committee] but some of mine are good, some are bad and some are plain stupid," she said.

Her last GMC had been inquorate, the activists, those she described as the "politicials," had turned up but those who had joined the party to be a councilor and the peak of whose ambition was to become Mayor and meet the Queen were more typical. "That's the kind of people we have as delegates. Yours might be totally intellectual, ours are not," she said to laughter. "So when the GMC meets we have very little political debating."

To those that argued that the decision should be left in the hands of the GMC delegates she said: "That is the biggest laugh. We don't debate anything except drainage and repairs. So the idea that it is so democratic for these delegates to come and give their wisdom over the heads of ordinary members is ridiculous." She earned the biggest ovation of the day.

Source: *The Guardian*, September 29, 1987, reporting the remarks of Mrs. Mary Duffy—a delegate to the Labour conference—in support of party reforms. Used by permission.

eral Party and the relatively new Social Democratic Party.

The Liberal Party, the senior partner in the merger by virtue of its age, embraced a participatory approach when the pressures for democratization were the most intense. The Liberal Party Assembly, as the annual conference was called, played an important role in the discussion and formulation of key policies. However, the party leader and his principal colleagues in Parliament ultimately decided the exact lines of the Liberal agenda. This became clear in the buildup to the 1987 election. The assembly took an abolitionist stance re-

garding nuclear weapons in the autumn of 1986. Nonetheless, David Steel, the leader, worked out a compromise with David Owen, his Social Democratic Party opposite number. Here the Alliance platform adopted by both parties allowed for retention of a British nuclear capability.

The assembly consisted of an amalgam of constituency, parliamentary party, and national organization delegates. A special convention elected the leader. This included constituency representatives chosen by mail ballots and rank-and-file members. Because of the lack of prominence of the parliamentary party in the House of Commons, the central party organization held relatively little sway over constituency associations.

The Social Democratic Party followed a similarly participatory line of governance. A postal ballot to the entire membership selected the chairperson who presided over the Council for Social Democracy, an executive body that debated the major issues associated with policy and organization. On the other hand, representatives of constituencies selected the leader. As with the Liberals, the leader could take stances on the substance and timing of policy objectives that ran counter to the council.

Although the Liberal Democratic Party formed in 1988 inherited its democratic structure from the two parties that established it, the rise of a younger leadership transformed the philosophy of the party. While in 1987, the combined platform of the Liberals and the Social Democrats—under the Alliance banner—promised all types of intervention like high public spending and income policies, the 1992 Liberal Democrats platform promised choice, competition, quality, and enterprise.

Platforms

As we have seen, the British vest considerable importance in the process whereby parties ar-

In the buildup to the 1992 election, the Tories made hay of Labour's plan to raise taxes. Here, then Chancellor Norman Lamont celebrates the unveiling of the Tories' latest weapon.

rive at their policy platforms. Annual conferences ratify the central elements of a party's policy agenda. In the case of the Conservatives, the leadership holds very tight rein on proceedings; thus, substantial divisions between the stated policy objectives of the leadership and those of the conference rarely occur. In the other parties, democratization has greatly increased the likelihood of major differences between the two levels.

The higher democratization of the Labour and Liberal Democratic parties in comparison to the Conservative Party comes at a cost of electoral appeal. This is largely due to the fact that the very menu of issues that receives attention in Conservative platforms tends to reflect more faithfully the concerns that might serve as focuses of public debate. In short, the Conservatives occupy the natural center in the United Kingdom. The other parties must work harder

to demonstrate to the electorate that they too can lay claim to the moderate middle between extremes. The process of democratization has made this task increasingly difficult.

British political scientists have found that the bulk of voters tend to focus on family-centered issues.[1] In this respect, economic issues like the cost of living, prices, and employment always loom large. Politics starts with bread-and-butter issues. Even other matters that might become important in the wider community—like housing, crime, and immigration—take a back seat to whether the family lacks adequate take-home pay or finds its future economic security threatened.

Within the complex array of issues contending for attention from individual parties, thematic emphases have emerged over the years. For example, a study of party manifestoes between 1924 and 1983 revealed that the Conservatives consistently played up the Commonwealth, regional priorities, individual enterprise, and efficient administration. Labour, on the other hand, stressed control of the economy, social justice, and support of international cooperation.

Another study examined to what degree the two parties' platforms resonated with the public preoccupations of the day during elections between 1950 and 1979. It found that the Conservatives adopted positions that corresponded to the public mood more often than did Labour. However, two issues, if looming large in a given election, could lessen the Conservatives' natural advantage: redistribution of wealth and social welfare.

The re-emergence of the Liberal Party as a significant political force and the launching of the Social Democratic Party substantially changed this bipolar competition for the center. As we will see in the section following, these two parties—separately in 1983 and together under the Alliance in 1987 and the Liberal Democrats in 1992—began to appeal to a sizable proportion of middle-of-the-road voters. Their presence on the electoral scene began to crowd both of the main parties out of the center. To date, however, Labour has had the greatest difficulty by far in retaining at least some of its presence there.

A comparative look at the 1992 platforms of the three parties (Conservative, Labour, and Liberal Democrats) underscores this point. Several matters addressed in the platforms hardly rated as burning issues to the bulk of the electorate. Thus the Conservatives chose in many instances to eschew bold promises of any kind. The government party piously ruminated about its intention to run a national lottery to maintain the level of public support for the arts and to encourage contributions from the private sector. Both Labour and the Liberal Democrats felt compelled to call for major reforms—including creation of a ministry for the arts. Did they ask themselves how many rank-

and-file voters worry about the arts? Did they also anticipate the electorates' view of proposals for another department? Have not many of Margaret Thatcher's and John Major's successes stemmed from stroking the general public by earnestly agreeing that government needs to shrink?

Other fields suggest themselves in which the two opposition parties came across as overly innovative in areas where most of the electorate seemed decidedly complacent. The prospects of reforming the electoral system had an important place in the Liberal Democrats' platform and in Labour rhetoric; yet the public has paid scant attention to this issue. Nonetheless, both opposition parties argued vigorously for some kind of reform favoring regional and proportional representation. The Conservatives under Major favored, in general terms, a more active environmental policy. The two opposition parties introduced proposals carefully crafted to appeal to people concerned with pollution and nuclear power.

In all of this, it appears that the opposition forgot a bitter reality of politics: If the electorate has come to the conclusion that there has been too much change on too many fronts, then the maintenance of the status quo will become the center position. This immediately forces calls for elaborate remedial action out of the mainstream. Thus the 1992 campaign saw many issues in which both Labour and the Liberal Democrats found themselves splitting hairs over reform proposals that proved less than compelling to most voters.

To be sure, several issue areas commanded enough attention that the Conservatives had to put forth specific plans of action. Table 7.1 summarizes the positions staked out by the Conservative and opposition party manifestoes in three such policy fields: the economy, education, and local government. In each case, the Conservatives, banking on the fact that the public has broadly supported the thrust of their policies, simply advocated more of the same. In

Table 7.1   HOW THE 1992 PARTY MANIFESTOES COMPARED

	Conservatives	Labour	Liberal Democrats
Economy	—Share of national income spent on the public sector to be reduced to unleash enterprises. —Further privatization—British Coal, Docklands Light Railways, the trust ports, and local bus companies. —More competition for British Gas and the Post Office. —More power to the regulators. —Performance-related pay and compulsory competitive tendering.	—Aims to "ensure that the market works properly." —Utilities to be regulated to stop excessive price rises. —Electricity grid and water to be renationalized. —Coal industry to be supported by "reducing imports" and British Railways to stay in public sector. —Minimum wage to be introduced and EC social chapter to be approved. —Industrial policy to give investment incentives to small business and high-tech firms. —Technology trusts to link business with academia and investment bank for the public sector.	—Extra public spending to create 600,000 jobs over two years, based on "a prudent increase in borrowing." —British Gas and BT to be broken up. —British Rail and British Coal to get private railways. —A new competition agency to regulate financial raids and takeovers. —An operationally independent Bank of England. —Medium-term savings targets.
Education	—Measures to make it easier for schools to become grant-maintained. —Grant-maintained schools to be given more freedom to change their character and being sponsored by private contributors. —More City Technology Colleges for inner cities. —More rigorous testing and more practical teacher training. —The number of students in higher education to be increased and the student loans scheme expanded.	—An extra 6 billion pounds to be spent. —Reducing primary class sizes to 30 or fewer. —More books and equipment. —National curriculum and testing to stay. —New Education Standards Commission to work with inspectors. —Assisted places, opted-out schools, City Technology Colleges, and student loans, all to end. —Schools to keep their budgets and education authorities to get "new strategic role." —Work-experience schemes for the unemployed.	—An extra 2 billion pounds for schools within a year. —Grant-maintained schools and City Technology Colleges to go. —A new curriculum for teenagers. —A levy on companies (at 2% or less of their own training budget) for staff spending on training. —Student loans to be abolished and student entitlement to housing benefit and income support to be restored.

Table 7.1 Continued			
	Conservatives	**Labour**	**Liberal Democrats**
Local Government	—Poll tax to be replaced by a council tax with local spending capped where necessary. —The Audit Commission to publish league tables ranking the performance of councils, and councils to publish more information on their services. —More council properties to be handed over to housing associations. —More money and new quangos, national and local, for inner-city regeneration. —London government to be better coordinated via cabinet subcommittee, and Welsh local government to be reformed.	—Poll tax to be abolished and replaced by "fair rates" taxes based on revalued property; poor to get rebates. —Council-house sales to continue with a housing bank to release their receipts for new buildings. —Part-buy part-rent schemes to be introduced, councils to rent empty property to the homeless. —London to get elected authorities. —Plan to revitalize inner cities through "enterprise partnerships."	—Councils to be organized within a unitary structure. —Whitehall grants to be topped with a local income tax. —The uniform business rate (property tax) paid by business to be replaced by rates based on land values. —More power for councils over education, health, and planning—including road pricing.

Source: *The Economist,* March 21, 1992. © 1992 The Economist Newspaper, Ltd. Used by permission.

the economic field, they promised further moves toward reducing government's direct ownership or regulation of economic sectors. They also outlined further efforts to treat chronic unemployment with retraining rather than payment of benefits. The proposals touching on education and local authorities both built on the Conservative commitment to less latitude, in which local authorities might pursue and fund their own policies, and greater reliance on the private sector in provision of services—including schools and hospitals.

Thus in the 1990s the Conservatives have once again positioned themselves as custodians of the perspective on the role of the state that had dominated the 1980s—the view that much of what government does should be left to the free market. This strategy gave the opposition parties two choices. First, they could try to convince the public that they would pursue a better blend of government intervention and encouragement of the free market than would the Conservatives. Second, they could refute the Conservatives' stance and recommend further efforts on the part of government to direct the operation of the economy.

For the most part, the Labour and Liberal Democratic manifestoes leaned toward the second approach. As Table 7.1 suggests, the Labour Party in particular put forward mainly a wish list of programs and expenditure proposals. These harked back to Keynesian views of management of the economy, and revealed little effort to accommodate the shift in the public mood toward market-oriented solutions.

The Liberal Democrats followed much the same approach. However, their proposals came out in nearly every instance as cheaper—in expenditure terms—than Labour's. This left the impression that they had simply split the difference between the Conservatives, who made few proposals entailing additional spending, and Labour. Both parties had tried to shift the public's focus back to economic intervention and the social agenda. However, they faced an intractable difficulty: most Britons, even many who had yet to partake in the good times, believed—as John Major and the Conservative Party have maintained—that a return to some kind of social intervention will further hurt the economy.

ELECTIONS

The Rules of the Game

Unlike the United States, Britain has no fixed schedule for national elections. However, each Parliament comes to an end five years after the most recent general election. Prime ministers can ask the monarch to dissolve Parliament at any time during this five-year interval. Dissolution automatically starts the wheels in motion for an election, which must take place within seventeen days (not including Sundays and holidays). Normally, prime ministers wait until a Parliament approaches its fourth year before seriously considering whether they should ask for dissolution. In case of a minority government—that is, one formed by a party that does not have a majority of seats in the House of Commons, the opposition parties might force the prime minister to ask for dissolution.

One of the most contentious issues surrounding the British electoral system concerns the practice whereby a candidate for the House of Commons need only obtain more votes than any opponent to win a seat. This rule, which is identical to the applicable rule in U.S. congressional elections, is known as the "first-by-the-post" system. Its opponents include Fred Ridley, a professor of politics at Liverpool University. After the 1987 election, Ridley published a newspaper article in *The Guardian* asserting that Britain now had the least democratic society in Europe (see Table 7.2). He used,

Table 7.2 BRITAIN RANKED THE LOWEST AMONG EUROPEAN DEMOCRACIES WITH RESPECT TO THE PROPORTION OF VOTERS WHO SUPPORTED THE PARTY/PARTIES THAT FORMED THE GOVERNMENT AFTER THE 1987 ELECTION.

Switzerland	77.5%
Luxembourg	68.4%
Italy	57.4%
West Germany	55.8%
Austria	52.9%
Netherlands	52.0%
Denmark	52.0%
Belgium	50.2%
Sweden	50.0%
Norway	49.0%
Finland	48.9%
Ireland	47.3%
Greece	45.8%
France	44.9%
Spain	44.1%
Portugal	44.0%
United Kingdom	42.3%

Source: Fred Ridley, At the Bottom of The Democracy League, *The Guardian*, August 10, 1987. Used by permission.

Table 7.3 PERCENTAGE OF VOTES AND SEATS OBTAINED SINCE 1974

Party	1974 (Feb. 28) Votes	Seats	1974 (Oct. 10) Votes	Seats	1979 (May 3) Votes	Seats
Conservative	38%	47%	36%	44%	44%	53%
Liberal	19%	2%	18%	2%	14%	2%
Social Democratic	*	*	*	*	*	*
Liberal Democrat (under "Alliance" in 1987)	*	*	*	*	*	*
Labour	37%	47%	39%	50%	37%	42%
Other	6%	4%	7%	4%	5%	3%

Party	1983 (June 9) Votes	Seats	1987 (June 11) Votes	Seats	1992 (April 9) Votes	Seats
Conservative	42%	57%	43%	58%	44%	53%
Liberal	14%	3%				
Social Democratic	12%	1%				
Liberal Democrat (under "Alliance" in 1987)	(26%)	(4%)	23%	3%	19%	3%
Labour	28%	32%	32%	35%	35%	43%
Other	4%	7%	2%	4%	2%	1%

*Did not exist in this election.

as his definition of democracy, "government by the whole people of the country, especially through representatives whom they elect." His article simply underscores the fact that the first-by-the-post system in Britain distorts the will of the electorate. With multiple parties, it all too often awards seats to those who draw less than 50% of the vote.

Many other European systems make at least some accommodation for the votes given to parties that do not win pluralities. For example, Germans select members of their lower house half on the basis of single-member districts and half on the basis of the proportion of voters supporting a party list devised at the *Land* (state) level. The latter element of the German system is called *proportional* representation.

A further feature of the British system deepens the unrepresentativeness of British governments. The distribution of votes throughout the country makes it too easy for a party to win an absolute majority of seats in the House of Commons without obtaining the same level of support in the electorate. In many other European systems, the strongest parties rarely obtain an absolute majority of seats in the lower house. Therefore, they form coalitions with other parties to secure majority assent on their legislative program. Such alliances broaden the support among the electorate for the current government.

Table 7.3 indicates some distortions that come from the current electoral system. In the six elections since 1974, no party has formed a government with more than 44% of the votes. In fact, Labour won the February 1974 election with only 37% of the national vote—a figure that translated into 47% of the seats. In elections of February and October 1974 and May 1979, the Liberals garnered, respectively, 19%, 18%, and 14% of the vote. This support, however, gave them only 2% of the seats in each instance.

The participation of the Social Democratic Party in the 1983 and 1987 elections produced a combined drawing power of 26% and 23% respectively; the merged party—Liberal Democrats—generated 19% of the votes in 1992.

Under whichever banner, the center failed to gain more than 4 percent of the seats in the respective elections. At the same time, the center "factor" disturbed the balance in the relative yields of Conservative and Labour votes. The 1983 election saw the Conservatives gain 57% of seats with 42% of the vote. The comparable Labour figures were 28% and 32%. A similar pattern emerged in 1992 with the Conservatives getting 53% of the seats for 43% of the vote and Labour realizing 43% of the votes for 35% of the seats.

Both Alliance parties—now the Liberal Democrats—had grasped the nettle and proposed replacement of the first-by-the-post system. In view of the "lost" votes of the Liberals and the Social Democrats in the 1983 and 1987 elections, we can certainly understand their position. However, the Liberal Democrats will not readily win over the Conservatives and Labour to their view. Even though Labour's recent gains have been slight, it still benefits from the current arrangement. Notwithstanding its poor showing in 1983, 1987, and 1992, it continues to style itself as a contender for the windfalls that have frequently enough bestowed the party with working—even large (in 1945 and 1966)—majorities from electoral pluralities. Proportional representation appears to be, as the British say, a "nonstarter."

Recent Elections and the Legacy of Thatcherism

For Labour and the Alliance parties, many dire predictions emanated from Margaret Thatcher's resounding victory in 1987. Some commentators viewed it as a total realignment heralding a period of Conservative domination of British politics all the way into the next century. Before assessing the significance of the election and how the opposition parties have responded to the grim scenarios, we should look back into the Thatcher years to discover the origins of this resounding success.

We begin our account before the 1983 election. Thatcher emerged from the 1979 election with 339 seats—22 more than she required to control the House of Commons. Considering the radical nature of her policies, this majority provided less than an optimal cushioning. In fact, Thatcher had to reverse herself on some stances to avoid embarrassing revolts on the part of her own backbenchers.

Economic policy proved to be one area in which Thatcher refused to flinch. We have already noted in Chapter 4 the degree to which Thatcher's increase in the value-added tax, deep cuts in public expenditure, and exceedingly tight control of the money supply combined to depress the economy. These seemingly draconian policies stemmed from the view of her most trusted advisers that only shock treatment would jolt British industry out of its lethargy.[2]

The shock produced some severe side effects. At the outset, inflation rose to over 20% (Figure 7.1). However, by early 1980 it began a gradual decline to only slightly above 10% by the end of the year. On the other hand, unemployment started a sharp upward trajectory early in 1980, rising from under 1.5 million to nearly 2.5 million by the end of the year. Both trends continued through 1981—with unemployment approaching 3 million and

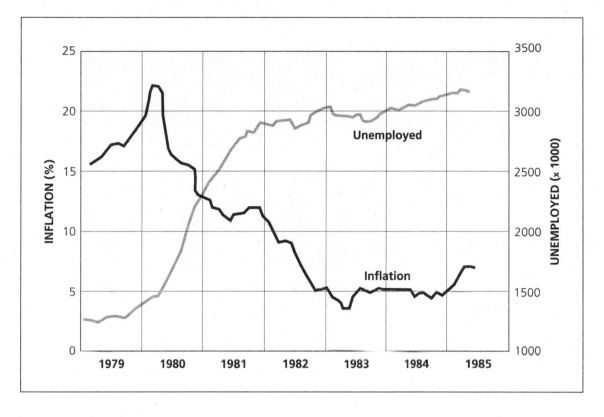

Figure 7.1 Two Sides of British Economic Performance under Thatcher. Source: Helmut Norpoth, "Guns and Butter and Government Popularity in Britain," *American Political Science Review,* 81 (1987), 951. Used by permission of American Political Science Association.

inflation dipping close to 10% by the end of that year.

During the first two full years of Margaret Thatcher's government, the public seemed to repudiate the Thatcher program. By the end of 1981, their approval of her performance had plummeted to 25% (Figure 7.2). Analysts believe that voters' disenchantment came from the unprecedented rise in unemployment. They chose not to give credit to Thatcher for reducing inflation.[3] Some observers believe that this state of affairs was turning around by early 1982—that people were beginning to give Thatcher credit for bringing down inflation.

And a slight improvement in Thatcher's support did reveal itself early in 1982.

At this point, we must account for an event that turned the public mood around completely. On April 2, 1982, Argentina occupied two British possessions: the Falkland Islands and South Georgia Island. Over the next two months, Thatcher led the country through the arduous process of regaining the islands by military means. In the process, her public support rocketed to just shy of 60%. This political ascent was as sharp a restoration of public confidence as a leader in any democracy had ever experienced.

Figure 7.2 Satisfaction with Thatcher's job as Prime Minister.   Source: Helmut Norpoth, "Guns and Butter and Government Popularity in Britain," *American Political Science Review*, 81 (1987), 951. Used by permission of American Political Science Association.

Thatcher's handling of the crisis did more than simply rehabilitate her standing as a decisive and effective leader. It also enshrined her credibility. Over the next twelve months ending with the election of June 9, 1983, not even continued concern about relentless unemployment—the number of jobless people by then hovering around 3 million—could erode the immense Falklands factor. Of course, Michael Foot, the leader of the Labour Party through the 1983 election, contributed greatly to a Conservative appeal based on leadership ability. He seemed increasingly to embody indecisiveness

and ineffectiveness. The Thatcher legacy began to take shape as leadership that actually led.

The 1987 Election in Perspective

The rocky road to Thatcher's third election victory was incongruous with her resounding success. However, her eventual triumph was predictable when we recall the depth of Labour's defeat in the 1983 election. Its 28% of the 1983 vote was 14% below the Conservatives and only 2% above the Alliance parties. Eyes began to focus on whether the Alliance would overtake Labour as the second leading party. Many observers began to speculate about the emergence of a three-way struggle in which the Conservatives, Labour, and the Alliance would ultimately draw roughly the same proportion of voters.

The Conservatives did not maintain a consistently high level of support throughout the second Thatcher term. The county election results in May 1985, for example, pointed up the potential appeal of the Alliance (these results excluded Scotland, London, and the metropolitan boroughs, none of which went to the polls that spring). The proportion of seats held by the Conservatives in the shires holding elections slipped from 48% to 44%. Labour experienced a decline from 35% to 32%. The Alliance, on the other hand, doubled its share of seats from 10% to 20%. Did this mean that it would finally be able to translate its national support into seats in the House of Commons, come the next general election?

Later in 1985, the MORI poll began to track a period of doldrums for the Conservatives. In the early autumn, for example, their support dipped almost to 30%—below Labour's and almost equal to the Alliance's. The summer of 1986 saw a particularly fickle mood in the electorate. An early July poll put the Conservatives 5% behind Labour. In the midst of a poll taken between July 18 and 22, Buckingham Palace made it plain that the Queen objected to Thatcher's refusal to entertain proposals to stiffen sanctions against South Africa for its apartheid policies.

The issue loomed so large because the government's stance was driving a wedge between Britain and the rest of the Commonwealth. The interviews taken by MORI before this "Palace row" indicated that the Conservatives had switched positions with Labour and enjoyed a modest lead. Those conducted after the row revealed that Labour regained all of its losses. A subsequent poll, taken on July 30 and 31, put

Labour 9 points ahead of the Conservatives at 41%. And the Alliance had enjoyed a shorter spurt, placing it at 25%.

As we have seen before, the October party conferences radically altered Labour's and the Alliance's prospects. Initially, the effects showed themselves in a dramatic decline in the appeal of the Alliance. This was bad news for Labour as well. Labour, more a party of resort than the natural government party, actually stood the best chance of winning if the Alliance captured just enough moderate constituencies to make the Conservatives vulnerable to a Labour surge.

Analysts can actually work out the probable outcomes in seats for various combinations of support for the three main parties. They project the likely results in each seat based on previous voting behavior in the constituency and the likely effects of national swings toward and away from the parties. For example, two British authors writing in the leading assessment of the 1983 election noted that the Conservatives enjoyed on average a 16-seat edge in the various percentage shares of support that they held in relation to Labour.[4] This bias in favor of the Conservatives was largely due to the fact that they won their seats with smaller margins— thus more efficiently—than did Labour.

An elaborate array of such projections appeared in *The Guardian* newspaper in May before the 1987 election. It demonstrated the degree to which Labour had to catch up with the Conservatives. It also underscored the fact that Labour would have to benefit from an exceptional Alliance performance.

The Guardian predicted that the worst case for Conservatives, while still winning an absolute majority of seats, would be 38% of the popular vote. In this situation, they would survive a 26% to 33% vote for Labour and a 27% to 34% vote for the Alliance and still form majority governments of 326 to 334 seats. On the other hand, Labour could form a majority government of 326 to 331 seats with only 37% of the vote. However, the electorate would have to keep a tight harness on the Conservatives—between 27% and 30% of all votes—while giving between 31% and 35% to the Alliance—an unlikely prospect.

Will Conservatives Reign Forever?: What the 1992 Election Tells Us

The actual 1987 election results—43% of the vote and 375 seats for the Conservatives, 32% and 229 for Labour, and 23% and 22 for the Alliance suggested two things pertaining to the length of Thatcher's and the Conservative Party's hegemony. First, Labour regained some of the ground it lost when routed by the Conservatives in 1983, while still falling short of the votes that would give it even a bare majority. In fact, some revised projections incorporating the 1987 results suggested that Labour would have to take 8% from the Conservatives in order to emerge from the next election with a majority of one. Second, the inroads made by the Alliance were inadequate to weaken the Conservatives or make them vulnerable to Labour gains.

The question arose as to whether 1987 had set in stone Conservative rule into the next century. Some data from the Gallup election survey (June 10 and 11, 1987) presented some clues to what would have to happen before Labour would stand a chance of forming a government. When respondents were asked to name two important issues, the four concerns receiving the most mention were unemployment (49%), defense (35%), the National Health Service (33%), and education (19%). In the case of the three "social" issues, respondents actually believed that Labour would do a better job than the Conservatives. The party held 34%, 49%, and 15% edges among people who cited unemployment, the National Health Service, and education, respectively, as important. However, when defense was a key issue, the Conser-

vatives won by a margin of 63% over Labour. The softening of Labour's stance on nuclear disarmament in the autumn of 1989 helped to make it more competitive in this regard. More critically, the collapse of communism in Europe shifted voters' focus away from national security.

A study of the tremendous success of Ronald Reagan in the U.S. election of 1984 has highlighted the degree to which fate dealt the president a lucky hand.[5] That is, the public mood about economic performance reached an apogee at the optimal time for a landslide victory. The 1987 Gallup election poll suggested a similar effect in Thatcher's victory.

Notwithstanding unemployment that remained close to 3 million, Britons had taken a bullish turn on their futures. In fact, Gallup had recorded a dramatic swing in the voters' view of the economy and their own prosperity. In September 1986, 32% more people thought the economy was getting worse than believed it was getting better or staying the same. By election day, the balance had swung to +15% on the side of those who saw light at the end of the tunnel. With respect to respondents' views of the finances of their household, a 12% skew in the direction of pessimism had become a slight—2%—bias toward optimism.

Observers who projected a Conservative dynasty from the 1987 election results engaged in a risky speculative enterprise. Several factors must continue to carry weight. First, Thatcher did not repeat the nearly flawless performance of her past periods, and this contributed to her demise. If her government had run the entire life of the parliamentary term—till 1992—Thatcher would have almost turned 67 and have served as prime minister for more than 13 years.

Pierre Elliott Trudeau, the immensely adroit and popular Canadian prime minister, recognized as he approached 65 and had served for more than 15 years, that it was time to step down. Clearly the Canadian electorate and the Liberal Party notables alike had tired of the

"Not so fast, children!" We're ahead of schedule so we'll wait for an emptier one!"

The leaders of the opposition wait on a near-empty underground train as Thatcher makes it clear to her party that she will determine when the time (for the election) is auspicious (*The Guardian,* April 8, 1987).

prime minister. Grapes ripen more slowly than strawberries, but if left on the vine too long, they shrivel. The departure of Margaret Thatcher and the succession by John Major left the party with weaker leadership.

Second, interpreters of what 1987 had meant could not assume that voters' views of the economy and their stake in it would remain static. Like Ronald Reagan in 1984, Thatcher in 1987 faced the electorate at a time of relative optimism. British prime ministers enjoy the benefit of greater maneuverability in this respect. Like presidents, they can pursue policies that will work toward desirable economic conditions at election time. However, they also enjoy the luxury of choosing the date for the next election. Still, prime ministers can get the economy, the timing for the election, or both, wrong.

One key consideration about individuals' feelings about the future and the Conservatives' performance in 1987 related to privatization. The Conservatives pursued this policy—discussed in greater detail in Chapter 6—with a vengeance in the buildup to the election. It involved selling off shares in state enterprises, well below market rates. This allowed average citizens to realize windfall returns when they resold these shares. Historically, Keynesian governments have greased the palms of voters with increased spending in social programs just before elections. The Conservatives used the stock market to accomplish the same end.

The question arises whether there are limits to the pursuit of this strategy. In time, a government will run out of state enterprises suitable for delivery to the public sector. For example, between the 1987 and 1992 elections, the Conservatives privatized the distribution of water and electricity. Yet, selloffs in both these cases produced a backlash from people who support privatization but still believe that the government must maintain control over core service industries. Indeed, the Conservatives, under such pressures, abandoned plans to privatize nuclear power plants. To this day, they face strong public skepticism over the ability of cost-conscious private companies to provide good-quality water. Indeed, in the summer of 1993, some of these companies continued to lobby for an extension of their exemptions from producing water that fulfilled European Union standards for quality. On this subject, some analysts probed election survey data to assess whether the Thatcher years saw an erosion of voters' perceptions of the baseline role of government.[6] They failed to confirm any such slippage.

Events immediately following the stock market crash on October 19, 1987, also gave pause. As it turned out, the Conservatives had scheduled a major sale of British Petroleum shares for the week after the crash. They doggedly refused to call off the sale, averting a disaster by propping up the offer with staggered payments and Bank of England guarantees so that the sale did not deepen the crash itself.

The whole experience proved a failure as a demonstration of "popular capitalism." The purchases by private citizens fell far short of anticipated levels, and merchant bankers had to come to the rescue. The episode underscored two obvious facts that had apparently escaped the promoters of privatization. First, every market has a saturation point. Second, the attractiveness of shares expands or contracts in relation to whether the stock market is bullish or bearish. Investors reminded us—and that proved true in the 1992 campaign—that the Conservatives were not able to use privatiza-

tion in future elections to the degree that they did in the buildup to 1987.

In spite of all the problems the Conservatives inherited from the Thatcher era, Labour was unable to capitalize on them. If there is a chance for Labour to become a government in the future, the new leadership has to do more than run an effective political campaign—Labour's 1992 campaign was widely regarded as first-rate. The newly elected leader Tony Blair has to promote a more democratic Labour Party by eliminating unions' bloc voting and promoting a revitalized party leadership with fresh ideas about Britain's future. He must also enshrine his own image as a potential prime minister.

Finally, the Liberal Democrats got off to a slow start as successor to the Alliance. The 1987 electoral verdict drove home the fact that the Alliance could not survive as a loose federation of the Liberal and Social Democratic parties under two heads. Even if the unitary party projected less ambiguity, its actual operation proved as cumbersome as its original name— "The Social and Liberal Democrats."

The merging of the two parties in the Alliance proved more difficult than anticipated. To start with, David Owen, the former leader of the Social Democratic Party, refused to join the merged party; a remnant, dubbed the "Owenites," clung to him too long after the Social Democratic Party had become history. The conferences in which the respective parties decided upon union without Owen were still not so smooth. In particular, the Social Democrats had to make embarrassing policy concessions in order to adopt the Liberal Democratic manifesto. The new party's rocky merger contributed in February 1988 to Labour's attaining 42% in a Marplan poll—the highest level of support that it had attracted in six years. Although the Liberal Democrats have subsequently performed well in by-elections, they underachieved—much as the Alliance did in 1987—in the 1992 general election.

"Vote your pocket and do the economy a favor" was the Conservative slogan in the decisive issue of taxation in the 1992 election. While Labour relentlessly pursued the issue of health care and the Liberal Democrats presented education as the center of their campaign, the Tories pressed the idea that a Labour government—or a Labour-Liberal Democratic coalition—would introduce extra taxes, higher prices, and higher mortgages. On March 10, 1992, the Conservative government presented a skillfully crafted budget that boxed Labour into a corner. The budget cut the standard rate of income tax and raised the level below which individuals would not pay tax. Both measures aimed to favor people with low incomes. Instead, this strategy flew in the face of fiscal responsibility—even given the fact that the Conservatives planned to hold the line on spending. The strategy effectively pushed John Smith—then Labour's shadow chancellor—to introduce an alternative budget containing higher taxes that would finance traditional Labour positions in social programs.

The importance of the tax issue was not obvious before the last months of the campaign; in fact, public polls showed that health, education, and unemployment were the most important issues. And the Labour Party held a big lead on each. Tax as an issue remained lower on the list of the electorate's concern. Thus Smith's position on taxation reflected a fiscally responsible Labour ready to reject the easy route of public borrowing to finance new expenditures—an argument that, if well played, could become an asset showing the party's new acquired responsibility. The Conservatives found in the inevitable tax increase, if Labour was elected, an invaluable focal point for an otherwise lackluster campaign.[7] The Conservative strategists—without taking into account any distributional nuances—argued that Labour's tax increase would amount to an extra £1,000 for the average taxpayer. This fig-

ure thereafter appeared in Conservative billboards, posters, and speeches as "Labour's Tax Bomb." The success with which the Conservatives painted Labour as a tax-and-spend party set the stage for Major to resort to Thatcherite scaremongering. In the latter days of the election, the prime minister raised the specter of Britain turning socialist just as Europe had abandoned the left.

Meanwhile, Labour—trying to underline its proposal's redistributive consequences—unsuccessfully proclaimed that eight out of ten families would be better off under John Smith's budget. Unfortunately for Labour, voters more readily grasped the Tories' "Tax Bomb" motif. A Gallup postelection survey showed that only 30% of the voters said that they would be better off under Labour's tax and budget proposals; 49% maintained the contrary. The outcome of the 1992 campaign presented yet another lesson for the opposition parties: in spite of the electorate's professed preference for more social spending and its concern for social issues, the pocketbook motivation almost invariably proves decisive when it is time to cast the ballot. The failure of the pre-election polls to show the tax issue in its real dimension alerts us to the people's inclination to give "socially correct" answers to certain issues. Although few people are ready to reveal selfish motives for their voting intentions, individual interests play a big role in their voting decisions.

In 1992, the Liberal Democrats' strategy was almost single-minded in its concentration on education and electoral reform. This strategy did not hamper the Conservatives'—and to a lesser extent Labour's—ability to dominate the agenda by launching expensive campaigns that displaced the Social Democrats from sufficient press coverage and reduced their possibilities for communicating their message. The Liberal Democrats' hope for the immediate future would be a "hung" Parliament in which neither the Conservatives nor Labour would gain a

majority. Under such circumstances, the Liberal Democrats could trade their participation as junior partners in a Labour–Liberal Democratic coalition in exchange for the promise of electoral reform. As we have seen before, proportional representation would enhance the Liberal Democrats' electoral potential.

CONCLUSION

This chapter has examined party organization and the electoral process in the United Kingdom. It has assessed the effects of democratization in the Labour and Liberal parties on their electoral viability. It has also traced the development of the Liberal Democrats from the emergence of the Social Democrats and through the Alliance period.

It appears that interest in democratization has ebbed due to less demand from the general public. Labour and the Liberal Democrats have had to learn lessons about the costs of implementing participatory reforms too quickly or in ways that alarm relatively nonattentive voters.

Labour and the Liberal Democrats stand a better chance of appearing as attractive and disciplined parties in the next several years. We might also expect Thatcherite conservatism to lose some appeal with age. In addition, as our discussion has suggested, the Conservatives under Margaret Thatcher enjoyed tremendous luck in the timing of and circumstances surrounding the 1983 and 1987 elections. John Major experienced the same good fortune in 1992. Will this luck hold in the next outing?

NOTES

1. Ian Budge and David McKay et al., *The New British Political System: Government and Society in the 1980s* (New York: Longman, 1985), p. 90.

2. William Keegan, *Mrs. Thatcher's Economic Experiment* (Harmondsworth: Penguin, 1984), pp. 119, 158.

3. Helmut Norpoth, "Guns and Butter and Government Popularity in Britain," *American Political Science Review,* 81 (1987), 951.

4. John Curtice and Michael Steed, "Appendix 2: An Analysis of the Voting," in Davis Butler and Dennis Kavanaugh, *The British General Election of 1983* (London: Macmillan, 1984), p. 361.

5. D. Roderick Kiewiet and Douglas Rivers, "The Economic Basis of Reagan's Appeal," in *The New Direction in American Politics*, eds. John E. Chubb and Paul E. Peterson (Washington, D.C.: Brookings Institution, 1985), pp. 71–72.

6. Harold D. Clark, Marianne C. Stewart, and Gary Zuk, "Not for Turning: Beliefs About the Role of Government in Contemporary Britain," *Governance: An International Journal of Policy and Administration,* 1 (1988), 271–288.

7. David Butler and Dennis Kavanagh, *The British General Election of 1992* (London: The Macmillan Press Ltd., 1992). Anthony King, *Britain at the Polls* (New Jersey: Chatham House, 1992).

REFERENCES AND SUGGESTED READINGS

Alt, James E. 1984. "Dealignment and the Dynamics of Partisanship in Britain," in Dalton, R. J., Flanagan, S. C., and Beck, P. A., eds. *Electoral Change in Advanced Industrial Societies*, eds.

Anderson, Bruce. 1991. *John Major: The Making of the Prime Minister.* London: Fourth State, 1991.

Beer, Samuel J. 1967. *Britain Against Itself: The Political Contradictions of Collectivism.* New York: Norton.

———. 1982. *Modern British Politics: Parties and Pressure Groups in the Collectivist Age.* New York: Norton.

Beloff, Max, and Gillian Peele. 1985. *The Government of the UK: Political Authority in a Changing Society.* London: Weidenfeld and Nicolson.

Butler, David, and Dennis Kavanagh. 1984. *The British General Election of 1983.* London: Macmillan.

Clarke, Harold D., Marianne C. Stewart, and Gary Zuk. 1988. "Not For Turning: Beliefs About the Role of Government in Contemporary Britain." *Governance: An International Journal of Policy and Administration* 1: 271–288.

Crewe, Ivor, Bo Sarlvik, and James Alt. 1985. "How to Win a Landslide Without Really Trying: Why the Conservatives Won in 1983," in Ranney, A., ed.

Britain at the Polls, 1983. Durham, N.C.: American Enterprise Institute and Duke University Press.

Curtice, John, and Michael Steed. 1984. "Appendix 2: An Analysis of the Voting." In Butler and Kavanagh.

Franklin, Mark. 1985. *The Decline of Class Voting in Britain.* Oxford: Clarendon Press.

Forman, F. N. 1985. *Mastering British Politics.* London: Macmillan.

Keegan, William. 1984. *Mrs. Thatcher's Economic Experiment.* Harmondsworth: Penguin.

Kavanagh, Dennis. 1987. *Thatcherism and British Politics: The End of Consensus.* Oxford: Oxford University Press.

Kiewiet, D. Roderick, and Douglas Rivers. 1985. "The Economic Basis of Reagan's Appeal," in Chubb, J. E. and Peterson, P. E., eds. *The New Direction in American Politics.* Washington, D.C.: Brookings Institution.

Norpoth, Helmut. 1987. "Guns and Butter and Government Popularity in Britain." *American Political Science Review* 1992 81: 949–959.

Norpoth, Helmut. 199x. *Confidence Regained: Economics, Mrs. Thatcher, and the British Voter.* Ann Arbor: University of Michigan Press.

8

The Prime Minister, Cabinet, and Whitehall

ondon is a very different town from Washington. It more nearly resembles New York and Washington rolled into one. London thus serves as the hub for virtually every type of activity in Britain. In fact, London knows few rivals as a world-class center. In some respects, it remains a more important city for finance, the performing arts, and the media than it does for politics. Although Britain has lost ground in the sphere of international affairs, London remains among the most powerful and influential cities in many fields of human endeavor.

Unlike Washington, the political side to London comes across as subdued. Buckingham Palace provides a clear enough landmark for tourists. However, most visitors recognize that the building, the people who occupy it, and the soldiers who guard it are all busy with ceremonial functions. Except in rare and isolated instances, the monarchy plays no substantive role in British politics. For the most part, only relatively modest statues that crop up randomly in squares and circles commemorate the great political leaders—including prime ministers. Washington remembers presidents in the same idiom that Rome used to give homage to gods and former emperors. Britain does not even honor its greatest monarchs this way.

Of course, Westminster Palace occupies a special place in the minds of Americans. This august building along the banks of the

No one can approach to an understanding of the English institutions, or of others, which, being the growth of many centuries, exercise a wide sway over mixed populations, unless he divide them into two classes. In such constitutions there are two parts (not indeed separable with microscopic accuracy, for the genius of great affairs abhors nicety of division): first, those which excite and preserve the reverence of the population—the *dignified* parts, if I may so call them; and next, the *efficient* parts—those by which it, in fact, works and rules. There are two great objects which every constitution must attain to be successful, which every old and celebrated one must have wonderfully achieved: every constitution must first *gain* authority, and then *use* authority; it must first win the loyalty and confidence of mankind, and then employ that homage in the work of government.

Source: Walter Bagehot, *The English Constitution*, 1867.

Thames contains both the House of Commons and the House of Lords. Its famous tower stands as a worldwide symbol for parliamentary democracy. Yet its architecture and environs do not leave the impression given on Capitol Hill in Washington of a mighty and energetic legislative branch. Lords in Britain have no private offices and staff. A member of Parliament usually shares an office with at least one other colleague, and together they all occupy various nooks and crannies they have found in several buildings close to Parliament. These facilities were not designed for their current function. And no uninitiated passerby could imagine that they have a role in the great scheme of governance.

Westminster Palace is located in a large square. With our backs to the palace, Parliament Street begins at our right and becomes Whitehall one block to the north. In Washington, the main government departments line broad boulevards. Whitehall, on the other hand, is a narrow canyon. For a few blocks to

the north, most of the buildings on the right are nondescript commercial structures. On the left, we find in huge edifices, mostly of Victorian vintage, Her Majesty's Treasury, the Foreign and Commonwealth Office, and the Cabinet Office. About halfway up, the Ministry of Defence and the Ministry of Agriculture, Fisheries and Food rise to the right.

All these structures bespeak bureaucratic power. Two of the departments along this corridor—the Treasury and the Cabinet Office—function as nerve centers for the entire state apparatus.

But only a small fraction of *Whitehall*—a term applied to the entire standing bureaucracy and to all departments—lays claim to this cherished address. The rest of Whitehall brigades itself in buildings spread throughout London. Except for Inland Revenue, which occupies a former palace several blocks down the Thames along the Strand, other departments have found utterly functional accommodation. Often this is in modern office towers that could just as easily pass as the headquarters of banks or other businesses.

One final address deserves mention. In the midst of Whitehall, one finds a narrow alleyway guarded by iron gates and a picket of police constables—both accoutrements of the Thatcher era. It bears the name *Downing Street*. Peering in, one can see a row of Georgian townhouses. One of these—No. 10—serves both as the office and residence of the prime minister.

Less than fifteen years ago, visitors could move freely through this passageway. And to

The Queen is only at the head of the dignified part of the Constitution. The Prime Minister is at the head of the efficient part. The Crown is, according to the saying, the "fountain of honour"; but the Treasury is the spring of business.

Source: Walter Bagehot, *The English Constitution*, 1867.

get into No. 10, individuals simply presented themselves to the police officer, or bobby, standing at the door. He or she either would already expect you or duck his or her head in the door to see if you had an appointment. Even with the barrier and the police guards barring free access to Downing Street, No. 10 stands in stark contrast to the White House. How like the British: they enshrine the ceremonial head of state in Buckingham Palace behind massive fences secured by crack troops; but the person who actually wields the executive authority over the government works and resides in a lightly guarded townhouse.

This chapter will examine what actually happens in No. 10 Downing Street and Whitehall—in the inclusive sense of the term. The next chapter will look at Westminster. In addition, Chapter 9 will consider the degree to which all three centers of power and political activity—No. 10, Whitehall, and Westminster—must take into consideration other factors that impinge on British governance. We will look at the role of the judiciary insofar as it touches on policy. We will also examine relations between Whitehall and local governments. Finally, we will assess the significance of the European Union as an international body whose functions and legitimacy increasingly provide an overarching context for British domestic and foreign policies.

The Cabinet System of Government

After the debacle of Watergate, several incumbents to the American presidency asserted that they wish to achieve a higher degree of "cabinet government" in the executive branch. Presidents Ford, Carter, and Reagan all took up this theme. They argued essentially that the president could not run the U.S. government all on his own. He required some devolution of his decision making. This could take two forms. Presidents could make it clear to individual cabinet secretaries that they should use greater discretion and refer fewer issues to the White House. They also could foster the development of cabinet-level bodies in which department heads work out as many matters of detail as possible before bringing policy proposals to the president.

The Iran-Contra affair stands as the most egregious instance of the inadequacy of U.S. cabinet government in recent years. Collective consultation failed. President Ronald Reagan's administration surreptitiously pursued a policy that was bitterly opposed by two cabinet officials with an inherent stake in the issue—the secretaries of state and defense. Further, individual discretion and integrity simply disappeared. National security adviser John Poindexter felt justified in embarking on highly questionable activities without direct presidential approval. Poindexter argued that Reagan would have wanted the actions carried out, but would not have wanted to know about them.

Neither President George Bush nor his successor, Bill Clinton, took up these themes to the degree that Presidents Ford, Carter, and Reagan did. However, analysts have observed that Bush could have benefited from a more systematic handling of cabinet decision making. Indeed, some have characterized the poor handling by the United States of Iraqi leader Sad-

---

So, although I was convinced that we could properly do it [divert profits from arms sales to Iran to aid the Contras], and that the president would approve, if asked, I made a very deliberate decision not to ask the president so that I could insulate him from the decision and provide some future deniability for the president if it ever leaked out.

Source: Rear Admiral John Poindexter in testimony to the U.S. Senate and House of Representatives hearings on the Iran-Contra affair, 1987.

---

dam Hussein's threats to invade Kuwait as a classic case of inadequate collective management of a mounting crisis. Similarly, Clinton's administration has failed several times to coordinate the handling of both domestic and national security issues adequately.

Keeping in mind the timeliness of this issue to American politics, we examine closely what is meant by cabinet government in the United Kingdom. In many respects, the British system serves as an archetype of collective cabinet government. Under constitutional convention, all British executive power resides in the cabinet. This body, while acting in the name of the monarch, in fact exercises all of the monarch's executive authority.

The prime minister presides in cabinet as first among equals: making the final judgment in preparation of its agenda, chairing its deliberations, discerning what ultimately the consensus is, and taking the lead in assuring that departments actually follow through on cabinet decisions. Yet the cabinet, as tradition goes, determines collectively all major policy positions of the government. The conventional view of the British system also assumes unwavering loyalty among the members of the government party in the House of Commons. In theory, this assures that cabinets can attain parliamentary approval of their legislative programs with relative ease.

Changes in the Conditions for Cabinet Government

Of course, no system—even a model for the rest of the world—would operate so smoothly in practice. And developments over the past two decades have not spared British cabinet government. First, despite victory at the polls, a winning party may fall short of an absolute majority in the House of Commons. In fact, they have done just this in 6 of 25 elections between 1900 and 1992.

The emergence of the Social Democratic Party and its alliance and ultimate merger with the Liberals has presented the specter of a "hung" Parliament. Such a Parliament would emerge from an election result in which no party clearly obtained even a viable plurality of seats. No one party would be able to form a government on the basis of an informal understanding whereby another party would agree to support its legislative program. A "hung" outcome would force a series of negotiations whereby two parties would ultimately have to come together in a coalition. This arrangement would necessitate the assignment of cabinet posts to members of Parliament from each party on some agreed-to provision for the division of these positions.

Especially in the buildup to the 1987 election, some public opinion polls pointed to a very close election through much of 1985 and 1986. These poll results engendered a great deal of debate about how readily this process of coalition building would work in a country that is used to relatively clear verdicts from the electorate. In turn, Britons would take time getting acclimatized to coalition government. For example, cabinets would not be able to maintain anywhere near their accustomed discipline if they included members of Parliament from more than one party. We have already noted in Chapter 4 that party discipline has weakened in the British House of Commons even under majority governments. This has increased the frequency with which prime ministers must retreat from public stances because their cabinet colleagues urged caution in the face of resistance from disgruntled backbench members of Parliament.

The solidarity that we associate with cabinet government does not come as naturally to the British as many American observers have thought. Prime ministers increasingly find themselves absorbed with the task of teasing consent from their colleagues. In the meantime, running Britain has not become any easier.

When John Major formed his new cabinet after his election in 1990, it brought in 22 cabinet members. In addition, 29 ministers assumed day-to-day responsibility for chunks of departments but did not belong to the cabinet. There were 17 departments of state in Whitehall.

All this adds up to an immense coordinative task. It requires that the prime minister spend a very large part of the time making sure that the various goals of his or her administration mesh. A prime minister must also see to it that the programs that implement these policies function effectively and efficiently. In other words, some issues require that the prime minister take the lead in coordination and not simply defer to his or her cabinet colleagues' perceptions of when and how they should resolve the matter. The prime minister shoulders ultimate responsibility for assuring that Whitehall adopts and adheres to sound management principles.

In response to the demands of the position, recent prime ministers have assumed increasingly high profiles and accumulated more and more staff resources. These trends have occasioned complaints that prime ministers have gradually transformed cabinet government into a variant of presidentialism—dubbed *priministerialism*—with prime ministers usurping the authority of the cabinet. Allegedly, they can so manipulate cabinet deliberations and the machinery of government that they can operate as if all executive power centered on themselves. This being the case, the critics say, prime ministers effectively enjoy the same latitude as presidents in deciding the central positions of their administrations.

Within the debate about the current nature of the British system rests an irony: it appears that neither Britons nor Americans understand one another's systems very well. Presidents hardly enjoy the immense power to act on their own, although British critics of the modern prime ministership attribute this to them. This fact becomes manifest when we look at the degree

[The prime minister] is now the apex not only of a highly centralised political machine, but also of an equally centralised and vastly more powerful administrative machine. In both these machines, loyalty has become the supreme virtue, and independence of thought a dangerous adventure. . . . The post-war epoch has seen the final transformation of Cabinet Government into Prime Ministerial Government. Under this system the "hyphen which joins, the buckle which fastens, the legislative part of the state to the executive part" becomes one single man.

Source: R. H. S. Crossman, "Introduction" to Walter Bagehot, *The English Constitution*, 1967 (1963 edition).

to which presidents fail to work their will with Congress. It also comes to the fore in the innumerable circumstances in which presidents cannot win agreement on major issues from their cabinet secretaries and the bureaucracies that they are supposed to direct. Further, on this side of the Atlantic, Americans continue to romanticize the collective nature of cabinet government in Britain. Many even think that British cabinets take votes and the majority inevitably wins the day—impressions that have rarely reflected reality. We can engage in much more productive inquiry if we remember that both systems differ in very substantial ways. Often it helps to remember that both the presidency and the prime ministership have changed in response to the complexities of executive leadership in our current era. Britons perhaps would correctly note that American presidents have adapted to the requirements of modern executive leadership more quickly than have their own prime ministers. They probably should refrain, however, from labeling British developments toward modernization of the prime ministership as "presidentialization."

The British Cabinet in Perspective

Americans and Britons alike should take greater care to place their respective executive systems into a wider context. We style presidents as "chief executives." Of course, a president also serves as the head of state—a ceremonial function that the queen assumes in the United Kingdom. We construe the prime minister's position as that of "first among equals." In the cases of both presidents and prime ministers, we are talking about the principal executive authority of the land: the effective head of government. Both individuals have to appoint colleagues who will advise them and run parts of the state apparatus.

On the one hand, prime ministers and presidents want to give these political authorities a voice in matters that do not fit neatly into a single "portfolio" and require wider consultation. On the other, both presidents and prime ministers want to maintain the ability to decide things on their own when chronic impasses and severe emergencies justify such interventions. The British have tended to stress the necessity of wide consultation and the Americans to favor the prerogatives of the chief executive. Britons have not always placed themselves in the same spot on the continuum between collective and concentrated executive authority. This becomes clear when we examine the ebbs and flows of cabinet government in history.

Cabinets first emerged in Britain as informal instruments of monarchical rule, developing under a system in which executive authority was—as is the case today with the U.S. president—effectively concentrated in one person. This individual was the sovereign. The term *cabinet* did not gain currency until the early 1600s. Indeed, constitutional writings did not fully acknowledge the cabinet's legitimacy and functions until the mid-1800s.

The first cabinets operated essentially as executive committees of the Privy Council. The latter body had only emerged in the fifteenth century as the recognized designation for the coterie of the monarch's most trusted advisers and government officers. Cabinets began to develop when the Privy Council became too large and unwieldy. They allowed monarchs to consult in relative secrecy with their most trusted and powerful privy councilors. The cabinet focused only on the most sensitive and prickly problems faced by the monarch. Members of this body obtained and retained their positions at the pleasure of the monarch. Thus they enjoyed their authority only when monarchs chose to share their regal prerogatives. Apart from the obvious fact that they were not elected, British monarchs related to their cabinets more as presidents than as prime ministers.

British monarchs' use of cabinets did not always follow even lines.[1] James II (1685–1688) convened his cabinet every Sunday and even assigned a clerk to arrange its business. George I (1714–1727) ushered in a period in the eighteenth century in which the regularity both of cabinet meetings and the king's attendance fell off. Thus even as coordinative tools that worked at the pleasure of the monarch, cabinets played significant roles only for sovereigns capable of giving coherent direction to the myriad affairs of state.

During the nineteenth century, the monarchy declined considerably. Concomitantly, Parliament's power rose at the expense of the executive. Initially, these developments resulted in the enhancement of the most prestigious ministerial domains to the point that some departments became virtual baronies.

Two areas where this was clearly the case were foreign policy and defense. The foreign secretary, the chancellor of the Exchequer, and the ministers of the two military services—the Army and the Navy—worked out many matters either within their own departments or between themselves with little or no reference to the cabinet or the prime minister. During the last half of the nineteenth century, various mili-

. . . For practical purposes after 1717 the Cabinet ceased to be a body meeting with the King.

The reasons for this change have not been pinpointed but a number of motives are fairly evident. The old explanation that George's [I, (1714–27)] inability to speak English led to the withdrawal has been abandoned since the problem of communication had evidently been overcome for the best part of three years after George's accession. The chief reason was that George's personality altered the situation. He was both ignorant of English affairs and stupid and could never be at ease presiding over a wide-ranging discussion among ten or twelve Cabinet ministers. Like many stupid men he was suspicious and preferred to lean on his German advisers and mistresses and perhaps one or two Englishmen. The politicians, for their part, sensing this situation, preferred to consult with the King in private and not at the Cabinet where misunderstandings and animosities could so rapidly arise and flourish.

Source: John P. Mackintosh, *The British Cabinet*, 1977.

tary crises and disasters sparked efforts to institutionalize consultation on foreign policy and defense. However, the principals of the key departments continued to frustrate such efforts by refusing to coordinate their activities beyond technical matters.

The baronial pattern persisted through to 1916 when David Lloyd George became prime minister. He broke the logjam over the coordination of Britain's war effort by bracketing the cabinet and creating a new body, the War Cabinet, which assumed the coordinative tasks that the prime minister could not fulfill on his own. Only one member of this new body administered a department as well. Of course, the urgent circumstances of a brutal and seemingly intractable war greatly aided Lloyd George's ability to override cabinet government.

Significantly, Lloyd George's approach to the prime ministership simply quickened a process that had already begun. Since the late 1800s, the degree to which the electorate identified parties with their leaders had already begun to undermine the baronial positions of ministers. Prime ministers were using more discretion in the selection of cabinet members and more exertion of personal authority within the executive. After the war, they increasingly mandated ad hoc groups of ministers to prepare the especially sensitive elements of policy initiatives for presentation to the entire cabinet.

The use of such bodies can spark resentments in cabinet. Ministers consistently not included in key ad hoc groups that touch on their domains can become obstructionist—even obstreperous—in meetings of full cabinet. In recognition of this fact, prime ministers eventually moved toward the institutionalization of cabinet committees. In this regard, Lloyd George also proved himself a man ahead of his time. Close to the end of the war, he created standing committees for economic defense and development, home affairs, and postwar priorities. The period between world wars saw only sporadic adherence to this level of regularization.

Since World War II, all prime ministers have adhered more or less to a system of routinized

War in the twentieth century has raised the problem of co-ordination in an acute form by bringing about sudden increases in the scope of government action. At the highest level, the need to impose coherent policy without undue recourse to the interdepartmental bargaining typical of peacetime Cabinets has led in both wars to the creation of small bodies with supreme authority to direct the war.

Source: John Turner, *Lloyd George's Secretariat*, 1980.

cabinet consultation through a network of standing cabinet committees—although the longer Margaret Thatcher stayed in power the less she worked through formalized groups. The canons of secrecy that enshroud the operation of the British executive keep us from obtaining exact knowledge of every part of the system. For example, the names and membership of cabinet committees remained a state secret until John Major—in a gesture toward open government—released them in the summer of 1992.

Some prime ministers have indulged themselves in committees of all sorts.[2] Clement Attlee (1945–1951) had 148 standing and 313 ad hoc committees operating at various stages of his administration. Harold Wilson's first government (1964–1970) saw more than 230 ad hoc groups by early 1969. Thatcher, on the other hand, displayed relative parsimony. By the end of her term, she had only used between 30 and 35 standing committees and some 140 ad hoc groups.

As in so many other things, John Major has broken from Thatcher tradition when it comes to committee use. From the outset, he made it clear that he planned to rehabilitate cabinet-style government. An attitude change has taken place, as well as a move toward division of labor through committee establishment. Cabinet ministers feel at ease discussing policy options with Major. Under Thatcher, ministers were told what policy would be and often were tentative about offering even constructive suggestions. Major made a pledge to listen to his fellow Conservatives, cabinet colleagues, committee heads, and even opponents—and make decisions on a collective, informed level. He has largely lived up to this commitment.

Whatever the preferences of individual prime ministers, we can expect that any government will operate standing committees in some specific areas that always require careful coordination. These include planning for legis-

The method adopted by Ministers for discussion among themselves of questions of policy is essentially a domestic matter, and is no concern of Parliament or the public. The doctrine of collective responsibility of Ministers depends, in practice, upon the existence of opportunities for free and frank discussion between them, and such discussion is hampered if the processes by which it is carried on are laid bare. For these reasons it is also the general practice to avoid, so far as possible, disclosing the composition and terms of reference of Cabinet Committees and, in particular, the identity of their Chairmen.

Source: Winston Churchill in a 1952 confidential directive to Cabinet.

lative sessions and management of parliamentary affairs, economic strategy, overseas and defense policy, relations with the European Union, home and social affairs, and security and intelligence. And we can assume that networks of regularized subcommittees function under each of these umbrellas.

THE PRIME MINISTER AND THE RESOURCES AT THE CENTER OF GOVERNMENT

As noted above, Britons do not normally employ the term *chief executive* when referring to prime ministers. Conventions integral to the British unwritten constitutional system require that prime ministers—unlike presidents—exercise their authority only after consultation with the cabinet colleagues. In their capacity as head of government, however, prime ministers fulfill a host of functions that, taken together, make observers wonder whether in practice they operate as chief executives. We can best examine the multiplicity of the prime minis-

Few people in Britain would know John Hunt. However, as secretary of the cabinet from 1973 to 1979, he was the power behind the throne for four prime ministers—Heath, Wilson, Callaghan, and Thatcher.

ter's roles by looking at what the staff and cabinet do. The prime minister draws upon two resources, his personal staff in No. 10 Downing Street and the various secretariats operating out of the Cabinet Office.

No. 10 Downing Street

The closer we get to power, the more crowded the office facilities. This certainly applies in Washington. Deputy assistants to the U.S. president ensconce themselves in huge accommodations in the Old Executive Office of the president across an alley from the White House. Their bosses—assistants to the president and above—trade opulence for proximity. Thus they vie for relatively cramped offices in the West Wing annex to the White House. The same pattern holds in Whitehall. To be under the same roof as the prime minister, some 70 people tolerate conditions that otherwise would border on insufferable.

Prime ministers pretty much determine the specific contours of their No. 10 staff on their own. However, some positions appear to be permanent features of the organizational chart. These include the private secretaries, a foreign affairs adviser, a political adviser, a policy adviser, a press secretary, a secretary for governmental appointments, and a member of the House of Commons who serves as parliamentary private secretary.

The private secretaries—five officials all told—cram themselves into two small rooms immediately adjacent to the prime minister's office. These assistants are all permanent civil servants on loan from various Whitehall departments. In the White House, such career officials would never be trusted to work so directly for the president. In No. 10, the private secretaries essentially run the switchboard for the prime minister's communication with cabinet secretaries and various parts of Whitehall. They make abundant use of their highly developed networks of contacts in departments. They also can gain entry to virtually any Whitehall meeting of cabinet ministers or officials in which the prime minister has an interest.

Through these means, private secretaries gather an immense amount of intelligence on what is happening with various policy proposals or what has gone wrong with controversial programs and why. They brief the prime minister directly and do not hesitate to suggest the major issues at hand and how the prime minister might resolve them. Even when the prime minister communicates wishes directly to a cabinet minister, private secretaries, as often as not, explain the prime minister's mind when departments come back to No. 10 for further clarification. One or another private secretary will sit in on all of the prime minister's meetings with groups and individuals, and likewise will monitor all telephone calls. This makes it extremely difficult for people who have discussed matters with the prime minister privately to distort the substance of what was said.

Private secretaries virtually always return to their civil service departments after serving two or three years in No. 10. Margaret Thatcher departed from this custom with regard to her private secretary from the Foreign and Commonwealth Office who assumed responsibility for supporting her in matters concerning foreign affairs. That man, Charles Powell, joined the private office in 1984 and stayed there until Thatcher resigned the prime ministership. He emerged as one of the main players in the government's foreign-policy-making proc-

ess—sometimes even eclipsing the foreign secretary's influence on Thatcher. Powell's influence grew with the years, while other private secretaries came and went. Much to the chagrin of his original department, he often pressed counter-conventional positions in his advice to the prime minister. For example, he fanned her suspicions on European integration, her fears about German unification, and her enthusiasm for supporting George Bush in the Persian Gulf crisis. He also successfully pursued a strong Atlantic foreign policy in opposition to the Eurocentric Foreign Office.

What happened to Powell once Thatcher left office served as an illustration of the continued strength of the permanent civil service culture in Whitehall. An unwritten rule holds that officials must serve loyally but not overly enthusiastically. Certainly they should not make themselves into free agents operating against the bureaucratic culture that has selected and nurtured them with great care (and attention to one's aptitude for conventionality).

Participating in the high politics of countervailing the advice of the Foreign Commonwealth Office went beyond the normal role of a fairly junior civil servant who did not even head the prime minister's private secretary office, much less the foreign affairs establishment. Predictably, Powell's old department indulged in a bit of nonconventionality when he left No. 10. Usually when private secretaries depart No. 10 they collect a juicy post that will sustain them on their track to the very top of their departments. Powell, on the other hand, received offers of jobs so unattractive that he chose to leave public service. Others crossed the line during the Thatcher era in many other parts of Whitehall and found that the mandarins at the top of their departments would not soon forget such transgressions.

Two other career officials who are fixtures in No. 10 are the *secretary for appointments* and the *press secretary*. The former person manages the process whereby the prime minister exercises a

Now someone has to tell the prime minister that this is what you have got, and suggest to her the sequence in which she should read these in order to make sense of them, to draw together the salient points that they are making—hopefully they are all moving in some kind of direction—bring out the points of conflict and so lead the prime minister to the point where she is able, without having herself to write an essay, to give specific directions as to what she wants done on the issues that are now before her.

Source: A member of the prime minister's private office as quoted in Colin Campbell, *Governments under Stress*, 1983.

key prerogative: recommending to the queen the names of recipients of government appointments and honors. Such awards, of course, comprise a major source of patronage to party faithful. However, many jobs and honors in fact go to individuals more on the basis of their being among "the great and the good"—people with distinguished careers in one walk of life or another. As a deferential society, Britain takes special pains to formalize belonging to the establishment with board memberships and honorific titles.

Although not a private secretary, the *foreign affairs adviser* warrants mention here. The position emerged in the wake of the Falklands crisis. It acknowledged the fact that the prime minister required in No. 10 someone very eminent within the foreign affairs field. The presence of such an adviser there would give permanent officials in Whitehall a highly credible point of contact when and if threatening developments had failed to get sufficient attention from their ministers. However, the incumbents of this position have never exerted much influence on the prime minister—even less did they have much impact in the days when Charles Powell had the ear of Margaret Thatcher.

The role of the press secretary as a career official simply on loan from Whitehall has come into question of late. Two recent occupants of this position—Tom McCaffrey under James Callaghan and Bernard Ingham under Margaret Thatcher—both became so attached to their prime ministers that their nonpartisanship came into question. McCaffrey in fact went with Callaghan to head his office when he lost the election in 1979 and became the leader of the opposition. Ingham served Thatcher from 1979 until her resignation in 1990. His approach was not only partisan, it was politicized in a manner loyal only to Margaret Thatcher. Before Thatcher's resignation and in the face of attacks from Michael Heseltine and regrouping by John Major and Douglas Hurd, Ingham stood steadfast and nearly alone behind the prime minister. He openly questioned whether Heseltine was fit to serve as prime minister. When Margaret Thatcher left No. 10, Ingham did also. His was the first resignation accepted by John Major.

The press secretary plays a vital role. The emphasis on secrecy in Whitehall contributes to this; through it, the press secretary can—much more effectively than his opposite number in the White House—control the timing and substance of most statements and information flowing from ministers and government departments. Secrecy also allows him to make maximum use of his briefings of lobby correspondents (see Chapter 6) as a way to put the prime minister's "spin" on media coverage of conflicts within the cabinet and between departments.

All of the remaining assistants in No. 10 are "party-political" advisers. This means that they gain and hold their positions at the pleasure of the prime minister on the basis of their political loyalty. Two of these officials center their work largely on mending fences in the party. The parliamentary private secretary, a member of the House of Commons, maintains a liaison between the prime minister and backbench members of Parliament. The political secretary monitors the prime minister's party-political affairs, including relations with the party organization, and assesses the electoral benefits to or fallout from prime ministerial actions. These might range from high-order policy decisions to seemingly trivial (though potentially sensitive) issues such as whether No. 10 should receive a delegation of party members or voters.

A third official, the policy adviser, heads a unit—usually ranging between five and ten officials—that has taken one form or other in the No. 10 organization chart since 1970. Bernard Donoughue, who headed the policy unit from 1974 to 1979, earned a reputation as a policy professional who, though a party-political appointee, developed strong links with the major figures of the permanent bureaucracy. The heads of the policy unit under Margaret Thatcher became a hidden hand that made sure that policy commitments of great importance to the prime minister were resolved in a satisfactory and timely way. The relevance of this position increased with the appointment of Sarah Hogg, the head of John Major's policy unit. Hogg brought to the government people firmly linked to the Conservative Party's center and left, and has tried to make a distinct shift from Thatcherism. She and her staff have expertise in business, economics, and social issues and directly influence items like Major's Citizen's Charter; market testing and privatization initiatives; and the budget in health, social security, local government, and taxation. Hogg's management style is seen as systematic and organized while also open to ideas and argument—a noticeable departure from the established prejudice and ideology of the Thatcher era.

Under both parties, the policy unit's effectiveness depends primarily on the resourcefulness of its members. These advisers must learn how to obtain access to key committee meetings and tap into the private office for a steady flow of essential documents. They do not always achieve this degree of maneuverability. However, they can exert considerable leverage when they do.

The Cabinet Office

Next door to No. 10 is the Cabinet Office. This organization represents a resource unlike anything American presidents can tap. To be sure, it incorporates some units that do not play vital roles in policy formulation. However, if we isolate attention on the secretariats that support the cabinet committee system, we find that its staffing vastly exceeds comparable resources in the U.S. executive branch.

The National Security Council staff and the parallel domestic offices perform the same functions in the United States as the Cabinet Office does in the United Kingdom. In a 1981–1982 comparison, however, the U.S. agencies claimed only 110 staff and spent about $7 million.[3] The Cabinet Office policy secretariats employed 331 staff and spent more than £10 million in the same period.

These figures highlight the substantially greater emphasis placed by the British executive branch on the task of supporting collective decision making. The contrast becomes even more stark when we consider that all of the officials working in the Cabinet Office are permanent civil servants on loan from Whitehall departments. The U.S. offices responsible for coordination, on the other hand, consist largely of political appointees—many of whom have accumulated relatively little experience in government.

In principle, the Cabinet Office works first for the cabinet. In this respect it has several central roles in the process whereby cabinet governs over policy issues:

1. It advises officials from elsewhere in Whitehall on how to prepare issues for interdepartmental and cabinet consideration.

2. It monitors this preparation to ensure that departments have adequately consulted with other interested agencies—especially the Treasury, which controls the purse strings.

3. It advises when an issue is ready for consideration by a cabinet committee.

4. It transmits committee recommendations to the prime minister and to the entire cabinet.

5. It drafts cabinet minutes and communicates decisions to all concerned parties.

6. It takes the lead in ensuring that decisions are actually implemented.

You have probably already noticed that these functions relate as much to the prime minister's role as the head of government as they do to the cabinet's standing as the ultimate locus of executive authority. Fulfillment of the last three functions in particular requires that members of the Cabinet Office work very closely for and to the prime minister.

In this country . . . we haven't got a prime minister's department. In theory, the Cabinet Office serves all ministers; in practice, it serves the prime minister a good deal more than anyone else. But he hasn't got a department to serve him. He has, at No. 10, very efficient private secretaries who can deal with his daily life and his mail and that sort of thing. But, they, when they want advice, almost always look here. I mean I don't want to pretend we are a prime minister's department under another name, because we're not. We haven't got that position yet, and the prime minister isn't the chief executive. He can't overrule his colleagues just like that. He's got to get his consensus in cabinet. But we are the department that services him.

Source: A member of the Cabinet Office as quoted in Colin Campbell, *Government under Stress*, 1983.

We saw above that a great deal of controversy surrounds the issue of whether prime ministers have reached the point where they effectively operate as chief executives. Astute use of the Cabinet Office certainly places any prime minister at a clear advantage in situations where personal leverage and institutional resources count the most. However, no Cabinet Office would retain effectiveness and legitimacy if it became totally a captive of the prime minister. It does have a special relationship to the prime minister. But it also must remain responsive to requirements of the cabinet so that secretariats can facilitate its decision-making processes in a relatively detached way. The Cabinet Office that loses its capacity for neutral brokerage will decline in legitimacy.

Whitehall Departments

Whitehall departments function under the direction of individual cabinet secretaries— *not* the prime minister. All of the major departments have ministers of state and undersecretaries of state who assist their cabinet secretaries in overseeing policy development and the operation of programs. For example, before Thatcher split it up in 1988, the Department of Health and Social Security had one minister each for Health and Social Security, plus three undersecretaries of state. All such officials belong to either the House of Commons or the House of Lords and owe their appointments to the prime minister.

The prime minister's influence over departments does not end with the power to appoint, shuffle, and dismiss cabinet secretaries and ministers. The prime minister has general responsibility for the management of Whitehall. He or she maintains overall authority for the development of the civil service. Thus prime ministers ultimately determine personnel policies that concern major changes in the duties, privileges, and compensation of permanent officials. The official responsible for the Cabinet Office—the secretary of cabinet—serves, in a formal capacity as head of the civil service, as the prime minister's principal adviser on these matters.

Prime ministers tend to focus their involvement with Whitehall personnel issues on those that pertain to the uppermost groups. For example, prime ministers must personally approve all promotions to the top two rungs: permanent secretaries and deputy secretaries. The former officials stand at the very top of Whitehall departments.

In many respects, permanent secretaries rival ministers in their power over departments. They normally bring a wealth of departmental experience to their work. As well, they control the careers of the permanent officials whose cooperation cabinet ministers must have if they are to achieve their goals. As for deputy secretaries, they enjoy considerably greater leverage than do ministers of state or undersecretaries of state. The former shoulder hierarchical responsibility for major clusters of departmental activities; the latter simply receive delegated responsibility from cabinet ministers to monitor the development of policies and the operation of programs within the department.

In comparison to the U.S. president, the prime minister can reorganize the bureaucracy with relative ease. Notwithstanding his strong support of Vice President Al Gore's plans for "reinventing" the public service, President Clinton must still seek congressional approval for many key initiatives contained in the proposal. And it is by no means clear that this will be forthcoming.

Strictly speaking, John Major can redistribute responsibilities to and between departments without any more than perfunctory consultation of the cabinet. He certainly does not have to spend much time winning parliamentary approval for such changes—in fact, many can be made by mere cabinet approval. Realistically, the prime minister would have to assure

Robin Butler's career reflects the "neutrality" of Whitehall mandarins. Butler, the handsome young man behind Prime Minister Harold Wilson, served as a private secretary to both Edward Heath and Wilson, and secretary of the cabinet and head of the civil service for both Thatcher and Major.

that key colleagues agreed with his major initiatives. Yet no prime minister would face the inherent intractability that a president wishing to reorganize the U.S. executive branch does. As well, Parliament invariably passes most required enabling legislation with barely a comment.

The prime minister's influence over Whitehall structure allows indirect benefits as well. In

One of the reasons why no rigorous reconsideration seems to have been given to the qualities needed by senior officials or to the grading system may be the need felt by senior officials to select "leaders." . . . Leadership has the quality of a "hurrah" word among certain sections in British society, particularly the middle and upper classes which have provided the core of officers in the armed forces and senior officials in the higher civil service.

Source: Richard A. Chapman, *Leadership in the British Civil Service*, 1984.

election years, the prime minister's party often uses Whitehall to cost out campaign promises made by the opposition parties—although this activity must cease the moment the election campaign formally starts. For example, during the buildup to the 1992 election, Labour proposed introducing a statutory minimum wage if they formed the next government. The Conservative government looked to the bureaucracy for a response. Michael Howard, John Major's secretary of state for employment, had civil servants calculate possible job losses resulting from Labour's proposition. Howard's original estimate was 750,000 jobs lost, but with the help of Whitehall staffers and a Treasury model, the number reached 2 million. Conservatives wasted no time in taking their new ammunition to the battlefront, casting further doubt on Labour's economic competence. All of this came courtesy of "nonpartisan" career civil servants in Whitehall.

It would take an entire chapter to begin to describe the bureaucratic cultures operating within various Whitehall departments. By any standards, the world of the British civil servant is exceedingly closed and stratified. The strong secrecy norm limits the degree to which officials can speak with outsiders interested in the policies and programs for which they are responsible. Consultation with interest groups

normally takes the form of structured sessions, often in the presence of a cabinet minister or a minister of state. One finds virtually no informal, day-to-day interaction with backbench members of Parliament and the House of Lords. However, parliamentary committees increasingly call upon officials to give testimony.

The stratification of the British civil service is due largely to the sharp distinction between the *administration group* and the rest of the nonclerical or non-blue-collar workers. The former work within a separate corps of officials who, even if they have not achieved sufficient rank, have been selected and trained to assume substantial roles in policy-oriented positions. The others—executive officers, specialists, scientists, and senior technicians—only by rare exception take on major policy positions.

The administration group has received a great deal of critical comment over the years. Many view it as an anachronistic holdover from Victorian times. The selection of these officials certainly raises serious questions. Most of them are chosen in their final year of university or soon after. Selection involves a series of exams and interviews that, it is thought, give an edge to candidates from Oxford and Cambridge. Critics therefore believe that it encourages candidates who have an air of intellectual and social superiority. When we consider the fact that most members of the administration group are generalists without graduate or professional education, we can see how their special status grates against the sensitivities of civil service groups with advanced credentials. Min-

You have to have a view of what the British economy can stand. Ministers left to themselves would do things which would not be consistent with the proper management of the economy.

Source: A Treasury official as quoted by Colin Campbell, *Government under Stress*, 1983.

isters also often resent these mandarins' tendencies to behave as if only they could discern the long-term interests of Britain.

THE IMPORTANCE OF THE THATCHER PRIME MINISTERSHIP

Margaret Thatcher shared with former U.S. President Ronald Reagan the reputation for having reversed the tide of the welfare state and entrenching a host of market-oriented policies. Some assessments of President Reagan attributed his success in enshrining his central policies—reduced taxes and domestic spending, and increased defense expenditure—to the speed with which he essentially overrode the permanent state apparatus.[4]

These analyses urge that future presidents must focus much more on their "responsive competence." They should, if necessary, forget about trying to make certain that they make decisions on the basis of the most rigorous analysis available or ensure that the public service operates with optimal efficiency and effectiveness. The point is to centralize decision making as much as possible in the White House and allow only people who pass stringent loyalty tests to assume appointive positions in the agencies.

Other students of the presidency adopted what, before the Iran-Contra affair, had become the minority view.[5] Bert Rockman argued, for example, that executive leaders must blend public standing, intra-elite relations, organizational and management ability, and policy knowledge and analysis. Through this they achieve both political responsiveness *and* creative engagement of the state apparatus, or "policy competence." Reagan's lack of interest in detail and engagement in the day-to-day affairs of state simply exacerbated the negative consequences of overriding the standing bureaucracy.[6] He occupied the office of "president" without fully understanding, let alone utilizing, the institutional resources of the presidency.

Margaret Thatcher demonstrated the same attributes. Yet apart from the Falklands crisis, which she pulled out of the fire, her approach failed to produce a debacle. She proved most successful at responsive competence. In the process, she altered the model for prime ministerial leadership.

John Major wants to conduct a more collective and less decisive government. However, he has to buck the popular appeal of personalized leadership and strong direction. The public became fearful of the consequences of some of the strong medicine prescribed by Thatcher to get the country back on the right track. And they objected to her strident language concerning the rest of Europe. This does not mean that they repudiated her leadership style. (In fact, it was her Conservative colleagues in Parliament—and not the voters—who ousted Thatcher.) She was no Mussolini. However, just as many Italians still admire this fascist leader for making the "trains run on time," many Britons see Thatcher as a model democractic leader from the standpoint of staking out stances and getting things done. This legacy will remain in the British national psyche for a long time.

In some respects, Thatcher's leadership bordered on rule by fiat.[7] She established a cabinet system in which conviction had become nine parts of the law. She regularly browbeat ministers when they disagreed with her. Cabinet met less regularly and considered fewer submissions. Charmed circles of ministers in especially good grace with the prime minister often resolved issues that then received only *pro forma* discussion in standing committees or the entire cabinet.

The prime minister took exceptional liberties with Whitehall by introducing personalized criteria into the selection and advancement of senior permanent officials. In other words, she advanced officials who adopted a "can do" approach to her agenda and priorities over

Ministers increasingly voice concern . . . about the way key decisions are being taken by Mrs. Thatcher and small groups of ministers without reference to the full Cabinet—a practice which they say has contributed to failings in the presentation of policies. One minister said privately last week that Mrs. Thatcher probably has used Cabinet less than any prime minister since the war. Some MPs are calling for a return to genuine *Cabinet Government.*

Source: *The Times*, March 5, 1984.

more traditional civil servants who might stress the obstacles and pitfalls to her policies. She also brought about sweeping reorganizations with little or no consultation of her cabinet colleagues and virtually no regard for civil service morale.

Even during her second term, observers began to wonder how long the system would withstand the immense strains placed on it by the force of Margaret Thatcher's personality. In late 1985, an uproar arose over the prime minister's handling of a dispute between her defense minister, Michael Heseltine, and her trade and industry minister, Leon Brittan, over the future of the Westland helicopter manufacturers. Heseltine ultimately resigned in protest over Thatcher's highly manipulative approach. Her tactics—according to Heseltine—involved alternating between ad hoc groups and the appropriate standing committee in search of the right mix of ministers, conveying to the press distorted accounts of ministers' preferences and expunging from cabinet minutes any record of dissent.

Only the release of the salient cabinet documents—30 years or more from now—will help us establish whether Heseltine rendered an accurate account of his treatment by the prime minister. We do know, however, that the secretary of trade and industry resigned his post in late January 1986. He had been caught red-handed in having his information officer select highly prejudicial excerpts of a letter from the solicitor-general to Heseltine and leak them to the press. The entire episode contributed significantly in the government's slide in the polls through the next six months. But questionable competence of the opposition contenders and hype about the performance of the British economy eventually obscured memories of the incident. Nothing succeeds like success. And notwithstanding her imperial style, Thatcher had maintained her credibility as the leader for the times.

Her approach to governance reemerged as an issue midway through her third term. In October 1989, it led to the resignation of the chancellor of the Exchequer, Nigel Lawson, over whether Britain would enter the European Monetary System. This episode even provoked a decline in Thatcher's popularity to the lowest point of any prime minister since polling began fifty years ago.

Sir Geoffrey Howe's resignation in November 1990 proved to be the episode that began the complete collapse of her leadership. For seven years, Howe had served as foreign secretary until July 1989 when Thatcher kicked him upstairs to deputy prime minister—a post that the prime minister created for him. Thatcher had removed him from the Foreign Office because of his alliance with Lawson over the European Exchange Mechanism. Thus, not coincidentally, the controversy over Europe was his reason for leaving the government. His departure exposed a growing rift in the Conservative Party that went beyond the European Monetary System issue and to the very nature of Thatcher's leadership style. One of the great and good of her nation and party had given an unequivocal thumbs down to her continued rule.

I now realize that the task has become futile; of trying to stretch the words beyond what was credible; or trying to pretend there was a common policy when every step forward risked being subverted by some casual comment or impulsive answer. . . . I fear that the Prime Minister increasingly risks leading herself and others astray in matters of substance as well as style. The tragedy is—and is for me personally, for my party, for our whole people and for the Prime Minister herself, a very real tragedy—that her perceived attitude towards Europe is running increasingly serious risks for the future of our nation.

The conflict of loyalty to the Prime Minister and the loyalty I perceive to the true interest of this nation has become all too great. I no longer believe it possible to resolve that conflict from within this government. The time has come for others to consider their response to the tragic conflict of loyalties with which I have myself wrestled for perhaps too long.

Source: Sir Geoffrey Howe in his resignation speech to the Parliament. The speech was considered by backbenchers of all parties as the most devastating critique of a serving prime minister in living memory. Quotations from *The Independent*, November 11, 1990.

As we saw earlier, Thatcher's tenacity was paralleled only by her intransigence and her doctrinaire stance on Europe. These traits alienated several of her allies, allowing a leadership challenge that finally culminated with Thatcher's resignation in December 1990. The challenge was mounted by Thatcher's former defense minister, Michael Heseltine, who was perceived to be to the left of the party and a potential threat to her legacy. Although Heseltine was not able to oust Thatcher in the first round of ballots, he denied her the mandate required for her to maintain control of the party. Thatcher never fought the second vote, a widespread belief of an imminent defeat

spread among the members of her cabinet, and she was forced to step down. Helped by Thatcher's sympathizers and the center of the party, John Major defeated Heseltine in the second ballot.

Major Renovations

Just as Margaret Thatcher shares some dynamics of history with Ronald Reagan, John Major has brought about changes in Britain similar to those that George Bush brought to the United States. Major assumed the prime ministership midway through the Gulf Crisis and engaged himself next to President Bush in expelling the Iraqis from Kuwait. Through that process, however, Major never publicly revealed the vindictiveness that increasingly characterized Bush's rhetoric surrounding the buildup for the war and its actual execution.

On the home front, just as Bush rewarded the loyalty of campaign supporters like Dan Quayle and John Sununu, Prime Minister Major wasted no time in recognizing people who stood steadfastly by him in the leadership race. Major's first action as prime minister was to appoint a cabinet full of friends who played an active role in bringing him to power. Norman Lamont, David Mellor, and Richard Ryder received positions for their support, as did Michael Heseltine—Major's principal rival in the leadership bid—for his loyalty to the Conservative Party.

Like Bush, and Reagan before him, John Major has continued a shift away from the old-boy network toward national popularity. He and his handlers tend to keep a weather eye on the polls and increasingly "go public" in their bids for policy support.

At the hand of Majorites, the 1992 election bore all the marks of recent presidential campaigning. This included a personalization both of efforts to draw support—that is, drawing

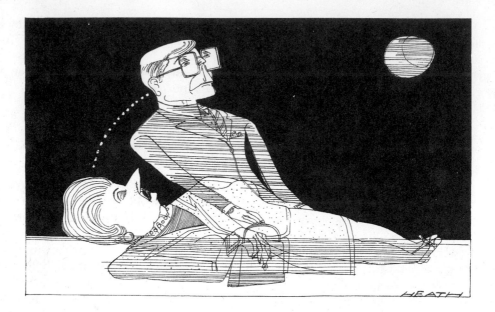

When John Major rose as the main contender in the second ballot for the Tory leadership, many believed that he was simply Thatcher's ghost. While he has surprised many by plying an independent course, he still has to contend with Thatcherism.

voters' attention to the decency and simplicity of Major—and to attack the opposition. For example, they based attacks on Labour on Neil Kinnock's personality rather than on his party's specific policy proposals. When the 1992 Bush campaign began to flounder, top aides went to the United Kingdom to find how the Conservatives had snatched a victory from the jaws of defeat in the election of the spring of 1992. This action stood as no small tribute to the genius of the Conservative campaign in shifting the focus to Neil Kinnock's negative attributes.

John Major also created a "kinder and gentler" government—based on his Citizen's Charter initiatives whereby government departments and agencies must view members of the public as customers to be served. With regard to leadership styles, this prime minister may receive the popularity points that he does

have for who he is *not* rather than who he is. Margaret Thatcher is synonymous with confrontation and divergence; John Major stands for consultation and unity, not to mention courtesy. As noted earlier, the atmosphere in Parliament and the cabinet has improved. According to Edward Heath—the former prime minister—Tories, "when talking together no longer have to look over their shoulders all the time to see if there is somebody waiting there to report them to Number 10."

Major still suffers from one important liability—namely, indecisiveness. We find that this comprises a significant hazard to those following a dominant prime minister. People might have objected to Thatcher's imperiousness. However, she did get things done. Many competent world leaders have been lost in the annals of history simply because they did not live up to the brilliance of their immediate prede-

Some have taken John Major's more conciliatory approach to leadership as weakness.

cessors. Major lacks Thatcher's brand of high authority that goes beyond competence to reach seemingly unattainable goals sometimes. Even after the 1992 election, Major's approval ratings slipped almost immediately. He continues to be buffeted by Thatcherites and Europhobes. He seems never entirely capable of taking charge and getting his own party under control. The very harsh economic times have compounded his difficulties. Indeed, they have contributed to his approval ratings reaching all-time lows.

CONCLUSION

This assessment of the role of the prime minister, cabinet, and Whitehall has attempted to put our understanding of the British executive branch in a sharper perspective. Looking from across the Atlantic, we might tend to romanti-

cize how exactly the British system functions. In particular, we might give excessive credence to the British constitutional conventions whereby executive authority is supposed to be exerted collectively by the cabinet.

The case of Thatcher perhaps overdemonstrates the point. Today there can be little question that a "conviction" prime minister can operate as monocratically as the most powerful president. However, we have to recognize that personalities rarely introduce such huge distortions into the operation of cabinet government. Most prime ministers stay within the conventional parameters of their prerogatives. We can say this while still acknowledging that recent prime ministers have found themselves much more capable of providing central direction to their administrations than did their predecessors. Still, the Thatcher legacy has raised the standard for people who choose to live by decisive action. This presents special difficulties for prime ministers like John Major who still uphold the tradition of collegial governance as the ideal.

NOTES

1. John P. Mackintosh, *The British Cabinet* (London: Stevens, 1977).
2. Peter Hennessy, *Cabinet* (Oxford: Blackwell, 1986), pp. 100–101.
3. Colin Campbell, *Managing the Presidency: Carter, Reagan and the Search for Executive Harmony* (Pittsburgh: University of Pittsburgh Press, 1986), p. 19.
4. Terry M. Moe, "The Politicized Presidency," in *The New Direction in American Politics*, eds. John E. Chubb and Paul E. Peterson (Washington, D.C.: Brookings Institution, 1985).
5. Bert A. Rockman, *The Leadership Question: The Presidency and the American Political System* (New York: Praeger, 1984). Campbell, *Managing the Presidency: Carter, Reagan and the Search for Executive Harmony.*
6. Campbell, *Managing the Presidency: Carter, Reagan and the Search for Executive Harmony*, pp. 5–6, 20–22.
7. Hennessy, Ch. 3.

REFERENCES AND SUGGESTED READINGS

Aberbach, Joel D., Robert D. Putnam, and Bert A. Rockman. 1981. *Bureaucrats and Politicians in Western Democracies.* Cambridge: Harvard University Press.

Bagehot, Walter. 1867. *The English Constitution.* 1963 edition by R. H. S. Crossman. London: Fontana.

Campbell, Colin. 1983. *Governments under Stress: Political Executives and Key Bureaucrats in Washington, London and Ottawa.* Toronto: University of Toronto Press.

Campbell, Colin. 1986. *Managing the Presidency: Carter, Reagan and the Search for Executive Harmony.* Pittsburgh: University of Pittsburgh Press.

Chapman, Richard A. 1984. *Leadership in the British Civil Service.* London: Croom Helm.

Grant, Wyn. 1989. *Pressure Groups, Politics and Democracy in Britain.* Hertfordshire: Simon and Schuster.

Gray, Andrew, and William Jenkins. 1991. "Administering Central Government," in Jones, B., ed. *Politics UK.* New York: Phillip Allen.

Heclo, Hugh, and Aaron Wildavsky. 1974. *The Private Government of Public Money: Community and Policy Inside British Politics.* Berkeley: University of California Press.

Hennessy, Peter. 1986. *Cabinet.* Oxford: Blackwell.

———. 1991. "Mrs. Thatcher Impact upon Whitehall," in Jones, Bill. ed. *Politics UK.*

Hogwood, Brian W., and Thomas T. Mackie. 1985. "The United Kingdom: Decision Setting in a Secret Garden," in authors, eds. *Unlocking the Cabinet: Cabinet Structures in Comparative Perspective*, eds. Hogwood and Mackie. London: Sage.

Jones, George W. 1987. "The United Kingdom," in Plowden, W., ed. *Advising the Rulers.* Oxford: Blackwell.

Mackintosh, John P. 1977. *The British Cabinet.* London: Stevens.

Moe, Terry M. 1985. "The Politicized Presidency," in Chubb, J. E. and Peterson, P. E., eds. *The New Direction in American Politics.* Washington, D.C.: Brookings Institution.

Pearce, Edward. 1991. *The Quiet Rise of John Major.* London: Weidenfeld and Nicolson.

Plowden, William. 1984. "The Higher Civil Service in Britain," in Smith, B. L. R., ed. *The Higher Civil Service in Europe and Canada: Lessons for the United States.* Washington, D.C.: Brookings Institution.

Rockman, Bert A. 1984. *The Leadership Question: The Presidency and the American Political System.* New York: Praeger.

Rose, Richard. 1980. "British Government: The Job at the Top," in author and Suleiman, E. N., eds. *Presidents and Prime Ministers.* Washington, D.C.: American Enterprise Institute.

———. 1984. "The Political Status of Higher Civil Servants in Britain," in Suleiman, E. N., ed. *Bureaucrats and Policy Making: A Comparative Overview.* London: Holmes & Meier.

Turner, John. 1980. *Lloyd George's Secretariat.* Cambridge: Cambridge University Press.

9

An Increasingly Crowded Field:

Players Beyond the Executive

e now step out of the vortex of power in the United Kingdom. In this chapter we will examine the roles of Parliament, the judiciary, and local governments. We will also assess how Britain's membership in the European Union affects the exercise of sovereign authority over the various affairs of state. Finally, we will look at the role of interest groups in the process by which government policies take shape.

All of this is a very tall order for one chapter. A book entirely dedicated to Britain could productively examine each of these topics in its own separate chapter. We essentially are focusing here on elements of the policy process that would easily sustain free-standing treatment. However, cabinet and the bureaucracy still give by far the greatest added value in the process in which policy and programs emerge in the British system. This chapter simply attempts to make the reader cognizant of how exactly other elements of the process might work very significant effects as well.

Obviously, we have touched on many of the constitutional issues connected to the legitimacy and power of these various elements of the governmental process and political processes in earlier chapters. Some points, however, bear repeating. These matters effectively overarch the entire operation of the relationships among executive power, parliamentary authority, jurisprudence, local autonomy, and European unity.

In Chapter 5, we saw how the elements of central government derive their legitimacy and authority from interlocking channels. The genius of Britain's cabinet system of government rests on cooperation among people who control Parliament, those who assume executive authority in the principal posts of the land, and those who administer justice.

Among parliamentary legislatures, Westminster enjoys almost paragon status. This owes in no small part to the eloquence and dispatch with which it considers and treats the great affairs of state. This "efficiency," of course, means that backbench members of Parliament within the governing party must frequently bite their tongues. The judiciary, until very recently, has maintained an external posture of obeisance to the letter of the law and the intent of Parliament. It eschews interpretation based on broader principles like fundamental civil liberties. We have seen in Chapter 5 that cracks have developed in communality of authority in the central government. This chapter will probe the dimensions of these fissures.

In Chapter 6, we briefly examined efforts to accommodate the distinctive characters of Scotland, Wales, and Northern Ireland, with respect to the devolution of some of the administrative apparatus of the central government to the regions. We touched as well on the changing status of local governments that has stemmed largely from Margaret Thatcher's efforts to circumscribe their ability to extract their own revenues. We will in this chapter focus more closely on the characteristics of provincial and local governance.

Finally, as we found in Chapter 5, Europe plays an enhanced role in the United Kingdom—especially with respect to civil liberties and economic policy. We will now inquire more deeply into the dynamics whereby British political leaders and institutions must now take much greater cognizance of Europe while developing and administering policies and programs.

WESTMINSTER IN TRANSITION?

The British Parliament divides into two chambers, the House of Lords and the House of Commons. The former body consists of some 1,200 members. The number is not fixed because the institution includes four groups that vary in size: hereditary lords, peers appointed for life, the law lords (senior members of the judiciary), and archbishops and bishops representing the Church of England. Except for hereditary lords, all members of the House of Lords receive their appointments from the queen on the advice of the prime minister. With respect to life peers, accession to the upper house often serves as a reward for political service either within the House of Commons or through contributions to and work for a party. The practice of appointing life peers began in 1958. Even the relatively conservative constitutional authority Walter Bagehot had advocated life peerages in the latter part of the nineteenth century.

The House of Lords is an anachronism in a democratic era. It harks back to the oligarchical times. With the rise of the House of Commons throughout the nineteenth century, people wishing to preserve the upper house sought a restraint against the unbridled popular will as expressed by the majority in the lower house. At the time, only members of the nobility belonged to the chamber. The current House of Lords boasts a more eclectic complement— thanks to the institution of life peerages. And it no longer views itself as a bulwark against excessive democracy. However, the existence of the institution still provides leverage for the British establishment in the political process— leverage that other segments of society lack.

An assembly in which the mass of the members have nothing to lose, where most have nothing to gain, where every one has a social position firmly fixed, where no one has a constituency, where hardly any one cares for the minister of the day, is the very assembly in which to look for, from which to expect, independent criticism. And in matter of fact we find it. . . . But such criticism, to have its full value, should be many-sided. Every man of great ability puts his own mark on his own criticism; it will be full of thought and feeling, but then it is of idiosyncratic thought and feeling. . . . There ought to be many life peers in our secondary chamber capable of giving us this higher criticism. I am afraid we shall not soon see them, but as a first step we should learn to wish for them.

Source: Walter Bagehot, *The English Constitution*, 1867.

Efforts to reform the House of Lords have come slowly. Despite deadlocks between the upper and lower houses throughout the nineteenth century, Parliament did not limit the legislative powers of the former until 1911. From that year, money bills—that is, those concerning taxation and expenditure—automatically received royal assent one month after reaching the House of Lords. According to the 1949 Parliament Act, the upper house cannot delay other public bills passed by the House of Commons for more than two successive sessions (with the exception of cases in which less than one year has elapsed between the second reading of the bill in the first session and its third reading in the next session).

The House of Lords can produce some embarrassing reversals for the government party, although few of these touch at the very heart of bills. The Thatcher and Major governments often have rankled lords. In these circumstances, bipartisan movements within the upper house have forced amendments in a great deal of government legislation. A count cover-

ing ten years of Margaret Thatcher's tenure in office, from 1979 to 1989, put such amendments at 115. This relatively intense activity tended to center on legislation covering schools and local government. For example, one such occasion was a government defeat in a 1984 bill that paved the way for the abolition of the Greater London Council—legislation that eventually was enacted and implemented. More recently, in 1990 the Lords twice defeated a bill that would have given local authorities responsibility for coordinating community care for the elderly, handicapped, and mentally ill. The Lords demanded that the government earmark cash for these services to ensure minimum standards of provision.

The House of Commons takes in 650 members of Parliament, all of whom represent single-member constituencies. Most of the governments' legislation passes through the House of Commons before proceeding to the House of Lords. The executive introduces the overwhelming majority of bills that ultimately gain royal assent. Only the executive can originate bills that involve taxation or spending. This stands in stark contrast with Congress in which individual senators or representatives put forth a large proportion of legislative initiatives that then appear under their names. The House of Commons does make a very modest provision in its schedule for "private-member" bills. However, precious few of these ultimately become law.

As with any legislature, bills must pass through several stages. "First reading" constitutes formal introduction of the measure and does not entail debate. "Second reading" allows for a lengthy debate on the policy and programmatic merits of the proposed legislation. After second reading, the bill goes to standing committees consisting of 16 to 50 members. These bodies examine bills clause by clause. However, they really do not deserve the title "standing." Rather they come into being on an ad hoc basis in response to specific initiatives. The leadership of the various parties will exert considerable control over the membership of these bodies. The government party in particular will want to avoid embarrassing criticism from one of its members of Parliament.

Standing committees can introduce amendments to legislation. However, these must concern technical matters associated with the implementation of policy and not the principles behind it. Governments themselves introduce many amendments at this stage, virtually all of which will receive endorsement from the respective standing committees. Only a minuscule proportion of amendments proposed by individual members without explicit government backing gain the support of standing committees. If the bill has been changed, it must proceed through the report stage in the House of Commons before the amendments are accepted. Whether revised or not, the bill must pass through "third reading." However, it will receive additional consideration in debate only if six members of Parliament have submitted a motion beforehand calling for further discussion.

Formal divisions—occasions in which members file out of the house to register their votes for or against a bill or an amendment—occur relatively frequently. In the four parliamentary sessions between 1984 and 1988, the total number of sitting days ranged between 109 and 218; meanwhile, between 196 and 468 divisions took place.[1] In all but one session, the ratio of divisions to sitting days was at least one-and-a-half to one. It is not unusual for members to congregate in the house at 1:00 or 2:00 in the morning in response to the division bells.

The number of these votes that see Conservative or Labour members taking stands at variance with their party has increased dramatically in the past two decades. There were seven parliaments from 1945 to 1970. Only under the parliament between 1959 and 1964 did members of Parliament cast dissenting votes in more than 10% of divisions.[2] In fact, three parliaments witnessed 3% or fewer such divisions. The three parliaments between 1970 and 1979 produced dramatically different figures. The divisions with dissenting votes rose to 20%, 23%, and 24% in the 1970–1974, 1974, and 1974–1979 parliaments, respectively.

This trend did not spare Thatcher—despite her forceful leadership and her large majorities in the House of Commons. For example, the first session of the 1983–1987 parliament produced divisions with dissenting votes that came to 25% of the total. Of the 115 divisions that produced defections, 62 included Conservative members of Parliament. Philip Norton has examined 18 of the more significant divisions in the 1979–1983 parliament.[3] In these cases, the number of Conservative dissenters ranged between 6 and 51. Seven of the revolts resulted in no effects on the bill; three led to withdrawal of the offending provision; four ended with the government accepting an amendment; and four led to a government commitment to review its policy—in three cases the review accommodated the dissenters' concerns. We can see, thus, that recalcitrance among a substantial number of government members of Parliament led to large concessions even from the likes of Margaret Thatcher.

According to parliamentary procedure that prevailed until the 1970s, the loss of a vote in a major division would spell the end of the government. That is, it would constitute *prima facie* evidence that the prime minister and cabinet could no longer rely on the support of the House of Commons. However, Edward Heath suffered five losses on such items between 1970 and 1974 and the succeeding Labour government absorbed defeats on expenditure, tax, Scottish devolution, and wage restraint measures.[4] Indeed, in 1978 James Callaghan lost a major pay guideline provision that—notwithstanding its status as a center-piece of his economic policy—failed to win the support of the house.

In today's practice, a government can come to an end in one of two ways. The government must take a stand as a matter of "confidence" and lose the motion to sustain it, whereupon there is pressure to ask the queen to dissolve Parliament.[5] Or the opposition could force the government's hand with a motion of "no confidence." That is how John Major lost the battle but won the war in the 1993 vote over the Maastricht Treaty. He lost the ballot on the treaty itself but defeated the no-confidence motion that the opposition put forward in the aftermath.

In American minds, perhaps "question time" stands out most vividly as the opportunity for holding the government accountable for its actions. From Monday to Thursday each week, members of Parliament address questions directly to ministers in an effort to force the government to explain its policies and administration. The approach especially appeals to American observers who are used to open hearings on issues like the Watergate and Iran-Contra scandals. The process in Britain, however, seems to allow members of Parliament to get to the bottom of executive branch wrongdoing much more directly than the avenues open to Congress.

The significance of question time falls somewhat short of the myth built up on this side of the Atlantic. For one thing, the entire practice follows a strict routine. It takes place only between 2:30 and 3:30. The prime minister will take questions for only fifteen minutes on Tuesdays and Thursdays. By the same token, other ministers know precisely which days they may be called upon. Members must give advance notice in writing of their interventions, which they may follow up with oral supplementary questions. Frequently, ministers appear armed with thick briefing notes from which they read

canned answers. If they become flustered, they can receive support from the officials in their departments who can slip notes from the official box in the corner of the house to the right of the speaker's chair.

Ministers, of course, must uphold the policies of the government no matter how reasonable the opposition criticism. In fact, they often offer themselves freely as lightning rods or human shields to protect the prime minister from admitting to some embarrassing stance or incident.

These procedures contrast sharply even with practices in other parliamentary systems that follow the Westminster model. For example, Canadian ministers—including the prime minister—must accept questions whenever they appear during "question period," and they enjoy no right of prior notice. And the substantially less decorous Canadian house would not suffer gladly anything but ad lib responses that display clearly the ability of the ministers to think on their feet about the issues for which they hold executive and administrative responsibility. They have no ready recourse to their official staff while fielding questions.

Notwithstanding its defects, question time in the British House of Commons still plays an instrumental role in the parliamentary process. In an adversarial system, much of the power of the opposition hinges on its ability to undermine trust in the government party. Also no opposition party will attract sufficient popular support to loom as a contender for the government mantle unless it appears to be a viable alternative. Question hour is the main occasion for the opposition to drive home the points necessary to swing the electorate toward its policies. Nevertheless, the use of question hour to force the government to account for its actions falls short of the cleansing power ascribed to it by some American observers.

One difference between the House of Commons and Congress in their pursuit of accountability is the failure of the question hour in Commons to attain its presumed objective. Too often the opposition parties pry open a can of worms, only to find that the government can frustrate their efforts to go further. Thus they can expose ineptitude or venality, but they often find it extremely difficult to bring people who are implicated in wrongdoing to account for their actions.

This situation is possible largely because of the weakness of parliamentary committees. The opposition can harp about government misdeeds as long as it wants. Yet the government itself must support efforts to launch formal committee inquiries before any serious investigations can take place. Even if a committee examines a question exhaustively, the government ultimately determines whether the House of Commons will debate its report and act upon its recommendations.

Developments since 1979 have made it easier for members of Parliament to press for inquiries into the actions of ministers and officials. In that year, the newly elected Conservative government completely revamped the committee system. In the process, it created fourteen new select committees. Each of these covered a major policy field that paralleled the departmental structure in Whitehall. These included Agriculture, Defence, Education, Employment, Energy, Environment, Foreign Affairs, Home Affairs, Industry and Trade, Social Services, Transport, Scottish Affairs, Welsh Affairs, and Treasury and Civil Service.

Working from these specialized committees with responsibilities for shadowing various departments, members of Parliament can more readily convince the government that they should hold formal inquiries into clear instances of negligence or wrongdoing.

Committee positions and chairmanships go to parties in proportion to their representation in the House of Commons. Before the 1992 election, seven out of fourteen committees were chaired by Conservatives. Although after the

election Labour captured two more chairmanships and seventy of its members of Parliament became committee members, this change did not alter the government's capacity to influence the depth of committee inquiries and the tone of their resulting reports. To dilute backbench members' influence in committees, the Conservatives invoked an obscure parliamentary rule that no member of Parliament can serve on a select committee for more than three parliamentary terms. With the application of the rule, the government has been successful not only in reducing Labour's power but also in removing outspoken Conservative members who opposed the government's policies.

However limited, the select committee system has revamped the leverage of backbenchers in the House. All but the Scottish Affairs Committee have only eleven members. This imparts great status to committee membership. While party whips play a role in allotting positions, they can only with difficulty remove members of Parliament from their assignments during a parliamentary session. Select committees, unlike standing committees, can operate when Parliament is not in session. This greatly reduces the pressure for members to bring special inquiries to a quick conclusion, just because Parliament will soon adjourn. Each committee retains the assistance of a senior member of the parliamentary staff and has a budget for outside expert advice.

The perceived effectiveness of the committees and the members' eagerness to be part of them—attendance in the commons often falls to 5% while special committees register a 70% attendance rate—have favored the expansion of the system. Today the number of committees has grown to sixteen. Two new select committees have been created since 1992, the National Heritage Committee (1992)—in charge of cultural issues and the Northern Ireland Committee (1994).

Committees have not turned the House of Commons into a Congress-style legislature.

Discipline still prevents unbridled criticism by members of Parliament who belong to the government party. Parliament still lacks the powers vis à vis the executive to subpoena cabinet secretaries or senior officials, the way legislative committees do in the United States. As well, members of Parliament must play an endless game of cat and mouse with Whitehall bureaucrats who do testify. In observance of the secrecy conventions of the British system, such permanent civil servants pretty much confine themselves to elaboration of technical details. They will not delve into issues associated with the conduct of ministers and Whitehall colleagues.

Notwithstanding the emergent nature of committees in the House of Commons, they have made their impact felt. Senior Whitehall officials increasingly find themselves testifying before these bodies. In fact, in a single parliamentary session in 1987–1988, 276 civil servants appeared before select committees.[6] This constituted no small development, in view of the fact that most of them would have experienced virtually no such exposure to the House of Commons throughout their careers had the system not been changed. The committees have also been very prolific in issuing reports: they published 197 reports in the 1979–1983 parliament and 306 in the 1983–1987 parliament.

Indeed, some investigations have dug deeply into executive affairs. These include the Defence Committee inquiry into the events surrounding the resignations of the secretaries of defence and trade and industry over two incidents. One was the Westland affair, which prompted the Foreign Affairs Committee to investigate the sinking of the Argentinean cruiser *General Belgrano* during the Falklands War. The other was the Industry and Trade Committee examination of the causes of the 1985 collapse of an international tin cartel that the British government had helped to maintain. More recent cases include the Industry and Trade Committee investigation of the exportation of steel tubes to Iraq by a British company during 1989 and 1990. The tubes, to be used for military purposes, were part of a ballistic test bed and its ultimate purpose was previously known by the British Department of Trade and Industry. In addition, the Treasury and Civil Service Committee inquired into a case of financial fraud and money laundering by the Bank of Credit and Commerce International (BCCI), a Pakistani institution with British branches and management.

In all of these cases, the respective committees ran into numerous roadblocks in their efforts to uncover all of the pertinent facts. In each instance, however, the committees' hearings helped to establish the legitimacy of such studies, even within the constraints of the parliamentary system. Institutional changes take a long time to work their effects. Gradually, however, members of Parliament are learning how to use astutely their power to examine in detail the conduct of the government. With each success, the case builds for an expansion of members' ability to obtain the testimony of officials and to get them actually to cooperate.

THE JUDICIARY

We have noted that courts play a different role in the United Kingdom from that of their counterparts in the United States. Britain has not enshrined the fundamentals of its constitutional system in a single written document. Nor has it enumerated the rights of citizens in a formal charter. Thus the will of Parliament, as embodied in statutes, comprises the most authoritative source of the law of the land.

Traditionally, this fact has sharply constrained judicial interpretation. Judges lack the higher references, such as the Constitution or the Bill of Rights in the United States, with which to pass judgment on the legal standing of statutes. In case of ambiguity, they focus their deliberations on discernment of what Parliament intended. There are no "founding fathers" whose original intention judges could attempt to divine.

We cannot conclude from this that the judiciary does little that affects the contours of policy and administration in the United Kingdom. The activity of courts permeates British society. Further, they deliberate on a host of issues that do not involve conflicts over the meaning of statutes but still require active interpretation. These include the status of enactments of local authorities, the standing of government regulations insofar as they draw upon ministers' discretionary powers imbedded in acts of Parliament, the validity of specific applications of statutes in individual cases, and applicability of *common law* to a huge load of cases that cannot be resolved by recourse to specific statutes.[7] Common law here reflects the accumulated precedents for the administration of justice, including many matters that relate to fundamental rights dating date back to Anglo-Saxon times.

The judicial system operates at five levels. On the lowest tier, we find *magistrates' courts.* Here local justices of the peace—appointees who are not lawyers—try minor criminal cases. They also preside at the remand hearings in which all criminal prosecutions, regardless of the gravity of the offense, receive preliminary examination. On the next rung, two different courts handle separate branches of law. *County courts* hear the vast majority of civil cases; *crown courts* handle all criminal offenses that are too large for magistrates to try on their own. Professional judges staff both courts. An overlap exists between crown courts and the next level, known as *High Court,* where the major criminal cases are heard.

The High Court is the first of the next three levels that take us to the elite of the British judiciary. The High Court is based in London, and includes some 100 judges and divides into three units. The *Chancery Division* rules on matters concerning trusts, inheritance, property,

corporate law, and taxes. The *Family Division* judges the more difficult contested divorce cases. The *Queen's Bench*—the largest division by far—handles three types of cases: the most important criminal trials, civil disputes that involve statutory law as opposed to common law, and administrative matters touching on the behavior of officials of state toward individuals.

On the next tier up, we find the *Court of Appeal.* This body, presided over by the *master of the rolls,* functions in two divisions, namely Criminal and Civil. Consisting of about thirty members, the court considers cases in three-judge panels, some of which—in criminal cases—would include one or more members of the Queen's Bench. Civil cases may be taken beyond the Court of Appeal to the House of Lords *Judicial Committee.* Here some twelve *lords of appeal*—members of the upper house especially appointed for their judicial experience—break into panels of five to share a workload in the neighborhood of fifty cases per year.

We should not lose sight of the limits of judicial interpretation in the United Kingdom, fixed as it is on divining the intent of acts of Parliament. However, judicial review has become an area of significant growth. The tortuous route of the Peter Wright case—discussed briefly in Chapter 4—demonstrates the degree to which some issues engage the judiciary profoundly. The various opinions rendered by judges along the way also point up the extent to which courts increasingly venture judgments about the prerogatives of the executive branch; they will assert themselves in cases where they find that ministers and officials have taken actions against individuals that overstep statutory authority or their attached discretionary powers.

As we saw in Chapter 4, the Wright case involved a retired member of the British security and intelligence agency MI5. This man sought in 1986 to publish a book, *Spycatcher,* that would disclose serious wrongdoing and security lapses in the agency. Since Wright resided in Australia and had been able to publish the offending book in that and other countries, the case focused on the right of British newspapers to report on his book.

In June of 1986, a High Court judge granted the government an injunction against publication of either the book or newspaper accounts of its contents. However, a series of subsequent rulings began to whittle away this very sweeping order. These were handed down by the High Court and the Appeal Court in July 1986, and by the latter in July 1987. All three judgments quarreled in particular with the government's efforts to restrict newspapers' coverage of judicial proceedings in the United Kingdom and in Australia.

On July 30, 1987, a five-member panel of law lords upheld the original court injunction against the newspapers in a 3-to-2 decision. In fact, they added a further constraint by prohibiting newspapers from reporting allegations made by Wright in Australian courts. One minority opinion, however, involved a momentous change of heart from no less than the senior law lord. This judge, Lord Bridge of Harwich, had previously earned a reputation for deference to the executive. In fact, he had, while he was chairman of the Security Commission, taken only three days to examine more than six thousand phone tap warrants and rule that they all had been properly authorized. This feat had drawn the bitter complaint that he was the "poodle of the executive" from Roy Jenkins, a former Labour cabinet minister and a cofounder of the Social Democratic Party.

In his judgment on *Spycatcher*, Lord Bridge raised poignantly serious second thoughts about his view of the British constitution. He noted the fact that Britain, even though a signatory to the European Convention on Human Rights, still has not adopted this code formally as part of British law. For himself, he had taken the view that such charters place rights such as the freedom of speech on "too lofty a pedestal." He also trusted "in the capacity of the common

Freedom of speech is always the first casualty under a totalitarian regime. Such a regime cannot afford to allow the free circulation of information and ideas among its citizens. Censorship is the indispensable tool to regulate what the public may and what they may not know. The present attempt to insulate the public in this country from information which is freely available elsewhere is a significant step down that very dangerous road. The maintenance of the ban, as more and more copies of the book *Spycatcher* enter this country and circulate here, will seem more and more ridiculous. If the Government are determined to fight to maintain the ban to the end, they will face inevitable condemnation and humiliation by the European Court of Human Rights in Strasbourg. Long before that they will have been condemned at the bar of public opinion in the free world.

Source: Lord Bridge of Harwich, 1987.

law to safeguard the fundamental freedoms essential to a free society." In the strongest possible terms, he then offered the caveat that totalitarian regimes strike first at freedom of speech when they begin to establish themselves. He noted too that the government's decision could not survive either "the bar of public opinion in the free world" or the inevitable condemnation of the European Court on Human Rights.

Three newspapers, *The Guardian, The Observer,* and *The Sunday Times,* all defied the government injunction by proceeding with detailed accounts of *Spycatcher.* Smuggled copies of the book were freely available throughout the United Kingdom. The government continued its prosecution in the High Court. However, it lost its case there in December 1987. In February, it then faced a resounding rejection of its arguments in a unanimous ruling by a three-judge panel of the Court of Appeal that included the master of the rolls.

All of the opinions gave weight to the view that the executive cannot completely suppress allegations of "iniquity" in the very services that avowedly dedicate themselves to national security. One of these even recommended a proper sequence for legitimate disclosure of misdeeds. If the executive clearly refuses to deal with these, then those concerned may seek remedies in Parliament and, failing these, resort to publication in the press.

On October 13, 1988, the government lost its final appeal. A panel of five law lords ruled that the papers could proceed with publication of the allegations contained in *Spycatcher*. On behalf of his colleagues, Lord Keith of Kenkel explained that all possible damage to national security had already occurred through the publicity that Wright's allegations had thus far received. Thus a continuation of the injunction would not make sense. The law lords made it clear that they did not base their ruling on broader issues such as balancing the various interpretations of public interest or the nature of freedom of the press.

The last word on *Spycatcher* serves to illustrate that notwithstanding ferment within the judiciary over the proper role of the executive and the protection of democratic freedoms, the most senior judges in the land will dodge these issues when the opportunity presents itself.

The fallibility of the courts as they relate to the rights of the individual has of late been a matter of great controversy. Three appeal reviews in the course of eighteen months beginning in late 1989 show that judicial review in the United Kingdom, especially in England and Wales, proves at times to be more concerned with the integrity of the court than the individual's right of freedom from wrongful prosecution. The Guildford Four (the basis of the film *In the Name of the Father*), Maguire Family, and Birmingham Six cases question the ability of the Court of Appeal to catch and redress miscarriages of justice.

Police officers had testified that the Guildford Four carried out terrorist bombings and the defendants were convicted and imprisoned. The Appeal Court chose not to hear the case, but officials later discovered that the police had withheld evidence and individual officers had committed perjury. Members of the Maguire family had received convictions for allegedly running a bomb factory in the basement of their London home. The Court of Appeal rejected the family's petition for a new trial. An inquiry into the prosecution's handling of the case, however, exonerated the family.

In the Birmingham Six case, the authorities wrongfully accused six men of a terrorist bombing. The police brutally arrested the men, threatened them with snarling police dogs, physically assaulted them during interrogation, and told each suspect that the others had implicated him. The constables finally coerced the men into signing confessions. In 1975, the authorities successfully convicted the six men on twenty-one counts using what Lord Justice Bridge called "the clearest and most overwhelming evidence . . . ever heard."

A judicial system is only as good as the evidence that individuals put into it, and sometimes individuals make mistakes. But the test of a system's integrity is the zeal with which it detects miscarriages of justice and goes about correcting them. In the Birmingham Six case, the courts failed that test.

The freedom of the press is not an optional extra. It is a right to be recognised unless compelling reasons for restraint are shown. Here [in the Peter Wright case] they were not.

Source: Lord Justice Bingham, 1988.

Only after three attempts at appeal, a failed civil suit against police, public campaigning, recognition of wrongdoing by the police, and sixteen years of imprisonment were the men exonerated. Lord Penning, a former master of the rolls, when faced with public outcry in support of the men, said, "We shouldn't have all these campaigns to get the Birmingham Six released if they'd been hanged." Finally, in March 1991, Lord Justice Lloyd ruled, "In the light of fresh evidence which has become available since the last hearing in this court, your appeal will be allowed and you will be free to go as soon as the usual formalities have been discharged."

In the United Kingdom, it is only for the courts to decide when decisions it makes are incorrect. Unfortunately, the mechanism for detecting and correcting blunders is not intact. The Birmingham Six and other cases bring to light a need for judicial reform and creation of a bill of rights while they question the equity of the United Kingdom's present system of justice.

GOVERNMENT AT THE PROVINCIAL AND LOCAL LEVELS

We discussed the operation of government beyond the central apparatus in Chapter 6. We noted that the British government administers many programs through the Scottish Office, the Welsh Office, and the Northern Ireland Office rather than through Whitehall. We also observed that nationalists seeking devolution of legislative powers to these regions have faced decisive setbacks. Devolution referenda for Scotland and Wales failed in 1979, and civil unrest in Northern Ireland led to the suspension of that province's separate legislature, Stormont, in 1972. Chapter 6 also pointed up the degree to which the Conservatives under Thatcher and Major have curtailed the powers and authority of local governments throughout Britain.

National Regions

Notwithstanding the lack of patriated legislative powers, considerably different administrative structures manage the affairs of the three provinces from those functioning directly out of Whitehall. In the case of Northern Ireland, a distinct civil service operates numerous departments. These include six major agencies—Agriculture, Economic Development, Education, Environment, Finance and Personnel, and Health and Social Services—each of whose functions parallels those of Whitehall departments.

A Whitehall-based department, the Northern Ireland Office, supports the secretary of state for Northern Ireland in developing and overseeing the policies administered by Northern Ireland Civil Service. It also maintains special responsibility toward law and order in the province.

Neither the Scottish Office nor the Welsh Office maintains large establishments in London. The former enjoys a sounder base than does the latter. The secretary of state for Scotland draws, in fact, on separate statutory authority in several policy areas, administering laws passed by the British Parliament but that applying specifically to Scotland. The counterpart for Wales overwhelmingly executes statutes that pertain both in England and Wales.

We might ask whether these various structural features mean anything to the average citizen in the provinces. For the most part, they simply provide a context in which civil servants can gear the administration of policies to the peculiar requirements of a national region. Yet, even this must be done within limited parameters. For instance, none of the offices exerts a great deal of discretion over budgeting;

the expenditure of an office in specific areas must, with few exceptions, follow broadly the contours of that in England. For example, the Scottish Office cannot decide unilaterally to reduce expenditures on new bridges so as to pour additional funds into its health services.

In the case of Scotland, the separate statutory authority for many governmental areas does improve the chances that programs will be administered differently. The organization of the legal system, schools, universities, and local government, to name the most obvious areas, has followed substantially different paths in Scotland from the rest of the United Kingdom. Thus, one derives a more palpable sense of administrative discretion in the Scottish Office than one discerns in the Welsh Office. A similar pattern might have prevailed in Northern Ireland had not the deep divisions between Protestants and Catholics, coupled with the imposition of direct rule, militated against quasi-autonomous provincial governance even in matters of administrative practice.

Local Government

The British refer to their local governments as "local authorities." These entities suffered a huge bloodletting of power under Margaret Thatcher. And the process has continued under John Major. As we noted in Chapter 6, this dramatic turn of events has resulted from five Conservative policies:

1. relying more on cabinet authority and less on Parliament in instigating change;

2. limiting local authorities' discretion in implementing statutes;

3. sharply constraining their spending powers;

4. curtailing their ability to raise revenues; and

5. abolishing the Greater London Council and six metropolitan counties.

There are some 500 main local authorities in England and Wales.[8] These include the governing bodies of metropolitan districts, county councils, and county districts. Within this very complex system, the larger authorities assume responsibility for local administration of much of education, social welfare, police, and regional and town planning. Before Thatcher, the central government operated alongside local authorities in many areas. In postsecondary education, for instance, polytechnical institutes came under the jurisdiction of local authorities, whereas universities came under the sway of Whitehall. The Conservative government ended local authorities' control of polytechnics.

With the exception of the provision of housing, smaller local authorities look after the less significant activities that metropolitan districts and county councils choose not to take under their umbrellas. The Scottish system operates in more hierarchical terms than does that in England and Wales.[9] Scotland divides into nine regions with clearer overarching responsibility for the districts below them. The regions assume functions associated with public services that do not fall within the compass of local authorities in England and Wales. Due to the unrest in Northern Ireland, the more significant operations of local government have become almost totally absorbed by the central government administrative apparatus in Northern Ireland.

By the late 1980s, local governments were spending approximately £40 billion a year—about one-quarter of public expenditure. A 1980 study reports that local authority employees accounted for close to 40% of those working in the public sector in 1977.[10] Obviously, any government in London, especially a market-oriented Conservative one like Thatcher's, would have taken on the task of limiting local spending authority and the size of its labor force.

Thatcher waited until her third term before introducing a package of radical reforms of

The Conservatives under Thatcher and Major have pressed for a dramatic increase in places at tertiary education institutions in Britain. However, increases in resources have fallen far behind what is required for these institutions to keep up with the added burden. Polytechnics—former local-authority-run schools that became universities in 1992—have experienced an especially severe resource crunch. This photo captures how Staffordshire Polytechnic tried to cope with student overload—housing students in a gym.

local government financing. Until then, local authorities relied on three main sources of revenue. These were "rates"—the tax levied upon property, charges for specific services, and various grants from the central government. The latter included aid based on entitlement to support for specific programs, funds for housing, and the Rate Support Grant. In addition to providing a baseline for the infusion of funds from the central government, the grant sought to maintain relative parity in the resources available to local authorities. It entailed an elaborate process for negotiations between the Department of the Environment in Whitehall and the various local governments.

The intricate Rate Support Grant consultations took especially formal shape with the institution in 1975 of the Consultative Council on Local Government Finance. The negotiation process became important to Whitehall's macroeconomic policies. The consultations yielded a series of fiscal years in which aggregate local authority spending came very close to target.[11] In fact, local authorities' spending more frequently fell short of the agreed figures than it exceeded them.

During its second term, the Thatcher government truncated the Rate Support Grant consultative regime by imposing mandatory ceilings on local authority spending. This closed out many options for councils to decide on their own what level of service to maintain in their area. In fact, local authorities actually lost some of their Rate Support Grant if their expenditure exceeded the limits imposed by the central government.

As we saw in Chapter 6, Major's government terminated the poll tax, replacing it with the council tax—a form of property tax. Despite the government's professed intention of providing a renaissance in local government, the council tax has not returned control over local services spending to local authorities. On one hand, as a consequence of the implementation of the new tax, the central government provides 85% of all local government revenues. As well, it retains the power to establish ceilings on local expenditures. In some areas such as education, the central government has even impinged on discretionary power. Local authorities find themselves very constrained under these circumstances. We might reasonably ask whether local governments will retain any significant capacity to discern and respond to the needs of their communities under the strictures imposed by the Thatcher and Major governments.

ON BEING EUROPEAN

Many Americans view England as the gateway to Europe. Certainly, a large proportion of them pass through London, even if business or pleasure takes them to the continent. Yet U.S. visitors will find that Britons do not automatically consider themselves European. As an island people, they still feel somewhat remote from the mainland. Until the tunnel under the English Channel was completed in 1994, Britons still had to fly or take a ferry to reach their closest mainland neighbor—France.

In addition to the physical barrier, Britons have not advanced greatly in overcoming a psychological block about foreigners and different languages. Precious few Britons—even leaders in politics, business, and the scholarly world—are fluent in a second language. This contrasts with the French political, economic and educational elite, many of whom can at least struggle through a conversation in English. Of course, the Dutch, Germans, and Scandinavians count a large proportion among their leadership who speak English fluently.

Britain did not jump at the chance to integrate itself more fully into Europe as the movement for greater unity built up steam on the continent. In 1949, the United Kingdom joined the Council of Europe, an organization for advancing European unity (not to be confused with the European Economic Community, which was established in 1957), as a founding member. However, the leaders of both the Conservative and Labour parties encountered domestic resistance in marshaling support for British entry into the European Economic Community, or Common Market. Not all of the blame rests on Britons' dithering about joining the Common Market. In 1963, the French president, General Charles de Gaulle, brought entry negotiations to an abrupt end by vetoing British admittance. De Gaulle thwarted Britain once again in 1967.

De Gaulle's resignation as president cleared the way for renewed negotiations that began in 1970. The Conservative government of Edward Heath (1970–1974) managed to win a House of Commons endorsement of entry by 356 votes to 244 in October 1971. It obtained this large victory—notwithstanding 39 Conservative defections—due to the support or abstentions of nearly 90 Labour members of Parliament. The issue did not stop there. The Labour Party under Harold Wilson forced a renegotiation of the terms of Britain's entry in 1974. Ultimately, the Wilson government put the revised terms to a national referendum in June 1975. This carried with a 67 percent "yes" vote. However, doubts reemerged occasionally in both parties, especially Labour. For instance, its national conference overwhelmingly supported a withdraw-from-Europe proposition in 1980. Membership in the European Community (the new name after a merger with two other communities in 1967) did not rank as a top issue in either the 1983 or 1987 general election.

As we saw in Chapter 3, the successor to the European Community—the European Union—has become a formidable executive, bureaucratic, legislative, and judicial complex in its own right, and Britons have played an active role in all four arenas. Thatcher gained almost unrivaled standing among Community political leaders, much as she had established herself as one of the more dominant governmental leaders in world affairs. Following in her footsteps, John Major has combined his more diplomatic approach with the influence won by his predecessor to establish an impressive position for the United Kingdom in an integrated Europe.

This is not to say that Major's government has solved the more intractable policy issues related to Britain's integration into the European Union framework. Although the outcome of the 1991 Maastricht Treaty negotiations was regarded as favorable for the British government, the results translated neither into internal harmony nor in electoral gains for the Conservative Party. Britain won concessions from the European Community in three areas. First, Major gained an exemption from the social chapter of the treaty—a provision that would have required Britain to align its employment laws with those of the more labor-friendly member countries of Europe. Second, Britain imposed its view that existing defense organizations such as the North Atlantic Treaty Organization, or NATO, should be maintained as the basis for European military security. Third, the other European Union members accepted the British view that joint foreign policy would continue to be made by consensus at the level of the Council of Ministers and not by a qualified majority.

In pressing for these concessions, Major sought to appease the Thatcherite flank of the Conservative Party opposed to further integration. He was also banking on the expectation that the Labour Party, seeking to be the "party of Europe," would not lightly advocate rejec-

Prime ministers spend a great deal of time consulting with their European opposite numbers. In this 1991 photo, French Prime Minister Edith Cresson joins in a press conference with John Major in front of No. 10 Downing Street.

tion of the treaty—even with the exemption of Britain from the social chapter. In fact, these assumptions held true in the early months. As a consequence, the Maastricht Treaty did not play a meaningful role in the 1992 elections. Many believed that Major had chalked up a coup in the treaty negotiations.

Subsequent events elevated the treaty to an exceedingly divisive status. Treaty agreements do not require enactment of legislation in Britain. Normally they receive ratification through the queen acting on the advice of her ministers in an "Order in Council"—equivalent in the United States to an executive order. And normally the two houses of Parliament pass resolutions approving only the drafts of a treaty. However, the government first judged that the Maastricht Treaty affected the powers of the European Parliament. According to the 1978 European Assembly Elections Act, any treaty altering the powers of the European Parliament must receive approval by an act of the British Parliament.

Major's difficulties stemmed from the fact that he went beyond this formal requirement and sought an act of Parliament approving the entire treaty. This proved to be a mine field. Both Euro-skeptics in the Conservative Party and left-leaning Labourites stanched support of the legislation. The former sought to reject the bill outright; the latter tried to reinsert Britain into coverage by the social chapter.

At the eleventh hour—the end of the 1992–1993 legislative session in July 1993, the opposition parties in the House of Commons, supported by Tory Euro-skeptics, passed an amendment to the government bill reinstating British participation in the social chapter. However, a subsequent motion that the government inform the European Union that it would participate in the social chapter failed by one vote—cast by the speaker of the House of Commons.

Next, Major played the "confidence" card. Making it clear that he would ask the queen to dissolve Parliament and call an election if the vote failed, he called for a motion of confidence. The uncertainty of an election—including the prospect of a Labour or coalition government—sent the dissident Tories scurrying back to the fold. The motion was not a bill. Instead, it was a simple resolution, "That this House has confidence in the policy of the Government on the adoption of the Protocol on Social Policy." This meant that the house supported the opt-out of the social chapter that Major had negotiated for Britain in Maastricht. The Maastricht Treaty bill never passed in the House of Commons. The

government acquired ratification the good old-fashioned way—by Order in Council.

The British secretary of state for foreign and Commonwealth affairs belongs—along with his counterparts from other member states—to the Council of Ministers. As we saw in Chapter 3, this body serves as the continuing executive council of the European Union. Various "technical councils," including ministers from member countries responsible for specialized policy areas such as agriculture, hammer out policy and programmatic details. In this respect, they function somewhat the way ministerial committees in the United Kingdom operate in relation to the cabinet.

British ministers from various Whitehall departments participate fully in these bodies. Indeed, some have begun to interact with their European Union colleagues almost as much as they do with fellow cabinet secretaries in Whitehall. As well, officials work closely with opposite numbers in Brussels and other European Union bureaucracies on myriad issues of mutual concern. Increasingly, a duty tour in European Union bureaucracy in Brussels comprises an important stop in one's rise to the upper levels of Whitehall departments. Learning to deal with Brussels has become an important part of one's training for the top jobs in Whitehall.[12]

Britain has not proven to be an exemplary member of the European Union. Part of the difficulty stems from the fact that the country gains little if anything from the Common Agricultural Policy, which until 1992 was the only functioning part of the trade community. It simply lacks sufficient numbers of the small and relatively inefficient farms that benefit so much from the policy elsewhere in Europe. On other fronts, the British have developed a reputation for driving hard bargains. Thatcher proved especially effective on negotiations over the European Community budget.

Britain recused itself from the European Monetary System since its inception in 1978 until finally entering in 1990. Under Labour, the

British Treasury worried about pressures on the pound—upward from the United States or downward from Germany—that would make it extremely difficult to keep the currency within its own set limits. Thatcher's strong monetarist views kept her from allowing British entry into the system until just before her fall from power.

The Treasury had long before this come around to the wisdom of full membership. It had kept the pound within limits compatible with full participation through much of the mid-1980s. This tacit policy led ultimately to the dispute in October 1989 between Thatcher and Nigel Lawson, the chancellor, resulting in Lawson's resigning from the government.

Britain ultimately joined the European Monetary System in October 1990, only to abandon it during the September 1992 "Black Wednesday." It had become clear that the United Kingdom could no longer sustain the value of the pound as European currencies generally encountered pressure from a strengthening dollar. Commentators noted at the time of Britain's departure that it had entered the system with the pound at an artificially high level. When Britain bolted, the system began, piecemeal, to collapse. The late 1980s' vision of a single European currency now appears to be very far off indeed.

On other fronts, Britain appears to be odd-man out in more than its share of European/European Union disputes. For instance, it isolated itself in two key discussions in 1987: development of a joint policy on technological change, and the Community contribution to an international effort to address the crisis about the diminishment in the earth's ozone layer. To people who chalk up these obstructionist reflexes to coincidence, a document leaked to the press in 1987 gives pause for thought. The chairmanship of European Community bodies rotates in six-month terms. Britain assumed the chair for the second half of 1986. A confidential British directive issued in anticipation of assuming the chair re-

A booklet, *Guidance on the Exercise of the Presidency,* was circulated last May to those British officials who were chairing EEC committees in Brussels during the second half of 1986.

. . . Paragraph 10 of the chapter on "tactics" explains how to block progress if agreement would be counter to British interests.

"The UK's objective may be to delay a decision (e.g., until after the UK Presidency). As long as the UK is not isolated, the simplest device will be for the chairman to let delegations ramble on.

"Provided that agreement is not actually staring him in the face, he may be able to conclude that a number of new issues have been raised which require consideration in capitals and reflection by the Commission."

When the day comes to resume the discussion "meetings can then be cancelled because another group needs the meeting room . . . and so on."

The guide concedes that it is the chairman's duty to be "even-handed in his dealings with all delegations" and that the "task of promoting the UK's objectives" falls, in theory, to another official occupying the UK chair.

But it goes on to suggest the possibility of discreet collusion. "It is not uncommon for the national delegation to take an extreme position at one end of the spectrum, leaving the Presidency scope for an apparently even-handed compromise which is actually highly acceptable to the national delegation."

Source: From *The Independent*, February 6, 1987. Used by permission.

vealed that Whitehall even coaches its officials in obstruction.

Prime Minister Major has demonstrated a more amiable approach to European politics. Where in the past Thatcher may have spoken *for* Europe, Major now speaks *through* the European Union. However, as we have seen in his troubles with Euro-skeptics over Maastricht, Major was not without opponents regarding

SUBSIDIARITYMAN

The irony of John Major pleading that rights of subsidiarity for Britain within Europe, while heading a government that has trammeled the autonomy of local authorities in Britain, provoked this cartoon.

the Community matters. The Conservative right, including Margaret Thatcher—now a member of the House of Lords—has fought tooth and nail before the public and in the papers to keep Britain from committing to a "federal" European Union. Major stands strong, but the old guard is not dead yet.

WHITEHALL, PARLIAMENT, AND INTEREST GROUPS

Just before he left office, President Ronald Reagan spoke of "iron triangles" that dominate politics in Washington. These are coalitions of key players that can prevent the government from responding in a timely way to the most urgent problems faced by the nation. He noted that these iron triangles consisted of interest groups, Congress, and the media.

In fact, Reagan took liberties with a tried and true political science concept in the United

States: that subgovernments develop within specific policy sectors through which people with the highest stakes work out deals with one another to protect the status quo. Frequently innovators (including presidents) find it virtually impossible to dislodge these iron triangles. Reagan departed from the usual understanding of the three sectors that form subgovernments by including the media and excluding government departments. The classic statement of the theory holds that the myriad specialized offices and bureaus of departments and agencies form cozy relations with their clients—that is, interest groups and their patrons: congressional committees and subcommittees. Held together by mutual political advantage, these subgovernments cohere in such a way that they can thwart most efforts on the part of a president to change policies or to withdraw resources.

We find little evidence of iron triangles in Britain. A look at the relations between interest groups, Parliament, and the bureaucracy in the United Kingdom suggests that one of the elements, Parliament, simply does not play a substantial enough role in the policy process. This is largely due to the weakness of committees in the House of Commons and the House of Lords. Above all else, iron triangles run on monopolies of information. With only a nascent tradition of specialized committees, Parliament finds itself greatly hampered in finding out enough about the issues it considers to gain leverage with the other players. In addition, the House of Commons performs little detailed review of the resources that the government has earmarked for various programs. Thus neither British interest groups nor departments spend anywhere near the amount of time explaining themselves to legislative committees as their counterparts do in the United States.

Interestingly, British members of Parliament indulge in one practice that most Americans would view as fraught with conflict of interest. Over 100 members of Parliament receive retainers from corporations and interest groups. Members must report these arrangements in a public register. They must also note all such relationships whenever they speak on issues of concern to people from whom they receive retainers. Normally members of Parliament who take retainers also assume titles in the firms or organizations they represent. That is, they usually become "directors" or "consultants."

Parliament has begun to recognize conflicts of interest when a member of Parliament is a member of a Commons select committee. As we saw above, select committees review the operation of government departments that in turn regulate and grant contracts to businesses. Some committee members connected with outside interests have recently failed to mention their business links during committee proceedings. As a result, Westminster is toughening rules on member interests by requiring further disclosure, and at times, urging divestiture.

According to a 1987 agreement, members' salaries must stay within the range of those for principals in the career civil service—officials who work as far as seven levels down in departmental hierarchies. In 1991, the salary assigned to members of Parliament came to some £30,000. In dollar terms, this figure would come to less than one-half of what members of the House of Representatives make. We can therefore see that retainers can make the difference between a strapped and comfortable standard of living for members who are not independently wealthy.

Retainers do more than simply allow members to augment their relatively meager salaries. The House of Commons supplies members neither with adequate funds for staffs nor suitable offices. An affiliation with a company or interest group, then, can provide a member with the amenities necessary to function effectively. Taken together, the retainers and amenities make many members of Parliament somewhat beholden to their clients. One must therefore ask whether the disclosure rule alone acts as an adequate check on conflict of interest in the House of Commons. The tighter rules proposed to curb conflicts of interest apply only to select committee members. Some members of Parliament have become so dependent on directorships and consultancies that one can hardly conceive that they have retained much latitude for independent judgment. Conservative members tend to enter into retainer arrangements more readily than do the members of the other parties. Thus the practice works a subtle effect toward reinforcing the pro-business bias of the Conservatives.

On the other side of the House of Commons, a long-standing Labour practice helps maintain the special relationship between the party and trade unions. We saw in Chapter 7 that the Labour Party started in 1900 as a committee that encouraged members of the working class to run for election to the House of Commons.

Currently, unions sponsor the candidacies of about 50% of Labour members. This does not mean, however, that half of all Labour members are working class. For the most part, Labour members are university graduates and/or have worked in white-collar jobs before running for the House of Commons. Still, people wishing to obtain nomination in heavily working-class constituencies must come to terms with local trade union organizations. And this fact—along with the formal links between the party and trade unions—tends to galvanize individual Labour members' attentiveness to the claims of the unionized worker.

As indicated previously, individual backbench members of Parliament do not play a very significant role in determining the actual contours of government policies and budgets. Even if some members have established very close links to outside groups and interests, we cannot inflate these to iron-triangle status. Here we come to an ancillary reason for the relatively low salience of members' roles in the policymaking process. Generally, permanent civil servants in Whitehall departments avoid any direct contacts with members of Parliament. This is with the exception of providing testimony or accompanying their ministers to parliamentary committees. So the links between members and the outside lack strength, regularity, and durability. Thus the ties between members and Whitehall officials fall considerably short of what *iron* connotes.

When we search for where outside groups and interests go when they want to influence government, we have to focus on the process by which Whitehall gathers advice and information. To be sure, the prime minister and cabinet secretaries fashion policy agendas that they busy themselves trying to fulfill during their term of office. And along the way, backbench members can weigh in from time to time either to support the government's plans or to caution it about how best to proceed. However, minis-

ters overwhelmingly rely on permanent civil servants to examine the likely consequences of various policy proposals, to advise on the timing and approach of new initiatives, to recommend how resources might be allocated so as to reflect the government's priorities, and to implement resulting programs.

Within this framework, it becomes crucial that outside groups and interests try to influence the advice that permanent civil servants give to ministers. It becomes equally critical that they engage in discussions with officials on ways in which the latter will exercise the discretion to judge on their own many of the fine points of implementation. Whitehall departments have proven over the past two decades to be increasingly receptive to establishing ongoing consultative ties with individuals and groups that take a keen interest in their activities. Obviously, these ties vary according to the status of the outside clients and the extent to which high-level civil servants perceive that they require the groups' cooperation in developing and administering policies and programs. The point is that a significant cultural change has taken hold in Whitehall. Twenty years ago, officials would confine their direct encounters with outside groups and interests either to formal meetings, usually presided over by a minister, or to social engagements. Now many senior officials in Whitehall maintain relatively well-developed networks of contacts whom they regularly consult.

Some interest groups enjoy easier access to Whitehall than others. Two factors influence access more than any others. It helps immensely if a group "has a letter box," meaning that a significant bureaucratic organization concentrates its activities in an area that corresponds to that of an outside group. For example, business organizations can develop relations with the Department of Trade and Industry; oil producers with the Department of Energy; farmers and fishermen with the Ministry of Agriculture, Fisheries and Food; and physicians with the Department of Health.

Other obligations might limit a department's commitment to the positive agenda of specific groups. Environmentalists will find that the Department of Environment shoulders responsibility for a host of government programs that might conflict with their goals. The Ministry of Defence does not refuse to speak with representatives of the Campaign for Nuclear Disarmament; however, we could hardly expect its officials to embrace the group's objectives.

The second factor is how much leverage the group enjoys when it presses its appeals. Some groups speak for virtually all the people within their area. For instance, the British Medical Association, the National Farmers' Union, and the National Union of Mineworkers brigade more than 90% of their potential members within their organizations. Others, such as environmentalists and consumer groups, incorporate as paid members just a relatively small proportion of the people who identify with their causes.

Britons tend less than Americans to involve themselves in movements not directly associated with their livelihoods. This makes mobilization of support more difficult for groups dedicated to a cause that cuts across occupational interests. And in the same vein, groups attain different levels of legitimacy in the eyes of officials. Some organizations that engage in demonstrations and strikes might offend the codes of propriety that prevail in Whitehall. Others might simply press viewpoints that officials know articulate positions held only by fringe groups.

Some sectors of interest group activity become so complex that overarching organizations form. These institutions try to give greater continuity to the process of influencing government from the standpoint of a major segment of society. For the business community, the Confederation of British Industry tries to hammer out and communicate to the government common positions on issues affecting the economy. The confederation consists of some 12,000 corporate members—many of which have fewer than fifty employees. For workers, the Trades Union Congress serves as ringmaster for nearly 150 unions' collective efforts to influence government.

During the 1960s and the 1970s, governments around the world tried to develop ways of bringing business and union leaders more regularly into consultation on the management of the economy. In this period, both the Labour and Conservative governments tried to devise mechanisms whereby Britain could follow this approach. They believed that they could improve the performance of the British economy through a direct transaction. By teasing concessions from business and union leaders on prices, production, wages, and trade practices, the government would gain a more stable environment for planning the economy. For their part, the business and union leaders would benefit from having a direct say in the contours of government policies.

The various consultative processes arising from this approach produced less than satisfactory results. It became clear that neither the confederation nor the Trades Union Congress could actually deliver their memberships' support of the policies that emerged from consultations with the government. This was substantially due to the fact that neither organization could exert tight control on the actions of its members. The trade unions came off especially poorly in the congress's efforts to get unions to adhere to its agreements with governments on pay. The resulting disillusionment and—by 1979—chaos contributed to Margaret Thatcher's resolve not to attempt to manage the economy through consultative mechanisms.

Labour has not given up on the approach. Labour has mentioned in its platforms a return to wage accords when and if they come to power. Labour believes that consultation is essential in a cooperative social economy.

CONCLUSION

This chapter has followed a treatment of the role of the prime minister, cabinet, and Whitehall that perhaps left readers wondering whether any other elements of the policy process matter. On closer inspection, we can say that improvements in the leverage of Parliament and the judiciary, as well as the exigencies of belonging to the European Community and its succeeding entity, the European Union, have all complicated the lives of political executives and bureaucrats. Domestically, the executive branch—especially under lopsided Conservative majorities—still can get its way most of the time. It simply has to explain itself a great deal more both to Parliament and the courts. Meanwhile, officials interact more frequently with individual interest groups—notwithstanding the fact that formal consultative processes involving the Confederation of British Industry and Trades Union Congress have played a greatly reduced role. When Britain entered the European Community, the nature of such an alliance immediately imposed constraints on the British executive—constraints that slow down dramatically the process of developing and implementing policies. Finally, local authorities have, of course, faced a sharp diminution of power, the extent of which still remains to be fully revealed.

NOTES

1. Philip Norton, *The British Polity* (London: Longman, 1991), p. 298.
2. Philip Norton, "Behavioural Changes: Backbench Independence in the 1980s," in ed. author, p. 24.
3. Norton, "Behavioural Changes: Backbench Independence in the 1980s," p. 30.

4. Leon D. Epstein, "What Happened to the British Party Model?" *American Political Science Review,* 74 (1980), 19.
5. J. Harvey and L. Bather, *The British Constitution and Politics* (London: Macmillan, 1982).
6. Andrew Adonis, *Parliament Today* (Manchester University Press, 1990), p. 108.
7. Ian Budge and David McKay et al., *The New British Political System: Government and Society in the 1980s* (London: Longman, 1985), pp. 164–165.
8. George W. Jones, "The Crisis in British Central-Local Government Relationships," *Governance: An International Journal of Policy and Administration,* 1 (1988), 167.
9. Budge and McKay, p. 118.
10. Richard Parry, "The Territorial Dimension in United Kingdom Public Employment," *Studies in Public Policy,* 65 (1980), as cited by Budge and McKay, p. 112.
11. Jones, p. 172.
12. James B. Christoph, "The Effects of Britons in Brussels: The European Community and the Culture of Whitehall," *Governance,* 6 (1993), 518–537.

REFERENCES AND SUGGESTED READINGS

Arthur, Paul. 1984. *Government and Politics of Northern Ireland.* London: Longman.

Bagehot, Walter. 1867. *The English Constitution,* 1963 edition by R. H. S. Crossman. London: Fontana.

Birch, Anthony H. 1977. *Political Integration and Disintegration in the British Isles.* London: George Allen & Unwin.

Bruce, Steve. 1992. *God Save Ulster: The Religion and Politics of Paisleyism.* Oxford: Oxford University Press.

Budge, Ian, and David McKay et al. 1985. *The New British Political System: Government and Society in the 1980s.* London: Longman.

Burton, I., and G. Drewry. 1981. *Legislation and Public Policy.* London: Macmillan.

Christoph, James B. 1993. "The Effects of Britons in Brussels: The European Community and the Culture of Whitehall." *Governance* 6:518–537.

Downs, Stephen J. 1985. "Structural Changes, Select Committees: Experimentation and Establishment," in Norton, P., ed. *Parliament in the 1980s.* Oxford: Blackwell.

Epstein, Leon D. 1980. "What Happened to the British Party Model?" *American Political Science Review.* 74:9–22.

Griffith, J. A. G. 1981. *The Politics of the English Judiciary.* London: Fontana.

Harvey, J., and L. Bather. 1982. *The British Constitution and Politics.* London: Macmillan.

Hennessy, Peter. 1991. "How Much Room at the Top? Margaret Thatcher, the Cabinet and Power-Sharing," in Norton, P., ed. *New Directions in British Politics.* Aldershot: Edward Elgar.

Jackson, R. M. 1977. *The Machinery of Justice in England.* Cambridge: Cambridge University Press.

Jones, G. W., and J. Stewart. 1983. *The Case for Local Government.* London: George Allen & Unwin.

———. 1988. "The Crisis in British Central-Local Government Relationships." *Governance: An International Journal of Policy and Administration,* 1:162–183.

Kavanagh, Dennis. 1977. "New Bottles for New Wines." *Parliamentary Affairs.* 31:6–21 [a treatment of intergovernmental affairs in the European Community].

Moran, Michael. 1991. "Britain and the European Community," in Jones, B., ed. *Politics UK.* New York: Phillip Allan.

Norton, Philip. 1980. *Dissension in the House of Commons, 1974–79.* Oxford: Oxford University Press.

———. 1984. *The British Polity.* London: Longman.

———. 1985. "Behavioural Changes: Backbench Independence in the 1980s," in Norton, P., ed.

Parry, Richard. 1980. "The Territorial Dimension in United Kingdom Public Employment." *Studies in Public Policy* 65.

Radice, Lisanne, Elizabeth Vallance, and Virginia Willis. 1987. *Member of Parliament: The Job of a Backbencher.* London: Macmillan.

Ridley, Nicholas. 1991. *My Style of Government.* London: Fontana.

Rose, Richard. 1982. *The Territorial Dimension in Government: Understanding the United Kingdom.* Chatham, N.J.: Chatham House.

Sbragia, Alberta. 1991. *Euro-Politics: Institutions and Policymaking in the New European Community.* Washington, D.C.: Brookings Institution.

Schwartz, John E. 1980. "Exploring a New Role in Policy Making: The British House of Commons in the 1970s." *American Political Science Review* 74:23–37.

Wallace, Helen, William Wallace, and Carole Webb. 1977. *Policy-making in the European Community.* Chichester: Wiley.

Wilson, Tom. 1989. *Ulster: Conflict and Consent.* London: Blackwell.

10

How Policy is Made:
A Look at Economics and Foreign Affairs

*S*o far, this consideration of British government and politics has attempted to identify and discuss the dimensions crucial to any understanding of the United Kingdom system. Broadly speaking, we have examined the following issues:

1. the problem of economic, institutional, and political decline in Britain;

2. the important themes that emerge with respect to the system's efforts to adapt to adversity;

3. the inherent limitations of the British political culture;

4. parties and elections in a period of realignment;

5. guidance in the heart of the British government—the roles of the prime minister, cabinet, and Whitehall; and

6. the significance of elements less central in policy arenas, including Parliament, the judiciary, local governments, the European Union, and interest groups.

Obviously, each of the above issues contained many subtopics. We have also taken special pains in each chapter to relate various structural and behavioral features of the current British system to individual cases. In other words, we have tried to keep in perspective what we have found about the underlying principles of the British polity, putting them in bold relief by examining how our assertions about structure and behavior actually manifest themselves in specific circumstances.

Following this approach, we now move on to an effort to illustrate how the British system works in two policy areas. We have chosen economic and foreign policy. Both of these merit close attention because major decisions in each sector affect the entire political system. A focus on these areas enables us to observe the exertion of power and authority in matters where there is no question about the importance of the stakes. In this respect, they provide us with an opportunity to glimpse how the system functions in relation to two dimensions fundamental to its survival and adaptation to new circumstances.

ECONOMIC POLICY: A NATURAL MONOPOLY OF THE TREASURY?

Managing the economy is not an easy task. The difficulties go beyond simply coming out with the right solutions to the various economic problems faced by a country. Often relatively clear options present themselves. But solutions must work their way through mazes filled with bureaucratic and political obstacles. In the process, even straightforward problems become mind-bogglingly complex.

Suppose we were to rank the United Kingdom's economic policy-making process in terms of complexity. We would find that it appears relatively streamlined, particularly if we keep in mind the intricacy of the American system. Even when an administration in the United States is at the stage of developing its economic forecasts, it must negotiate these through the Department of the Treasury, the Office of Management and Budget, and the Council of Economic Advisers. The same organizations will compete intensely in developing an administration's macroeconomic policies. These policies form the broad framework that guides the administration's stances on the use of various economic instruments like exchange and interest rates, tariffs and other trade restrictions, managing the national debt, spending, taxation, and regulation.

When we look at how an administration actually resolves conflicts over the use of these instruments, we find innumerable constellations of countervailing interests. For instance, the early years of Ronald Reagan's presidency frequently found the Department of the Treasury and the Office of Management and Budget at loggerheads over the proper balance between taxation and spending restraint necessary to cut the deficit. The separation of powers greatly exacerbates the difficulty of achieving unity in U.S. economic policies. Even if an administration achieves relatively strong consensus on a particular policy, Congress will almost invariably have another view that will very often prevail to the point where it completely obfuscates the policy intentions of the administration.

A Less Complicated World

Unlike the United States, one British department, Her Majesty's Treasury, controls most of the bureaucratic levers affecting the economy. In fact, we find that all the key elements to economic management function under one roof in Britain. That is, the Treasury houses the central operations in the British government responsible for tax policy, financial institutions and markets, monetary policy, overseas finance (including matters involving the European Union), macro- and microeconomic analysis, public expenditure control, and policies pertaining to both private and public enterprises.

Obviously, other departments actually implement many of the policies established by the Treasury. For instance, Inland Revenue and Customs and Excise collect the taxes. Departments like those actually can give the Treasury

I'm not terribly keen personally on setting up deliberately a countervailing force. That was part of the idea of the Department of Economic Affairs, creating tension and all that kind of thing. But it tends to waste an awful lot of time. If it's institutionalized, sooner or later perhaps one or the other tends to win.

Source: A Treasury official's reflections on the advantages of having all the economic levers under one roof. Colin Campbell, *Government under Stress*, 1983.

a run for its money in the sway they exert within their own domains. For example, the Department of Trade and Industry usually plays a very substantial role in any Whitehall discussions about policies that affect commerce and the development of specific industries. However, the Treasury usually dominates the central agency community in the field of economics. *Central agencies* are government departments that shoulder comprehensive responsibility for one or another element of guidance and control functions affecting the whole bureaucracy. In this respect, neither No. 10 Downing Street, which serves the prime minister exclusively, nor the Cabinet Office, which supports the prime minister and cabinet, enjoys the staffing levels and the direct access to levers necessary to play consistent roles in the economic policy making. This does not suggest, however, that they do not make substantial inputs from time to time.

This chapter studies the British adoption of such a streamlined apparatus for economic policy making. It followed several efforts in the 1960s and 1970s to break down the Treasury's hegemony. For instance, in 1964 Harold Wilson's first Labour government created the Department of Economic Affairs that was supposed to take the lead in macroeconomic analysis and the development of medium-term economic plans. However, its minister was

never able to command the attention from the prime minister that the Treasury's head—the *chancellor of the Exchequer*—does. Further, the Treasury maintained control of the "sharp end"—that is, all instruments necessary actually to shape economic policies.

The peculiar nature of the Whitehall culture buttresses the Treasury's hegemony over economic policy. Unlike the U.S. bureaucracy, Whitehall maintains a "village life."[1] A common *esprit de corps* permeates the senior ranks of the British civil service. Thus officials, whatever their differences, work behind a veil of secrecy in developing the necessary consensus to resolve differences between departments. During the period of policy gestation, this secrecy many times prevents interdepartmental squabbles from attracting any substantial public attention to the details that might have engendered bureaucratic infighting. It is worse than "poor form" to violate the village norm of secrecy.

Incidents like the Ponting and Westland affairs, which we discussed in previous chapters, raised questions about the effectiveness of the tradition of secrecy and the power of the oath of confidentiality. After losing in the Ponting case, the government amended the Official Secrets Act by loosening restrictions on information like cabinet minutes, but more clearly defining other areas of secrecy like defense, security, and intelligence. Ultimately, this made it easier for the government to punish violators. Dissenters who decide to go public expose themselves to prosecution under the Official Secrets Act or, minimally, place their promotion prospects in severe jeopardy.

Cabinet ministers behave within this context in an entirely different way from political appointees in the United States. They will argue their departments' cases in the cabinet and its committees. The press might become aware of individual ministers' reservations about a policy; however, only very rarely will ministers register their concerns publicly. Normally, when the cabinet decides a matter, that is it. This is especially the case in the economics policy field.

Strictly speaking, the Treasury is the prime minister's department. This is the basis of the special reporting relationship that the chancellor of the Exchequer has to the prime minister. Chancellors might strongly disagree with the prime minister. However, a failure on the part of the chancellor to adhere to the policy preferences of the prime minister would constitute *prima facie* evidence that the latter had lost control of his or her government.

The process whereby a government wins Parliament's approval of key economic policies presents a still starker contrast with that by which an American administration obtains congressional assent to similar initiatives. As we saw in the preceding chapter, backbench members of Parliament on the government side of the House of Commons increasingly brave the threat of reprisals and vote against their party. However, they usually pick social issues, such as the level of welfare benefits or the unpopular poll tax, in which to assert their independence. A backbench revolt on a central element of economic policy would cut too close to a government's viability to attract a substantial numbers of dissenters.

As reported in the previous chapter, several Conservative Euro-skeptics made considerable mischief by supporting a Labour amendment for inclusion of Britain in the social chapter of the Maastricht Treaty. However, the vast majority of the dissenters abandoned their cause when John Major put forth a motion of confidence whose loss would lead to an election. Issues whose core is economics invariably concentrate minds in this way. And since economic policies set the context for resolution of so many social issues, the influence of backbench members on these serves as a fairly good indicator of their capacity to obtain change on the issues that really count for a government. Members of Parliament chip away at the

edges. But they only rarely work their way down to the core of the process in which matters are decided.

In a less dramatic way, members of Parliament can significantly influence public discussion of economic policy through the *Treasury and Civil Service Committee*. This committee emerged in 1979 at the time that Margaret Thatcher's new government authorized creation in the House of Commons of select committees that would monitor the activities of each of the main Whitehall policy sectors.

The Treasury and Civil Service Committee has proven to be one of the most active of these new bodies. For instance, during the 1987–1988 session of Parliament, it produced twelve reports—more than any other select committee.[2] In the same session, this committee also made full use of a provision in which select committees may contract the services of outside experts, retaining nine advisers on short-term consultancies. Only the Foreign Affairs and the Social Services committees exceeded this level of utilization of external advice.

The Treasury and Civil Service Committee does not change the Treasury's mind on many economic issues. However, it does command its attention. It cannot order ministers or officials to testify, nor can it insist upon seeing specific documents. However, Treasury ministers and officials have usually agreed to meet with the committee upon request. Thus committee hearings have exposed to scrutiny the thinking behind the Treasury's policies and actions to a degree that substantially enhances the ability of members of Parliament to enter public debates on economic issues intelligently.

A Tale of Two Prime Ministers and Some Observations on John Major

Since the prime minister and the chancellor of the Exchequer hold economic policy so closely to themselves, we should find it instructive to compare briefly the decision process that operated under the two recent governments. In the case of James Callaghan's government, we will focus on its efforts to limit wage increases; in that of Margaret Thatcher, we will examine the effects of its commitment to monetarism. We will also discuss John Major's handling of economic policy.

James Callaghan. James Callaghan served from 1976 to 1979 as prime minister in the Labour government that Harold Wilson had formed in 1974. During this period, Britain—like most other long-standing political systems—struggled with a protracted period of stagflation. That is, it encountered simultaneously persistent unemployment and inflation.

Callaghan spent a great deal of his time on economic policy. He intensively used the machinery in the center of government that was designed to assist coordination of economy policy. In this period, the economics and European secretariats of the Cabinet Office began to assume stronger than usual roles as integrating agents for coordinated economic policies. They did this in support of the cabinet committee system within the economics sector, which had become more active than normal.

To cite one area of especially grave concern in the attempt to control inflation, the government created a cabinet committee that reviewed all wage settlements between employers and unions. This body would often meet twice a week and eventually became hopelessly snarled in the minutiae of pay policy.

In an effort to impose greater discipline on the unwieldy complex of cabinet-level committees, Callaghan, supported by the cabinet secretary, ultimately struck a macroeconomic policy group that became known as "the seminar." This included the chancellor of the Exchequer, a trusted adviser to the prime minister who belonged to the cabinet but did not have a department, the head of the Cabinet Office

think tank, the top permanent official from the Treasury, and the governor of the Bank of England.

Public knowledge of the seminar might have placed in question the degree to which Callaghan was adhering to the principle of collective decision making. The seminar's limited membership, after all, precluded the direct participation of several ministers in discussions about key elements of the government's economic policies. The committee also gave a few strategically placed civil servants greater access—when compared to that afforded the excluded ministers—to crucial deliberations on the future of the economy. Thus Callaghan kept the very existence of this body a closely guarded secret.

Notwithstanding the heightened activity in the center, the actual decision process under Callaghan still relied very heavily on received wisdom coming from the Treasury. During the Callaghan government, wage controls had become a fashionable policy as advanced economies struggled with efforts to reduce inflation. The approach followed the reconstructed Keynesianism of John Kenneth Galbraith's *Economics and the Public Purpose,* which held that mandatory wage and price controls must make up for the manifest inability of the free market to restrain inflation.

The Treasury had embraced this view enthusiastically, focusing the bulk of its attention on pay controls. Initially, it considered these simply as urgent measures designed to dampen demand. In time, however, it developed the view that a permanent structure for achieving wage restraint would greatly stabilize the economy. Meanwhile, the Labour government's mandate would run out by May 1979. In the summer of 1978, Callaghan began to come around to the Treasury's view that the government should extend the pay policy to another phase.

Inflation had declined to the point that unions began to champ at the bit in anticipation

The Treasury . . . is more or less the classical White-hall department where advice is embodied in folk-lore. That is, the Treasury actually has its own line on different subjects independent of its ministers . . . however, constitutional that might be. . . . Advice, in the first instance at least, will almost 80–90 per cent consist of folklore: "Our line on flexible exchange rates is this and here it is." . . . [Cabinet Office involvement in these cases is] pretty superficial. You mainly have to deal with "The brief has to be up by then, the meetings, the what did they decide for heaven's sake."

Source: A member of the Cabinet Office as quoted in Colin Campbell, *Government under Stress*, 1983.

of a return to free collective bargaining. To the Treasury, however, controlling inflation involved political and psychological warfare as much as economics. A 5% pay increase limit would provide a smoother transition to a "freer" wage policy. That is, it would send the signal to the unions that there would not be an immediate return to unrestricted collective bargaining.

By his nature, Callaghan tended to take the longer view of policy issues. He could thus readily grasp the Treasury point that an extended restraint program would deepen the process of re-education whereby the unions might ultimately accept a permanent regimen for wage negotiations. More important, the specter of a Labour prime minister extending the pay limits, despite the decline of inflation and the protests of unions, might send just the right message to middle-class voters. Callaghan saw in continued restraint an opportunity to broaden his electoral appeal.

The entire strategy anticipated an election in the autumn of 1978. However, the polls took a dramatic turn for the worse in September. Callaghan, who only a few months before had sold reluctant ministers on the Treasury's plan as an election ploy, sprung on his cabinet the news that an autumn vote was off. The Labour government now faced what would become known as the Winter of Discontent.

Unions militantly resisted the further imposition of wage restraint and an endless succession of strikes ensued. Further, in December, Parliament—in which Labour held less than an absolute majority of seats—refused to continue sanctions against private-sector firms that reached wage settlements violating the 5% limit. By January, strikes had just about brought the country to a standstill. To make matters worse, Britons faced winter weather as bitter as they had ever experienced. Callaghan, abetted by the Treasury, had proved too clever by half. Had he listened to his cabinet rather than the Treasury in the summer of 1978, Britain might never have had a Thatcher government. Even if Labour had lost an autumn 1978 election, Margaret Thatcher would have lacked a Winter of Discontent to run against in 1983 and 1987!

This case exemplifies several points. First, the bureaucracy can press its policy preferences to the point that it gives the government advice

[Direct] incomes policy . . . started as a . . . shock exercise in round one back in '75. Having proved successful with that round, they [Labour] tried it again and then moved into a slightly different idea, not of regarding what had happened as being a once-and-for-all shock exercise but now "Let's try a transition gently into something freer." The present operation is not only a further step in that transition, tightening the thing down further, but—as we made absolutely clear in our white paper—really this government is now persuaded that some permanent framework of a direct attempt to influence the way that leg of the economy goes is part of the scheme of things.

Source: A Treasury official as quoted in Colin Campbell, *Government under Stress*, 1983.

that falls short of political viability. Notwithstanding their special prerogatives toward economic policy, prime ministers should "roundtable" their decisions sufficiently to canvass political mine fields. Callaghan erred in this regard both by taking the Treasury's hardline advice and then by calling off the anticipated election with virtually no collective consultation—including a reassessment of his economic policy. Finally, Parliament's curtailment of sanctions took an enforcement tool from the government without diverting it from its core policy. Of course, the minority status of the government, an unusual situation in the postwar era, provided the context in which Parliament could assert itself to this degree.

Margaret Thatcher. If James Callaghan displayed a penchant for pay policy, Thatcher developed an ardor for *monetarism.* As we noted in Chapter 4, this came from her close attachment to Sir Keith Joseph, who had converted to monetarism after the debacle of the Heath government. Sir Keith believed that imposition of tight restraint on the money supply offered the only means to control inflation and get British industry back into competition.

Thatcher imposed immense discipline over the economic policy apparatus. She began with herself. From the outset, she eschewed personal involvement in microeconomic issues. She preferred instead to focus on the fundamental tenets of the monetarist view. If she got her macroeconomic policies right, her assumption went, the rest would fall into place. In some respects, this comprised a self-fulfilling prophecy. Tight monetary policy would greatly limit the degree to which ministers could press claims for tax exemptions or additional spending for their clients and pet programs.

Thatcher lacked total consensus on the monetarist approach. However, she adroitly employed the devices at her disposal for rigging the Whitehall machine so that it would follow her leadership. She packed the key economy

One Cabinet minister, a member of the Economic Strategy Committee but not of this most secret inner group, which was meeting straight afterwards, was a bit slow to gather his papers. As he was about to leave, Sir Geoffrey Howe, then Chancellor of the Exchequer, launched into his paper on the plan to abolish exchange controls. "Oh," says the laggardly minister, "are we going to do that? How very interesting." Embarrassed silence. Then Sir Geoffrey says, "X. I'm afraid you should not be here." X departs Cabinet door left.

Source: Peter Hennessy, *Cabinet,* 1986.

strategy committee with monetarist ministers. Indeed, she took a leaf from the Callaghan administration and created a still more elite group through which she worked when she anticipated or encountered difficulties in the larger committee. She also used her appointive powers most imaginatively. For instance, she retained dedicated monetarist advisers in No. 10. She also allowed the chancellor of the Exchequer to develop a small team of party-political economic advisers in the Treasury. Finally, she took the unprecedented step of appointing an outsider and committed monetarist as chief economic adviser in the Treasury and head of the economic service for the entire permanent bureaucracy.

In this regard, we encounter a truly remarkable feature of the Whitehall system. The Treasury has long recognized that it must adapt its overarching view of how the economy runs to the times. In the 1960s, it preserved its hegemony in Whitehall because it marshaled its resources behind setting the policy agenda in ways that comported with prevailing neo-Keynesian notions. During the late 1970s, it went through an extremely painful process of responding to the growing attractiveness that monetarism held for the world's ranking economists and politicians. As early as 1977,

We . . . had a framework for the economy [that was] basically neo-Keynesian. We set the questions which we asked ministers to decide arising out of that framework, so to that extent we had great power. . . .

Source: Sir William Armstrong (former permanent secretary of the Treasury) as cited by Richard Chapman, *Leadership in the British Government*, 1984.

the monetarist sympathizers within the Treasury began to prevail in some crucial battles. At the advent of the Thatcher government, they had positioned themselves to take over the leadership of the department. In classic Treasury form, time healed the wounds and many neo-Keynesians even converted to the monetarist faith.

Notwithstanding Thatcher's very capable maneuvers and the Treasury's adjustment to

We have still got undercurrents of this Keynesian-Friedmanite dilemma. Those are the extremes. . . . On some of these things it becomes difficult to talk because really quite basic gut feelings about the way the economy works are not consistently shared. . . . It came perhaps most forcefully to the top a year ago [1977] when it just happened to focus on the question of whether the exchange rate should be let go in the interest of stopping an inflow of funds. . . . It was resolved not by agreement but by one of those kinds of drifts of opinions where you suddenly found that a minority had become a majority and so a decision was taken that way. [The pound was allowed to float up in an effort to keep the British money supply down.] This left a certain amount of unhappiness behind among people who felt it was the wrong decision.

Source: A Treasury official as quoted in Colin Campbell, *Government under Stress*, 1983.

monetarism, the government did not always find it easy to adhere to its macroeconomic policies. Under the rubric of monetarism, it focused its efforts on working through the Bank of England to manipulate the *minimum lending rate* (the rate of interest at which the Bank of England lends money to discount houses in which banks borrow and lend on the short term). A high minimum lending rate will decrease the supply of money; a low one will increase it.

Although the government did set its sights on targets for the money supply and kept them there, it encountered greater difficulty in deciding what other levers to pull in managing the economy. When she came into power, Thatcher granted a substantial tax cut. A persuasive segment of the cabinet talked her into balancing this move with an increase in the consumer value-added tax. They argued that people would otherwise simply spend the added disposable income accruing from the tax cut, rather than investing it. The public went on a spending spree anyway. The combined effects of the tax cut and the increase of the value-added tax soon pushed inflation beyond 20%.

Presented with an economy awash with money, the Treasury kept increasing interest rates. In due course, this strategy priced British goods out of the international trade market. Whenever interest rates in one economy attain a level dramatically higher than those in other nations, foreign investors will seek the most opportune rates and flood that country with money. If this trend persists, it might trigger a vicious circle in which policy makers in the money-flooded country continually raise interest rates to reduce the money supply. In fact, such responses simply attract more outside money.

Eventually, the country's currency will break through a threshold whereby potential importers of goods and services will no longer be able to tolerate the adverse rates of exchange. This is precisely what happened to the

. . . There was quite a lot of resistance to ideas of the new government in the early stages, there was certainly a very strong feeling among the skeptics that . . . there would have to be U-turns . . . around November, December [1979], when things began to look very dirty and they were having great pain and grief over public expenditure discussions and the skeptics would say "Oh, we've seen this before, which way will the U-turn go and hadn't we better start some contingency planning for the things that we ought to be doing." . . . That died away because they did indeed soldier on. . . . The MLR [Minimum Lending Rate] went up from 12 to 14 percent and that of course has an effect on mortgage rates and mortgage rates are a well-known political Pavlovian problem and we all read the prime minister in the newspaper as saying she didn't like this at all, we were losing control and she didn't want mortgate rates going up and so forth. In November we put the MLR up from 14 to 17 percent and those who had not been close to the situation were fearful of a tremendous lambasting from the prime minister for letting interest rates go up so high, though of course what was proposed certainly accorded with the views of the hawks on monetary policy and it was a confirmation to some and a salutory surprise for others that the prime minister didn't make any fuss about it. She accepted it. She said, "You've got it wrong but since we are where we are, you'd better change it."

Source: A Treasury official in interview with Colin Campbell, 1980.

British economy in the immediate aftermath of Thatcher's policies. With seriously dampened demand for British goods, manufacturing industries (as we saw in Chapter 4) suffered a precipitous decline and unemployment began to increase exponentially. Whether the government would flinch—that is, modify its mone-

tarist approach—began to loom as the question of the day.

As we noted in Chapter 4, in 1981 the government began to ease its policies. However, it resisted taking any action that clearly would amount to a U-turn—a clear departure from monetarism. And the eventual decline of inflation below double-digit figures allowed for considerable reductions in the minimum lending rate.

Interestingly, conflicts over the degree of monetarist observance arose again in Thatcher's third term. In this respect, it is important to recall that the government created a mini-boom in the economy in 1986. It did this by allowing interest rates to fall to a point where the declining value of the pound began to place British goods in a relatively competitive position.

In Chapter 9 we discussed the often bitter controversy over whether Britain should enter the European Monetary System. The system limits the inflation or deflation of the currencies of individual nations according to agreed parameters established by the value of a "basket" of European currencies. By 1986, the Treasury had brought the prime minister far enough along that she agreed to allow the pound to participate *de facto* in the European Monetary System by staying within specified values in relation to the other currencies. Thatcher refused, however, to agree to formal membership in the system.

This amicable arrangement suited the Treasury until 1988. As a result of the October 19, 1987 crash, investors began to lose confidence in the U.S. dollar and to cut back on their financial holdings in the United States. Under these circumstances, the pound began to inflate to the point that only limits on interest rates—along with interventions from the Bank of England—could keep it within the informally adopted European Monetary System parameters. Ultimately, the prime minister and the chancellor of the Exchequer could no longer

Thatcher yielded to pressure for Nigel Lawson—the chancellor—and Sir Geoffrey Howe—the foreign secretary—to control the rise of the pound through the spring of 1988.

conceal the fact that they disagreed on membership in the system. Further, it became clear that the prime minister again poised herself to fight any pending inflationary pressures with high interest rates.

Meanwhile, the chancellor, Nigel Lawson, worried more about good citizenship within the European Community and the danger of dampening the British economic recovery with excessive monetary controls. He found support in sympathetic statements by the secretary of state for foreign and commonwealth affairs, Sir Geoffrey Howe. It appeared as if a damaging cabinet storm was brewing. By May 1988, however, Thatcher yielded to the council of the Treasury and the chancellor and the urging of the foreign secretary. She allowed that, even if the pound had exceeded its European Monetary System limits, it would not, contrary to her previous assertions, rise to the level determined by the monetary markets. However, the issue re-emerged in the spring of 1989 when Thatcher came under pressure from other European leaders to commit herself to joining eventually the European Monetary System. After making a vague agreement, she turned around and demoted Howe, in her summer cabinet shuffle. Further efforts to renege on her undertaking with other European Community leaders led in October 1989 to the resignation of Chancellor Lawson from the cabinet.

Tension over the European Monetary System re-emerged in mid-1990. European leaders were making progress toward full European monetary union. Many members of Thatcher's cabinet believed that Britain should not miss the latest train toward a united Europe. Thatcher did not agree, and adopted a strongly anti-European tone at the Rome summit of October 1990 and later in the House of Commons. This cabinet rift was the last straw for then Deputy Prime Minister Howe. He followed in the steps of Michael Heseltine and Nigel Lawson and, to the surprise of almost everyone in government, resigned from the cabinet. His resignation brought into question the amount of support Thatcher commanded and, in part, inspired Heseltine's leadership challenge.

What lessons can we derive from this case? The Treasury adjustment from Keynesianism to monetarism—though well on its way before Thatcher—became complete under her leadership. And based on the advice it proffered, the department simply replaced one form of groupthink for another. For a while, it became more Catholic than the pope—urging Thatcher to adhere to the most stringent aspects of monetarism.

The sticking point became the Treasury's fears for Britain's long-term relations with the rest of Europe. Economic integration forms part of the neo-liberal catechism. The continued ambiguity of Britain's relationship to the European Monetary System made its position in an integrated European economy unclear.

So the Treasury cultivated Nigel Lawson. He quietly altered British policy to the increased agitation of Thatcher. The monetarist prime minister and the monetarist Treasury increasingly saw the economy through European spectacles—but the colors of the lenses clashed.

This case illustrates how even an internecine (they were both arguing monetarist views) battle between the bureaucracy and the political leadership can lead to a political impasse. Significantly, the Conservative caucus and cabinet ultimately had to step in as referees. To be sure, this occurred only when everyone began to fear that Thatcher's intractability was destroying the party's electoral prospects.

The Heseltine-led challenge sent the signal that she had outworn her welcome. Still, if members of the cabinet had not individually gone to her and pointed to the writing on the wall, she might have still tried to stand up to her opponent. Prime ministers should never forget that their immense power rests on their maintenance of the confidence of the House and the allegiance of their cabinet colleagues. There are limits to each of these. The unceremonious ejection of Thatcher gives us a good notion of what these are.

John Major. In succeeding Margaret Thatcher, John Major radically changed the policy toward monetary union, pledging to make the European Monetary System the cornerstone of his economic policy. By linking the pound to stable, non-inflationary currencies like the German mark, the new government hoped to avoid the cycles of boom and bust that plagued Britain under Thatcher's experiment with monetarism. A commitment to the European Monetary System entailed reducing active fiscal management to combat recessionary forces and the floatation of exchange rates with free capital movements in favor of establishing the value of the mark as the anchor of the system. These conditions were bound to induce high interest rates that would hurt homeowners, cost jobs, and bankrupt businesses. The politically dangerous cocktail of these factors and the lingering recession of the 1990s precipitated sterling's bolt from the European Monetary System in September 1992. Since then, Major has managed the economy in a gradualist fashion, introducing cuts in interest rates and tightening fiscal policy.

Thus, while Major's approach to Europe has been much more congenial, he and the members of his cabinet remain cautious, at best, about full monetary union. Despite attempts by European Commission officials to appease Britain and curb British vetoes, the Conservative government is still hesitant about expanding union to include a common currency. In addition, Margaret Thatcher and some powerful Conservative backbenchers continue to oppose European monetary union. As discussed in the previous chapter and noted earlier in this chapter, the Maastricht Treaty's encounter with the House of Commons suggests that members of Parliament increasingly will press publicly their objections to government legislation. However, they will pull up short of life-threatening predicaments—such as a failed motion of confidence leading to an election that might cost them their jobs.

FOREIGN POLICY

The Iran-Contra affair reminded Americans about the need to coordinate decisions concerning foreign policy. There are at least four important players in any major presidential decision on foreign policy: the secretaries of State and Defense, the assistant to the president for national security affairs, and the director of the Central Intelligence Agency. Issues with major budgetary implications will almost inevitably involve the director of the Office of Management and Budget. Issues touching on substantial economic and commercial interests will draw in the Treasury secretary, and perhaps even the Commerce secretary and the U.S. trade representative. Especially strong relationships between the president and individual cabinet members can affect national security deliberations, even in cases in which the departments headed by those cabinet members would not normally concern themselves with foreign affairs. For example, President John F. Kennedy relied very heavily on his brother Robert, the attorney general, during the 1962 Cuban missile crisis. Ronald Reagan allowed Edwin Meese, his counselor (1981–1985) and attorney general (1985–1988), to attend meetings of the National Security Council on a regular basis.

Some might wonder why so many cabinet secretaries—each of whom might press an array of departmental concerns that might simply complicate the decision process—find such ready access to national security affairs. After all, the departments of state and defense control the two instruments—diplomacy and military force—by which the nation pursues its foreign policy. Yet, we certainly know that most problems do not fit completely into one or both of these departments. Besides, the president often will side with one or another secretary, or stake out a position at variance with both. Even in the U.S. system, in which executive authority ultimately rests with the president, situations

arise that remind us once again that coordination does not just happen, but requires some regularization of the process of consultation by which presidents reach their decisions.

Interestingly, people who advocated creation of the statutory body that bears responsibility for coordination of foreign policy decisions in the United States—the National Security Council—used as their pattern Winston Churchill's War Cabinet.[3] Of course the U.S. Constitution does not compel the president to consult widely before making foreign policy. However, observers of the British cabinet's handling of the war discerned instrumental advantages to some sort of regularized machinery for decision making in national security.

The result was creation of the National Security Council by an act of Congress in 1947. Most assessments of what brought about the Iran-Contra affair suggest that the United States must relearn the lesson brought back from the United Kingdom in 1945. For this reason, it is instructive for us to examine more closely how the collective decision-making apparatus for national security actually operates in Britain. We will examine and contrast James Callaghan's and Margaret Thatcher's handling of the Falklands crises in, respectively, 1977 and 1982. First, however, we should study the structural features of the British national security policy process.

The Apparatus

Strictly speaking, the cabinet must decide major foreign policy issues. The prime minister, who enjoys neither the status of a chief executive nor the title "commander-in-chief," must give due deference to the convention of cabinet consultation. In practice, prime ministers have departed from literal adherence to this principle. We noted in Chapter 8 that David Lloyd George, who became prime minister in the middle of World War I, created a war cabinet consisting of only five ministers.[4] Interestingly, only one of these actually had direct responsibility for a department. The rest essentially functioned as prime ministerial overseers of key elements of the war effort. Even though peace came in November 1918, Lloyd George did not reconstitute a traditional cabinet until October 1919.

During World War II, Winston Churchill also adopted the war cabinet format. However, his was a more inclusive body than was Lloyd George's: it ranged in size between 8 and 11 members.[5] Further, most of these ministers maintained specific responsibilities for departments. And Churchill held a weekly "cabinet parade" that included ministers who did not belong to the war cabinet. These meetings attempted to apprise the entire ministry of major developments in the war effort.

The institution of war cabinets during the two world wars built upon a practice that emerged in the late nineteenth century. Although it operated under different titles, some sort of defense committee had functioned through most of the past 100 years. The current body is known as the Oversea and Defence Committee. Unlike the National Security Council, the committee enjoys no statutory base. It owes its existence entirely to conventional practice. Until the summer of 1992, its exact membership—along with that of all other cabinet committees—remained an official secret. However, the committee claims the distinction of being the first such body whose existence the government admitted—an action taken in the early 1920s because the media tended to fan speculation over impending military engagements every time they saw the chief of defence staff enter No. 10 for a meeting. It became necessary to assuage public anxieties by revealing why the chief of staff was visiting No. 10 so much!

The prime minister chairs the Oversea and Defence Committee and its membership includes the secretaries of state for foreign and commonwealth affairs and for defence, and the chancellor of the Exchequer (the minister in charge of the Treasury). Currently only the chief of defence staff regularly attends committee meetings. However, the committee will request the presence of the chiefs of staff of individual services whenever this seems necessary.

Additional ministers often attend—simply because issues requiring their involvement arise with considerable regularity.[6] We would certainly count among the most regular of these ad hoc participants the lord president of the council, by virtue of that role as leader of the government party in the House of Commons; the secretary of state for home affairs, especially because of the responsibility for MI5, the domestic intelligence agency; the secretary of state for Northern Ireland, because of the instability of that province; the secretary of state for trade and industry, since diplomacy often entails trade issues and the development of a defense system relies heavily on British industries; and chief secretary of the Treasury, because many foreign affairs and defense issues will require the allocation of new funds. We might assume that ministers who do not formally belong to the committee will press the case that they should attend ad hoc when committee discussions concern their departments' mandates.

You have probably already concluded that the Oversea and Defence Committee, whatever its formal membership, does not prove to be any better bounded than the National Security Council in the United States. Both presidents and prime ministers find it difficult to exclude interested cabinet secretaries from official and widely known deliberations that have widespread repercussions. Pressures for inclusion in formal bodies play almost as heavily on prime ministers as they do on presidents. Almost inevitably, such pressures force them to treat the most sensitive and potentially intractable foreign policy decisions in exclusive groups that might even operate without the knowledge and consent of other interested cabinet secretaries.

Although we should not inflate its role, Parliament can influence the course of foreign affairs decisions in some cases. We have already noted in other chapters instances in which this has happened. In May 1980, Thatcher succumbed to backbench pressure and withdrew a provision that would have imposed retroactive trade sanctions against Iran. Before the Argentinean invasion of the Falkland Islands, British governments had moved very cautiously in negotiations—partially because they feared that ultranationalists among Conservative members of Parliament would label any type of disengagement "capitulation." When it became clear that the Thatcher government had not adequately anticipated the possibility of the 1982 Argentinean invasion, howls of protest in the House of Commons forced the resignations of three ministers. These included the secretary of state for foreign and commonwealth affairs, Lord Carrington.

After the Falklands War, members from both sides of the House of Commons raised enough questions about the way in which the crisis occurred and how it was handled to prompt the government to create the Franks Committee. Subsequently the House Select Committee on Foreign Affairs brought to light many embarrassing circumstances surrounding the war. Similarly, deep skepticism of government actions surrounding the Westland affair, which concerned the rescue of Britain's only military helicopter manufacturer, led to two ministerial resignations and a prolonged inquiry by the Select Committee on Defence.

Two Approaches to Similar Crises

The Falklands War lasted from the time of Argentina's attempt to establish its long-standing claim by invading the islands on April 2, 1982,

until their recapture by the British on June 14, 1982. This marked the 150th year of continuous British occupation of the islands—against Argentina's protests. While the Falklands issue had simmered throughout this period, the two parties had engaged themselves in especially serious negotiations since 1965. Britain appeared to be inching toward acceptance of Argentinean sovereignty over the islands. However, Conservative and Labour governments alike feared the appearance that the residents of the islands, most of whom are Britons, had been forsaken by a negotiated settlement. If not handled very delicately, any arrangement that would cede sovereignty would outrage Parliament. The view developed that a middle ground would be to transfer sovereignty to Argentina and then lease back the islands so that the colony might remain British.

James Callaghan. To begin our examination of Callaghan's handling of the 1977 Falklands crisis, we should first outline how the Oversea and Defence Committee process normally would work in response to new developments in the Falklands.[7] Each Monday committees known as "current intelligence groups" meet in the Cabinet Office. These bodies focus on various sectors of the world and include representatives from the intelligence-gathering agencies and the departments with especially strong interests in the area. For the Falklands, known as Islas Malvinas among its Argentinean claimants, the relevant committee was the Latin American Current Intelligence Group.

The Joint Intelligence Committee of officials meets Wednesdays to assess the material gathered by the current intelligence groups and to compile a Red Book summarizing their findings. The Red Book circulates to ministers on the Oversea and Defence Committee on a "need to know" basis. When the system functions properly, the evidence of impending military action that would endanger the Falklands would prompt one or more ministers to call for a meeting of the committee.

Throughout the period of negotiations that began in 1965, British governments kept a weather eye open for any indications that Argentina might attempt to invade the islands. In the autumn of 1977, the military regime in Argentina had made several threatening moves indicating that it might take military action. Notwithstanding resistance from the Ministry of Defence, which argued that it could not spare the required sea power, the foreign secretary under the Labour government, David Owen, eventually convinced the prime minister, James Callaghan, that circumstances called for a "trip wire" against a possible invasion.[8] Eventually, Callaghan called a meeting of the Oversea and Defence Committee that authorized the deployment of a nuclear submarine and two frigates in the Falklands area.

The government kept this mission a secret, and analysts cannot demonstrate with certainty that the Argentineans knew about the force, much less that they canceled an impending invasion on the basis of its proximity to the islands.[9] Such a force probably would not have thwarted a determined invasion attempt. However, it would have proscribed smaller actions and even given pause for consideration of a full-scale military initiative. In this respect, the Oversea and Defence system worked. It had brought early warnings of possible aggression to the attention of the appropriate parties. Further, it had facilitated a commitment of resources in a timely fashion.

Two factors explain why the Callaghan government acted so decisively in 1977. The first relates to prime ministerial focus. Callaghan had served in the Royal Navy during World War II. While prime minister, he took a passionate interest in the fleet—right down to maintaining his own records on the positions of various vessels.

The second factor behind the government's performance stems from process. We already have noted the degree to which Callaghan relied upon cabinet consultations. In the buildup to the 1977 crisis, the Oversea and Defence process engaged itself much more vigorously than it did in 1982 under Thatcher.[10] In a February 1976 meeting of the Oversea and Defence Committee, Callaghan had requested a full assessment from the defense secretary of the military options, should Argentina take direct action in the Falklands. In March, he called for a full committee review of British policies toward Argentina. This study engendered a revamped stance toward negotiations that received full discussion in subsequent meetings of Oversea and Defence.

Notwithstanding the renewed overtures, the situation began to deteriorate rapidly in the

---

But I have no doubt in my mind from my own experience over many years on this subject that that was a war that could have been avoided if we had taken the proper and prudent precautions at the time when the signs became evident, and it was the neglect of Ministers which led to the Falklands war. . . . Matters of this sort should be put on the Cabinet agenda, if they seem to be of that importance. . . . Because of my background, I asked the Admiralty every week to send me a map of the world, about the size of this blotter in front of us here, which set out the position and disposition of every ship in the British Navy, including all the auxiliaries, so that I could know exactly what we could do and how long it would take us to get to the Falklands and where we needed to be. That is the kind of thing that I think a Prime Minister must do. There are small things he must do, and large things. That's one of the small things he must do that can save a very large catastrophe.

Source: James Callaghan interview with Peter Hennessy, entitled "All the Prime Minister's Men," produced by Brook Productions for Channel Four Television Limited (May 1986), used by permission of Channel 4 International.

autumn of 1976. It was during this period that the foreign secretary requested the paper on military options that formed the basis for the request of a "trip wire." Further, this account only covers the activities of Oversea and Defence. Through 1976 and 1977, the Joint Intelligence Committee frequently updated the interdepartmental assessment of the Falklands' situation.

Margaret Thatcher. In contrast to the Callaghan administration, the Thatcher government's handling of similar signs of a brewing crisis provides a textbook case of failure of the Oversea and Defence system. Thatcher found the committee's highly routinized processes a bit tedious. Thus she was loath to have set times for committee meetings. She much preferred engaging herself when specific crises emerged. Besides, Foreign Secretary Lord Carrington disliked ministerial meetings. Rather than pressing for committee sessions, he normally would try to transact his business through correspondence with his cabinet colleagues. Further, the government had imposed a series of cuts on the defense program that had absorbed much of the Oversea and Defence community's time during the first three months of 1982. This process—along with the usual menu of major issues that present themselves—pretty much preordained that the Falklands would remain on a back burner.

In early 1982, the United Kingdom found itself in a similar position regarding the Falklands to that which had emerged in 1977. The Argentineans were trying to speed up the pace of negotiations, yet it was clear that the Thatcher government would encounter extreme difficulty in selling a settlement to the islanders and their advocates in the House of Commons. Talks between the two nations in New York in late February had resulted in little progress. An Argentinean hardliner, General Leopoldo Galtieri, had assumed the presidency in December 1981. Further, the regime began to

play up the Falklands issue, perhaps to divert public attention from human rights concerns and rising alarm over the poor performance of the economy.

The Franks Report chronicles just how little the Oversea and Defence system had taken note of developments in the Falklands. The Joint Intelligence Committee had conducted a full assessment of the Falklands situation in July 1981. It concluded that only severe provocation by Britain or an abandonment of trust in the negotiation process would induce Argentina to invade the Falklands.[11] The Latin American Current Intelligence Group had failed even to discuss the Falklands in its eighteen meetings between July 1981 and March 1982.[12] Notwithstanding developments during the three months leading to the invasion, neither the committee nor the cabinet focused on the Falklands until Argentina took concrete military actions. That is, the cabinet did not discuss the situation until March 23, when Argentinean forces occupied South Georgia Island, one of the Falkland Island Dependencies. Oversea and Defence did not examine the issue until April 1, the day before the invasion of the Falkland Islands.[13]

If the Argentineans were determined to invade the Falklands, we cannot say that any British move, short of timely deployment of a full naval task force, would have prevented such an action. However, the Thatcher government made errors in its handling of the Falklands. Some of these badly miscued the Argentineans about Britain's resolve to protect the Falklands. Others involved failure to take the military precautions necessary to prevent an actual invasion. Two examples point up the magnitude of some of these errors.

The first of these concerns Britain's resolve. For years, the ice-patrol ship *HMS Endurance* had provided a token but symbolically important naval presence in the waters surrounding the Falklands. However, the *1981 Defence Review* had judged that the vessel was not cost effective.[14] In June 1981, the government announced that the *Endurance*'s 1981–1982 voyage would be her last. The foreign secretary had protested this decision on several occasions. However, the defense secretary would not reverse himself. The Foreign Office had become particularly distressed that the Argentinean press had trumpeted the move as abandonment of the Falklands. However, the foreign secretary's protests fell short of actually bringing the matter to the Oversea and Defence Committee—although he did suggest in a letter to the defense secretary dated February 17, 1982, that he might do this. We can safely conclude that Lord Carrington was not especially enthused about fighting the Ministry of Defence on the issue—especially since the budget-minded prime minister would probably side with the plans to withdraw the *Endurance.*

The second error of judgment was a failure to take advantage of an opportunity to improve Britain's preparedness in response to clear indi-

---

Mr. James Callaghan

. . . is the Prime Minister aware that the Government's decision to withdraw and pay off HMS "Endurance" . . . is an error that could have serious consequences?

The Prime Minister

I recognize that this is a very difficult decision for my right honourable Friend the Secretary of State for Defence. . . . There are many competing claims of the defence budget, even though we are increasing it substantially . . . the defence capability of that ship is extremely limited. My right honourable Friend therefore felt that other claims on the defence budget should have greater priority.

Source: Parliamentary questions on the withdrawal of the *Endurance,* February 9, 1982.

I think it is reasonable to observe that the major issues of the Falklands War were more or less written in the stars. There wasn't actually a great sense of option or choice. It was clear the task force had to go. Having gone, it was clear that, if it reached there before any kind of serious and sensible peace proposal could be offered, . . . the task force then had to do something. It was clear that . . . fudge proposals from the Argentinians which amounted to saying "We've done what we've done now let's negotiate from here" were quite unacceptable and it was clear that the task force had to land and do its bit. So I think, of course, it was right and proper that these things came to Cabinet. But I think it would be glorifying things a bit to say that re-created Cabinet government in its full glory.

Source: David Howell, secretary of state for transport at the time of the Falklands War, as quoted by Peter Hennessy in *Cabinet,* 1986.

---

cations of a possible invasion.[15] After a disappointing round of negotiations in New York on February 26 and 27, the Argentinean regime began to signal the fact that it planned to take military action if the impasse continued. It did this first in a terse, unilateral communiqué at the end of the New York meeting. Following this, the seemingly informed Argentinean press reported that unnamed official sources in Buenos Aires had spoken explicitly of plans for direct military intervention.

On March 3, the British ambassador to Argentina cabled London about the press commentary on the significance of the unilateral communiqué. The prime minister wrote on her copy of the telegram "we must make contingency plans." However, her private secretary did not get around to conveying the prime minister's comments to the Foreign and Commonwealth Office—with copies to the Ministry of Defence and the Cabinet Office—until March

A triumphant Margaret Thatcher visits troops in the Falkland Islands.

8. On the same date, the prime minister asked the defense secretary how quickly the Royal Navy could deploy ships to the Falklands. According to the Franks Report, the window of opportunity had already shut.[16]

Even if the government had made a small deployment—similar to Callaghan's—it would have had to act by March 5 in order to play any role in deterring the invasion of April 2. Ironically, on precisely that date, J. B. Ure, a senior career official in the Foreign and Commonwealth Office, asked the permanent head of the foreign service for permission to depart from Whitehall practice.[17] Normally, career officials do not disclose to ministers the secret actions of their predecessors. Ure requested and obtained clearance to tell Lord Carrington about Callaghan's deployment of the nuclear submarine and two frigates to the Falklands area in 1977. Lord Carrington did not register much interest in this option. Indeed, the government dithered and only vaguely anticipated a Oversea and Defence Committee meeting in

which it would fashion an appropriate response to Thatcher's request for military contingency plans.

Of course, Thatcher acted decisively once the invasion took place. In fact, she chaired a war cabinet that met almost daily to coordinate the war effort. This included the home secretary, the new foreign secretary, Francis Pym, the defense secretary, and the paymaster general—who, more importantly, served as the chairman of the Conservative Party. The committee, thus constituted, viewed its coordinative task as harmonizing the various diplomatic and military moves *and* garnering and maintaining the support of the cabinet, Parliament, and the public.

Thatcher, already under harsh scrutiny over her economic policies, had just fumbled the ball badly. She had done so by failing to pay attention to a volatile situation. She had also allowed the apparatus designed to compensate for limits to prime ministerial attention span run down. Ministers simply had not come together at a timely moment to exchange views on the brewing crisis. Perhaps the Falklands did not mean much to the United Kingdom. However, their loss to the Argentineans due to an invasion which the government had failed to anticipate would comprise a devastating blow to the prime minister's fortunes. Thatcher's political future and the recapture of the Falklands became inextricably linked. There would be no room for a negotiated end to hostilities. The ultimate British victory over the Argentineans covered a multitude of sins of omission. It also handed Thatcher proof positive that she provided just the type of tough leadership that many Britons believed their country required.

Foreign Policy under Major

As he does in most other areas, Margaret Thatcher's hand-picked successor differs greatly from her regarding foreign policy. While the United Kingdom still has a "special relationship" with the United States, John Major did not possess the special "special relationship" with George Bush, or more recently with Bill Clinton, that Margaret Thatcher had with Ronald Reagan. Major is less likely to exploit Britain's connection with the United States than his predecessor. At home, Major does not use foreign affairs to score party points as readily as Thatcher did. Prime Minister Major's approach to foreign policy is characterized by consultation, both with his cabinet and with his fellow world leaders.

Major's biggest foreign policy challenge so far has been managing Britain's role in helping the Allied force ultimately move to push Iraqi troops out of Kuwait and pursue them all the way back into their own country. In handling the affair, Major demonstrated his penchant for collective cabinet government. Once the shooting had started, he assembled a war cabinet similar to Margaret Thatcher's and consulted it regularly. Since the Desert Shield force and the coalition upon which it was based were dominated by President Bush, there was limited room for initiative on the part of other leaders, but John Major was included in the inner circle of allied chiefs.

During the Persian Gulf crisis, even John Major's war-theater demeanor proved palpably different from that of Margaret Thatcher during the Falklands War.

When Major did have a chance to initiate policy, he first consulted his European Community counterparts. In lobbying for a safe area for Iraqi Kurds after the Gulf War, Major rallied the support of his European counterparts, and *then* approached the White House. Thatcher would most probably have picked up the "hot line" and asked the president of the United States directly—without prior consultation with Europe. Whether either leader's approach would have worked is not of consequence; what matters is that Major chose to stress collaboration and approached Europe first.

Outside the cabinet, the prime minister reinforced his role as first among equals by appearing unfaltering and in control, soothing the British public in a time of crisis. After the war, Major was more popular in the polls than any prime minister before him. But never in the course of events did he resort to the jingoism and saber rattling that Thatcher had employed both during the Falklands War and the first stage of the crisis in the Persian Gulf. However, Major's popularity never translated into electoral support for his party. Together, the deplorable consequences of the war for the Kurds and the Shi'ites, the dominant role of the American forces, and Britain's apparent irresponsibility in providing arms to Iraq before the war determined that the Gulf War had far less beneficial impact on Tory electoral prospects than had victory in the Falklands nine years earlier.

CONCLUSION

This chapter has attempted to flesh out what we learned in chapters 8 and 9 about the roles of various institutions within the policy process. We focused our attention on how economic and foreign policy are made. We also contrasted the approaches taken under James Callaghan and Margaret Thatcher, and we made some preliminary observations of John Major's approach in the respective fields.

We saw, of course, that the personalities and interests of prime ministers influence the way in which the policy process operates. For instance, Callaghan's reliance on collective decision making helped bog his government down in seemingly interminable deliberations over pay policy. However, his consultative approach paid dividends in his handling of the Falklands crisis in 1977. Thatcher's tendency to tire of cabinet government got her into perilous straits in the 1982 Falklands crisis. However, her assertive leadership style helped her act decisively, once she was confronted with an actual invasion. This character trait also enabled her to adhere to popular policies such as monetarism and privatization, even when she encountered resistance because they departed from the received wisdom in the political and bureaucratic establishments.

We have seen in this chapter that not all the institutions involved in the policy arena enjoy the same leverage in various decision processes. The more urgent and sensitive the matter, the greater the likelihood that ad hoc groups will form in cabinet to seek a solution that can then be presented as a *fait accompli* to the rest of the government. Some departments are more equal than others. Even in Thatcher's struggle with the Falklands, we found that the Foreign and Commonwealth Office was deferring to the Ministry of Defence over whether *HMS Endurance* should be withdrawn and whether further vessels should be sent to the Falklands. In turn, the Ministry of Defence found that economy measures imposed by the *1981 Defence Review* sharply constrained its ability to provide a presence in the area. Of course, the Treasury had imposed the fiscal constraints operating behind the *Defence Review*.

We examined the ways in which debates in the House of Commons and specific committee inquiries can influence decision making on both the economic and foreign policy fronts. To date, Parliament has not developed to the point where it consistently earns a place at the table in the major debates within the policy arena.

Too many issues are resolved within Whitehall—by the cabinet and the bureaucracy—and then referred to Parliament as a virtual *fait accompli*. However, the loosening of party discipline and the strengthening of the committee system have worked to improve Parliament's role appreciably. Certainly incidents such as Thatcher's ouster and Major's difficulties with Parliament over the Maastricht Treaty remind all concerned that ultimately everything rests on the confidence of the House of Commons and the solidarity of the cabinet. Prime ministers take either for granted at their peril.

Notes

1. Hugh Heclo and Aaron Wildavsky, *The Private Government of Public Money: Community and Policy Inside British Politics* (Berkeley, Calif.: University of California Press, 1974).
2. A. Adonis, *Parliament Today* (Manchester: Manchester University Press, 1990), p. 108.
3. Anna Kasten Nelson, "National Security I: Inventing a Process (1945–1960)," in *The Illusion of Presidential Government*, eds. Hugh Heclo and Lester M. Salamon (Boulder, Colo.: Westview Press, 1981), p. 231.
4. John P. Mackintosh, *The British Cabinet* (London: Stevens, 1977), pp. 371, 382.
5. Mackintosh, pp. 492–493.
6. Richard Crossman, *The Diaries of a Cabinet Minister*, vol. 3 (London: Hamish Hamilton and Jonathan Cape, 1977); and Peter Hennessy, *Cabinet* (Oxford: Blackwell, 1986).
7. Hennessy, pp. 114–115.
8. Simon Jenkins, "Britain's Pearl Harbour," *The Sunday Times*, March 29, 1987, p. 29.
9. Franks Report, 1983, pp. 18–19.
10. Franks Report, 1983, pp. 14–18.
11. Franks Report, 1983, pp. 26–27.
12. Franks Report, 1983, p. 83.
13. Franks Report, 1983, p. 79.
14. Franks Report, 1983, pp. 33–34.
15. Franks Report, 1983, pp. 40–45.
16. Franks Report, 1983, p. 82.
17. Franks Report, 1983, p. 43.

References and Suggested Readings

Adonis, Andrew. 1990. *Parliament Today*. Manchester: Manchester University Press.

Beloff, Max, and Gillian Peele. 1985. *The Government of the UK: Political Authority in a Changing Society*. London: Weidenfeld and Nicholson.

Campbell, Colin. 1983. *Governments under Stress: Carter, Reagan and the Search for Executive Harmony*. Toronto: University of Toronto Press.

Chapman, Richard A. 1984. *Leadership in the British Civil Service*. London: Croom Helm.

Clarke, Michael. 1992. *British External Policy-making in the 1990s*. London: Macmillan Press.

Coutts, Ken, and Wynne Godley. 1990. "The British Economy under Mrs. Thatcher," *Political Quarterly*, 60 (April–June).

Crossman, Richard. 1977. *The Diaries of a Cabinet Minister*, vol. 3. London: Hamish Hamilton and Jonathan Cape.

Donoughue, Bernard. 1987. *Prime Minister: The Conduct of Policy under Harold Wilson and James Callaghan*. London: Jonathan Cape.

Elles, Diana. 1987. "The Foreign Policy of the Thatcher Government," in Minogue, K. and Biddiss, M., eds. *Thatcherism: Personality and Politics*. London: Macmillan.

Ellis, Nesta W. 1991. *John Major: A Personal Biography*. London: Futura Press.

[Franks Report] Committee of Privy Councillors. 1983. *Falkland Islands Review*. London: Her Majesty's Stationery Office.

Heclo, Hugh, and Aaron Wildavsky. 1974. *The Private Government of Public Money: Community and Policy Inside British Politics*. Berkeley, Calif.: University of California Press.

Hennessy, Peter. 1986. *Cabinet*. Oxford: Blackwell.

Jenkins, Simon. 1987. "Britain's Pearl Harbour." *The Sunday Times*, 29 March:29.

Keegan, William. 1984. *Mrs. Thatcher's Economic Experiment*. Harmondsworth: Penguin.

Mackintosh, John P. 1977. *The British Cabinet*. London: Stevens.

Patten, C. F. 1987. "Mrs. Thatcher's Economic Legacy," in Minogue, K., and Biddiss, M., eds. *Thatcherism: Personality and Politics*.

Riddell, Peter. 1985. *The Thatcher Government*. Oxford: Blackwell.

ATLANTIC OCEAN

Reykjavik
ICELAND

NORWAY

FINLAND

Oslo

SWEDEN

Helsinki

Stockholm

Tallinn

St.
Petersbu

ESTONIA

North Sea

DENMARK

Baltic Sea

Riga

LATVIA

Copenhagen

LITHUANIA

IRELAND
Dublin

Vilnius

Minsk

UNITED
KINGDOM

KALININGRAD
(RUSSIA)

BELARUS

London

Amsterdam

Berlin

Warsaw

NETHERLANDS

Brussels

GERMANY

POLAND

BELGIUM

Bonn

Prague

Paris

LUXEMBOURG

CZECH
REPUBLIC

SLOVAKIA

Chisina

FRANCE

Vienna

Bratislava

MOLDOV

Berne

AUSTRIA

Budapest

SWITZERLAND

SLOVENIA

HUNGARY

ROMANIA

Ljubljana

Zagreb

CROATIA

Belgrade

Bucharest

PORTUGAL

Lisbon

Madrid

ITALY

Adriatic Sea

BOSNIA
AND
HERZEGOVINA

Sarajevo

YUGOSLAVIA

BULGARIA

SPAIN

Rome

MONTENEGRO

Sofia

Tirana

Skopje

MACEDONIA

ALBANIA

GREECE

Aegean Sea

Athens

Mediterranean Sea

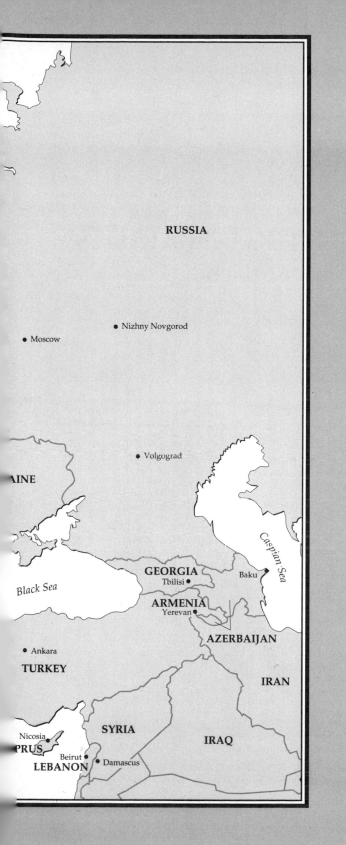

III

France

RUSSIA

• Nizhny Novgorod

• Moscow

• Volgograd

AINE

GEORGIA
Tbilisi •
Black Sea
ARMENIA
Yerevan •

Baku •

Caspian Sea

AZERBAIJAN

• Ankara

TURKEY

IRAN

Nicosia •
PRUS

SYRIA

IRAQ

Beirut •   • Damascus
LEBANON

11

The Current Situation:
Between a Rock and a Hard Place

*L*ike the other countries of the industrial world, France has been troubled by the major changes in the world economy that have occurred since World War II and especially since the oil crisis of 1973–1974. The persistent stagnation that all economies have known since the crisis has made traditional approaches to economic problems obsolete. After twenty-three years of postwar conservative rule, France elected François Mitterrand and a Socialist team to reduce unemployment and to rejuvenate a decaying industrial base. They were not successful and political conditions became volatile. In 1986, voters elected a conservative majority in Parliament, not only rebuffing Mitterrand, but creating conditions that many political scientists thought would make France ungovernable. Two years later, French voters re-elected Mitterrand and a Socialist plurality. Five years after that, they turned his Socialist Party out of power in a landslide unequaled in the French Fifth Republic.

DIVIDED GOVERNMENT

The French parliamentary elections held in March 1993 brought a crushing defeat to the French Socialists and effectively transferred power to a coalition of conservative parties. The right wing returned to the previously dominant position that it occupied from 1958 to 1981.

Well, not exactly. For the second time, Gallic voters opted for a power-sharing arrangement which they call *Cohabitation*. Under France's unusual political system, power is shared among the president, prime minister, and Parliament in ways that, under some conditions, are not clearly defined by the Constitution of 1958. The president appoints the prime minister, who must, in turn, enjoy the confidence of the Parliament. In situations where the president and prime minister are from opposing parties, executive authority is essentially a matter of negotiation and maneuvering. This in turn depends on the relative strength of the prime minister's parliamentary majority and on the political skills of the president. Unlike the president of the United States, the French president does not have veto power over legislation. On the other hand, a crafty politician occupying the Elysée Palace (the French equivalent of the White House) can employ a host of subtle tools to undercut the thrust of policies and politicians with which and with whom he or she disagrees.

This all happened before, when the conservatives came to power during Mitterrand's first presidential term, when they won the parliamentary elections of 1986. At that time, Mitterrand outmaneuvered them, winning re-election and dismissing the conservative government in 1988. The second period of Cohabitation gave the conservatives a stronger hand. They had an overwhelming majority in the Parliament, unlike their two-seat victory margin in 1986, and could claim to have a mandate for change. Unfortunately for the French conservatives, however, they have very little economic space in which to maneuver.

BACKGROUND

France is a country whose ways of doing business and government's relation to the economy have been long established. Above all, it is a country where government has traditionally had the responsibility of assuring the well-being and growth of the French economy. The various institutions that constitute the French government—that is to say, the state—have long had a special place in directing the progress of French society. This was especially true after World War II, when seemingly tireless government officials worked long hours to open various bottlenecks, effectively use scarce resources, and push past production obstacles to bring France, sometimes kicking and screaming, into the twentieth century. By the 1960s, France was a full and contributing member of the world economy.

Of course, the French growth experience had much in common with that of other industrial countries. Like the other countries of Western Europe, France was a recipient of U.S. aid under the Marshall Plan immediately after World War II. Indeed, West Germany, Italy, France, and even Britain all experienced "economic miracles" as they rebuilt their economies from the devastation wrought by the war. The injection of capital from America was put to good use in Europe, as its highly educated work force turned investment into a sixfold increase in productive capacity. The universal acceptance of Keynesian policy techniques—that is, using governmental taxing and spending power to influence the overall demand for goods and services—led to a smoothing-out of each nation's business cycle. This made recessions more tolerable and quickened the return to prosperity. In fact, recessions were so inconsequential during the first two postwar decades that E. J. Hobsbawm, the dean of British economic historians, referred to the period as "the Long Boom."[1] Figure 11.1 shows the overall growth of the French economy since 1949.

A host of international factors all contributed to the tremendous European resurgence, not the least of which was the liberal economic order established with the enthusiastic support of the United States. In 1944, at Bretton Woods,

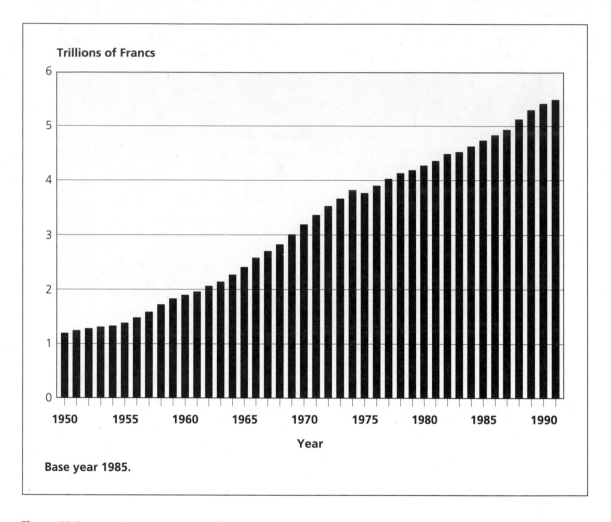

Trillions of Francs

Base year 1985.

Figure 11.1 Gross Domestic Product of France.   Source: International Monetary Fund, *International Financial Statistics,* vols. 32, 45 (Washington, D.C.: 1979, 1992).

New Hampshire, the victorious allies laid plans for a set of international institutions that would lower trade barriers and facilitate exchange between countries. Among these, the International Bank for Reconstruction and Development performed just as its title suggested: it helped to finance European reconstruction. The International Monetary Fund financed the short-term needs of its member countries. Eventually, an international set of rules regulat-

ing trade—the GATT (General Agreement on Tariffs and Trade)—was developed, enhancing trade between all developed noncommunist countries. Figure 11.2 shows the growth of French imports and exports.

At the European level, the Office of European Economic Cooperation, the European Payments Union, and eventually the European Economic Community all facilitated intra-European exchange and mutual economic

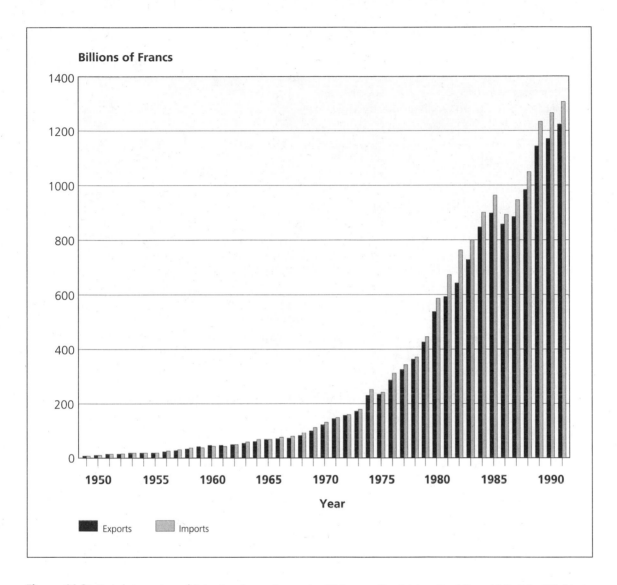

Figure 11.2 French Imports and Exports. Source: International Monetary Fund, *International Financial Statistics* (Washington, D.C.: various years).

growth. France, like its neighbors, grew robust in a favorable international climate. Like its neighbors as well, its growth figures were stupendous after World War II. But unlike the other countries of Europe, there were peculiarly French reasons for the country's economic success.

One of the most important French mechanisms for promoting growth was national economic planning, performed by the *Commissariat au plan*. Well within the "statist" tradition (that is, the traditional role of the French government to intervene in markets), economic planning was a procedure whereby government officials met periodically with private sector representatives to compare notes, avoid production bottlenecks, and jointly develop market projections for the entire French economy.[2] The idea was to maximize the opportunities for French firms, to facilitate their growth, and to increase the employment possibilities for all French citizens. This partnership of government and private industry has been largely credited for the success of the French economy after World War II. It was, however, a partnership that would become increasingly troubled.

Part of the reason for the troubled partnership is that large numbers of people were excluded from the policy process. France's democracy was not rebuilt as quickly as its economy. Not only was policy made by an extremely small number of public and private elite, but the interests of labor were almost entirely excluded from meaningful representation in policy circles.[3] This meant that France's tremendous economic growth was partially financed by keeping wages artificially low. This kept the costs of French products down, and made profit margins correspondingly attractive to investors. But there was a political price to be paid. French workers could look across the border at Germany and see that their salaries had not kept pace. Their disgruntlement with the political system dominated by conservative elites made them ripe for change.

Thus in 1968, when students demonstrated for reform of the French educational system, workers also took to the streets in another kind of partnership: an alliance with the students. A proliferation of workers' strikes and student demonstrations spread throughout the country. France in May 1968 was closer to a genuine social revolution than at any time since the Great Revolution of 1789. General Charles De Gaulle called new elections in the face of the upheavals. Middle-class and small-town French voters were frightened by the specter of a left-wing revolution, and supported the conservatives *en masse*. But the newly elected conservative economic managers had learned a valuable lesson. Wages were permitted to rise, and this presented the country with a new set of problems.

The Road to Decline

For a short period (1969–1973) France reconstituted its productive forces and groped back toward its postwar habits. The world, however, had changed. The very openness and freedom of exchange that had promoted economic growth for so long began to backfire. Japan began to dominate world markets with cheap, high-quality goods. Newly industrializing countries, such as South Korea and Brazil, penetrated many of Europe's markets for traditional manufacturing. It was hard for countries whose workers had gained higher living standards to compete with the new, low-wage producers.

The *coup de grâce* was the oil crisis of 1973–1974. While the increased competition and saturation of world markets had occurred gradually, the sudden disruption of oil supplies and accompanying meteoric price increases dealt a final blow to the postwar system. The huge increase in the price of oil sent all industrial prices skyrocketing. The tremendous price rises (that is, inflation) proved highly resistant to traditional Keynesian management techniques. Immediate reactions to increased prices led to a precipitous decline in world demand for goods and services. The world economic pie ceased expanding, and competition grew even more intense for that which remained. The stagnant growth exaggerated conflicts of interest between social groups within countries as well as intensifying the basis for conflict among the industrial countries.[4] In short, the halcyon days of seemingly limitless expansion, where all seemed possible and a better tomorrow seemed inevitable, were gone forever. The industrial world, Europe especially, and France inevitably, appeared doomed to decline.

The industrial stagnation of the 1970s and 1980s resisted the cures that had worked so well in the postwar years. Government spending created inflation without creating jobs. Inflation became so entrenched that it could only be controlled by draconian measures that reduced employment to levels reminiscent of the Great Depression of the 1930s.

ECONOMIC DECLINE AND POLITICAL CHANGE

From 1958 to 1981, French politics was dominated by conservative politicians. The combined phenomena of an electoral system that gave narrow majorities a long lease on power, an extended period of economic growth, and the existence of a strong Communist Party that struck fear into potential supporters of the left-wing opposition, all acted to reinforce the hegemony of the Gaullists and their conservative allies. However, economic growth slowed significantly—and was sometimes negative—after the onset of the first oil crisis in 1974. This was the year that Valéry Giscard d'Estaing was elected president. In the meantime, Socialist Party leader François Mitterrand's strategy of luring away Communist voters by moving his party to the left bore fruit. By 1981 the Communists were no longer a threat and voters were willing to express their dissatisfaction with the Right's economic policies by voting for the Left. Mitterrand won the presidency and dissolved Parliament to obtain a working majority (the French constitution allows the president to call legislative elections to obtain a favorable majority before the expiration of the normal five-year term, so long as he does this no more than once a year).

The ensuing Socialist landslide allowed Mitterrand and his friends to implement all the cherished policy ideas that the Left had advocated since the end of World War II. The policies turned out to be, at best, insufficient—and, at worst, counterproductive (depending on which critic was commenting). The Socialists, with the Communist Party as a junior partner, nationalized a large number of competitive corporations and most of the country's banks, raised the minimum wage, and embarked on a course of Keynesian deficit spending.

The real problem, as it turned out, was not the nationalizations—which, for the most part, became more profitable after falling under state ownership. The problem was the Keynesian deficit spending, which injected money into the economy and increased the demand for goods and services. Unfortunately for the Socialists, French companies did not expand production, so people turned to buying imported goods. As more and more people demanded marks, pounds, and dollars to purchase goods from abroad, the Bank of France ran out of foreign currency reserves. This foreign exchange crisis forced the government to borrow huge sums of money and the amassed debt then formed a constraint on the government's ability to intervene actively in the French economy. To restrain demand for foreign goods, the Socialists inaugurated an austerity program that then vitiated any possibility of fighting France's already substantial unemployment. The economic malaise eroded the popularity of the Socialists and led to the conservative parliamentary victory in the 1986 elections.

Unfortunately for the conservatives, they based their economic strategy on privatizing the nationalized industries. This was not the problem, as the companies were already profitable and efficient, and the privatizations did nothing to solve France's persistent unemployment. Unluckily for the right-wing parties, after the failure of the initial Socialist strategy, the Socialists then began implementing a very conservative set of economic policies, focusing on expansion of financial markets, liberation of prices, and a strong franc. The conservative policy preferences of the Right had been implemented by the Left. From the perspective of the former, privatization policies were the only thing that distinguished conservatives and Socialists, and these were clearly no solution to the country's 10% unemployment levels. Like the Socialists before them, the conservatives were defeated by the economy in the presidential and parliamentary elections of 1988. Figure 11.3 illustrates the unemployment problem.

The lackluster performance of the French economy in the next Socialist administration quickly eroded support for Mitterrand, despite the surge in support he received for France's participation in the Persian Gulf War. Things went from bad to worse. Mitterrand's legen-

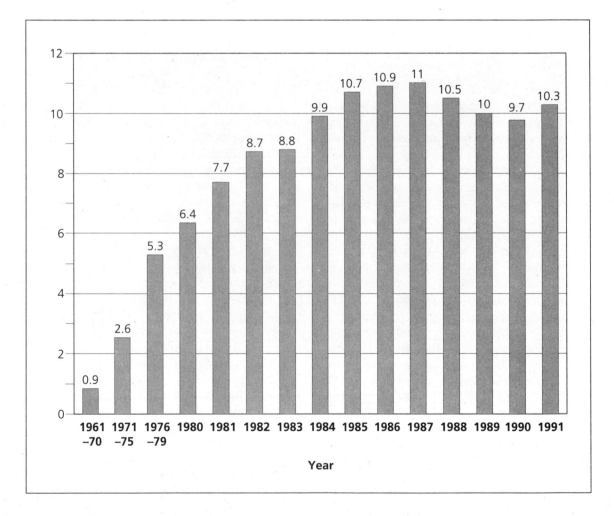

Figure 11.3 Unemployment in France, in Percent.   Source: Tom Peirce, "The Politics of Employment Policy in France" (Washington, D.C.: George Washington University, December 1993), unpublished paper, p. 2. Used by permission of the author.

dary political acumen seemed to fail him in his choice of Edith Cresson to succeed the popular Michel Rocard as prime minister. Cresson, a close personal friend of the president, seemed quixotic and prone to an increasing number of political gaffes. The disastrous performance of the Socialists in the local elections of March 1992 were attributed—rather unfairly—to the country's first female prime minister, who resigned from office and was immediately replaced by Pierre Bérégovoy, a very moderate Socialist with a pronounced preference for financial orthodoxy.

The strict monetary policy of Bérégovoy, which favored fighting inflation over fighting unemployment, was probably enough to do the Socialists in at the 1993 elections. But to add insult to injury quite literally, a series of scandals came to light as the election approached. Most of the scandals involved illegal party financing, where the Socialists appeared to be at least as sullied as the parties that came before them. Some scandals were personal, and even Bérégovoy himself—who had invited the derision of France's elite in the remark "You can tell he's an honest man: just look at his socks!"—was found to have accepted an interest-free loan from a tainted financier. A month after the 1993 elections, wounded by the accusations of impropriety and despondent over the crushing defeat of his party, Bérégovoy committed suicide.

The ironic effect of all this political volatility was to stabilize the kind of policies that politicians from both the Left and the Right actually implemented. The experience of power had a moderating influence on the Socialists. After 1982, when the initial results of their program became clear, they retracted many of their reforms. By 1986 the differences between the Socialists and their conservative opponents was more rhetorical than real. By 1993 the difference in the positions of the political parties was barely even rhetorical.

SOCIAL CHANGE

If the various governments of France had been unsuccessful in fighting economic stagnation, they did better in the area of social policy. While the economic difficulties of the country aggravated the already substantial inequalities of French society, in some ways the policies of both conservatives and Socialists improved the lives of most French people. Although a country where most people consider themselves to be Catholic, and where women gained the right to vote only in 1944, the conservative presidency of Valéry Giscard d'Estaing (1974–1981) brought France one of Western Europe's most liberal abortion laws. The Socialists passed tough laws against sexual harassment and pursued an active policy of assuaging racial tensions among the French and newly arrived immigrants from the former French colonies.

On this latter issue of immigration and racial tensions, the French governments were less successful than in the enfranchisement and empowerment of women. Most of the countries of Western Europe have seen a significant increase in such social disturbances. This is especially a problem in Germany, which not only has had to absorb all the problems of the former German Democratic Republic, but has had to deal with large numbers of foreigners remaining on its soil, despite a deep recession and consequent rising animosities. But France has also had its problems.

Large numbers of immigrants were brought into the country to avoid labor shortages during the period of expansion after the Second World War, and especially since the 1960s. The first waves of immigrants, from southern and eastern Europe, integrated relatively easily into French culture. However, the Moslem North Africans and people from sub-Saharan Africa and the Caribbean were not as easily accepted. Their cultures were considerably different from the Europeans' and the newcomers found it even more difficult to blend in as peoples of color. The period of stagnation that followed the oil crisis of the 1970s aggravated the situation. Poor white French citizens, rarely in a position to be generous to foreigners, were especially fretful when they saw the immigrants competing for their jobs. This was fertile ground for the neofascist National Front Party, which made inroads into both the small-business constituencies of the Right and the blue-collar voters of the Left. Conservative genuflections to the National Front became worrisome during the first period of Cohabitation (1986–1988). But their huge margin of victory in 1993 gave them the political space to ignore the far right fringes of the political spectrum. However, immigrants clearly did better under the Socialists than during periods of rule by the conservative coalition.

EUROPEAN INTEGRATION

The problems of growing unemployment seemed increasingly intractable. While there was no dearth of politicians eager to take charge, most were aware that there was little room for maneuver and huge penalties to pay for experiments that did not pan out. Increasingly, it seemed that economic problems could no longer be addressed by national governments. Europe-wide problems seemed to call for European solutions. Thus in 1992, the countries of the European Community (excepting Denmark, which endorsed the movement a year later) voted for greater integration. The treaty signed in Maastricht in the Netherlands at the close of 1991 was a tacit admission of defeat of national economic policy. But the treaty itself also spelled trouble for French do-

François Mitterrand addresses a meeting in Strasbourg, May 1988.

mestic politics. President Mitterrand had taken as the theme of his second term the "building of Europe"—that is, the advancement of European integration under the auspices of the then European Community. While Mitterrand had been a supporter of the Common Market and its subsequent accoutrements, the cause of European unity had distinct political advantages. Most importantly, it divided the French conservatives in much the same way it did the British Tories. The Gaullists especially have been more inclined to economic nationalism than have been other conservative parties on the continent. Moreover, the extent to which future European integration would involve a transfer of powers from Paris to Brussels was deeply feared, and consequently strongly opposed, by many on the Right. Mitterrand's call for a referendum on the Maastricht Treaty in 1992 embarrassed conservative leaders while tainting the "European ideal" with the odor of partisan politics. While it is certainly proper that any dramatic shift in power from national to supranational institutions deserves to be publicly debated and carefully considered, the way in which the Maastricht Treaty was politicized probably made the finding of cooperative, international solutions to the economic problems of the 1990s more difficult.

France and Our Five Propositions

Chapter 2 announced five propositions that in many ways form the themes of this book. Broadly, all of the propositions involve the political consequences of long-term economic decline to industrial polities. The first and second propositions argue that industrial decline encourages increased skepticism directed especially at parties that held power during the period of government expansion, and that state interventionism itself becomes the victim of this skepticism. These are somewhat slippery

questions in France, since the state has had such a large role for such a long time (almost three centuries!). Nevertheless, the state expanded dramatically under the Socialists after they took power in 1981. The failures of their program certainly led to grave doubts about their economic philosophy. While this evaluation was clouded by the various scandals that were certainly more instrumental in coloring public attitudes, there is no question that state intervention in the economy is no longer given the credence it used to have among French voters.

The economic context has indeed altered the way groups and alliances shift their forms of association, as posited in the third proposition. The conservative landslide of 1993 could only have been possible if rank-and-file union members deserted the Socialist and Communist parties *en masse*. The decline in manufacturing activity led to a reduction in levels of unionization, reducing the influence of blue-collar workers. At the same time, the rise of immigration and racism created a new menace to the electoral chances of the traditional conservative parties, which were confronted by the extremist National Front. We shall discuss this evolution in the ensuing chapters.

The fourth proposition, which notes the increasing role of European integration, as it promotes economies of scale and greater efficiency, is no doubt as important to France as any other European country. It is equally true that the disquiet demonstrated in the French referendum on the Maastricht Treaty is not transitory. Defenders of a more developed European Union will no doubt have a tougher row to hoe.

The final proposition, that events in Eastern Europe demonstrate a recrudescence of ethnic and national particularisms, is not completely inapplicable to France. France, as we shall see in the next chapter, is a composite of regional identities that for the most part have been superseded by a national French culture. Yet it is this very national culture that is at the root of a broad, anti-immigrant reaction that has had profound impact on French politics. When the economic pie ceases to expand, people feel less generous toward people they identify as outsiders.

CONCLUSION

The economic stagnation of the last part of the twentieth century offered no easy solutions. All countries in Europe, as in the United States and Japan, would need leaders of consummate skill and imagination to extract their populations from what seemed to be a morass. Such leaders are always scarce. For its own future, France—like its neighbors—would depend on finding them; ultimate success would depend, like so many other things, on skill, luck, and politics.

NOTES

1. E. J. Hobsbawm, *Industry and Empire* (Baltimore: Penguin Books, 1966).
2. See especially Andrew Shonfield, *Modern Capitalism* (New York: Oxford University Press, 1969), chap. 5; and Stephen S. Cohen, *Modern Capitalist Planning: The French Model* (Berkeley and Los Angeles: University of California Press, 1977).
3. On the collaboration of public and private elite, see Ezra N. Suleiman, "Industrial Policy Formulation in France," in Ezra N. Suleiman and Stephen J. Warnecke, eds., *Industrial Policies in Western Europe* (New York: Praeger, 1975); on the exclusion of labor from macroeconomic planning, see Mikkal Herberg, "Planning, Politics and Capitalism: National Economic Planning in Britain and France," *Political Studies,* 29 (December 1981). While on the whole labor was a junior partner in French economic growth, workers in industrial sectors did not do as poorly as those in agriculture or services. I am grateful to Michael Loriaux for pointing this out.
4. On the intensity of interest group conflict and its effects on public policy, see Lester Thurow, *The Zero Sum Society* (Baltimore: Penguin Books, 1978).

REFERENCES AND SUGGESTED READINGS

Cerny, Philip G., and Martin A. Schain, eds. 1985. *Socialism, the State and Public Policy.* New York: Methuen.

Cohen, Stephen S., and Peter A. Gourevitch, eds. 1982. *France in the Troubled World Economy.* London: Butterworth Scientific.

Foglesong, Richard, and Joel Wolfe, eds. 1989. *The Politics of Economic Adjustment.* New York: Greenwood.

Gourevitch, Peter A. 1986. *Politics in Hard Times.* Ithaca, N.Y.: Cornell University Press.

Hall, Peter A. 1989. *The Political Power of Economic Ideas.* Princeton, N.J.: Princeton University Press.

Katzenstein, Peter J., ed. 1978. *Between Power and Plenty.* Madison: University of Wisconsin Press.

Lauber, Volkmar. 1983. *The Politics of Economic Policy: France 1974–1982.* New York: Praeger.

Pinder, John. 1991. *European Community.* Oxford: Oxford University Press.

Piore, Michael J., and Charles F. Sabel. 1984. *The Second Industrial Divide.* New York: Basic Books.

Sbragia, Alberta M., ed. 1992. *Euro-Politics: Institutions and Policymaking in the New European Community.* Washington, D.C.: Brookings Institution.

Shonfield, Andrew. 1969. *Modern Capitalism.* New York: Oxford University Press.

12

Historical Background:
A Legacy of Instability

*I*n the period immediately after World War II and the two decades that followed, American political scientists were especially concerned with the issue of democratic stability. Having recently emerged from a period in which much of continental Europe had succumbed to fascist dictatorship, and threats from the political extremes were very real, it is easy to understand this preoccupation. In this context, the situation of France was viewed as especially precarious. Not only did France emerge from the war with a fragile political system where left and right extremes were generously represented, but there was little in French history that allowed one to predict with any confidence that democracy would survive. Indeed, between the French Revolution of 1789 and the oil crisis of 1973–1974, France had known five republics, two monarchies, two empires, and a fascist dictatorship. This was not a track record to inspire confidence. In this and the next chapter, we shall examine competing explanations for such a shaky history.

POLITICAL RESPONSES TO SOCIAL CONFLICT

In fact, while turbulence was frequently the norm, it would be a distortion to view the history of French political institutions simply as spontaneous responses to intermittent chaos. If there is any thread tenuously uniting the series of political regimes, it is that the very deep divisions in French society led to responses on the part of political elites that both reinforced and undermined the power of central political institutions.

All political institutions are, in a very basic sense, the result of preceding political conflict.[1] They are efforts to routinize patterns of behavior in response to previous conflicts so as to resolve (or suppress) those conflicts. Political institutions are mechanisms aimed at facilitating specific kinds of social behavior. Thus the development of the absolutist kings at the end of the sixteenth century was a response to the conflicts engendered by a decaying feudal order and an attempt to shore up an agricultural system of manors and estates ruled by an aristocracy that benefited from traditional privileges. The Revolution of 1789 was a response to the inequities of absolutism. And so on, down the line.

These statements, of course, could easily be rejected by historians as glib and simplistic, an injustice to French history. Certainly, they paint complex events with a very broad brush. But it may be useful to view those events as intricately interwoven in a way that suggests a pattern—a pattern that makes present political institutions more comprehensible.

THE DECAY OF FEUDALISM AND THE ORIGINS OF MODERN FRANCE

The borders of modern France were principally achieved by the eighteenth century and are perhaps the most enduring achievement of the absolutist kings. By "absolutist" one means that these kings were able to rule without sharing power. During the feudal period, administrative and political authority was shared among kings and vassals (that is, aristocrats) so that each had reciprocal rights and obligations. Kings were frequently dependent on the aristocrats for financial and military support, and the constellation of power and authority was decentralized at best and fragmented at worst. Sovereignty was parceled out among competing power centers. Indeed, kings often had more to fear from potential rivals among their own aristocracy than they did from foreign powers. The French kings were quite aware of this, and the history of France during the feudal period was one not only of extending the borders of control of the royal house outward from Paris, but also of increasing the subjugation of aristocratic vassals. It should be noted that even in the heyday of absolutism, Louis XIV was less powerful than Napoleon would be. This was because the king never completely dominated the aristocracy.

The development of absolutism was both the product of a long period of consolidation and the immediate result of the crisis of feudalism in the seventeenth century.[2] The deep structural challenge to feudalism throughout Europe was the extension of the market system. This allowed new groups to grow wealthy and to command the resources necessary to challenge aristocratic power.

The immediate causes of feudal erosion in France were military and political: . . . the history of the construction of French Absolutism was to be that of a "convulsive" progression towards a centralized monarchical State, repeatedly interrupted by relapses into provincial disintegration and anarchy, followed by an intensified reaction towards concentration of royal power, until finally an extremely hard and stable structure was achieved. The three great breakdowns of political order were, of course, the Hundred Years' War in the 15th century, the Religious Wars in the 16th century, and the Fronde in the 17th century. The transition from the medieval to the Absolute monarchy was each time first arrested, and then accelerated by these crises, whose ultimate outcome was to create a cult of royal authority in the epoch of Louis XIV with no equal anywhere in Western Europe.

Source: Perry Anderson, *Lineages of the Absolutist State*, p. 86.

The Bourgeoisie

The origins of the term *bourgeoisie* are found in the French word *bourg*, or town, which in turn derives from the German *Burg* ("fortress"). Towns in the Middle Ages were fortified, and it was there that goods could be safely bought and sold. Townspeople then derived their living from commerce; hence the later association of *bourgeoisie* with the founders of capitalism. They were a "middle" class in that they were weaker than the aristocrats but stronger than the peasants.

The Achilles' heel of absolutism was, paradoxically, the feudal order it was meant to preserve. Louis XIV and his successors conceived of their role in the terms of their feudal precursors. The traditional way for monarchs to increase their power was territorial aggrandizement. Attempts at military expansion against England, Spain, and Holland greatly burdened the financial resources of the country. The king's attempt to pay for his military program with higher taxes alienated important groups, especially the middle classes or *bourgeoisie*, and undermined his overall domestic support. An attempt to tax the aristocrats led to the convening of the *Estates-General*. The ultimate result would be the world's most democratic revolution. But first, some background is necessary.

CIRCUMSTANCES LEADING TO THE FRENCH REVOLUTION

The French Revolution, even more than its American predecessor, was the seismic event of the eighteenth century. It was the cataclysm that shattered European feudalism and marked the genuine beginning of modern politics. The reasons for that revolution can hardly be reduced to a few factors, or *variables*, as we call them in social science. Nevertheless, tracing the impact of a few important influences on political events is a useful and illuminating exercise.

An important study completed in the 1960s by Barrington Moore, Jr., sheds much light on French history.[3] Moore's study focused on the transition from feudalism to modern political regimes in England, France, America, India, Japan, and China. It was his contention that the political institutions that eventually developed were especially shaped by the development of agricultural markets. Commercialization of different agriculture products generated different economic incentives, and these incentives had political ramifications.

An important contrast here was found between England and France. In England, aristocrats developed an interest in the commercial benefits of raising sheep. Aristocrats influenced friends and relatives in Parliament to pass enclosure laws abrogating the traditional rights of peasants to common pastures so that lords could use the land exclusively for sheep. The resulting wool was marketed by the urban commercial classes (the bourgeoisie), and thus a mutuality of interest developed between the aristocrats and their allies in the towns. By depriving peasants and small farmers of their livelihoods, the enclosures disrupted the countryside, and the growing wealth of the aristocrats disturbed the king. The king found himself in opposition to the powerful allied interests of the bourgeoisie and aristocracy. The victory of this alliance restricted the growth of the monarchy. In legal terms, the confrontation resulted in the supremacy of Parliament (an aristocrat-dominated institution) over the crown. By the time of the Glorious Revolution of 1688, the principle of constitutional monarchy had been established.

In Britain, successive economic conflicts were also solved politically, usually by giving new groups the vote. Thus, the bourgeoisie was given a stake in the political system by the Great Reform of 1832, and the skilled workers gained entrance into the system after the Great Reform of 1867. Critically, political conflicts were solved at each major crisis by extensions of British democracy.[4]

The French responses to the commercialization of agriculture were entirely different, and with their own dramatic consequences. Whereas the product that launched British democracy was wool, France would suffer the consequences of an economy based on wine, Moore tells us. French markets for wine were smaller than those for wool in Britain, and the incentives generated by its production and sale would lead the country down a very different path to political democracy. Broadly, the development of the wine trade would fuse the interests of the aristocracy and the king and would solidify the forces hostile to democracy.

First, it is important to note that commercial agriculture was much slower to develop in France than in England. To the extent that wine was produced for markets at all, most was destined for local consumption. This meant that concern about the king's regulations or any other aspect of economic policy would not engender much interest on the part of the French, especially the aristocrats and bourgeoisie.[5] Most importantly, wine production had economic characteristics that had very different political ramifications than the production of wool. Unlike wool, wine production did not force peasants off their traditional lands. There are no significant *economies of scale* in the making of wine. This means that there was no incentive to amalgamate the small holdings of peasants into large estates for reasons of efficiency. There was, therefore, no reason to depopulate the countryside.

Furthermore, wine production did not have what economists call "spread effects." Wool production generated the possibility for related industries such as weaving, textile industries, and, eventually, steam engines. Aside from bottles and corks (the latter were produced in Portugal), and a modest distribution system, wine could not fuel an industrial revolution. Profits were relatively small, aside from the prestigious wines we know today, and implementation of new wine technologies as generators of greater profits were rare—read, negligible.

What this means from the point of view of a contrast with England is that French aristocrats continued to live from peasant dues. As the economic possibilities for improving the peasants' lot were relatively meager, this meant that any improvement in the aristocrats' income would come at the expense of the peasants. This was further aggravated in periods of bad harvests or during occasional periods of inflation, when the bite of the lord of the manor was especially painful. Moreover, feudal traditions limited the possibilities for enrichment of even the prosperous peasants. All of these conditions provided the foundation for peasant hostility to the feudal order. That order was enforced at the top by the king of France.

The fate of the French aristocrats, unlike those in England, was closely tied to the fate of the king. Importantly, the bourgeoisie also had an economic interest in maintaining royalty. The French bourgeoisie was smaller than that of England and had a very different commercial outlook. This was because much of this class depended for their livelihoods on the sale of luxury goods and weapons. Since their principal clients were royal and aristocratic families, they had a clear stake in the absolutist system. As France entered the eighteenth century, the forces behind absolutism seemed insurmountable.

The power of the king was reinforced by the way in which the state was financed. Feudal traditions generally limited the ability of the king to tax the aristocracy. Thus the king tended to finance governmental activities by taxing other classes and by selling positions in the bureaucracy to affluent members of the middle class. This "venality of offices" had several effects. It reduced the efficiency of the royal administration, created a quasi nobility from the upper reaches of the French bourgeoisie as officeholders passed their bureaucratic titles and rents to their children, and reinforced the loyalty of that class to the royal establishment.

The constant wars of the absolutist kings continued to put a strain on royal finances. With aristocrats unwilling to shoulder more of the burden, offices and taxes proliferated. Ultimately, the overtaxed segments of the bourgeoisie became alienated from the system, and many began to favor radical change. Here they found allies in the disaffected peasants and the urban poor. By the time Louis XVI called a meeting of the Estates-General, the traditional feudal assembly necessary to legitimize new levies, the country was ripe for change. In 1789 France exploded.

For the next ten years the country experienced unprecedented instability as different sectors of French society grappled for power. In its initial period (1789–1792), the revolution was dominated by the bourgeoisie in alliance with liberal aristocrats and clergy, institutionalized as the *Constituent Assembly*, a constitutional but still monarchical regime. Urban dissatisfaction and mass uprisings pushed the revolution to form the first republic, the *Convention* (1792–1795), that voted the execution of Louis XVI. The Convention, dominated by a left-wing faction of the bourgeoisie, the *Jacobins*, and especially by a group of Jacobins called the *Girondins*, led France into war with the surrounding aristocratic regimes. The latter were, in fact, poised to attack anyway under the leadership of Prussia and Austria. This led to the formation of a war cabinet, the Committee of Public Safety, under the leadership of Maximilien Robespierre. The Committee of Public Safety, though much maligned later for its abuses, was clearly sympathetic to the demands of the urban poor as well as reasonably competent in running the war effort. Their abuses were considerable, however, as Robespierre (originally the author of a bill abolishing capital punishment) and his allies used the genuine internal and external threats to the revolution as an excuse to wipe out their enemies. More than 40,000 went to the guillotine during the Reign of Terror. This ultimately led to the revolt of the Convention against its own

executive and the establishment of a new constitutional republic, the *Directory*.

NINETEENTH-CENTURY FRANCE: IMPERIAL AND REPUBLICAN EXPERIMENTS

The Directory oversaw the first genuinely free elections under republican auspices in France. However, after years of violent left-wing rule, peasant sympathies turned conservative and a pro-royalist assembly was elected. This prompted one of the country's most able generals, supported by many republicans, to initiate a coup d'état.

On the Eighteenth Brumaire, Year VIII (November 9, 1799; see "The Revolution Calendar"), the general Napoléon Bonaparte took control of the government and launched France on the road to modernity.

Bonaparte initially organized his dictatorship as a reorganization of the First Republic, calling it *The Consulate*, with himself as first consul. Later, in 1804, with victories abroad and confidence at home, the first consul transformed himself into Napoleon I, Emperor of the French.[6]

The Revolutionary Calendar

The revolutionaries were so committed to break with the past that they renamed the calendar. Dating the calendar from the founding of the First Republic (September 22, 1792), the months were: Vendémaire, Brumaire, Frimaire, Nivôse, Pluviôse, Ventôse, Germinal, Floréal, Prairial, Messidor, Thermidor, and Fructidor. They were especially concerned with breaking the power of the church by eliminating the daily reminder of the Christian calendar.

Source: R. R. Colton and Joel Palmer, *A History of the Modern World to 1815,* 5th ed. (New York: Alfred A. Knopf, 1978), pp. 341–382.

Napoleonic France

Alexis de Tocqueville in a famous study noted that the preceding efforts of the French kings to centralize power in the capital facilitated the work of the revolutionaries.[7] By seizing Paris, the rebels were able to seize the entire country, and that is exactly what they did. The class content of power changed in 1789, but the organization of administration remained intact. Even under the revolutionaries, France remained highly centralized, and that centralization would greatly affect the stability of French politics down to the present day.

It was Napoleon, however, who is credited with giving France its modern centralized form. Under the Constituent Assembly and the Convention, the revolutionaries returned power to local elected authorities, after first abolishing the old aristocrat-dominated provinces and redrawing constituencies into 96 roughly equal *départements*. Under Napoleon, the departments lost their independence and fell under the tutelage of prefects appointed by Paris. The system very much resembled that of the Old Regime, where the king's *intendents* performed the same role.

The Centralization of France

Writing in 1855, Tocqueville described the Napoleonic system as an iteration of the Old Regime: "We find a single central power located at the heart of the kingdom and controlling public administration throughout the country; a single Minister of State in charge of almost all the internal affairs of the country; in each province a single representative of government Supervising every detail of the administration. . . . Is not this exactly the highly centralized administration with which we are familiar in present-day France?"

Source: *The Old Regime and the French Revolution*, p. 57.

Yet Napoleon's innovations went much further. He established France's first *meritocracy*, where government positions were filled by virtue of talent and intelligence rather than by aristocratic origin or venality. The heart of the government was the Council of State, which advised the emperor and exists to this day as the country's highest administrative court. To train such talent for public work, the university system was reorganized, and specialized "great schools" were established such as the École Polytechnique, France's top engineering school. Under the emperor's guidance, the Council of State overhauled the nation's legal system, giving France a systematic and egalitarian set of laws, known collectively as the *Code Napoléon*, that were the most progressive of their day.

The regime was, of course, still a dictatorship. The quasi-elective legislative body that replaced the Constituent Assembly and the Convention had no powers of deliberation and served largely to legitimize Napoleon's rule. The Tribunate, a kind of senate, had no power to enact legislation, although it could openly discuss proposed legislation.

Ultimately, the regime was undermined not by its exclusion of popular will, but by the emperor's external expansion. Napoleon's attempt to extend the French empire to the limits of Europe menaced all aristocratic regimes, and they fought back. Led by Britain, Prussia, and Austria, the aristocratic alliance finally defeated Bonaparte in 1815 and restored the Bourbons to the French throne.

The Restoration and the July Monarchy

The victorious aristocratic powers successfully replaced Napoleon with the brother of Louis XVI, Louis XVIII, the son of the old king having died in prison. Yet the restoration did not mean a re-establishment of feudalism. The French bourgeoisie had grown stronger in the period from 1789 to 1815. Lands that had belonged to the aristocracy and the church were purchased by many bourgeois and well-to-do peasants. This made them a significant obstacle to the re-establishment of the Old Regime. Louis XVIII had to settle for a constitutional monarchy guaranteeing freedom of speech and property. Wealthy nonaristocrats were allowed to vote and serve in the legislature. Thus, while the French system was somewhat less democratic than even the unreformed British Parliament of the same period, formal aristocratic privileges were not restored.

The kings took an active role in government during the restoration. Both Louis XVIII and his successor, Charles X, became closely identified with specific policies. The latter's close association with ultraroyalist Prime Minister Auguste Polignac proved to be his undoing. The king's refusal to appoint a different head of government after the 1830 elections, which overwhelmingly repudiated the Ultras, alienated the bourgeoisie and parts of the aristocracy. When riots in the streets of Paris broke out as a reflection of the economic crisis, the bourgeoisie and liberal aristocrats threw their support to the Duke of Orléans, a descendant of Louis XIII. Charles X abdicated, and the July Monarchy was established under Louis-Philippe of Orléans. Because of its economic base of support, the regime also became known as the Bourgeois Monarchy.

THE BOURGEOIS MONARCHY: 1830–1848

The character of the new regime was perhaps best summed up by the British historian Alfred Cobban:

> The so-called "bourgeois monarchy" was in fact an oligarchy of landowners. In the absence of a more detailed analysis of Orleanist society, we must not read too much into this statement; but at least it suggests that the landed wealth of the country was no longer mainly in the hands of old legitimist [pro-Bourbon] families, but partly in those of a class of new men, who had doubtless made their wealth in many ways in the course of the ancien régime and the Revolution. Their figures, like that of Père Grandet, dominate the novels of Balzac. Their new wealth had largely been invested in land, and they were now a well-established propertied class, with a sufficiently strong sense of its own interests to use the revolution of 1830 to oust the legitimist-clerical regime of the restored Bourbons, and at the same time prevent the republicans from acceding to power.[8]

Befitting its title, the bourgeois monarchy's main successes and ultimate failure were to be found in the French economy. While the king mainly concerned himself with foreign policy, the government presided over the beginnings of industrialization. Most notably, the beginnings of modern industrial infrastructure were promoted by the regime. Canals and roads were improved. Railways began to make an appearance. Importantly, state-sponsored schools overtook the older parochial (church-run) schools as the vehicle for mass education.

As France slowly became industrial, a new class of urban workers gradually assumed political importance, especially in the city of Paris. A bad harvest in 1846 and a deepening economic crisis created hardship, particularly for these workers. The regime of Louis-Philippe, based on the support of landed wealth, was not especially sensitive to the workers' needs, nor to the needs of those whose livelihood depended on commerce. Parisians took to the streets again in 1848, and this time the result was the Second Republic.

THE SECOND REPUBLIC AND THE SECOND EMPIRE

The street riots of 1848 coincided with the increased audacity of the republican opposition to Louis-Philippe. With the sympathy of the National Guard supporting them, the republicans formed a provisional government in Paris. Men of democratic ideals, their actions would ultimately undermine democracy in France. The republicans instituted universal suffrage. This shifted formal power to the largely illiterate peasants, who were especially amenable to the leadership of local notables and a conservative clergy. Peasant votes assured the creation of a conservative constituent assembly.

The assembly wrote the constitution of the Second Republic, which allowed for a powerful, popularly elected president. Knowing that this would mean the election of a conservative to the post and given the proclivities of peasant voters, the Left fulminated and Parisian workers once again rioted. This frightened the bourgeoisie, no less than it did the peasantry who recalled the Red Terror of Robespierre, and feared confiscation of their property. This time the army, composed mainly of peasants, stepped in to quell any possibility of a socialist revolution. In the succeeding election, a conservative was indeed elected to the presidency. His name was Louis Napoléon Bonaparte.

Louis Bonaparte was Napoleon I's nephew. He had grown up mostly in exile and was rather more of an adventurer than a politician. In his youth he had been active in Italian revolutionary politics, and he spoke French with something of a German accent. He was, however, more interested in power than in principle. At the time of his election he had already served time in a French jail for having led an abortive coup attempt. His talents, in fact, lay more in public relations than in intellect. His speeches were especially seductive to the peasantry, while the French elite, as well as other Europeans, were more circumspect (Otto von Bismarck, the "Iron Chancellor" of Germany, would later call him "the greatest mediocrity in Europe").

While Louis Bonaparte owed his election to the French peasantry, his eventual power would be exercised as a result of divisions in the French bourgeoisie. The conflicting interests of agriculture and industry, land and capital, were not easily reconciled in the Parliament of the Second Republic.[9] Bonaparte was able to take advantage of these conflicts in a period of economic recession and crisis. When, once again, the streets of Paris promised to erupt, he led a coup d'état against the Republic and declared himself emperor. Thus began the Second Empire, with Louis Bonaparte dubbing himself Napoleon III.

FRANCE INDUSTRIALIZES

The fact that the peasants were on the winning side of the French Revolution and the subsequent acquisition of large amounts of land by the French bourgeoisie were significant factors retarding the spread of industry. The political clout of the peasants during periods of universal suffrage and the bias toward landed interests during the Bourbon and Orleanist monarchies greatly inhibited industrialization along the lines of the British model. Napoleon III, however, broke with these trends, and his regime established the political conditions necessary for economic change. Influenced by the writings of the social scientist Saint-Simon, who saw French backwardness as a product of a lack of credit, Napoleon III adopted policies favorable to credit expansion that not coincidentally were also favorable to his friends in banking circles.[10]

More importantly, the state took an active role in promoting industrial expansion. New financial institutions were established to promote industrial investment. The state guaranteed a 4% return on railroad investment, which in turn created a demand for the products of heavy industry such as steel and coal. Tariffs were lowered to stimulate competition. By the end of the 1860s, France was the European continent's largest industrial power.[11]

Industrialization reinforced the central role of Paris. Paris was the natural hub of the railroads. Investment tended to flow to Paris, where the largest consumer market existed and where an educated work force could most easily be found.

With some important exceptions, firm size tended to remain small, however. Companies were family-owned, and those that employed more than a handful of workers were relatively rare. This not only limited economies of scale and thus restrained French firms from being internationally competitive, but also made them more difficult to unionize. French society, therefore, remained alienating for the urban workers. While Napoleon III was not wholly unsympathetic to the plight of the worker, he had other priorities. Moreover, the emperor could count on the support of both the peasantry and the bourgeoisie. He could afford to let the workers go. It was not unnatural, therefore, that French workers should gravitate toward socialism at a very early stage in the country's industrial development. This phenomenon would come back to haunt future regimes.

Ultimately, Napoleon III's undoing, like that of his uncle, came from outside French borders. Rising competition from Prussia and the expansionist ambitions of Bismarck and his supporters eventually came into conflict with France. After a demoralizing French defeat at Sedan, with Napoleon III leading troops in the field, the initial phase of the Franco-Prussian War came to a close when the emperor of France surrendered.

Although the emperor was in prison, and subsequently deposed, the war continued for a few months more because the French had installed a provisional government. A lengthy siege of Paris and a failed counteroffensive led to a final and ignominious end to the war. Conditions were ripe for another attempt at republican government. This time the attempt would succeed.

THE THIRD REPUBLIC

The Third Republic would ultimately prove to be France's most successful attempt at parliamentary government. It started, however, inauspiciously. Not only was the new assembly faced with the immediate task of suing for peace, but initial elections, dominated once again by the peasant vote, brought to power a very conservative assembly, mostly of monarchists. The new government attempted to disarm the left-wing city guard and passed new laws requiring workers and the lower-middle class to pay tremendously inflated rents. This led Parisians once again into an uproar. The national government simply abandoned the capital for nearby Versailles, with Parisians left to their own devices, much as had been the case during the Prussian siege. Resentful Parisians, mostly from the lower and middle classes, formed an independent municipal government, which they dubbed the *Commune* (March 28, 1871). It was named after the radical experiment in city government of 1792. The Commune of 1871 actually did very little that was radical except resist the authority of the national government in Versailles. This was enough. Under the leadership of the conservative prime minister, Adolphe Thiers, the *Versaillais* ruthlessly and barbarously repressed the *Communards*. Paris was defeated, but the Commune entered permanently into the mythology of the French Left.

The monarchist assembly, though divided among Legitimists, Orleanists, and Bonapartists, managed to elect a conservative general, MacMahon, to the presidency in 1871. By 1875, the mood of the country had changed considerably, and a majority of republicans were elected to the new *Chamber of Deputies*, the principal house of the French Parliament. MacMahon immediately dismissed the assembly and attempted to rig new elections to return a royalist majority. However, the republican tide was too strong for even a corrupt electoral system.

The republican majority was renewed and the presidency fell into disrepute. From then on, until 1958, the legislature would dominate French democratic regimes.

The period from 1871 to 1914 is generally considered the high point of French parliamentary government. Though dominated by conservatives, the Third Republic even recognized organized labor by 1884, although workers were far from integrated into the political system.[12] While politics remained highly polarized between right and left, most of the country's problems were handled reasonably effectively by democratic solutions worked out in the context of a representative assembly. Not without interludes of crisis, such as the Dreyfus affair (see boxed insert, Chapter 13, page 234), by and large the Third Republic was successful until World War I. After that watershed, France's problems became more difficult and the ability of the country's political institutions to solve them became more questionable.

The beginning of the end came in 1929, and once again the source of France's problems was external to the country's borders. The source was, of course, the world economic collapse announced by the New York stock market crash. Because protectionist measures had kept France isolated from the world market during most of the life of the Third Republic, the Great Depression did not begin to affect most of the French until 1931. Then it struck with a vengeance. Unemployment climbed to more than 3 million and was probably much worse than it appeared on paper, as underemployment was greatly disguised by the large numbers of people still living (wretchedly) in the countryside. Government policies only made things worse, as orthodox economic solutions prescribed reduced government expenditure and reductions in real wages.[13]

Government ineptitude as well as popular perception of official corruption led to increasing discontent, which once again spilled into the streets. The ranks of both left- and right-wing organizations were swelled by the misery of the Depression and its intractability in the hands of centrist politicians. Tension reached a high point when fascist leagues, such as the *Croix de Feu*, marched on the Chamber of Deputies on February 6, 1934. The attempted coup d'état was foiled by loyal companies of police, but the situation appeared to be touch-and-go during the six hours of street fighting.[14]

THE POPULAR FRONT

The near catastrophe of February 6, 1934, traumatized the various factions of the French Left enough to patch up their differences to form an alliance for the coming elections. On the other hand, the failure of the coup disoriented the forces on the Right. The result was a victory for the left-wing parties in the elections of 1936. A cabinet of Radicals (who were actually centrists, despite their name) and Socialists, supported by the Communists, was formed under the leadership of Léon Blum, a moderate socialist. The coalition took the name *Popular Front.*

In the desperate conditions of the Depression, factory workers interpreted the Left's electoral victory as the first step in a social revolution. Some began occupying factories, while others took the occasion to strike. The highly charged atmosphere frightened the industrialists, who also thought a social revolution was at hand. Representatives of both sides of the class divide met at the Hôtel Matignon, the prime minister's official residence, and hammered out an agreement that gave significant concessions to the French working class. Not only were wages raised, unions recognized, and the forty-hour week conceded, but for the first time, workers received paid vacation. That summer many workers saw the ocean (only three hours from Paris by train) for the first time in their lives.

The Matignon Agreements were a milestone for blue-collar workers, but the millstone of the

Depression was too heavy to be buoyed by such measures. Revolution was averted, but the Popular Front was unsuccessful in bringing France out of the Depression. Attacked on both left and right, the Blum government resigned thirteen months after its electoral victory.

WORLD WAR II AND VICHY

If the deep causes of the collapse of the Third Republic were rooted in the world depression, the *causa proxima* of its demise was World War II. France declared war on Germany after the latter attacked Poland, a French ally, in September of 1939. Organized by the general staff to fight a trench war, France was poorly equipped to repel the highly mobile and mechanized German war machine. It was only a matter of time before the French were defeated on humiliating terms. The end came on June 22, 1940, with the signing of an armistice.

The defeat gave the French right, many of them fascist sympathizers, the opportunity they had been denied on February 6, 1934. After the armistice, the north of France was occupied by German troops. At the same time, a fascist state was set up in the South; fearful of an urban proletariat, its leaders chose the sleepy resort of Vichy as the new capital and inaugurated a dictatorship under the personalistic rule of Marshal Henri Pétain. Pétain had been a hero of the battle of Verdun during World War I and had been a figure with considerable right-wing support during the 1930s. The conservative last Parliament of the Third Republic had turned to him to negotiate the armistice and he, in turn, had no clear ideas about the kind of conservative regime he would head. The building of a fascist state owed more to his underlings than to Pétain himself. Much of its construction would rely on the efforts of Pierre Laval, a right-wing politician during the 1930s, and on Admiral Darlan, commander of the navy during the war.

While the high echelons of government were subject to considerable intrigues by various politicians of the Right, the fascist government was, in fact, managed by the French bureaucracy. The French bureaucracy had been a traditional source of employment for the bourgeoisie, and most of the higher officials were not only from upper-middle class or even aristocratic origins, but frequently sympathetic to the far right. They were all too willing to suppress labor, enforce racist legislation, and implement a quasi-Nazi regime. Indeed, partially due to these activities, the upper administration would be a target for reform immediately and continually after the liberation of France.

THE RESISTANCE AND THE LIBERATION

The advent of the Vichy government was a new phenomenon for France. Fascism, as an ideology that attempts to popularize an oppressive form of capitalism by playing on nationalist feelings, found fertile ground in much of the country.[15] Indeed, opposing fascism, which, as in Germany, had come to power legally, took a good deal of courage. Vichy turned traditional patriotism on its head.

The Rationale of the Resistance

In the Second World War republican France passed from the humiliation of total collapse to the moral ambiguity of divided allegiance. Sabotage and rebellion were the needs of patriots, loyalty and obedience the virtues of defeatists and collaborators, murder and torture part of the normal machinery of government and assassination the method of "opposition."

Source: Alfred Cobban, *A History of Modern France*, vol. 3, pp. 199–200.

June 1945: the liberation of France. On French soil for the first time since the German occupation, General de Gaulle walks through the streets of Bayeux accompanied by enthusiastic crowds of his fellow countrymen.

Two main groups resisted Vichy: the Communist Party and the followers of General de Gaulle. De Gaulle had been undersecretary for war briefly before the armistice, and fled to England when defeat was apparent. From the very beginning he urged the French to resist Vichy and set up an exile government in London. He also organized a nationalist resistance to sabotage the German war effort from within France. The Communists formed the other major group after the invasion of the Soviet Union in 1941.

While the Gaullists and Communists cooperated in the face of the common enemy, in fact they competed, each wanting to impose a specific vision of postwar France. It has, in fact, been argued that defeating the Communists was de Gaulle's principal goal, which he subtly pursued by closely cooperating with them.[16]

While the Resistance was actually quite small and its military achievements debatable, its political importance was supreme. The organization was sufficiently large and active to make it impossible for the Allies to ignore. De Gaulle used the organization to replace local governments as different regions were liberated, and thus the Resistance formed the natural nucleus of the postwar government. In 1944, a provi-

Table 12.1 IMPORTANT DATES IN FRENCH HISTORY

58–5 B.C.	Julius Caesar conquers Gaul
486 A.D.	Clovis, King of the Franks, defeats Roman governor of Gaul
800	Charlemagne becomes Emperor
987	beginning of the Capetian dynasty in France
1302	Philip IV calls the first Estates-General
1337–1453	France defeats England in the Hundred Years' War
1789–99	the French Revolution
1792	establishment of the First Republic
1799	Napoleon's coup d'état
1804	establishment of the First Empire
1815	defeat of Napoleon at Waterloo and Restoration of the Bourbon dynasty
1830	establishment of the July (Bourgeois) Monarchy
1848	establishment of the Second Republic
1852	Napoleon III's coup d'état and establishment of the Second Empire
1870–71	Franco-Prussian War
1871	establishment of the Third Republic
1899	retrial of Dreyfus
1914–18	World War I
1936	Popular Front forms government
1940	defeat of France in World War II
1940–44	Vichy regime in south of France, Germany occupies north, then entire country
1944–46	de Gaulle head of Provisional Government
1946	Fourth Republic established
1946–54	French Indo-Chinese War
1954–62	Algerian War
1957	Treaty of Rome signed, establishing the Common Market
1958	establishment of the Fifth Republic
1981	Mitterrand elected, first Socialist government of the Fifth Republic
1986–88	"Cohabitation" of conservative prime minister and Socialist president
1988	re-election of Mitterrand, first president to be re-elected in the Fifth Republic
1993–95	Second period of "Cohabitation"

sional government began the task of restoring republican and democratic government to France. A new Constituent Assembly was elected, and the wheels of the Fourth Republic were set in motion.

THE FOURTH REPUBLIC

For all practical purposes, the Fourth Republic was simply a continuation of the Third. This was not the original intention of either its founders or the French people. A referendum held after the liberation rejected resuming the Third Republic and mandated a new constitutional convention. The first draft of the new constitution, which included a change to a unicameral legislature, was rejected by French voters, and the second draft restored most of the institutions of the Third Republic. The new regime was still a parliamentary republic, with executive power in the hands of a prime minister and cabinet responsible to the lower house. With France still divided into many political parties, none large enough to dominate, coalitions remained fragile and cabinet stability was difficult to achieve. De Gaulle, refusing to participate in an enterprise dominated by parties, withdrew from the government and, gradually, from politics as well.

The principal achievement of the Fourth Republic was economic reconstruction. The discrediting of the Right because of its collaboration with the Nazis left French government in the hands of socialists, socially oriented Catholics, and communists. While these three groups would eventually come to loggerheads, they agreed in the early years on a high level of government intervention to rebuild the economy (see Chapter 11). The results, supported by U.S. economic aid, were stunningly successful. By the end of the 1950s the economy had totally recovered.

It was, however, the crumbling French Empire that would instigate the demise of the Fourth Republic. The communists broke with their partners over voting war credits to quash the revolt in French Indochina (Laos, Cambodia, and Vietnam). It was the revolt in Algeria, though, that provided the *coup de grâce*.

French colonization of Algeria dated from 1830. The large territory had been divided into three *départements* with ostensibly the same political status as any departments in metropolitan France. In fact, the Arab natives, by far the numerical majority, were vastly underrepresented and given the inferior status of French "subjects" rather than citizens.[17] In 1954 a bloody revolt began, using terrorist methods, which invited ruthless repression from Paris. In 1958 the ignominious battle, with torture used by both sides, greatly divided the sympathies of metropolitan France. Political leadership in the French Parliament was weak, as governments were paralyzed over how to conduct the war. Fearing that a left-of-center government would grant Algeria its independence, French

army garrisons in Algiers revolted on May 13, 1958. The army revolt soon spread to Corsica, and French politicians began to fear the possibility of a right-wing coup d'état in Paris. There seemed only one way out: Charles de Gaulle.

The French habit of looking to a single man to save the country from trying times had a long set of precedents: the two Bonapartes, Pétain, and de Gaulle during World War II. A military man and a traditionalist, de Gaulle was expected to have the confidence of the army and the Right. His credentials from the Resistance made him acceptable, albeit reluctantly, to the Left.

De Gaulle's participation carried a price. Long convinced that a parliamentary system could never provide the stability that France needed, de Gaulle demanded that the institutions of republican government be changed if he were to again enter politics. The desperate politicians of the Fourth Republic reluctantly agreed. Working in close cooperation with Michel Debré, a close colleague from the Resistance, de Gaulle created a set of institutions that allowed for a strong presidency and a submissive Parliament. A new republic was being born, the Fifth Republic. Political life under these new institutions will form the subject of the coming chapters.

NOTES

1. See, for example, John Zysman, *Governments, Markets and Growth* (Ithaca, N.Y.: Cornell University Press, 1983).
2. This argument draws heavily on Perry Anderson's *Lineages of the Absolutist State* (London: Verso, 1974), chaps. 1, 2, and 4. In the strictest sense, feudalism had seriously decayed by the fourteenth century. I am grateful to Michael Loriaux for making many helpful suggestions to improve this chapter.
3. Barrington Moore, Jr., *Social Origins of Dictatorship and Democracy* (Boston: Beacon Press, 1966), chap. 2.
4. Moore, chap. 1.

5. However, Alexis de Tocqueville pointed out that by the late eighteenth century, there was considerable concern about the regulation of guilds and industry, especially in Paris. See his *The Old Regime and the French Revolution*, trans. Stuart Gilbert (New York: Doubleday, 1956; originally published in 1856).

6. This was with some ambivalence, however, and in deference to his original Jacobin sympathies, the original coinage bore the inscription: "French Republic; Napoleon, Emperor."

7. De Tocqueville.

8. Alfred Cobban, *A History of Modern France. Volume Two: From the First Empire to the Second Empire. 1799–1871* (Harmondsworth: Penguin, 1965), p. 98.

9. The most famous version of this argument was articulated by Karl Marx in his essay "The Eighteenth Brumaire of Louis Bonaparte," originally published in 1852. Marx wrote his analysis as a series of newspaper articles for a German-language weekly published in New York.

10. Most notably, the Péreire brothers.

11. For a highly readable account of French economic history during these years, see Tom Kemp, *Industrialization in Nineteenth Century Europe* (London: Longman, 1969), chap. 3.

12. On this point see Gregory M. Luebbert, "Social Foundations of Political Order in Interwar Europe," *World Politics,* 39 (1987):452–456. Luebbert relies for much of his information on Val Lorwin, *The French Labor Movement* (Cambridge: Harvard University Press, 1954).

13. For an examination of the influence of economic orthodoxy and its comparative impact on different countries during the Great Depression, as well as during other crises, see Peter A. Gourevitch, *Politics in Hard Times* (Ithaca, N.Y.: Cornell University Press, 1986).

14. On this, see Cobban, volume 3, pp. 137 ff.

15. See especially Robert O. Paxton, *Vichy France* (New York: Alfred A. Knopf, 1973). This point is also brought out dramatically in Marcel Ophuls's classic 1970 documentary *The Sorrow and the Pity*. For an analysis of fascism as a general category of political development, see Moore, chap. 8.

16. Cobban, volume 3, p. 201. This was a strategy that would be proven useful, three decades later, by François Mitterrand (see pp. 477–479).

17. Alfred Grosser, *La IVᵉ République et la Politique Extérieure* (Paris: Armand Colin, 1961).

REFERENCES AND SUGGESTED READINGS

Anderson, Perry. 1974. *Lineages of the Absolutist State.* London: Verso.

Bloc, Marc. 1968. *Strange Defeat,* trans. Gerard Hopkins. New York: W. W. Norton.

Cobban, Alfred. 1965. *A History of Modern France.* Harmondsworth: Penguin.

Keohane, Nanerl O. 1980. *Philosophy and the State in Modern France.* Princeton: Princeton University Press.

Lacouture, Jean. 1968. *De Gaulle,* trans. Francis K. Price. New York: Avon.

Moore, Barrington, Jr. 1966. *Social Origins of Dictatorship and Democracy.* Boston: Beacon Press.

Paxton, Robert O. 1973. *Vichy France.* New York: Alfred A. Knopf.

> *I denounce a sickness that gnaws us in every limb. . . . Profligate anarchy or reaction, it's all the same, since the sickness comes from the country itself, which has been incapable of organizing itself under any of the different forms of government it has successively tried in the past century.*
>
> GEORGES CLEMENCEAU
>
> *A man thinks differently in a palace than in a hut.*
>
> LUDWIG FEUERBACH

13

Political Culture:
A Fragmented One

The frequent failures of political institutions in France, especially when compared with the relative stability of structures in Britain and elsewhere in the English-speaking world, have intrigued political scientists. This chronic instability, as well as the interwar fascist experiences in Latin and Germanic Europe, led many political scientists to wonder if Anglo-Saxon culture were especially favorable to the growth and stability of democracy.

By most accounts, French society was deeply divided. Levels of trust between left and right and between religious and antireligious groups were extremely low. People were ambivalent about the role of democratic (or any) government and had mixed feelings about public officials and elected representatives. Such attitudes might explain why democratic governance had such a fragile hold on French society.

POLITICAL CULTURE AS A CONCEPT

The concept of "political culture" posits an important role for the attitudes and orientations that people hold toward authority. It

Is There a "Civic Culture"?

If the democratic model of the participatory state is to develop. . . it will require more than formal institutions of democracy—universal suffrage, the political party, the elective legislature. These in fact are also part of the totalitarian participation pattern, in a formal, if not functional, sense. A democratic form of participatory political system requires as well a political culture consistent with it.

Source: Gabriel Almond and Sidney Verba, *The Civic Culture*, (Boston: Little, Brown, 1963), p. 3.

describes a configuration of beliefs, values, and symbols common to a nation, or to large groups within a nation, that are directed toward political institutions. Symbols may be concrete, like the flag or the Arc de Triomphe. They may be historical figures such as Napoleon or George Washington. They may be ideas that take on a symbolic importance, such as equality or liberty.[1]

Borrowing from the literature on psychology and anthropology, political culture theory focuses on both the *cognitive* and *affective* orientations toward authority. The examination of cognitive orientations occurs when we ask such questions as: How aware are people of the political system? What is the expected role of government in their eyes? How far does government extend? Do they expect too much from government? What do children know about the political system?

Affective orientations concern the way people feel about their government. Do they like what they see? If people expect too much from government they may be disappointed by it, and that disappointment may easily turn to disaffection. These are important considerations if one is concerned with the problem of political stability.

Countries may often be constituted by people with diverse political orientations and values. The lack of a consensus as to the nature and powers of the political regime may also be a cause of instability. Thus the process by which political consensus develops about the basic rules of the game and basic agreement on who is to be considered a member of the political community is crucial to understanding the stability of a regime.

THE PROCESS OF NATION BUILDING AND OUR FIFTH PROPOSITION

We argued in Chapter 2 that events in Eastern Europe illustrated the trend toward highly particularistic concerns of people who perceived themselves divided along group, ethnic, and national lines. This is not a new problem. The process by which diverse ethnic groups develop sentiments of solidarity with each other is called "nation building." While we are accustomed to thinking of France as a single nation, a "nation-state," as it were, in fact links of solidarity among the French are of rather recent vintage. By and large, France could be considered a single nation only as of the late nineteenth century.

By almost any measure, France in the early nineteenth century was divided against itself. Regional, cultural, and linguistic cleavages, harking back to before the Middle Ages in some cases, divided France into many separate communities. Perhaps most important was the language cleavage.

Nations are people "shaped to a common mold by many generations of shared historical experience."[2] They have frequently been defined by the language they speak as well as the symbols they share. The German nationalist philosopher J. G. Fichte remarked that language ". . . developed continuously out of the actual common life of . . . people."[3] By this

"In 1863, according to official figures, 8,381 of France's 37,510 communes [local districts] spoke no French: about a quarter of the country's population. The Ministry of Public Instruction found that 448,328 of the 4,018,427 schoolchildren (ages seven to thirteen) spoke no French at all, and that another 1,490,269 spoke or understood it but could not write it, suggesting an indifferent grasp of the tongue. In 24 of the country's 89 departments, more than half the communes did not speak French, and in six others a significant proportion of the communes were in the same position. . . . In short, French was a foreign language for a substantial number of Frenchmen, including almost half the children who would reach adulthood in the last quarter of the century."

Source: Eugen Weber, *Peasants into Frenchmen* (Stanford, Calif.: Stanford University Press, 1976), p. 67.

measure, France was hardly a nation in the early or even mid-nineteenth century.

Until the nineteenth century, France was really a collection of nations rather than a single entity. More often than not, people spoke a regional dialect derisively called a *patois* by Parisians. In some cases people spoke entirely different languages. In the south and southeast, people spoke *Occitan* or *Provençal*, Latin-based languages that were as similar to French as to Spanish or Italian. In the northeast, they spoke *Alsacien*, a dialect of German. In the northwest *Breton*, a Celtic language, was spoken. Near the Spanish border, *Basque* predominated. Originally, only the people of *Île de France* (the region around Paris) and the region north of the Loire river, as well as the aristocracy generally, spoke French.

The French had fierce loyalties to these ethnic regions. Such loyalties were largely tolerated or ignored by the kings of France, so long as such diversity posed no threat to royal administration or power.[4] While there was indeed a

France before the Revolution, there was no French nation.

The nationalism that characterized the French Revolution was, in many ways, an idea ahead of its time. The notion of a country populated by citizens united by sentiments of solidarity, and loyal to a government that was an expression of their will, preceded the political reality. In modern terms, it was Napoleon who set in motion the process that would lead to the final creation of a single French national entity.

Initially, the principal mechanism of national integration was the army, with the nationwide conscription innovated by Napoleon to preserve the fledgling French Republic. Not only did service in the army allow Frenchmen of different regions to meet and depend on each other, increasing their mutual levels of trust, but it forced them to speak a common language. Once the military men were demobilized, they returned to their homes, taking their acquired language with them.

The returning soldiers not only brought French back to the hinterlands, but brought Napoleonic values with them as well. Such Napoleonic ideals as liberty and equality before the law often accompanied the provincials' initiation into the French language. Of course, the principal inculcation of republican values had to await the spread of mass education under the Third Republic.

CENTRALIZATION

Liberty and equality were not the only values given a special impetus by Napoleon. Administrative centralization was equally a part of the Napoleonic heritage. While Tocqueville was quite accurate in remarking that the centralization of political life predated the Revolution (see Chapter 12), it was the administrative apparatus of Napoleon that channeled the development of mass politics. Napoleon organized the administration of France in such a way as to put certain revolutionary ideas into practice. These ideas reflected the thoughts of the Jacobins (see Chapter 12). The Jacobins argued that an egalitarian society required centralization. If different regions of France were free to pass their own laws, citizens of one part of the country would be subject to different requirements from those of another section.[5] Equality required standardization, and standardization required centralization. Thus, Napoleon, for his own reasons and because he was the quintessential Jacobin, located all power of decision in Paris. Administration became so thoroughly centralized that it was only a slight exaggeration to say that, for instance, the minister of education could look at his watch at any given moment and know what page of the standard history text every French student in the country was studying.

Napoleonic administration forced a kind of unity on France, but it was a unity that demanded a price. The price was grassroots democracy. Tocqueville is perhaps the most well-known proponent of decentralization as a guardian of personal liberties. For him, the creation of competing centers of power was the best guarantee against the abuse of authority. Thus the creation of a federal structure in the United States with powerful state and local governments, as well as a separation of powers at the national level, assured that no one arm of government would get out of hand. The lack of power at the local level in France not only deprived citizens of such safeguards, but also limited the democratic experience of the French population. This has had consequences for both the political elite and the citizenry in general. As Suzanne Berger noted,

> Democratic politics requires that the political system provide experiences of conflict and compromise. . . in sum, a political education, both for political activists and for the interested but less active citizenry. . . . By controlling or eliminating the possibilities for local initiative, the state does

> limit the risk of having incompetent or corrupt local officials, but at the same time it stunts the growth of responsible local leadership.[6]

Thus the effect of centralization, itself intended as a correction to the problems of diversity, was to increase the instability of French politics. Lacking experience in compromise, losers in political battles expected, and often received, the worst. Thus the consequences of defeat in national contests were frequently considered too dire to accept. Potential losers were more than receptive to achieving by coup d'état what they were unable to achieve electorally. Such thoughts were all the more likely in view of the various deep cleavages that divided the French.

HISTORICAL DIVISIONS OF THE FRENCH POLITY

One of the longest-lasting issues over which the French were divided concerned the role of religion in French politics. While over 80% of the population was born into nominally Catholic families, the number of those who viewed religion as an appropriate influence on secular politics was considerably smaller. The hostility or preference for religious intrusion had much to do with French history.

By and large, the church in France has traditionally been associated with conservatism. This harks back to the original association of the Catholic Church with the *ancien régime*. The links of the church with conservative rule were, of course, common in many countries (see Chapter 35 on the role of the church in Italy and Spain, for example), if only because the doctrine of an afterlife tended to encourage temporal passivity vis-à-vis the institutions of the time. The doctrine of divine right of kings, which maintained that royalty was the anointed of God, also continued the association of the church with reactionary regimes. Most importantly in France, the high ecclesiastical positions tended to be filled by the aristocracy, and a considerable amount of land was held by the church. All of these links did not endear the church to the opponents of absolutism.[7] What is interesting about France is the persistence of these associations long after absolutism was overthrown. From the time of the Revolution onward, the church tended to be associated with royalists and the later manifestations of the French Right.

What made the church the most enduring opponent of the Republic was the nature of the rest of the anti-Republican opposition. Fragmented as the opposition was among the supporters of different dynasties (Legitimists [pro-Bourbon], Orleanists, Bonapartists, etc.), affection for the church seemed the only commonality. Moreover, the response of the Vatican to the gradual secularization of French society was extremely rigid. Republican deputies to the French Parliament were consistently excommunicated until 1892.[8]

Sociological and geographical factors reinforced the antipathy of pro- and antichurch forces. The principal support for the church was located in the countryside. By the mid-nineteenth century the peasantry had lost its revolutionary fervor. Largely uneducated and fearful of that which they did not understand, French peasants were often dependent upon priests for temporal as well as spiritual guidance. It was not unusual for them to take their cues from the village *curé* (priest) when it came to politics.[9] Conversely, anticlerical sympathies were to be found primarily in the cities, especially Paris. Thus given the degree of centralization, hostilities that formed around the role of the church in politics tended to coincide geographically with the resentment of the special influence of Paris. Paris viewed from the countryside was secular, industrial, and, until defeat of the Commune, left wing. The peasants, viewed from Paris by the partisans of the Republic, were rubes unwittingly manipulated by

the priests and by Rome. Not surprisingly, geographic and secular cleavages became most politicized over the issue of public education.

Education, of course, is the process by which not only information but also values are transmitted from one generation to the next. The issue of who would control the schools was perhaps the most vehemently politicized of the nineteenth century. The Restoration and Second Empire, based on conservative support, left the church an influential role in the education of French youth. It was the Third Republic that really took the lead in secularizing public education. That secularization not only educated but often alienated the agricultural population in the provinces. But it was the full-scale effort to establish mass education by the Third Republic that not only finally unified France linguistically, but inculcated democratic values at the same time.[10]

REGIONAL AND ECONOMIC CLEAVAGES

The centralization and economic integration of the country also had a divisive effect on the French political culture. Economic unification of the country actually occurred under the absolutist kings, especially under the guidance of Louis XIV's minister Jean Baptiste Colbert. Colbert took the lead in encouraging the construction of infrastructure like canals and roads. By the mid-nineteenth century the railroads not only completed the unification of the French market, but also stimulated the demand for industrial goods, putting France on the road to a modern economy.

It might, however, be argued that France became a single economic unit too early for its own good. It is a natural tendency for business people to invest near preexisting infrastructures, as well as near markets and suppliers. Just as in the case of the unification of the Italian *Mezzogiorno* (southern Italy) with the more prosperous north, the integration of some of the poorer French departments with the rest of the country distorted economic growth.[11] The major French cities, and especially Paris, grew richer, while less-developed regions stagnated. Had the latter areas not been politically integrated into France, they might have been able to erect tariff barriers to protect infant industries. As it was, resources flowed to the center.

The political result of this economic distortion was resentment. Previous regional tensions were compounded by the effects of poverty. It was not an accident that persistent separatist sentiment ran highest in the economic backwaters of Brittany and Corsica.

Even where conditions were less extreme, resentment of Paris ran high. This was partially a heritage of the religious split between the anticlerical workers and intellectuals in Paris and the religious peasants in the countryside. However, even as religious differences faded, the monumental differences in cultural and economic opportunities between the capital and the provinces did not. The situation was accurately described as "Paris and the French Desert."[12] We shall return to this problem in Chapter 16.

CLASS CLEAVAGE IN FRANCE

Economic differences between haves and have-nots are certainly not greater in Europe than in the United States. However, cleavages between socioeconomic classes have traditionally been more politicized on the eastern shores of the Atlantic. Nowhere, with the possible exception of Great Britain, have economic distinctions served more to rally citizens to political purposes than in France. If France is a country of two political cultures, one of the Left and one of the Right, then that distinction owes much to the division of social classes.

The greater hostility that social classes hold for each other is at least partially due to the conditions under which France industrialized. These in turn were affected by the political role of the French peasantry. The French Revolution could not have taken place without the active support and participation of the peasantry. All successive regimes were obliged to take into consideration the needs and demands of this most numerous social class. The result was almost a century and a half of protectionist legislation aimed at sheltering the peasants from economic competition, allowing generations to remain on small, inefficient farms.

Unlike England, where common pastures were enclosed and forbidden to peasants, France gave few incentives to leave the land. Consequently, there were fewer people available for work in factories, and industrialization proceeded slowly. Manufacturing firms that did arise tended to be small, inefficient, and conservative. The high costs of production and the slow growth made the bourgeoisie's hostility to wage demands especially rigid. As a working class gradually emerged, with a concomitant rise in industry, it found itself surrounded by hostile forces. As factory owners, the bourgeoisie, of course, had interests that directly conflicted with those of their workers. Moreover, at the political level, the bourgeoisie found ready allies in the peasantry. Both groups were committed to the defense of property and were hostile to the socialist sympathies of the workers. Numerically, this conservative coalition could control the state, making radical, antigovernment ideologies all the more appealing among the workers.

Tragically, the economic lines that divided the French coincided with religious sympathies. Workers perceived the church as the icon of the peasantry and the ally of the bourgeoisie. Workers were by and large secular, while the faithful were essentially drawn from the ranks of the peasants and bourgeoisie. The impact of this lack of "cross-cutting cleavages" was to reduce levels of trust among the social classes. By contrast, the United States, with high levels of religiosity among all social strata,[13] benefited from "overlapping memberships." Workers and management might be divided on economic issues, but be on the same side of the fence on religious issues. They might disagree on the shop floor, but meet socially at church events. Thus disagreement on some issues was mitigated by agreement on others.

In France, social classes were polarized on religious as well as economic beliefs. Where in the United States mobilized groups would change depending on the specific issue, in France the opponents were always the same. The result was a very low level of trust between Right and Left and a genuine fear on each side that if the other were elected to office it would not willingly give up power. Such conditions made support of a coup d'état and other kinds of extraconstitutional action appealing to "out" groups. This was a formula for political instability, and many social scientists attribute the volatility of French politics to this factor.

POLITICAL CULTURE AND THE ROLE OF THE STATE

Not only do political scientists look to French political culture for an explanation of recurrent constitutional (and extraconstitutional) changes, but they also see the culture as explaining the persistently large role citizens have accorded the state. That is, the French state performs many tasks that in other countries are left to the private sector. Part of the reason for this is that French people are said to dislike dealing with each other face to face, and thus require intermediaries to a greater extent than other cultures. So, for example, where labor-management bargaining is a private matter in the United States or Britain, in France both sides look to the state to solve disputes.[14] It was in this long tradition that the Socialists legislated a fifth week of vacation for all French workers when they achieved power in 1981.

The Dreyfus Affair

Political culture is fraught with symbolism. Perhaps the most dramatic symbol of France divided into Left and Right is the "Dreyfus affair."

Alfred Dreyfus (1859–1935), a French army officer of Jewish extraction, was arrested on October 15, 1894, on charges of spying for Germany. He was convicted the following December and sentenced to life imprisonment on Devil's Island. In 1896 a member of the French general staff, Georges Picquart, found evidence that Dreyfus was innocent, but the army maintained a cover-up.

Many on the French Left urged a retrial, including the author Émile Zola, who spelled out the case in his famous article, "J'accuse!" ("I accuse!"). The eventual retrial in 1899 had all the characteristics of a kangaroo court and Dreyfus was again found guilty, but he was pardoned by President Émile Loubet a few days after the verdict. Finally, the case was reviewed in 1906 by France's highest court of appeal, and Dreyfus was found innocent.

The importance of the case had less to do with the turpitude of the army than with the political battle outside the courtroom. Divisions of Left and Right crystallized around the affair. Socialists and republicans favored Dreyfus, while the Right argued that to question the army was unpatriotic and villainous. As historian Barbara Tuchman put it, "Rent by a moral passion that reopened past wounds broke apart a society and consumed thought, energy and honor, France plunged into one of the great commotions of history."

Source: Barbara Tuchman (*The Proud Tower.* New York: Bantam Books, 1966, p. 196).

(Vacations are a matter of private contract in the United States and Britain.) Similar actions had been taken by the Popular Front government in the Matignon Accords of 1936, and by the Gaullist government in the Grennelle Agreement of 1968. A law limiting layoffs was passed by the conservative Giscard d'Estaing government in 1975 (and repealed by the Conservative government of 1986).

These, of course, are examples of state intervention in only one area of human activity. More important for the purposes of this book is a consideration of the cultural foundations underlying the activities of the state in all areas, but especially the economy. Much of the state's influence has to do with the high prestige accorded it by most of the French. Moreover, the state frequently became interventionist because of the lack of French people adventurous enough to start new firms.

French culture, then, produced few real entrepreneurs. It was therefore left to the state to proceed where businessmen feared to go. Thus the culture of French businesspeople reinforced the impact of interpersonal behavior in France: both encouraged a greater role for the state.

The concept of free enterprise, as developed in the England of the nineteenth century and transplanted to the United States, with its postulate of a competitive struggle for markets and drastic penalties for failure and with its emphasis on earning more and more for producing more and more for less and less, has never really been accepted in France. Instead, France [until the latter part of the Fourth Republic] . . . continued to cherish the guild organization of the pre-Revolutionary period. This ideology may be summed up briefly as follows: every man has his place in society, should produce enough goods and services of quality to maintain his place, and has a right to the living earned in this manner. In other words, the justification of survival lies not in the ability to make a profit, but in the correct performance of a social function.

Source: David Landes, "French Business and the Business: A Social and Cultural Analysis," *Modern France: Problems of the Third and Fourth Republics,* ed. Earl Meade (New York: Russell and Russell, 1964), p. 348.

Traditional French political theory also legitimized the role of the state. Jean-Jacques Rousseau, in his famous *Social Contract*, saw the importance of an all-powerful "elector" who alone could stand above the fray of personal interests to represent the general interest. This theme was also picked up in the Napoleonic state, the supremacy of which was justified because it was representative and, therefore, deemed democratic.[15] Moreover, a powerful state was acceptable to both left- and right-wing political traditions. Jacobinism saw the state as the great equalizer, while the Right saw the state as the national interest incarnate. No less a conservative than Michel Debré, a noted Gaullist and principal author of the Constitution of 1958, could write: "The State represents the national collectivity. The services under its charge are tasks it performs on behalf of the general interest."[16]

RECENT TRENDS AND OUR SECOND PROPOSITION

French culture seems to be at the root of the power of the state, yet, as we noted in Chapter 11, the extensive role of the French state in the nation's economy has recently come into question. Even before the conservatives came to power in 1986, the enthusiasm that greeted the Socialists' introduction of political decentralization in 1982 suggested that the cultural foundations of the Napoleonic state had considerably weakened (see Chapter 16).

The second proposition put forth in Chapter 2 argued that perceptions of the role of the state change according to the values that dominate a political system at a given point in history. This is certainly true of France. The popularity of neoclassical (that is, more *laissez-faire*) economic solutions advocated by Edouard Balladur, Giscard d'Estaing, Jacques Chirac, and other politicians of the Right among a growing segment of the French electorate also suggested that the assumptions of many French had changed. Certainly, the election of the conservative Parliament of 1986, after a campaign emphasizing denationalizations, indicated that the role of the state could now be safely questioned, although the conservative election victory of that year was more likely due to conjunctural elements than fundamental ideological changes among voters. This was also true of the parliamentary election of 1993, which probably had more to do with corruption scandals and high unemployment than it did with careful weighing of economic philosophies. Nevertheless, conservative writers such as Guy Sorman found a ready audience for his adulatory *La Révolution Reagan,* and Alain Cohen-Tanugi could advocate the increased use of private lawyers in a self-regulating *societé contractuelle* to replace many state functions without incurring the laughter that might have been reserved for such ideas a few years earlier.[17] Looking beyond the theorists, the increase in French venture capitalists, responding to changes in the tax laws made by the Socialists, strongly suggested that entrepreneurial lethargy could no longer be cited as an easy justification for state intervention.

While it has now become commonplace to discount the importance of the religious cleavage in French society, at least since the middle of the twentieth century, accounts of its demise may have been exaggerated. Certainly, like all modern societies, France has become more secular. Moreover, since the papacy of John XXIII (and even before), the church has become a less predictable political force, with many priests being as frequently associated with the Left as with the Right. Recent polls have shown that religious Catholics can no longer be expected to vote as a bloc for the parties of the Right. During the legislative election of 1978, 14% of practicing Catholics voted for parties of the Left. By the time of the 1988 presidential election, more than one in five ex-

pressed a preference for the Socialist candidate, François Mitterrand.[18]

However, the majority of practicing Catholics still vote to the right, and conservative religious sentiment can still be mobilized on some issues. This was especially true with the attempted educational reform of 1983. The Socialists, looking to rejuvenate the enthusiasm of the rank and file after losing considerable public support for their economic policies, introduced legislation aimed at bringing church-run schools under more direct control of the state. This provided an excellent opportunity for the conservatives to mobilize their supporters in massive street demonstrations to protest infringements on *l'école libre* (the euphemism for private, *viz.* Catholic, schools). Reaction against this proposed state intrusion on the religious prerogatives of the bourgeoisie was severe enough to force the withdrawal of the education reform bill.[19] However, when the conservatives came to power again in 1993, they rewarded their Catholic constituency by passing a new education bill that reinstated the nineteenth-century *Loi Filliou.* This law authorized local governments to subsidize parochial schools up to 10% of their costs. Predictably, this policy enflamed passions and enraged the (mostly left-wing) supporters of public schools.

Another religious issue has also become part of the political debate: the rise of Moslems as the country's second largest religious group. Primarily because of the high numbers of immigrants who came to France from the former colonies of North Africa, almost 2% of the population is Islamic. This number may seem small, but in a country unaccustomed to religious diversity, it is politically significant. Because the North Africans are physically, as well as culturally distinct, they are frequently targets of discrimination. Moreover, attempts to maintain religious habits have been politicized in the public school system. Islamic girls who have tried to attend classes while wearing *chadors* (body veils worn by traditional Moslem females) have been expelled for contaminating the secular character of public education. Politically, this issue has also served to alienate relations between French-Arab immigrants and their greatest potential allies, the Socialists, who on the one hand are the political party most likely to sympathize with the immigrants' plight, yet on the other hand see themselves as the historic defenders of secularism in France.

CONCLUSION

This chapter has examined the role of French political culture as an explanation for many of the phenomena noted in Chapters 11 and 12. Certainly, the fragility of French political institutions followed logically from an examination of the values and orientations of the citizenry. It was especially the lack of political consensus that made questionable the viability of any of the country's historical constitutional arrangements. Not only was France deeply divided along linguistic, religious, and economic lines, but these cleavages were politically reinforcing. Many of these divisions lasted well into the twentieth century.

Paradoxically, while some cultural characteristics weakened political institutions, others strengthened the role of the state. This was especially true of standards of interpersonal behavior as well as the habits of the French business class, who shied from risk and found shelter in the policies of the state.

More recently, government policies have suggested that some attitudes have changed, at least in terms of the economic demands voiced by some of France's traditionally conservative strata. On the other hand, the persistence of many old schisms, such as those of class and religion, suggest that announcing the death of France's fragmented political culture may yet be premature.

French Culture and Anti-Americanism

For many Americans encounters in France have been problematic. Even those who have not traveled there have nevertheless heard stories of French anti-Americanism. Historically, much of the reporting by French intellectuals reflected sentiments that, while focusing critically on the United States, were actually more revealing about French cultural attitudes, rather than about America:

> *Interwar observers like Georges Duhamel and André Siegfried announced the major themes that succeeding generations of America-watchers elaborated. They contrasted French civilization with American conformism. Americans, from this perspective, might be wealthy and powerful, but they were dominated by businessmen like Henry Ford who trained their fellow Americans to be mass producers and consumers—creating a society of comfortable conformists and cultural philistines.*
>
> *. . . [P]ostwar America appeared as both a model and a menace. The issue for the French was to find the way to possess American prosperity and economic power, yet avoid what appeared to be the accompanying social and cultural costs. The challenge was to become economically and socially "modern" without such American sins as social conformity, economic savagery, and cultural sterility. Cast in its grandest terms the issue was, how could France follow the American lead and yet preserve a French way of life?*

Source: Richard Kuisel, *Seducing the French: The Dilemma of Americanization.* Berkeley and Los Angeles: University of California Press, © 1993, pp. 2, 3. Reprinted by permission of University of California Press.

NOTES

1. Think, for example, of the word *freedom* as it is used in political discourse in the United States. The nation's highest civilian award is the Medal

of Freedom. Imagine the political impact of calling it the "Medal of Doing What You Want."

2. Rupert Emerson, *From Empire to Nation: The Rise and Self-Assertion of Asia and African Peoples.* Quoted in Samuel Beer, "Modern Political Development," in Samuel Beer et al., *Patterns of Government,* 3rd ed. (New York: Random House, 1973), p. 33.

3. Quoted in Elie Kedourie, *Nationalism* (London: Hutchinson, 1966), p. 66. Kedourie finds the equation of nation with language as an intellectual foundation of Nazism, for it is close to the images of "blood and soil" that fostered xenophobia and anti-Semitism among the German peasantry in the nineteenth and early twentieth century. Also evoking this theme is Alexander Getschenkron in *Bread and Democracy in Germany* (Berkeley and Los Angeles: University of California Press, 1943). However, for our purposes it is useful to point out the linkages between language and nation-building in the French context.

4. Eugen Weber, *Peasants into Frenchmen* (Stanford: Stanford University Press, 1977), p. 70. The parallels between the treatment of ethnic divisions in pre-Revolutionary France and the treatment of the various nationalities in the old Soviet Union seem clear.

5. Consider the situation in the United States as a way of examining the inequities of decentralization: welfare recipients receive much more in California, even taking into account a different cost of living, than they do in Mississippi.

6. Suzanne Berger, *The French Political System* (New York: Random House, 1974), p. 10.

7. To be fair, the absolutist kings had their differences with Rome. The former wished to control clerical appointments within France. Louis XV expelled the Jesuits from France, and many sectors of the clergy allied themselves with the Third Estate and against the king at the time of the Revolution.

8. See Berger, pp. 21 ff.

9. This was especially true in the underdeveloped west of France. Such proclerical attitudes were weakest among the peasantry of the Midi (south), many of whom had a strong anticlerical tradition.

10. Weber, pp. 330–338. Regrettably, this inculcation also laid the foundation for a rampant and rabid nationalism that would have horrid consequences in World War I and even later in the government of Vichy.

11. See Figure 11.2. Cf. Uwe Kitzinger's argument, cited in Jack Hayward, "The Prospects for British Regional Policy," *Journal of Common Market Studies,* 11 (1973):287.

12. Jean-François Gravier, *Paris et le Désert Français* (Paris: Flammarión, 1972).

13. Voting behavior studies show the United States to be much less secular than Europe or Japan. See, for example, Walter Dean Burnham, "The 1980 Earthquake. Appendix A. Social Stress and Political Response: Religion and the 1980 Election," in *The Hidden Election,* eds. Thomas Ferguson and Joel Rogers (New York: Pantheon Books, 1981), pp. 132–140.

14. See especially Michel Crozier, *The Bureaucratic Phenomenon* (Chicago: University of Chicago Press, 1964), pp. 213–237; and Stanley Hoffmann, "The Paradoxes of the French Political Community," in *In Search of France,* eds. Hoffman et al. (New York: Harper & Row, 1962).

15. Ezra N. Suleiman, *Power, Politics and Bureaucracy in France* (Princeton: Princeton University Press, 1974), p. 22.

16. Michel Debré, *Au Service de la Nation* (Paris: Edition Stock, 1963), p. 11, quoted in Suleiman, p. 21. See also Berger, p. 9.

17. Alain Cohen-Tanugi, *Le Droit sans L'État* (Paris: P.U.F., 1986).

18. Henri Tincq, "La Découverte d'Une Nouvelle Laicité," *Le Monde,* April 3–4, 1988, pp. 1, 6.

19. On the overall politics of this educational reform, see John Ambler, "Constraints on Policy Innovation: Thatcher's Britain and Mitterrand's France," *Comparative Politics,* 20 (1987): 85–107.

REFERENCES AND SUGGESTED READINGS

Almond, Gabriel, and Sidney Verba. 1961. *The Civic Culture.* Boston: Little, Brown.

Berger, Suzanne. 1974. *The French Political System.* New York: Random House.

Hoffmann, Stanley, et al. 1962. *In Search of France.* New York: Harper & Row.

Kuisel, Richard. 1993. *Seducing the French.* Berkeley and Los Angeles: University of California Press.

Peyrefitte, Alain. 1986. *The Trouble with France,* trans. William R. Byron. New York: New York University Press.

Tocqueville, Alexis de. 1955. *The Old Regime and the French Revolution,* trans. Stuart Gilbert. Garden City, N.Y.: Doubleday.

Weber, Eugen. 1976. *Peasants into Frenchmen.* Stanford, Calif.: Stanford University Press.

14

Decline, Alienation, and the Organization of Interest

While social harmony has always been in short supply in France, the economic stagnation of the 1970s and 1980s served to intensify conflict at many levels. Moreover, many of the traditional mechanisms for expressing organizational interest have lost their effectiveness. In this sense France is not very different from other advanced industrial countries. As in Britain and Germany, small business has declined. Napoleon's derisive description of Britain as a "nation of shopkeepers" not only misses its original target, but misses the mark in France and Germany as well. Labor unions have lost power almost everywhere. Most distressing of all, racism has waxed significantly in all three countries.

INTEREST GROUPS

Alexis de Tocqueville noted in his famous study, *Democracy in America,* that one of the principal differences between the United States and France was the relative abundance of interest groups in the former and their relative scarcity in the latter. Interest groups (or "secondary associations," in modern political science parlance), Tocqueville reasoned, were not only useful for articulating demands to government; they were also an important deterrent to possible abuse by the state. These watchful and politically sophisticated amalgams had their members' interests at heart and reduced the potential for demagogues to dupe the unwary. Such groups became a kind of buffer between citizen and state in America, while France remained relatively unprotected.[2]

France's aversion to intermediaries between citizen and state has had some logical historical grounding. During the era of Absolutism, the only semi-independent organizations in public life were the *parlements* (actually local courts run by aristocrats) that were notoriously corrupt and associated with entrenched privilege. When Louis XV finally abolished them, there were no regrets among the citizenry. In this context the comments of so enlightened a figure as Voltaire could be understood: "I consider it better to serve under a well-born lion . . . than under two hundred rats of my own kind."[3] Rousseau concurred: "It is essential, if the general will is to be able to express itself, that there should be no partial society within the State and that each citizen should think only his own thoughts."[4] This sentiment endured well after the Revolution. Thus part of the reason for France's occasional lapses into the caesarism of the Bonapartes, Pétain, and others has been attributed to this atomization of French society.[5]

To the extent that France has had interest groups, often they have been limited to those created, or at least officially recognized by, the French government. This kind of group organization reached its apogee during the Vichy period (1940–1944) and is often described as "corporatism,"[6] as illustrated by Figure 14.1. Under the fascist regime estab-

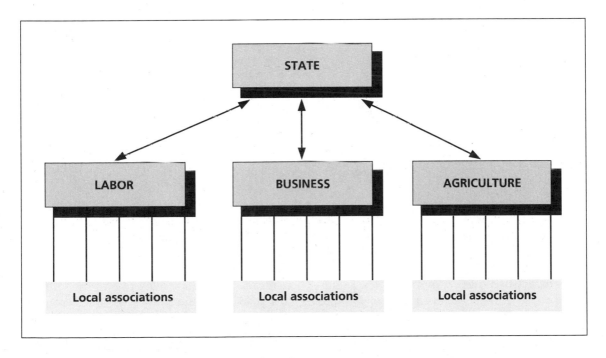

Figure 14.1 Corporatism. Under corporatist arrangements, such as the Vichy regime, all interest groups are organized into exhaustive "peak associations," which, in turn control membership through local associations. Under fascist regimes the state controls the leadership of the peak associations and corporatism becomes a mechanism of social control. Under democratic regimes like those in Austria or Sweden, the leadership is elected by their respective members and corporatism becomes a mechanism for democratic bargaining with the state. Corporatism facilitates the implementation of bargains made between interest groups and the state.

lished by the Vichy government, French society was officially organized by economic sector into "corporations" that, while nominally self-regulating, were controlled by progovernment officials at the top of each organization.

Even after Vichy, French governments sought to identify specific groups and offer them special access to policymaking in exchange for some measure of social control. This was especially true in agriculture, where Gaullist governments developed a special relationship with the *Fédération nationale des syndicats d'exploitants agricoles*.[7] Indeed, the French governments of the Fifth Republic have always played favorites, although this is nothing new. During the Third and Fourth republics preference was usually given to the needs of agriculture and small business, both notoriously inefficient, while labor and consumers were slighted. The Fifth Republic favored large enterprise. Labor was favored under the Socialists.

The weakening of parliamentary powers under the Fifth Republic did change the venue of interest group–government relations, however. To some extent this change actually occurred before the change in constitutions, but the biases of *hauts fonctionnaires* (higher civil servants) made themselves fully felt after 1958. Before that date, lobbies were oriented to the specialized parliamentary committees in relations that were not unlike the "iron triangles" of American policymaking.[8] Victories of the alcohol or private school lobbies were often spectacular when the influence of parochial deputies could be counted on.[9] After 1958, the bureaucracy became preponderant. The preferences of the Gaullist bureaucracy were simple: lobbies representing large enterprises were "*sérieux*" (serious); the others were not.[10]

Predictably, this situation changed somewhat under the Socialists, when organized labor joined the ranks of the *sérieux*. Business groups considered themselves adversaries of the government at this point, but in fact were treated in the same privileged fashion as under the conservatives. Indeed, this was of necessity, for

even though the Mitterrand government had significantly expanded the public sector, over 80% of the economy (and therefore the vast majority of jobs) remained in private hands.[11] After the conservative victories of 1986 and 1993, the situation returned to the pro-business norms of the Fifth Republic.

INDUSTRIAL DECLINE: THE *PATRONAT* AND THE CRISIS OF ORGANIZED LABOR

Unlike Germany or, to some extent, Britain, employers' associations were rather slow to form in France. This was primarily because the weakness of organized labor and the conservative policies of French government made such associations unnecessary.[12] Aside from government-sanctioned cartels to restrict competition in various sectors, industry associations as lobbies were rare, and were traditionally weak compared to the state.

The principal national employers' association in France is the *Conseil national du patronat français,* known usually as the *Patronat*. The organization was originally formed in response to the generalized labor unrest in 1936 as the Confédération générale de la Production Française.[13] However, as a centralized organization representing the united interests of French capital, the *Patronat* has never played the kind of role that similar federations have in central and northern Europe. Bargaining and lobbying have traditionally been at the level of the trade association. The role of the Patronat has been more one of loose coordination and general public relations. One author has refused to mince words and simply labeled the organization as "impotent."[14] Henry Ehrmann put it another way: "One cannot help asking if the CNPF [Patronat] did not exist, would anybody invent it?"[15]

Part of the reason for the weakness of the *Patronat* is that capital itself is divided. Business groups are divided into buyers and sellers, competitive and noncompetitive enterprises. They rarely have the same policy interests, except on such general issues as lower taxes, reduced labor costs, and the like. Even here, consumer industries wish their consumer-customers to be well paid, which means some other industries must accept higher wages, while export-oriented industries, which sell to the consumers of other countries, merely want low wages to reduce their costs.

Small businesses have traditionally been fearful of large enterprises, the latter having higher volume and lower costs, and they have formed their own organization of small and medium-sized firms, the *Confédération générale des petites et moyennes entreprises.* They have occasionally been successful in influencing legislation aimed at preserving small retailers.

The lower ranks of management have often seen their interests better defended by white-collar trade unions than by professional associations, and have been drawn to the *Confédération générale des cadres* (general confederation of executives).

If, however, the historic position of employers' organizations has been weak in France, organized labor has hardly been strong. France has five major trade union confederations that are ideologically divided. The largest is the *Confédération générale de travail* (general confederation of labor), which is closely associated with the Communist Party. The second largest confederation is the *Confédération française et démocratique de travail* (French and democratic confederation of labor), which was originally associated with the Catholic union movement and now is closer to the Socialist Party. The *Confédération française des travailleurs chrétiens* (French confederation of Christian workers) represents the remainder of church-associated unions. *Force ouvrière* (workers' force) is a traditionally conservative union organization focusing on narrow work-related issues similar to the American AFL-CIO (indeed, the AFL-CIO helped to create the force ouvrière) and has been the fastest-growing of the French labor organizations. The *Confédération générale des cadres* (see above) represents white-collar workers.

While the principal divisions between the unions are ideological, the absence of laws permitting union shops (enterprises where a single union is allowed to monopolize recruitment after an employee vote) has reinforced these divisions. For whatever reason, however, the fact of division has consistently meant that labor in general has been in a weak position *vis-à-vis* management. These divisions, added to the sobering statistic that less than one-eighth of the work force belongs to any union at all, have compounded the present crisis of French unionism. Moreover, the decline in the effectiveness of Keynesian policies and the popularity of neoconservative calls to "roll back the state"—in this case, the unions' traditional ally when the Left comes to power—have made labor especially vulnerable (see Figure 14.2).

French unions have historically been weak, partially as a consequence of late industrialization. Retarded industrialization meant that French firms were usually smaller than those in more industrially organized countries and were frequently family-run. Smaller firms meant that unions had to organize more enterprises to reach the same percentage of the work force as in other countries, and family-run firms often meant greater management resistance to union demands. This was especially true if demands were viewed as encroaching on management prerogatives (almost always the case), but occasionally family-run companies did tend to improve working conditions in a kind of paternalistic way, providing recreation facilities and child care, for example. The Michelin tire company, to name one such family-run company, though hardly small anymore, fit this description.

The stagnation that affected Europe starting in the 1970s was especially problematic for organized labor. Traditional industries—such as steel, coal, and textiles—that had the highest

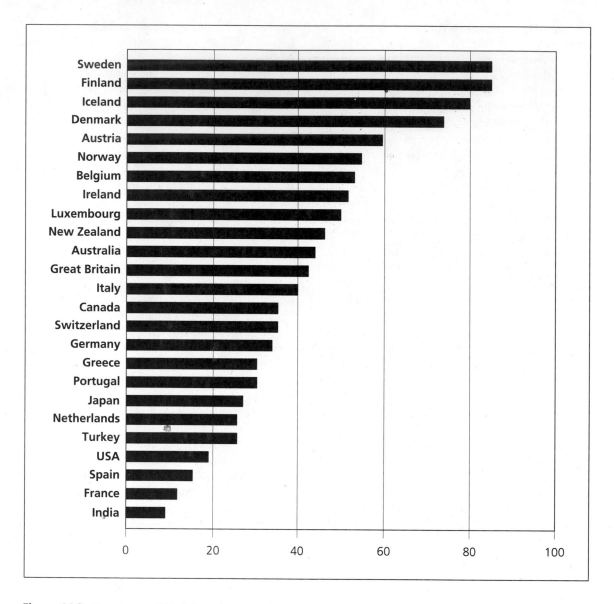

Figure 14.2 Percentage of Work Force in Unions (1991). Source: French Embassy, Washington, D.C.

levels of union membership were especially affected. Stagnating demand and increasing competition from the newly industrialized countries, as well as from Japan, created pressure for layoffs, wage reductions, and other givebacks. While jobs were being lost in old industries, some were being created in service industries, but these were notoriously poorly paid and sufficiently dispersed so as to inhibit unionization. This situation was of course not unique to France, but the strategies of French unions compounded their problems. Union leadership was slow to adapt to the new situation and often tried to apply leverage more appropriate to an expanding economy.[16]

The position of labor in general and unions in particular improved briefly under the Socialist administration of 1981–1986. However, even some of the Socialist reforms actually reduced the bargaining effectiveness of organized labor. The *loi Auroux* of 1982 was intended to give workers more control over their working conditions and in many ways was similar to the Wagner Act in the United States, requiring employers to participate in collective bargaining and guaranteeing workers' rights. But the new law also guaranteed employers' rights and often had consequences unintended by its Socialist authors. As Mark Kesselman put it, "By guaranteeing the right to strike under certain conditions strikes become illegal under all other conditions."[17] Bargaining shifted from sector-wide negotiations to enterprise-level negotiations, shifting worker identification to the prospects of the company rather than reinforcing class solidarities. Also as a consequence of the *loi Auroux*, the role of the state as an intermediary between labor and management was reduced. In short, industrial relations in France have become much more collaborative and much more like those in more conservative countries like the United States (and even Japan).[18]

YOUTH UNEMPLOYMENT

Another way in which class solidarities have broken down in an era of economic decline can be seen by examining the role of young people in the work force. Young people, and especially young women, have borne a disproportionate share of the burden of unemployment in France. Roughly twice as many young people are unemployed as the rest of the population. In 1993, 22.2% of young men under 25 were unemployed, while 31.3% of young women of the same age could not find jobs. These statistics do not include young people who chose to remain in school rather than confront the job market.[19] The figures improved slightly between 1986 and 1990, but began to rise again after 1992 (see Figure 14.3). These unhappy statistics suggest that the potential for a youth rebellion along the lines of the uprising of 1968 (see Chapter 11) are hardly out of the question.

THE DECLINE OF AGRICULTURE?

Agriculture has always been a very important part of the French political scene. Because France was a late industrializer, a very large proportion of French people remained on the land well after the farmers ceased to be influential in Britain, the first industrializer. During the Third and Fourth republics, politicians ignored the interests of farmers at their peril. Over 25% of the active population was rural until just after the Second World War, and this fact of life spelled agricultural protectionism as a major part of all French economic policy.

During the Fifth Republic, the Gaullists courted agriculture by giving special treatment to the *Fédération nationale des syndicats d'exportants agricoles*, which was perhaps the most conservative of the professional agricultural organizations. When the Socialists came to power in 1981 they tried to promote agricultural pluralism by according equal treatment to other agricultural organizations, but the head start of the federation was simply too great and for this interest group egalitarianism was a failure. Today the federation retains its privileged position.

The protection of agriculture has had a major effect on the costs of not only the French, but all of Europe. When the European Union was formed in 1957 (as the European Economic Community, see Chapter 3) the Gaullists were able to protect rural interests through the crea-

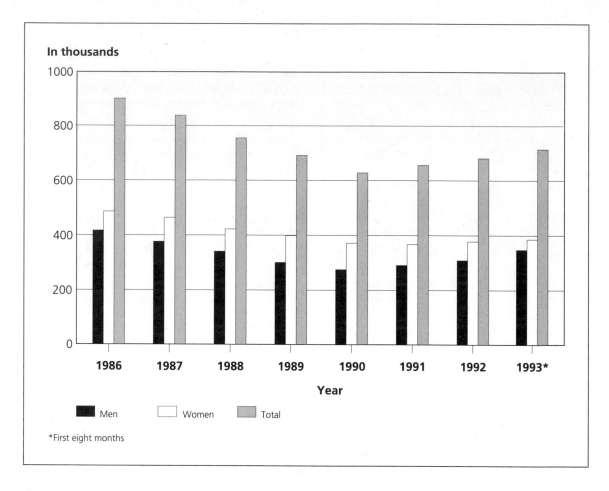

Figure 14.3 Youth Unemployment. Source: French Ministry of Labor, reprinted in *Le Monde*, December, 1993.

tion of the Common Agricultural Policy. This kept low-cost foodstuffs from entering the Common Market countries, and subsidized inefficient European farm exports, of which the French were the greatest beneficiaries. This added to the high-cost structure of French and European industry (workers demanded higher salaries to meet the higher cost of living) and reduced competitiveness.

Politically, protection of inefficient French agriculture has allowed more people to stay on farms. This has increased rural voting strength, which in turn bolstered the conservative par-

ties. Yet even the Socialists and Communists cannot ignore farmers. That is because most French people, even city dwellers whose families have not been rural for more than three generations, think of themselves as having rural roots and sympathize with farmers.

Not surprisingly, this situation has made it very hard for French public officials to agree to agricultural trade liberalization, which in turn has affected French relations with the rest of the European Union, and with the United States. It is very likely that the Uruguay Round of the General Agreement on Tariffs and Trade negotiations, would have concluded much earlier than December 1993 had not the French been so commited to their farmers.

It is an interesting fact of political life that farmers remain the most privileged interest group in France.

VOTING BEHAVIOR AND THE MARGINALIZATION OF FRENCH COMMUNISM

The economic stagnation of the 1980s and 1990s profoundly affected the behavior of voters as well as the interaction of interest groups. Voter turnout in France has always been higher than in the United States for several reasons. The high turnouts have in part been reflections of the lack of opportunity for other forms of legitimate political expression. Since power was concentrated in Paris, local elections were of little salience and, therefore, of little interest to voters. Low levels of collective bargaining and the crucial interventions of the state in industrial relations also underlined the importance of national elections. This was equally true for agriculture, given farmers' dependence on state subsidies and the traditional role of parliamentary deputies as ombudsmen for farmers' interests.

The transformation of the French economy after the Second World War from an agricultural to an industrial society affected the interests and voting patterns of French citizens. A second, more gradual transformation toward a service-oriented economy also made its mark on French politics.

The majority of French voters supported conservatives during much of the time after the war, although for the first few years the sorry record of the pro-Nazi collaborators and the association of the Resistance with the political Left tarnished the reputation of the Right. The charisma of de Gaulle and the special circumstances of the Algerian war did much to restore

Coal miners of the French leftist union CGT ask the French government to respect its promises. In March 1984 an estimated 10,000 miners protested the government's plans, marching to the coal board's headquarters in Paris.

the power of the Right, but deeper causes were also at work. The conservatives returned to popularity for two main reasons. First, late industrialization meant that much of the electorate earned its livelihood from agriculture or small business. These groups were threatened by the modernization of the economy and were attracted to candidates who announced fidelity to the status quo and who preached loyalty to traditional values with nationalist appeals. Moreover, these groups were terrified by the proclamations of working-class leaders and suspicious of the intellectuals associated with the Left. Canny politicians, especially de Gaulle, were able to parlay these sentiments into extended tenure of office. When the student and worker uprisings occurred in 1968 (see Chapter 11) de Gaulle was able to capitalize on the average French voter's fear of radicals, and especially the image of the Communist Party, to turn the subsequent elections into a landslide for the Right. Indeed, the Left could only come to power when the fears of a Communist-dominated government were allayed.

THE DECLINE OF THE COMMUNISTS

The decline of the Communist electorate had three broad causes: the transformation of the economy, errors in the political strategy of the Communists themselves, and an effective strategy by their rivals, the Socialists. The first explanation is sociological. The gradual decline of traditional industries and the increasing orientation of the French economy toward the service sector eroded the historic base of the Communist electorate. The high point of Communist sympathies was, of course, immediately after the war. Not only were the Communists among the bravest and most tenacious fighters in the Resistance, but the need to rebuild the economy from the postwar ruins lent credence to the productivist assumptions of the Communist economic strategy.[20] The base of Communist support has always been blue-collar workers. Thus the modernization of the French economy after the war guaranteed a significant source of support for the party, at least at the polls, if not on membership rosters. However, as blue-collar jobs were eliminated by both competition from abroad and the shift into services, the constituency of people who could most readily see the appeal of the Communist vision began to disappear.

As the base disappeared, the leadership of the party failed to see the need to find replacements. Partially this was because—unlike the Italian Communist Party—the leadership in France was more concerned with the demands of its present blue-collar membership than with the potential for victory at the polls by an appeal to other strata. Had they identified common interests with such groups as the newly emerging waves of white-collar workers, decline might have been forestalled, but the party would have been transformed.[21]

Another source of Communist support, totaling consistently about 25% (including members' votes) of the electorate until the 1970s, was the protest vote. This was the expression of voters alienated from the capitalist system as it operated in France or disaffected with the government of the day and its non-Communist opposition. Such voters did not vote for the Socialists because of the pivotal role they played in the Fourth Republic and the Algerian war, or because that party was not viewed as sufficiently radical.

It was the electoral strategy of François Mitterrand that eroded the protest vote destined for the Communists. Mitterrand almost single-handedly built a new Socialist Party from scratch (see Chapter 15). Not only did the new Socialist Party reject association with the old party of the Third and Fourth republics, but Mitterrand resolutely pushed the orientation of the party leftward so as to capture much of the Communists' former constituency. This was done by signing a common platform with the Communists in 1972, which called for most of the nationalizations that eventually took place ten years later. When the two parties broke the pact in 1978 because the Socialists refused to accede to additional Communist demands, the Socialists surpassed the Communist vote in the legislative elections of that year. This seemed to guarantee that not only would the Socialists not cave in to the Communists for the sake of an election, but that in any future leftist government, the Communists could never be more than junior partners.

DEALIGNMENT

Most of the recent research on voting behavior in France suggests that a process of dealignment is taking place.[22] While party identification has never had quite the same meaning in France as in the United States, fidelity to at least a general conception of left or right has been a consistent trait of the French voter.[23] However, in the words of one analyst, "The French voter is increasingly up for grabs, unsettled over his or her party loyalties, or indeed over whether to participate in the electoral game at all."[24]

Nevertheless, French voters are still more self-consciously ideological than voters in the United States. In one study, only 5% of respondents refused to place themselves on a seven-point left-right scale, where right correlated with Catholic religious affinity in the traditional manner (see Chapter 13).[25]

Sociologically, the makeup of the French electorate has moved in a direction that should have favored the French Left. The country has become more urban, secular, and economically modern. Indeed, François Mitterrand averred that in his election of 1981, "The French political majority has just identified itself with its sociological majority."[26]

Political changes happen more slowly, however. Often people whose low income might suggest left-wing voting voted conservative. Frequently, this was because they had other characteristics, such as inherited property, that suggested an interest identified with the Right. In 1978, 31% of people with an income of 1,500 francs per month (less than $300 at 1978 exchange rates) voted for the Communists, but only 3% of people in the same income group (but who had a significant inheritance) voted for them.[27] Indeed, the left-wing landslide of 1981 might well have been a fluke, owing more

to divisions in the Right than a shift of voter allegiances to the Left.[28]

RACISM AND THE NATIONAL FRONT

Perhaps one of the most distressing changes in French voting patterns is the recrudescence of overt racism. This is, unfortunately, a common occurrence now in Europe, and is related to the present economic crisis in the industrial world. "Paky-bashing" and football hooliganism have been on the rise in the poorer neighborhoods of Britain for some time, while "Ausländer 'raus!" (Foreigner, go home!) can be seen scrawled on many public places in Germany. Immigrant groups that were invited into these countries to supply cheap labor in more prosperous times are now seen as competing for scarcer jobs. Figure 14.4 illustrates recent immigration trends. While the overall number of immigrants has been decreasing in recent years, as the government has tried to reduce the inward flow in a period of recession, the percentage of new immigrants who have come from Africa, especially North Africa, has actually increased. Culturally distinct groups have become pariahs and the focus of resentment. In France, this has meant, above all, racist attacks on the country's large Islamic community.

Racism is not new in France. The anti-Arab racism is not very different, at least in its clientele, from the anti-Semitism of the early twentieth century and Vichy. People caught in the closing vise of a shrinking economy often look to the simplest explanation for their predicament, and racism is commonly found among groups that are already at the margins of their society: unskilled workers, small business people on the precipice of bankruptcy, and peasants who understand little of the world outside their immediate surroundings. Disaffection with the traditional right-wing elites has also drawn local politicians to the extreme right.[29]

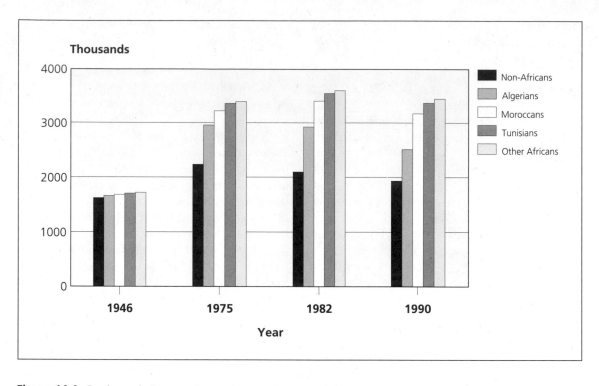

Figure 14.4 Foreigners in France. Source: Annuaire Statistique de la France, 1992–92, vol. 96 (Paris).

In the past, this segment of the electorate has frequently been vulnerable to the appeals of parties on the far right. Such groups supported the various fascist extraparliamentary organizations in the 1930s (see Chapter 12). In the 1950s these groups supported the Gaullists (then espousing an antiparliamentary philosophy) and Pierre Poujade, who led a small shopkeepers' movement in reaction to modernization and European integration. By 1984, supporters of racist and anti-immigrant policies coalesced behind Jean-Marie Le Pen and his National Front. This was essentially a single-issue party demanding "France for the French," but also sharing many economic assumptions of the traditional Right in calling for a *laissez-faire* economy. In the 1984 and 1986 elections, some former Communist voters turned to the National Front out of protest, but the bulk of supporters had voted for the Gaullists in previous elections. The National Front tends to do best in the south of France, where the French repatriated from Algeria after independence tend to have settled.

At the national level, the Front reached its highest level of support in the first round of the 1988 presidential election, with 14.4% of the popular vote going to Jean-Marie Le Pen. At the local level they did almost as well during the elections of March 1992, where they achieved over 13.9% of the vote. Some French analysts were unperturbed by this score, noting that traditionally 20–25% of the French vote as a protest against the political establishment and that the combined Communist and National Front vote was just over 21%. The fact that the ecologically oriented parties did as well as the Front in the 1992 local elections reinforces the notion that the vote for all of these marginal parties is a form of protest. However, others put more emphasis on the sociological context and saw alarming parallels with the rise of fascism during the Great Depression of the 1930s.[30]

On the opposite side of the immigration question, there are now more than 800,000 young voters, known as "les beurres," who are the sons and daughters of North African immigrants. Not surprisingly, they tend to vote for the Left. Up to this time, however, the "beurres" (butters) had not been intensively studied.

CONCLUSION

This chapter has examined the behavior of interest groups and voters in France. Interest groups, a traditional focus of political scientists, were found to be less numerous in France, with vestiges of corporatism found in those that do exist. The power of organized labor has been especially weak, and the French Communist Party, often touted as powerful, is a mere shadow of its former self. While French voters have become disaffected and are "dealigning" from traditional parties, partially in response to increased economic uncertainties, these same economic forces have encouraged a recrudescence of racism in the French electorate, especially among groups that have voted for the far right in the past.

NOTES

1. Quoted in Ezra N. Suleiman, *Politics, Power and Bureaucracy in France* (Princeton: Princeton University Press, 1974), p. 316.
2. Cf. William Kornhauser, *The Politics of Mass Society* (New York: Free Press, 1958).
3. Quoted in Pierre Avril, *Politics in France*, trans. John Ross (Baltimore: Penguin, 1969), p. 131.
4. Quoted in Suleiman, *Politics, Power and Bureaucracy in France*, p. 319.
5. Marx's description of the French peasantry as a "sack of potatoes" in *The Eighteenth Brumaire of Louis Bonaparte* implicitly offered a similar kind of reasoning.
6. Philippe Schmitter calls this "state corporatism" to distinguish it from the more benign kind of interest group organization found in countries like Austria or Switzerland, where officially recognized groups are nevertheless democratic and independent of government control. This latter kind of organization Schmitter calls "societal corporatism." State corporatism is normally associated with fascism. See Schmitter's "Still the Century of Corporatism?" in *Review of Politics*, January 1975. On democratic corporatism, see Peter J. Katzenstein, *Small States in World Markets* (Ithaca, N.Y.: Cornell University Press, 1984).
7. John T. S. Keeler, "Corporatism and Official Union Hegemony: The Case of French Agricultural Syndicalism," in Suzanne Berger, ed., *Organizing Interests in Western Europe* (Cambridge: Cambridge University Press, 1981). Cf. David Wilsford, *Doctors and the State: The Politics of Health Care in France and the United States* (Durham: Duke University Press, 1991).
8. The notion of the "iron triangle" represents the mutual interdependence of congressional committees, relevant bureaucrats, and lobbies in the formulation of public policy.
9. Bernard E. Brown, "Pressure Politics in the Fifth Republic," *Journal of Politics*, 24 (1963); Susan Berger, *The French Political System* (New York: Random House, 1974), chap. 4.
10. Suleiman, *Power, Politics and Bureaucracy in France*, chap. XII.
11. Cf. Charles E. Lindblom, *Politics and Markets* (New York: Basic Books, 1977), chap. 13.
12. The "Chapelier Law" inspired by early nineteenth-century liberal economics even made associations illegal.
13. The classic examination of the French employers' association is Henry W. Ehrmann, *Organized Business in France* (Princeton: Princeton University Press, 1957).
14. Henri Weber, *Le Parti des Patrons. Le CNPF (1946–1986)* (Paris: Seuil, 1986).
15. Ehrmann, review of Weber, *Le Parti*, in *French Politics and Society*, 5, 3 (June 1987):46.
16. George Ross, "French Labor and Economic Change," in Peter A. Gourevitch and Stephen S.

Cohen, eds., *France in the Troubled World Economy* (London: Butterworth, Scientific, 1982).

17. Mark Kesselman, "Conclusion" in Kesselman and Guy Groux, eds., *The French Workers' Movement* (London: George Allen and Unwin, 1984), p. 316.

18. Guy Groux, "Organized Labor and Industrial Relations," paper presented to the panel *Changing Patterns of French Political Economy: An End to French Exceptionalism?*, Sixth International Conference of Europeanists, October 30–November 1, 1987.

19. "Le chômage des jeunes augmente à nouveau," *Le Monde*, December 1, 1993.

20. By "productivist" we mean an economic philosophy that has as its principal goal the production of more and more goods for lower and lower costs. These goals were broadly shared and contributed to the consensus necessary to make French economic planning a success. Cf. Peter Hall, *Governing the Economy*, chap. 6; and Stephen S. Cohen, *Modern Capitalist Planning: The French Model* (Berkeley and Los Angeles: University of California Press, 1977). This contrasts with the antiproductivist goals of the late 1970s represented by the "Green" movements across Europe. These activists emphasized quality-of-life issues over simply increasing production. See Volkmar Lauber, "From Growth Consensus to Fragmentation in Western Europe: Political Polarization over Redistribution and Ecology," *Comparative Politics*, 15 (1983); and especially, Ronald Inglehart, *Culture Shift* (Princeton: Princeton University Press, 1990).

21. George Ross, "Destroyed by the Dialectic: Politics and the Decline of Marxism, and the New Middle Strata in France," *Theory and Society*, 16, 1 (January 1987).

22. W. Rand Smith, "Plus ça change. . . ? Elections and Electoral Behavior in France, 1978–86," *French Politics and Society*, 5, 3 (June 1987). Much of the following argument is derived from this article.

23. Philip E. Converse and Roy Pierce, *Political Representation in France* (Cambridge, Mass.: Harvard University Press, 1986), chap. 3.

24. Smith, "Plus ça change. . . ?," p. 40.

25. Colette Ysmal, *Le Comportement Électorale en France* (Paris: Decouvett, 1986).

26. Quoted in Smith, p. 43.

27. Elisabeth Dupoirier and Gerard Grunberg, eds., *Mars 1986: la drôle de défaite de la Gauche* (Paris: Presses Universitaires de France, 1986); Smith, pp. 42–43.

28. Alan Lancelot, ed., *1981: Les élections de l'alternance* (Paris: Fondation Nationale des Science Politiques, 1986).

29. James Hollifield, "Immigration, Race and Politics," *French Politics and Society*, 13 (March 1986):16.

30. *Le Monde*, April 26, 1988.

REFERENCES AND SUGGESTED READINGS

Berger, Suzanne, ed. 1981. *Organizing Interests in Western Europe*. Cambridge: Cambridge University Press.

Cheles, Luciano, Ronnie Ferguson, and Michalina Vaughan, eds. 1991. *Neo-Fascism in Europe*, New York: Longman.

Converse, Philip, and Roy Pierce. 1986. *Political Representation in France*. Cambridge, Mass.: Harvard University Press.

Dalton, Russel J. 1988. *Citizen Politics in Western European Democracies*. Chatham: Chatham House.

Ehrmann, Henry W. 1957. *Organized Business in France*. Princeton: Princeton University Press.

Gourevitch, P., A. Markovits, A. Martin, and G. Ross. 1984. *Unions, Change and Crisis*. London: Allen and Unwin.

Keeler, John. 1987. *The Politics of Neo-Corporatism in France*. New York: Oxford University Press.

Kesselman, Mark, and Guy Groux. 1984. *The French Workers' Movement*. London: Allen and Unwin.

15

The Party System as a Moveable Feast

*P*arty systems are a traditional interest in political science. There are, of course, many varieties of such systems. The two-party system, characterized by parties ideologically close together and by a pendulumlike alternation in power, as in the United States, is a relatively rare phenomenon. The single-party system such as existed in communist countries (until 1989) has been more common, and typically served as an instrument for elite recruitment. Another kind of single-party system, such as is still found in several African countries, tends to be used as an instrument to mobilize popular support. France has a multiparty system, as do all other countries of Europe.

There are, of course, many different kinds of party systems even within the broad "multiparty" category. There are systems with grossly unequal parties such as in Germany or the United Kingdom, and systems with several roughly equal parties (in terms of membership and votes), as found in central and northern Europe. Systems may be stable (that is, they experience few changes in government between elections), as in Germany, or unstable,[1] as in most of Latin Europe—at least historically. What is intriguing is why such different categories of party systems come about, and why they change. Historically, France has had relatively unstable multiparty systems during the Third and Fourth republics and a relatively stable multiparty system during the Fifth Republic. More recently, there has tended to be a convergence of the parties into two opposing coalitions. Since the 1980s, the ideological divisions between the two camps have become eroded. The focus of this chapter will be on explaining this evolution of the French party system.[2]

Explaining Party Systems

The Institutional Approach

Perhaps the most well-known explanation for the variety of party systems in Western democracies is the institutional approach contributed by the French political scientist Maurice Duverger.[3] Duverger argued that the principal reason for the divergence between two- and multiparty systems was the electoral system. In a nutshell, countries that employed a system of single-ballot, single-member district voting were more likely to tend toward a two-party system, and countries employing proportional representation were more likely to have multiparty systems.

The United States and Britain use a system of single ballots and single-member districts. There is only one representative or member of Parliament for each district. Only one ballot is held for that seat and the candidate receiving the plurality is awarded the seat. In such an electoral system supporters of small parties will tend to "vote usefully" by abandoning their first choice if the candidate is unlikely to be among the top two and to vote instead for the "lesser of two evils." Thus small parties tend to disappear and a two-party system emerges.

There are various kinds of proportional representation mechanisms. The purest, perhaps, are found in the Netherlands and Israel, where each party is accorded seats in the Parliament according to the percentage of votes it receives in a single national election. More common is the system used in various countries, and occa-

sionally in France, where each electoral district is presented with opposing slates of candidates (scrutin de liste) and the seats of each district (each district is a "multimember district" with more than one representative) are apportioned to the parties in accordance with their respective percentages of the vote. Under a system of proportional representation, supporters of small parties have an incentive to remain loyal to their favorites because they are usually assured of at least some representation in the national Parliament. Moreover, supporters of small centrist parties have an even greater incentive to remain loyal, because centrist parties are often necessary to the formation of coalition governments. Indeed, this has been the constant role of the Free Democratic Party in Germany and was the historic role of the Radical Party in France during the Third and Fourth republics. France employed a proportional representation system during most of the Fourth Republic, and again in 1986.

Political parties are well aware of the effect of such voting systems. The Liberal and Social Democratic parties (merged in 1988) in Britain have been extremely vocal in their demands for a proportional representation system that would favor these small, centrist parties. In France, there can be little doubt that the Socialists reintroduced proportional representation in 1986 so as to allow the small, extreme right-wing National Front Party to gain seats in the Parliament and gnaw at the expected majority of the traditional conservative parties. Indeed, because of the success of the National Front, which then earned about 10 percent of the seats in the National Assembly (the lower house of the French Parliament), proportional representation eroded the traditional conservative representation to a winning margin of only two seats. The National Front lost all but one seat when proportional representation was abandoned in the 1988 legislative elections.[4] In the legislative elections of 1993 the Front won 12.41% of the vote in the first round, but only

5.66% in the second and did not qualify for a single seat in the National Assembly.

The normal voting mechanism of the Fifth Republic has been the single-member district, two-ballot system. If no candidate receives an absolute majority, a runoff election is held one or two weeks later where voters must choose again, but where a plurality accords victory. The effect of this system is to encourage coalitions of parties on the second ballot. Frequently, for example, left-wing parties would form agreements to allow withdrawals (*désistements*) of progressive parties in favor of the best-placed left-wing candidate, so that they would not be divided on the second ballot. (A lot depended on whether the Communist Party wished to play the role of a spoiler.) Parties on the Right have done the same. Thus it was no surprise to Duverger, who was the first to articulate this phenomenon, that the many parties of France have tended to converge into two broad coalitions of Left and Right since the formation of the Fifth Republic.

Explaining the Party System as a Reflection of Social Cleavages

A second broad category of explanations for party systems relies on an examination of the diverse cleavages in French (or any) society to explain the appearance of the many parties. Political institutions, such as parties, take on their particular shapes because they are, in fact, reflections of deeper social conflict. Thus the deep fissures in the French social fabric that we examined in Chapter 13 became the basis for divisions in the party system. Differences among social groups over the exclusion of the church from public life led to the formation of pro- and anticlerical parties, especially during the Third Republic. As France industrialized, the new economic cleavages between peasants, workers, and the bourgeoisie also affected the party system.

This explanation does not, of course, exclude the institutional approach. Proportional representation made it easier for new parties to appear. The two-ballot elections gave incentives for parties to cooperate, and that cooperation made it possible for the allied parties to survive, rather than fade—as third parties traditionally have in the United States.

While electoral mechanism tells us something about the tendency of the party system to fragment, it is the social cleavage approach that informs us about the kinds of demands parties are likely to make. Most importantly, it helps us understand why, in France, new parties have tended to appear on the political Left, a process Duverger called *"sinéstrisme."*[5]

Basically, the historical tendency of parties to appear at the left of the political spectrum is related to France's late industrialization. The rise of the working class made the old party disputes over the role of the church seem irrelevant.[6] But it was the lateness of industrialization that helps explain the intensity of ideological commitment that would characterize French socialism.

The late industrialization retarded the development of the union movement, as we noted in Chapter 14. This meant that a party representing workers' interests would have little financial support in its early years, and this in turn meant that a strong grassroots organization would have to suffice in the absence of funds. Organization is, of course, the traditional weapon of the Left. Commitment to a chain of command, when short-term material incentives are lacking, requires a common perception of problems and a powerful set of shared goals; in short, an ideology. Marxism proved to be that ideology.

French socialism was militant from its inception (Marx's daughter, in fact, married one of the country's early socialist leaders, Lasalle). The French Workers' Party (*Parti ouvrier français*) was the first real socialist party to form, in 1867, and it gradually evolved into the militant

Marxist *Section française de l'internationale ouvrière*, the French section of the (First) Workers' International.

By the turn of the century, the political expression of French workers was already facing a fissure as social conditions began to change. A significant improvement in the standard of living of some of the workers, and especially among their intellectual allies, such as teachers and journalists, led to divergences in strategy among the leadership. The Dreyfus affair raised the issue of defense of the "bourgeois republic" from right-wing attack. A current arose professing class collaboration and, eventually, participation in World War I. Others remained militantly anticapitalist. The issue of militarism versus moderation finally came to a head in 1920 at the Socialist Congress of Tours. There, two-thirds of France's Socialists voted to affiliate with the Third International and became known as the French Communist Party. The minority, under Léon Blum, a schoolteacher, retained the name SFIO. The party had divided over participation in the First World War and, most importantly, over the issue of support of the Soviet Union, whose recent revolution was a proximate product of that bloodbath. Sociologically, the blue-collar socialists remained radical, while the white-collars became reformist.[7]

The sociological origins of the right-wing parties are more problematic. This is partially because as new parties appeared on the Left, the old left-wing parties moved right. The classic case was the old Radical Socialist Party. In the nineteenth century this party represented the bourgeois Left and was the standard-bearer of secularists. Despite its name, the party advocated a classic liberal philosophy, including a preference for free markets. As the Socialist and Communist parties gradually appeared, the party was pushed to the center—its clientele, as ever, the enlightened middle classes. To its right were parties representing traditional rural interests (*Indépendants*). In the nineteenth century there were also diverse royalist factions, with occasional Bonapartists and Boulangistes.[8] Some of these became protofascist organizations, supporters of which were similar sociologically to the present advocates of the National Front (unemployed, lower-middle class, and other economically marginal groups; see Chapters 12 and 14).

THE PRESENT PARTY SYSTEM

The present party system, that is, the system that has more or less stabilized since the advent of the Fifth Republic in 1958, has gradually come to resemble the British and American models. The multiparty system has not disappeared, but under the incentive structure of the two-ballot system, and under the economic conditions of advanced industrialism, the parties have tended to coalesce in a bipolar way, with both poles being more moderate than extreme. The Left is less radical and the Right is neither antiparliamentary nor an advocate of primitive capitalism.

The Right: *Rassemblement pour la République*

Perhaps the most stunning transformation of the party system was the development of a majority party under the charismatic spell of General Charles de Gaulle.[9] Unlike all previous republics, the Fifth coasted without the usual coalition governments, and with a powerful executive at its disposal; conservative rule became the norm. The coattail effect of de Gaulle gave the Gaullist party hegemony over French politics for more than two decades.

Of course, coattails were not all. Georges Pompidou, de Gaulle's hand-picked successor, worked tirelessly to give the party substance beyond de Gaulle's shadow. Under his stewardship the party became implanted at the local, as well as national, levels.

While the party has changed names several times,[10] it has consistently led the other conservative parties. It is now known as the *Rassemblement pour la République*, "Rally for the Republic." Philosophically, the party has changed considerably. In the Fourth Republic the party was further to the right and had resemblances to the rightist movements of an earlier period, being antiparliamentary (at least anti-Fourth Republic), deeply nationalist, and favoring an imperial foreign policy.[11] The attitudes changed during the Algerian war, although the emasculated Parliament of the Fifth Republic is a product of earlier Gaullist suspicions. Unlike conservatives in the United States or Britain, the Gaullists were also committed to substantial government intervention in the economy, when that intervention was thought to be in the national interest. Much like the Jakob Kaiser wing of the German Christian Democrats immediately after World War II, there was also a Left Gaullism with affiliated labor unions, flourishing during the first decade or so of the Fifth Republic.

This has changed. The Gaullists under the leadership of Jacques Chirac have become much more like conservative parties elsewhere in the world, advocating a rollback of the state (with the exception of the police) wherever possible.[12] In fact, the change in philosophy became so pronounced under Chirac that the appellation "neo-Gaullist" became more appropriate.

Union pour la Démocratie Française

The political ally of the Rally for the Republic is the Union for French Democracy. The *Union pour la Démocratie Française* is actually a coalition of three small parties and two political clubs, united originally to support President

Prime Minister Jacques Chirac presides over the opening session of the National Assembly, April 1986.

Giscard d'Estaing in the legislative elections of 1978. The most important of the three, the *Parti Républicain*, was Giscard's own party. It is a small party with little articulation at the local level, whose philosophy was and is classically liberal (conservative, or perhaps "libertarian," in the American sense), favoring free markets and small government wherever possible.

The other members of Union are the tiny vestiges of parties that were important in the Third and Fourth republics. The *Centre des Démocrates Sociaux*[13] is a remnant of the old *Mouvement Républicain Populaire*, a Christian Democratic party that occupied the center of the political spectrum during the Fourth Republic. The *Parti Radical* is the rump of the old *Parti Radical Socialiste*, the anticlerical party of the Third Republic. The party split over whether to support the Common Platform of the Left (signed by Communists and Socialists in 1972), with the Left sympathizers leaving. The other two affiliates of the Union are "political clubs," small groups of elites that have not tried formally to create a mass base of support, and are ideological centrist. They are the *Club Perspectives et Réalités* and the *Mouvement des Démocrates Sociaux*.

The Front National

The party furthest to the right on the French political spectrum is the National Front. The party is in fact more of an interest group in the sense that it really only focuses on one issue: immigration. It does, however, have local as well as national organizations, and it rules in coalition with the traditional conservatives in many local governments, especially in southeastern France, where large numbers of former French Algerian settlers were repatriated. These local coalitions have been formed despite the fact that the latter parties have refused to enter into formal alliance at the national level (see Chapter 14).

Led by Jean-Marie Le Pen, a well-known figure on the far right since the Algerian war, the party has sought to capitalize on the frustrations of working- and lower-middle-class French by advocating expulsion of France's mostly Islamic immigrant population. Other than thinly disguised racism (see Chapter 14),

the party has only a vague ideology emphasizing a free market economy linked to pronounced jingoism.

The Left: The *Parti Socialiste*

The *Parti Socialiste* is, after the Rally for the Republic, the greatest success story in French politics. If the Rally was the first majority party democratic France has ever known, the *Parti Socialiste* is the first majority party that the Left has ever known. It came to that position both through favorable circumstances and through the strategy of its leader and founder, François Mitterrand.

In the 1970s, Mitterrand took the remnants of the old french section of the Workers' International (SFIO), which had fallen on hard times because of its failures during the Fourth Republic, especially *vis-à-vis* Algeria, and combined it with several left-wing political clubs to produce the new *Parti Socialiste*. As recounted in the previous chapter, Mitterrand moved the party in a leftward direction to capture the protest vote normally accruing to the Communist Party, and was spectacularly successful. Not only did the Socialist Party become the largest party on the Left, it became the largest party in the country after 1981.

The victory in 1981 was as much serendipitous as the product of strategy, however. The Right split over supporting the reelection of President Valéry Giscard d'Estaing, the Union candidate. The Gaullists, led by Jacques Chirac, Giscard's rival, afforded the Union president only lukewarm support during the second ballot in 1981. Moreover, the poor performance of the French economy since 1974, when Giscard had first been elected, alienated many voters, while fear of a Communist-dominated Left simply disappeared. Mitterrand won, bringing the Socialist Party on his coattails as the majority party in the National Assembly. Even after the defeat of the Left in 1986, the Socialist Party remained the largest single party in France. The legislative elections of 1993 were another story, however. After eleven years in power, and tainted by scandals concerning party financing (see Chapter 11) the Socialists took their worst drubbing since they became serious contenders for power. They received only 28.25% of the vote and many in the party, particularly former prime minister Michel Rocard, began to consider forming a new left-wing party that would incorporate the non-Socialist Left.

Even so, without such a major reconfiguration as envisioned by Rocard, the Socialists very much fit Otto Kirchheimer's notion of a "catch-all party."[14] Its left wing is decidedly Marxist; its middle, the *Mitterrandistes,* is pragmatic; and its right wing, the *Rocardiens* (supporters of former prime minister Michel Rocard), is social-democratically in favor of a mixed economy. There are small factions as well, linked to specific leaders and based on theoretical differences within the socialist family.

The *Parti Communiste Français*

The Communist Party of France (PCF) was one of the largest in Western Europe, second only to Italy's, but is now only a shadow of its former self. It may well be argued that it was the size of the Communist Party that kept the conservatives in power for so long. The Red Menace (often pictured on conservative French posters as a grimacing Bolshevik with a knife in his teeth) was adroitly used by de Gaulle and his successors to keep the Left at bay. For much of the postwar period, voters needed no reminding: the case of Eastern Europe, and especially that of Czechoslovakia, where the local Communist Party took advantage of its ministries in a coalition government to take over the state in 1948, loomed large in most French memories.

Nor did the French Communist leadership help matters by their continual and slavish endorsements of all Soviet actions.

For a while, during the 1970s, the French Communist Party leadership indulged the party's intellectuals by distancing themselves from the Soviet Union and adopting a "Eurocommunist" independent stance, even dropping the term "dictatorship of the proletariat" from their list of goals. This was a short-lived attempt to expand the electoral base despite reservations from an "un–de-Stalinized" rank and file. The ultimate failure of this electoral strategy led to a break with the Socialists in 1978, the departure of many intellectuals from the *bureau politique* (the ruling committee) of the party, and renewed voter confidence in the Socialists as the latter refused to cede to Communist demands for revision of the Common Platform, signed in 1972. If demographics would ultimately lead to the decline of France's Communists (see chapter 14), the party leadership seemed to make every effort to seal their collective fate, with a Soviet-style comportment repellent to most voters.[15]

The party enjoyed a short revival when, in 1981, Mitterrand asked them to join a united government of the Left. Mitterrand's reasons were not announced, but more than likely, his invitation was intended to assure the cooperation of the Communist-dominated labor confederation, and to make sure that the Communist Party would share the blame for any mistakes the new government might make. Indeed, as unemployment soared under Socialist economic restructuring, the Communists left the coalition to enter into official opposition. They regained some influence after the 1988 legislative elections. The Socialists, forced to form a minority government, required at least tacit Communist acquiescence in order to govern.

The Communists continued to decline in the 1993 elections, receiving only 4.61% of the vote in the second round. Because their supporters are concentrated in a few constituencies, mostly outside Paris, the Communists did retain 23 seats, enough to constitute a formal caucus. Moreover, their influence actually increased because of the poor showing of the Socialists, who retained only 54 seats in the 1993 elections. This small number meant that by themselves the Socialists could not legally constitute the formal opposition to the ruling conservative government. Most importantly, they would need Communist support to introduce a "motion of censure" (that is, "no confidence") against the government.

Mouvement des Radicaux de Gauche

A few words need to be said about the final member of the Left. The *Mouvement des Radicaux de Gauche* is the other half of the old *Parti Radical Socialiste* that broke up over the decision to join the Common Platform of the Left, signed

---

A Communist's Point of View

Being a Communist has brought me many things. It has brought me friends, a way to reflect on both political and personal life. It has permitted me to have confidence in myself and believe in myself. I couldn't think of not being a Communist. It's my life. I don't make an effort to be a Communist. I live it. . . .

I am proud to be a Communist and have always been proud to be a Communist. There were difficult times on the international front, Afghanistan, for example, but I was never embarrassed to call myself a Communist. People did leave the French Communist Party at that time, but many are coming back.

Source: Jean-Pierre Quilgars, Renault factory worker, quoted in the *New York Times*, January 23, 1989, p. A-11.

---

in 1972. Indeed, the breakup of the party is perhaps the best indicator that French politics has bifurcated in the last two decades. In a society that divided all issues into right and left, there was no room for a party at the center. Like the old American labor song, the society asks, "Which side are you on?!" Forced to choose, these members of the Radical Party found more in common with the Socialists than with the Union. While the Radical Left Movement is small, it has captured a few city halls, bearing testimony to effective local organization as a party, and does not quite fall into the "political club" category. Ideologically, the Left Radicals, despite their misleading name, are closest of the left parties to the center.

THE ECOLOGISTS

The newest parties in France have grown out of the environmental movement. This movement has been smaller in France than in other countries at least partially because their tenets could not easily be classified in the left/right terms that categorize political debate in France and with which most voters identify themselves. However, while the movement was small, it grew rapidly. After the Socialist victory of 1988, President Mitterrand named Brice Lalonde, leader of the French branch of Friends of the Earth, as minister. However, Lalonde fell out with the Socialists after three years and formed one of the two environmental parties. Lalonde's party, *Génération Écologique* (Ecological Generation) is the more pragmatic pro-environmental party, while *Les Verts* (The Greens) under the leadership of 1988 presidential candidate Antoine Waechter is the more idealistic (or "purist") party. Thus the divisions that the German Green Party experienced as part of its internal debate (*Realos* versus *Fundis*) were encapsulated in two separate parties in France. For a while, it appeared that both parties would take off. Together they scored better than the *Front National* in the local elections of 1992, while the mainstream parties declined. However, when the time came for the legislative elections of 1993, despite an electoral pact between the two parties, the environmentalists did not achieve enough votes to gain even one seat in the new National Assembly. Clearly, they still have a way to go before they can be considered anything more than an avenue for protest votes.

RECENT TRENDS

The overall trend of the French party system has been for the various parties to coalesce into two broad coalitions of right and left, much the way Duverger predicted. However, this coalescing was a long time in coming. While the Fifth Republic was inaugurated in 1958, and was antedated by most of the parties, the Common Platform of the Left was not signed until 1972, and the conserva-

---

Perhaps the less attractive side of party politics, in France or anywhere else, is the way in which parties finance their operations. In France, there have traditionally been few holds barred, and all parties have tended to abuse their positions when elected. Some examples illustrate the problem.

While left-wing parties have tended to rely on membership dues and union contributions for financing throughout Western Europe, the weakness of the union movement has made French leftist parties more reliant on other funding sources.

The Socialists and Communists have often had more success at the local levels during the Fifth Republic and have used city halls to obtain funds. For example, companies awarded public contracts at the local levels are often expected to pay for "studies" conducted by members of the mayor's party. These kinds of shady dealings, along with other scandals, led to the Socialists' defeat in the national parliamentary elections of 1993.

On the Right, which has more frequently occupied national office, parties have raised money by having intermediaries linked to the party take part of the commissions on national government contracts, recorded as payments to go-betweens. Also, according to the *Canard Enchaîne*, the closest thing France has to investigative journalism, conservative parties have used double billing tech-

niques, where businesspeople are encouraged to take out advertising in the party journal (at expensive rates) that, in fact, never appears.

The French Parliament met in special session in late 1987 to introduce more "transparency" into the system, to make financing a matter of public record, and to introduce some spending limits. Copying many of the reforms from U.S. law, a relatively cosmetic law was passed. It should be added that this, like the bipolarization of the party system and reduced ideological distinctions between the parties, suggests another way in which French politics are becoming Americanized. The funds, however, are relatively small compared to those in the United States, mostly because television time is free to all parties. In a way that is perhaps amusing to Americans, French politicians tend to worry about the cost of posters.

Whereas much talk was devoted to the issue of financial reform, it is not as yet clear whether the changes in the "transparency" law had much of an impact, as revelations of financial abuse still appeared during the 1993 parliamentary campaign.

Source: *Washington Post*, November 27, 1987; *Le Monde*, November 14, 1987; Jean Claude Masciet and Pierre Mutignon, *"Le Financement Publique des Partis et la Règlementation de leurs Ressources et Dépenses," Problemes Politiques et Sociaux*, no. 527 (January 10, 1986).

tives' "Liberal" alliance[16] did not formalize until 1986.

Two factors seem to explain the delay. On the Right, the charisma and coattail effect of de Gaulle obviated the necessity for Gaullists to formalize relations with other conservative parties, though the latter were invited into government under Georges Pompidou and Giscard served as de Gaulle's finance minister without joining the party. On the Left, the pariah status of the Communist Party, coupled to its significant following, hindered the possibilities for any successful electoral alliance to be formed. Logically, the disappearance of de Gaulle and the withering away of the Communist Party removed these obstacles to coalition politics.

The other major trend in the party system is the convergence of the two coalitions. That is, the policies of Left and Right have tended to converge in recent years. As the differences between the parties tend to be defined in economic terms, the best explanation for this convergence is the economy.

France has become increasingly locked into the web of interdependencies that have characterized the economies of the advanced industrial countries since the end of World War II.[17] This means that the pursuit of an independent economic strategy has become increasingly difficult. As we mentioned in Chapter 11, the Socialists discovered that they could not reflate the French economy when the rest of the world was deflating. Government deficits intended to stimulate demand, and thus jobs ended up only stimulating imports. That is, French companies did not produce enough goods to absorb the increase in demand generated by government spending. French consumers, who now had more money, thanks to government programs, tended to purchase goods from abroad, as there were not enough French goods to meet the demand. The Socialists turned to more market-oriented solutions, such as deregulating capital markets to stimulate investment,[18] and began to look much more like the conservatives. On the other hand, French conservatives were loath to call for the dismantling of the welfare state.[19] With the stock market crash of October 1987, the privatization program of the conservatives ground to a temporary halt and market solutions lost much of their attraction for French voters. (When the conservatives resumed power in 1993, they justified their privatization program not in terms of the superiority of private enterprise and the market, but simply as a way to obtain funds for new jobs programs.) Indeed, the policy disasters of both Left and Right pushed the policy debate to the center—or rather, out of sight: in the presidential debate of 1988 between François Mitterrand and Jacques Chirac, a total of two minutes was devoted to the problem of unemployment.

OUR FIVE PROPOSITIONS AND THE FRENCH PARTY SYSTEM

As we noted in chapter 2, the phenomenon of industrial decline has had a major impact on the political landscape. Our *first proposition* argued that parties associated with the expansion of the state would encounter significant skepticism from voters. This is true of the Socialists and Communists, but it is also true of the Gaullists. Since there was such a large consensus on state intervention in the past, the current industrial malaise wounds both right- and left-wing coalitions and adds to the volatility of the electorate, a phenemenon we already noted.

Our *second proposition*, that perceptions of the state will change according to changes in the current values of the political system gives the edge to the conservatives. However, the shift toward the center of the political spectrum that occurred among the Socialist leadership after its disastrous first two years in office has made the market more popular among Socialist adherents and allows them to compete on this terrain with the conservatives.

The shifts in groups allying with parties, however, our *third proposition,* has not yet occurred, probably because historic voter identities with either Left or Right (see Chapter 14) are very durable. Neither unions nor business have shifted their allegiances. However, they have all become more circumspect about associating with a particular political party. This makes conditions more volatile and realignment a distinct possibility.

Our *fourth proposition,* about the slowing of European integration, cuts across parties with supporters and detractors of the European Union in both camps. The only parties that are wholeheartedly pro-integration are those of the Union for French Democracy. Every other party has pro- and anti-European Union factions. This lack of unified opinion should, in itself, slow the move toward a United States of Europe.

Our *fifth proposition,* emphasizing the rise of particularism, is no doubt most clearly manifested in the rise of the National Front. The fact that extreme right, anti-immigrant parties have gained ground in most of Europe should give no comfort to the supporters of the more enlightened parties. Conservative parties especially have felt the need to move in the direction of the National Front, but many of its supporters are found in blue-collar constituencies that have frequently voted Left. This is the least sanguine marker of Europe in the nineties.

CONCLUSION

The bifurcation of the French party system into two opposing coalitions and the convergence of the Left and Right suggests that French politics is becoming more like that of the United States. Mitterrand's overtures to the Union for French Democracy after the 1988 elections sug-

gest the possibility of politics along the German model by creating a center-left government similar to Helmut Schmidt's Free Democrat-Social Democrat alliance, but the strategy did not work.

After the legislative elections of 1993, the move toward an American system of two broad parties taking turns in the exercise of power seemed to be stymied. The Left lost so many seats that the political model the country was approaching seemed less like that of the United States and more like that of the Japanese, with a single Conservative coalition dominating politics. However, one election by itself does not announce a trend. (Even in Japan the long rule of the Liberal Democratic Party came to an end in 1993 in the wake of a series of scandals.) In both broad ideological and institutional terms, the French party system retains many traits that characterize politics in the United States. It is certainly much different from the picture of French politics painted in textbooks as late as the 1970s.

Not only have the announced policies of the parties converged, but the trend toward pragmatic policies and away from solutions dictated by traditional ideologies has made present-day France rather different from the country that was so politically idiosyncratic through much of the modern era.

The principal factors conditioning the change were, of course, first, the advent of the institutions of the Fifth Republic. The electoral system and the institutions themselves have reduced the role for the political center and encouraged Right and Left coalitions. The poor showing of the ecological parties demonstrates this. Moreover, the suppressing of proportional representation is likely to relegate the more radical parties, the Communist Party and the National Front, to the political sidelines, despite persistent social reasons for their existence. This may, however, take some time. Finally, the general crisis of the industrialized economies in the world market has limited the options available to political groups. These conditions that have shaped the current French party system are not likely to disappear quickly.

NOTES

1. *Unstable* may be a deceptive term: while governments may change, policies often do not.

2. Much of my own thinking on the French party system was shaped by Maurice Duverger's course at the Institut d'Études Politiques, which I had the good fortune to take as an undergraduate during the 1969–1970 term. In addition, my discussion in this chapter is especially informed by Suzanne Berger's original analysis in her *French Political System* (New York: Random House, 1974), pp. 59–77. For a review of the more recent literature on political parties, see Kay Lawson, "Political Parties Inside and Out," *Comparative Politics,* 23, 1 (October 1990). For an innovative hypothesis on the development of party systems, see Ronald Rogowski, "Trade and the Variety of Democratic Institutions," *International Organization,* 41, 2 (Spring 1987).

3. *Les Partis Politiques* (Paris: Armand Colin, 1951).

4. Indeed, by the first round of the 1988 presidential election, the National Front received 14.4% of the vote. Many analysts attributed the growth of the National Front electorate to the legitimacy gained from its representation in the National Assembly; this, in turn, was due to proportional representation.

5. One of France's newest parties, the National Front, of course, appeared on the Right, although much of its social base was the same as that supporting the Communists. See pp. 204–205 of this text. The newest parties, *Les Verts* and *Génération Écologique,* are somewhat hard to define in terms of the traditional Left/Right spectrum, but are considered by most people to be left of center.

6. Berger, pp. 67–71.

7. Some further nuances are necessary here. Blue-collar workers in the North of France remained loyal to the SFIO, while the Communists ac-

quired the allegiance of many of the disadvantaged in the Midi.

8. General Georges Boulanger was a late-nineteenth-century charismatic populist whose ultimate preference for government by coup d'état led to his undoing.

9. See especially Ezra N. Suleiman, *Politics, Power and Bureaucracy in France* (Princeton: Princeton University Press, 1974), chap. XIII; Berger, pp. 72–77.

10. The names were, in succession: *Union nationale pour la République (UNR), Union pour la défense de la Vienne République (UDVeR), Union pour la défense de la République (UDR), Rassémblement pour la République (RPR).* The latest name, "Rally for the Republic," recalls the Gaullist party title under the Fourth Republic, *Rassemblement du Peuple Français (RPF),* "Rally for the French People."

11. It would be mistaken, however, to consider the party fascist.

12. For an analysis of this recent convergence in terms of policies, see Jeffrey R. Henig, Chris Hamnett, and Harvey B. Feigenbaum, "The Politics of Privatization: A Comparative Perspective," *Governance,* 1, 4 (October 1988).

13. The *Centre des Démocrates Sociaux* ran a separate slate of candidates for the 1989 elections to the European Parliament. It was then unclear whether it would remain a part of the Union.

14. Catch-all parties are broadly based parties that incorporate many factions and tendencies. See *Politics, Law, and Social Change,* ed. F. C. Burin and K. L. Shell (New York: Columbia University Press, 1969).

15. Longtime Communist Party leader Georges Marchais, who had much to do with the party's failure to modernize, finally stepped down in 1993.

16. The term *liberal* in France refers to proponents of free markets and to those who oppose state intervention in the economy. The Rally and the Union based their alliance on a common preference for low taxes, sale of nationalized industries, deregulation, and a general "liberation" of private enterprise. By 1993 the term *liberal* had lost much of its electoral cachet and the conservatives downplayed it in their campaign.

17. On the overall theory of "interdependence," see Robert O. Keohane and Joseph S. Nye, *Power and Interdependence* (Boston: Little, Brown, 1977). For the constraints on France, see Stephen S. Cohen and Peter A. Gourevitch, eds., *France in the Troubled World Economy* (London: Butterworth Scientific, 1982).

18. Old solutions tended not to work because the private sector anticipated government strategies and acted to counter them in advance. See especially Michael Loriaux, "States and Markets: French Financial Intervention in the Seventies," *Comparative Politics,* 20, 2 (January 1988).

19. Henig, Hamnett, and Feigenbaum, "Privatization." See also Harvey B. Feigenbaum and Jeffrey R. Henig, "The Political Underpinnings of Privatization: A Typology," *World Politics,* 46, 2 (January 1994).

REFERENCES AND SUGGESTED READINGS

Bell, David S. 1982. *Contemporary French Political Parties.* New York: Methuen.

Berger, Suzanne. 1974. *The French Political System.* New York: Random House.

Duverger, Maurice. 1953. *Political Parties.* New York: Methuen.

Frears, J. R. 1977. *Political Parties and Elections in the French Fifth Republic.* New York: St. Martin's.

Janda, Kenneth. 1980. *Political Parties: A Cross-National Survey.* New York: Free Press.

Ross, George. 1982. *Workers and Communists in France: From Popular Front to Eurocommunism.* Berkeley: University of California Press.

Ware, Alan. 1987. *Political Parties.* Oxford: Blackwell.

Wilson, Frank. 1982. *French Political Parties under the Fifth Republic.* New York: Praeger.

16

The Hierarchy of Government

rance is, as we have noted, a country of contradictions and paradoxes. Perhaps nowhere is this more true than in the transformation of the country's formal institutions of government. The parade of governments during the parliamentary Fourth Republic led to the transformation of national institutions into a highly stable presidential system. The centralization of the economy under the Socialists also occurred at the same time as the decentralization of the hierarchy of government. Paradoxically as well, the assumption of power by a Gaullist prime minister in 1986 (and again in 1993) led the Gaullists to undermine the strong presidential authority that their founder had struggled to create.

TRANSFORMATION OF THE NATIONAL GOVERNMENT

Parliament

For most of France's republican history, the chief expression of democracy was the election of deputies to the Parliament. Whereas France has oscillated between constitutions favoring a strong executive and those favoring a strong legislature, the *democratic* constitutions favored the legislature until 1958.[1]

Under the legislative constitutions of the Third and Fourth republics, there was a fusion of executive and legislative authority. That is, the prime minister and the cabinet served as the executive by virtue of their election by the lower house (the *Chamber of Deputies*). They also served at the pleasure of the legislature: if for any reason a majority of the deputies refused to support a policy of the government, a new government would have to be formed. We use the term *government* to mean the prime minister and the cabinet. (In French the cabinet is called the *conseil des ministres,* while under the Third and Fourth republics the prime minister was also known as the *président du conseil.*)[2] Any time a government lost the support of the deputies in a formal vote, it was said to have lost a *vote of confidence.* New elections were not necessary to form a new government unless a new majority could not be established, or unless five years had passed since the last election.

Majorities were difficult to form in both the Third and Fourth republics for two essential reasons. First, there were a large number of parties in the Chamber of Deputies because of the political divisions in the French electorate (see Chapter 11) and because of the frequent recourse to proportional representation as the chief voting system. The second essential reason for difficulty in forming majorities was the limited grounds for agreement between the parties—because they represented such diverse sections of the electorate (see Chapter 13).

A subsidiary reason for the instability of governments during the Third and Fourth republics was the lack of party discipline. Frequently, the collapse of a government meant that new ministers would be drawn from the rank-and-file deputies ("backbenchers," to use British terminology). This gave deputies an incentive to vote against the governments *of which their own parties were members,* knowing that their party leadership had few instruments to punish them, and that committee chairs especially were likely to become newly appointed ministers. This situation, in turn, was a result of the limited party funds to finance campaigns, leaving backbenchers to rely on their own resources and reducing the impact of any party threat to withdraw support ("withdrawal of the whip" in Britain).[3] Moreover, the refusal of both the Communists (after 1947) and the Gaullists (after 1946) to participate in governments left the potential candidates for ministers to be found among the weakly organized parties of the center.[4]

More often than not, adoption of controversial policies spelled the end of a government. The ever-present possibility that coalition members would defect, even for the most transitory gains, sharply constrained all governments, but especially those of the Fourth Republic. This made it hard to address the increasingly difficult problems facing the country. To some extent this *immobilisme* (deadlock) of parliamentary government meant that many of the problems of the country were simply left to the bureaucracy. But as crises arose, incremental bureaucratic solutions became inappropriate, and deputies developed a habit of investing plenipotentiary powers in the prime minister or, eventually, the president. Such was the case of the transitory "dictatorships" of Georges Clemenceau (World War I), Gaston Doumergue (the Great Depression), Henri Pétain (Vichy, tragically less transitory than originally expected), Pierre Mendès-France (the Indochina war), and Charles de Gaulle (the Algerian war).

It was the last crisis of the Fourth Republic and the parliamentary habit of investing powers in a single "savior" that led to the suicide of the last parliamentary regime. In 1958 France was torn by civil strife over government efforts to quell the Arab rebellion in Algeria, which many of the French considered a genuine part of France, and not merely a legal fiction of colonialism. Unable to extricate itself from this part of North Africa, while doubting the loyalty of the army to the republic should Algeria be granted independence, the leaders of the Fourth Republic turned to de Gaulle, who was, at least, a proven democrat whose nationalist credentials were assumed to be attractive to the army. De Gaulle accepted the post as prime minister on condition that the constitution be drastically revised. What resulted was, in fact, a new constitution.

The Fifth Republic

The essential thrust of the Constitution of 1958 was to circumscribe the authority of Parliament and to shift power to the executive. The assumption of de Gaulle and his supporters was that Parliament was immobilized because of the power of self-interested political parties and the national interest could not, therefore, be served. This was a typical conservative outlook that viewed representation as divisive and assumed that somehow, despite the fact that different segments of French society had conflicting interests (a "zero-sum game," in modern parlance), that a national interest could be found and served, if only political institutions could be placed above the fray. Members of de Gaulle's government therefore reduced the role of Parliament, whose very representative nature reflected the conflicts of French society, and attempted to shift authority to the executive. As Michel Debré, a close collaborator of de Gaulle's and principal author of the new constitution, expressed the basic philosophy of the document: "To be sure, the nation is composed of individuals and of groups. But this composition gives birth to an independent and animated body which is, in fact, the nation and, in law, the State."[5]

Power Under the Constitution of 1958

The Constitution of 1958 created three centers of authority: the Parliament, the government, and the president.

Parliament.   As with the Third and Fourth republics, the new Parliament was bicameral: the National Assembly (*Assemblée Nationale*) was the new name for the lower house, with deputies directly elected by districts. The Senate (*Sénat*) was the much less powerful upper house, with senators elected by local electoral colleges.

The powers of the Parliament were aimed at providing a democratic check on the government, but with additional clauses aimed at reducing potential instability:

◆ The government is appointed by the president but can be disavowed by the National Assembly through a "motion of censure."

◆ A "motion of censure" (that is, a vote of no confidence) was made difficult to pass: it must be initiated by 10% of the deputies, voted in 48 hours, and passed by an absolute majority of all deputies (not just those present); and passage of the motion requires immediate dissolution of the Assembly and new elections.

◆ Ministers may not be deputies. Deputies must resign their seats if named to the government.

◆ The legislative powers of the National Assembly are severely constricted: it may legislate only in areas of civil and political rights, crimes, taxes, elections, and nationalizations; it may decide only "basic principles" of defense, local government, property, work, and welfare; it may not pass detailed "regulatory" laws; only the government may initiate legislation that would increase public expenditure or decrease revenues; the Parliament may sit for only six months out of the year, unless called into special session by the president; it votes only on amendments to legislation that the government accepts; the government can demand package voting (for example, on the budget).

◆ The new constitution also reduced the role of committees, which were thought to be vulnerable targets for interest groups.[6] The number of standing committees was reduced from nineteen to six: the subject matter of each committee was intended to be so broad as to inhibit members from developing expertise as leverage against the government (knowledge is power!) and to have so many members as to become unwieldy. Ultimately, though, these reforms could be subverted: committees still have the power to create smaller, more specialized subcommittees, while special, ad hoc committees can also be created. However, the government's influence over the budget keeps these sub- and ad hoc committees from being adequately staffed.

The Senate.   The Senate, the upper house of the French Parliament, is somewhat more powerful than the House of Lords in Britain and considerably less powerful than the U.S. Senate. Like the German and American upper houses, it provides regional representation, with less populous regions being overrepresented. This overrepresentation was intentional. The indirect election of the French Senate (by local elites) and the exaggerated influence of rural areas were intended to make the Senate a conservative check on the National Assembly. To de Gaulle's chagrin, in the first decade of the Fifth Republic the Senate was composed of *anti-Gaullist* conservatives. For this reason, he sought to abolish the upper chamber by referendum in April 1969—only to lose, leading to the general's resignation.

If the government does not intervene, a bill must pass both the National Assembly and the Senate to become law. If the Senate is recalcitrant, the government can give the National Assembly the last word and ignore a negative vote in the Senate. The Socialists met constant opposition to their reforms from the Senate during the 1981–1986 session, and, like de Gaulle, were unfettered by this opposition. Conservative majorities emerged in both chambers in 1993.

The Senate can, however, serve to delay legislation: when the Socialists returned to the opposition in 1993, they were able, for example, to delay conservative education reforms by proposing hundreds of amendments when the bill reached the Senate at the end of the parliamentary session. The conservative government was forced to withdraw their reform until the next session.

The Government.   The power and the Achilles' heel of the Gaullist constitution is the government. The government—consisting of the prime minister, ministers of state, and secretaries of state (junior ministers)[7]—is appointed by the president, but can be voted out of power by a motion of censure in the National Assembly. Thus for the executive to be truly powerful, the president must not have a hostile majority in the lower house of Parliament. This situation of a powerful executive with a friendly majority existed from 1958 to 1986.

The Constitution of 1958 is unclear as to where ultimate executive power resides, whether in the presidency or in the prime ministry. Largely, the powers of the president and prime minister have been defined by practice, with most of the precedents being set by de Gaulle. De Gaulle took it upon himself to establish the main lines of public policy, and left day-to-day management of the executive to the prime minister. This has been a practice of each of his successors and was only modified with the advent of Cohabitation (see pages 273–274 of this text).

De Gaulle also established certain "reserved areas" of presidential policymaking: foreign policy, defense, and constitutional questions. This practice was maintained by his successors, and was extended to economic questions by

Valéry Giscard d'Estaing, who was trained in economics.

Finally, de Gaulle asserted the president's right to *fire* as well as appoint the prime minister and his cabinet. This right is nowhere in the constitution, but since parliaments were, until 1986, always friendly to the president, the practice became solidly established.

AN IMPERIAL PRESIDENCY?

For several reasons, there has been a worldwide trend of increasing executive power since (at least) the Great Depression of the 1930s. This has partially been a function of the globalization of politics and the increasing importance of foreign policy, a traditional bastion of executive authority. Moreover, the Keynesian economic revolution gave government a primary role in the management of the economy where, in the interest of comprehensive policy, the executive has emerged as the principal manager of the nation's economy. (Even when Keynesian economic theory lost popularity, executives were loath to give up their powers.)

Perhaps nowhere has the shift toward the executive been more pronounced than in France. Certainly, French history has provided both precedents and symbols that have facilitated this shift. Historically, both the kings and Napoleon I have provided heroic symbols and a positive view of executive authority. It is also certain that these historic cues have not been equally received in France, for the Right more than the Left has favored a powerful executive.

While it is essentially true that the constitutions of the Third and Fourth republics located power in the legislature, whereas the Fifth circumscribed the legislature in favor of the presidency, a look at French history reveals this dichotomy to be less than clear-cut. Presidents under legislative regimes had subtle powers, while the vagueness of the Constitution of 1958 leaves the door open for parliamentary assertiveness.

Role of the President under Parliamentary Regimes

The traditional role of the French president has been one of a national symbol, above the sordid fray of normal politics. In legislative regimes, the office has been both ceremonial and one of a sort of spare wheel, available should the machinery of government break down.

At the beginning of the Third Republic, the office of the president of the republic was primarily championed by royalists. Despite the debacle of Napoleon III, the republicans were too weak to oppose it, and throughout much of the Third Republic the office was occupied by conservative politicians. This was facilitated by the fact that the president was indirectly elected—a tradition in France until 1962, when de Gaulle urged the popular election of the president to legitimize the powers of the office.

While the prime minister was the constitutional chief executive in both the Third and Fourth republics, a clever president could wield his ceremonial powers to substantial effects. Jules Grévy, a conservative republican during the nineteenth century, did much to stretch his influence beyond the intentions of those who opposed the Second Empire, which the Third Republic had replaced. The French president, much like the queen of England, was vested with responsibility for naming a prime minister, subject to the approval of the Parliament. Grévy carefully chose weak leaders who, in the absence of strict party discipline, could often find a (transitory) majority to support them as prime minister. As the president's ceremonial function included presiding over cabinet meetings, Grévy then used his powers of persuasion to influence—and occasionally dominate—the cabinet, including its premier.[8]

While the president had no power to overrule the prime minister, frequent votes of no confidence served the interest of the president. With his seven-year term unaffected, the president remained while premiers came and went. Not only did the president serve as the institutional memory of the executive, but a strong-willed president who had failed to convince the prime minister needed to wait only a few months and he could try again with the next premier.[9]

Moreover, even though executive power was concentrated in the prime minister's office, it often served the interests of Parliament and the cabinet to leave certain powers with the president. This was especially true of foreign affairs, where deputies saw little value to their constituencies in pursuing specific foreign policies and consequently were content to let the president retain power to negotiate treaties and control the armed forces.

THE FIFTH REPUBLIC

The constitution of the Fifth Republic was intended, of course, to be emphatically presidential, although not to the extent of the American Constitution, where a complete separation of powers was defined. The ambiguous role of the government (prime minister and cabinet) made the new French constitution a hybrid of parliamentary and presidential systems. Why de Gaulle and his supporters preferred the hybrid form is not clear, although in 1985, as France was about to venture into Cohabitation, Michel Debré argued that the original intent was that the locus of power would shift between premier and president, depending on the nature of the parliamentary majority.[10] This, of course, was self-serving, as Debré backed the Gaullists, who were about to take over the

prime ministry while the Socialists retained the presidency.

It may well have been that the Gaullists originally backed the hybrid system both to avoid the appearance of imitating the United States and to avoid the genuine possibility of continual stalemate to which a separation of powers system is always vulnerable.[11]

Formal Powers

The president does have important formal powers. He or she may dissolve the National Assembly and call new elections, presumably to achieve a friendly majority, but may only do so once a year (to avoid instability).

Perhaps most dramatic to Americans, Article 16 of the 1958 Constitution allows the president to become a kind of temporary dictator if "the institutions of the Republic, national independence, [or] territorial integrity are seriously and immediately threatened and the regular functioning of constitutional public power is disrupted." The only checks on these powers are that the president must consult with the prime minister and speakers of each house and with the *Constitutional Council* (see page 274 of this text). Parliament must remain in session during the exercise of emergency powers, but cannot legislate.

While Article 16 appears antidemocratic, in fact it was invoked only once, in April 1961, when there was a genuine fear that generals unhappy with de Gaulle's Algerian policy would attempt a coup d'état. After the danger passed, de Gaulle returned to normal constitutional processes. In 1993 President Mitterrand proposed the elimination of the powers outlined in Article 16. Since, however, he proposed this reform just before the 1993 legislative elections, it was quickly dismissed as a ploy to deflect voters' attention from the Socialists' economic policies. It is, however, an indication

The National Assembly

of how little the French public is disturbed by the dictatorial potential of Article 16 that Mitterrand's proposal could be so easily ignored.

Also among the formal powers of presidents is the power to appoint three of the nine members of the Constitutional Council—the highest court in France on constitutional matters. They may also pardon prisoners, traditionally done at the beginning of the seven-year term—a power Mitterrand used extensively when he first entered office.

Significantly, the president does not have the power to veto laws passed by the Parliament.

Informal Powers

Among the president's informal powers is that which is conferred by the prestige of the office. The president is the only official elected by the nation at large, and this gives their demands great legitimacy. If the president is also charis-matic, like de Gaulle, or a clever politician, like Mitterrand, he can use this legitimacy to manipulate the other parts of government. In addition, the president has patronage powers, which allow control of the bureaucracy in much the same way that the United States' "spoils system" influences the American executive branch.[12]

The president, as in the parliamentary republics, presides over cabinet meetings (the cabinet is still called the *conseil des ministres*). For reasons of efficiency, decision making rarely occurs in the whole cabinet. Rather, just as in Britain and Germany, decisions are made in cabinet committees (*conseils restreints*), where only the ministers affected by a specific policy issue are admitted to the discussion. This division of labor served to keep the Communist ministers from joining in defense or foreign policy discussions during their participation in the government of the Left from 1981 to 1984. Presidents may chair, if they so desire, all *conseils restreints,* and also set the agenda of cabinet meetings.

Cohabitation

As we noted earlier, the hybrid nature of the 1958 Constitution means that the executive shares most of its powers with the Parliament. Essentially, this is because of the ambiguous position of the government. In that it is appointed by the president, but can be fired by the National Assembly, the government must be acceptable to both branches. Until 1986 the potential problems of this arrangement remained hypothetical, since presidents had always enjoyed friendly majorities in the Parliament. Party discipline assured that the National Assembly would accept whomever the president nominated to the government. In 1986, however, a conservative alliance (Rally for the Republic and the Union for French Democracy) won a narrow majority in the National Assembly. As parliamentary and presidential terms do not coincide (they are five years and seven years, respectively), this meant that a conservative National Assembly had to come to terms with a Socialist president.

While the president had the option of calling new elections, the political climate would simply have assured the re-election of the same conservative alliance, a return to a stalemate situation, and a severe loss of prestige (and therefore power) for the president.[13] Mitterrand chose to let the election stand.

This situation forced the Socialist president to name a conservative prime minister and cabinet, for no other would survive a motion of censure in the National Assembly. The problem then became: who would set national policies, the president or the prime minister? The constitution is not explicit on this point, nor was precedent helpful. The last time a serious divergence between president and prime minister took place was when Jacques

Chirac, Giscard's first prime minister (1974–1976), tried to eclipse the president. Giscard simply fired him. Though they were from different parties, both were of the conservative coalition, and the conservative deputies simply accepted the president's preeminence. Giscard's Union for French Democracy accepted the action because the president was head of the party, and the Gaullists accepted the firing of Chirac in deference to the principle of presidential government.[14]

What made the Cohabitation—as the uneasy Socialist-conservative coexistence was called—work was the decision by Mitterrand not to oppose the implementation of the conservative program. That program consisted mainly of denationalizing the companies taken over by the Socialists in 1982 (see Chapter 11). While Mitterrand announced his decision to accede to the "will of the people," more than likely it was based on a quite accurate calculation that the conservatives would fail to solve France's economic problems and thus would bear the brunt of public dissatisfaction in the 1988 presidential election. This established a precedent for the second period of Cohabitation after the election of 1993.

Moreover, there had been a convergence of Socialist and conservative policies since 1981. The Socialists, who had started deregulating the French economy after 1982, began to have their doubts about nationalizations when the overall economy failed to improve with the newly profitable nationalized companies.[15] The conservatives, for their part, were unwilling to abandon the welfare state (see Chapter 11). There were almost no differences on foreign policy. Thus, Cohabitation took on an air of American politics when the president and Congress are controlled by different parties: there were differences to be sure, but there were grounds for agreement on fundamentals.[16]

It was this agreement on fundamentals that made France's second experience with Cohabitation smoother than the first (see Chapter 11).

The conservative parties swept into the Parliament with a huge majority in the March 1993 election. Mitterrand then named Gaullist Edouard Balladur as prime minister, the candidate preferred by leadership of the new parliamentary majority. Balladur not only adopted an economic policy very similar to that of the previous Socialist government, but since he also seemed (at first) to harbor few aspirations for the presidency, his relationship with Mitterrand was quite cordial.

THE CONSTITUTIONAL COUNCIL

A brief word needs to be said about the role of courts at the national level. France, like the rest of continental Europe, has a civil law system based on Roman law. This means that jurists, unlike those in the Anglo-Saxon common law system, see themselves as interpreters rather than makers of law. In most cases there is no concept of judicial review as it exists in the United States. That is, most courts cannot rule on whether a law is unconstitutional. Usually, a court can only decide whether a law has been applied properly in a particular case.

The exception to this principle is found in the Constitutional Council. The Constitutional Council, which rules on constitutionality only *before* a law is promulgated, is an innovation of the Fifth Republic and is composed of three judges appointed by the president of each house of Parliament and three appointed by the president of the republic, totaling nine. Members enjoy nonrenewable terms of nine years. In addition, any living former president of the republic may also sit on the council. However, unlike the Supreme Court of the United States, there is no illusion in France that the council merely provides an objective interpretation of the constitution. Rather, recourse to the council is overtly political.[17]

During the first two decades of the Fifth Republic constitutional challenges were rare. Under Giscard d'Estaing, however, recourse to the council was made easier (sixty deputies or sixty senators could invoke the council) and the political opposition (the Left) began to use it to publicize their complaints (the conservative composition of the council made rulings in the Left's favor next to impossible). Use of the council became common after the Socialists achieved the majority in the National Assembly. Appeals by the Union and Rally for the Republic to the conservative council were used to block Socialist legislation. For instance, nationalization of major industries was blocked temporarily by objections to the mode of financing the government purchase (nationalizations are legal under the French constitution so long as they are adequately compensated).[18] The Socialists learned from this experience and began filling vacancies with their supporters as they arose.

LOCAL GOVERNMENT

The most significant statement to make about French local government is that until 1982 there was very little of it. As we mentioned in previous chapters, France has been highly centralized since the advent of the absolutist kings. While the kings centralized France to consolidate their power, even progressive reforms took the form of increased centralization. As we mentioned, Louis XVI abolished local courts to curb the corrupt practices of the provincial aristocracy. Napoleon created a highly centralized administration not only to consolidate his own power, but also to create a highly efficient instrument of public service.

Early on, of course, this highly centralized system had its detractors, most often in quarters advocating liberal reforms. Tocqueville, perhaps the best known of these when he wrote in *The Old Regime and the French Revolution*, said that it was the intense centralization of the monarchs that made them especially vulnerable to overthrow, for by seizing Paris one could easily seize the whole country. He was, of course, in favor of extending democracy rather than simply advocating a less vulnerable *status quo*. Most of the critics of centralization have essentially had the same democratic motives, but more recent critics, observing the fate of the even more extreme hypercentralization of the Soviet Union, have also argued that concentrating so much power in Paris is simply inefficient. Given the growing complaints about French centralization, what is perhaps a more interesting question is why there were no significant reforms until 1982, when the Socialists introduced new local powers in the *loi Deferre*.[19]

One reason for the maintenance of a highly centralized administration was ideological: as we mentioned in Chapters 12 and 13, centralization fit with the Jacobin notion of equality, assuring that citizens were subject to the same laws, no matter where in France they lived. This Jacobin ideology guided the thinking of the French Left, especially the Communists. On the Right, Bonapartists and later Gaullists saw a centralized administration as the best way to marshal the country's resources in the name of the nation and, eventually, as the best way to thwart subnational particularism such as the Breton or Corsican separatist movements. (The Spanish ultimately saw decentralization as a way to achieve the same purpose when they devolved powers on regional assemblies in the Basque and Catalan areas: half a loaf was better than none.)

Moreover, the centralized system functioned reasonably well. This was partly because of the virtues of centralized organization: economies of scale, coherent policymaking, gains from standardization, and so on. Although centralization might, on the face of it, lead to inappropriate policies because Paris ministries were ignorant of local conditions, in fact there was often a good deal of flexibility. Paris-appointed prefects would work with local officials, even if the latters' formal powers were weak.[20]

Nevertheless, by the 1970s, centralized administration had become quite unpopular. Elections could be won almost solely by promising more power to the localities. Some reforms did indeed take place, albeit in a piecemeal fashion. Under the *loi Frey* of 1972, metropolitan France was divided into twenty-one regions with elective regional councils (departments were considered to be too small to be viable economic units) with some taxing and spending powers; some other new units of government such as *communautés urbaines* or *syndicats à vocation multiple* ("urban communities" and "multipurpose associations") were also created.[21] Yet compared to American, German, or even Spanish local governments, the reform was paltry.

The major reform of France's local government had to wait until the entry of the Socialists into power. It appears that at least one main reason for the long delay in local government reform was partisan politics. An important analysis argues that any reform of local government during the Fifth Republic would have meant some power sharing with the political opposition. In this case, the conservatives, during their long period of hegemony, were reluctant to give significant powers to local governments that might be controlled by leftists, especially Communists.[22]

Understandably, the Left made decentralization part of their platform, although the Communists, for ideological reasons as well as a perceived weakness in electoral support, were less enthusiastic about the reform.

The reform came in the Deferre Law of 1982, with significant follow-up legislation in 1983 and 1984. The *loi Deferre*, followed by some twenty laws and two hundred decrees, increased the independent authority of the localities. Prior approval of local initiatives by the national government was no longer necessary, although Paris could disapprove actions *a posteriori*. The reform abolished the old prefect system (Paris-appointed departmental governors), and local executive power was transferred to the presidents of departments and to presidents of regional councils (representing several departments), both offices being elective. Working with local elected officials were local civil servants, independent of the national administration. The twenty-one regions, each composed of several *départements*, created by the *loi Frey*, were given significantly greater powers. However, as of the writing of this book, it was not obvious that local governments would have the financial resources to be truly effective.

CONCLUSION

Like all countries, France's formal political institutions have been constantly evolving. Most dramatically, France followed the worldwide trend toward strong executives by adopting the Constitution of 1958. Under the auspices of this document, the powers of Parliament were severely circumscribed. When the president has a friendly majority in the National Assembly, he enjoys constitutional powers greater than any other democratic executive. If, however, the majority in the lower house is opposed to the president, the precedent of Cohabitation suggests that power will revert to the prime minister.

If the hidden fragmentation in national government has become more apparent in recent years, power has become even more decentralized at the local level. Political forces finally coalesced in 1982 to grant significant powers to localities, yet the national scale of France's economic problems probably meant that serious policymaking options would still remain in Paris.

In fact, the overall direction of problem-solving has meant an international approach to macroeconomic policy. In this sense the European Union has offered French citizens a new range of possibilities in raising levels of prosperity, but administratively the European Union imposes a supranational level of constraints on the formulation and implementation of public policy.

NOTES

1. Cf. Suzanne Berger, *The French Political System* (New York: Random House, 1974), chap. 2; Pierre Avril, *Politics in France*, trans. John Ross, (Baltimore: Penguin, 1969), chap. 2.

2. I will occasionally use the term *premier* as synonymous with prime minister. The English word derives from the French *premier ministre*.

3. In this sense there were similarities between French and American party systems, both being what Duverger called "bourgeois" or nineteenth-century party systems. See Duverger, *Les Partis Politiques,* chap. 1.

4. The Communists originally joined the Socialists and Christian Democrats in the tripartite governments of 1946–1947, but entered quasi-permanent opposition after refusing to vote war credits for the French forces in Indochina. De Gaulle and his followers went into opposition with the adoption of a Parliament-centered constitution in 1946.

5. Michel Debré, *La Mort de l'État Republicain* (Paris: Gallimard, 1947), p. 35; quoted in Ezra N. Suleiman, *Politics, Power and Bureacracy* (Princeton University Press, 1974), p. 24.

6. Indeed, there is a cozy relationship between lobbies and committees in the United States. Along with relevant bureaucracies, these have been called "iron triangles."

7. Ministers of state are most senior. They always attend cabinet meetings. The others attend when invited.

8. Avril, *Politics in France,* chap. 4; Alfred Cobban, *A History of Modern France, Volume Three,* (Harmondsworth: Penguin, 1965), chap. 1.

9. Avril, *Politics in France,* chap. 4.

10. Interview with Debré, *Le Quotidien de Paris,* 11 June 1986.

11. For a contrast of presidential and parliamentary systems, see especially R. Kent Weaver and Bert

A. Rockman, eds., *Do Institutions Matter?* (Washington, D.C.: Brookings Institution, 1993).

12. Except, of course, that unlike America, French bureaucrats are guaranteed a job of equivalent status if they are ousted for political reasons. See Chapter 17.

13. In a similar situation in 1877, the royalist president MacMahon dissolved a republican assembly, only to have the republicans re-elected, leaving MacMahon deprived of prestige and influence. See Cobban, *A History of Modern France, Volume Three*, chap. 1.

14. On this episode, see Suleiman, "Presidential Government in France," in Suleiman and Rose, eds., *Presidents and Prime Ministers* (Washington, D.C.: American Enterprise Institute, 1980). For an extended discussion on the first period of Cohabitation, see Harvey B. Feigenbaum, "Recent Evolution of the French Executive," *Governance*, 3, (July 1990), pp. 264–278.

15. For an explanation of this failure of public enterprise, see Harvey B. Feigenbaum, *The Politics of Public Enterprise* (Princeton: Princeton University Press, 1985), chap. 6.

16. Many Socialists, however, did not share this convergence of views and, at least verbally, remained committed to a Marxist vision of social change. This was especially true of the CERES faction of the party.

17. Increasingly, scholars of the U.S. Supreme Court have recognized the intrinsic political nature of the body. See Martin Shapiro, "The Supreme Court: From Warren to Burger," in Anthony King, ed., *The New American Political System* (Washington, D.C.: American Enterprise Institute, 1978).

18. See John T. S. Keeler, "The French Constitutional Council," in Stanley Hoffmann and George Ross, eds., *The Mitterrand Experiment* (New York, 1987).

19. Cf. Peter A. Gourevitch, *Paris and the Provinces* (Berkeley and Los Angeles: University of California Press, 1980), *viz.* chap. 11.

20. Cf. Jean-Pierre Worms, "Le Préfet et ses notables," *Sociologie du Travail*, July–September, 1966; Mark Kesselman, "Over-Institutionalization and Political Constraint: The Case of France," *Comparative Politics*, 3, 1(1970).

21. See Gourevitch, *Paris*, pp. 226 ff.

22. Ibid., pp. 228 ff.

REFERENCES AND SUGGESTED READINGS

Ashford, Douglas E. 1982. *Policy and Politics in France: Living with Uncertainty.* Philadelphia: Temple University Press.

Feigenbaum, Harvey B. 1990. "Recent Evolution of the French Executive," *Governace*, 3, 3 (July).

Gourevitch, Peter A. 1980. *Paris and the Provinces.* Berkeley: University of California Press.

Kesselman, Mark. 1967. *The Politics of Uncertainty.* New York: Alfred A. Knopf.

Rose, Richard, and Ezra N. Suleiman, eds. 1980. *Presidents and Prime Ministers.* Washington: American Enterprise Institute.

Sbragia, Alberta M., ed. 1992. *Euro-Politics.* Washington, D.C.: Brookings Institution.

Schmidt, Vivien. 1990. *Democratizing France: The Political and Administrative History of Decentralization.* Cambridge: Cambridge University Press.

Tarrow, Sidney, Peter Katzenstein, and Luigi Graziano, eds. 1978. *Territorial Politics in Industrial Nations.* New York: Praeger.

Weaver, R. Kent, and Bert A. Rockman, eds. 1993. *Do Institutions Matter?* Washington, D.C.: Brookings Institution.

Williams, Philip M. 1968. *The French Parliament.* New York: Praeger (reprinted by Greenwood Press in 1977).

17

The State Apparatus

The economic uncertainties of recent years have engendered a lively and politically charged debate about whether the state's role in economic management should be increased or diminished. France's long history of state management of the economy has left the country both with a highly articulated apparatus for government intervention and with a convenient target upon which to pin blame for the poor economic performance of recent years. Although conservatives blame the state for the problems of the economy, many analysts have attributed France's meteoric postwar growth to a talented and highly trained bureaucracy. It is to that bureaucracy that we now turn.

THE BUREACRATIC STATE

All modern states have bureaucracies. Indeed, a well-developed bureaucracy is one of the principal characteristics that distinguishes modern polities from those that are termed "traditional." Only if power flows from an office rather than a person can one be assured that a political regime will outlast its founders. Moreover, governments develop bureaus and agencies to handle specialized problems.[1] Similarly, routines and standard operating procedures are developed by bureaucracies in the name of efficiency; such procedures arise because certain public problems recur frequently, and routine solutions free officials from having to reinvent the wheel each time a problem comes up. Of course, routinized behavior by bureaucracies often inhibits solving new problems if unimaginative officeholders refuse to depart from routines.[2]

The French bureaucracy has often been held up as a model of the positive role a state can play.[3] Within the country the bureaucracy enjoys high prestige. Public service has traditionally attracted the best and brightest of French society. Not only was the French bureaucracy the principal instrument of Napoleon, but the chronic instability of republican governments often left the bureaucracy as the main locus of state power, for it was unaffected by continually collapsing coalitions, and often exercised power by default.

THE ROOTS OF STATE POWER

Like almost every other aspect of French political organization, the roots of the bureaucracy's power can be traced to the lateness of industrialization, although some vestiges of that authority derive from earlier historical traditions. Briefly, economic conditions necessitated a strong state if France was to develop, and preexisting administrative structures facilitated the arrival of such a state.[4]

As noted earlier, even before the Revolution, France had a history of state involvement in the economy. Jean Baptiste Colbert (1619–1683), Louis XIV's minister of finance, did much to initiate the development of infrastructures (roads, ports, and canals, etc.). The highly centralized administration established by the absolutist kings facilitated the involvement of royal government in shaping the economy. But government involvement in the eighteenth century was common in all European countries. In fact, Adam Smith's famous *Wealth of Nations,* published in 1776, was originally written to persuade public officials and the educated classes of the day to abandon this common practice of mercantilism. Another factor besides a tradition of government economic intervention is necessary to explain the development of a power French bureaucracy.

Lateness of industrialization is one of the most significant factors explaining the power of the French bureaucracy. Briefly, the argument, based on the writings of the economic historian Alexander Gerschenkron, goes like this: by the time France industrialized, Great Britain, its principal competitor, had not only developed an industrial base in textiles, but had proceeded to develop significant, capital-intensive industries such as steel and railroads. If France were to catch up, it would need to amass huge amounts of capital. Given the predominance of agriculture and small-scale business, powerful, centralizing institutions would be necessary to collect highly dispersed savings from a conservative peasantry and middle class. Only the French state could fulfill this function.

Political culture reinforced this tendency. The absence of entrepreneurs meant that there would be little competition for the state as an economic actor. Indeed, most French business people feared competition among themselves as well, and they were all too happy to have the state regulate their respective markets. Moreover, the high prestige of public service facilitated public acceptance of state economic intervention and also served to attract the highest caliber of France's human potential to the state's task.

For all of these reasons, the role of the state grew substantially over the course of the nineteenth and twentieth centuries. However, the timing-of-industrialization argument does not explain why the bureaucracy grew at the expense of other state institutions like the Parliament. Part of the reason is cultural: the cleavages in French society, reflected in the party system, led to highly unstable parliamentary government. Thus if the tasks of the state were to be fulfilled, the bureaucracy was in a better position to do the job. Conversely, survival in Parliament led deputies to develop very different skills from those necessary to manage an economy. Avoiding decisions and providing services to specific constituencies were more important to the deputy, while the bureaucrats' promotions depended primarily on the efficient performance of assigned tasks. Consequently, to the extent that the economy developed (and many argue that true development did not take off until the mid-twentieth century), it tended to parallel the development of the bureaucracy.

THE RELATION OF STATE TO SOCIETY

The French bureaucracy has also played a robust role in French society because of its capacity to assist social mobility. Different strata of French society have been aided by the employment opportunities offered by the state. In many ways the upper ranks of the public service became the new aristocracy. While service in the military had been a traditional avenue for the gentry, the power of the bureaucracy in France attracted former aristocrats and the upper levels of the bourgeoisie to state service. The French of more modest origins could find employment in the lower ranks of the public sector (as letter carriers, railroad workers, teachers), and the sons and (eventually) daughters of peasants could rise in status by climbing the ladder of civil service promotions.[5]

While the different divisions of the bureaucracy were, in fact, almost as stratified as the society it reflected, the state preserved its image as a meritocracy, which in turn facilitated its acceptance by all strata. The principal mechanism for maintaining this image was and is the competitive examination. That is, entry to state jobs is determined by performance on competitive examinations that are open to all French citizens. Thus bureaucrats are presumed to hold their offices on the basis of merit.[6]

In fact, recruitment by competitive examination is so embedded in French culture that it sometimes reaches manic proportions. An advertisement from the *Journal Officiel*, the official journal of the French Parliament, illustrates the extent of the phenomenon vividly: "Authorized in three months following publication of the present notice, a competition for the recruitment of two cabinetmakers for the national establishment at Sèvres."[7]

THE CIVIL SERVICE AND THE *GRANDES ÉCOLES*

The reality of civil service recruitment is of course rather different from the myth, although, to be fair, the caliber of French functionaries is indeed quite high.[8]

Before World War II most senior civil servants were recruited from the *École Libre de Science Politique*. This was a private college in Paris where only people who were able to pay the tuition, as well as pass the entrance exams, could enter. The school was nationalized after the war, and a new *École Nationale d'Administration* was created with the intent of democratizing recruitment to the civil service as well as improving the training of the state's senior staff.

Students were required to pass rigorous examinations in order to enter ENA (successful graduates are called "*Énarques*," while the influence of these graduates on the whole of the public sector has facetiously been dubbed "*Énarchie*," playing on the French word for anarchy). As an additional aid to economically deprived candidates who might otherwise not be able to afford graduate study, students at the École Nationale d'Administration are paid a salary. In a parallel fashion, the best technically trained civil servants attend the *École Polytechnique*, France's premier engineering school (founded by Napoleon), and are paid a military salary.

The École Nationale d'Administration and the École Polytechnique, as well as a few other elite graduate schools, are known as *Grandes Écoles* ("great schools"). The prestige and competitiveness of these schools, if not the actual quality of instruction,[9] are far greater than in the regular university system (for example, the Sorbonne) and attendance is *de rigueur* if one is to ascend the ranks of the French elite.

The problem is that while the entrance examinations are theoretically open to all French citizens, it is extremely rare for students from poorer economic backgrounds to do well. This is partially the case because ENA demands essay exams, which tend to favor students whose families are well educated, where flowery French is well understood, and where self-confidence is a subtle product of class origin. Self-confidence is especially important, since prospective ENA students must pass a public oral exam in front of a jury of distinguished senior civil servants. Questioning is meant to prove the candidates' potential to think on their feet, but in fact, self-conscious working-class candidates rarely feel sufficiently comfortable to do as well as upper-class candidates. An example illustrates the panache needed: a jury member pulls out his pocket watch and says to the candidate, "Prove to me, Sir, that this watch exists."

Without losing a beat, the self-confident candidate sweeps up the watch, pockets it, and replies to the startled examiner, "*You* prove to *me* that your watch exists."

Economically less fortunate students who do make it to the Grandes Écoles tend to opt for the scientific track, in universities, where use of language and cultural comportment are less important.

Moreover, the reality of the examination process for both administrators and engineers requires previous attendance at the country's best secondary schools in order to prepare adequately for the ordeal. In the case of ENA, attendance at the country's competitive *Institut*

d'Études Politiques (the new name for the École Libre des Science Politiques), or less preferably, at one of the provincial political science institutes, is also required. Since most of the country's best *lycées* (academic high schools) and its most prestigious political science institute are in Paris, Parisians have an edge.[10] Provincial families wishing to send their children to Parisian schools must be able to afford to do so. This further biases the recruitment process in favor of the economically privileged.

DIVISIONS WITHIN THE BUREAUCRATIC STATE

The *Grands Corps*

The most prestigious of the positions in the French civil service are held by members of the *Grands Corps*.[11] These are self-governing groups of civil servants organized along functional lines. Examples are the Diplomatic Corps, the Financial Inspectorate, Mining Engineers, and Civil Engineers. While there are hundreds of corps, entry into the most prestigious of them is limited to the top graduates of the Grandes Écoles. Social links between corps members are not unlike the "old school ties" in Britain or the United States, but are rather more formalized.

Originally, the corps were established to accomplish specific governmental functions, as their titles suggest. Indeed, corps members do start their careers doing exactly the kind of government service that the title of the corps indicates: administering mines, inspecting finances, and the like. However, these elite functionaries rarely do such tasks for very long. Usually they are lent to ministerial cabinets (advisers to government ministers), they move into the directorates of public enterprises, or they leave government service altogether and move to princely salaries in the private sector. The French call this move into private business jobs *pantouflage*, or "putting on the soft slippers." The terminology alone suggests the French image of private sector versus public sector work.

Such interesting and, occasionally, lucrative alternatives to the boredom of routine administration not only attract France's best and brightest, but often lead to competition among the corps to capture the best jobs for their members. Different sectors of the French economy have been staked out by diverse corps. The result is that corps members still in the bureaucracy often advocate policies that are good for their respective corps, and the industries they dominate, rather than for the nation as a whole.[12]

Administrative Conflicts

While the existence of the *grands corps* makes the French bureaucracy rather unusual, other aspects of bureaucratic behavior found in France are common in other industrial countries. Conflicts among different departments and agencies over responsibilities and funding are evident in France, just as they are elsewhere.[13]

The most frequent conflicts within the French administration tend to arise over budgets. Each agency has a view of its own role and often requests additional funding to fulfill that role. This may involve creating new projects, hiring new people, raising salaries, or any of myriad ways to spend money. Usually this means coming into conflict with France's most powerful ministry, the Ministry of Finance. In times of contractionary budgets, when departments are expected to reduce expenses, conflicts, of course, become exacerbated.

Clientelism

Battles over policy often involve different agencies championing different alternatives to solve a particular problem. Sometimes this may simply be because of genuine differences of opin-ion about the best way to solve a problem. However, it is frequently the case that bureaucrats have ulterior motives. The most common such motive is protection of a client group in the private sector. The Ministry of Agriculture tends to champion the needs of farmers, the Energy Directorate defends the interests of oil companies, and so on.

The tendency toward clientelism is partially explained by the career patterns of French bureaucrats. Normally, they view their tenure in the bureaucracy as only the first stage in their career. They then hope to find jobs in the private sector, usually in an industry in which they have regulatory experience. Civil servants thus constantly have their ears to the ground waiting for opportunities to move into the industries they are regulating. They are not likely to want to alienate a prospective employer, and so they tend to favor policies that are in the best interest of their "clients."

Such clientelism is not specifically French. Similar situations arise in countries as diverse as America and Japan. In Japan, in fact, *pantouflage* is called *amakudari* or "descent from heaven."[14] Some groups have been especially adept at influencing the public sector. The notaries, a group in France that serves almost no useful function, have managed to survive by adroitly manipulating bureaucrats.[15]

Venality and manipulation, however, are not the only reasons for the close relationship between public and private elites. Bureaucrats also depend on the private sector for information and expertise. While graduates of the Grandes Écoles receive some technical training, schooling is short and bureaucrats are often less technically expert than their counterparts in the private sector. Thus, civil servants tend to rely on business executives for advice and gradually accept their point of view.[16] Moreover, the French bureaucracy very rarely has sources of statistics and information other than those provided by the industry being regulated. They are thus vulnerable to misinformation and manipulation.

Finally, clientelism is abetted by rivalries among the *Grands Corps.* Civil servants tend to advocate policies on the basis of the needs of an economic sector that a corps has "colonized." For example, through the mechanism of *pantouflage* the corps of mining engineers "colonized" the oil industry. Senior members of the corps now in the private sector subtly pressured junior members still in government service to support policies that would help the oil industry or, at the very least, create jobs for corps members in that sector.[17]

Influence of Political Parties

While various forms of administrative rivalries have divided the bureaucracy for a very long time, direct political influence of the administration has been dramatically transformed since the advent of the Fifth Republic. Specifically, what has changed is the way in which political parties have meshed with the administration.

Like all modern bureaucracies, the French administration is nominally independent of the government of the day. Career civil servants have guaranteed tenure of office; they are allowed to express their political opinions freely, although judiciously,[18] and may even run for office without losing their jobs. Under the Third and Fourth republics, however, the top posts in the bureaucracy were allotted according to political affiliation, a system not unlike that in Italy today. Different parties were accorded specific ministries despite changes in parliamentary coalitions. The Foreign Ministry, for example, was almost always headed by a member of the Christian Democratic Party (MRP), while the Division of Public Health was always left in the hands of the Radicals or Socialists.

All of this changed under the Fifth Republic. The reason was the novel situation of a majority party and the increased power of the executive. The condition of a strong, party-oriented executive made its mark on the bureaucracy,

the chief instrument of the executive. De Gaulle and his successors drew heavily on technically trained bureaucrats ("technocrats") to populate their cabinets. Technocrats learned that the key to influence was the proper party connections, and by the 1960s only members of the ruling majority found a ready ear in the bureaucracy.[19]

All of this changed again in 1981 when the Socialists came to power. Mitterrand dismissed more than four hundred department heads and replaced them with more sympathetic civil servants. Under French law, however, the dismissed bureaucrats could not be fired, and equivalent posts had to be found for them; at the very least, they retained their salaries. The result was an expensive experiment in something resembling the U.S. "spoils system." Ultimately, however, little changed. Dependence on the *Grands Corps* and the social biases in recruitment patterns produced a network of "socialist" bureaucrats that did not differ very much from the previous "conservative" ones.[20] Similar changes occurred after the conservatives came to power in the legislative elections of 1986 and 1993.

Two additional changes occurred after the conservatives came to power in 1986. In keeping with their (new) philosophy of "shrinking the state," the conservatives instituted reforms in the National School of Administration that effectively reduced the number of new students by about half. Although this did reduce the number of new high-flying bureaucrats, it effectively made the positions even more elite. Not only does reducing the supply of any item increase its value (even civil servants!), but the conservatives eliminated the possibility of a student's entering ENA after working in local government or the trade union movement, reforms that had been initiated by the Socialists to help "democratize" the administration school.

The second reform earned the enmity of the entire *Grands Corps:* the National School of Administration was moved to Strasbourg, ostensibly to be closer to the institutions of the European Union (the European Parliament is located in that lovely, albeit provinicial, Alsacian city). There are few tasks more thankless than encouraging the decentralization of the French administration (see Chapter 16).

CONCLUSION

Bureaucracies are necessary to rationalize authority and to depersonalize power. This insures the existence of a regime beyond the lifetimes of the people who found it. The French bureaucracy—for reasons of precedent, economic history, and political necessity—has been a strong and relatively independent force. While it has been the vehicle for some social mobility, recruitment patterns for the most powerful positions have tended to be biased in favor of those from the privileged segments of French society. Career patterns of bureaucrats also influence the bureaucracy in the direction of sectors that can offer the most in *pantouflage*. Finally, although the bureaucracy is powerful, it is limited by its own disunity, as divisions arising from administrative, clientelistic, and corps rivalries serve as an internal check on the power of the state.

Much of the thrust of our propositions in Chapter 2 have been to examine the decline in the legitimacy of the state. In this sense the French state has had further to fall than its counterparts in most of the other longtime capitalist countries. Thus it should not be a surprise that while the French state does not quite have the cachet of earlier days, it still enjoys the respect of most people in France. Nevertheless, even the French state has fallen in stature, while training of its *crème de la crème* has suffered the indignity of being shipped to the provinces.

Still and all, no one expects the National School of Administration to remain in Strasbourg for very long. Most observers deem it only a matter of time before the world's most prestigious school of public administration will find its way back to the City of Light. It is more than likely that a dynamic role for the French state will return as well.

NOTES

1. For the classic literature on bureaucracy, see Max Weber, *The Theory of Social and Economic Organization,* Talcott Parsons, ed. (New York: Free Press, 1964); *From Max Weber: Essays in Sociology,* H. H. Gerth and C. Wright Mills, eds. (New York: Oxford University Press, 1946), chap. VIII. On the division of labor, see Adam Smith, *Wealth of Nations.*

2. This fidelity to standard operating procedures was one of the chief sources of criticism in Graham Allison's famous study of the Cuban missile crisis. See his *Essence of Decision* (Boston: Little, Brown, 1971).

3. For example, John Zysman, *Political Strategies for Industrial Order* (Berkeley and Los Angeles: University of California Press, 1977).

4. On lateness of development see Alexander Gerschenkron, "Economic Backwardness in Historical Perspective" in his collection of essays by the same name (New York: Harvard University Press, 1962). On preexisting structures see Alexis de Tocqueville, *The Old Regime and the French Revolution,* trans. Stuart Gilbert (Garden City, N.Y., 1955), Combining these two analyses, see Peter A. Gourevitch, "The Second Image Reversed," *International Organization,* 32, 4 (Autumn 1978).

5. On the traditional role of aristocrats, see Stendhal, *Le Rouge et le Noir*; on the bourgeoisie and the bureaucracy, see Ezra N. Suleiman, *Politics, Power and Bureaucracy in France* (Princeton: Princeton University Press, 1974); oil, peasants, and teachers, see Eugen Weber, *Peasants into Frenchmen* (Stanford: Stanford University Press, 1977).

6. The reality, of course, is different. Candidates from more privileged backgrounds do better on entrance exams. See page 223 of this text.

7. Quoted in Pierre Avril, *Politics in France,* trans. John Ross (Baltimore: Penguin, 1969), p. 201.

8. For the best treatment of the French bureaucracy and the role of the *Grandes Écoles,* see Ezra N. Suleiman, *Politics, Power, and Bureaucracy in France* and his *Elites in French Society* (Princeton: Princeton University Press, 1978).

9. See Suleiman, "The Myth of Technical Expertise," *Comparative Politics,* 10, 1 (October 1977).

10. There are, of course, some excellent *lycées* in the large provincial cities, but even this avenue to social mobility is difficult for the inhabitants of small towns and villages.

11. See Suleiman, *Politics, Power and Bureaucracy in France* and *Elites in French Society*; see also Jean Claude Thoenig, *Ére des Technocrates: Le Cas des Ponts et Chaussées* (Paris: Éditions d'Organisation, 1973); and Harvey B. Feigenbaum, *The Politics of Public Enterprise* (Princeton: Princeton University Press, 1985), chap. IV. Most of the discussion below draws heavily on Suleiman and Feigenbaum.

12. See especially Feigenbaum, chap. IV.

13. The classic study of U.S. bureaucratic conflict is Allison's *Essence of Decision.* The evidence for French bureaucratic battles is drawn from Feigenbaum.

14. We are grateful to Dr. Martha Caldwell Harris for pointing this out.

15. Ezra N. Suleiman, *Les Notaires: Les Pouvoirs d'une Corporation,* trans. Martine Meusy (Paris: Editions du Seuil, 1987). The English version of Suleiman's book is *Private Power and Centraliza-tion in France* (Princeton: Princeton University Press, 1987).

16. See Feigenbaum, chap. IV.

17. Feigenbaum, chap. IV.

18. Civil servants are expected to refrain from criticizing policies that they must implement.

19. See Suleiman, *Politics, Power and Bureaucracy in France,* chap. XIII.

20. See Feigenbaum, chap. VI.

REFERENCES AND SUGGESTED READINGS

Aberbach, Joel, Robert Putnam, and Bert Rockman. 1981. *Bureaucrats and Politicians in Western Democracies.* Cambridge, Mass.: Harvard University Press.

Bottimore, T. B. 1964. *Elites and Society.* Harmondsworth: Penguin.

Crozier, Michel. 1964. *The Bureaucratic Phenomenon.* Chicago: University of Chicago Press.

Feigenbaum, Harvey B. 1985. *The Politics of Public Enterprise.* Princeton: Princeton University Press.

Keohane, Nanerl O. 1980. *Philosophy and the State in Modern France.* Princeton: Princeton University Press.

Suleiman, Ezra N. 1974. *Politics, Power and Bureaucracy in France.* Princeton: Princeton University Press.

———. 1978. *Elites in French Society.* Princeton: Princeton University Press.

18

Policy: Foreign and Domestic

erhaps what makes France so interesting are the contrasts it provides with both the United States and the other countries of Western Europe. These contrasts are evident in both foreign and domestic policies. France, more than any other country in Western Europe, has pursued a foreign policy aimed at maximizing independence from the other powers, while seeking a position of prominence in Europe and the Third World. In domestic economic policy, the French state has played an equally distinctive role, a role more pronounced than in any other capitalist country save Japan.

FRENCH FOREIGN POLICY

French foreign policy, especially during the Fifth Republic, has been more consistent than that of most countries, and even the Socialists, who had little else in common with de Gaulle, shared many of his foreign policy concerns.[1] Essentially, these are themes that emphasize French "greatness" and French "exceptionalism."

Influence of Geography and History

The geography of France, unlike that of Germany, provided certain defensible frontiers so that security, while always significant, never quite dominated the domestic politics of the country.[2] It was neither as isolated as Britain nor as vulnerable as Germany. Consequently, the importance of the army was greater than in the former and less than in the latter.

The heritage of the wars of the Middle Ages left France a tradition of rivalry with Britain that ultimately translated into a quest for global empire.[3] After the Franco-Prussian War (1870–1871) rivalry with Germany dominated French security concerns. Always there would be the crosscurrents of a European or a world vocation. Sometimes oriented toward Europe, sometimes oriented to the world at large, French foreign policy would find its ultimate expression in the vision of Charles de Gaulle.

Gaullist Foreign Policy

The defeat of France in World War II was a shock. Until 1940 France had been considered the greatest military power on the European continent. No one expected the rapid collapse of French defenses in the face of the German onslaught in the spring of 1940.

When the Allies finally won, the position of de Gaulle's government as coequal victor was, in fact, more of a fiction than a reality. However, it became de Gaulle's aim, throughout his period of leadership, to restore France's great power status. To do so required the achievement of three interrelated goals. De Gaulle had to solve the crisis of decolonization, establish France's independence from the superpowers, and restore the primacy of Europe.

Certainly the most traumatic foreign policy problem at the beginning of the Fifth Republic was that of decolonization (although some

French people would argue this was a *domestic* problem!). In the latter part of the nineteenth century, France established an empire in Africa for economic reasons, as well as to capture additional manpower and raw material resources in the event of another war with Germany.[4] France's rivalry with the other major powers led it to establish colonies (and "protectorates") in the far-flung areas of what is now referred to as the Third World. France's most important colonies were in Indochina (Laos, Cambodia, and Vietnam) and Africa (especially Algeria). France also exercised "trusteeships" in the Levant (Syria and Lebanon).

The victory of the democracies in 1945 made it very hard for them to deny democracy to the populations "of color" in the empire. Nevertheless, among the earliest acts of the French government after the war was the reassertion of the French presence on the periphery. Against American wishes, de Gaulle moved to re-establish French rule in Indochina, which had been occupied by Japan during World War II, as he headed the provisional government preceding the Fourth Republic (1944–1946). Almost at the very beginning of the postwar period, Vietnamese nationalists fought against the re-establishment of colonial rule as they had fought against the Japanese occupation during the war.

As the Cold War intensified, the communist ideology of the Vietnamese nationalists influenced the Americans to underwrite the French effort to re-establish their colony. A series of military defeats culminating in the rout of French troops at Dien Bien Phu led the Fourth Republic to give up, and the Chamber of Deputies voted plenipotentiary powers to Prime Minister Pierre Mendès-France to negotiate French withdrawal in 1954.[5]

Almost at the same time as France was leaving Indochina, the Arab population in Algeria began to stir against the inequities of French rule in North Africa. Algeria had formally been divided into three French *départements,* with the French government maintaining that Algeria was as much a part of France as was Provence. While it was true that Algeria, unlike the protectorates of Tunisia and Morocco, had never been an independent country in the European sense, it was equally true that Arabs did not enjoy even legal equality with Algerians of European extraction during French rule. Even under the relatively progressive constitution of the Fourth Republic, Arabs were dubbed French "subjects," while Algerians of European ancestry enjoyed the status of "citizens," a legally superior status.[6] The reality of Algeria was that of a privileged European minority and a deprived Arab majority.

The uprising of Arabs in Algeria grew into a protracted and bloody struggle. The insurgents used terrorist techniques to frighten the Europeans into leaving, while the French army replied with increased repression and, eventually, torture. Not only was the war a drain on French resources, but it also rent the social fabric of the nation. By 1958 the problem seemed intractable to the deputies of the Parliament. Political demonstrations grew more frequent and increasingly violent. Division over what to do about Algeria tore at the French polity like nothing since the Commune or perhaps even the Revolution.[7] As we have recounted in previous chapters, the ultimate impact was the demise of the Fourth Republic and the return of Charles de Gaulle.

De Gaulle saw the handwriting on the wall. He soothed rioting Europeans in Algeria with an enigmatic *"Je vous ai compris"* ("I have understood you") and promptly set the machinery in motion to extricate France from North Africa. In the resort town of Évian, the new French president granted Algeria independence while assuring France privileged economic relations with the new country.[8] While the Évian accords were signed in 1962, they in fact reaffirmed a set of relationships that France had already established with the majority of its ex-

colonies. Morocco and Tunisia had gained their independence in 1956, most of black Africa in 1960, and virtually all, with the exception of Guinea, maintained cordial—and economically privileged—relationships with France. Later, critics would call these relationships, which were quite beneficial to the former mother country, "neocolonialism."

Re-establishing French Independence

If de Gaulle had, once again, extricated France from difficult external circumstances while maintaining fundamentally democratic institutions, he is most remembered by Americans for his conflictive approach to the United States.

De Gaulle's conflicts with the United States went back to the Second World War. First, the United States did not take his London-based government in exile very seriously. When the Roosevelt administration did finally distance itself from Vichy, the Americans sought to promote another general as head of the Free French.

It was de Gaulle's return to power in 1958 that created the most friction, however. His vision of France's international role simply did not complement American foreign policy. Most difficult for Washington was de Gaulle's decision to withdraw France from the integrated command structure of the North Atlantic Treaty Organization in 1966. This did not mean that France withdrew from the Alliance, for de Gaulle maintained French commitment to defend its allies; but he refused to put French troops under the command of a foreign, that is, American, general, as the integrated military structure of NATO required.[9]

De Gaulle saw France as occupying the important role of mediator of East-West conflict. He pursued a rapprochement with the Soviet Union, despite his own fierce anticommunism, and directed France to become the first western country to recognize the People's Republic of China. For de Gaulle, these established French independence, but in an atmosphere emotionally charged with Cold War Manichaeism, Americans saw de Gaulle's conservative *Realpolitik* as immoral neutralism. Ultimately, however, France's independence served American interests, as France provided the diplomatic good offices that allowed the United States finally to withdraw from Vietnam.

Europe

Central to the Gaullist vision of an independent France was the reestablishment of Europe as a focus of world politics. While de Gaulle spoke of Europe "from the Atlantic to the Urals," in fact, the reestablishment of Europe meant the European Community (now called the European Union). While de Gaulle had no interest in a supranational organization of any sort, he saw the Common Market as the first step in the reconstruction of Europe as an independent force in international affairs. The Community would be centered in France and Germany, the continent's two most powerful countries. Moreover, de Gaulle firmly rejected Britain as a member of Europe, not so much because of its historic empire, but because of its special relationship with the United States.[10]

De Gaulle promoted the European Community largely because he felt that economic integration would not affect political independence. After 1966, the Treaty of Rome required that the Council of ministers decide issues on the basis of majority voting, rather than unanimity. For de Gaulle, this compromised France's sovereignty so much that he simply refused to accept this elimination of French veto power. Majority voting meant France might have to obey a Community decision that it had opposed, and this was unacceptable to the French president (the Treaty of Rome had, of course, been signed under the

Fourth Republic in 1957). The other members of the Community gave in, and each country retained a veto.

French Foreign Policy after de Gaulle

There are two major reasons why it has been useful to examine foreign policy under de Gaulle. First, it illustrates the importance of the president. Under the Constitution of 1958, foreign policy could, indeed, be made by one person. With party discipline in a National Assembly occupied by the president's party (and eventually by a pro-de Gaulle coalition), one need only examine the president's ideas to describe foreign policy. (Of course, it should be added that Gaullism was also favorable to the most powerful interest groups in the society, but we will return to this issue later in the chapter.) Second, it is worth going into Gaullist foreign policy because little has changed since the general left power in 1969.

De Gaulle's two conservative successors took less interest in foreign policy. Pompidou, president from 1969 until his death in 1974, was more interested in domestic politics, and devoted his efforts to building up a solid party apparatus and developing links to the local level where Gaullism had been weak. He did manage to continue irking the United States by redeeming U.S. dollars into gold, weakening the American currency and—for this was the point—weakening U.S. hegemony in monetary affairs.

Giscard d'Estaing, president from 1974 to 1981, was the first non-Gaullist president, although he had served as de Gaulle's minister of finance by virtue of his economic expertise. Giscard was more willing to pursue a rapprochement with the United States. Because his term of office coincided with the oil crises of 1974 and 1979, he was faced with tremendous disruptions in the world economy. This put a premium on cooperation with the other industrialized countries, and some agreements were worked out. However, France refused to join the International Energy Agency, an organization of industrialized oil-consuming countries that was paradoxically based in Paris. The agency was viewed by Giscard as potentially disruptive of France's warm relations with Arab states, and this refusal was strongly reminiscent of General de Gaulle.

The situation changed somewhat with the accession of François Mitterrand to the presidency. Mitterrand's own fierce anticommunism, as well as his intent to isolate the French Communist Party, brought anti-Sovietism back to a premier place on the foreign policy agenda. This gave France the appearance of being the warmest supporter of the policies of U.S. president Ronald Reagan's administration, a government with which it otherwise shared no common ground. Eventually, this anti-Soviet rhetoric also facilitated cohabitation, for the conservatives in Parliament after 1986 had little reason to challenge Mitterrand in foreign policy.

If the Socialists differed at all from their predecessors, it was in their policies toward the Third World. The Socialists were willing to make economic sacrifices to benefit less-developed countries. For example, they signed a very generous contract for Algerian natural gas at prices far in excess of the world market price. Socialists frequently supported Third World demands in international meetings for a "New International Economic Order." However, as the French economy continued to stagnate, there was little even a socialist France could do for its neighbors to the south.

AFTER THE COLD WAR

The end of the Cold War affected French foreign policy in important ways. First, with the collapse of the Soviet Union, France's strategic position as diplomatically independent of the superpowers lost its importance. However, the powerful military that France had nurtured to assure its independence made the country an even more important player in the conflicts that were to come. During the Persian Gulf War of 1991, French air power was an important element in the Allied invasion of Iraq. As the "new world order" gradually took shape, French forces played a key role in the interventionist actions of the United Nations. They contributed to the relief of Somalia and helped assure the peacefulness in the elections of Cambodia. Closer to home, they were perhaps most visible in assuring humanitarian assistance to Bosnia, where Mitterrand made a daring visit in 1992 and where French General Morillon commanded United Nations peacekeeping forces.

French policy with regard to the European Union grew more complex after 1992. President Mitterrand took an active role in promoting the Treaty of Maastricht, which aimed Europe toward greater unity, and especially toward a common currency. Here public support was more problematic. In the referendum on ratification of the treaty, the pro-Maastricht side won by the thinnest of margins. The conservatives, who took power in 1993, were deeply divided on the issue, with many fearing that the treaty would transfer too much of France's sovereignty to Brussels. Nevertheless, given the economic conditions of the time, it was increasingly difficult to implement the treaty, no matter how strong its domestic support might have been. The long, intense recession divided the interests of Union members. Germany, fearing inflation from its incorporation of the former German Democratic Republic, fought to keep interest rates high. France, and most of the other countries in the Union, preferred low interest rates so as to stimulate economic activity and job creation. The effect was to tear assunder the European Exchange Rate Mechanism, a device intended to help coordinate monetary policy and lead the way to a single currency. As of the writing of this textbook, plans to continue the unification of Europe were put on hold. Nothing appears truer than the *fourth proposition* of Chapter 2, which predicts that the path to greater European integration will become increasingly precarious.

DOMESTIC POLICY: THE MACROECONOMY

The dislocations in the world economy that became increasingly pronounced after the oil crisis of 1973–1974 have profoundly altered traditional practices in economic policy. Demand-stimulus policies that formed the bedrock of the conventional wisdom in the postwar era seemed only to stimulate inflation in the 1970s. More importantly, the relatively free trade of that era had served to link the industrial economies so that no country could easily go its own way. France discovered this belatedly, as the stimulative policies the Socialists inaugurated in 1982 increased the demand for imports so that deficit spending in France created more jobs abroad than at home (see Chapter 11).

The deadened economy of the early 1990s seemed a sad end to what had seemed to be one of the world's economic success stories. France had grown stupendously since the war, dwarfing the growth of Britain and making a very good case for the French style of economic policy, a style based on a concept of state-led growth.[11]

French political institutions, as we have seen, were especially well suited to state interventionism in the national economy. Almost all of French history seemed to justify it. The achievement of Jean Baptiste Colbert, Louis XIV's minister of finance, and his successors provided reference points for statist arguments. The innovations in banking and state-directed investment in the nineteenth century left France with a base upon which to build. As we noted in Chapter 17, France also developed an elite bureaucracy to carry out state development plans, a bureaucracy that for many reasons enjoyed the political clout to get things done. Moreover, after the Fifth Republic was established, the interest group-oriented Parliament was too weak to interfere with the projects of the executive and its technocratic bureaucracy.

The two major forces governing French economic policy in the postwar period were the Planning Commission (*Commissariat au Plan*) and the ministerial bureaucracies, especially the ministries of finance, the economy, and industry. All of these were coordinated by the office of the prime minister.

Planning

France's capacity to pursue long-range economic planning has frequently been credited with the country's tremendous growth after World War II.[12] This was not Soviet-style central planning, but rather "indicative" planning. Indicative planning was a kind of huge market survey done every five years, where major producer groups were invited by the French government to provide information on their market projections for the next five years and to elaborate their needs for inputs. Thus, auto makers would be asked how much steel and other materials they would need, and those material producers would be informed of the expected demand for their products so that they could prepare to produce adequate amounts. The idea was to avoid bottlenecks that might slow down industrial growth or force companies to look to foreign suppliers when jobs might be had by French workers. The French state, in addition, undertook the commitment to make capital available to key industries that would have spread effects on

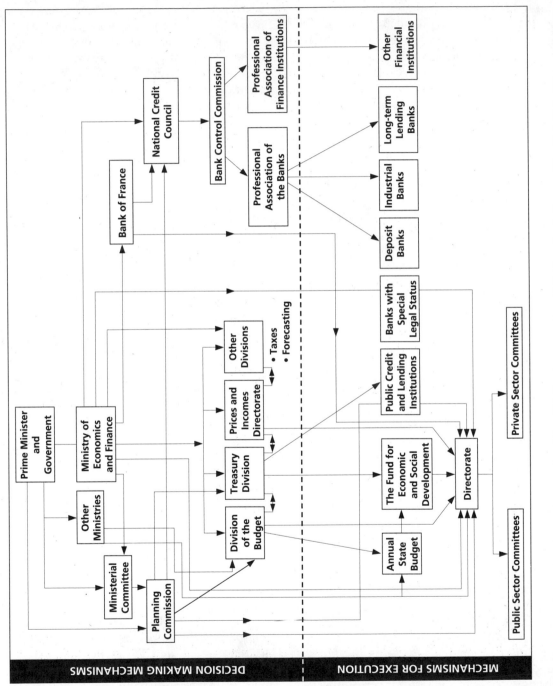

Figure 18.1   The Process of Implementing a National Plan (6th Plan).   Source: Peter Hall, *Governing the Economy* (New York: Oxford University Press, 1986). Copyright © 1985 by Peter A. Hall. Reprinted by permission of Oxford University Press, Inc.

Table 18.1 THE FORECASTS OF THE SIXTH AND SEVENTH PLANS COMPARED WITH THE ECONOMIC RESULTS

	Annual percentage increase in volume			
	Projections in Sixth Plan	Results 1970–1975	Projections in Seventh Plan	Results 1976–1978
GDP	5.9	3.6	5.2	3.8
Household consumption	5.4	5.1	4.7	3.7
Government consumption	3.3	3.0	2.0	3.8
Gross fixed investment:				
Corporations	6.6	3.4	6.9	2.5
Households	4.4	3.4	2.0	–0.9
Government	7.6	4.3	4.3	2.2
Imports	9.3	6.9	11.9	8.5
Exports	10.0	8.2	12.0	7.4
Consumer prices	3.2	8.7	7.2	10.3
Net number of jobs created (OCOs)	300.0	27.0	792.0	171.0

Source: Organization for Economic Cooperation and Development, *Economic Survey: France* (Paris: OECD, 1979), 47; Commissariat Général du Plan, *Dossier Quantitatif Associé au 7e Plan* (Paris: Documentation Française, 1975).

the rest of the economy, and to provide infrastructure where necessary.[13] Figure 18.1 illustrates how planning was organized.

Planning did well during the first two decades of the postwar period. Or at least, the best years of French economic growth occurred when planning was most active. However, as the economy grew, it became more complex. Options supporting one growth strategy would help some industries and hurt others. Consensus crumbled and conflicts became more intense among different segments of French society.[14]

Planning also became a kind of implicit criticism of the government. Establishing five-year targets only highlighted the government's failure when those targets were not achieved (see Table 18.1).[15] As France became increasingly integrated into the world economy, it became dependent on the outside world for markets and supplies. These were harder to predict and impossible to control. Finally, under Giscard d'Estaing, a president ideologically opposed to state intervention, planning receded to little more than a symbolic role.

The Bureaucracy and the Economy

French bureaucrats are among the most talented and well trained of all developed countries. It was, therefore, reasonable to expect that if state intervention would work well anywhere, it would work well in France. For a while, it did. This was not only because the French planning mechanism allowed the administrative apparatus to accurately target and assist potential areas of industrial growth, but also because the system of elite recruitment facilitated the task. The mechanism of *pantouflage* discussed in Chapter 17 meant that private and public sectors would be populated by executives who knew each other from school, who spoke the same language, and who more or less thought the same way. The tendency was to run French economic policy in the interest of big business.[16] This, however, was an improvement over the policies of the Third Republic, which favored the inefficient sectors of small-scale ("Malthusian," in French terminology) agriculture and manufacturing.

The Crisis

The oil crisis of 1973–1974 was only the most obvious manifestation of a series of relationships that were affecting the shape of the world economy. The oil crisis was, in fact, a price explosion that forced a transfer of resources to the oil-producing countries and the huge multinational oil companies. It could only have been accomplished by public and private cartels that limited competition and reduced output. This was a situation that was symptomatic of the general trend in the advanced industrial economies.[17]

Some analysts have argued that the stagnation that has become chronic since the oil crisis is, in fact, due to a crisis in a world economy based on mass production.[18] Briefly, with the rise of the newly industrializing countries such as Brazil, Taiwan, and South Korea, as well as the presence of the already industrialized producers in Japan, Europe, and North America, there are simply more goods being produced than can be consumed in mass markets. In a world of overcapacity, workers are laid off, and the advanced countries have run persistently high levels of unemployment. These, in turn, drive up the expenses of the welfare state and exacerbate the tax burden on industries that do manage to find markets for their products.

The present industrial crisis is unlike any in the past, and traditional economic theories have not offered very convincing clues as to what should be done. In this atmosphere of uncertainty, partisan politicians have returned to traditional ideologies to comprehend the world around them. Socialists looked to nationalization of major industries as a solution to the crisis, while conservatives argued for a return to free markets. The results of both the Socialist and conservative experiments in macroeconomic policy have not been encouraging.

The initial reaction of the Socialists to economic stagnation was nationalization. They reasoned that French industries were losing their competitive edge because French businesses were not investing. Plant and equipment were not being modernized and very little was being invested in research. Since businesses were not investing, the state had to do so, so it took over the lethargic private enterprises.

They soon discovered that modernizing meant replacing personnel with machines and closing down factories because demand had been reduced. This meant that unemployment became the principal cost of modernization. The levels of unemployment, unprecedented since the Great Depression, quickly disillusioned Socialist supporters, and the Right easily won control of the legislature in 1986.

As we mentioned in Chapter 11, the principal difference between Right and Left in economic policy was the issue of privatization versus nationalization. The Right argued that not only were private firms more efficient, but that by selling off the nationalized firms, the state would make enough money to reduce taxes. With a smaller tax burden, French industries could become more competitive, restore profits, and have money left over to reinvest. After two years in office, the Right sold off more industries than Britain's Margaret Thatcher did in ten. The industries were sold—by and large—for three times more than the Socialists paid for them, indicating, at least, that state ownership had hardly been injurious to the

Table 18.2 COMPARISON OF REVENUES OF NATIONALIZED AND PRIVATE COMPANIES (GROSS REVENUES IN MILLIONS OF FRANCS)

	1976	1979	1982	1983	1984	1985
Seven nationalized companies	24,441	42,027	68,622	83,129	109,314	130,481
Percent growth	—	—	—	+21.1	+31.5	+19.4
Private companies (non-financial)	195,122	283,530	377,126	419,028	469,092	521,924
Percent growth	—	—	—	+11.1	+11.9	+11.3
All companies (non-financial)	219,563	325,557	445,748	502,157	578,406	652,405
Percent nationalized companies of all companies	11.1	12.9	15.4	16.5	18.9	20

Source: Centre Européen d'Entreprise Publique, Annuales, 1987; Reprinted in Michel Durupty, *Les Privatisations en France,* Notes et Études Documentaires, no. 4857 (Paris: La Documentation Française, 1988), 16.

health of the firms. (In fact, Table 18.2 shows that nationalized firms were *more* profitable than private firms!)

Certain aspects of the French economy improved during the conservative interregnum from 1986 to 1988. Net capital investment rose and unemployment leveled off. Moreover, the privatizations were successful—in the sense that the conservative government was able to find buyers for the nationalized firms they chose to privatize. This was, at least partially, because shares in the newly privatized firms were sold at a substantial discount (see Table 18.3).

However, it is not clear that the improvements in the French economy had very much to do with the policies undertaken by the conservatives. Many of the improvements were a reaction to changes that had been initiated under the Socialists, especially deregulation and modernization of capital markets and industries.[19] Moreover, the "success" and popularity of the privatization program had more to do

with the fact that shares in the previously nationalized firms were sold at bargain prices. After the world stock market crash in October 1987, interest in privatization cooled.

When President Mitterrand was re-elected in 1988, he declined to renationalize the privatized firms, or to continue the privatization program. He cited the proximity of new developments in the European Union as a reason not to shake up the French economy any further. More than likely, he realized that neither nationalization nor privatization had much to do with curing the ills of the French economy.[20]

When the conservatives returned to power after the parliamentary elections of 1993, they once again placed privatization high on their economic agenda. However, unlike their 1986–1988 privatizations, they justified the new batch in a very different way.[21] Rather than preaching the superiority of private enterprise to public ownership (although many conservatives surely believed this to be true) the privatizations were defended as simply the least

Table 18.3 SHARE DISCOUNTS ON ASSET SALES IN FRANCE

Company	Gross Proceeds (FFrbn)	Discount End First Day (%)
Elf-Aquitaine (Sept. 1986)	3.3	30.5
Saint Gobain (Nov. 1986)	13.5	19.0
Paribas (Jan. 1987)	17.5	24.2
SOGENAL (Mar. 1987)	1.5	36.0
BTP (Apr. 1987)	0.4	23.1
BIMP (Apr. 1987)	0.4	21.4
TF-1 (Apr./Jun. 1987)	3.5	7.9
Credit Commercial (Apr. 1987)	4.4	16.8
CGE (May 1987)	20.6	11.4
Agence Havas (May 1987)	6.4	8.0
Societé Générale (Jun. 1987)	22.3	6.1
Suez (Oct. 1987)	19.6	−18.0
Matra (Jan. 1988)	2.0	14.0

Source: Jenkinson and Meyer, 1987, and *Regards sur l'actualité* 136, p. 9 (updated). Note that the value is not identical to proceeds as there was already private participation in some enterprises in France.

onerous way to raise money for the government's employment programs.[22] Other than these new privatizations, however, the conservatives' economic policies looked very much like those of the Socialists before them.

CONCLUSION

Both in foreign and domestic policies, France provides interesting contrasts. In foreign policy French decision makers, and especially Charles de Gaulle, have been preoccupied with asserting a special role for their country. France's concern for national independence has proved prickly for the United States and occasionally trying for its European allies. Since the end of the Cold War, however, France has been a powerful supporter of its allies and an active participant in United Nations peacekeeping activities.

Fundamentally, France has never deviated from its staunch and continuous defense of western values.

Economically, France's statist approach to the development of industry and commerce has earned kudos, while recently attracting criticism from politicians on the Right. Conservatives and Socialists agreed on the indicative planning associated with the postwar economic miracle, but the changes of the 1970s and 1980s emphasized that the old solutions of both Right and Left were inadequate to problems that have persisted since the oil crisis of 1973. As time has passed it is clear that the highly interventionist role of the state has enjoyed decreasing support. This finding is in keeping with the thrust of the *first two propositions* put forward in Chapter 2. Nevertheless, while the forms of intervention have changed, the notion that governance of the economy is a legitimate role of the state is an opinion still shared by most people in France.

NOTES

1. Stanley Hoffmann, "Gaullism by Any Other Name," *Foreign Policy*, Winter 1984–1985.
2. Cf. Perry Anderson, *Lineages of the Absolutist State* (London: NLB, 1974), pp. 113–142, 236–278. The notable exception to this description is that the Great Northern Plain, running from Moscow to Paris, created vulnerabilities not unlike those of Germany, and motivated a significant part of French foreign policy.
3. Arno Mayer argues that most of Europe was dominated by political relationships rooted in the Middle Ages until the end of the First World War. See his *The Persistence of the Old Regime* (New York: Pantheon Books, 1981).
4. This was one of the justifications for imperialism in Africa given by Prime Minister Jules Ferry at the dawn of the Third Republic. The importance of economic motives behind the last century's imperialism has been the subject of much debate. The classic work in this regard is V. I. Lenin's *Imperialism: The Highest Stage of Capitalism* (New York: International Publishers, 1939), originally published in 1916. For a critique see Benjamin J. Cohen, *The Question of Imperialism* (New York: Basic Books, 1973). My own preferred explanation is that of E. J. Hobsbawm, *Industry and Empire* (Harmondsworth: Penguin, 1969), although the author focuses primarily on Great Britain. Hobsbawm emphasizes the interconnection of political and economic goals.
5. For an excellent account of French foreign policy under the Fourth Republic, see Alfred Grosser, *La Quatrième République et sa Politique Extérieure,* (Paris: Armand Colin, 1961). See also Guy de Carmoy, *Les Politiques Étrangères de la France, 1944–1966* (Paris: La Table Rond, 1967).
6. Grosser, chap. 4.
7. Cf. Miles Kahler, *Decolonization in Britain and France* (Princeton: Princeton University Press, 1984).
8. These actions nearly cost de Gaulle his life, as disgruntled partisans of a French Algeria

formed a secret terrorist organization (*l'Organisation de l'Armée Secrète*) and attempted assassination several times.
9. Cf. Michael M. Harrison and Mark G. McDonough, "Negotiations on the French Withdrawal from NATO," *FPC Case Studies*, no. 5 (Foreign Policy Institute, School of Advanced International Studies, The Johns Hopkins University, Washington, D.C., February 1987).
10. Rebuffed by the United States when de Gaulle wished to share, as did Great Britain, the secret to the atomic bomb, the general gave the go-ahead for French construction of its own bomb. This ultimately led to the development of other areas of technology and indirectly led to France's becoming a major arms maker. It also led to French primacy in civilian nuclear power.
11. See especially John Zysman, *Governments, Markets and Growth* (Ithaca, N.Y.: Cornell University Press, 1983); Peter A. Hall, *Governing the Economy* (New York: Oxford University Press, 1986).
12. See especially Andrew Schonfield, *Modern Capitalism* (New York: Oxford University Press, 1969), chap. V. See also Stephen S. Cohen, *Modern Capitalist Planning: The French Model* (Berkeley and Los Angeles: University of California Press, 1977), and Hall, *Governing the Economy.*
13. See John Zysman, *Political Strategies for Industrial Order* (Berkeley and Los Angeles: University of California Press, 1977), chap. III.
14. Hall, chap. 6.
15. Feigenbaum, *The Politics of Public Enterprise* (Princeton: Princeton University Press, 1985), pp. 110–113.
16. See Ezra N. Suleiman, *Politics, Power and Bureaucracy in France* (Princeton: Princeton University Press, 1979), chap. XII.
17. This is a controversial analysis supported by the writings of such economists as John Kenneth Galbraith, and was also accepted by the Socialists when they came to power in 1981. Many American economists dispute these contentions and argue that the market, left to its own devices, would become more competitive.
18. See, for example, Michael Piore and Charles Sabel, *The Second Industrial Divide* (New York:

Basic Books, 1984). For a critical appraisal, see Robert Boyer, "The Eighties: The Search for Alternatives to Fordism," Sixth Annual Conference of Europeanists, Washington, D.C., October 30–November 1, 1987. See also Alain Lipietz, *Towards a New Economic Order,* trans. Malcolm Slater (New York: Oxford University Press, 1992).

19. Michael Loriaux, *France After Hegemony* (Ithaca: Cornell University Press, 1991).

20. In 1992 the members of the European Community were scheduled to implement the Single Market Act, which would eliminate all remaining trade barriers and consequently subject most French industries to very intense competition.

21. For an examination of the motives of the first privatization project, see Harvey B. Feigenbaum, "France: From Pragmatic to Tactical Privatization," *Business and the Contemporary World,* March 1993.

22. For an analysis of the new privatization program, see François Morin, "Privatisations: Onde de Choc," *Le Monde,* 29 June 1993, p. 33.

REFERENCES AND SUGGESTED READINGS

Cerny, Philip G., and Martin Schain, eds. 1985. *Socialism, the State, and Public Policy in France.* New York: Methuen.

Cohen, Stephen S. 1977. *Modern Capitalist Planning.* Berkeley: University of California Press.

Feigenbaum, Harvey B. 1985. *The Politics of Public Enterprise.* Princeton: Princeton University Press.

Hall, Peter A. 1986. *Governing the Economy.* New York: Oxford University Press.

Hoffmann, Stanley. 1968. *Gulliver's Troubles.* New York: McGraw-Hill.

Kamerman, Sheila B., and Alfred J. Kahn, eds. 1989. *Privatization and the Welfare State.* Princeton: Princeton University Press.

Kolodziej, Edward A. 1974. *French International Policy under De Gaulle and Pompidou.* Ithaca, N.Y.: Cornell University Press.

Loriaux, Michael. 1991. *France After Hegemony.* Ithaca, N.Y.: Cornell University Press.

Zysman, John. 1983. *Governments, Markets, and Growth.* Ithaca, N.Y.: Cornell University Press.

———. 1977. *Political Strategies for Industrial Order.* Berkeley: University of California Press.

IV

Germany

19

The Current Situation:
The Making of a New Germany, 1990

However miraculous, German reunification in 1990 is not a tale ending with the familiar line "And they lived happily ever after." Not until some monsters have been tamed and goblins banished.[1] Unity has come with a monstrous price tag that is taxing the generosity of western Germany. What is worse, it seems to have awakened goblins of xenophobia and right-wing extremism. In November of 1992, three Turks living in Mölln, a town near Hamburg, were killed in a firebombing of their home. In the city of Rostock, rioters wearing Nazi insignia and armed with stones and gasoline attacked a hostel for Vietnamese workers in broad daylight. Most jarring for Americans was the assault on a U.S. luge team member by skinheads in a winter resort in eastern Germany. Such acts of violence raise more pointed questions about Germany than almost anywhere else. They bring back the scariest ghosts of Germany's past. No sooner has the German Question been settled than it is back on the agenda in another format. It remains to be seen whether the making of a new Germany ends up as an inverted fairy tale, with a happy beginning and a grim ending.

WE, THE PEOPLE

To be sure, few moments in recent history have filled people with more joy than the opening of the Berlin Wall on November 9, 1989.

Berliners east and west celebrate the opening of the wall, November 9, 1989.

Whose heart could have remained cold at the sight of the delirious crowds of East Berliners streaming through what had been a lethal obstacle to freedom until just the day before? However ugly and cruel, the Berlin Wall had seemed destined to compete with the Chinese Wall for longevity. It was not in the hands of West Germany to tear it down. Former U.S. president Ronald Reagan, during his visit to Berlin, was right in addressing his call for such action to then Soviet president Mikhail Gorbachev. The Wall did not just divide Germany, it was the dividing line of the Cold War. But whether ending that war would be enough to overcome the German division was by no means certain.

West Germans had grown politically and economically secure in the Federal Republic, while their East German cousins appeared ever more distant and removed.[2] Reunification was no burning issue in the West, though when

asked about it in polls, most western respondents typically approved of the idea.[3] Meanwhile, the German Democratic Republic, the official name for what was popularly termed "East Germany," had taken major steps to flesh out its own separate identity, even bowing to previously despised icons such as Frederick the Great, the Prussian king (1740–1786). In 1989, the rulers looked forward to celebrating the German Democratic Republic's 40th anniversary with Socialist spit and Prussian polish. By then, half of its people had been born and reared there. Even many older ones had no personal experience with any other political order or had ever lived under a united German roof. East Germany had won recognition as a separate state all around the world. East Germans felt proud of the gold their athletes brought home from Olympic Games, adding excitement to a life where bread and other essentials were cheap. It appeared that the Democratic Republic had gained a measure of respect among its citizenry.

Cracks in the Wall

As is so often the case, however, reading the minds of a captive population from the outside is dangerous. The Wall had never managed to halt the escape of people disaffected with life in East Germany; it only bottled up that flow and diverted it. The probing for weak spots somewhere in the curtain of iron and concrete never stopped. In the spring of 1989, the curtain suddenly tore, though at some distance from the German Democratic Republic. The government of a socialist sister country, Hungary, decided to dismantle its barbed-wire fortifications along its western border. It did so in large part to ease a refugee problem caused by large numbers of migrants from Rumania pouring into Hungary, seeking transit to Austria. Word of this decision spread instantly to East Germany through West German television, one of the few things the Wall was powerless to avert. East Germans had long enjoyed the freedom to vacation in other socialist countries like Hungary, but were forbidden to exit to Austria or other western countries. Now thousands of East Germans streamed into Hungary trying to find unguarded spots to cross the border to Austria and then head for West Germany. Others tried the shorter detour through Czechoslovakia. When, soon afterward, Hungary also abandoned its policy of returning by force any East German caught trying to cross that border, scattered flight turned to a mass exodus toward a more promising land.

Meanwhile many East Germans staying behind offered little comfort or consolation to their rulers. Emboldened by their helplessness, political opposition now dared to sprout openly in groups called "New Forum" and "Democracy Now." Ironically, it was the celebration of the German Democratic Republic's 40th anniversary that handed them an unexpected opportunity to publicize their demands. Thousands called out to Soviet leader Gorbachev ("Gorbi!"), visiting East Berlin to participate in the celebration, for help in, well, getting rid of the one-party dictatorship. Lenin supposedly said that the capitalists would sell their enemies the rope with which to hang themselves. But now, oddly enough, it was his disciples' love of parades that mobilized the very discontent that would sweep them from power.

Chanting "We are the people," East Germans poured onto streets all across their country in the largest demonstrations of protest since the uprising in 1953, which almost toppled the Communist regime. But this time no Soviet tanks rolled out to crush the upheaval. In 1989, the protesters did not expect that Gorbachev would order them into action, and the East German rulers, to their chagrin, probably knew that for a fact. No longer propped up by the Soviet Union, East Germany's Socialists faced a dilemma: crush the uprising (a "Chinese solution") on their own or give in to the demands of the protesters. A bloodbath was averted through a party coup that forced out Erich Honecker, for eighteen years the party leader of the German Democratic Republic. If participants' accounts can be believed, Honecker's shoot-to-kill order was revoked by fellow politburo member Egon Krenz, who then went on to succeed Honecker.[4] Having decided against breaking the protest, the new rulers, though still of the same old party, now resolved to bend.

A German Revolution?

With little fanfare they granted the right to travel freely to the West. Instead of cracking down on protest, the new regime gambled that the freedom to travel would pacify the vast majority, assuming that this was all the free-

Table 19.1 A CHRONOLOGY OF GERMAN REUNIFICATION, 1989–90	
Sept. 10, 1989	Hungary permits East Germans free passage to the West.
October 7	The German Democratic Republic celebrates its 40th anniversary.
October 9	Mass protest in Leipzig against the regime.
October 18	Erich Honecker is ousted as the East German leader.
November 9	The German Democratic Republic opens the Wall and allows its citizens to travel freely to the West.
November 28	West German chancellor Helmut Kohl presents a 10-point plan for German unification.
December 7	The East German government promises free elections in 1990.
December 19	Chancellor Kohl visits Dresden.
February 10, 1990	Soviet president Gorbachev says unification is up to the Germans to decide.
March 18	The first free elections in the German Democratic Republic. The Alliance for Germany wins.
April 12	Lothar de Maizière is chosen as the new German Democratic Republic prime minister.
July 1	Monetary union between Federal Republic and Democratic Republic.
July 14–16	Gorbachev agrees to a united Germany staying in NATO. Soviet Union will withdraw its troops from East Germany in three to four years.
Sept. 20–21	The parliaments of West and East Germany approve the unification treaty.
October 3	Germany is unified.
December 2	First national election of unified Germany.

Source: *Inter Nationes,* "On the Path to German Unity: Chronology of Events," Bonn, 1990.

dom most people were clamoring for. Over the following weekend, more than four million East German residents, nearly one of every four, took advantage of this long-sought freedom and visited the nearest place in the West. And as the rulers had assumed, the vast majority returned, their pockets filled with what DM 100 ($60) of western welcome money could buy. But being free to visit the West was by no means the only demand. Why not enjoy a better life and political liberties, as the West obviously did? It proved impossible to deny political freedoms once the Wall had been opened. East Germany's rulers agreed to hold free elections, the first ones in the history of the German Democratic Republic.

With those steps, the Socialist regime in East Germany had drafted its political obituary. Shall we call this a revolution? If not abrogated, the promise of a free election meant more than a change of government. It would install a new political order, in the mold of a western democracy. One cannot imagine a more sweeping political transformation. Yet the old regime let this happen without a fight, after being tempted briefly to resort to force. As revolutions typically go, the overthrow of the government was remarkably nonviolent. As far as is known, not a single bullet was fired, or a drop of blood spilled, though many people suffered bruises at the hands of the police and spent time in jail.

Many protests against government policies in West Germany have turned out to be more bloody and violent. To visit Miami in a rented car might expose an East German to greater peril than taking his or her demand for free travel to the streets of Magdeburg. It is also worth noting that none of the formerly high and mighty paid with their lives, either—not even those who had issued shoot-to-kill orders. The people's wrath largely turned onto the Stasi (the state security police), but even its agents have had little to fear personally. No cry for blood, no back-alley executions, no revolutionary tribunals. It was almost too merciful to be a genuine revolution. Although the rulers surrendered without a fight, it was not speeches and declarations alone that made them step down. What did was an irresistible show of human force that swept aside the seemingly immovable Wall. The old rulers were sober enough to calculate the odds of winning a fight and decided to forfeit.[5]

Kohl's Unification Policy

Meanwhile the West German side moved from cheerleading to active participation in the revolution unfolding in the East. Among West German politicians, Chancellor Helmut Kohl took the lead and outlined a *ten-point plan*. It was a proposal for ultimate unification of West and East Germany in a federal union. One of the points not specified, however, was a date of national marriage; the end of the 1990s still looked like an optimistic target. One of Kohl's closest aides recorded in his diary that he kept throughout those days and weeks: "The Chancellor [Kohl] estimated that it would take five to ten years to achieve unification. We all agreed: even if unity were to be reached at the end of the century, it would be a historic stroke of luck."[6]

According to Chancellor Kohl's plan, the elaborate courtship would include cooperation, treaties, and confederate arrangements; all in an orderly, incremental process, much like the building of the European Community. Indeed, Kohl was quick to point to the international framework in which those steps were to be taken. A unified Germany, he reassured everyone, would not turn its back on Europe, leave the Atlantic Alliance, and pursue nationalistic aspirations. No call for a place in the sun or for territorial expansion anywhere. Having laid out his plan, Kohl visited East Germany for the

first time, unsure of what reception to expect. To his surprise, he was greeted in Dresden by the chant "We are *one* people." This was a not-insignificant change from "We are *the* people." It was a signal that unification was far more urgent and far closer at hand than most, including Kohl himself, had believed just a few weeks earlier. But there were other places to visit and the consent of others to obtain before that goal came into reach.

Throughout history, the German Question, as we shall see in greater detail in the next chapter, had always been too important a matter to be left to the Germans. So long as nobody thought reunification was likely to happen, foreign governments in the West happily endorsed the principle of self-determination for the German people. But it is doubtful whether deep down they favored that prospect any more in 1990 than they did 120 years ago. The Soviet Union held the key. The German Democratic Republic belonged to the Warsaw Pact, with nearly 400,000 Soviet troops stationed there. The Federal Republic, by contrast, belonged to NATO, with a quarter of a million U.S. troops, along with sizable contingents of British and French forces, stationed on its territory. Unless those four Allied Powers, who had conquered and divided Germany in 1945, arrived at an agreement about reunification, the road in that direction seemed a dead-end street. But how would they secure that agreement?

Allies and Adversaries

The key, so the conventional wisdom went, lay in Moscow, which had a huge military and security stake in the German Democratic Republic. There had been signs now and then that the Soviet Union might be interested in a unified Germany. But the conditions, namely neutral status (no NATO membership) and weak military, made those proposals utterly unacceptable to West German governments. If Gorbachev insisted on those conditions, the path toward unity would have remained blocked in 1989–1990. There was no doubt that Chancellor Helmut Kohl would refuse to pay that price for unity. The question was whether Gorbachev still had the power or the will to exact it. In dealing with fellow leaders in the Soviet bloc, he had made concessions that were simply unthinkable under his predecessors: the pull-out of troops in Afghanistan, free elections in Poland resulting in the ouster of Communist rule, and the chiding of East German rulers for being too unbending in their communism. By then, what had become unthinkable was for the Soviet leader to threaten military action to suppress the overthrow of Communist rule.

Oddly enough perhaps, it was a western ally who was most outspoken in opposing German reunification. British prime minister Margaret Thatcher made no bones about her animosity, fearing that a reunited Germany would turn into an aggressive power that would upset the balance of power. International politics does make strange bedfellows. Those views put her in the company of the German Greens and many left-wing critics in the Federal Republic, not her usual fan clubs.[7] In September of 1989, she went to Moscow to stiffen Gorbachev's resolve against reunification. In her memoirs, Thatcher recounts with astonishing candor:

> In Moscow . . . Mr. Gorbachev and I talked frankly about Germany. I explained to him that although NATO had traditionally made statements supporting Germany's aspiration to be reunited, in practice we were rather apprehensive. Nor was I speaking for myself alone—I had discussed it with at least one other western leader, meaning but not mentioning Mitterrand. Mr. Gorbachev confirmed that the Soviet Union did not want German reunification either. This reinforced me in my resolve to slow up the already heady pace of developments.[8]

Prime Minister Thatcher also tried, without success, to persuade U.S. president George Bush to slow the train of unification. Her final hope was the "creation of a solid Anglo-French axis" that she proposed to French president François Mitterrand to "check the German juggernaut."[9] She claimed that Mitterrand was tempted by her offer, but too fearful to try. While Chancellor Kohl faced a formidable adversary to his policy in the British government, he could count on firm support from President Bush. An unusually close rapport between Bush and Kohl did much to defuse Thatcher's attempts at sabotage. Yet, ultimately it was Kohl's success in his dealing with Soviet leader Gorbachev that settled the issue.

In their highly dramatic meetings with Gorbachev, Chancellor Kohl and his foreign minister, Hans-Dietrich Genscher, secured Soviet assent to a unified Germany. In one critical negotiation, on February 10, 1990, Gorbachev declared:

> There are no differences of opinion among the Soviet Union, the Federal Republic, and the GDR about German unification and the right of the people to achieve it. They have to determine for themselves which way they want to go.[10]

That concession was a historic breakthrough that stunned the West German side at the negotiating table—so much so that they asked Gorbachev to repeat it. He left no doubt that he agreed to the principle of unification without raising killer conditions such as neutrality or calling for a conference of the four Allied Powers to settle the German Question. In the summit with Kohl in July, Gorbachev pulled yet another surprise by allowing the future unified Germany to remain in NATO; he also pledged that the Soviet Union would withdraw its military forces from East Germany within three or four years. With enemies like Gorbachev, Kohl may have wondered about the need for friends like Thatcher.

There can be no doubt that a Soviet refusal to yield would have halted the train of unification. But it is highly doubtful that the Soviet

The Deal is Done: Chancellor Helmut Kohl (seated right) and German foreign minister Hans-Dietrich Genscher (left) with Soviet Leader Mikhail Gorbachev (center) in the Caucasus, July 15, 1990.

Union could have derailed it, short of massive military intervention, which no longer featured as a serious option of Soviet foreign policy. Gorbachev, it seems, proved to be a master of making a virtue out of necessity by letting the Germans themselves decide their own future, just as he did in Afghanistan, Poland, the Baltics, and other places. Moreover, in return for his generosity, he could count on German financial aid worth billions of Deutschmarks to assist him with *perestroika* at home.

THE EAST VOTES FOR UNITY

The first free election in East Germany, on March 18, 1990, sent the lame-duck German Socialist Unity Party rulers into political retirement. That was not much of a surprise. A patchwork of groups and parties called the *Alliance for Germany* scored a stunning victory. That was a surprise in so far as that alliance included a party that had served as a lackey of Communist rule, the eastern CDU (Christian Democratic Union). Its name notwithstanding, that party had long been despised by its western namesake (Chancellor Kohl's party).

Nonetheless, in the new age of competitive party politics, the eastern party adapted quickly and was adopted by the western CDU. Chancellor Kohl personally entered the East German campaign, just as if his own election were at stake. In front of hundreds of thousands he promised to "create a flourishing country within a short time." Whatever the eastern CDU may have been in the days before the Wall came down, in early 1990 it had succeeded in becoming the party of choice for East Germans who were bent on rapid unification with the West.

The March election was a bitter disappointment for the very groups who, at considerable risk to themselves, had spurred the protest and articulated the demands for freedom and democracy (New Forum and Democracy Now, in particular). As measured at the polls, their support proved pitiful, even smaller than that of the Communist rulers, now campaigning in more respectable attire as the "party of democratic socialism" (PDS). How come the planters of the seeds of revolution harvested so little electoral fruit?

No doubt, the winning parties got plenty of campaign help from their western patrons, rich in resources and electioneering experience. But it was also apparent that most people in East Germany did not so much demand civil rights and democracy in the abstract as that they wanted those goals in a highly tangible and familiar form. That form was the (western) Federal Republic, including the blessings of its economic system, to be sure. As it turned out, even with communism expunged, few East Germans cared about preserving a separate democratic republic. This must be disheartening both to democratic idealists as well as those believing that East Germany had acquired a distinctive national identity.

The outcome of the March election was also a bitter disappointment for the Social Democrats. People with long memories recall that so long as elections were free, the eastern German states (the area later subsumed as the German Democratic Republic) used to be a Social Democrat stronghold. The problem was that, like a plant without water, the party's roots in the East German electorate had withered in the absence of free electoral politics. Now, rushing to capture its share of the new electorate, the re-established eastern Social Democrats failed to regain a stronghold.

Opinion surveys showed that the vast majority of East German voters cast their votes based on which of the *West* German parties they liked best.[11] With its firm and quick offer of unification, Chancellor Kohl's party was more appealing than the western Social Democrats. The leaders of that party sounded more worried than pleased by the prospect of national unity. The election installed the newly chosen leader of the eastern Christian Democratic Union,

Lothar de Maizière, as the new head of the East German government. Being the German Democratic Republic's first freely chosen prime minister, he also intended to be the last. The revolutionary nature of his election is evident in his pledge not to preserve the constitution of his state, but to abolish it. Unification with the Federal Republic was his government's singular policy purpose.

A FRIENDLY TAKEOVER

The only prediction one can safely venture about the unification process is that everything happened much faster than expected. Hardly anyone expected the Wall to come down in 1989, or free elections to be held so soon afterward. Nor did many anticipate the groundswell for rapid unification in the East. The first formal step in that direction was economic and social union. A proposal to introduce the Deutschmark as a common currency in East and West Germany had been one of Kohl's promises in the campaign for the March election. The way the West German government saw it, either the Deutschmark went east or the East Germans would come west for the Deutschmark. The proposal to establish a currency union was no empty promise. It was delivered with a single stroke and under most generous terms for the Easterners. On July 1, they were able to exchange a substantial amount of East marks (4,000, equivalent then to $2,400) at a 1–1 rate for the treasured Deutschmarks. However happy that made the East Germans, who would have garnered only a few pfennigs (pennies) for their marks in an open market, the Bundesbank, West Germany's central bank, did not consider it an economically wise move. Political wisdom triumphed over economics—a dismal science, after all.

Along with the now worthless East marks, the German Democratic Republic also buried its socialist aspirations. From one day to the next, like a drunk put in detox, the East German economy was subject to the harsh rules of a market economy. That the German Democratic Republic would surrender its political sovereignty next was no longer an issue of controversy—only a question of when, and maybe how. The West German government proposed to rely on Article 23 of the Basic Law, West Germany's constitution. That article allows for the possibility that parts of Germany not belonging to the Federal Republic in 1949 may join later.

The East German government agreed to negotiate the details of a merger of the two Germanys on the basis of Article 23. Hence, political unification was less a union of two parties than of one party joining the other, comparable perhaps to new states like Kentucky in 1792 gaining admission to the Union. Some would put it in less flattering terms and call unification a takeover. A big and wealthy country of more than 60 million people took over a small and bankrupt country of barely 16 million on less than half the property. But if it was a takeover, it was not a hostile one. The East German electorate had loudly demanded it in the March election. The freely elected representatives approved the unification treaty by an overwhelming majority (299 to 80). If there was pressure, it was the promise of better times ahead.

More quickly than anyone could have imagined at the beginning of the year, the two Germanys united on October 3, 1990, under the red glare of fireworks and the sound of a replica of the Liberty Bell ringing. As *The New York Times* noted: "Forty-five years after it was carved up in defeat and disgrace, Germany was reunited today in a midnight celebration of pealing bells, national hymns and the jubilant blare of good old German oom-pah-pah."[12] With that, the East German Democratic Republic expired and its prime minister retired in a "farewell without tears." The old Federal Republic had comprised ten states, from Schleswig-Holstein in the North, bordering on Denmark, to Bavaria, bordering on Austria in the South. Now six "new" *Länder* in the East had been added: Mecklenburg-Western Pomerania (Vorpommern), Brandenburg, Saxony-Anhalt (Sachsen-Anhalt), Thuringia (Thüringen), Saxony (Sachsen), and a reunited Berlin.

Whatever consequences October 3, 1990, may have for Germany and the world at some future date, whether or not some of the dire predictions of opponents as varied as novelist Günter Grass, former prime minister Margaret Thatcher, or columnist William Safire will come true, it is worth keeping in mind how German unity was achieved. Above all, it was not by "blood and iron," the way Bismarck settled the German Question more than a hundred years earlier in the 1860s (the next chapter discusses that policy). It was unthinkable for Kohl to contemplate war or just the threat of military action to achieve his goal. To be sure, not all of Germany's neighbors were thrilled at the prospect of a larger and more powerful Germany. But peaceful negotiation was sufficient to secure the consent of both western allies and the Soviet Union, long an immovable obstacle. Second, the new, more powerful Germany would not be a stand-alone power, but remained firmly moored both in the European Community and in NATO. That was not a grudging concession of the kind that Germany was forced to sign in the 1919 Treaty of Versailles, and would be itching to abandon at the first opportunity. What is more, the commitment to Europe and NATO was not just the policy of the Kohl government, but the result of a deep and firm consensus shared by all major parties in the Federal Republic. It was not simply window dressing for naked power politics.

Finally, if what happened was a revolution, it certainly was not a revolution from above. Unification was not imposed by rulers on a reluctant public, let alone on one that was opposed. Even though the people in East or West Germany were not asked to approve of unity

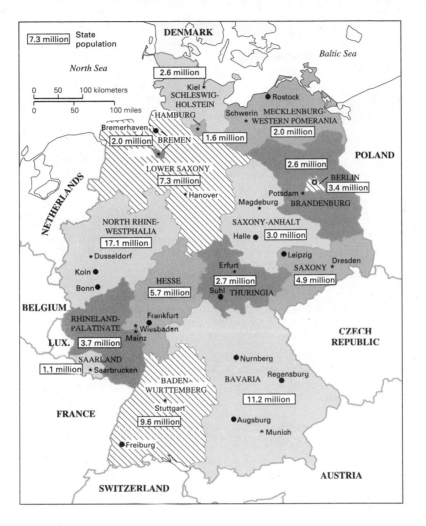

Figure 19.1 A reunited Germany.

through a formal referendum, they sent an unmistakable message through their votes in elections, and in public opinion polls as well. It was an act of democracy that finally, close to the end of this century, fulfilled the aspirations articulated in Germany's national anthem: *Einigkeit und Recht und Freiheit* (unity with law and freedom). A long and bloody chapter of German history had been quietly closed. While the next chapter examines that and other chapters of Germany's past, the final chapter turns to a discussion of the price of reunion.

NOTES

1. That is how *The Economist* put it, taking up the pen of the Brothers Grimm, those nineteenth-century collectors of German folk tales. See "A Survey of Germany: Not as Grimm as It Looks," *The Economist*, May 23, 1992.

2. See Gebhard Schweigler, *National Consciousness in Divided Germany* (Beverly Hills: Sage, 1975).
3. See Elisabeth Noelle-Neumann and Renate Köcher, *Allensbacher Jahrbuch der Demoskopie 1984–1992* (Allensbach Yearbooks of Public Opinion) (New York: K. G. Saur, 1993), p. 437.
4. See Craig R. Whitney, "Party Coup Turned East German Tide," *New York Times,* November 19, 1989.
5. For a more theoretical exploration of the sources of protest and revolution, see Edward N. Muller and Karl-Dieter Opp, "Rational Choice and Rebellious Collective Action," *American Political Science Review,* 80 (June 1986): 471–487; and Ronald A. Francisco, "Theories of Protest and the Revolutions of 1989," *American Journal of Political Science,* 37 (August 1993): 663–680.
6. Horst Teltschik, *329 Tage: Innenansichten der Einigung* (329 Days: An Insider's View of Unification) (Berlin: Siedler, 1991), p. 52. The entry in the diary was for November 27, 1989.
7. For a forceful West German dissent on unity, see the essay by the author of *The Tin Drum,* Günter Grass, *Two States—One Nation?* (San Diego: Harcourt Brace Jovanovich, 1990).
8. Margaret Thatcher, *The Downing Street Years* (New York: HarperCollins, 1993), p. 792. For Kohl's reaction to Prime Minister Thatcher's efforts and statements, see Teltschik, *329 Tage,* pp. 115–116.
9. Thatcher, *Downing Street Years,* pp. 796, 797.
10. As recorded by Teltschik, *329 Tage,* p. 140.
11. See Dieter Roth, "Die Wahlen zur Volkskammer in der DDR: Der Versuch einer Erklärung," *Politische Vierteljahresschrift,* 31 (1990), 369–393; also Helmut Norpoth and Dieter Roth, "Unification and Electoral Choice," in Russell Dalton, ed., *The New Germany Votes: Unification and the Creation of a New German Party System.* (Providence: Berg Publishers, 1993).
12. Serge Schmemann, "The Two Germanys Unite After 45 Years with Jubilation and a Vow of Peace," the *New York Times,* October 3, 1990.

REFERENCES AND SUGGESTED READINGS

Anderson, Christopher, Karl Kaltenthaler, and Wolfgang Luthardt. 1993. *The Domestic Politics of German Unification.* Boulder: Lynne Riemer.

Ash, Timothy Garton. 1993. *In Europe's Name: Germany and the Divided Continent.* New York: Random House.

Gedmin, Jeffrey. 1992. *The Hidden Hand: Gorbachev and the Collapse of East Germany.* Washington, D.C.: American Enterprise Institute Press.

Pond, Elizabeth. 1993. *Beyond the Wall: Germany's Road to Unification.* Washington, D.C.: The Brookings Institution.

Smith, Gordon, William E. Paterson, Peter Merkl, and Stephen Padgett, eds. 1992. *Developments in German Politics.* Durham: Duke University Press.

Wallach, H. G. Peter, and Ronald A. Francisco. 1992. *United Germany: The Past, Politics and Prospects.* Westport, Conn.: Greenwood Press.

20

Historical Background:
The Nation of the Middle

In Germany, politics comes with the territory. Lacking a moat of oceanic waters, Germany has not been allowed to thrive, or to wither, in splendid isolation from the outside world. A look at a map of Europe can leave no observer in any doubt of Germany's exposed location in the middle of the continent. Major north-south as well as east-west routes of trade and warfare have run through German territory. They brought in many foreign customs and armies and at the same time lured Germans away from home. Through all of this, the German people have rarely had the opportunity to nurture a sense of their own identity that was not either defensive or aggressive. The middle location has made them alternately obsessed with power and oblivious to it. Geography may not be destiny, but it does not deal its cards randomly.

In the first half of the nineteenth century, when both Britain and France had laid the foundations for a liberal political order, Germany was largely a "geographical expression." It was a patchwork of independent states held together by cultural attachments. Germany was a nation without a state or a modern constitution. It is said that both the nation-state and democracy were "late" in coming to Germany, and that it was "too little" in the case of democracy. The attempts to resolve the German Question—actually two questions—proved a traumatic experience, not only for Germans but also for their neighbors.

Figure 20.1 Europe after the Congress of Vienna, 1815.

Looking over the course of German history, one finds it hard to resist the temptation to ask what-if questions. What if Germany had become a democracy in 1848? What if it had remained the picturesque patchwork of political diversity? What if its rulers had shown more prudence and less impudence in 1914? What if the Weimar Republic had been spared the back-to-back shock of hyperinflation and mass unemployment? Most likely, Germany would not have been tempted to try the poison of National Socialism. However short-lived on the vast scale of historical time, Hitler's rule casts a long shadow both over Germany's past and its present.

ROMAN INFLUENCE

Questions about Germany have been asked as far back as 2,000 years ago. The defeat of Roman legions A.D. 9 northeast of the Rhine shook the Empire, while creating a German folk hero, Arminius, among the victors. The battle called attention to the "Germanic" tribes, whose life and character received an admiring notice in a book entitled *Germania* by the Roman historian Tacitus. Few outside influences have made a more lasting impression on Germany than did the Roman Empire. In time to come Germany's supreme ruler would claim the title Caesar Augustus—Kaiser in the vernacular—and his realm would be referred to as the Holy Roman Empire of the German Nation. In other words, Germany took the mantle of Rome, of a Rome to be sure that had converted to Christianity after the days of the original Caesar.

The First Empire

In A.D. 800, an easy date to remember, the Frankish king Charlemagne went to Rome to receive the pope's blessing as emperor of an area that covered large chunks of France, Germany, and Italy. In this extension, the empire did not survive its founder, although it remained an ideal; indeed, the European Economic Community formed in 1957 looks remarkably similar to the geographical outline of Charlemagne's realm. Its western part formed the nucleus of modern France, its eastern part that of Germany. There the imperial tradition continued when Otto, leader of the Saxons, was crowned emperor by the pope in A.D. 962.

From then on, as a rule, German-speaking monarchs wore the imperial crown. It is well to remember that this was not a German Empire but a Roman Empire. Germans were a part of it, among others. The empire lasted almost a thousand years, until 1806, when it was dissolved after the crushing blows of Napoleon's conquest. The empire was never a tightly centralized regime. More a confederation, it accommodated rival states, ranging from free cities along the North Sea coast to archdioceses along the Rhine, to independent counties, duchies, and even kingdoms like those of Bavaria, Saxony, Austria, and, later, Prussia. It arguably represented the most diverse confed-eration assembled under one political roof and sharing a vague sense of belonging to the same nation. How that sense survived at all amidst the relentless territorial splintering boggles the mind. Pluralism, to use a modern term, was an everyday experience within the empire.

The emperor was powerless, for example, to impose a common religion on his subjects when, in the sixteenth century, the Reformation challenged Roman Catholicism. While many territories in the North of Germany went Protestant, many in the South stayed with Roman Catholicism. What all the various princes were able to impose on their respective subjects the emperor could not do for Germany. Religion, it was resolved at the *Reichstag*, the gathering of the 240 or so independent states forming the empire, was a matter for subimperial authorities in Germany to decide ("cujus regio, ejus religio").

A World War in the Seventeenth Century

This privilege exacted a terrible price soon afterward. Lacking a powerful central authority, the empire was ravaged by a civil war that turned into a European showdown between the political forces and armies of the Reformation and those of the Roman Catholic Counter Reformation. With Sweden, Denmark, and France joining in—to undermine the empire as much as to assist their beleaguered religious brethren—the Thirty Years' War (1618–1648) left Germany scorched and bloodsoaked. Its population was decimated by a war of appalling cruelty, as related by Grimmelshausen in his novel, *Simplicissimus*. Already weak at the top, the empire now suffered from atrophy in its limbs as well. It took more than one hundred years for Germany to replenish the population losses.

The Westphalian Peace of 1648 sanctioned the sovereignty of the territorial lords of the

A joyous postilion announces the end of three decades of bloodshed.

empire, including the right to conclude alliances with one another and with foreign powers. By now there were roughly 350 independent territories, and their number would swell rather than shrink in the future. Yet one should not conclude that the empire had been read its last rites. After all, the key power within it, the Habsburgs of Austria, wore the crown. The rest of Europe nevertheless grew accustomed to a Germany that posed no threat to anyone. Any significant change in that status quo would not be accepted by them without a fight. That was the message between the lines of the Westphalian treaties.

PRUSSIA

While Germany as a whole lingered in a political coma, life on its eastern frontier began to stir. Centered in the border region around Berlin, Brandenburg—better known later as Prussia—rose in the eighteenth century to become the major challenger for supremacy within the em-

pire. Nevertheless, Prussia was no cradle of parliamentary government or democracy. It was a monarchy in which the king ruled, not just reigned, while others decided policy. "Reason as much as you like, but obey" was the motto. For many, Prussia was synonymous with military power. As the French put it sharply, Prussia was not a state with an army, but an "army that had a state." The landed nobility, the *Junkers* as they were called, buttressed the king's rule, their key payoff being leading positions in the army and the administration. A "smoke-filled cabinet" at times served as a council for the king to seek advice and consent from the *Junker* class.

Yet Prussia was also a beacon of enlightened and humane government. It fashioned the institution of a modern civil service: professional and free of corruption. Frederick the Great (1740–1786) abolished torture as well as censorship of the press. Rule of law became a hallmark of the Prussian state. The Prussian General Law of the Land spelled out limits of police authority and state power. Indeed, Prussia was a rare voice against religious fanaticism and for religious tolerance. In 1685, when the French king expelled the Protestant Huguenots, Prussia offered them a haven; it did the same for Jews driven from Austria. "Let everyone find salvation in his own fashion," Frederick the Great proclaimed. It was in Prussia where Jews, formally emancipated in 1812, felt welcome. True, tolerance paid dividends; the French Protestants and the Jews who settled in Prussia proved a boon to its economy and culture.[1]

Capable of sweeping reforms, the Prussia of the early nineteenth century was a country where servitude had been abolished, where economic feudalism was dismantled, where cities and towns enjoyed a wide measure of local self-government, and where eight years of schooling as well as military service for males were compulsory. In these domains, as well as before the law, equality made large and early strides in Prussia.

LIBERALISM AND NATIONALISM

News of revolution in America and then France strongly reverberated throughout Germany. "America, you are better off than our continent, the old one," intoned Johann Wolfgang Goethe (1749–1832) in a poem dedicated to the spirit of 1776. The ideals of political liberalism were beginning to gain a foothold in Germany. They included demands for human rights, a constitution limiting the power of rulers, and citizen participation in politics.

National Awareness

At the same time, the invasion by French troops during the Napoleonic Wars, while exporting some of those principles, also stirred up the dormant sense of national identity in German lands. The liberty that Germans began to taste was liberation from the French occupiers, akin to the liberty that the thirteen American colonies had demanded in their war against British rule. The "war of liberation," as the struggle against Napoleon's France was glorified, did not just rouse the Prussian military but also the German nation. Just as Napoleon led a *levée en masse,* those trying to defeat him also mobilized the masses. The military—especially in Prussia—and the German nation would never be the same again.

It was, of course, not just Napoleon's fault (or to his credit) that German nationalism stirred. A certain cultural awakening preceded him, with writers like Goethe and philosophers like Immanuel Kant making German literature and philosophy respectable for the educated in German lands. The Romantic poets revived respect for Germany's cultural heritage. The brothers Grimm went out to collect German folktales from their contemporaries and record them for posterity; few German children have been reared without hearing those often "grim" tales.

Meanwhile, economic development was tugging at the innumerable strings imposed by territorial divisions. Business and commercial interests demanded that tariffs hindering trade and commerce within Germany be removed. The goal was the creation of a common market or an economic community, to use language of the twentieth century with regard to Europe. There could be little doubt that industrialization was turning the wheels of Germany's political unification. It was a question of "coal and steel," as the British economist John Maynard Keynes later said. Industrial power would plow under the old agrarian world.

The Revolution of 1848

Pressures to create a German nation-state went hand in hand with demands for a liberal form of government. The monarchical rule prevailing in most German territories, including Prus-

By going to war against France—and excluding Austria—Otto von Bismarck created a new German empire.

yet-to-be-united Germany. The proposal envisioned a German nation-state that excluded Austria and stipulated a parliamentary monarchy, with the lower house to be chosen by popular elections. The Prussian king was to serve as emperor of the new German nation.

But during the time that it took the deputies to agree on that proposal, the old rulers recovered their strength and quashed the revolution. The Prussian king contemptuously refused the "honor" of the imperial crown, branding it as reeking of the gutter. Even so, the spirit of 1848 did not perish. Denied and suppressed, it nonetheless created nearly irresistible pressures for change. The yearning for national unity and the demands for a liberal form of government confronted the old order with an inescapable challenge.

The Prussian Solution

Even Prussia bent, and imposed, as it was called, a constitution on its subjects barely a year after the king turned down the imperial crown. True, it did not yield on the principle of parliamentary responsibility or mass suffrage, but it granted an elected parliament, which soon would flex its muscle. The constitution also provided for a prime minister. The incumbent of that office would soon tie Prussia's destiny to that of Germany. Full of bravado, Otto von Bismarck (1815–1898) made his debut as Prussian prime minister in 1862 with his "blood-and-iron" speech to Parliament:

> It is not through speeches and majority resolutions that the great questions of our time are decided— that was the big mistake of 1848 . . .
> —but through blood and iron.

It sounded ruthless and menacing, but probably did not miss the historical truth of nation-building by much. Neither Britain nor France owed the creation of their nation-states mainly to speeches or resolutions. It should also not

sia, stood in the way of both at the beginning of the nineteenth century. It is sometimes not clear what those rulers feared more: German nationalism or liberalism. In 1848, a revolution led by middle-class liberals shook that rule and paved the way for a constitutional convention, emulating the example of the convention that drafted the U.S. Constitution in Philadelphia in the 1780s. Meeting in the Paulskirche in Frankfurt, the assembled deputies proposed a constitution, but it was a constitution for a be overlooked that just as Bismarck was speaking, the United States was in the midst of a civil war that would make the Union a nation. In any event, Bismarck held more cards than brute military force. By deft diplomacy he divided and conquered part of the opposition to unification.

Nonetheless, a German nation-state could only be formed in defiance of the international order that had prevailed since the end of the Thirty Years' War. International politics, as much as domestic problems, had thwarted the noble aspirations of 1848: the rumbling of the Russian bear, the huffing of the British fleet, and the rattling of Austrian sabers had intimidated the unifiers. Sensing a weak moment among those powers, Bismarck felt that history offered Prussia a rare opportunity in the 1860s.[2] He bought himself the favor of Russia first, found a convenient ally in unification-eager Italy, and then, from 1864 to 1871, fought Denmark, Austria, and France—one at a time, while leaving England with no chance to intervene.

Revolution from Above

The war against France in 1870–1871 also brought in line the reluctant southern German states and swayed an unenthusiastic Prussian king to accept the imperial crown. So the nation-state came about by a "revolution from above," as opposed to the "revolution from below," as it was envisioned in 1848. The princes of the sovereign German states agreed to a confederation. The constitution did not open with anything like "We, the people." In fact, it never even mentioned the word "nation." To many, this new empire looked suspiciously like a Greater Prussia, what with king, prime minister, and bureaucracy of Prussia in charge of the German empire, not to mention the Prussian army. No matter. The national dream, which briefly came to life in 1848, had

been fulfilled; constitutional demands had been met, halfway in some respects, more than expected in others. Bismarck's counterpart in Britain, Prime Minister Benjamin Disraeli, called the German unification of 1871 a "greater political event than the French Revolution [of 1789]."[3]

THE MONARCHICAL EMPIRE (1871–1918)

The new empire had a national parliament, named after the institution of the previous empire, the *Reichstag,* with legislative and fiscal powers. Its members, moreover, were elected by universal and equal male suffrage, a move that few had demanded and that shocked many. It was Bismarck who pressed for this unprecedented grant of the franchise. Why? Because like U.S. president Abraham Lincoln, who also waged war in the name of national unity, he believed in "government of the people, by the people, for the people"? Undoubtedly not. Those words would not come over Bismarck's lips. Not approvingly. Like all good Prussians, Bismarck believed that government was service, that monarch and prime minister were the top servants of the people. He believed that the franchise would endear the people to the new empire. Moreover, he was confident that he would win their partisan hearts for his side. In that regard Bismarck thought very much like his Conservative counterpart in Britain, Benjamin Disraeli.

Political Fault Lines

No matter the motive, he and his successors had to contend with a growing mobilization of the masses. Political parties, which had been taking shape since the 1840s, quickly made their presence felt in the new state. Several of them were not much to Bismarck's liking, and he tried his utmost to suppress and harass them. The extreme diversity of the German party spectrum laid bare the numerous fault lines dividing the newly unified nation. With at least six major entries, the party system resembled a hexagon. Two corners were occupied by conservatives: one kind deeply unhappy with Prussia's loss of identity in the new Germany, the other agreeable. There were also two kinds of liberals: the National Liberals, ardent champions of German nationalism, and the Progressives, thwarted by Bismarck in their quest for a more liberal constitution. In addition, fearful of their minority status, the Catholics had their own party, the Center, which resembled a political action committee of German Catholicism. And finally, there was a party preaching social revolution, the Social Democrats.

Strong Executive, Weak Parliament

Without much preparation, by historical standards, the latecomer entered the modern age of mass politics. How useful would the old authoritarian recipes for governing prove in such a pluralistic system? True, the head of the government, the *Chancellor,* was accountable to the *Kaiser,* the emperor. And it was the emperor who could fire him, not the Reichstag. There was no provision for a vote of no confidence, the essential characteristic of a parliamentary system. Still, it must be recognized that the chancellor could not expect to get much done without or against Parliament. Like it or not, the chancellor had to build coalitions, not in any formal sense, but certainly in an ad hoc manner, like an American president dealing with Congress. The lack of a no-confidence vote notwithstanding, chancellors had to secure majority support for their policies in Parliament.

While influential, the political parties nevertheless did not govern. They stayed in the waiting room, especially when it came to making foreign policy and military policy. In the Prussian bureaucracy, which administered the empire, a proper Conservative orientation was a must for a career. Liberals and Catholics needed not apply, let alone Socialists. Much has been made of the missing parliamentary responsibility of the chancellor; with it, the empire would have steered in a different, less catastrophic direction. But the truth is that the political parties never pressed this demand to the breaking point—and some opposed it in principle. It must also be acknowledged that the parties would have faced a formidable task in forming a government. They were deeply split among themselves, with none near a majority of seats. As it was, the parties in the Reichstag got used to wielding influence without having to shoulder responsibility. That is too comfortable to stir up revolutionary fervor.

A Place in the Sun

On the eve of World War I, the Germany that had been the least among equals of the European powers laid claim to the number one rank. The furious pace of industrialization, technological progress, and social upheaval in the half century since 1871 turned the gingerbread Germany into a "restless empire." The heady sensation of sudden political prowess was hard to restrain. Gone was the day when a Bismarck could execute cold-blooded, though rational *Realpolitik.* In 1897, accompanied by cheers in the Reichstag, the foreign secretary, and later chancellor (1900–1909), Bernhard von Bülow, promised a more hot-blooded and adventurous course:

> The times when the German conceded one of his neighbors the earth [Russia], and to another the sea [England], and reserved for himself the heaven where the pure doctrine presides—these times are over . . . We do not wish to put anyone in the shadow, but we demand our place in the sun.

With his demand for a "place in the sun," he probably sounded to German ears very much like his contemporary Theodore Roosevelt did to American ears. Certainly, von Bülow was brandishing a big stick, although he was not speaking very softly. Impudent and imprudent, as it must look to a neutral observer, Germany discarded the restraints that Bismarck had urged for a nation hemmed in by "envious and distrustful neighbors." A big and boastful buildup of the navy challenged British supremacy on the high seas and sank any hope of an Anglo-German alliance, which would have calmed German fears of encirclement. Their frequent colonial skirmishes notwithstanding, Britain and France agreed to an *entente cordiale,* aimed against Germany. Add to that the alliance between autocratic Russia and democratic France, and a volatile Germany was left with the moribund Austro-Hungarian Empire as its sole friend.

WORLD WAR I

Obsessed by fear of encirclement, Germany adopted a military strategy that envisioned a lightning strike against France before England could land on the continent and before Russia could put armies into the field. With timing all so critical, Germany believed it had to strike first in order to have any chance of winning a war that was widely expected all over Europe to come sooner or later. That strategy was a desperate gamble that would risk not just military defeat but destruction of the unified Germany and of its political order. Bismarck would have shuddered. Add to that the recklessness in drawing the United States into the war in 1917, and one gets a foretaste of Hitler's military strategy twenty years later.

After fours years of stalemated trench warfare, on November 11, 1918, Germany had to admit defeat of its high-risk strategy.[4] The awesome empire found itself in the doghouse of world politics instead of the sun. Nonetheless, although few realized it, Germany was lucky not to be occupied and carved up by the victors.

Instead, mutiny on the front and turmoil in the streets stirred up a revolutionary brew that simmered until 1933. Behind the lines of combat, the war had sundered a tenuous alliance of domestic forces. The extremes on right and left grew noisier, while the prospects for governing this unruly empire dimmed. When the Kaiser abdicated, political authority fell into the laps of the political parties. The strongest of them was the Social Democratic Party, led by a very pragmatic figure, Friedrich Ebert, who abhorred revolution. The Social Democrats quickly joined forces with the army high command to quash a Bolshevik-type revolution as well as uprisings from renegade military units (*Freikorps*).

THE WEIMAR REPUBLIC (1919–1933)

As the victorious Allies drafted a peace treaty in Versailles, Germans elected a national assembly to draft a new constitution for what was now a republic. The delegates convened in Weimar, far from the din of the revolutionary fighting still going on in Berlin, and evoked the spirit of Germany's most illustrious poets, Goethe and Schiller.

An Unworkable Constitution

The constitution that they designed was a curious hybrid. On one hand, it emphasized the parliamentary principle: the chancellor would be responsible to the Reichstag through the vote of no confidence. On the other hand, the constitution also set up an American-style president, popularly elected and invested with sweeping powers, including the hiring and firing of the chancellor, dissolution of the Reichstag and the emergency powers (Article 48), on which government would heavily rely in times of crisis.

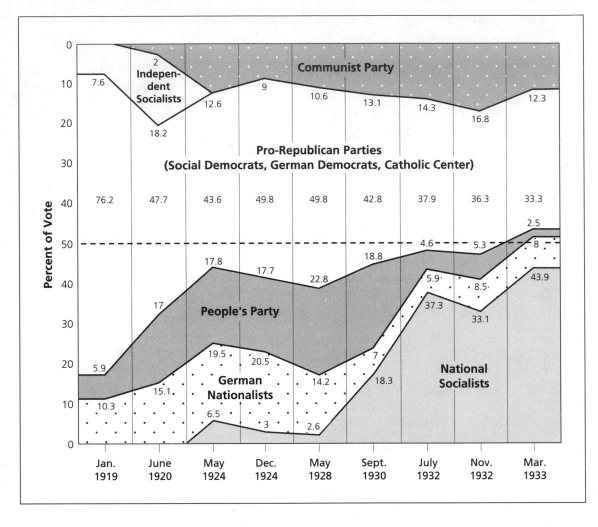

Figure 20.2 Parliamentary Elections in the Weimar Republic.   Source: Hagen Schulze, *Weimar* (Berlin: Severin & Siedler, 1982).

Oddly enough, the constitution makers appeared oblivious to the problem of creating majorities in Parliament that would make the republic governable. The electoral system mandated "proportional representation" of an extreme kind. It allowed for parliamentary representation of even the tiniest party fragments. For an already badly splintered party system, more of the disease was prescribed instead of a cure. Far from aggregating political interests, the Weimar party spectrum magnified and multiplied the divisions of German society (see Figure 20.2).

An Ungovernable Republic

What had been covered up under the monarchy now broke into the open: the inability of the parties in the Reichstag to form authoritative governments. Chancellors in the Weimar Republic lasted less than one single year in

office, on the average, compared to nearly a decade in the monarchy until the outbreak of World War I. For the most part, not two, not three, but four parties had to come to terms to give any chancellor majority support in the Reichstag. The old Conservatives, now running under the German-National banner, and the newly formed Communist Party each cast a spell on the republic. Thus the republic could only be governed if the following parties agreed to lend their support: Social Democrats, Catholics, and the still unreconciled two liberal parties.

At best, it was government by a bickering middle against an implacable opposition from both extremes; at worst, it was caretaker government without parliamentary support. The extremist parties could gloatingly outbid each other in exploiting popular dissatisfaction with the succession of makeshift governments. Surprisingly perhaps, right-wing coups of one sort or another did not overthrow the vulnerable republic, nor did Communist uprisings. The army high command stayed on the sidelines, and the bureaucracy, though mourning the loss of the monarchy, grudgingly stuck to the republican state when a right-wing putsch threatened it in 1920. Hitler's attempt of a coup in 1923 ended ignominiously, although the judiciary let Hitler off with a slap on the wrist. He received an unusually short sentence and was able, in comfortable conditions and aided by trusted assistants, to write *Mein Kampf* while incarcerated.

Unbearable Mortgages

What saddled the new republic with a crushing mortgage right from the start was the Treaty of Versailles, unveiled to a stunned German public in 1919. The treaty stripped Germany of territory in the East, shrank its army to a force suitable for parades but not war, and imposed reparations amounting to more than 100 billion marks. Instead of rallying public support

around an embattled government, that treaty polarized Germany, poisoned public debate, and was grist for the nationalist propaganda mills. "Weimar" and "Versailles" became hated synonyms in wide segments of the German public, two sides of the same coin of national humiliation. The nationalism that had been aroused before 1914 and was wounded by the defeat of 1918 would attack relentlessly any effort to comply with the provisions of the treaty.

If not Versailles, two economic disasters doomed the republic. First the hyperinflation of 1922–1923, fueled by reckless deficit spending aimed at retiring the war debts, ruined countless families whose fortunes were held in savings (see Figure 20.3). Then the Depression of 1929–1932 devastated the German economy. As one business after another tumbled into bankruptcy, unemployment soared to unprecedented levels in Germany: from 6% of the work force in 1928, to 12% by September 1930, to 30% by July 1932, and to 34% by early 1933.

An Undemocratic Triumph

In eerie tandem with those figures climbed the vote share of a party that had languished at the extremist fringe. The party was named incongruously and cumbersomely the National Socialist German Workers Party. Its leader was Adolf Hitler, who had joined it after infiltrating it as a spy. From less than 3% in 1928, it jumped to 18% in 1930 and doubled that share to reach 37% in the July 1932 election. With his party being by far the largest one in the 1932 Reichstag, Hitler justifiably demanded to be appointed chancellor. There was no other party or combination of parties left that commanded a majority in Parliament anymore. Despite strong reluctance and deep disdain for the Nazi leader, President Paul von Hindenburg, a Prussian conservative and World War I hero, finally obliged in January of 1933.

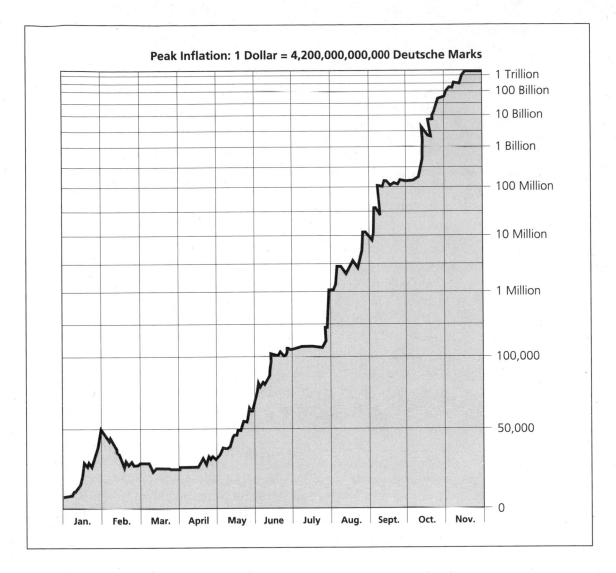

Figure 20.3 Ruinous inflation in Germany, 1923. (Note: the vertical scale is logarithmic). Source: Hagen Schulze, *Weimar* (Berlin: Severin & Siedler, 1982).

Von Hindenburg had just defeated Hitler in the presidential election of 1932. The former general probably felt he could handle the former private. Moreover, the president saw to it that enough Conservatives joined the cabinet to restrain the new chancellor. The plan proved futile, however, as Hitler quickly swept aside his inept and too gullible chaperones, though he was careful to stay in the president's good graces until his death a year later.[5]

THE NAZI APPEAL

What was it about Hitler's party that made so many Germans flock to it in free elections?

Trying to capture the appeal of a party that ultimately delivered mass murder is a painful task. Did Hitler dupe people about his true intentions? He certainly spoke in blunt and, in the ears of upstanding middle-class listeners, offensive language. Nazi propagandists like Joseph Goebbels were not biting their tongues in lashing out at their enemies.

The Charismatic Leader

One need not subscribe to the great-man theory of politics to recognize the personal appeal of Hitler. It hurts to dignify him as "charismatic," but nobody can deny his talent for galvanizing a devoted following and rousing mass audiences with his intoxicating speeches. Other than the war hero, President von Hindenburg, nobody among the many chancellors, ministers, or party leaders can measure up to Hitler in raw personal appeal. This is all the more astonishing since Hitler had few accomplishments in his résumé. No experience in government, or in any walk of private life. He was no war hero himself; no successful entrepreneur; an artist whose paintings neither sold nor won rave reviews. It was easy for reasonable people to underestimate him. And too many did.

Above all, Hitler was a master at appealing to the fears and hopes of people shaken by military defeat and economic depression. He practiced what he preached: "If you want to win the masses you must know the key that opens the door to their heart. It is not objectivity, thus weakness, but will and force."[6] If he gave people a reason to support his party it was largely the promise of a glorious tomorrow to come. But like a religious leader, Hitler asked people to trust him with their hearts rather than their heads. As Gordon A. Craig, an acclaimed American historian with no sympathy for the Nazis, wrote:

Among all the prominent figures of the Weimar period, [Hitler] is the only one of whom it can be said unequivocally that he possessed political genius . . . In his person were combined an indomitable will and self-confidence, a superb sense of timing . . . the intuitive ability to sense the anxieties and resentments of the masses, and to put them in words . . . a mastery of the arts of propaganda, great skill in exploiting the weaknesses of rivals and antagonists, and a ruthlessness in the execution of his designs that was swayed neither by scruples of loyalty nor by moral considerations.[7]

The Message

The better tomorrow Hitler promised to deliver envisioned a nation with power and glory far beyond anybody's dreams (or nightmares). At home, it would be a nation unified in solidarity. There was no room for class warfare in National Socialism. And the other kinds of socialism (Marxism and bolshevism) were to be fought tooth and nail.[8] Abroad, it would be a nation expanding its *Lebensraum* eastward in a vast *empire,* following a German version of "manifest destiny." Hitler made no secret that this called for war and conquest. To him, politics was nothing but the continuation of war by other means. Above all, one group was singled out with unrelieved hatred: the Jews. Hitler blamed them in most lurid terms for every misery Germany had endured. As he thundered incessantly and put in writing in *Mein Kampf,* it was the Jews who had betrayed the nation in 1918 and ruined its economy. He would show no mercy in dealing with them.

It was an intoxicating mixture of hatred and hope that left many sensible observers uncomprehending. But that appeal captured a wide segment of the general public, wider than any other German party ever had. To be sure, the Nazi Party did better among middle-class voters than among the working class. But its electoral support cut to an unprecedented degree across social classes, regions, and religions. Some have called the National Socialist Party the first "people's party" in Germany.[9]

HITLER'S STATE (1933–1945)

With blazing speed, availing himself of emergency powers, Hitler consolidated his grip on power after being named chancellor on January 30, 1933. A new political order, whose classification defies familiar categories, took shape within less than a year. All political parties other than the Nazi Party were banned unless they dissolved themselves. Not having been too adept at using power, those parties now proved no more successful in avoiding their own extinction. The Third Reich, as the new political order was often called, was a one-party state.

But it was also a system that centralized power to an unprecedented degree in the *Führer,* a single leader, around whom it built a quasi-religious worship. For all practical purposes, Hitler's word, often without a written record, was the law. This was not a monarchy restored, or a Napoleonic dictatorship. Perhaps the closest model was the fascist state under Italy's Benito Mussolini, whose attempt to seize power Hitler had tried to copy in 1923, or else the Soviet system. Yet for all of Hitler's singular power, or maybe even as a result of it, the structure of government was by no means as orderly as was claimed. In a curious way, the Third Reich fashioned a panoply of rival institutions alongside established structures of government.

Whatever the organizational structure, the new rulers aimed far more deeply than any other political order had before at politicizing the population. In the proper new spirit, of course. Great effort was devoted to instilling Nazi ideals in the young, through such organization as the Hitler Youth. This state did not just give orders, it wanted people to participate, albeit without asking their opinions or tolerating dissent.

Rearmament and Economic Recovery

It was all part of a mobilization for war and conquest. From day one, Hitler embarked on a gigantic rearmament: in personnel, armaments, navy, air force, and so on. Military spending in 1933 already tripled the 1932 amount, rose threefold again by 1936, and once more by 1938. This buildup quickly resulted in a welcome consequence for the German public, although that was not the primary objective: the collapsed German economy revived. Hitler was no economic genius, but his drive to restore Germany as a great power spelled economic recovery, just as the U.S. entry into World War II finally led the American economy out of the Depression. Here and there, more guns also meant more butter (or maybe just margarine).

By 1936 already, German industrial production surpassed the pre-Depression level of 1928; three of every four who had been unemployed in early 1933 had jobs again by 1936. It does not seem far-fetched to imagine that Hitler could have won re-election in 1936 by a landslide in a free election. Most Germans might have given a favorable response to the question "Are you better off now than you were four years ago?" At least on the economy, the Nazis had succeeded where the Weimar Republic had failed miserably.

MEANS OF CONTROL

But apart from bread or circuses—like the 1936 Olympic Games in Berlin—the Third Reich also impressed its will by means of intimidation, torture, and murder. Citizens' political rights, like freedom of speech or assembly, were suspended. It was not wise to mock the regime in private and downright suicidal to defy it in public. Opponents of the regime, including many who were only suspected of disloyalty, experienced one of the chillier inventions of the Nazis: *concentration camps*.

Although being carted off to one of those camps did not mean certain death in the prewar period, the acronym KZ and whispers of the blood-curdling conditions there would send a chill up anyone's spine. That was part of the purpose, to intimidate opposition and discourage even the thought of resistance. This was true, too, for the *Gestapo* (secret state police), whose officials were recognizable by their trademark ankle-length black leather coats. It was no secret that this police force operated torture cellars right in the center of towns.

The Holocaust

All of this pales, however, compared to the fate of the Jews in the Third Reich. What began with harassment escalated to legalized discrimination by 1936. As the Nazi rulers tightened the vise of economic deprivation and publicly stigmatized the Jews as an alien group, a large number of them saw an ominous handwriting on the wall and left Germany, where they had felt welcome for generations. Those who stayed awaited an unimaginable horror. With the attack on Poland in September of 1939, Hitler did not only start World War II, but embarked on the Holocaust. The "final solution," as the Nazis euphemistically called this horrific deed, was a policy of genocide. With an efficiency that was only possible in the modern age, they rounded up the Jews in occupied territories as well as Germany and delivered them to certain death in killing camps like Auschwitz and Treblinka. How was this possible, many have asked and keep asking.

Admittedly, the final solution was treated like a state secret in Nazi Germany. This was not a matter of public discussion, nor did the regime boast of it. Responsibility for it was entrusted to a special organization, the dreaded SS (*Schutzstaffel*, security units), which carefully screened its recruits. Even within that organization, a great number probably never saw a single person put to death. Leading officials like Adolf Eichmann executed people as if they executed papers dealing with some harmless business. They were bureaucratic killers, not necessarily people whose hearts were filled with murderous desires.

Several brave souls in Germany tried to defy this evil empire of death, among them a group of college students in Munich called the White Rose. The most serious and best-organized attempt on Hitler's life was by German army officers on July 20, 1944. When that attempt failed, it was left to the Allies to liberate the world from National Socialism and reimpose civilized government on Germany.

DEMOCRACY RESTORED

Defeat in 1945 placed Germany's destiny in the hands of the United States, Britain, France, and the Soviet Union. This time, unlike 1918, the nation was occupied and carved up. What is more, defeat now brought to light the shameful horror of the Holocaust and the abominable treatment of people in countries occupied, enslaved, and worked to death by Germany during the war. A nation that disgraced itself and any ideal of civilized government was not fit to govern itself. But before the full measure of Germany's crimes could be taken by the Allies, disputes between the western powers and the Soviet Union soon turned into a warlike conflict, the Cold War. The United States, Britain, and France increasingly pooled their administrative efforts and permitted the creation of common institutions across their zones of occupation. By 1948 those three zones formed a union with a government, for all practical purposes to handle economic matters, albeit under western tutelage.

Politics soon followed economics as the Cold War threatened to grow hot. In 1948, a week after Joseph Stalin imposed a blockade against Berlin, the western powers gave the go-ahead for a constitution to be drafted for a new German state comprising the three western zones. Delegates from regional parliaments, which themselves had been elected as early as 1946, convened what was modestly called a "parliamentary council." The council met in Frankfurt, the city of the 1848 national assembly. And just as national unity proved to be an elusive goal then, it did again, almost exactly 100 years later. But what turned out to be attainable this time was the making of a democratic constitution, at least for the western part of Germany.

Afraid, however, that this would jeopardize Germany's national unity, the parliamentary council did not call its work a "constitution," only a "Basic Law." It was meant for the interim until the eastern part could join in the deliberation for a new national constitution. On May 8, 1949, exactly four years after Germany's unconditional surrender to the Allies, the delegates approved of the draft for a basic law. The vote was 53 in favor and 12 opposed. The broad coalition of support included Christian Democrats, Social Democrats, and Liberals. Once accepted by the Allies, the draft was also ratified by all state parliaments except in Bavaria, which objected to what it considered too little authority for the states.

Anyone reading the text of the Basic Law against the backdrop of German history cannot help but notice the efforts of the framers to put their history lessons to use. Fearful of the threat posed by political parties hostile to freedom and democracy, the framers expressly permitted the banning of such parties. Blaming President von Hindenburg for Hitler's coming to power, they sharply downgraded the authority of the president. The president is not to be chosen by popular election or willed emergency powers; the presidential role in hiring and firing chancellors is narrowly circumscribed, and so is authority for dissolving Parliament.

The new constitution, in turn, strengthens the authority of the chancellor, who will have less to fear from parliamentary intrigue and party conflict. Though not revoking the no-confidence vote, the framers curtail it sharply. Parliament can no longer oust a chancellor unless it can agree on a successor. The Basic Law also introduces judicial review of government acts and vests such authority in a constitutional court. And the election system adopted later on makes great strides to avoid the partisan fragmentation that had bedeviled Germany both under the monarchy and the Weimar Republic. Whatever those provisions may be worth for practical politics, one must admire the devotion of the framers to create a political order that would ease rather than hinder the formation of effective government, while at the same time remaining faithful to the ideals of democracy.

DEMOCRACY DENIED

No sooner had the Federal Republic come to life in the western part of Germany than a separate republic was proclaimed in the eastern part occupied by the Soviet Union after 1945. It was called the German Democratic Republic, but it struck many as neither German nor democratic. For years, most westerners referred to it as the "Soviet zone" or "East zone." The German Democratic Republic was a Soviet-type political system, in which Communists ruled the state without a legal opposition. To be sure, other parties existed, some with names like parties in the West, but they did not compete with one another in free elections. Republic, democratic, civil rights, Christian Democrat, Liberals—many names were the same, but their meanings in East and West had nothing in common. It began with the landing of a small group of German Communist exiles during the

Enraged but powerless: In June, 1953, the East German people could only defend themselves against Soviet tanks with stones.

last week of World War II. Led by Walter Ulbricht, a former member of the Reichstag who
had spent the Nazi years in the Soviet Union,
this group acted under the directive of the Soviet high command. Their assignment was to
establish local self-government in Soviet-occu-
pied Germany. As one of its members later
revealed, Ulbricht instructed them as follows:
"It must look democratic, but we must have
everything in our hands." They took great
pains to appeal to the democratic ideals of 1848,
promised the free operation of political parties,
and disavowed any attempt to impose a Soviet-
style system on East Germany.

Yet their acts soon belied those assurances.
The parties admitted by the Soviet military
government were compelled to join an "antifascist–democratic unity front" in which nothing could be decided against the will of the

Communists. Moreover, in the style of a shot-
gun wedding, the Communists married the Social Democrats, adopting the name of the
German Socialist Unity Party for this forced
partnership. By the end of 1946, the party
indeed enjoyed a monopoly position in East
Germany, buttressed by the Soviet military
government. As in the twelve years before, it
was, once again, not wise to speak freely, even
in private, or to defy the ruling party in public.
East Germans rose against this oppression on
June 17, 1953, and nearly toppled the regime.
As they would do a few years later in Hungary,
Soviet tanks crushed the popular uprising. It
was obvious then that the "people's democracy," as the Communists called their system,
enjoyed little, if any popular support with the
East German public. As the playwright Bertolt
Brecht, by then residing in East Germany, bit-

ingly suggested, the best solution would be for the East German rulers "to dissolve the people and elect a new one." They never quite managed to accomplish that, and so, almost 40 years later, the people dissolved them, as we have seen in the previous chapter, and elected to join the Federal Republic.

NOTES

1. See Christian Graf von Krockow, *Warnung vor Preussen* (Warning of Prussia) (Berlin: Severin & Siedler, 1981).

2. See Michael Stürmer, *Das Ruhelose Reich: Deutschland 1866–1918* (The Restless Empire: Germany 1866–1918). (Berlin: Severin & Siedler, 1983).

3. As quoted in Hagen Schulze, *Weimar: Deutschland 1917–1933* (Berlin: Severin & Siedler, 1982), p. 19.

4. The United States adopted November 11 as Veterans Day.

5. Contrary to much polemics, there is little evidence that German business was a major contributor to the rise of the Nazi Party. Financial support from business did not flow to the party until it had become the strongest party in elections. See Henry Ashby Turner, Jr., *German Big Business and the Rise of Hitler* (New York: Oxford University Press, 1985).

6. Adolf Hitler, *Mein Kampf,* as quoted by Schulze, *Weimar,* p. 338.

7. Gordon A. Craig, *Germany, 1866–1945* (New York: Oxford University Press, 1978), p. 544.

8. The relationship between National Socialism and Communism is a matter of intense dispute. One thesis is that National Socialism is a reaction against Communism. See Ernst Nolte, *Three Faces of Fascism* (New York: Holt, Rinehart and Winston, 1966), p. 323. Also see his highly controversial book, *Der europäische Bürgerkrieg 1917–1945: Nationalsozialismus und Bolschewismus* (The European Civil War 1917–1945: National Socialism and Bolshevism) (Frankfurt: Propylaen, 1987). An article summarizing the hypothesis of that book in the *Frankfurter Allegmeine Zeitung* touched off the "Historians' Dispute." The dispute is discussed in the next chapter.

9. Jürgen W. Falter, *Hitler's Wähler* (Munich: Beck, 1991), p. 371.

REFERENCES AND SUGGESTED READINGS

Craig, Gordon A. 1983. *The Germans.* New York: Putnam.

Hamilton, Richard F. 1982. *Who Voted for Hitler?* Princeton: Princeton University Press.

Krisch, Henry. 1974. *German Politics under Soviet Occupation.* New York: Columbia University Press.

Mayer, Arno. 1989. *Why Did the Heavens Not Darken?* New York: Pantheon.

Merkl, Peter. 1963. *The Origin of the West German Republic.* New York: Oxford University Press.

Stern, Fritz. 1989. *Dreams and Delusions: National Socialism in the Drama of the German Past.* New York: Vintage Books.

Turner, Henry Ashby, Jr. 1987. *The Two Germanies since 1944.* New Haven: Yale University Press.

> *For a prince it is necessary to have the people friendly; otherwise he has no remedy in adversity.*
>
> NICCOLÒ MACHIAVELLI

21

Political Culture:
Citizens and Authority

t times, German princes have proved remarkably deaf to Machiavelli's advice. However devious and ruthless, East Germany's red princes fell from public grace in the fall of 1989. Their only remedy in adversity was to let their "unfriendly" people go, and these people promptly voted them out. Similarly, Germany's last real prince, Kaiser William II, fled from his people amidst mutiny and popular unrest some seventy years earlier. If lessons are needed, these instances demonstrate that politics is more than the actions of rulers. Democracies, of course, guarantee the right of the people to have a say over the actions of rulers. The people's participation is not simply allowed; it is expected. Indeed having a "government by the people" makes it hard to tell who governs and who is being governed.

There is no denying that attitudes and actions of ordinary people matter greatly for government and politics, in Germany as elsewhere. People are no mere spectators of a game played by political professionals. To be sure, many may confine their involvement to cheering on their favorites or booing the other side. But they also may, at any moment, decide to join in the game, trying to alter its outcome in the direction they desire. Hence it is important to determine what the German public thinks about politics. How friendly are Germans toward the rules by which their political game is played? What role do they believe they can play on the political stage? What influence do important social groups have on their political orientations? How do Germans learn what they believe about politics?

CULTURAL PREDISPOSITIONS

Political scientists like Gabriel Almond and Sidney Verba use the concept of "political culture" to call attention to attitudes of the mass public that have an important bearing on the working of the political system.[1] In their view, a democracy is not likely to thrive unless a "civic culture" has taken root in the general population. This is a culture where, among other things, citizen participation is highly valued and the political system enjoys a broad measure of good will among the citizenry.

Cultural False Starts

Germany is a case, as we have seen, where an experiment with democracy failed miserably, in 1933. No doubt, the Weimar constitution had flaws; the burden of Versailles and the Depression were crushing; elites in agriculture and industry despised the republic; intellectuals disparaged it; and political leaders tried to subvert it. But it can also be argued that Germany lacked the requisite civic culture to make a democratic system work. It does not libel Wei-

mar to call it a "republic without republicans." There seemed to be few citizens whose hearts beat faster at the thought of the republic or the sight of its symbols. The death of the republic did not touch off a massive show of public mourning, whereas Hitler's inauguration was greeted by delirious crowds.

For that reason, many observers worried about the success of replicating the experiment with democracy after World War II. The convening of a constitutional assembly was not by popular demand. Nor did people celebrate the fruits of that convention, the Basic Law, with fireworks, parades, and a lot of cheers. Opinion polls confirm the lack of popular enthusiasm for either the Weimar or the Federal Republic early on. The Allensbach Institute has been asking people to indicate the time period "when in this century do you feel things have gone best for Germany?" (see Table 21.1). The first glimpse of those feelings is available in 1951. The answers could not have been more discouraging to the friends of democracy.

In 1951, hardly any German thought Germany was best off at that moment. The creation of a democratic constitution in 1949 apparently counted little, compared with the country's de-

Table 21.1 OPINIONS OF WEST GERMAN PUBLIC ABOUT THE TIME IN THIS CENTURY WHEN THINGS HAVE GONE BEST

	1951 (%)	1959 (%)	1963 (%)	1970 (%)	1980 (%)
At present	2	42	63	81	80
Between 1933 and 1939 (Third Reich before World War II)	42	18	10	5	3
Between 1920 and 1933 (Weimar Republic)	7	4	5	2	2
Before 1914 (Kaiser Reich)	45	28	16	5	4
Don't know	4	8	6	7	11
	100	100	100	100	100

Source: Elisabeth Noelle-Neumann, *The Germans: Public Opinion Polls 1967–1980* Copyright © 1981. Reprinted with permission of Greenwood Publishing Group, Inc., Westport, CT.

feat and present-day deprivations. Likewise, the Weimar Republic evoked few pleasant memories. Its promise of democracy meant little, certainly less than its practice and performance, especially at the end. We begin to understand why this republic fell without a whimper or much weeping in public.

The Illiberal Culture

One of Germany's most celebrated novelists of the twentieth century once wrote that "the German people will never love political democracy."[2] He was by no means distraught by this lack of love. Nor was he alone taking intellectual shots at democracy. German political thinkers neither pioneered nor helped popularize the ideal of liberal democracy in the way that Locke, Montesquieu, or Jefferson did elsewhere. Many intellectuals of his time held democracy to be a western import alien to the spirit of German culture. Thomas Mann was just one of the most eloquent voices of Germany's cultured elite defending the virtues of a special brand of political order separate both from western democracy and eastern despotism.

The kind of political system that Mann called, with a mix of awe and affection, the *Obrigkeitsstaat*, was not oppressive or capricious. It revered the rule of law and tolerated freedom of speech. But this political order was firm in keeping the people at bay, especially the modern form in which they expressed their views and organized themselves, namely the political parties. What Mann extolled in ringing phrases, others, saw in less benign terms. Critics deplored what they regarded as a dangerous "illiberalism," which was bound to lead Germany into catastrophe.

Strangely enough, in Germany this illiberalism is said to have conquered the social class that elsewhere led the fight for liberal values: the educated and prosperous middle class. Why this bizarre twist in Germany? According

Thomas Mann (1875–1955)—His family saga, *The Buddenbrooks*, earned him the Nobel Prize for Literature in 1929..

to the historian Fritz Stern, in Germany national chauvinism and fear of social revolution triumphed over liberal aspirations.[3] The sociologist Ralf Dahrendorf draws the image of a "faulted nation."[4] Rather than adopt the values of the American and French revolutions and embark on the road to the modern age, middle-class Germans turned backward in ardently embracing the feudal order that delivered order at home and a place in the sun abroad. As part of the bargain, they were happy to accept an "apolitical" role for themselves in that system.

The Good Old Days of the Empire

Indeed, even a quarter century after it was gone, the empire of the good old days before 1914 was much beloved. This was a system whose passing was mourned and whose re-establishment would have seemed quite welcome in 1951. Even allowing for some nostalgia, it is safe to say that the empire commanded a strong "system affect" at its time. Whatever that may tell us about the support for an authoritarian regime, it must be acknowledged that this empire had some democratic features. The general (male) population was able to participate in politics. And people were not averse to making use of their political rights. Their partisan choices were as diverse as anywhere in the world, and one political party, the Social Democrats, had attracted more than one million members by the turn of the century. The experiment with democracy had begun long before 1918.

What is more, voters increasingly flocked to political parties that favored the expansion of democracy or, at least, were amenable to democratic reforms. In 1919, with women now equal in political rights, the German people elected a national assembly that drafted a democratic constitution with overwhelming support. It was not a choice that had to be forced down people's throats, although few risked their necks later on to save it.

The Popularity of National Socialism

What is truly shocking about the opinions in 1951, however, is that 42 percent picked the Nazi period (Third Reich) as the best time for Germany. One hates to ponder how many more West Germans felt that way, but were too uncomfortable to admit it face-to-face to an interviewer. To be sure, the reference is only to the prewar years of Nazi rule, which brought recovery from the Depression and a return to

great-power status. These are no small accomplishments, if one can simply ignore the fact that they were deliberate preparations for a war of conquest. But even with that qualification set aside, were those accomplishments worthy enough to outweigh the lack of political freedom, widespread oppression, torture, and murder in concentration camps, and the blatant segregation of Jews, marking them for some ominous fate to come? Did those Germans just close their eyes and ears? Or did they accept the dark sides as the inevitable costs of those benefits? Or, perish the thought, did they happily approve of the darker side of National Socialism?

Whatever the answer, it is no longer utterly mysterious how the Nazi regime managed to carry out its policies. It could count on strong "system affect" in the German public. There can be little doubt but that the Third Reich was genuinely popular; popular enough for people to shrug off or rationalize ghastly deeds. It was not simply full employment and Germany acting like a great power, again, that won applause. Even as Hitler, at the end of the war, condemned his own people to total destruction, they remained friendly enough not to rise up against this system. One hates to contemplate how Germans would have reacted to a successful attempt to overthrow Hitler: with cheers for the plotters or with wrath?

The many brave souls who paid with their lives for resistance notwithstanding, it is undeniable that a large portion of the German people liked a political order that ruled with an iron hand, put "enemies" in their place, and got rid of the irritations of public debate and competing party interests. Indeed, considerable public support for a one-party state survived the end of the Nazi tyranny. In 1950, according to another Allensbach survey, one-quarter of the respondents favored such a system. In a large segment of the West German public, the Nazi culture was quite alive throughout the 1950s. Even at the end of the decade, as Table

21.1 shows, nearly one-fifth still rated the pre-war Third Reich as Germany's best years.

If anything, this share must be regarded as a low estimate, given the growing pressures of socially desirable responses and "political correctness." To display Nazi sympathies openly in the Federal Republic was, and still is, against the law. Oddly enough, the democratic state has to resort to abridging political freedoms to protect itself from people deemed "unfriendly" to the political order. In view of the attitudes of a good number of the people, that caution was not without reason.

ACQUIRING A TASTE FOR DEMOCRACY

Under the watchful eyes of the western powers, democratic institutions had been re-created in 1949 in the western part of Germany. Would a civic culture follow this time? The Allies helped with programs of de Nazification and re-education. And the Germans themselves engaged in what they called, in ugly bureaucratese, *Vergangenheitsbewaltigung* (coming to grips with the past, i.e., the crimes of the Nazi period). In the long run, generational change was bound to alter the complexion of the political culture. The age groups with fond memories of the empire would die out in the next twenty years, and the age groups with Nazi sympathies somewhat later. Indeed, by 1980, according to Table 21.1, hardly anyone expressed fondness for either of those eras anymore.

Output Orientation

But the rapid decline of that support and the steep rise of support for the present Federal Republic stemmed from more than generational turnover. Already by the end of the 1950s, Germans were able to pass judgment on a democracy that had achieved fabulous pros-

perity and a quick return of what was now West Germany to the ranks of major powers. Furthermore, the government in Bonn had shown an impressive staying power and resolve in handling the big postwar issues. The first chancellor of the Federal Republic held office longer than the whole Weimar Republic lasted. All of this must have dispelled any fear that democracy could deliver neither (a) prosperity, (b) international respect, nor (c) orderly government. It was a set of lessons apparently not lost on the West German public. By 1963, almost two-thirds picked the Federal Republic as the period when things had gone best for Germany.

On the other hand, Almond and Verba's study of political culture failed to uncover much evidence for a "general system affect" in the German public, who took great pride in the country's economic system, but little pride in the governmental system. The one did not necessarily carry over into the other. Germans were seen to be "output-oriented." They judged the value of a political system by how well it delivered the goods. Almond and Verba concluded that:

> Germans tend to be satisfied with the performance of their government, but to lack a more general attachment to the system on the symbolic level. Theirs is a highly pragmatic—probably overpragmatic—orientation to the political system.[5]

To moralists that attitude reeked of opportunism, bordering on moral corruption. It is a major theme of a novel like *Billiards at Half Past Nine* by Heinrich Böll, one of Germany's best-known postwar writers and also a winner of the Nobel prize for literature.[6] Without the slightest qualms of conscience, key figures in that novel make their peace successively with an authoritarian regime, a totalitarian regime, and finally a democracy, all in a single lifetime. Poetic license turns the executioners of yesterday into the executives of today, letting them proclaim their sincere support for the principles of the regime of the day. It is less the devotion to an evil empire at one time than the faithlessness of such people that galls Böll. An unrepentant Nazi, or Communist nowadays, would seem more appealing than a *Wendehals* (rubber neck), the latest brand of deft U-turn artists. The term was coined for East Germans who managed to convert from socialism to capitalism the moment the Wall fell.

Falling Satisfaction with Democracy

It is one thing to think highly of democracy when times are good. It is another to be faithful to it in times of sickness and strife. In particular, given the German experience, what happens to support for democracy when the economy falters? So far, four economic recessions have occurred since 1949, including the latest one in 1992–1993. To be sure, none of them was even remotely comparable to the Depression of the 1930s. Even the Weimar Republic might have survived any of them unscathed.

The first economic setback, in the mid-1960s, stirred the dormant right-wing extremism back to life. The National Democratic Party, whose name sounded ominously similar to that of the Nazi Party, captured close to 10% of the votes in some state elections. It was enough to sound a loud warning that only receded when the party failed to win representation in the federal election of 1969. The next recession, in the mid-1970s, failed to trigger a right-wing revival or any other challenge to the democratic order. Germans, it seemed, had learned to take such setbacks in stride and not lose faith in their democracy. Perhaps system affect had by now grown so strong as to be immune to economic colds. In the early 1980s, the recession was accompanied by the rise of new social movements and the Green Party, although they were more concerned with ecology than economy. In the early 1990s, economic tribulations again have coincided with a resurgence of extremist parties on the right, but the dominant concern appears to be more with the influx of foreigners than with the domestic economy.

Still, by some measure, support for democracy appears to have slipped in recent years. Throughout most of the 1970s, nearly eight of ten West Germans typically expressed "satisfaction" with the democracy of the Federal Republic, according to *Forschungsgruppe Wahlen* surveys. In the next three years, as the West German economy suffered its worst recession since the 1930s, that support level slipped toward the 50% mark. As the economy recovered, democratic support rose only slightly, rarely topping 65%. Strangely enough, that may be a healthy sign for democracy. It might be wrong to think that satisfaction with the existing democracy is the same as support for the principles of democracy. Indeed there are numerous critics who argue that the Federal Republic is not very democratic at all, that it camouflages autocratic rule with democratic rhetoric. It is no coincidence that the drop in satisfaction with democracy corresponded with the rise of new social movements and the Green Party. As we shall see, one of the key motives for their growth is the demand for more citizen influence over government decisions. They press for a more direct form of democracy. It would not be correct, however, to say that demands for a more perfect democracy come only from the quarters of the new politics.

NATIONAL ALLEGIANCE

Few Americans would see any problem in holding both a strong belief in democracy and warm feelings about one's national identity. Likewise, among political liberals in the Germany of the early nineteenth century, the two went hand in hand. The spirit of 1848 held both democracy and nation dear. Bismarck severed that harmony, and from that time on, nationalism increasingly became a cause of the anti-democratic right, all the way to National Socialism. Germany is a country where nationalistic fervor turned to hubris, and where the past raises more painful questions about the nation than it provides comforting answers. Critics on the left, like Jürgen Habermas, assert that a "conventional form of national identity" does not suit the Federal Republic: "The only patriotism that does not alienate us from the West is a constitutional patriotism."[7] In the 1920s, advocates of such an attitude were known as *Vernunftrepublikaner* (loosely translated as "republicans without passion"). They were no match for the power of Hitler's appeal to people's emotions.

Calls for More Patriotism

Opinion polls have consistently shown that, compared with other countries, West Germany has indeed been short on national pride. One rather typical finding was that whereas 87% in the United States, 58% in Britain, and 42% in France said they were "very proud" of being citizens of their respective nations, only 21% did in the Federal Republic.[8] The mid-1980s witnessed a scattered chorus calling for a more unabashed attitude toward the nation. One of the loudest voices among established politicians was that of the late Franz-Josef Strauss: "We don't want totally fanatical nationalists ... but instead we don't want a nation of 60 million nihilists either!"[9] Likewise, Chancellor Kohl has made it a point to appeal to national symbols, frequently invoking the "Fatherland" in his speeches, and calling for a "normal patriotism."

Critics read such calls as code words for closing the book on Germany's (Nazi) past. They suspect that such flag-waving is intended to sweep away the question of guilt, to help people feel better about the present by letting them forget the past. In 1986, an article by the histo-

rian Ernst Nolte entitled "The Past that Will Not Pass" ignited a firestorm of controversy.[10] This "quarrel among historians," just like the one in the 1960s over Germany's responsibility for World War I, was much less a scholarly debate than a cultural street fight waged on the pages of papers like the *Frankfurter Allgemeine* and *Die Zeit*. Nolte insinuated that the preoccupation with the Nazi past served political interests, with the Left using it to detract attention from mass killings committed by Communist regimes. But that was only a firecracker compared to the bomb he tossed by suggesting that the Holocaust was a preventive measure against the threat posed by Stalin's murderous communism. Critics angrily rejected this argument as a lie and a clumsy attempt of political cleansing.[11]

The Nazi past remains a topic in which even the purest intentions may easily lead to career-ending slips of the tongue. An effort to explain comes across as an attempt to excuse, to ask for forgiveness as a plea to forget, and to blame particular groups and parties as self-serving. How difficult this task can prove, even for a well-meaning speaker devoid of any personal responsibility, was demonstrated by the fate of Bundestag speaker Philipp Jenninger. His speech on the fiftieth anniversary of *Kristallnacht* (the Nazi pogrom of 1938) touched off such a furor that he was forced to step down as speaker.[12]

The Good Feeling of Home

These issues have also played themselves out in popular culture. Movies and television turned bolder in addressing the issue of national identity. A strong popular resonance greeted the television series "Heimat," that untranslatable German expression connoting "area where one feels at home," where the land and the people are familiar and sweet. The 15-part series, which also aired on American television (PBS), is the saga of life in a fictional village, poor but picturesque, near Coblenz on the Rhine. It portrays its characters leading their daily lives through this century with political fallout from the empire to the Federal Republic raining on them like a faint drizzle.

Yes, the Nazi era also intrudes in their lives, but that is just one among many other events. Moreover, it passes through without leaving much of a trace. The Nazis remain an alien force that fails to diminish the basic goodness of the people in "Heimat." The viewer feels more inclined to sympathize with the characters than pass judgments on their actions, however questionable they may seem. American viewers may follow with special fascination the fate of one of the main characters, who early in the series heads for the road to a place far away, leaving an uncomprehending childhood sweetheart behind. Much later it is revealed that he made his way to the United States, where he prospered in business. After several visits back to Germany, never quite able to reconcile with his former love, he returns home for good in his old age. Though unmistakably American in mannerism, he is heartsick for the Heimat he abandoned as a young man looking for adventure far from home.

THE POLITICAL GERMAN

What had been extolled as a virtue by some and decried as a vice by others, the "apolitical German" must nowadays be placed in the category of endangered species. Interest in politics has risen dramatically since the unenthusiastic reception of the Basic Law by the West German public. In 1952, according to Allensbach surveys, barely one of four Germans was reported to be interested in politics, while twenty years later one of every two did.[13] Likewise, the inclination to talk about politics has surged, to a point where over 80% report discussing politics during election campaigns.[14] And what is most reassuring, "the politically interested in the Bonn Republic are the most emphatic opponents of a reemergence of the totalitarian past."[15] More interest in politics goes hand in hand with greater support for democratic institutions.

Group Membership

In one regard, Germans have always matched up well to requirements of good citizenship. Germans are joiners. Above all, in sports. The country that won the 1992 Soccer World Cup (its third trophy) has 5.2 million members in soccer clubs, a sport with a distinctive working-class connotation. The country-club sport of yesterday, tennis, has rapidly expanded to attract nearly 2 million members nowadays, inspired by the successes of Steffi Graf and Boris Becker. Even more belong to clubs pursuing the most traditional form of physical exercise in Germany—gymnastics.[16] Physical fitness was part of the agenda of the patriotic movement in the nineteenth century. Sports and politics have been closely married in Germany since then, through Hitler's 1936 Olympic showcase of Nazi superiority, the greenhouselike raising of athletes in the former German Democratic Republic, and the passionate nationalism of soccer fans at national games in the Federal Republic.

In small towns and in the countryside, *Schützenvereine* (rifle clubs), with their colorful attire, their parades and local festivals, are the heart of social life. At work, nearly one of every three Germans belongs to a labor union. That share has been achieved without the coercive benefit of the "closed shop" and has not changed much in recent years. The political parties count their dues-paying membership in the hundreds of thousands, with the Social Democrats exceeding one million in 1976.

Aloofness from social groups certainly is no characteristic of German society. Group activity pervades everyday life to a remarkable degree, even though the school system does little, by American standards, to foster the group spirit through extracurricular activities.

Civic Orientations in the West

Political interest and group activity go hand in hand with a sense that the individual is not a passive subject in politics, but an active participant. A question asked of Germans in 1959 and again in 1974 indicates that West Germans have acquired a considerable sense of "civic competence." That is the feeling that citizens can do something about influencing political decisions at the top. Whereas in 1959, barely four in ten Germans felt they could do something about an unjust national regulation, by 1974, nearly six in ten felt that way.[17] The gap that separated Germans from Britons in this regard has been virtually closed. If anything, Germans under 30 years of age have moved ahead of their contemporaries abroad. The young, after all, are being brought up in a thoroughly democratic climate that tolerates not the slightest espousal of authoritarian alternatives.

As a result, Germany today represents an exception in reverse. Whereas the United States and Britain witnessed a decline of such attitudes as civic competence, political efficacy, and trust in government, the trend line for those attitudes in the Federal Republic pointed upward. Whatever deficits may have afflicted the German political culture have been largely erased. Yet ironically, it is the growing citizen competence that provokes frustrations with the existing democracy. The political system is not responsive enough to civic-minded citizens pressing their demands on policymakers. This is especially true for politics at the federal level. Hence, Germany nowadays has a political culture where increased citizen confidence may diminish one's confidence in the political order.

Democratic Values in the East

If ever a generation of Germans proved their credentials of democratic citizenship not in opinion polls or hypothetical situations, but by sticking their necks out, it was the one that rose against their rulers and overthrew them in East Germany in 1989. They earned their political rights for themselves and the rest of society in a way that had never happened in Germany before. In view of that, it is almost beside the point to inquire about the attitudes of East Germans toward democracy and the citizen role. The behavior of East Germans, however, raises some puzzling questions about political culture. For one thing, if East Germans exhibit democratic attitudes to a high degree, how could they have acquired them, given the non-democratic system in which they lived for more than 40 years? Second, if it turned out that they did not hold democratic attitudes, what prompted their actions?

Table 21.2 shows that the eastern German public, in fact, espouses democratic values to an astonishing degree. It would do the citizens of any democracy proud. The support matches almost point for point the support exhibited by the western German public. How did the eastern Germans come to those beliefs? One possibility is that those beliefs represent the lesson of their own experiment with democracy. You preach what you practice. Another possibility is that eastern Germans have learned that those beliefs are now the "politically correct" ones to express. Both suggestions strain our assumption of how fast people learn. It took western Germans a long time, as we just saw, either to keep mum about politically incorrect opinions or to espouse honestly democratic principles.

Table 21.2 DEMOCRATIC ATTITUDES IN WESTERN AND EASTERN GERMANY

Percent who agree that	West	East
Everyone should have the right to express an opinion even when the majority disagree	92	92
A viable democracy is not possible without an opposition	92	95
In principle, every democratic party should have a chance to govern	91	88
Citizens have the right to demonstrate, if necessary, for their convictions	90	90
It is the responsibility of the opposition not to criticize the government, but to support it	61	47

Percent who would		
Sign a petition	87	87
Participate in a demonstration	53	60
Join a citizen initiative	75	83
Use violence	14	18
Occupy construction site	21	21
Damage buildings	6	2

Source: Rudolf Wildenmann, "Some Aspects of the German Revolution of 1989," paper presented at the 1990 meeting of the American Political Science Association, San Francisco. Manfred Berger, Matthias Jung, and Dieter Roth, *Einstellungen zu Aktuellen Fragen der Innenpolitik 1992 in Deutschland*, 1992. Used by permission from American Political Science Association.

The alternative is that East Germans had come to espouse democratic values for quite some time and were acting upon them in overthrowing the Communist regime. Indeed, seen from that perspective, the East German revolution would be proof that a political culture can sweep away a political system (authoritarian) that is at odds with that culture (democratic). The question, then, is how that culture was able to take root right under the nose of a hostile and highly intrusive state apparatus. The answer must be that East German citizens were living a "virtual reality" kind of life in the West by way of daily television exposure to western culture. These are tantalizing prospects that future research will have to illuminate more fully.

POLITICAL SOCIALIZATION

In the typical case, political beliefs are learned from one's parents and affected by education and life experiences. We do not become political citizens just by entering adulthood. By that time, most of our political orientations have taken shape. We are inclined to stick to them unless strong pressures compel us to think otherwise.

Family Ties

Unfortunately, by the time Germans typically reached late adolescence during this century, strong pressures were pushing them in a different direction from what their parents had pointed them to. Only the Federal Republic has lasted long enough to permit one generation reared under it to bring up its offspring without major political upheavals. And even that can be safely said only about the western part of that republic. Given the widespread allegiance to nondemocratic systems in the German population of the early postwar years, it is doubtful that many growing up in the 1950s and even 1960s learned to love democracy at mommy's knee or from dad at the dinner table. If mom and dad talked politics with the kids, it might have been more about the good old days than about the republic today.

Even the good old days was a tricky topic, however, since they had ended in defeat and shame. Children being bundles of curiosity, what youngster could resist needling parents with the question "And what did you do in those years?" Hence, it seemed most prudent for parents to keep politics out of family discussions. After all, as a German saying goes, politics ruins family life. One way or the other, political socialization in German families could do little to kindle an appreciation for democracy and good citizenship.

Political Learning in Schools

The schools found themselves in very much the same situation as the parental generation. But they had some ways to avoid it, especially in the West. First of all, civics or social studies were not taught until the late 1960s. Politics surfaced in history classes. But that subject of study was burdened with a long agenda ranging from the ancient cultures on the Nile and Euphrates to the balance of power of the Bismarck era. There was often not enough time left at the end of the school year to cover the Third Reich. Let alone the Federal Republic, which was simply the present, and thus not history anyway.

The study of German literature like Heinrich Böll's *Billiards at Half Past Nine,* Bertolt Brecht's *Life of Galileo,* or Thomas Mann's *Magic Mountain* was apt to illuminate political issues, though perhaps leaving the student with a more cynical than cheerful attitude toward German politics, past and present. To be sure, social studies has become a recognized subject, but its focus is more wordly

than simply the political order of the Federal Republic.

Moreover, schools in the Federal Republic are not required to engage in the democratic rituals familiar to American schoolchildren. In Germany you do not start out the day with a pledge of allegiance; and you don't sing the national anthem before a school concert or football game. Nor do you conduct mock elections for president; or have school teams in sports or much in the way of extracurriculaur activities. Many Germans would scoff at such rituals as reciting the Pledge of Allegiance as being either ridiculous or dangerous. Many, especially on the political Left, are leery of any flag-waving patriotism. Democracy may have captured the minds of German students, but not their hearts. It is significant that national pride is especially low among the Germans under 30 years of age with *Abitur.* These are the most highly educated of the younger generation, brought up by parents and teachers—many of whom were themselves reared after 1945. Whatever it is they learn in school, it is not to love their republic; nor, in the absence of any extracurricular activities, how to be a good republican.

Class Stratification in Schools

One inadvertent lesson, however, not lost on many students is a lesson in social stratification. In the Federal Republic, the typical teenage student does not attend a comprehensive school. The best and the brightest attend the Abitur-awarding *Gymnasium.* Lest the name confuse you, this is a place for much mental, but little physical, exercise. The chief mission of this vaunted institution has always been, and still is, to prepare youths in their teens for university study in their twenties. It is a college-preparatory high school, in other words, but with a nine-year curriculum.

Entering a *Gymnasium* at age 10 is a tense rite of passage, with your parents making the key decision. Caught between parental expectations and the pressures of a demanding and not-too-forgiving scholastic environment, you are facing a moment filled with anxiety. Middle-class parents would send their offspring to the *Gymnasium* as a matter of course, while working-class parents would not think of it. A steelworker's son would continue in the *Volksschule* (now *Hauptschule*), or maybe *Realschule*, and then learn a trade afterward.

This class bias has spurred controversial demands for reform. The most radical reform proposal is aimed at dissolving the *Gymnasium* and creating a unified type of secondary school, the *Gesamtschule*, instead. This would be an American-style high school, in other words. The *Gymnasium* survived this onslaught, but at a price. It is easier now to enter this type of school as well as to survive the first few critical grades. As a result, a much larger and more diverse student body nowadays attends the *Gymnasium* and what it prepares for, the university. The social class lines of (West) German society have become more permeable.

But with educational opportunities expanded, *Gymnasium* graduates are often getting a bitter taste of equality and competition. Many of them find their favored major closed out; the most popular majors of German university students remain, in this order, law, medicine, and business administration. Moreover, a rejection slip from the central admission office means being rejected not just by the favored university, but by every single one within the Federal Republic. The expansion of university enrollment has raised expectations that have gone unfulfilled. Ironically, "as more and more people take advantage of educational expansion, they . . . discover that opportunities for social promotion through education have declined."[18] For many students admitted to their favored major, the bitter taste may come after university graduation. In particular, students who now graduate with a degree in Ger-

man literature or political science will find the door closed where they hoped to find employment: in the educational system, especially the *Gymnasium*. The state is not hiring. A shrinking population fills fewer classrooms—which require fewer teachers to staff them.

CHURCHES AND STATE

Germany is the country where the Reformation originated some 500 years ago and where the political traces of religious divisions are visible to this day. The North is predominantly Protestant, the Rhineland and the South mostly Catholic. The regional religious split dates back to the policy of "cujus regio, ejus religio." It meant that the religious preference of the ruler of a territory prescribed the proper religious faith for all subjects. Religion came with the territory of the ruler, though rulers like Frederick the Great of Prussia (1740–1786) were known for their tolerance of different religions.

In the unified Germany of 1990, Protestants and Catholics hold a rough parity, with each of them commanding roughly 40 percent of the population. That leaves quite a large proportion unaccounted for. Most of them are in eastern Germany, which used to be predominantly Protestant. Religious allegiance appears to have withered during the years of communism. Is that a tribute to communism's heavy-handed efforts to stamp out religion and instill atheism in the population? If so, it would rate as one of the few "accomplishments" of communist indoctrination.

It is quite apparent that Germans in the West, baptized though they may be, are attending church services in dwindling numbers. Formal membership, yes—participation, no. In the western part, barely three in ten Catholics and only one of ten Protestants appear to go to church every Sunday.[19] Churchgoing Catholics form the most dependable pillar of electoral support for the Christian parties. Those voters cannot help but miss the sermon on election day—always a Sunday—exhorting them to go and vote for candidates upholding Christian principles. This is truly a case of preaching to the converted.

Yet regardless of whether they attend services every Sunday, or just at Christmas, or never, nearly all of them dutifully make their financial contributions to the church of their baptism. How do the churches manage to count on such generosity and cooperation from their members? Is this the ultimate proof of the civic-mindedness of German citizens? Well, anytime everyone contributes, you might guess that it is a tax withheld from your paycheck. That is indeed how it works. Any baptized German is assessed a "church tax." That is the name for it. It is one of the arrangements between state and church in the Federal Republic that the state collects an amount close to 10% of one's income tax liability and forwards that to one's church.

With some exaggeration, one might say that the Federal Republic recognizes both Protestantism and Catholicism as alternate state religions, each enjoying privileges. In addition to serving as tax collector for them, the state allows each religion to be taught in schools, provides for theology departments in the universities, and treats church employees as civil servants. There is no sharp separation of church and state, as called for by the U.S. Constitution. A potentially explosive issue, the linkage stirs little political conflict in Germany.

Quietly, many Germans are solving the problem personally by terminating their church membership, which requires a visit to the courthouse, not the church rectory. Unification apparently has spurred a withdrawal movement. The imposition of a unification tax prompted a good number of inactive church members to take a closer look at their pocket-

books than at their prayer books.[20] By saving the church tax, roughly the same amount as the unification tax, they wind up with little net loss of income. As is so often the case, politics is a double-edged sword for religion.

Notes

1. See Gabriel Almond and Sidney Verba, *The Civic Culture* (Boston: Little, Brown, 1965).

2. Thomas Mann, *Betrachtungen eines Unpolitischen* (Reflections of an Apolitical) (Berlin: S. Fischer, 1922), p. xxxiv.

3. See Fritz Stern, *The Failure of Illiberalism* (Chicago: University of Chicago Press, 1971).

4. See Ralf Dahrendorf, *Society and Democracy in Germany* (Garden City, N.Y.: Doubleday, 1967).

5. Almond and Verba, p. 313.

6. Heinrich Böll, *Billiards at Half Past Nine* (New York: Avon Books, 1975).

7. As quoted in *The New York Times*, September 6, 1986.

8. See E. J. Dionne, "Government Trust: Less in West Than U.S.," *New York Times*, February 16, 1986. Also see Elisabeth Noelle-Neumann and Renate Kocher, *Die Verletzte Nation* (The Injured Nation) (Stuttgart: Deutsche Verlags-Anstalt, 1988), p. 50.

9. As quoted in *The New York Times*, January 13, 1987.

10. See Ernst Nolte, "Vergangenheit, die nicht vergehen will," *Frankfurter Allegmeine Zeitung*, June 6, 1986.

11. For an overview of this controversy, see Konrad H. Jarausch, "Removing the Nazi Stain? The Quarrel of the German Historians," *German Studies Quarterly* (1988): 285–301; also *Forever in the Shadow of Hitler? Original Documents of the Historikerstreit, the Controversy Concerning the Singularlity of the Holocaust* (Atlantic Highlands, N.J.: Humanities Press, 1993).

12. See Serge Schmemann, "Bonn Speaker Out after Nazi Speech," *The New York Times*, November 12, 1988.

13. Elisabeth Noelle-Neumann, *The Germans: Public Opinion Polls 1967–1980* (Westport, Conn.: Greenwood Press, 1981), p. 150.

14. Kendall Baker, Russell Dalton, and Kai Hilde-brandt, *Germany Transformed: Political Culture and the New Politics* (Cambridge, Mass.: Harvard University Press, 1980), p. 40.
15. David P. Conradt, "Changing German Political Culture," in *The Civic Culture Revisited*, Gabriel Almond and Sidney Verba, eds. (Boston: Little, Brown, 1980), pp. 239–241.
16. *Facts about Germany* (Frankfurt: Societäts-Verlag, 1992), p. 309.
17. See Samuel Barnes and Max Kasse, *Political Action: Mass Participation in Five Western Democracies* (Beverly Hills: Sage, 1979). The figure for 1959 was reported by Almond and Verba, *The Civic Culture*.
18. Heiner Meulemann, "Value Change in West Germany, 1950–1980," *Social Science Information*, 22 (1983), 777–800.
19. *Forschungsgruppe Wahlen*, February 1987 survey.
20. See Craig R. Whitney, "Church Tax Cuts German Fold," *The New York Times*, December 27, 1992.

References and Suggested Readings

Boynton, G. Robert, and Gerhard Loewenberg. 1974. "The Decay of Support for Monarchy and the Hitler Regime in the Federal Republic of Germany," *British Journal of Political Science*, 4: 453–488.

Braunthal, Gerard. 1990. *Political Loyalty and Public Service in West Germany: The 1972 Decree against Radicals and Its Consequences*. Amherst: University of Massachusetts Press.

Laqueur, Walter. 1985. *Germany Today: A Personal Report*. Boston: Little, Brown.

Merritt, Richard L. 1994. *Democracy Imposed: U.S. Occupation Policy and the German Public, 1945–49*. New Haven: Yale University Press.

Rueschemeyer, Marilyn, and Christiane Lemke, eds. 1989. *The Quality of Life in the German Democratic Republic*. New York: E. M. Sharpe.

Scheuch, Erwin K. 1990. "Die Suche nach der Besonderheit der Deutschen," *Kölner Zeitschrift für Soziologie und Sozialpsychologie*, 42: 734–752.

22

Parties and Ideologies

Political parties are orphans in the life of most constitutions. Such organizations were unknown when political theorists first thought of designing governments that would guarantee liberty and prevent tyranny. Yet nowadays, wherever free people are exercising their political rights they invariably encounter political parties offering a hand to shake, guide, and lead people looking for political directions. One need not be a cynic to suspect that those helpful guides are driven by impulses other than charity. Political parties seek to capture control of government by gaining the people's support in elections. They are more than debating clubs, groups of like-minded people, or lobbies. It is in their very nature to reach for political office and exercise it for partisan goals, but that makes many observers uncomfortable.

The Federal Republic has put political parties under both the shield and the sword of the constitution. Right after listing the basic rights of citizens and before introducing the governmental institutions, the Basic Law grants political parties the right of participation (Article 21). Parties have legal standing as representatives of the popular will. The blessing, however, has some strings. The right is restricted by duties. Parties "must" obey democratic rules and open their pocketbooks for inspection. Moreover, a party not willing to play by the constitutional rules will be disqualified. Antidemocratic parties face the prospect of being banned by the Constitutional Court, another innovation of the republic's founders. With ideological even-handedness, the Court banned one party each of the extreme right and left in 1952 and 1956, respectively.

As always, there is more to political reality than meets the eye of someone reading a constitution. In the Federal Republic, the parties have seen to it that they get hefty subsidies for their services to "form the people's will." The headquarters of German parties are no beggar's quarters; they are edifices as imposing as those of government departments. Some complain that the parties have entrenched themselves so deeply in government as to block popular influence and to corrupt the political process. The Federal Republic is called, with increasing disapproval lately, a *party state.* There is growing concern that collusion among the parties is depriving the public of the benefits of party competition.

THE GERMAN PARTY SYSTEM

In 1953, with the Federal Republic barely four years old, the Christian Democratic Union/ Christian Social Union won 45% of the votes. With that, the alliance of Christian parties captured a majority of seats in Parliament.[1] That had never been done in Germany before in a free election. That year, 1953, has all the earmarks of a "critical" or "realigning" election with far-reaching consequences for the governance, party system, and political culture of Germany. It was the dawning of the age of people's parties in Germany.

From *Weltanschauung* Parties to People's Parties

From 1871 until 1933, the nation that Bismarck unified, the parties divided. Those cleavages, as students of parties call social divisions, ran along constitutional, economic, social, religious, and regional lines.[2] Or to put it positively, it was a time when parties were different and offered choices. They related to distinct social worlds with their own values, ideologies, and subcultures—what Germans call *Weltanschau-*

ungen. To be a Conservative, National Liberal, Progressive, Socialist, or (Catholic) Centrist was less a partisan affiliation than a confession of political faith.[3] In a sense, those parties did exactly what the Basic Law stipulates for today's parties: "participate in forming the political will of the people." At the same time, those parties did not do what comes naturally to today's parties: govern. Until 1918, they lacked the constitutional prerogative to select or remove the chancellor; but they were also not subsidized. That was how the constitution of the empire was designed. Still, it is hard to imagine how those parties would have governed if the constitution had allowed it. When they were put to the test during the Weimar Republic, they flunked it with disastrous consequences not only for Germany, but for the world.

The point is that a party system that is good at representing the diversity of social interests need not be good at governing. In 1928, perhaps the best year of the Weimar Republic, the largest party received fewer than 30 percent of the vote. It needed help from three other parties for a workable government, which would dissolve with the next political rain. Individual preferences are not easily integrated into majorities. Some theorists believe it is a miracle that it happens at all without violating democratic principles.[4]

The transformation of the West German party system during the 1950s into one dominated by *Volksparteien,* literally "people's parties," sharply distinguishes the Federal Republic from the Weimar Republic. American readers will have no difficulty grasping the meaning of this term since it describes their own parties. The rise of people's parties is part of the Americanization of German politics. Unlike the German parties prior to 1933, this new type of party appeals to the broad electorate as a whole. Perhaps not to all voters, as the catch-all label suggests, but enough potentially to capture a majority. The Christian alliance proved the success of this party type in 1953. Ironically, in so doing it compelled its strongest rival, the Social Democratic Party, to transform itself into the same type. Only one other party survived this Darwinian selection process, the Free Democrats; how they managed to do so is an intriguing question. There can be little doubt that the process of government has run more smoothly and effectively with people's parties. Largely because of that, Bonn—and soon, Berlin—are not Weimar. But that is no guarantee, in the eyes of many, that democracy is in good hands, or that important issues get the attention they deserve.

New Values and Movements

Without much doubt, the grip of people's parties on the political system of the Federal Republic has weakened in recent years. Some observers claim that one of the key pressures comes from changing values. A *silent revolution*, as Ronald Inglehart argues, is slowly replacing concern with such material values as economic well-being and security with concerns relating to the quality of life.[5] For lack of a better term, the new value priority is called "postmaterialism." Ironically, it is the very success of achieving a sense of security, economically and otherwise, that is said to promote the demise of materialist values. The people's parties are punished for the very success they have achieved.

As always in times of revolution, the young are the most likely recruits. The cohort of young people attending college in the late 1960s is identified as the vanguard of postmaterialism. The second half of the 1960s is a period of tumult and ferment after the staid 1950s. Attitudes toward work, religion, education, and the citizen's role in politics changed dramatically.[6] The cohorts growing up amid and in the wake of this value change found the established parties either inhospitable, hostile, or just irrelevant. The veterans of the student revolt, the "extraparliamentary opposition," and the counterculture, which flourished on college campuses, were looking to create a political party of their own. Their natural partisan home, the Social Democratic Party, was too fixated on materialist concerns and run with too much of an authoritarian hand to attract a generation bent on self-realization and participation. At best, the Social Democrats offered a "long march through the institutions."

The upheaval of the 1960s also launched a new political phenomenon that challenged the established parties. The debate over the deployment of nuclear missiles in West Germany stirred up a vocal "peace movement." Meanwhile the construction of nuclear power plants ran into vocal protest from "citizen initiatives." The protest against nuclear missiles or nuclear plants grew extremely violent in some instances, with opponents occupying construction sites and engaging the police in pitched battles. Less dramatically, feminist groups threw a gauntlet at the male-dominated political establishment that denied women equality. Those causes became popular rallying cries that challenged the established political parties, whether they were in office or not. None offered recipes that were palatable in the 1970s to a growing segment of the West German public. Discontent began to be vented through an array of new initiatives. They bypassed the established political parties and tried out new forms of "unconventional" participation.

Partly because some of the issues were new and partly because of the unconventional forms of action, the term *new social movement* has been coined to describe this phenomenon.[7] At the core of such a movement is a network of activists, zealous in pursuit of their cause and out in public. Beyond that circle of activists, there is a larger segment of people feeling concerned without taking an active hand in an organization or action in the street. The loose attachment of a large number of people to a

Protest against nuclear weapons, West Berlin, 1982.

particular cause merits the term "movement." As we shall see below, these upheavals have transformed the system of parties established in the postwar era.

The Christian Democrats

The strongest of those parties is the Christian Democratic Union/Christian Social Union, though calling this alliance "one" party will offend Bavarians. From 1949 until 1969, all West German chancellors were Christian Democrats. And since 1982, under Chancellor Helmut Kohl, the party has been at the helm in Bonn again. In all but one federal election did the Christian alliance capture the largest share

of the votes; once (in 1957) it actually exceeded the 50% mark (see Figure 22.1).

Breaking the Mold

Founded right after World War II, the Christian alliance is not a revival of one of the former parties that went under in 1933. On the contrary, it represented a gamble to forge something new. To be sure, old hands of the former (Catholic) Center Party, like Konrad Adenauer, played leading roles in this venture. But their aim was to break the Catholic mold that had stunted the growth of the old Center Party. What the founders of the Christian parties did not want was to revive a party that attracted a

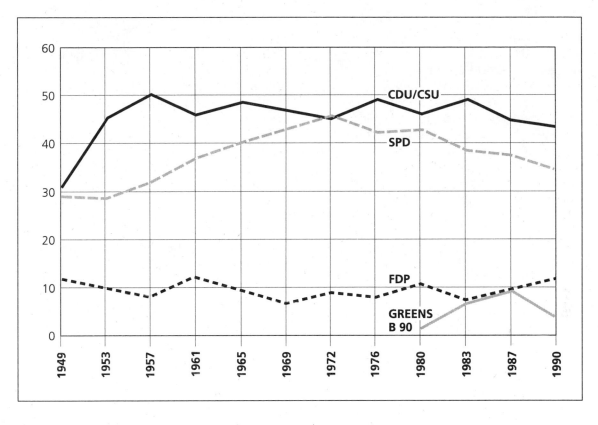

Figure 22.1 Bundestag Elections (Percent of Party List Votes).

minority as firmly as it repelled the majority. In other words, no more party serving as a PAC (political action committee) for German Catholicism. Instead they set their sights on rallying the nonsocialist majority of the German electorate behind a single party banner.

The conditions for such a venture to succeed were probably uniquely favorable in the immediate postwar years. In a perverse way, even the Nazi regime played a helpful hand. The destruction of all German parties, except their own, in 1933 gave attempts to work from scratch in 1945 a fighting chance. Moreover, Allied licensing stipulations, followed by the constitutional provisions of the Basic Law, checked any resurgence of neo-Nazi or other-

wise nationalist-authoritarian parties. Voters leaning that way found themselves without a partisan home after 1945. Thus, an historic opportunity presented itself to political entrepreneurs willing to gamble on a political party with a broad enough appeal to attract a majority of German voters. None seized this opportunity more eagerly than Konrad Adenauer.

Ideology

The "Christian" label permitted the fledgling party to adopt broad segments of the Protestant population now left in a state of political orphanage. At the same time, that label also allowed it to woo the Catholic clientele of the former Center Party. The result was a marriage of political Catholicism with Protestant conservatism. In political colors, this was a "black-blue" configuration. Whatever its internal shades, the party was stamped by Adenauer and Ludwig Erhard, his longtime economics minister (1949–1963), in several distinctive ways: market economy, family values, anti-communism, and western integration. The Christian Democratic Union/Christian Social Union was a party that was:

> socialist and radical in Berlin, clerical and conservative in Cologne, capitalist and reactionary in Hamburg, and counterrevolutionary and states-rights in Munich.[8]

In foreign policy, the party's overriding goal has always been an unambiguous tie to western Europe and the United States. The Federal Republic was to seek its role as a part of an integrated Europe instead of teetering between East and West. When the attempt to form a European army failed in 1954, the party became a strong advocate of the Federal Republic's joining NATO. The party pressed for the rearmament of West Germany, though as an integrated part of NATO. Opponents argued that such a policy was bound to close the door to reunification, but the Christian alliance was not prepared to cut the ties with the West for the sake of that goal.

The domestic equivalent of its western orientation is a strong advocacy of a market economy, though without antigovernment zealotry. The party not only tolerates, but has initiated far-reaching social legislation. This balancing of conflicting goals is aptly captured by the concept of the "social market economy" (see Chapter 26). To be sure, the popularity of this concept owes less to its ideological appeal than to the "economic miracle" of the 1950s and 1960s. Nonetheless, the "social" modifier makes it possible for an avowedly Christian party to embrace capitalism without pangs of guilt.

On many other matters, however, the Christian party is more comfortable with traditional orientations, be it on questions relating to the family, education, public morality, individual liberties, or the place of religion in public life. No friend of strict church/state separation, though no mouthpiece of the Catholic Church either, the party will rise to the defense of the churches against their challengers. By American usage of the term, the Christian Democratic Union/Christian Social Union could be called conservative, with its emphasis on the market, defense, and traditional values. But American conservatives might consider the party's social-welfare orientation close to socialism.

One Party or Two?

Strictly speaking, the CDU/CSU—as it is commonly known in Germany—is not one, but two parties. You will look in vain for a Christian Democratic Union office in Bavaria, or a Christian Social Union office outside Bavaria. There is no such thing as a federal chairman of the CDU/CSU. So it is presumptuous to speak of "one" party. The justification is that, at the federal level, the Christian Democrats and the Christian Social Union do form a single parliamentary party and nominate a single candidate for federal chancellor. All the while, very much in the vein of fratricidal warfare between Southern and non-Southern Democrats in the United States, the two Christian "sister parties" often get in each other's hair. Such spats were routine so long as the ebullient Franz-Josef Strauss led the Christian Social Union. Once, the spat almost turned into a split. Fed up with the "wimps" in the Christian Democratic Union, Strauss toyed with a plan for a nationwide Christian Social Union in 1976. But when the Christian Democratic Union flexed its maligned muscles and threatened to do likewise, the Christian Social Union forced Strauss to relent.

Nonetheless, proving that politics is short on memory and long on forgiveness, the two parties joined in nominating Strauss as their chancellor candidate for the 1980 federal election. His electoral strategy was of the all-or-nothing sort: either win a majority outright or stay in opposition, but no coalition with the Free Democratic Party (which would have no part with him either). The drubbing the CDU/CSU suffered in the 1980 election paved the way for Kohl's return as chancellor-candidate. Yet Strauss kept up a high profile for the Christian Social Union, as he governed his state with the pomp, longevity, and reverence due a Bavarian king until his death in 1988.

Table 22.1 PARTY MEMBERSHIP (IN THOUSANDS) IN THE FEDERAL REPUBLIC

Year	CDU/ CSU	SPD	FDP	Greens
1968	361	732	57	—
1972	530	954	58	—
1976	798	1,022	79	—
1980	865	987	85	18
1984	914	916	71	32
1991	970	935	162	41[a]

[a]West only, 1989.

Source: Bundeszentrale für politische Bildung, *Parteiendemokratie* (Bonn, 1985); *Facts about Germany* (Frankfurt: Societätsverlag, 1992).

Organization and Leadership

Oddly enough, the Christian alliance scored its stunning electoral victories in the 1950s and 1960s without the benefit of the organizational apparatus and membership base of a modern party. A mass party in electoral appeal, the CDU/CSU was not a mass-membership party. Because of that, some observers were quick to dismiss it as a genuine political party, calling it instead a *Kanzlerwahlverein* (chancellor campaign organization). Adenauer's departure from the political scene, however, did not prove fatal to the alliance. What the exercise of power did not accomplish, the loss of power at the federal level in 1969 apparently did. Both the Christian Democratic Union and the Christian Social Union turned to organization-building. Membership rolls nearly tripled between 1968 and 1984 and supplied the two parties with a combined membership base rivaling that of the Social Democratic Party.

At the same time, the leadership of the Christian Democrats passed on to someone who, as of 1994, has led the party longer than many of the readers of this text are old. Helmut Kohl took over a Christian Democratic Union that had been crushed by its defeat in the 1972 election and faced more than seven lean years out of government. The joint parliamentary caucus of the two Christian parties chose him as their candidate for the chancellorship in the 1976 election, and did so again after the 1980 election, when Strauss failed to lead them to victory. With the expanding party apparatus behind him, Kohl was able to weather the stretch of lean years for the Christian alliance in the federal capital. What is more, to fortify his standing in federal politics, he also secured the chairmanship of the CDU/CSU Bundestag caucus. No one since Adenauer has wielded as much control over the party as has Kohl, or has kept it in office longer.

THE SOCIAL DEMOCRATS

Of all the parties making claims to shape the politics of a democratic Germany, none ever felt to be more justified than the *Sozialdemokratische*

Partei Deutschlands (SPD); and none has been more deeply disappointed each time, be it in 1919, 1949, or 1990 in the eastern part. History has not been kind to this party that demonstrated its democratic credentials with its heroic "No" to Hitler in 1933 and its patriotism with its "Yes" for Kaiser and country in 1914. More recently, the first political party to challenge the East German regime during the revolution of 1989 was a newly founded party of Social Democrats. To little electoral avail, as it turned out, in the first free election a few months later. The party must also curse history for saddling it with government responsibility just as the Great Depression of 1929 plunged Germany into unprecedented misery. And likewise for the deepest recession since then, in 1982. Both times, the Social Democrats fell from power and remained shut out of national office for years to come.

Socialist Roots

The Social Democratic Party is one of the world's oldest political parties still operating. Like the Republicans in the United States, Germany's grand old party dates back to the middle of the nineteenth century. By 1900, when similar parties barely existed in England or France, it already commanded the largest voter support in German elections. It held on to that rank until 1930. Two patron saints have inspired the party's faithful, but have also torn them in opposite directions: Karl Marx, on one side, preaching the doctrine of proletarian revolution and Communist utopia; and Ferdinand Lassalle, organizing worker associations and seeking more immediate changes through political action. From the outset, disputes between revolutionary and reformist wings have afflicted this party.

During World War I, the revolutionary wing broke away, ultimately forming Germany's Communist Party. The split deprived the So-

cial Democratic Party of one-quarter of its electoral support and kept this party looking nervously over its left shoulder. But the split also underscored that the party was not predominantly a revolutionary one, its strident Marxist rhetoric notwithstanding. The party did not hesitate, in fact, to suppress Bolshevik uprisings in the early years of the Weimar Republic. In all fairness, this party never was a friend of the "socialism" practiced by one-party Communist regimes.

From Class Party to Mass Party

Yet no matter what brand, socialism was definitely no winning card in the game of politics played in the Federal Republic. With the horror show of socialism in the East, and the market performing economic magic in the West, pleas for socialism fell on deaf ears. Nor did the Social Democrats fare any better with their foreign policy proposals. The party opposed the western orientation pursued by the Christian alliance, fearing that this would jeopardize German reunification. The Social Democratic Union said "No" to membership in the Atlantic military alliance, "No" to rearmament, and "No" to the European Economic Community.

Steeped in tradition, the Social Democrats found it painful to adapt to the demands of mass-party politics. Ironically, it was in the affluent and scenic resort town of Bad Godesberg near Bonn, the new federal capital, where the party took an ideological bath in 1959. The party congress unveiled a new policy platform. It announced, in effect, the great policy compromise with the Christian Democratic Union and the Christian Social Union. Out went the rhetoric of the class struggle, the goal of nationalizing industries, state planning of the economy, and other Marxist-inspired schemes of socialist transformation. Instead, private initiative and economic competition were praised, and the party reached out to be recognized as a people's party rather than as the party of the working class. The Social Democrats subsequently also endorsed the Federal Republic's ties to the western alliance, including a military role within NATO. Still, the party did not stifle all of its old impulses. It pressed for more flexibility in dealing with the other Germany and the Soviet Union; this approach later became known as *Ostpolitik*. The Social Democratic Party also proposed bold programs of domestic reform.

The rigidly stratified German educational system had long irked Social Democrats, who accused it of blatantly favoring the well-to-do. Access to higher education, they felt, ought to be a civil right for the sons and daughters of all families instead of a privilege, in effect, of those born to affluent families. Likewise, large industrial companies ought not to be controlled exclusively by owners and executives. Though eschewing nationalization, the party pushed for a program of equal partnership between stockholders and employees on the supervisory boards of companies (*Mitbestimmung*). This was a key concern of the labor unions, the core supporting group of the Social Democratic Party.

Membership and Organization

The Social Democratic Party is widely credited with pioneering an organizational form called the "mass-membership" party. Making a virtue of necessity, the party of the workers raised capital by formally enrolling large numbers. Each member pays regular dues, akin to dues paid to a labor union. But the party did not simply take over the unions or allow itself to be taken over by them; though united spiritually, unions and party followed more a divide-and-conquer strategy. In return for regular dues, a member of the Social Democratic Party is issued a party book. While looking like a passport, such a membership book also contains a

synopsis of Social Democratic ideology. The opening words strike a solemn, almost religious, tone:

> *This is the contradiction of our time,*
> *that man has unleashed the power of the atom,*
> *and now fears the consequences;*
> *that man has perfected the productive capacity,*
> *has amassed awesome wealth,*
> *without providing a just share*
> *of those accomplishments for all.*[9]

The party membership book is a ticket to attend party gatherings as well as proof of good standing. A party book contains much empty space for documenting entries. In this case, entries into the party's treasury. The party expects members to contribute 1% of their gross incomes. That makes it less expensive than religious membership. Party dues are also easier to evade since they are not withheld like a tax, unless you hold a patronage job. All in all, the Social Democratic Party has long led other parties in the competition for dues-paying members. By 1914 already, its rolls exceeded one million.

Though happy to take their money, the party has proved less than forthcoming in giving the rank-and-file members either a voice in deciding issues or a choice in selecting candidates for office. One of the classic studies of political parties chose the Social Democratic Party as its case for documenting the lack of democracy within parties.[10] Michels coined his *"iron law of oligarchy"* to apply not to some reactionary party defending the privileged few or the interests of business, but to a party loudly espousing liberty and equality for the masses. His point was that organization, however noble and democratic the motives of its creators, inevitably breeds oligarchy—that is, rule by the few for their own interests. Leaders of party organizations worth their salt will be able to control the flow of demands from below. Americans familiar with party machines will have no trouble following Michels's analysis of a foreign party.

The New Left

In the early 1970s, the party faced demands from a generation whose key political experience had been the student revolt of 1967–1968. Driven by a desire for social "transformation," not just piecemeal corrections of consensus politics, this rebellious group revived the Marxist spirit that the Social Democrats had forsworn in Bad Godesberg. Radicals captured control of numerous local party branches, especially in cities like Munich and Frankfurt, where mainstream Social Democrats were eased out of their positions. The most receptive forum for the new ideas was the party's youth organization. The Young Socialists cared little for the all-too-moderate brand of social democracy practiced by Chancellor Helmut Schmidt. But they found a sympathetic ear in Willy Brandt, who stayed on as the party chairman even after stepping down as chancellor. In fact, the older he got, the more receptive he grew to new issues and movements. A beloved figure among the party's Left, Brandt often spoke warmly about the Greens and the prospect of a new majority to the left of the Christian alliance.

One issue, in particular, aroused the Left's ire: the defense policy of Chancellor Schmidt. With him out of office in late 1982, the Left had won the battle. The Social Democratic Party repudiated its support for stationing a new type of missile in West Germany. It also became a vocal critic of Ronald Reagan's tough talk and action in confronting the "evil empire." Neutralist and pacifist tones gained strength among the Social Democrats as never before since the 1950s. At the same time, on issues of domestic policy the party moved increasingly toward the agenda of the Greens. The choice of Oskar Lafontaine as

the Social Democratic chancellor-candidate for the 1990 election signaled how much the red party had turned green.

Prospects

Going into the federal election of 1994, the Social Democratic Party has spent twelve years in opposition. And like another party having been shut out of the federal executive that long, the Social Democrats turned to a 46-year-old governor of a small state, a moderate in his ideological outlook. He is Rudolf Scharping. His "political calculus is much the same as Bill Clinton's: he will be the next chancellor of Germany if he can convince the public he's not too much of a risk."[11] Not only does his candidacy bear a striking resemblance to Bill Clinton's, but Scharping also hails from the same state as Chancellor Kohl, Rhineland-Palatinate. Scharping has succeeded in wresting control of the state from the Christian Democratic Union in Kohl's home state. His strategy for the electoral conquest of the federal government is not a frontal ideological assault on Kohl, but a reassuring embrace of his policies. If that has a familiar ring for the Social Democrats, it is that it sounds like an echo of the Bad Godesberg conversion in 1959. Still, such conversions take time to pay electoral dividends. More troublesome perhaps, Scharping must bring his own party, which has veered to pacifism and anti-Americanism, in line for such a course. And he will also have to contend with a revitalized Green Party and rumblings on the Right. The problem is that at a time of profound disappointment with politics as usual, more of the same may not be the winning ticket.

THE FREE DEMOCRATS

The *Freie Demokratische Partei* (FDP) is a paradox in more ways than one. Its position in the

German party system is "at once so fragile and so advantageous."[12] The Free Democratic Party is not one of the big parties, but has held government office longer than either the Christian alliance or the Social Democratic Party. The Free Democrats are located in the center of the political spectrum, where the median voter is located, but the party does not win elections. Perhaps the one paradox compensates for the other: in the end, the party speaking for the median voter governs. It is a life full of risks for the Free Democrats nonetheless. This party has been married in coalition government to both the Christian alliance and to the Social Democrats, though not at the same time. And the Free Democratic Party has divorced both of them, several times in the case of the Christian alliance. Both partners have, on occasion, been mad and jealous enough to contemplate political murder. But the Free Democratic Party has been shrewd enough to prevent the two from ganging up on it. Or else perhaps just lucky enough in an age of easy divorce and frequent remarriage.

Liberal Roots

The Free Democratic Party claims the heritage of Germany's "liberal" tradition, whose roots reach back to the early nineteenth century. This liberalism is not the New Deal liberalism associated with the Democratic Party in American politics. Instead, it is the liberalism of the American Revolution: popular sovereignty, limited government, individual rights, separation of church and state, free enterprise, and nation-building. In 1848, German liberals were near triumph, having shaken the old monarchical order and laid the groundwork for a constitutional system of government in a German nation-state. But they did not succeed, and the liberal movement soon split into rival partisan formations. The National Liberals

Rudolf Scharping, the Social Democratic Chancellor Candidate in 1994, trying not to be too sober.

favored the empire founded under Bismarck's leadership in 1871, whereas the Progressives opposed it for not meeting the liberal ideals.

Under new names, both kinds of liberals resumed their rivalry during the Weimar Republic. In fact, the National Liberals were so presumptuous as to call themselves then the German People's Party. No matter the name, this party could not count on many people at the moment of crisis. Neither did the other one. How strange to see the electoral support of the liberal parties vanish as the Nazi Party surged in 1932.

From FDP to F.D.P.

With their special talent to shrug off defeat, liberals rose from oblivion after 1945. This time they huddled under a single partisan roof, called the Free Democratic Party. It was a remarkable achievement for such a fractious bunch. Almost miraculously, the party alone captured as much electoral support in the first Bundestag election, in 1949, as its predecessors did combined in the last "normal" Weimar election, in 1928. True to liberal form, the Free Democrats stood for free enterprise and against government tutelage. In other words, for a market economy without any modifiers. That made the party compatible, though not perfectly, with the Christian alliance, and kept the Social Democrats at arm's length. A Social Democratic Party wedded to socialism was plainly unacceptable for the Free Democrats. On the other hand, the Free Democratic Party's antichurch attitude and its nationalistic tone in matters of foreign policy irritated the Christian alliance. The Free Democratic Party was happy to help the Christian alliance govern while serving as a "liberal corrective."

A spell of nonparticipation in government in the 1960s prompted the Free Democratic Party to rethink its policy goals. It abandoned its fixation on the Christian alliance. The new strategy was one of being the "third force." That is to say, the Free Democrats would be open to either side, depending on where the liberal prospects looked brighter. The party adopted a "social-liberal" platform, emphasizing social reform more than economic *laissez-faire*. Along with that, the leadership of the party changed. Party chief Erich Mende, who bore some resemblance to Kaiser William II, gave way to the easygoing Walter Scheel. Even the party name underwent modernization.

American-style dots were added to the initials FDP, the common term for the party. So technically it is now the F.D.P. instead of just FDP.

To people paying close attention to the body language of politics in the late 1960s, it was clear that the Free Democratic Party was signaling its availability to the Social Democratic Party. Indeed, the two parties forged a coalition after the 1969 election. For the next 13 years the bond held. Having chosen a new partner, the Free Democratic Party would henceforth serve as its "liberal conscience": partner of the Social Democratic Party but also a check on that party's suppressed instinct for socialism. The strategy proved successful in the next three elections (1972–1980), which rewarded the Free Democrats with comfortable margins above the 5% minimum. German politics was set for a long "social-liberal" era under Chancellor Schmidt, who seemed not unhappy with the Free Democrats for making him keep the more radical elements in his own party on a short leash.

The Pivot in Action

The Free Democratic Party has become the key agent of government change in the Federal Republic. The decision in 1969 to align itself with the Social Democratic Party produced the first *Machtwechsel* (changing of the guard) in the Federal Republic. In 1982, the liberal party helped engineer one again. Under the leadership of Hans-Dietrich Genscher and prodded by a strong believer in the free market like Count Otto Lambsdorff, the Free Democrats left the coalition with the Social Democrats and forged a new one with the then opposition party, the Christian alliance. Although holding on to its share of government, the liberal party could not be sure about its share of votes in the next election. Voters who previously supported it because of its alignment with the Social Democratic Party had little use for it anymore.

In their eyes, the Free Democratic Party had committed treason. On the other hand, how many voters were prepared to trust it to be a loyal partner of the Christian alliance? The peril of electoral extinction is the price the Free Democratic Party must pay for its thrills on the coalition high wire.

The voters have learned to appreciate the rigors involved. They do not want to see one party control the government. Even when supporting a major party themselves, they tend to approve of a minor party like the Free Democrats sharing in government. In the voting booth a good number will split their ticket, as we shall see in the next chapter, to achieve that goal. It is also worth noting that for the leader of a major party the presence of another party in government is not without advantages. It helps restrain the more extreme elements of one's own party. Just as the Free Democratic Party helped Schmidt hold off the left wing of the Social Democrats, it helped Kohl stand his ground against such demanding rivals as Franz-Josef Strauss.

THE GREENS

What would politics be without colors? The left has long been fond of red while parties allied with the Catholic Church have been painted black, though not by their own choice. Now Germany has a political party called the Greens, *Die Grünen*. It's not a catchy label foisted on it by the media. It's their own given name. Formed in 1979, this party gained enough votes in the 1983 election to enter the Bundestag. It was the first time a new party had proved a success since 1953. The party's name literally refers to something that is, to a large extent, green: nature. Protection of the natural environment has become a powerful concern in the general publics of western democracies. It is like prosperity and peace, a commonly valued goal. The adoption of the "green" label was

a clever maneuver. But the German Greens are no single-issue party.

From Movement to Party

The Greens are the partisan offshoot of various social movements relating to a broad scale of causes ranging from the environment, nuclear power, disarmament, urban housing, gay and lesbian rights, Third World politics, multiculturalism, and more. "Rainbow Party" might have been a more suitable name. However far-ranging the policy concerns and however large the constituency for them, the birth of a political party was not preordained. In fact, it is quite rare for social movements to launch political parties. Most movements keep their distance from parties, and for good reasons. A movement thrives on being able to articulate demands without having to undertake the arduous task to implement them and be responsible for the consequences. A movement can remain pure at heart and true to its ideals, neither tempted nor corrupted by the enticements of power.

A political party, on the other hand, is hard pressed to evade the messy process of compromise and avoid the temptations of power. To be a political party that just says "No" all the time is not very rewarding for either the representatives or their constituency. So you will have to partake in the deal making that you so abhor and that is bound to turn off parts of your constituency, too. So why form a political party? The rational-choice answer is that in Germany, in particular, you cannot afford not to do so. The privileges provided for political parties make it irresistible for powerful movements to constitute themselves as parties. Paradoxically, the "party state" both breeds challenges and entices them to join the system:

The transformation of the West German new social movements that emerged in the 1970s into the Green party . . . testifies to the overwhelming

The Green leadership, 1990.

attractiveness of the institutional mode of normal politics. . . . Because of the . . . peculiarities of German political institutions, the decision not to adopt the party form would amount to the decision to forgo significant resources.[13]

It remains debatable, however, whether such a rational interpretation captures a political phenomenon that thrives on espousing unpopular causes.

Radical Democracy

To be sure, the Greens fight hard to avoid the fate of the moth that is being consumed by the flame that attracts it. Aside from new issues and new answers to them, the Greens also aspire to a new mode of politics. They reject the model of a "people's party." They do not mind being small since that allows them to speak up for unpopular causes. While critical of the practice of democracy in the Federal Republic, they extoll the virtues of democracy. Greens want to take "democracy" literally: as grassroots rule, not as rule by representatives beyond the reach of their constituencies. Like Jean Jacques Rousseau (1712–1778), the author of *The Social Contract*, and Robert Michels, who coined the *iron law of oligarchy*, the Greens see representation, organization, and leadership as inimical to democracy.

To ensure that their party is not run by an elite, the Greens have tried several innovations. One is not to vest the top leadership in any single person; another is what may be called a one-half-term limit, requiring elected representatives to give up their offices halfway through the term; yet another is the rule that representatives are bound by the instructions of extraparliamentary party bodies. Needless to say, the implementation of some of these rules has caused the Greens much pain, and the most radical ones have been abandoned. As is so often the case, a party organization outside Parliament, trying to bend parliamentary representatives to its will, ends up cutting off its nose to spite its face.

Fundis and *Realos*

The Green Party, by its very nature, is a model of diversity. Green Party conventions are contentious and contested, not designed to dull a sense of excitement about politics the way conventions of the other parties typically do. The clash between the "fundamentalists" and the "realists" is practically a birthmark of the Green Party. The *"fundis"* are more enamored of movement politics than of governmental responsibility, whereas the *"realos"* are more comfortable with party politics and less averse to the governmental route.

Even the *realos* consider but one coalition option, one with the Social Democratic Party. In terms of color coordination, that is quite a clash: red and green. Still, in more and more states, this coalition is being tested, though with more friction than success. For the federal election of 1987, the Green Party convention narrowly approved a resolution that signaled a willingness to forge a coalition with the Social Democrats in Bonn. Given the declining fortunes of the Social Democratic Party since then, however, red-green does not look like a winning combination at the federal level. To be able to govern in Bonn (or Berlin, soon), the Social Democrats and Greens would need to draw also on the Free Democrats. Colorwise, that would be a red-yellow-green combination, a traffic-light coalition. It would be as confusing

for the German voter as for a driver: stop, caution, go?

Surge and Decline

The surge of Green success came to an abrupt halt in the 1990 federal election. The party flatly rejected reunification as a bad idea. "Everyone else talks about unification; we talk about the weather" (like the ozone hole and the greenhouse effect), said one of its leaders. True to their convictions, the Green organizations in East and West refused to merge. The price for this refusal was a heavy one. Only the eastern Greens in conjunction with Alliance '90, the partisan umbrella of civil rights groups, won enough votes in the 1990 national election to get into Parliament. The western Greens were shut out. In mid-1993, western Greens and the eastern Alliance '90 finally merged. As erstwhile opponents of reunification, however, the Greens/Alliance '90 have reaped the benefit of popular disappointment with the consequences of unity. Going into the election year of 1994, the Greens claimed the voting support of nearly 15% in all parts of Germany, one of the highest levels ever.[14]

The remarkable flowering of Green politics in Germany, compared to France and Britain, has steered some observers to specifically German explanations. Could it be another case of a romantic, and deeply irrational, protest against the modern world? Or another attempt in German history to follow a *Sonderweg* (special path separate from other western democracies)? Or a case of youthful rebellion against the sins of the parental generation under Hitler? Others suspect that the Green agenda is simply recycled red politics, cleverly packaged to appeal to popular concerns. To a degree, these interpretations have a point. Compared with England and France, there is more Green politics in Germany; some Greens would turn back the industrial clock; and left-socialists are bound to find the Greens an inviting vehicle for promoting their agenda. But that should not obscure the fact that Green politics is a European-wide phenomenon.

Parties in Eastern Germany

The former German Democratic Republic, among other things, was a party state, owned and operated by the Socialist Unity Party (SED) and its subsidiaries. The constitution of the German Democratic Republic accorded monopoly power to the party in state and society. The fall of the Berlin Wall knocked this party from power and freed the subsidiary parties, called "bloc parties," from captivity. They were quickly adopted by their respective western counterparts, including the newly launched eastern Social Democrats. The eastern Greens/Alliance '90 took somewhat longer, as we saw. Political reunion has done surprisingly little to reshuffle the party system of the Federal Republic.

The only addition is a remnant of the former Socialist Unity Party. It was not buried under the rubble of the Wall. With new leaders and a new name, the Party of Democratic Socialism (PDS) managed to hold on to a formidable party machine. Many consider it the best-organized party in eastern Germany; it has the largest membership. It is also the party of choice of people who believed in and benefited from socialism. That is not a small constituency in areas like East Berlin and Brandenburg. What is more, the Party of Democratic Socialism is reaping the benefit from disappointment with national unity in the East. Voters who thought unification was a good idea in 1990, but not anymore, are flocking to the PDS, as it is best known in Germany.[15] In local elections in the state of Brandenburg in December 1993, the party won more than 20% of the votes, edging the Christian Democratic Union for second place. In a strange twist between East and West, voters in the new states in the East turned to the Party of Democratic Socialism to vent their anger while voters in the old Federal Republic in the West turned to extremist parties on the Right.

Rumblings on the Right

It would be nice if this topic could be safely skipped. But the rumblings on the extreme right are too audible to be ignored. In fact, if something is surprising, it is not that the extreme right in Germany makes noises but that its electoral resonance has been so weak. The electoral potential of the extreme right should not be underestimated. Recall that in 1951 almost nine of every ten West Germans rated either the prewar Nazi period or the pre-1914 empire as Germany's best years; by 1963, still one in four felt that way. It took a near-miraculous combination of favorable conditions plus Allied prohibition and constitutional restrictions to prevent a partisan expression of that potential during the first twenty years of the Federal Republic. It also meant that the major parties were getting the votes of many Germans whose political hearts or minds they had by no means captured.

The Old Nazis

A mild economic recession in the mid-1960s, coupled with political disarray in the federal government, contributed to a swell of electoral support for the National Democratic Party (NPD). It was not only the party's initials that sounded like an echo of Hitler's NSDAP (the National Socialist German Workers' Party). This was neo-Nazi revival, prompting the suggestion that it ought to banned. The party, however, failed to win enough votes in 1969 to enter Parliament. The return of prosperity and stable government, as well as the turn to the Right by the Christian alliance after that election, stopped the momentum of the National Democrats' potential. No doubt, it's not just the economy that makes voters turn to and from extremist parties. Even more, it depends on the ability of the democratic parties to offer inspiring and capable leadership. Witness the pitiful showing of the National Democrats in the mid-1970s, when the government was led by the forceful and popular chancellor Helmut Schmidt, who was not averse to wrapping his policies in the national flag.

The Republicans

To the surprise of most, the extreme right surged again in the late 1980s, this time without the trigger of economic distress. Moreover, these were not some born-again National Democrats, but a newly formed party with the respectable name of Republicans. The party was founded in 1983 by a Bavarian defector from the Christian Social Union, Franz Schönhuber, unhappy with the lack of a moral and spiritual turn to the Right after the Christian alliance returned to power. Still, it was easy to place this party in neo-Nazi company because Schönhuber was unapologetic about his wartime service in the army SS.[16]

Of all places, it was in West Berlin in 1989 where this party stunned the public by winning 7.5% of the votes in their first election there. The vote share was more than enough for the Republicans to enter the city council. The same year they also did well enough in the European Parliament elections to enter that arena as well. The fall of the Wall and the decisive handling of reunification by the Christian alliance and the Free Democrats put a damper on the Republicans, but support for it returned in state election soon afterward. In the state of Baden-Württemberg, the Republicans won almost 11% of the votes in 1992, one of the best results for a party on the right fringe.

Searching for clues for the electoral success of this party, analysts have pointed to resentment and hatred of foreigners.[17] Oddly enough, the foreigners in question originally were people of German heritage being resettled from the Soviet Union and Eastern Europe. More recently, they were foreigners entering Germany to seek political asylum. In the wake of reunification, the influx of asylum-seekers has fueled the electoral engines of extremist parties on the Right. But foreigners are only part of the story. They provide convenient scapegoats for a bundle of insecurities at a time of rapid political change, gloomy economic prospects, and diminishing confidence in established political parties.

A Divided Fringe

At the same time, the Republicans have had to contend with internal splits and external competition. The National Democratic Party has come back to life, but more threatening is the German People's Union (DVU). It was founded in 1971 by the publisher of the *National Zeitung* (National Newspaper), Gerhard Frey, who also happens to be a good friend of Vladimir Zhirinovsky, the leader of Russia's extreme nationalists. If anything, the German People's Union is more virulent and extremist than the Republicans. Yet when both the German People's Unionists and Republicans enter electoral campaigns on their own, they are more likely to divide than to conquer their target. In 1993, voters in Hamburg gave the two a combined share of 7.6%, but neither won enough to enter the city council (4.8% for Republicans, and 2.8% for the German People's Union).

Unlike the Nazi revivals in the 1950s and 1960s, this new wave shares characteristics with such groups as the National Front in France and similar movements in other European countries. Just like postmaterialism and the new social movements, it is not a unique

German phenomenon. Is it a backlash against this value revolution and movement politics? What can the established parties do to keep voters from defecting to the extreme right? Thus far, the federal government has refrained from calling on the Constitutional Court to ban either the Republicans or the German People's Union, though both are under close surveillance by the authorities. In any event, the proliferation of new parties is so rapid that legal measures may prove ineffective. Yet short of banning those parties, how are the established parties planning to fend them off? So far the main strategy seems to be to deprive them of the main issue, the asylum problem. The governing parties secured the support of the Social Democratic Party in 1993 for strict measures to stem the asylum tide.[18] But one step alone is rarely enough to dry out electoral support for extremist parties. At the same time, the threat of extremist parties always looms larger at midterm than at general election time—more a nuisance than a peril to the established parties.

Notes

1. The CDU/CSU held 244 seats out of 487 (excluding the Berlin representatives), but one of those seats was captured by a CDU candidate running on the platform of the Catholic Center party. See Richard L. Merritt, "The 1953 Bundestag Election: Evidence from West German Public Opinion," *Historical Social Research,* 16 (October 1980), p. 5.

2. See Seymour Martin Lipset and Stein Rokkan, *Party Systems and Voter Alignments* (New York: Free Press, 1967).

3. See Gerhard Loewenberg, "The Development of the German Party System," in *Germany at the Polls,* ed. Karl H. Cerny (Washington, D.C.: American Enterprise Institute, 1978).

4. This refers to the famous "paradox of voting." See Kenneth J. Arrow, *Social Choice and Individual Values* (New York: Wiley and Sons, 1951).

5. See Ronald Inglehart, *The Silent Revolution: Changing Values and Political Styles Among West-*
ern Publics (Princeton: Princeton University Press, 1977); also his *Culture Shift in Advanced Industrial Society* (Princeton: Princeton University Press, 1990). Inglehart's theory has sparked a lively scholarly debate over the concept of value change, the persistence of change, and its impact on party politics. See Ferdinand Böltken and Wolfgang Jagodzinski, "Postmaterialism in the European Community, 1970–1980: Insecure Value Orientations in an Environment of Insecurity," *Comparative Political Studies,* 17 (1985), 453–484.

6. See Meulemann, "Value Change," p. 789.

7. See Russell J. Dalton and Manfred Kuechler, eds., *Challenging the Political Order: New Social and Political Movements in Western Democracies* (New York: Oxford University Press, 1990).

8. As quoted in Heino Kaack, *Geschichte und Struktur des deutschen Parteiensystems* (Opladen: Westdeutscher Verlag, 1971), p. 172.

9. SPD Membership Book in 1976.

10. See Robert Michels, *Political Parties: A Sociological Study of the Oligarchical Tendencies of Modern Democracies* (New York: Free Press, 1962; originally published in 1915).

11. Joe Klein, "What's German for 'Ross Perot'?" *Newsweek,* January 31, 1994, p. 46.

12. Christian Soe, "The Free Democratic Party," in *West German Politics in the Mid-Eighties,* ed. H. G. Peter Wallach and George K. Romoser (New York: Praeger, 1985), p. 120.

13. Claus Offe, "Reflections on the Institutional Self-transformation of Movement Politics," in *Challenging the Political Order,* pp. 241–242.

14. Forschungsgruppe Wahlen, *Politbarometer December 1993.*

15. See Matthias Jung and Dieter Roth, "Die Ewig Gestrigen" (Forever in Yesterday's World), *Die Zeit,* December 10, 1993.

16. The *Waffen* SS (army SS) was a rival army set up by Hitler alongside the regular *Wehrmacht* (armed forces). The SS was Hitler's elite organization that operated the concentration camps and directed the final solution. The issue of the army SS arose in 1985 during the visit of former president Ronald Reagan in 1985 to the Bitburg cemetery, where, as it turned out, former members of the army SS were buried.

17. See Matthias Jung and Dieter Roth, "Der Stimm-zettel als Denkzettel" (The Ballot as a Mailed Fist), *Die Zeit*, April 10, 1992.
18. In May 1993, the constitutional guarantee of asylum (Article 16) was severely restricted. The change was approved with the support of the major opposition party, the Social Democratic Party.

REFERENCES AND SUGGESTED READINGS

Braunthal, Gerard. 1983. *West German Social Democrats, 1969–1982: A Profile of a Party in Power.* Boulder, Colo.: Westview Press.

Dalton, Russell J., ed. 1993. *The New Germany Votes: Unification and the Creation of a New German Party System.* Providence: Berg Publishers.

Frankland, E. Gene, and Donald Schoonmaker. 1991. *Between Protest and Power: The Green Party in Germany.* Boulder: Westview Press.

Kolinsky, Eva. 1993. *Women in Contemporary Germany: Life, Work and Politics,* 2nd ed. Providence: Berg Publishers.

Padget, Stephen, and Tony Burkett. 1986. *Political Parties and Elections in West Germany.* New York: St. Martin's Press.

Stööss, Richard. 1991. *Politics Against Democracy: The Extreme Right in West Germany.* Providence: Berg Publishers.

Wildenmann, Rudolf. 1987. "The Party Government of the Federal Republic of Germany: Form and Experience." In Richard S. Katz, ed., *Party Government: European and American Experiences,* ch. III. Berlin and New York: Walter de Gruyter.

23

Campaigns and Elections

*E*lections have given rise to much hope but also despair in German history. In 1990, the first national election in almost 60 years, the public celebrated a unification nobody had thought possible a few years earlier. In 1848, it was a popularly elected assembly that gave Germany its first democratic constitution, but the venture proved short-lived. Elections helped integrate the masses into the empire of 1871, but their representatives did not govern. A popularly elected assembly in 1919 drafted a democratic constitution, but voters in 1932 handed the Nazis the leverage to erase it. Nowadays an election is a commonplace event in Germany. It is no longer a life-or-death question. What difference do elections make in Germany? What opportunity do they offer the electorate to decide who governs the Federal Republic?

THE ELECTORAL RULES

To begin with, note for whom Germans cannot vote: the chancellor, the president, and the members of the *Bundesrat*, the constitutional body representing the states. All they can choose in federal elections are members of the federal Parliament, the *Bundestag.* But to elect them, each voter is allowed to cast two votes. Take a look at the ballot shown in Figure 23.1. On the left side, where it says *Erststimme* (first vote), the voter is asked to choose a candidate from his or her district. On the right side, where it says *Zweitstimme*

Stimmzettel

für die Wahl zum Deutschen Bundestag im Wahlkreis 194 Tübingen am 02. Dezember 1990

Sie haben 2 Stimmen

hier 1 Stimme (X)	(X) hier 1 Stimme
für die Wahl **eines/einer Wahlkreisabgeordneten**	für die Wahl **einer Landesliste (Partei)** – maßgebende Stimme für die Verteilung der Sitze insgesamt auf die einzelnen Parteien –
Erststimme	**Zweitstimme**

#	Erststimme		#	Zweitstimme	
1	**Grotz, Claus-Peter** Regierungsrat zur Anstellung Hechingen Fred-West-Straße 3	**CDU** Christlich Demokratische Union Deutschlands	1	**CDU** Christlich Demokratische Union Deutschlands Dr. Wolfang Schäuble, Matthias Wissmann, Dr. Lutz Stavenhagen, Anton Pfeifer, Udo Ehrbar	◯
2	**Dr. Däubler-Gmelin, Herta** Bundestagsabgeordnete Rechtsanwältin Dußlingen, Geierweg 20	**SPD** Sozialdemokratische Partei Deutschlands	2	**SPD** Sozialdemokratische Partei Deutschlands Dr. Herta Däubler-Gmelin, Harald Schäfer, Hans Martin Bury, Wolfgang Roth, Dr. Liesel Hartenstein	◯
3	**Keske, Hermann** Rechtsanwalt Tübingen Hundskapflingo 40	**FDP/DVP** Freie Demokratische Partei/ Demokratische Volkspartei	3	**FDP/DVP** Freie Demokratische Partei/ Demokratische Volkspartei Dr. Helmut Haussmann, Georg Gallus, Martin Grüner, Dr. Wolfgang Weng, Dr. Olaf Feldmann	◯
4	**Vogt-Moykopf, Christian** Journalist Rottenburg/N. Heuberger Hof 1	**GRÜNE** DIE GRÜNEN	4	**GRÜNE** DIE GRÜNEN Christa Vennegerts, Oswald Metzger, Ursula Eid-Simon, Dr. Thilo Weichert, Monika Knoche	◯
			5	**LIGA** CHRISTLICHE LIGA Die Partei für das Leben Karl Simpfendörfer, Bettina Schega, Ewald Jaksch, Wilhelma Schmidts, Marion Gotthardt	◯
			6	**CM** CHRISTLICHE MITTE Anny Stärk, Peter Bella, Michael Platt, Erna Schönstein, Werner Keller	◯
			7	**DIE GRAUEN** DIE GRAUEN Initiiert vom Semieren-Schutz-Bund »Graue Panther« e.V. (»SS8-GP«) Wolfgang Häffner, Martha-Elisabeth Fischer, Marga Höffgen, Walter Meyer, Dr. Ursula Körner	◯
8	**Schaal, Karl-August** selbständiger Kaufmann Tübingen-Pfrondorf Zollernstraße 35	**REP** DIE REPUBLIKANER	8	**REP** DIE REPUBLIKANER Dr. Rolf Schlierer, Leo Thenn, Michael Herbricht, Arnold Bräutigam, Dietmar Donnerstag	◯
9	**Maßler, Erwin** Rentner Ulm Ravensburger Straße 20	**NPD** Nationaldemokratische Partei Deutschlands	9	**NPD** Nationaldemokratische Partei Deutschlands Jürgen Schützinger, Waltraud Mussgnug, Dr. Michael Franck, Siegfried Härle, Erwin Maßler	◯
10	**Pfaffenritter, Hans-Jürgen** Werkssanitäter Horb-Altheim Am Haldenrain 20	**ÖDP** Ökologisch-Demokratische Partei	10	**ÖPD** Ökologisch-Demokratische Partei Hella Heuer, Maria Opitz, Bernd Richter, Hermann Bentele, Herbert Alexander Gebhardt	◯
			11	**PDS/Linke Liste** Partei des Demokratischen Sozialismus/Linke Liste Dr. Helga Bunke genannt Königsdorf, Dr. Theodor Bergmann, Dr. Heidi Knake-Werner, Dr. Günter Kehrer, Ilse Weinzieri-Dean Rubio	◯
			12	**Patrioten** Patrioten für Deutschland Dr. Helmut Böttiger, Edmund Belle, Bernd Schulz, Irene Belle, Karl Bauer	◯

Figure 23.1 Sample Ballot.

(second vote), the voter is asked to mark his or her preference for a party. Consider this second vote first.

Proportional Representation

Whatever percentage of these votes a party obtains entitles it to a commensurate share of seats in the Bundestag. Thus a party receiving 10% of the party votes will get roughly 10% of the Bundestag seats. However, not every party on the ballot will be rewarded with seats. In order to enter the seat-allocation sweepstakes, a party must garner at least 5% of all party votes cast in the Federal Republic. Note, however, that for the 1990 election, this requirement was applied separately in the old Federal Republic and the former German Democratic Republic.

By comparison with other countries using the proportional representation method, Germany imposes a fairly high threshold for entry. The 5% hurdle was introduced with the deliberate intention to forestall the splintering of the party system that had made Germany ungovernable in the 1920s. It has certainly helped make Germany more governable in the 1950s and beyond. Since 1953, when the rule was instituted, only one new party has succeeded in joining the Big Three in the Bundestag, the Greens. There would have been a lot more with, say, a 2% rule, like the National Democratic Party (NPD) in 1969 with its 4.3% of the vote. Even the minor party that has managed to clear the 5% hurdle in all federal elections, the Free Democratic Party, could not always be certain about that prospect.

Who Gets Elected?

Having cleared the 5% hurdle, how does a party decide who in particular will take the seats allocated to it? This is not a simple matter, and most Germans would be hard pressed to

explain it to a foreigner. For one thing, in voting for a party a voter endorses a list of candidates prepared by that party. The ballot does not actually itemize that list; only the names of each party's top warhorses are printed. The voter does not have the option of adding or deleting names, or of altering the rank order. It's a straight-ticket vote. Say a party is entitled to 50 seats based on its share of second votes. That means that the top 50 people on its list can enter the Bundestag. Many of those candidates, however, also run in local districts, where voters cast their first vote. Remember the left side of the ballot, where voters choose an individual candidate to represent their district. This part works exactly the same way as electing a member of the U.S. House of Representatives. Whichever candidate wins the most votes, not necessarily a majority, will go to Bonn for that district.

In 1990, 328 members of the Bundestag were chosen from as many districts. In theory, this should be half of the seats of the legislative body, with the other half being filled from the party lists. But as you can see from Table 23.1, the Bundestag elected in 1990 comprises a few more members than 656. That is because the Christian Democratic Union was able to win six more seats in district elections by way of first votes than it was entitled to from its share of second votes, all of them in the new eastern states. This "overhang" phenomenon is not unusual, but rarely amounts to more than a handful of seats.

This embarrassment of riches afflicts only the big parties. It is extremely rare for small parties like the Free Democrats or the Greens to carry any districts. In 1990, the Free Democratic Party succeeded in doing so in the new eastern state of Saxony-Anhalt, and the Democratic Socialist Party in what was East Berlin. For the most part, however, all of their seat allocations derive from lists, as can be gathered from Table 23.1. If all members of the Bundestag were elected in districts, with the winner being deter-

Table 23.1 HOW THE PARTIES IN THE 1990 BUNDESTAG WON THEIR SEATS

Party	District Contests	Party Lists	Total
CDU/CSU	235	84	319
SPD	91	148	239
FDP	1	78	79
Alliance '90/ Greens (East)	0	8	8
PDS	1	16	17
Total	328	334	662

Source: Forschungsgruppe Wahlen, *Bundestagswahl 1990*, p. 17.

mined each time by the first-past-the-post rule, parliamentary politics in Germany would be strictly a contest between just two parties: the Christian alliance and the Social Democratic Party. Just as congressional politics in the United States is a contest between two parties. And as there, the majority party would take the lion's share of seats.

Candidate Nomination

All candidates on the ballot with any chance of getting elected owe their nominations to political parties. That applies to district candidates no less than to list candidates. As you can see from the ballot in Figure 23.1, the local candidates competing for first votes carry party labels that are far bigger than their own names. To become a party's candidate in a Bundestag district, you must obtain the nomination from the district branch of a party. The local party guards this privilege jealously and frowns on interventions from state or federal party headquarters. Technically, the nomination lies in the hands of all the members enrolled in the district party organization. But neither one of the big parties conducts anything like a primary election among those members to select the party's favorite to run for the Bundestag. Instead, it is by small party committees that district candidates are typically chosen. Party regulars dominate the process. The ordinary member, who rarely attends local party meetings in the neighborhood and may be delinquent in dues payments anyway, takes little if any part in this process.

The local party activists, on the other hand, do not like to play rubber stamp. It is not unheard of for an incumbent seeking another term to be challenged for renomination and lose. There have been years in which almost one in ten incumbents have been denied renomination.[1] The Social Democratic Party has witnessed some bloody battles in big-city districts where the left wing gained the upper hand in the early 1970s. In several such instances, mainstream Social Democrat incumbents decided to quit rather than risk being dumped by their own party. The choice of candidates for a party's list is not in the hands of local organizations, but neither is it in the hands of the national organization, which plays a quiet role in the whole nomination process. The lists are drawn up by the *Länder* (state) party organizations. They decide who gets on the party list, and in which order. Only the better-placed candidates have any chance of entering the Bundestag, so it is for those places that competition is fiercest. Much behind-the-scenes bargaining takes place among party factions as well as among organized groups supporting the party. Drawing up a party list always tests a party's balancing skill.

It is a common practice for a candidate to get a place on the party list and be nominated in a district as well. All leading party figures buy themselves electoral insurance, so to speak, with highly placed positions on the list. Chancellor Helmut Kohl, for example, never carried his local district in Ludwigshafen until 1990. He owed his Bundestag seat to his top place on the Christian Democrats' list in his state of Rhineland-Palatinate. Yet he suffered no shame for not winning his district. Of course, Kohl could have sought nomination in a safe district elsewhere. Instead, he prefers to run in his *Heimat* (home place), the district where he grew up and feels at home—even though he had trouble winning it.

CAMPAIGNS FOR OFFICE

No sooner have the local and state organizations of a party settled the business of candidate nomination than the federal headquarters of each party takes over the campaign for office. Without much doubt, Bundestag campaigns are fought over which party or party coalition should run the federal government, not which representatives should serve in the Bundestag. The incumbent coalition of parties asks the electorate to be given another term in office, while the opposition parties hope to obtain enough votes to oust that coalition. In that sense, though indirectly, the electorate chooses the chancellor.

Hence, a Bundestag campaign is more than the sum of 300-odd local races or a dozen state races. These races are not conducted with many local or state considerations in mind; nor is there much emphasis on the personal qualifications of the local or list candidates. Instead, campaigns for Bundestag office are national party campaigns, conducted under the same party banners, colors, and slogans throughout the Federal Republic. Just about the only personal flavor comes from the party leaders, especially the incumbent chancellor and the chancellor-candidate put forward by the major opposition party. Of course, the Christian Social Union will emphasize some nuances in contrast to the Christian Democratic Union and prominently display its blue-and-white

(Bavarian) colors alongside the black-red-gold federal flag.

The Issues of the 1990 Campaign

While all election campaigns are unique in some ways, focusing on the peculiar issues and the leading characters of the day, the one in 1990 stands out in several respects. One, a single issue lit up the arena as few issues have ever done before, burning nearly all others. This was a campaign over unification. Nothing else mattered very much. Unification was the topic candidates talked about on the stump, and what voters wanted to hear about. Second, it was arguably the longest campaign, beginning with the fall of the Wall in November 1989. Almost like an American presidential campaign, there were primary skirmishes, like the first free election in the German Democratic Republic in March 1990. Third, while a date for the 1990 Bundestag election had long been set, it was not clear until a few months before that the citizens of the former East Germany would participate in it as well.

An external event, namely the revolution in East Germany, overturned the campaign scripts diligently prepared by the West German parties for just another normal election in the old Federal Republic. Those parties suddenly had to stake claims on an issue that had lain dormant in public consciousness for decades.

The Strategies of the Governing Parties

The Christian alliance happily seized on this opportunity. Helmut Kohl did not look like someone who had to pretend all of a sudden that he cared about a unified *Fatherland*, a term he had been using often in his speeches while critics sneered. Whatever else he and his party had prepared for the 1990 campaign, they were glad to tie their electoral destiny to promoting

A newspaper advertisement of the Free Democratic Party, 1990 federal election. The ad exhorts voters to "prevent an absolute majority" by a single party and to give the Free Democrats their "second vote."

unification. What is more, being in office at that very moment of opportunity, Kohl's party was in a position to fashion policies to accomplish that goal.

For his partner in governing, the Free Democratic Party, any electoral campaign is a high-wire balancing act. On one hand, this party must prove its worth by emphasizing where it differs from the bigger partner in government. Why bother voting for a copy when you can have the original? On the other hand, the Free Democrats cannot go too far in drawing distinctions, lest they raise questions about their loyalty to their partner. No Free Democrat leader has performed this acrobatic act more impressively than Hans-Dietrich Genscher. As the foreign minister, he was always in the spotlight during the year of unification. Whatever credit was due, he could claim as much as did Chancellor Kohl. But beyond all that, Genscher possessed an immense popular appeal. In purely personal terms, neither Kohl nor the Social Democrats' Oskar Lafontaine could beat Genscher in a popularity contest.

His personal standing mattered all the more in 1990 since that was the first election as long as anyone can remember that Franz-Josef Strauss of the Christian Social Union was not around anymore. His never-ending vendetta against the Free Democrats was always a boon for this party. For voters favorably inclined toward the Christian Democrats but wary of Strauss, the Free Democratic Party was the best insurance policy. Electoral survival dictates that the Free Democrats make a special appeal for the second vote, the party vote; the first vote being something for the big parties to contest. Having made a coalition commitment to the Christian alliance, the Free Democrats can unabashedly ask for supporters of the other party to split their ballots: go ahead and vote for the Christian Democrat in your district, but "lend" the Free Democrats your party vote! Since the government is run by a coalition anyway, don't worry so much about which particular party to support but make sure your most preferred coalition wins!

The Strategies of the Opposition Parties

The original strategy of the Social Democratic Party for 1990 had been to preempt much of the Green agenda and gain enough electoral support to oust the incumbent coalition. It was a daring course, but not without prospects of success. The environment had become an

Oskar Lafontaine, the Social Democratic Chancellor candidate in 1990.

found a way to reconcile old economic and new environmental concerns. Oskar Lafontaine, the successful premier (governor) of the Saar state, was tailored to lead this party, right down to his fashionable dark silk shirts and his irreverent wit, a youthful candidate from the postmaterialist generation.

Ideologically and temperamentally, this party, however, was not equipped to deal with the issue of unification. With its *Ostpolitik* twenty years earlier, the Social Democratic Party had accepted Germany's national division. Even though the father of that policy, Willy Brandt, warmly embraced the prospect of unification ("what belongs together will grow together"), the younger generation in charge of the party now mustered little enthusiasm. They preferred to take their time with it, hoping the question would remain open at least until after the election.

It was a strategy of ambiguity. The Social Democrats did not say "No" to unification, but when they said "Yes" to the policies designed to accomplish the goal they did so with more reluctance than conviction. In particular, chancellor-candidate Oskar Lafontaine harped mostly on the costs of unification and had fun mocking the patriotic posturing of Chancellor Kohl. It was his undeniable right as opposition leader to warn the West German voters of pending deprivations as a result of unification. His negative campaign appealed to voters' worries about the future, whereas Kohl appealed to their joy about the present. To the extent that those worries were widespread in the West German electorate, Lafontaine's strategy was by no means doomed to failure.

With no ambiguity at all, the Greens rejected unification. This was not an item on the post-materialist agenda. The Greens saw it as a throwback to an era of nationalistic politics that had brought much misery to Germany and the world. Moreover, unification by way of takeover, however friendly, went against the desire for self-determination on the part of the East

issue of immense salience in Germany. Moreover, the West German electorate was losing faith in the Kohl government over issues like housing, immigration, and unemployment. One could sense an it's-time-for-change mood in the electorate.

One year before the election, opinion polls showed a substantial lead for the Social Democrats over the Christian alliance. The Social Democratic Party was hopeful about returning to office after almost a decade out of it. This was a "new politics" party that appeared to have

Chancellor Helmut Kohl at a rally in Ludwigshafen, 1990.

German civil rights movement, with whom the western Greens felt the strongest kinship. Preoccupation with national unification was a most unwelcome distraction from the major concerns of the Greens. But showing their disdain for it and speaking loudly against it placed the party in great electoral danger. Not wanting to be a people's party is risky business in a democracy.

A Case Study in Contrasts

In the course of the 1990 election campaign, both Kohl and Lafontaine gave stock performances to the party faithful on two successive nights in the same arena. This happened in Ludwigshafen, which is Kohl's home district, but one he had never carried.[2] It was apparent that the Social Democratic Party was sending

its top gun into Kohl's backyard to beat him at least locally, if not nationally. Both candidates spoke to partisan audiences with little disturbance from hecklers. The indoor rally with thousands of partisan supporters listening to "the speech" of the main candidate, lasting well over an hour, is still an indispensable campaign device in Germany.

Kohl certainly had the easier time firing up his audience with his message of national pride and joy. His biggest applause came when he thanked Gorbachev for supporting unification. With both Bush and Gorbachev as your good friends, how can a German leader lose his own people? The tune of a German folk song about a hunter from his home region greeted Kohl's arrival in the hall as he wound his way through the crowd missing no hand to shake. It is the kind of corny, provincial touch that makes Kohl's detractors wince. By contrast, Lafontaine entered the hall from backstage, evading the crowd, to the tune of a jazz band.[3] His message of radical policies to deal with the environment failed to rouse the audience of this very industrial town, where BASF is the major employer.

MASS MEDIA

Electoral campaigns in West Germany are still geared to large partisan crowds, assembled in party strongholds. Larger-than-life pictures of Kohl, Lafontaine, and Genscher, with their party autographs in bold letters, adorn billboards across the country. The Greens eschew this personality cult, as did the Party of Democratic Socialism and the Republicans. In return, posters of the Greens and the Democratic Socialists are eye-catching, no matter whether you like the message or not, let alone understand it. Some are genuine works of (modern) art.

The Press

While professing nonpartisanship and political independence, many newspapers and weeklies are not too shy to make their case for one party or another. They do so through the tone of their stories and the tenor of their editorials. It is uncommon, however, for them to endorse a particular party or candidate outright. The *Frankfurter Allgemeine Zeitung,* widely regarded as the most prestigious national paper in Germany, minces few words about the benefits of a Christian alliance–Free Democratic government and the dangers of a Social Democratic Party in government, with or without the Greens. So does *Die Welt.* By comparison, the *Süddeutsche Zeitung* takes a less charitable view toward the Christian alliance, and the *Frankfurter Rundschau* leans toward the Social Democrats and the Greens. A newcomer to this illustrious round, the *TAZ,* sides most firmly

Table 23.2 GERMAN DAILY PAPERS AND WEEKLIES IN 1991

Daily Papers (City)	Circulation
Bild (Hamburg)	4,506,700
Westdeutsche Allgemeine (Essen)	724,900
Hannoversche Allgemeine (Hannover)	513,000
Sächsische Zeitung (Dresden)	499,400
Rheinische Post (Dusseldorf)	396,000
Frankfurter Allgemeine (Frankfurt)	391,000
Süddeutsche Zeitung (Munich)	389,000
. . .	
Die Welt (Bonn)	225,000
Frankfurter Rundschau (Frankfurt)	190,000
TAZ (Berlin)	61,000

Weeklies (City)	
Bild am Sonntag (Hamburg)	2,665,000
Der Spiegel (Hamburg)	1,083,000
Die Zeit (Hamburg)	495,000
Welt am Sonntag	406,000

Source: *Facts about Germany,* p. 327.

with the Greens. Most Germans, however, as can be gleaned from table 23.2, read none of these papers but prefer tabloids like *Bild* that dwell on more titillating fare than politics.[4]

Television

These days, however, the majority of Germans rate television by far the most important source of political information. This medium also offers the political parties unique opportunities not available in the printed press. By law, the two major networks, public corporations operating like the American PBS in a way, are required to make air time available to the parties for their campaign broadcasts, free of charge.

The parties may use the time allocated as they please. They may feature interviews with their leading figures or commercials produced by public relations firms. In return for the free allocation, the parties may not purchase any additional air time, although they are not barred from taking out paid advertisements in the print media.

The parties also benefit or suffer from the way the media cover them. The television coverage of politics frequently arouses the ire of the Christian alliance. This party feels that especially the first network (ARD) puts a leftist spin on the news and in so doing hurts the party's electoral prospects. It is no secret that the political sympathies of television journalists lie not particularly with the Christian Democratic Union/Christian Social Union. And their political preferences may color their reporting of political news and create an "opinion climate" unfavorable to the Christian alliance.[5] Still, it is a big step from there to changing people's votes. As so often happens, the most attentive voters also happen to be the ones who feel most strongly about their parties, candidates, and issues. They are the least likely to be swayed by media coverage.[6]

Campaign Debates

One of the staples of media coverage in the Federal Republic is a television debate a few days before election day. From 1972 to 1987, the two West German networks have jointly broadcast this event. However, these television confrontations have never featured a straight duel between the two chancellor-candidates. Instead, those two have had to share the limelight with the leaders of the other parties in the Bundestag, including the Greens in 1987. Germany does not, after all, have a two-party system, and when it comes to television, the Christian Social Union proudly hoists its own partisan colors.

With four or five participants and only two moderators in charge, these debates tend to turn into verbal free-for-alls, with participants interrupting one another and questioning each other's good manners. Altogether, this is quite an unruly spectacle, lacking in the supposedly German virtues of discipline and self-restraint. The participants, so it seems, treat the debate as their last chance to settle their accumulated campaign grudges; to test the thickness of the opponents' political skins; and to tag them as liars, crooks, and incompetents in front of a national audience bereft of something else to watch. Even the best prepared and most attentive viewers probably despair of discerning shades of policy differences among the various parties to the debate. But what one cannot fail to notice is the visceral animosity between the leaders of the government and those of the opposition. These debates appear to be waged on the strategic premise not to win converts but to hold on to one's supporters, keep them in line, and cheer them on.[7]

CAMPAIGN FINANCES

Campaigns cost money, even with generous allowances of free time for advertisement on television. By dues and donations, German parties have long tried to finance their own operations. A mass-membership party like the Social Democratic Party has traditionally relied on the dues paid by its members. On the other hand, a party with few but wealthy backers, like the Free Democratic Party, depends more heavily on donations. Unlike the case in the United States, there are no limits on the amount that one can contribute to a political party in Germany. Nor are business corporations barred from making such contributions. In fact, until a recent change, business contributions were tax-deductible. Despite all this, neither dues nor donations have kept up with the ever-growing financial appetite of political parties. With imagination and a touch of deviousness, the German parties found the perfect solution to their money problem. Or so they thought.

Public Subsidies

The answer was so close at hand as to be hard to miss. The parties tapped the public treasury. To justify subsidies, the parties claimed they were simply asking for "reimbursements" of electoral expenses. After all, the Basic Law asks them to perform a constitutional role. To keep the bookkeeping simple, the rule adopted was that a party bills the government a specified amount for every vote the party gained in the last election—proportional representation, financially speaking. In 1990, each party was legally entitled to receive DM 5 ($3) for each second vote it received.[8] Oddly enough, a party had to obtain only 0.5% (not 5%) to qualify for this reimbursement. An unintended consequence of that rule was to provide an irresistible incentive for any organization with some following to launch a political party. Indeed, it is the Greens whom public financing has greatly benefited—hardly a consequence intended by the established parties, which designed the law.

As Table 23.3 indicates, between one-third and one-half of party income came from the public trough in 1990. It was the single largest source of income for every party, surpassing the amounts raised from member dues. In 1990, the federal treasury paid out DM 500 million ($310 million) in subsidies to the political parties. And that is in a country with less than a third of the U.S. population. That went too far, the Federal Constitutional Court ruled in 1992 (more on this institution in Chapter 25). While not rejecting the principle of government subsidies, the court argued that subsidies could not exceed the amount a party raised by itself. The verdict ordered that a new law meeting various stipulations be drawn up before the next election. In so many words, the court wrote the new law, passed dutifully and promptly by the Bundestag a year later. The 1993 law drastically lowered the per-vote reimbursement to DM 1.30 ($.80) from the previous DM 5.[9] It remains to be seen how the German parties will manage to live with this diet welfare.

Money Scandals

With regulations guiding donations to parties being so loose, political money occasionally

Table 23.3 THE SOURCES OF PARTY INCOME IN 1990 (%)

Source	CDU	CSU	SPD	FDP	Greens[a]
Member Dues	26	18	38	13	17
Donations	21	39	11	26	18
Election Reimbursement	44	39	40	52	33
Other	9	4	11	9	32
Total	100%	100%	100%	100%	100%
Income (DM mill.)	340	91	343	89	60

[a]The "other" category for the Greens includes largely contributions from local groups (citizen initiatives).
Source: *Week in Germany,* April 17, 1992 published by the German Information Center, 950 Third Avenue, NY, NY 10022.

spices German politics with scandal. The biggest scandal involved a gigantic, though obscure company, the Flick concern. It gave Germany a case of "Flickgate." This scandal landed two former economics ministers, and almost Chancellor Kohl himself, in court on charges ranging from bribery, through tax evasion, and all the way to perjury. The two cabinet ministers, Hans Freidrichs and Count Otto Lambsdorff, were accused of granting lucrative tax waivers in return for Flick contributions to their party, the Free Democratic Party. In 1987, both were found guilty, though only on the lesser charge of evading taxes on the donations. Chancellor Kohl was accused by a prominent Green legislator, Otto Schily, of having accepted Flick donations that were never reported, and of lying about the channeling of donations through dummy party foundations. No indictment against the chancellor was handed up, however, because of "insufficient evidence." With no further court action, talk of Flickgate subsided, but a smell of impropriety lingered.

VOTER DECISIONS

In the 1990 Bundestag election, German voters handed a resounding victory to a governing coalition that had delivered unification barely two months earlier. It was perhaps no landslide of historic dimension, but with 55% of the (second) votes, the Christian alliance and the Free Democrats together mustered practically the same support among the new voters in the East as among the established ones in the West (see Table 23.4). For the major opposition party, the 1990 election was deeply disappointing. With barely 36% of the vote in the old Federal Republic, the Social Democratic Party took its worst drubbing since 1957. Nor did the other opposition party on the Left fare especially well. The western Greens failed to win 5% of the votes and thus missed entry into the new Bundestag.

Table 23.4 THE PARTIES' VOTE PERCENTAGES IN THE 1990 BUNDESTAG ELECTION (SECOND VOTES)

Party	West	East
CDU/CSU	44.3	41.8
FDP	10.6	12.9
SPD	35.7	24.3
Greens (West)	4.8	—
Alliance '90/ Greens (East)	—	6.0
PDS	0.3	11.1
Republicans	2.3	1.3
Others	2.0	2.6
Voting Turnout (%)	79	75

Source: Forschungsgruppe Wahlen, *Bundestagswahl 1990*, pp. 8–9.

Also noteworthy was the poor showing of the right-wing upstart, the Republicans. National reunification took the wind out of their electoral sails. The key difference between voters in East and West was the strong showing of the Party of Democratic Socialism in the former German Democratic Republic, where it captured more than 10%; in contrast, the party was practically invisible in the West, where it gleaned less than a single percent.

Voting Turnout

Oddly enough, the excitement over unification did not prompt an especially large number of Germans to turn out to vote in 1990. Slightly fewer than 80 percent of voting-age Germans went to the polls. While that would be a record for a U.S. presidential election in this century, it was the lowest in the Federal Republic since 1949. Voting participation has been traditionally high in Germany, dating back more than a hundred years to the days of the empire. Equal voting rights were given to men in 1871 and extended to women in 1919.

The high rate of voting turnout has often been attributed to the Germans' deeply ingrained sense of duty. Voting is like paying taxes and not crossing the street on a red light. The prevailing national stereotype certainly points in that direction, and many have discounted the high turnout in Germany as a sign of civic maturity. Indeed, there is strong evidence that a sense of duty is the key motive force in exercising the right to vote. But the evidence comes from American, not German, voters.[11]

A more compelling reason for high turnout is the absence in Germany of onerous registration requirements. A German citizen need not make a special trip to register to vote. Unbeknownst to most Germans, they are automatically registered to vote by means of their residence registration, which they must file under penalty of law. Voting, moreover, is always on a Sunday, in a polling station close enough to walk to; and the act of voting does not take long, since there are only two votes to be cast. The inconvenience costs of voting are truly minimal in Germany.

Yet recent experience shows that the low cost of voting is no guarantee for high turnout. West Germans have lately shown an increasing aversion to voting. From a postwar high of 91% in 1972, turnout has fallen in almost every election, to 79% in 1990 in the old Federal Republic. The reasons for this drop are a matter of dispute. Some blame it on deepening disaffection with the established parties. Others point to the erosion of the traditional milieux that spawned and nurtured political parties. In a curious coincidence, East German turnout slid from 93% in March to 75% in December 1990. East Germans are fast learners, it seems. To be sure, the pre-election polls left little doubt that the governing parties would win a sweeping victory,

but predictions of landslides in the past have not kept Germans, or voters elsewhere, from the polls. Closeness, as the saying goes, counts only in horseshoes and dancing.

Partisanship in the West

When going to the polls many voters take a strong sense of partisanship with them. The symptoms of partisan behavior are unmistakable. Since 1961, the Christian alliance has never received less than 44%, or more than 50%, in West Germany, while support for the Social Democrats has ranged from 36% to 46%. For many voters, the partisan choice on election day is not a matter of a long and arduous search through a forest of alternatives, but a case of brand-name loyalty, known as "party identification" in the United States. In the aggregate, voter identifications with political parties constitute a built-in stabilizer for any party system.[13] Without them, new parties will find it relatively easy to appeal to large segments of the electorate. It may be argued that it was lack of widespread identification with established parties that made the electoral surge of the Nazi Party so irresistible between 1928 and 1933. It seems that the parties that had cornered a share of the electoral market before 1928 lost little in the political crash following the economic collapse. On the other hand, those parties whose support had greatly wavered in the decades before 1928 were decimated in the Crash.

Surveys taken by the Forschungsgruppe Wahlen throughout the 1970s and early 1980s found roughly seven of ten West Germans expressing a long-term attachment to one of the parties. If anything, during the turbulent 1970s, when the United States and Britain experienced partisan dealignment, the curve of party attachment pointed upward in the Federal Republic. In the early 1990s, however, the signs of such dealignment have been unmistakable in the Federal Republic.[14] Partisan attachments are cooling and, as with religion, more people are opting out of partisan commitments altogether.[15]

Partisanship in the East

East Germans, on the other hand, just entered the electoral process in 1990, and without the preparation afforded by the usual forms of partisan socialization. Deprived of the experience of a competitive party system for nearly sixty years, East Germans had few opportunities to form partisan attachments. It is doubtful that more than a handful learned about the party of their 1990 choice from mom or dad at the dinner table, or from membership in labor unions or churches.

While opportunities to forge lasting partisan attachments in East Germany were undoubtedly limited, most East Germans did not live in a partisan vacuum. As with their general political attitudes described in a previous chapter, they may have focused their partisan feelings on the parties west of the border. Being heavily tuned into West German television, many East Germans must have felt quite at home in the party politics of the Federal Republic. Indeed, given how remote politics is for most people in western democracies, many easterners may have been as familiar with those parties as were their western contemporaries.

Short of forging an outright identification with one of those parties, East Germans had their favorites among the western parties. Barely a few months after the first free election in March 1990, practically all East German respondents in a survey picked one of the four well-known West German parties when asked which one they liked best.[16] In a fledgling electorate, a flood of responses like "don't like any of them," or "not sure about which one I like best," or even "don't know enough about them" would not have been surprising at all. Yet hardly anybody offered any of these

responses. Far from groping uncomfortably with the problem of sorting out the various political parties of another political system, East Germans seemed surprisingly sure-handed in their choices.

The Social Background

Unlike the fledgling party ties of East German voters, the more established partisanship of West Germans is rooted in social influence. Being a Catholic, and especially a Catholic attending church regularly, spells "CDU/CSU" in the dictionary of electoral choice, just as it spelled "Center," the name of the Catholic Party, until 1933. A Catholic going to church on election day, a Sunday of course, would be exhorted from the pulpit to vote for candidates favoring Christian principles. Likewise, for more than a century, to be a blue-collar worker with a union card has spelled "SPD."

Churchgoing Catholics and unionized workers define the respective electoral bedrocks of the two big parties. These group connections guarantee each a base of support and ensure against electoral extinction. But they do not encompass the full sweep of electoral support each of those parties enjoys. The Christian alliance could not win 20% of the vote with only regular Catholics, and the Social Democratic Party could not do so with unionized workers only. The recipe of success for the Christian alliance has been its ability to attract Catholics while not repelling Protestants. Among Protestants with at least some tie to their church, the Christian alliance draws roughly even with the Social Democratic Party. That party's recipe, in turn, has been its appeal to the growing ranks of white-collar and civil service voters, especially the unionized in those ranks.

Both major parties, moreover, face the problem that their core constituencies are shrinking. Barely one of three Catholics nowadays attends church regularly, compared to nearly two in three in the 1950s. Likewise, the ranks of blue-collar workers have declined from one-half of the electorate in 1950 to four-tenths by 1985. Unification has added few churchgoing Catholics to the German electorate. Although the ranks of unionized workers may have increased, in the East these people are not strongly inclined to the Social Democratic Party. The social alignments of the past are fraying for German parties. In 1987, the two big parties both lost ground for the first time in the Federal Republic. In 1990, they both lost ground again.

Issue and Candidate Evaluations

Even though Germans cannot vote for chancellor, the candidates for that office dominate the campaign limelight. Both major parties choose their nominees with an eye on the electoral bottom line. In rating the two candidates for chancellor, the West German public has typically given the incumbent chancellor a decided

edge (see Table 23.5). This is true even for incumbents who trailed far behind when they headed the opposition in earlier campaigns, like Brandt in 1961–1965 and Kohl in 1976.

The key to these ratings, however, is not a purely personal magnetism, but success at settling important issues or presiding over good times. Early in the election year, when unification was an uncertain prospect, the West German electorate did not favor Kohl over Lafontaine. What gave Kohl a decisive edge and the Christian alliance the lead over the Social Democrats was the fact that he accomplished the unification of Germany. It was the spectacular chain of international events from the summit with Gorbachev in mid-July to the signing of the unification treaty that turned the balance of West German opinion in Kohl's favor. This sweeping reversal also blunted the edge that the Social Democrats had enjoyed on such issues as the environment, housing, and social security.

By comparison, the East German voters already had staked their future on the Kohl gov-

---

Table 23.5 WHOM WEST GERMANS PREFER AS CHANCELLOR (PRE-ELECTION OPINION POLLS)

Year	Incumbent	Challenger	Percent for Incumbent	Percent for Challenger
1961	Adenauer (CDU)	Brandt (SPD)	47	34
1965	Erhard (CDU)	Brandt (SPD)	57	33
1969	Kiesinger (CDU)	Brandt (SPD)	55	22
1972	Brandt (SPD)	Barzel (CDU)	61	27
1976	Schmidt (SPD)	Kohl (CDU)	53	40
1980	Schmidt (SPD)	Strauss (CSU)	61	29
1983	Kohl (CDU)	Vogel (SPD)	53	42
1987	Kohl (CDU)	Ray (SPD)	46	46
1990W	Kohl (CDU)	Lafontaine (SPD)	56	37
1990E	Kohl (CDU)	Lafontaine (SPD)	57	40

Source: 1961–1976: Helmut Norpoth, "Kanzlerkandidaten," *Politische Vierteljahresschrift,* 18 (1977): 563; 1980–1990: Forschungsgruppe Wahlen surveys.

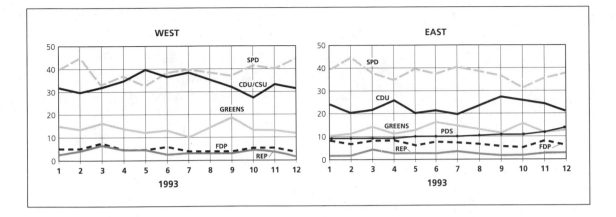

Figure 23.2 Party Support in East and West Germany, January–December 1993. Source: Forschungsgruppe Wahlen, *Politbarometer 1993.*

ernment in the March 1990 election. The prospect of rapid unification appeared far brighter to them with his government than with one led by the Social Democrats. By the middle of the year, the vast majority was desperate for unification ASAP. The Christian Democratic Union and the Free Democratic Party were the partisan beneficiaries of the fulfillment of those expectations in December. The result was a remarkable symmetry of electoral behavior in East and West, as the governing parties captured just about the same share of electoral support in the old Federal Republic and in the new eastern states. It was a reward for an historic accomplishment, tendered with the hope that the costs would be tolerable.[17]

Outlook

The year 1994 will test the Germans' stamina for electoral endurance. The "super election year," as it is billed, features elections in most of the sixteen states; the election of the European Parliament; of a new German president; and of a new Bundestag. It is almost like a U.S. presidential election year with primaries. The outcomes of early contests are bound to create momentum for some parties, disappointment for others, and endless speculation of how the final and most decisive contest will wind up, the election of a new Bundestag. The governing coalition is not entering 1994 with a high approval rating. Promises have been broken or left unfulfilled. The eastern states are not flourishing, and the westerners see economic gloom ahead after the booming 1980s.

There can be little doubt that the German electorate is in a throw-the-rascals-out mood. What is far less certain is whom they favor to take over. The years in opposition have done no wonders for the Social Democratic Party. To the contrary, this party has steadily lost electoral ground after being driven from power in 1982. The liabilities of the Christian alliance and the Free Democratic Party do not convert to credits for the Social Democratic Party. In search for more promising alternatives, Germans have scattered in all directions, from the Greens to Ross Perot–like organizations all the way to neo-Nazi groups. Only one thing is certain in 1994: the parties will have to woo the voters with a much smaller allowance from the public hand.

NOTES

1. See Gerhard Loewenberg, *Parliament in the German System* (Ithaca: Cornell University Press, 1966), p. 73.
2. The following is based on the author's observations of the two candidates during those events.
3. It must be noted, however, that Lafontaine had been the target of an attack on his life earlier in the year. He was stabbed in public, but not seriously injured.
4. For an analysis of media coverage of the 1990 campaign, see Holli A. Semetko and Klaus Schonbach, "The Campaign in the Media," in *The New Germany Votes: Unification and the Creation of a New German Party System,* ed. Russell J. Dalton (Providence: Berg Publishers, 1993); also Max Kaase and Peter R. Schrott, "Political Information in the 1990 German General Election," APSA paper (Washington, D.C., 1991).
5. These charges of media bias apply specifically to the 1976 election, in which the SPD-FDP coalition defeated the CDU/CSU by a very narrow margin. See Elisabeth Noelle-Neumann, *The Spiral of Silence* (Chicago: Chicago University Press, 1984), pp. 157–169.
6. See Helmut Norpoth and Kendall L. Baker, "Mass Media Use and Electoral Choice in West Germany," *Comparative Politics,* 13 (October 1980): 1–14; for the 1990 election, see Steven E. Finkel and Peter R. Schrott, "Campaign Effects on Voter Choice in the German Election of 1990," APSA paper (Washington, D. C., 1993).
7. See Kendall L. Baker and Helmut Norpoth, "Television Debates and Press Coverage in the 1980 and 1983 West German Elections," in *Germany at the Polls,* ed. Karl H. Cerney (Durham, N.C.: Duke University Press, 1990); also Peter R. Schrott, "Electoral Consequences of 'Winning' Televised Campaign Debates," *Public Opinion Quarterly,* 54 (1990): 567–585.
8. The per-vote rate was even higher than that. In a bizarre way of accounting, each party was also reimbursed for its percentage share of non-voters.
9. *The Week in Germany,* November 19, 1993, p. 7.
10. See, for example, Ralf Dahrendorf, *Society and Democracy in Germany* (Garden City: Doubleday, 1969). He entitled the chapter discussing voting turnout (21) as "The Unpolitical German."
11. See Angus Campbell, Philip E. Converse, Warren E. Miller, and Donald E. Stokes, *The American Voter* (New York: Wiley, 1960), pp. 105–106; also Angus Campbell, Gerald Gurin, and Warren E. Miller, *The Voter Decides* (Evanston: Row, Peterson and Co., 1954), pp. 187–199.
12. See the article bearing that title by John A. Ferejohn and Morris P. Fiorina, *American Political Science Review,* LXIX (September 1975): 920–925.
13. There is much debate over the merits of the concept of "party identification" in Germany. See Helmut Norpoth, "Party Identification in West Germany: Tracing an Elusive Concept," *Comparative Political Studies,* 11 (April 1978): 36–61.
14. See Helmut Norpoth, "The Making of a More Partisan Electorate in West Germany," *British Journal of Political Science,* 14 (1983): 53–71.
15. See Russell J. Dalton, "Two German Electorates?" in *Developments in German Politics,* ed. Gordon Smith et al. (London: Macmillan, 1992).
16. Forschungsgruppe Wahlen, Politbarometer-East, August 1990.
17. See Helmut Norpoth and Dieter Roth, "Unification and Electoral Choice," in *The New Germany Votes: Unification and the Creation of a New German Party System,* ed. Russell J. Dalton (Providence: Berg Publishers, 1993), pp. 209–230.

REFERENCES AND SUGGESTED READINGS

Dalton, Russell J. 1988. *Citizen Politics in Western Democracies.* Chatham: Chatham House.

Forschungsgruppe Wahlen. 1990. *Bundestagswahl 1990.* Mannheim.

Jesse, Eckhard. 1990. *Elections.* Providence: Berg Publishers.

Klingemann, Hans-Dieter, and Max Kaase, eds. 1993. *Wahlen und Wähler: Analysen aus Anlass der Bundestagswahl 1990.* Opladen: Westdeutscher Verlag.

24

Parliament and Coalitions

*I*n Germany, Parliament has long struggled to get respect, and continues to struggle for popular approval. Parliamentary government arrived late, compared with Britain, and the first experience with it, during the Weimar Republic, did more to douse than to rouse popular enthusiasm for it. The framers of the Federal Republic then adopted a trimmed version of a parliamentary system in 1949. While many agree that it has worked well, one can argue whether that owes more to what has been trimmed than to what is left of the parliamentary form of government. Meanwhile, whatever parliamentary claims the German Democratic Republic may have made were negated by the monopoly status of the Socialist Unity Party. With East Germany adopting the governmental institutions of the western Federal Republic in 1990, the *Volkskammer* (people's chamber) has ended up as a footnote of history, or as Communists liked to say, on the ash-heap of history. Since the first national election in that same year, the Bundestag (Federal Assembly) can finally claim to be the body of representatives of the whole German people. Note that in referring to the "Parliament" of the Federal Republic we mean the *Bundestag*, the body of representatives who are popularly elected, as described in the previous chapter. There is another institution, the *Bundesrat* (Federal Council), that has a voice in lawmaking, but should not be confused with an upper house or a second chamber of Parliament.

Meeting of the German Parliament in Bonn.

THE PLACE

For most of the last forty years, the Parliament of the Federal Republic has been housed in temporary quarters, actually a former teachers' college. The building always looked as new and functional as the Federal Republic. It inspired neither awe for the institution of Parliament nor exuded any warmth, although the purpose of educating people may have been an appropriate mission for Parliament in postwar Germany.

In the late 1980s, as the building was renovated so as to suit better a Parliament getting on in years, the deputies had to find another temporary refuge in—well, Bonn's waterworks. An unprepared visitor looking for Parliament may be forgiven for mistaking the city hall, with its baroque style, or the university for the site of the German Parliament. Now, with Berlin having been chosen as the capital of the reunified Germany, the former *Reichstag* building may have to have suit up once again to house an institution still looking for a permanent home. That, however, may prompt confusion as to whether the German Parliament should be called *Reichstag* or *Bundestag*.

Given its location in a former college, the Bundestag has held its floor sessions for most of the last forty years in what has the unmistakable look of a lecture hall. The only concession to ornament is a gigantic emblem of an eagle hovering over the podium. Members are assembled in a semicircle around the podium, each having a seat and a desk along with it. A visitor attending a floor session on an important issue will also notice that the podium seats not only the presiding officer but also the "federal government"—namely, the chancellor

Reichstag in Berlin.

along with the other members of the cabinet. The chancellor needs no special dispensation to attend the meetings of the Bundestag. No strict separation-of-power doctrine keeps him at arm's length. He is free to speak up and would be chastised for missing sessions or keeping mute whenever important issues are debated. Of course, the price for taking part in meetings of the Bundestag is that the chancellor is subject to relentless attacks on the government's policies by the opposition.

Prior to unification in 1990, the Bundestag typically comprised 496 or so popularly elected representatives as well as 22 nonvoting and not popularly chosen representatives from West Berlin. Unification raised the membership to 662. A regular Bundestag term runs to four years; early elections may be called, but only under very closely prescribed circumstances. Elections have rarely handed a single parliamentary party a majority of seats in the Bun-

destag, although the Christian Democratic Union/Christian Social Union is never far away from it (see Table 24.1). Only once, in 1972, did the Social Democratic Party outnumber the Christian alliance. Besides those big parties, only one other party, the Free Democratic Party, has consistently captured enough votes to be represented in the Bundestag. Though small, the Free Democratic Party controlled enough seats between 1961 and 1983 to supply each of the big parties with a winning margin.

THE MEMBERS

Neither in Germany nor anywhere else are members of Parliament chosen like a random sample from a nation's population. Instead, the people's representatives constitute an elite. They define a nation's political elite more closely than any other imaginable group. To be

Table 24.1 DISTRIBUTION OF SEATS BY PARTY IN THE BUNDESTAG

	1949	1953	1957	1961	1965	1969
CDU/CSU	139	244	270	242	245	242
SPD	131	151	169	190	202	224
FDP	52	48	41	67	49	30
Greens	—	—	—	—	—	—
Other	80	44	17	—	—	—
Total	402	487	497	499	496	496

	1972	1976	1980	1983	1987	1990
CDU/CSU	225	243	226	244	223	319
SPD	230	214	218	193	186	239
FDP	41	39	53	34	46	79
Greens	—	—	—	27	42	—
Other	—	—	—	—	—	25
Total	496	496	497	498	497	662

Source: Peter Schindler, *Datenhandbuch zur Geschichte des deutschen Bundestages 1980 bis 1987* (Baden-Baden: Nomos, 1988), p. 989, updated. Used by permission of the publisher, Nomos Verlagsgesellschaft.

sure, presidents of large corporations and banks, chiefs of labor unions, church officials, newspaper publishers, key journalists, among others, have a rightful claim to political-elite status, but for few of them is politics the primary occupation.

A Men's Club

Like most parliaments, the Bundestag is a predominantly male institution. Not until the election of 1987 did the share of female members of the Bundestag exceed 10%; by comparison, women captured 7% of the seats in 1949. The trend has been extremely slow to rise. The sudden increase to 15% in 1987 stemmed largely from the Greens. As Table 24.2 indicates, more than half of their members in the 1987–1990 Bundestag were women. No other party came close. While the Christian alliance seems most

inhospitable to women in politics, the Social Democratic Party also falls way short of gender equality in the Bundestag.

The problem is not that many women run for office and are spurned by the voters. It is that few women are nominated for Bundestag seats by local and state party organizations, except for the Greens. The big parties, in particular, are averse to nominating female candidates to run in Bundestag districts, which fill half the seats. In 1987, districts sent 18 women into the Bundestag, compared to 62 who were elected through party lists.[1] In Germany, the chance of a woman's entering the Bundestag is vastly higher by way of the party list than the local constituency. Once in the Bundestag, the chances of women occupying leading positions vary considerably by party. Since 1983, they have been highest among the Greens, and lowest among the Free Democrats. The Christian alliance improved its below-average rating through the choice of Rita Süssmuth, their most prominent female representative, as president (speaker) of the Bundestag in 1988. Throughout the 1980s, the best-known woman in the Social Democratic Party, Annemarie Renger, held the position of Bundestag vice president. Yet it is still true that no woman has been chosen to fill a key cabinet post, let alone the chancellorship. Such a prospect seems brightest if and when the Greens come to power. First, of course, the Greens of the old Federal Republic have to make it back into the Bundestag.

A Parliament of Academics

Aside from gender, education sharply sets the Bundestag membership apart from the general population. In Germany, roughly six of ten members of the Bundestag hold a university degree. It almost seems that an academic title is a prerequisite for entry into the Bundestag, especially in the Christian alliance and the Free Democratic Party (see Table 24.2). Surprisingly enough, the party that draws so much strength from the college-educated, namely the Greens, does not recruit its representatives disproportionately from those ranks. By far the most frequent university degree is in law. Hence, as in the U.S. Congress, lawyers are quite conspicuous in the Bundestag. But there is an important difference: few members with law degrees have had much experience in private practice. Aside from law, other common degrees are in areas (economics, political science, history, sociology) that can be said to have prepared their recipients for a political career.

Table 24.2 CHARACTERISTICS OF THE PARTIES' REPRESENTATIVES IN THE BUNDESTAG, 1987–1990

	Representatives of			
	CDU/CSU (%)	FDP (%)	SPD (%)	Greens (%)
Women	8	13	16	57
University Graduate	71	69	49	57
Government Official	17	23	7	0
Civil Servant	27	15	46	43
Interest-Group Official	8	15	22	9
Professional, Self-Employed	37	33	12	11
White Collar (private sector)	10	6	5	11
Blue Collar	0	0	4	2
Homemaker	1	4	2	7
Union Member	17	2	97	48
Freshman	11	23	21	75

Source: Peter Schindler, *Datenhandbuch zur Geschichte des deutschen Bundestages 1980 bis 1987* (Baden-Baden: Nomos, 1988), pp. 187–205, updated. Used by permission of the publisher, Nomos Verlagsgesellschaft.

By any yardstick of social standing, members of the Bundestag are thoroughly middle class. Even in the ranks of the Social Democrats, one has to look long and hard for someone with a blue collar (see Table 24.2). Whatever class warfare takes place in the Bundestag requires considerable role playing by middle-class actors. The lack of blue-collar workers in its Bundestag ranks notwithstanding, practically every Social Democratic member belongs to a union. It suggests that the Social Democratic parliamentary caucus is a "closed shop." The polar opposite of this is not so much the Christian alliance, but the Free Democratic Party. There, hardly any member belongs to a union. One wonders how Social Democrats and Free Democrats ever managed to agree on economic and social policy.

A Paradise for Bureaucrats

It is a cliché to refer to the Bundestag as a Parliament of civil servants. But there is considerable truth to it. Nearly half of the members are civil servants or government officials (including past service). Part of this is inherent in the parliamentary system, with members doing double duty as ministers and secretaries in government departments. But that is only a small part. More important, Germany is a country that provides nearly irresistible incentives to civil servants to embark on a parliamentary career. Note that, unlike the United States, a civil servant is allowed to serve as an elected representative without having to resign from the service. He or she may take a leave of absence for such a purpose, and the leave has no time limit. What is more, there is no loss of any perks that would accrue if the person did not venture into parliamentary politics. Hence, running for and serving in the Bundestag is a no-risk proposition for German civil servants. In other words, they can eat their cake in Parliament and have it too in the civil service. Or to paraphrase another saying, in Germany parliamentary politics is the continuation of bureaucratic politics with other means. One wonders why not all members of the Bundestag are civil servants.

Besides civil servants, employees of interest-group associations are a conspicuous presence among members of the Bundestag. That does not leave a large share for representatives with a nonpolitical, private-sector background. For them, a political career is fraught with far greater risks. Even in the ranks of the Christian alliance and the Free Democratic Party, where they are more prominent, the self-employed and professionals encompass barely one-third. Other than civil servants, nobody seems happy with this skewed recruitment of members. Politics already is bureaucratic enough to give civil servants a head start in the parliamentary race as well. Whatever happened to the idea that Parliament ought to be the place where "representatives of the whole people" meet and serve as an effective check against, well, the bureaucracy?

The Financial Reward

Whatever the past occupation of a member of the Bundestag, being a member long ago ceased being a part-time job. In fact, it's more like holding two or three full-time jobs, given the demands of committee work, party caucuses, the party back home, and, at least for half of them, errands for the constituency. No doubt, the pay is attractive: the equivalent of roughly $100,000 a year (at the rate of 1.6 Deutschmarks to the U.S. dollar), with a good portion of it tax-free. Few members are able to devote any time to the occupation they held before entering the Bundestag. For many, as we have seen, trying to do so would raise some constitutional questions.

COMMITTEES

Visitors to the Bundestag are often chagrined to find the chamber nearly empty on any given day, with those members who are present as alert as students in an early morning class. The simple truth is that the German Bundestag is a parliament of committees and party caucuses. As a rule of thumb, an individual member spends only as much time on the floor as in either committee meetings or party caucuses. The roughly twenty standing committees have well-defined jurisdictions, attract stable memberships, and are often chaired by members who make a career out of that job. After a bill has had its first reading on the floor, it is taken up for detailed discussion in one of the standing committees. Here, in a much more confidential setting, without the public intruding, the individual member can make a difference. Expertise, specialization, and hard work count.

This is also the place where members of the opposition have a chance to affect the shape of legislation, and where much give-and-take across party lines occurs. Unlike the U.S. Congress, the Bundestag majority does not claim all committee chairs. Winner-take-all is an un-German principle. Instead, opposition parties receive a proportional share of those posts. Even the anti-establishment Greens get their share, and they do not leave those chairs unoccupied. Once a committee has concluded its work on a bill assigned to it and reports it back to the floor for final consideration, floor debate is dominated by members of the reporting committee. The Bundestag approximates what is called a "working" parliament, like the U.S Congress, far more than a "debating" parliament, like the British one. In the latter type, more time is spent on addressing big issues of policy on the floor than on settling the details of legislation in committees. Observers enamored of the ideal of the British Parliament typically find the Bundestag wanting.

PARTY INFLUENCE

Unlike most other constitutions, the Basic Law takes account of political parties. It recognizes their role in the political process (Article 21). Yet, the Basic Law also endorses principles that are bound to collide with the idea that collective organizations like political parties have rights. According to Article 38, members of the Bundestag are supposed to represent the *whole people*, not specific groups (like political parties); to make decisions based on their *consciences*, not on orders or instructions.

Parliamentary Parties

In reality, of course, the individual member gets into the Bundestag by virtue of a party label and, once there, belongs to a *Fraktion*, a parliamentary party caucus. Much of a member's legislative life is spent in activities of that party caucus. It underscores the prominent role of party caucuses in the Bundestag that leading party figures serve as caucus leaders. It is not unusual to find a member with chancellor aspirations taking on the job as caucus chairman. From 1976 to 1982, Helmut Kohl led the Christian alliance inside the Bundestag, aside from being the federal chairman of the Christian Democratic Union organization outside the Bundestag as well. In the Social Democratic Party, it was Hans-Jochen Vogel who combined the same two jobs in that party from 1987 to 1991.

Party caucuses meet often, and the average member spends nearly as much time in caucus meetings as on the floor of the Bundestag or in its committees. It is in meetings of the whole caucus and of caucus committees that each party attempts to fashion a party consensus on all key issues to be taken up by the Bundestag. The caucus leadership prepares the agenda and steers the discussion. To be sure, these are meetings behind closed doors. Internal disagreements can be freely voiced and various organized groups within the parties can plead their cases on legislation affecting them specifically. No doubt, the line adopted by the caucus will not please all caucus members, at least not equally. But so long as the caucus has the opportunity to discuss the matter, each member knows what is expected on the floor: to vote for the party line. This process "permits the parties to negotiate their internal differences in private and to reach a caucus decision which its Members are willing to support in public."[2] Not everyone always does, but overall the percentage of party-voting averages in the upper 90s, just a shade short of a perfect 100.

Sticks and Carrots in Parliamentary Politics

Party discipline is a well-understood norm in the Bundestag. It is the glue that holds each party together and, if the coalition partners in government stick together, assures the chancellor a secure tenure in office. For a member of a governing party to vote with the opposition is to jeopardize that tenure. Repeated acts of such disloyalty will not endear the rebels to their leaders or colleagues. It will jeopardize their political careers, and they had better look for another party or quit parliamentary politics altogether.

One famous rebel within the Christian alliance, Gustav Heinemann, switched to the Social Democratic Party in the 1950s and later became federal president, but this is an exceptional case. More common is the fate suffered by rebels within the Free Democratic Party in the early 1970s. Strongly opposed to their party's coalition with the Social Democrats, those dissenters in the end left the Free Democratic Party. Some sought a new partisan home with the Christian alliance. But for most of them, the defection was a ticket to political

oblivion. The new party was as wary of the defector as the former was unforgiving. The lesson is that party rebellion (usually) does not pay. How compatible is that lesson with the constitutional guarantee of free representation of the whole people?

Well, nobody has ever filed suit over this issue. If someone did, much would depend on how the party in dispute went about establishing its party line and how it enforced it. Say a party made you deposit, at the beginning of the term, an undated but signed letter of resignation of your Bundestag seat. This device, which was common in the Communist Party (KPD), would certainly be ruled unconstitutional. In fact, the whole party was so ruled in 1956 by the Constitutional Court of the Federal Republic.

The truth is that the leaders of party caucuses in the Bundestag have few penalties to impose on rebels within their ranks. It is not up to those leaders, for example, to decide on a member's renomination. They may, on the other hand, see to it that he or she does not receive a ministerial position, a choice committee assignment, or other perks at their disposal. Seldom is a rebel expelled from the party caucus. Only members who make a big spectacle out of their dissent and rub their party's nose in it have to fear expulsion. For the most part, party leaders have to be able to rely on a shared ideology in their ranks to count on unity in action. Each party recruits candidates for the Bundestag who profess support for basic tenets of the party's values and goals to begin with. For most members, a vote with the party is more a matter of instinct than of an agonizing struggle to reconcile one's conscience with party dogma.

LAWMAKING

For anyone weaned on a strict separation-of-powers doctrine, it is strange to note that the

Bundestag must share a classic parliamentary role, lawmaking, with a body that is more bureaucracy than parliament. That body is the Bundesrat (Federal Council). It is composed of representatives of the *Länder,* which might suggest a similarity with the U.S. Senate. However, the members of the Bundesrat are not popularly elected. What is more, they are not free to decide matters as they see fit. Instead, the Bundesrat is composed of state officials acting in the name of their respective state governments. Hence, members of the Bundesrat fit the role of "instructed delegates," not that of "trustees" that the Basic Law, in Article 38, accords the members of the Bundestag. What some observers, with little justification, call the upper house of Parliament in Germany turns out to be a less-than-equal body of state government delegates. But like its namesake in Bismarck's constitution of 1871, the present-day Bundesrat gives the governments, not the people, of the federal states a voice in federal policymaking.

Legislative Initiative

Bills to be considered by Parliament, for the most part, originate in the federal government. Of the 522 bills submitted during the 1983–1987 Bundestag term, 280 originated that way (see Table 24.3), with 183 coming from members of the Bundestag, including the opposition, and 59 from the Bundesrat. Government bills are first considered by the Bundesrat, but can be taken up by the Bundestag after a certain period, regardless of whether the Bundesrat has taken action on them. As may be expected, member bills have a far lower chance of being enacted than government bills, and rare is the passage of a bill submitted by members of the opposition. Yet the German Parliament is no rubber stamp for government bills. During the tenth Bundestag, 237 of the 280 bills introduced by the government were passed, which equals the 85% rate of passage for such bills since 1949.

Table 24.3 REPORT CARD FOR THE 10TH BUNDESTAG: 1983–1987

	Number
Meetings	
Floor	256
Committees	1,724
Party Caucuses	900
Controlling the Government	
Interpellations	
Big	175
Small	1,006
Questions	
Oral	7,028
Written	15,836
No-Confidence Motions	0
Disapproval Motions against	
Chancellor	3
Motion to Dismiss a Cabinet Minister	6
Legislation	
Introduced by (Passed)	
Government	280 (237)
Members of Bundestag	183 (42)
Bundesrat	59 (32)
Meetings of Conference Committee	6
Average Time Required for Passage of Legislation (Days)	259
Roll Call votes	128

Source: Peter Schindler, *Datenhandbuch zur Geschichte des deutschen Bundestages 1980 bis 1987* (Baden-Baden: Nomos, 1988), pp. 993–1001. Used by permission of the publisher, Nomos Verlagsgellschaft.

And during the 1970s many that passed only did so after an eventful passage through conference committees.

The Power of the Purse

The biggest and most important "bill" introduced by the federal government each year is the annual budget. The budget debate affords the Bundestag an unrivaled opportunity to discuss the policies of the government. There are three separate deliberations of the budget on the floor of the Bundestag. However extensive the debate, the federal government does not have to contend, the way an American president may have to, with alternate budget proposals coming from Parliament. Any proposal by members to spend more than provided by the government budget is futile, since the government can veto the request and the Bundestag cannot override that veto. But the Bundestag, especially in the budget committee, takes a close look at increases in proposed spending and not infrequently slashes them in incremental fashion.

Like the U.S. Congress, the German Parliament developed the habit of rarely completing action on the budget in time for the new fiscal year. A good portion of the blame, however, belongs to the government for being late in submitting its budget. This has changed since 1983. The budgets for the years 1983 through 1988 were all submitted in time by the government and passed in time by the Bundestag and Bundesrat. In the event of late passage of the budget, however, no special parliamentary action is required to avoid a shutdown of the government. Instead, the finance minister alone can authorize expenditures necessary to meet fiscal obligations.

Technically, the constitution mandates a balanced budget, with Article 110 requiring that the budget must be balanced as regards revenue and expenditure. But the requirement is less than ironclad. The budget may include a deficit large enough to cover "expenditures for investments," according to Article 115. Moreover, a "disturbance of the overall economic equilibrium" allows for further exceptions. Still, the Bundestag is in no position to take advantage of those provisions against the objections of the government.

Conflict and Cooperation

With party discipline being as strong as it is, the Bundestag is often an arena of merciless enmity between governing and opposition parties. That is certainly the way Bundestag debates sound. If dueling were still legal, the Bundestag would be a dangerous place, or else, given that sanction, a most civilized one. On the big issues, especially concerning foreign policy, the parties attack one another with venom and vituperation. The debates over such questions as western integration in the 1950s, *Ostpolitik* in the 1970s, and missile deployment in the 1980s exposed deep disagreements between the Christian alliance and the Social Democratic Party.

Nonetheless, much of the verbal dueling in the Bundestag is partisan posturing. Statistically speaking, both sides agree with each other more often than they disagree. It is quite rare to witness all members of the Christian alliance voting one way and all Social Democrats voting the opposite way. In the first Bundestag (1949–1953), for example, which charted the postwar course of the Federal Republic, the opposition Social Democrats voted with the Christian alliance on 84% of the bills, its public furor over many key measures and its socialist ideology notwithstanding. Likewise, the Christian alliance voted for 93% of government bills during the first Bundestag in which it was the opposition (1969–1972).[3]

Compared to the "adversary model" of parliamentary politics, as practiced in Britain, the German system contains strong elements of a "cooperative model." A "grand coalition" between the two major parties is an important fact of everyday political life. The Unification Treaties in 1990 would not have passed without backing from the opposition Social Democratic Party. In 1993, the Social Democrats supported the governing parties in passing an asylum bill that severely curtailed the flow of foreigners from countries outside the European community. It must be noted, however, that passage of these laws required a two-thirds majority, which meant that the major opposition party played a part in fashioning the legislation long before the final vote.

Divided Government

The Basic Law puts the Bundesrat on an equal standing with the Bundestag only in matters affecting the states (Article 77). As a rule of thumb, roughly every other law requires the approval of the Bundesrat. In the event that the Bundesrat refuses to approve a bill passed by the Bundestag, the mediation committee will be called to iron out the difference. Yet even on matters not affecting the states, the Bundesrat need not fall silent. Should it object in such a case to a bill passed by the Bundestag, the latter can override the veto by majority vote. However, a Bundesrat protest by two-thirds of its members requires an overrule by two-thirds in the other house as well.

Thus, should the opposition somehow muster a two-thirds majority in the Bundesrat, it could practically block any proposal put forward by the federal government, which almost never commands a two-thirds majority in the Bundestag. No opposition has yet been so lucky. From 1972 to 1982, however, the Christian alliance did control the Bundesrat while being in opposition in the Bundestag. Divided control became a thorny fact of life for the Social Democrat–Free Democrat government. On matters requiring Bundesrat approval, the governments headed by Willy Brandt and Helmut Schmidt had no choice but to compromise with the Christian alliance opposition. Likewise, lack of Bundesrat control has dogged the government of Chancellor Kohl since early 1991. It must have been especially galling for Kohl to see his home

state of Rhineland-Palatinate fall to the Social Democrats and give that party a majority in the Bundesrat.

Divided control makes for a busy mediation committee. That is a committee, akin to conference committees in the U.S. Congress, that must find a compromise between Bundestag and Bundesrat. During the 1976–1980 parliamentary term, for example, this committee had to deal with seventy-seven legislative proposals, almost one-fifth of all proposals that were passed. By contrast, during the 1983–1987 term, when the governing parties in the Bundestag (the Christian alliance and the Free Democratic Party) also controlled the Bundesrat, the mediation committee was called only six times (see Table 24.3) and none of those bills failed to pass. The formal role of the mediation committee notwithstanding, under conditions of divided control it is negotiation between chancellor, plus coalition partner, and party leader of the opposition that will settle (or not) the disagreements.

OVERSIGHT

Making laws is one thing, seeing to it that they are faithfully executed is quite another. To hold the federal government and its administration accountable, the Bundestag can resort to a variety of devices. For the day-to-day work, interpellations and questions prove most effective in overseeing the work of the government. An interpellation is a device that compels the officials named to address the issues raised in the Bundestag and leads to a discussion on the floor of the Bundestag. Close to a thousand interpellations are handled by a typical Bundestag during a four-year term.

These exchanges are seen as tests of the mettle of officials and questioners. At the end, the Bundestag may conclude the exchange with a vote of approval or disapproval. While the Bundestag entertains occasional motions to dismiss a cabinet minister, such votes have no legal consequence. They do not compel the chancellor to fire a minister. Interpellations serve the opposition in the Bundestag as a device to engage the government in debates over basic policy issues. Individual members, interested in specific and often technical items, may avail themselves of "oral questions," which in most cases will be answered by civil servants and in front of empty benches. In many such instances members act as errand-runners for their constituencies, to settle a matter with the federal bureaucracy arising in their districts. The device of the oral question may also suit the purpose of raising issues not scheduled for parliamentary discussion, especially in instances where something happened literally overnight, as in the *Spiegel* affair in 1962. That affair involved the magazine *Der Spiegel*, top-secret NATO defense plans, and Franz-Josef Strauss, then serving as minister of defense. While the federal government accused the news magazine of treason, the government's own actions to arrest reporters and search the magazine's premises raised constitutional issues.[4]

Special investigative committees have been set up by the Bundestag on occasion to probe charges of corruption. This was done recently in a case involving financial contributions to party treasuries that put even Chancellor Kohl and his predecessor, Helmut Schmidt, on the spot. To be sure, the government parties control those committees as they do the Bundestag as a whole, and their representatives are not likely to reach conclusions that would embarrass the government; to do so would be a form of political suicide. Still, an investigative committee provides the opposition with an opportunity to file a minority report and see its findings publicized in the media, especially in *Der Spiegel*.

COALITIONS IN THE *BUNDESTAG*

No single parliamentary party typically commands a majority in the Bundestag. That makes coalition politics inescapable. Most party coalitions are marriages of convenience rather than love. If there is any love that keeps the parties together, it is love of power—not for each other. Each coalition government contains the seeds of its own destruction, from differences between the coalition parties over policies, to personal rivalries, to barely suppressed suspicions of each other's fidelity. What is surprising, given the sorry spectacle of coalition politics in the Weimar Republic, is that the Basic Law is mute on the topic of coalitions. Happily, the oversight proved negligible as the parties in the Bundestag proved far more adept than those in the Reichstag.

Forging a Coalition Government

Let us take the normal case where an election has just taken place and the various parties in the Bundestag eye their government prospects. Their actions typically unfold according to the following script:

◆ Two or more parliamentary parties (the Christian Democratic Union and the Christian Social Union count as one party here) decide to negotiate the formation of a government coalition.

◆ The negotiators fashion the policy agenda of the prospective government and distribute the cabinet posts (which party and which politician gets what federal department?).

◆ A "coalition contract" is drafted and submitted for approval to each party's executive committee.

◆ The president is consulted on the progress of the coalition negotiations.

◆ The president nominates the chancellor-candidate agreed upon by the coalition partners.

◆ The Bundestag votes on that nominee; no vote is required for the would-be ministers in the cabinet.

◆ The chancellor-elect presents the names of ministers agreed on during the coalition negotiations to the president, who formally appoints them and the chancellor.

This script has been enacted without a hitch after each federal election. The parties who initiate the coalition bargaining after a given election have never failed to connect. It's like scoring a touchdown on the first down. Moreover, the initial partners have always come up

with a coalition commanding majority support in the Bundestag (see Table 24.4). The typical coalition is one that contains no party that could be dropped without jeopardizing that majority. In fact, in many cases the margin above the mimimum majority has been breathtakingly slim (in 1949, 1969, and 1976). But living on the edge does not spell disaster. The smaller the margin, the stronger the pressure to hold on to each other.

The ease with which rival parties have forged majority coalitions, more than any stipulation of the Basic Law, has given the president a low profile in the process of government for-

Table 24.4 CHANCELLORS, COALITIONS, AND BUNDESTAG SUPPORT

From	To	Chancellor (Party)	Coalition Partners	Seat Margin
1949	1953	Adenauer (CDU/CSU)	FDP, DP	+6
1953	1957	Adenauer (CDU/CSU)	FDP, DP, GB/BHE	+89
1957	1961	Adenauer (CDU/CSU)	DP	+38
1961	1962	Adenauer (CDU/CSU)	FDP	+59
1962	1963	Adenauer (CDU/CSU)	FDP	+59
1963	1965	Erhard (CDU/CSU)	FDP	+59
1965	1966	Erhard (CDU/CSU)	FDP	+45
1966	1969	Kiesinger (CDU/CSU)	SPD	+198
1969	1972	Brandt (SPD)	FDP	+5
1972	1974	Brandt (SPD)	FDP	+22
1974	1976	Schmidt (SPD)	FDP	+22
1976	1980	Schmidt (SPD)	FDP	+4
1980	1982	Schmidt (SPD)	FDP	+22
1982	1983	Kohl (CDU/CSU)	FDP	+30
1983	1987	Kohl (CDU/CSU)	FDP	+28
1987	1990	Kohl (CDU/CSU)	FDP	+20
1990		Kohl (CDU/CSU)	FDP	+66

Source: Adapted and updated from Helmut Norpoth, "Coalition Government at the Brink of Majority Rule," in Eric C. Browne and John Dreijmanis (eds.), *Government Coalitions in Western Democracies* (New York: Longman, 1982), pp. 12, 13. Used by permission of Professor Eric C. Brown.

Note: The 1953 government lost the support of the GB/BHE (the All-German Bloc-Federation of Refugees and Expellees) in 1955 and the support of the FDP in 1956, but neither defection jeopardized Adenauer's majority in the Bundestag. "Seat margin" indicates the number of Bundestag seats held by the coalition above the requirement of a bare majority.

mation. His role (on which more will be said in the next chapter) is limited to naming as chancellor that person upon whom the parties commanding a majority coalition in the Bundestag have agreed.

Coalition Payoffs

In fashioning coalition governments, the partners have reached agreement on the prospective chancellor, the policy agenda, and the allocation of ministries. Of these three items, the chancellor question has always provoked the least controversy, and the filling of cabinet posts the most. While prospective chancellors have the last word on who joins the cabinet, they weigh not only the requests of the coalition partner, but also the requests from various groups in their own party. Even more than the party lists in federal elections, the assembly of cabinet lists requires an uncanny sense of balance.

Furthermore, since 1957, no coalition has included more than two parties (counting the Christian Democratic Union and the Christian Social Union as one party). The coalition parties are always the ones who, before the election, agreed to forge a coalition afterward, although the Social Democrats and Free Democrats admittedly were quite coy, even devious, about their plans in 1969. The typical coalition is truly an odd couple, to be sure. It seems to pair a giant (the Christian alliance or the Social Democratic Party) with a dwarf (the Free Democratic Party). What the dominant partner treasures the most is the chancellorship, while the small partner is content with exercising selective vetoes, be it on a matter of a policy or personnel that the small party finds objectionable. For the Free Democrats, the coalition deal has always been quite generous, providing it with more cabinet posts than its seat share would require, and with choice selections as well, especially since 1969.

Under Helmut Kohl as chancellor, the Free Democratic Party has controlled, among other things, the foreign office and the economics ministry. And Franz-Josef Strauss of the Christian Social Union, its nemesis, was kept out of the cabinet.

Coalitions and Political Change

The coalitions formed among parties in the Bundestag have lasted longer than many marriages these days. Heading into the election of 1994, the Christian alliance and the Free Democratic Party have shared power for twelve straight years; before that, the Social Democrats and Free Democrats stayed together for thirteen years. In the Federal Republic, coalition politics never degenerated into a game of musical chairs. At least, not a game played every year. The cycle of coalitions is more one of decades. There have been three memorable instances of government turnover. The first took place in 1966. Budgetary squabbling tore apart the coalition of the Christian alliance and the Free Democrats, as it confronted a darkening economic horizon. With Chancellor Ludwig Erhard proving incapable of resolving those differences, the Christian alliance scouted for both a new chancellor and a new coalition partner. By then, the Christian alliance and the Social Democrats were agreeable on key issues of economic and foreign policy. There was little resistance in the Christian alliance to embrace a willing Social Democratic Party as its new partner in government and forgo any attempt to repair relations with the Free Democrats. It must be added that the West German electorate was not unhappy with this grand coalition.[5] Voters loyal to the Christian alliance resented a Free Democratic Party they felt had been overplaying its hand. Similarly, Social Democratic voters had long yearned for a place for their party in government alongside the Christian alliance.

The second instance, called a *Machtwechsel* (changing of the guard) by some, took place in 1969. It was the most adroit coalition maneuver witnessed in the Federal Republic. But this time no economic crisis strained the incumbent coalition, nor did it suffer from lack of public confidence. The major change had occurred in a party outside government, the Free Democratic Party. With a new leader and ideological outlook, the party now calling itself the F.D.P. wooed the Social Democratic Party. For them, a coalition with the Free Democrats opened the prospect of capturing the chancellorship and being senior rather than junior partner in government.

Thus, by 1969, a Social Democrat–Free Democrat coalition was an outcome that offered both partners a better deal than the available alternatives (opposition for the Free Democrats, junior government status for Social Democrats). As the returns came in on election night, showing a narrow majority for that coalition in the Bundestag, Social Democrat leaders quickly accepted the advances of the Free Democrats and abandoned a dumbfounded Christian alliance. It was a backroom decision that went against the coalition preferences of most Social Democratic voters, happy to continue with the grand coalition. Nonetheless, many of them quickly fell in line with their leaders' coalition switch when the deal was done.

The third instance of government turnover was the familiar *Wende* (turnaround) of 1982, which brought Helmut Kohl to power. As in 1966, bad economic news confronted the government with some grim choices. The two governing parties sharply disagreed over the best way to handle the economic crisis: The Social Democrats wanted to raise taxes, especially on higher incomes, and spend more on jobs; the Free Democrats, led by Lambsdorff, a free-market advocate, preferred supply-side solutions like cutting taxes and reining in the welfare state. Moreover, the bubbling turmoil within

the Social Democratic Party over the issue of missile deployment made the Free Democratic Party nervous about its partnership with that party. While Schmidt could count on the Free Democrats, key figures in that party did not count on the Social Democrats anymore, and began to scout for an alternative. With public opinion polls showing an all-time low of public confidence in the Social Democrat–Free Democrat government, the Free Democrats abandoned the Social Democrats and quickly came to terms with the Christian alliance.

But this time, unlike 1966, the parties did not get away with backroom deals. Public pressure was such that the new partners in government agreed to hold a new Bundestag election so as to give the voters the last word on who governed. In so doing, the parties recognized that a parliamentary license was not enough to operate a government; popular approval was needed as well. But the Free Democratic Party's survival instinct dictated that the Bundestag had to take the first step before the electorate would be asked. As a result, the governing parties had to bend and twist the constitution. They enacted a charade, with the connivance of the president. What Chancellor Kohl did was to lose a vote on purpose and, on that basis, request that the president call new elections. A new Bundestag was elected in March 1983.

OUTLOOK

The first Bundestag of the unified Germany debated and settled a bundle of thorny issues: a tax increase to pay for unification costs; campaign finance reform; the Maastricht Treaty on European Union; and the change of the asylum law. It was not a do-nothing Parliament, or one hamstrung by gridlock, even though the opposition Social Democratic Party has controlled the Bundesrat since early 1991. Nor did the addition of some 140 members from the five new eastern states complicate the business of

Parliament. So one might think that the Bundestag enjoys a glowing rating in the general public. Wrong. Popular esteem for this institution has fallen sharply. The decline preceded reunification, but appears to be accelerating. Far more Germans, in East and West, have an unfavorable than a favorable opinion of the job done by the Bundestag.[6] That it takes great ability to become a member of the Bundestag, not even four in ten think so these days; twenty years ago, almost two in three said so. Trust in politicians, their competence and their integrity, is on the wane. The political parties have felt the brunt of *Verdrossenheit* (that sick-and-tired feeling), and so have leading politicians, including Chancellor Kohl. The Bundestag has not escaped it either. Perhaps that is not all bad, if it is a sign of critical maturity in the general public rather than one of brooding hopelessness.

NOTES

1. Peter Schindler, *Datenhandbuch zur Geschichte des deutschen Bundestages 1980 bis 1987* (Bonn: Nomos, 1988), p. 180.
2. Gerhard Loewenberg, *Parliament in the German Political System* (Ithaca: Cornell University Press, 1966), p. 360.
3. See Wolfgang Kralewski and Karlheinz Neunreither, *Oppositionelles Verhalten im ersten deutschen Bundestag, 1949–1953* (Opladen: Westdeutscher Verlag, 1963); and Hans-Joachim Veen, *Opposition im Bundestag* (Bonn: Eichholz-Verlag, 1986).
4. See Otto Kirchheimer and Constantine Menges, "A Free Press in a Democratic State? The *Spiegel* Case," in *Politics in Europe*, ed. Gwendolyn M. Carter and Alan F. Westin (New York: Harcourt Brace Jovanovich, 1965).
5. See Helmut Norpoth, "Choosing a Coalition Partner," *Comparative Political Studies*, 12 (1980): 424–440.
6. These and the following findings are based on surveys conducted by the Allensbach Institute. See Elisabeth Noelle-Neumann and Renate Köcher, *Allensbacher Jahrbuch 1984–1992*, pp. 652–661.

REFERENCES AND SUGGESTED READINGS

Braunthal, Gerard. 1972. *The West German Legislative Process.* Ithaca, N.Y.: Cornell University Press.

Hoffman-Lange, Ursula. 1989. "Positional Power and Political Influence in the Federal Republic of Germany," *European Journal of Political Research*, 17: 51–76.

Kolinsky, Eva. 1991. "Political Participation and Parliamentary Careers: Women's Quotas in West Germany," *West European Politics*, 14: 56–72.

Thaysen, Uwe, Roger Davidson, and Robert Livingston, eds. 1990. *The U.S. Congress and the German Bundestag: A Comparison.* Boulder: Westview Press.

25

Chancellors, Bureaucrats, and Courts

*M*odern democracies have little patience for the neat distinction between legislative and executive branches of government. Those branches have grown more like a bush in the wild than a plant in a nursery. That is especially true for parliamentary systems like the Federal Republic, where the top personnel of the executive is drawn from and accountable to the legislative institution. Moreover, political parties are pervasive in both—the oil, as it were, that lubricates both the gears and the engine of government. In addition, the executive has sprouted several branches and must contend not only with the Bundestag and the Länder (state) governments, but also increasingly with judicial checks.

CHANCELLOR DEMOCRACY

It is by a formal vote of the Bundestag that chancellors come into office (Article 63). And what the Bundestag giveth, it can taketh away if it wants to by means of a no-confidence vote (Article 67). The Federal Republic thus meets the key criterion for a "parliamentary system." By contrast, the monarchy (1871–1918) did not, since it failed to provide for a no-confidence vote. The Weimar constitution of 1919 made the chancellor accountable to Parliament by giving the latter the device of a no-confidence vote. But while the

Reichstag could bring down a chancellor, its role in installing one in office remained ambiguous. Many believed that constitutional reform was needed to make the parliamentary system work.

Electing the Chancellor

The election of a chancellor is not an everyday activity. A visitor to Bonn would have to pick a lucky day to witness it. A sure bet would be a few days after a federal election. At that time the newly elected Bundestag would take a vote—by secret ballot, that is—on who will be chancellor. Never mind that the incumbent chancellor may have led the parties in government to a victory in that election. Parliament will not be denied taking a vote on the chancellor question, just as a re-elected American president will have another inauguration. Heading into the election year of 1994, Helmut Kohl has been elected chancellor four times, the last three times as the head of a coalition winning reelection (in 1983, 1987, and 1990).

None of those three Bundestag votes was in any doubt, no more so than the votes of the Electoral College in the United States after a presidential election in November. Once the German voters have spoken and a coalition of parties has obtained a majority of seats in the Bundestag, the suspense is gone from the Bundestag's chancellor vote. Why? The reason is that on the chancellor vote, the coalition parties can count on enough discipline in their ranks to pull their chancellor-candidate through. Those who like to bet on things would be hard pressed to get any odds on most chancellor votes in the Bundestag.

Other than immediately following a Bundestag election, there have been few occasions for a chancellor vote. The first such occasion arose in 1963, when Konrad Adenauer (Christian Democratic Union/Christian Social Union) stepped down in the middle of the

legislative term after serving fourteen years as chancellor. The Bundestag promptly elected Ludwig Erhard as the new chancellor. It was a smooth decision since Erhard belonged to the same party as Adenauer and the transition had been arranged ahead of time by the parties in the government coalition. A few years later, the need arose again, but under far more taxing and uncertain circumstances, as Chancellor Erhard lost his parliamentary majority in 1966. This time two parties that had never governed together in Bonn (the Christian alliance and Social Democratic Party) forged a coalition government with a new chancellor, Kurt-Georg Kiesinger (Christian alliance). The third occasion was more like 1963. When Chancellor Willy Brandt (Social Democratic Party) resigned in the middle of a term in 1974, the same Bundestag majority that had supported him elected Helmut Schmidt (Social Democratic Party) to succeed Brandt.

Removing a Chancellor

While placing the right to choose a chancellor squarely in the hands of the Bundestag, the Basic Law severely ties those hands with regard to removing a chancellor from office. Of all the constitutional innovations, none appears more consequential than the stipulation that a parliamentary vote of no confidence must be "constructive." As Article 67 of the Basic Law spells it out, the Bundestag cannot simply dump an incumbent chancellor. Instead it must first agree on a successor. This provision says to Parliament, in effect, that you cannot beat somebody with nobody. There can be no more votes of no confidence that leave a vacuum in government. In other words, a bad government is better than none. So unless you have a successor ready to take over, don't bother submitting a motion of no confidence.

The drafters of the Basic Law meant to spare the Bonn Republic the follies of the Weimar

Republic, when chancellors rarely stayed in office longer than nine months. As it turned out, the chancellors of the Federal Republic have averaged almost that many years in office after their initial election, approximating the tenure of a two-term American president. In the forty-some years of the Federal Republic, only six chancellors have held office thus far. Even more important, the basic policy configurations and coalition alignments have been even fewer. This is not to say that constitutional reform alone deserves the credit for government stability.

Article 67 was the constitutional vehicle by which the Bundestag first installed Helmut Kohl as chancellor. In September of 1982, as we saw in the previous chapter, the governing coalition of the Social Democrats and Free Democrats broke apart amid bickering over economic and defense policies. Having lost majority support in the Bundestag, the then incumbent chancellor, the Social Democrat Helmut Schmidt (SPD), could have resigned and made room for a successor. He did not resign, however, but tried to seek a dissolution of the Bundestag and new elections. That move was pre-empted when the Bundestag voted on the motion submitted by the Christian alliance and the Free Democratic Party in accordance with Article 67:

> The Bundestag may resolve: The Bundestag expresses its lack of confidence in Chancellor Helmut Schmidt and elects Representative Dr. Helmut Kohl to succeed him as Chancellor. The Federal President is called upon to dismiss Chancellor Helmut Schmidt.[1]

On October 1, 1982, 256 members of the Bundestag voted for this motion, seven more than the required majority of 249. Without a lengthy transition, Helmut Kohl took Helmut Schmidt's place as chancellor. What set the stage for the successful use of Article 67 in 1982 was a rare coalition realignment in the Bundestag, as described in the previous chapter.

Winners and losers: newly elected Chancellor Helmut Kohl (CDU/CSU) is congratulated by the defeated incumbent, Helmut Schmidt (SPD), October 1982.

The Free Democrats decided to join a coalition with the Christian alliance at the very moment it left the coalition with the Social Democratic Party, which had been in office for thirteen years. Perhaps most important was the decision of the parliamentary caucus of the Free Democrats in the Bundestag, voting 33–18 in favor of a coalition with the Christian alliance; then the leading body of the Free Democrats' federal party organization also endorsed the decision. The two-thirds support among the Free Democrats in the Bundestag for a coalition with the Christian alliance was enough to guarantee Kohl a majority in the Bundestag.

Besides 1982, the Bundestag has tried the constructive vote of no confidence only one other time. That occurred almost exactly ten years earlier, and was also directed against a Social Democratic chancellor. In 1972, the Christian alliance moved to oust Chancellor Willy Brandt (a Social Democrat) by electing Rainer Barzel (Christian alliance) as his successor. The governing coalition of the Social Democratic and Free Democratic parties, so it appeared, had lost its majority in the Bundestag due to defections of several of its members. The vote taken by the Bundestag, however, failed to give the challenger the required majority. Since this was a secret ballot, it has long remained a mystery, feeding endless speculation as to who failed to deliver the missing votes and why. Documents recently released showed that officials of the former German Democratic Republic bribed a Christian Democratic Union representative (Julius Steiner) to switch his vote.[2]

Chief Policymaker

The Basic Law names the federal chancellor as the head of the federal government and entrusts that person with the authority to make policy. Article 65 specifies that the chancellor shall determine the "general policy guidelines." At the same time, the chancellor is singled out as being accountable to the Bundestag for the consequences of that policy. In plain English, the chancellor can be fired for purely political reasons. The chancellor therefore needs to maintain support of a majority in the Bundestag in order to keep the job.

Thus, of all the resources a chancellor needs for success, none is more critical than the support of the party. Lose that support and a chancellor will not be able to govern effectively or much longer. It is an article of faith, though not of the Basic Law, that chancellors be the chiefs of their respective party organizations. This was true for Adenauer and Brandt, and presently holds for Kohl. But two other chancellors,

Erhard and Schmidt, left the top party job to others. That may have cost those two their chancellor's jobs, many believe. Whatever the formal arrangement, a chancellor must constantly work to nurture and secure support in his party for his policies and leadership.

The staff and resources of the chancellory lend a formidable apparatus for exercising policymaking authority. With its five hundred or so staffers, this is one of the largest executive offices in western democracies, rivaling the personnel of a midsize government department in Bonn. It mirrors the organization of the federal bureaucracy in miniature format and allows the chancellor to keep up with the work of federal departments. The office grew rapidly in the early years of the social-liberal coalition (Social Democrats and Free Democrats), but fell short of turning into a policy-planning superdepartment. It has not succeeded in taking command of the activities of the various government agencies, but acts more like a brokerage house mediating between them.

Cabinet Government

The chancellor has a free constitutional hand to choose the members of the cabinet. No vote of approval is required from the Bundestag. And the president, who has to sign the letters of appointment, exercises no "advise and consent" role either, though he may grumble about certain appointees. The ministers have the constitutional authority (through Article 65) "to conduct the affairs of their departments autonomously and on their own responsibility," subject to the guidelines set by the chancellor. Individual cabinet ministers cannot be removed from office by a vote of the Bundestag, only the whole cabinet can by a constructive no-confidence vote directed at the chancellor. The twenty-member cabinet formed by Kohl after the 1990 election reflected the partisan composition of the governing coalition, with the junior partner of the Christian alliance receiving a better-than-fair-share of posts. As before, the Free Democratic Party took Foreign Affairs, Economics, and Justice, along with two other departments.[3] The cabinet included three politicians of the eastern states: Angela Merkel (Women and Youth), Günther Krause (Transportation), and Rainer Ortleb (Education and Science). The cabinet included four women, though none was picked for a high-prestige department. In addition to Merkel, they were Gerda Hasselfeldt (Health), Irmgard Adam-Schwaetzer (Regional Planning and Urban Development), and Hannelore Rönsch (Family and Elderly). By early 1994, only seven ministers appointed after the 1990 election still held their portfolios. That was a remarkable turnover.

The cabinet, with the chancellor presiding, meets approximately once a week to discuss policy matters and reach decisions. In particular, the cabinet agenda includes bills to be introduced in Parliament, the annual budget, defense and foreign policy measures, and senior appointments in the bureaucracy. By the time matters get to the full cabinet, most of the work has been done. But the cabinet is no rubber stamp for the chancellor, the "guideline" authority notwithstanding. For one thing, cabinet ministers "identify more with their roles as heads of departments than with their cabinet functions."[4] Backed by the expertise of their respective departments and dependent upon their loyalty, they see themselves as promoters and protectors of their domains. In addition, the cabinet includes not only members of the chancellor's own party, but of a coalition partner as well. While that partner can be outvoted in the cabinet, to do so would be foolish since it would jeopardize the government's tenure in office.

While it is a routine operation that a cabinet undergoes every year, the preparation of the annual budget preoccupies much of its time and cannot fail to remind the government of its

political mortality. Recall that the two chancellors forced out in midstream, Ludwig Erhard in 1966 and Helmut Schmidt in 1982, in large part fell because of disagreements between the coalition parties about the budget. First among equals among the ministers is the finance minister. In the Federal Republic that office combines two that are kept separate in the United States: the budget office and the treasury. The German finance minister is responsible, among other things, for the preparation of the annual budget. That job requires diplomatic as well as accounting skills. What must be done is to secure agreements with the various departments in the federal government on their spending proposals. Most of that work is done before the full cabinet ever meets on the budget. In those meetings, the finance minister is in a strong position to block attempts to reinstate cuts unless the chancellor deserts him. But the chancellor depends on the finance minister to get much of that work on his own.

THE FOUNDING CHANCELLOR: ADENAUER

The history of the Federal Republic, like few other periods, has been stamped by its chancellors. The era of postwar reconstruction, both in an economic and political sense, is closely identified with Konrad Adenauer as chancellor (1949–1963). To be sure, Adenauer was an unlikely candidate for that distinction. Already 73 years old, the former longtime mayor of Cologne was elected chancellor in 1949 by a one-vote majority (his own vote, of course, as he always insisted). But despite his narrow base and advanced age, Adenauer led the fledgling republic from defeat and destruction to unprecedented prosperity at home and recognition abroad. The "economic miracle," the western integration of the Federal Republic, and a firm hold on democratic government are the legacy of Adenauer's tenure. Age did not deter Adenauer from serving longer as chancellor than the Weimar Republic and the Third Reich each lasted.

Like Bismarck, whom Adenauer still remembered from his youth, the first chancellor of the Federal Republic was noted for a "will to power" and a sure hand at playing *Realpolitik.* Adenauer struck many as no less autocratic than the "iron chancellor." Critics dubbed his style of governing as "chancellor democracy." In meetings with his cabinet or party, Adenauer neither put up with much dissent nor suffered fools gladly. He was fond of quoting Article 65 of the Basic Law, the "guideline" power, and relished taunting critics within his own party to try Article 67, the no-confidence vote, against him.

The American president with whom Konrad Adenauer dealt the most was Dwight D. Eisenhower (1953–1961). One of the first encounters between the U.S. president and the German chancellor, whose names even rhymed, illustrated Adenauer's Machiavellian qualities. Ike, who was a hobby painter and had given Adenauer one of his artworks, wondered about Adenauer's appraisal of the painting. Adenauer was quick to send off a gushing note, claiming that many visitors admired the painting and were awed by Ike's artistic talent. In return, Ike instructed his secretary of state on his first visit to Bonn to see for himself. So here is John Foster Dulles meeting with Adenauer and asking to see the painting afterward. Of course, the painting hangs nowhere. So how does Adenauer avoid a touchy incident? He scribbles a note instructing an aide to "frame painting and hang in the state room" while continuing his conversation with Dulles. Carrying on long enough to get the confirmation "Painting hangs," he escorts Dulles into the stateroom, where both see the painting for the first time. Adenauer to Dulles: "You won't believe what a source of inspiration, strength, and confidence this painting has been to me!"[5] No wonder relations between Adenauer and Ike were harmonious for the next eight years.

But aside from being a political fox, Adenauer also was an electoral lion, leading the Christian alliance to the most resounding electoral victories a German party has ever scored. No other German chancellor has ever enjoyed a more secure parliamentary base. Adenauer made parliamentary government work. Curiously, a man of traditional values in his personal life and commonly derided as a staunch conservative politically, Adenauer nonetheless broke with several molds of old politics. In the realm of party politics, he abandoned the Catholic-center concept and gambled on a mass-party venture; in domestic policy, he took his chances with a free market economy; in foreign policy, he took a bet on European integration and the western alliance. A successful innovator far more than a follower of conventional formulas, he put a stamp on the new republic that has not faded yet.

CHANCELLORS OF REFORM: BRANDT AND SCHMIDT

The first Social Democratic chancellor of the Federal Republic, Willy Brandt, was widely greeted in 1969 as the champion of a new era, evoking the New Frontier imagery of the Kennedy presidency. "To dare more democracy," was a memorable rallying cry. In foreign policy, the new government introduced *Ostpolitik:* reconciliation with Eastern Europe and the Soviet Union, and more neighborly relations with the other Germany. Brandt became the first West German chancellor to meet with his East German counterpart, Prime Minister Willi Stoph. Brandt also visited Poland and paid homage to the victims of German atrocities in World War II by kneeling in front of a memorial to the Warsaw Ghetto. The gesture evoked a mixed reaction in the West German public. Half of it warmly applauded it, but the other half was furious.

The reactions to this event sharply illuminated the new battle lines of conflict in the

Willy Brandt (far right) with John F. Kennedy in Berlin, 1963.

Federal Republic. Outbursts of partisan acrimony not heard since the early 1950s over Adenauer's western policy now shattered the era of good feelings fostered during the 1960s. The new policy toward East Germany and Eastern Europe met with ferocious opposition from the Christian alliance. It was denounced as a national sellout and as acceptance of German partition. As his Bundestag majority began to buckle, with a handful of Free Democratic Party deputies defecting to the opposition, Brandt became the first chancellor to face the scourge of Article 67, the constructive vote of no confidence.

Just barely and amid charges of vote fraud, Brandt weathered this challenge. He won the Nobel Peace Prize for his Ostpolitik and led the Social Democrat–Free Democrat coalition to a triumphant victory in the Bundestag election of 1972, called one year ahead of schedule. Yet as he appeared safely in control, Brandt faltered. Domestic problems, especially economics, proved less tractable and captured Brandt's interest less than did the more grandiose task of international reconciliation. When a close personal aide was unmasked as an East German spy, Brandt immediately stepped down.[6]

Fortunately for the Social Democrats, an eager heir and one with a stronger interest in domestic policy was waiting for his turn to govern. Few chancellors have come with better preparation for the job than did Helmut Schmidt. A veteran of Bundestag politics and at one time leader of the Social Democratic Party's parliamentary caucus, Schmidt also distinguished himself as minister of finance as well as minister of defense. He personified *Durchsetzungskraft* (resoluteness) and political savvy. Cut from a tougher cloth than Brandt, Schmidt displayed a muscular leadership and an ease in wielding power not seen since Adenauer. "Chancellor democracy" was definitely back in fashion.

Schmidt was among the founders of the annual summits of western industrial powers beginning in 1975. Though short in size, he stood out as a dominating and domineering figure. Here was someone who acted as the leader of an economic giant, not as a self-doubting representative of a defeated nation. Schmidt touted the way Germany maintained a competitive economy while simultaneously preserving social peace under his stewardship as *Modell Deutschland*, an example for others to follow. Campaign posters in 1976 made generous use of the national colors in proclaiming that slogan.

Yet in his own party, Chancellor Schmidt was fighting a battle that threatened his grip on power. Never on good terms with his party's left wing, he had little patience with the concerns of "postmaterialists" and the "new social movements." Especially his policy of seeking the deployment of intermediate missiles, to offset Soviet missile production, met with mounting criticism. He was barely able to prevent his own party from disavowing that policy. This was one of those instances where the Social Democratic Party in government found itself under siege from its activists outside. Those activists looked far more favorably toward Willy Brandt, still the party chairman, than to their man in the chancellor's office.

Chancellor of Reunification: Kohl

His policy of reunification has earned Chancellor Kohl a place in the history books. Nonetheless, he remains a maddening puzzle to many observers. He looks, sounds, and acts like a most unlikely person to succeed as chancellor. His detractors miss the intellectual prowess, sharpness of wit, and worldly style of a Helmut Schmidt. They wince when they hear Kohl speak. They see a provincial bumbler hawking

corny recipes. Kohl has learned to relish being underestimated by his critics and adversaries: "I have been underestimated for decades . . . I've done very well that way."[7]

To be sure, Kohl's background is in party politics, and in an Arkansas-like state of the Federal Republic, Rhineland-Palatinate. Elected to the state parliament while still in his twenties, he became governor (prime minister) of the state in his thirties, and leader of the Christian Democratic Union in his early forties. In 1976, he came within a whisker of winning the chancellorship. Through his whole political career, Helmut Kohl has proved to be a master of the subject of his Ph.D. dissertation—party politics. He revived the Christian Democratic Union after its defeat in the 1972 election and led it back to power ten years later. He would never let the party forget it.

Through the revolving door of the constructive vote of no confidence, Helmut Kohl entered the chancellorship when Helmut Schmidt was tossed out. However unflattering the comparison with the other Helmut, Kohl settled the two issues that brought down Chancellor Schmidt's government, the economy and missile deployment. Germans called it a *Wende*, a turnaround. But the next *Wende*, namely German reunification in the wake of revolution in East Germany, was even more memorable, as we have seen in Chapter 19. Yet as Kohl's chancellorship enters the twilight phase, some of the problems (economic recession, declining public confidence, uncertainty about Germany's international role) sound eerily reminiscent of the conditions that doomed his predecessor in the early 1980s. It remains to be seen whether Kohl will be remembered more for achieving reunification than for the problems it brought.

A Ceremonial Presidency

Like the United States, Germany has a president, but he is not the person President Clinton would call or meet to discuss policy matters with; nor would he kid him about a likeness to a sumo wrestler. The German presidency is an office above politics with almost no policy-making role. Not only a poor descendant of the monarch of the old days, the federal president also compares poorly with his Weimar predecessor. The framers of the Basic Law abhorred the idea of the president being chosen by the people and wielding dictatorial power, as the Weimar constitution provided. Some wanted to get rid of the presidency altogether during the deliberations of the Basic Law.

Presidential Elections

German presidents are chosen by a special convention, composed of the Bundestag and of an equal number of representatives of state parliaments (not the Bundesrat). Political considerations weigh heavily in those choices. Prior to being chosen, all German presidents were well-known partisan figures. The choice of a new president invariably flashes a strong signal across the political horizon. In 1949, the election of a Free Democrat, Theodor Heuss, with Christian alliance support, set the stage for a government of Christian Democrats and Free Democrats under Chancellor Adenauer. Similarly, the election in 1959 of a Christian Democrat (Heinrich Lübke), known for his leanings toward the Social Democratic Party, raised the stock of a grand coalition. During the coalition crisis of 1966, President Lübke did his utmost to help along such a configuration.

Most prophetic was the election in early 1969 of a Social Democrat (Gustav Heinemann) with the support of the Free Democratic Party. This took place at a time when the Social Democrats formed the government in Bonn with the Christian alliance, which still held the chancellorship, and with the Free Democrats out of government. Many read Heinemann's election as a dress rehearsal for the new social-liberal play to be staged in the federal government after the Bundestag election later that same

year. For the presidential election in 1994, the Christian alliance planned to nominate a leading East German. But Steffen Heitmann, the justice minister in the eastern state of Saxony, proved too controversial with his opinions on women, foreigners, and the Nazi past.[8]

Presidential Powers

It is easier to say what German presidents are not than what they are. Not popularly elected, they are also *not* chief policymakers; commanders-in-chief of the armed forces; or potential dictators with Article 48-like emergency powers. Moreover, presidents lack veto power against legislation passed by Parliament, although they may exercise their right to sign legislation to voice objections. Occasionally the chancellor has withdrawn bills as a result of presidential opposition. Furthermore, presidents may not dissolve the Bundestag on their own initiative, but only at the request of the chancellor. Twice the president received such a call, in 1972 and 1982. Both times he obliged.

Even their role in selecting a chancellor is more a straitjacket than a stately robe. Presidents may only nominate a candidate to be voted on by the Bundestag. And then they must appoint the Bundestag's choice. A refusal to do so would precipitate impeachment proceedings against the president unless something was clearly suspicious about the vote in the Bundestag. No president, in fact, has ever submitted a chancellor-candidate to the Bundestag who was not subsequently elected. In 1961, however, when Adenauer's quest for a fourth term as chancellor met with opposition from the Free Democratic Party, President Lübke asked for, and received, the result of a secret poll of Free Democratic deputies that showed Adenauer with enough support to be re-elected by the Bundestag.[9] It is not beyond presidents now and then to probe the bounds of their conventional influence.

Richard von Weizsäcker, president of the Federal Republic, 1984–1994.

The president's authority largely pertains to noncontroversial, almost nonpolitical matters: to serve as a monarch pro tem, as a representative of the nation, and not of just one interest, ideology, or party. The presidency is an institution requiring dignity and a more spiritual tone than any other one. The incumbents have the standing to appeal to the conscience of the nation as no politician could. Richard von Weizsäcker, who served from 1984 to 1994, was known for speaking in bold language about the Nazi past. His speech on the fortieth anni-

versary of the end of World War II chided the German people for closing their eyes when there were unmistakable signs of the Holocaust. He also did not depict 1945 as a "defeat" of his country but hailed it as "liberation." However unpopular that may have been among some Germans, the presidency has invariably enjoyed a high public standing.[10] No other political institution comes close. With political parties, the Bundestag, chancellors, and state governments all slipping, Germans may wish to see some form of presidential rule.

A POLITICAL BUREAUCRACY

In Germany (nearly) everything is possible in the bureaucracy. Take civil servant Luise, a three-hundred pounder, speaking not a word of German, never having passed a written examination, but serving the state with honor and distinction. Luise happened to be a wild hog with an uncanny sense of smell for narcotics and explosives. The hog's sniffing performance alongside West German police in the mid-1980s led to a civil service job in the state of Lower Saxony. She retired with a generous retirement package after only two years on active duty. Let nobody say that German bureaucracy is hamstrung by silly rules in doing its job.

German Federalism

Besides the animal world, the federal government relies heavily on the states to administer its policies. Germany remains a country with a relatively weak central administration. The "federal" in Federal Republic means that the Länder (the federal states) do much of the administering. Article 30 of the Basic Law stipulates that:

The exercise of governmental powers and the discharge of governmental functions shall be incumbent on the Länder insofar as this Basic Law does not otherwise prescribe or permit.

Only a few agencies are wholly owned and operated by the federal government. These include the Foreign Office, the Defense Administration, the Federal Railroad System, the Postal Service, and the least liked of all, the federal tax office. Not many federal departments have much of an infrastructure beyond the city limits of the capital. Instead those departments depend on the administrative apparatus of the Länder to do the job for them. To use a metaphor, the federal departments simply provide the upper deck of an administrative ship anchored in the various Länder. Altogether, the federal bureaucracy in the narrow sense—excluding railroads, postal service, social security, and armed forces—is not the major employer in the public sector. The Länder and the municipal governments are. All in all, however, quite a few Germans earn their paychecks in the public sector, roughly one in every five.

Unlike the United States, the federal government and the states in Germany share the most lucrative taxes instead of raising separate ones. The receipts from the income tax, the value-added tax (VAT), and corporate taxes are distributed among Bonn and the state capitals (and the local governments, to some degree) according to a fixed key. This is institutionalized revenue sharing. One may also call it an example of "cooperative federalism" that can get quite contentious when one of the partners is pressed to renegotiate the distribution contract. All in all, the sixteen states taken together handle almost two-thirds as much tax revenue as the federal government (see Table 25.1).

Bureaucrats and Politicians

Whether federal, state, or local, bureaucrats are supposed to be professional, nonpartisan, apolitical, impartial, and impersonal hands of the government. Reliable implementers of policy, but neither critics nor initiators of policy. However applicable this Prussian ideal type may

Table 25.1 SHARES OF TAX REVENUES, 1991

Tax Revenue Going To	DM	%
Federal government	318	48
State governments	228	34
Local governments	84	13
European Community	31	5
Total	661	100

Source: *Facts about Germany,* p. 155.

have been in the past, it certainly misses the point in the Federal Republic today. The distinction between politicians and bureaucrats is blurred beyond recognition. Begin right at the top of the hierarchy. A federal department (ministry) is headed by someone (a minister) who is invariably a member of the Bundestag and a member of one of the parties forming the government. The nonpartisan, nonpolitical minister is an extinct species in the Federal Republic. Ministers have made their careers in party and legislative politics. They are not expected to leave all that behind, once the chancellor puts them in charge of ministries. They retain their seats in Parliament and had better maintain close rapport with their parties as well. Ministers are political appointees, through and through.

The highest-ranking civil servants in ministries are the *state secretaries.* They are part bureaucratic fish and part political fowl. Along with a few other high-ranking civil servants they can be removed (albeit at full pay) for such reasons as not getting along with new ministers or the new government. Below that level, tenure is a bureaucrat's best friend. In the late 1960s, the *parliamentary secretary,* British-style, was introduced. Like their ministers, these secretaries also hold seats in the Bundestag and belong to one of the governing parties. They serve as the ministers' temporary understudies and probable successors. Still, compared with the United States or even Great Britain, the slots available to be filled by a new government are not many.

In Germany, members of Parliament and bureaucrats operate more like partners in a joint venture than as checks and balances. As we saw in discussing the Bundestag, many members of Parliament are, in fact, civil servants on leave. Hence a "community of interest between German civil servants and parliamentarians is nourished in [Bundestag] committees."[11] The degree to which this happens in Germany is unique compared to other European countries. It is also a sea change compared to the old days in Germany (1871–1933), when civil servants were steeped in conservative political traditions that tried to keep parties and politics (other than conservative) at bay.

The favorable inclination nowadays of German bureaucrats toward the political game accords well with the demands of the job. Federal bureaucrats are not solely preoccupied with implementing policies decided by politicians. Instead, what preoccupies the civil servants' time and attention far more is the formulation of policy—formulation and revision of existing policy by way of federal legislation and federal spending programs, to be precise.[12] Odd as it may sound, the federal bureaucracy is more involved in shaping policy than in carrying it out. The detailed proposals that fill the agenda of cabinet meetings, and then become the grist of government bills introduced in Parliament, are largely the work of bureaucrats.

AN ASSERTIVE JUDICIARY

Question: what do same-sex marriages and the Maastricht Treaty have in common?

Answer: both were the subject of rulings by the Federal Constitutional Court in October of 1993.

Judicial review of laws and policies is thriving in Germany, but this is quite a recent experience and the practice differs in many ways from the one in the United States. To begin with, judicial review in Germany is no older than the Federal Republic. The framers of the Basic Law in 1949 embraced this concept as part of their efforts to create safeguards for the democratic system. For that purpose they set up a special court, the Federal Constitutional Court in Karlsruhe, to resolve what is and what is not constitutional (Article 93). That court is not the highest court in a judicial hierarchy, unlike the U.S. Supreme Court. Other federal courts handle the appeals of last resort in criminal, civil, and other cases.

What also distinguishes the German system is that an individual citizen may take a case to the Constitutional Court, claiming that a certain law or regulation at issue violates the constitution. Such "constitutional complaints" make up the overwhelming number of cases handled by the Constitutional Court. From 1951 to 1988, of a total of 71,132 cases on the docket, 67,834 were such "complaints."[13] The court has become a constitutional ombudsman. To be sure, a citizen must first exhaust legal remedies in the regular courts, which are not empowered to rule on the constitutionality of a law. To be heard by the justices in Karlsruhe, the plaintiffs must make a convincing claim that a particular act of government violates some provision of the Basic Law.

It is through a constitutional complaint that the issue of same-sex marriages landed at the doorsteps of the Constitutional Court. With local marriage offices refusing to allow homosexual partners to get married, and regular courts upholding that refusal, numerous homosexual couples took their cases to the Constitutional Court, complaining that their constitutional "freedom to marry" was abridged by current law.[14] The judges denied the complaint, saying that "marriage," as understood by the Basic Law (Article 6), referred only to heterosexual partnerships.[15]

Beyond reviewing the constitutionality of disputed laws, the Constitutional Court may also engage in "abstract review." This refers to:

cases of differences of opinion or doubts on the formal and material compatibility of federal law or Land law with this Basic Law, or on the compatibility of Land law with other federal law, at the request of the Federal Government, of a Land government, or of one-third of the Bundestag members. (Art. 95, 3)

Opposition parties like this provision, which gives them a handy tool to get in court what they cannot achieve in Parliament. This also goes to show that warfare (in the Constitutional Court) is the continuation of partisan politics with other means. Almost all historic foreign policy issues—from rearmament in the 1950s, through the Ostpolitik Treaties in the early 1970s, to the Maastricht Treaty in 1993—had to be settled in court before becoming law. In a sense, the court is called upon to render an advisory opinion on whether or not a proposed policy is constitutional even before the policy has been implemented. Only the advice is binding. In the case of the Maastricht Treaty, opponents argued that the treaty violated German sovereignty as well as democratic principles. The court upheld the treaty, but gave it a very narrow interpretation. As the *Süddeutsche Zeitung* put it in an editorial, the German judges acted "as if the European Council were nothing more than a harmless conference of national governments."[16]

Sweeping judicial verdicts are nothing new in German politics. While upholding the law in the two instances cited above, the court is by no means reluctant to strike down federal or state law and take on powerful chancellors as well as the political parties. Chancellor Adenauer, for example, had his federal television project overturned in court in 1961. Laws to subsidize political parties have been nullified several times, most recently in 1992, when the court imposed a deadline on Parliament to revise party financing legislation to meet the court's requirements. In a significant instance of cross-national contrast, the German Constitutional Court invalidated liberal legislation on abortion soon after the U.S. Supreme Court, in *Roe v. Wade* (1973), liberalized abortion. All in all, the German constitutional justices have nullified legislation at a rate that "makes the U.S. Supreme Court look timid by comparison."[17] However unhappy, the affected parties have generally complied with the court's rulings. Given the high respect that the legal system has long enjoyed in Germany, that may not be altogether surprising.

NOTES

1. Peter Schindler, *Datenhandbuch zur Geschichte des deutschen Bundestages 1980 bis 1987* (Baden: Nomos, 1988), p. 355.
2. *The Week in Germany,* November 19, 1993, p. 7.
3. See *The Week in Germany,* January 18, 1991; and February 11, 1994.
4. Renate Mayntz and Fritz Scharpf, *Policy-Making in the German Federal Bureaucracy* (New York: Elsevier, 1975), p. 43.
5. This account is taken from Hans-Peter Schwarz, *Adenauer: Der Staatsmann: 1952–1967* (Stuttgart: Deutsche Verlags-Anstalt, 1991), pp. 62–64. The major source was the memoirs of the translator present during the Adenauer-Dulles meeting.
6. See Arnulf Baring, *Machtwechsel: Die Aera Brandt-Scheel* (Stuttgart: Deutsche Verlags-Anstalt, 1982). Like the failed no-confidence vote against Brandt in 1972, the circumstances of his resignation in 1974 keep the rumor mills and conspiracy mavens busy, especially now that documents from the *Stasi,* the former East Germany's secret police, are available. The late chancellor's third wife recently claimed that it was the Social Democratic Party parliamentary leader, Herbert Wehner, who conspired with the East German Communists to bring Brandt down. See Craig R. Whitney, "Brandt Dispute Unsettles German Socialists," *The New York Times,* January 27, 1994.
7. As quoted in *The New York Times,* January 21, 1987.

8. See Stephen Kinzer, "A German Crash Course: It's Public Etiquette 101," *The New York Times*, January 19, 1994.

9. See Gerhard Loewenberg, *Parliament in the German Political System* (Ithaca, N.Y.: Cornell University Press, 1966), p. 227.

10. See Elisabeth Noelle-Neumann and Renate Köcher, *Allensbacher Jahrbuch 1984–1992*, pp. 652–653.

11. Joel D. Aberbach, Robert Putnam, and Bert Rockman, *Bureaucrats and Politicians in Western Democracies* (Cambridge, Mass.: Harvard University Press, 1981), pp. 231–232.

12. See Mayntz and Scharpf, *Policy-Making*, p. 63.

13. Donald P. Kommers, *The Constitutional Jurisprudence of the Federal Republic of Germany* (Durham, N.C.: Duke University Press, 1989), p. 12.

14. See "Germany's Constitutonal Court Rules Out Same-Sex Marriage," *The Week in Germany*, October 22, 1993, p. 6.

15. The court actually declined to accept that complaint for deliberation, but explained its refusal at some length.

16. Reprinted in *The Week in Germany*, October 15, 1993, p. 3.

17. Arnold J. Heidenheimer and Donald Kommers, *The Governments of Germany*, 4th ed. (New York: Crowell Harper & Row, 1975), p. 273.

REFERENCES AND SUGGESTED READINGS

Blondel, Jean, and Ferdinand Müller-Rommel, eds. 1988. *Cabinets in Western Europe*. New York: St. Martin's Press.

Gunlicks, Arthur. 1986. *Local Government in the German Federal System*. Durham, N.C.: Duke University Press.

Heidenheimer, Arnold J., Hugh Heclo, and Carolyn Teich Adams. 1990. *Comparative Public Policy: The Politics of Social Choice in America, Europe, and Japan*. 3rd ed. New York: St. Martin's Press.

Kirchhof, Paul, and Donald P. Kommers, eds. 1993. *Germany and Its Basic Law*. Baden-Baden: Nomos.

26

The Politics of Economic Policy

ermany is a country where democracy was destroyed and tyranny triumphed when an economic depression thrust millions into misery and despair in the early 1930s. By contrast, after World War II, the fledgling democracy in West Germany thrived amid unprecedented prosperity. When the Berlin Wall fell in 1989, it was largely the "turbocharged" Western economy, or as some critics sneered, its abundant supply of bananas—so scarce in the East—that led many East Germans to embrace political union. In this chapter we examine the German economic system, the policies that created and changed it, and the political struggle over those policies. In particular, we ask what made the economy of West Germany so appealing, and the economy of the former East Germany so unlovable. Is it proof that capitalism works best? How has the (West) German economy handled the transition to the postindustrial age? How important is the European Union for the German economy? Who are the key players in the game of economic policymaking? Has Germany undergone a conservative turnaround like Britain under Thatcher or the United States under Reagan? And what has been the economic price of German unification in 1990?

THE SOCIAL MARKET ECONOMY

Defying the strict logic of economics, the economic system of the Federal Republic goes by an oxymoron. The *social market economy,*

Ludwig Erhard, the Federal Republic's first and longest-serving economics minister (1949–1963).

as it is called, is a concept closely attached with Ludwig Erhard, the Federal Republic's first and longest-serving economics minister (1949–1963).[1] It is an economic order that mixes cutthroat capitalism with red-tape socialism. Like other seemingly contradictory formulas, the social market economy proved to be a recipe for political success. Initially a partisan idea put forward by the Christian Democratic Union/Christian Social Union, it entered the hall of consensus when the Social Democrats en-

dorsed it in 1959. From then on, partisan conflict was no longer about being for or against this economic order, but about which party was most loyal to that ideal. The consensus on the social market economy helped the political order of the Federal Republic gain popular acceptance to a much higher degree and far sooner than did the constitution defined in the Basic Law.

On one hand, the social market economy wholeheartedly champions the idea of competition and is hostile toward government takeover of economic enterprises (nationalization) or central planning. Government ownership and management of industries and banks is minimal—compared, say, with France or pre-Thatcher Britain. It is largely limited to such traditional domains as postal service, telecommunications, railroads, and air transportation. Yet these days even those domains are facing privatization, at least in part. Most of the renowned German firms, like Mercedes-Benz, BMW, Krupp, Siemens, Deutsche Bank, and BASF, are privately owned and operated. The hand that guides those enterprises to success or failure is primarily the invisible one of the market.

On the other hand, that market operates with the aid of a dense social safety net, whose first threads were woven over a century ago. Nowadays, for almost every German the state provides practically womb-to-tomb coverage, the quality of which in many areas exceeds that of former Communist systems. It begins with maternity benefits, ranges through child allowances, tuition-free university education, unemployment payments, old-age social security, all the way to burial costs. Surprisingly perhaps, it was conservatives like Chancellors Bismarck (1871–1890) and Adenauer (1949–1963) whose governments fashioned many of those policies.[2] Indeed Germany might be the odd case in which the welfare state predates the opening of the free market economy. For decades, apostles of *laissez-faire* economics fought conservatives as much as they did socialists.[3] Note that Germans have an affectionate expression for government: the "public hand." The image evoked is one of a benefactor, not of a predator, and calls to mind the *Obrigkeitsstaat* of yesterday.

The beneficial influence of the public hand goes beyond social protection. Even though the government (federal or others) may own and manage few economic enterprises, it regulates their operation with a vengeance. As even a casual visitor to Germany quickly finds out, all stores fall under uniform closing hours. The rules are, with minor exceptions, that stores must close by 6:30 P.M. on weekdays and by 2:00 P.M. on Saturdays, and must stay closed on Sundays. Standards for performance of anything technical are maddeningly stiff, as anyone knows who has tried to get a not-so-new car through the TÜV, the technical inspection service.

Job training is another domain where government intervenes in distinctively German fashion. The German apprenticeship system is one that relies on business doing the training under close tutelage and authorization by government.[4] The main type of German school, from which students graduate at age 15 or 16 nowadays, supplies the recruits for this vocational program. The state sets the guidelines, provides accompanying in-class education, and supervises the examinations. The private sector does the hands-on, on-the-job training. In a given year, the private sector in western Germany makes available some 700,000 apprentice slots for just as many applicants. Successful trainees receive a *Facharbeiter* diploma. It is a certificate of high prestige and an assurance of a well-paying job. This program is widely credited with instilling in the work force an appreciation for getting a job done well and on time.

Such government-mandated and supervised collaboration of the private sector is typically referred to as "corporatism." The roots of corporatism are even older than the welfare state, dating back to the medieval days of crafts and guilds, hence long before the advent of the industrial age. It seems some traditions prove quite useful in the modern age. All in all, Germany's social market economy is a far cry from a pure model of *laissez-faire* capitalism. But that has helped rather than hurt its popularity.

FROM ECONOMIC MIRACLE TO POSTINDUSTRIAL PAIN

It also helped that the social market economy delivered fabulous prosperity—an "economic miracle," as it was called. Digging out from the rubble after 1945, West Germany piled one bumper year upon another, as never before in history. In the first decade of the Federal Republic's life, economic growth averaged a staggering 7%; growth then tapered off to an average rate of 5% in the 1960s, before settling into a more normal pace of 3% in the 1970s. That breathtaking recovery inspired the hope in 1990 that East Germany would also make quick economic strides after unification. West Germany's postwar boom was by no means a short-lived surge doomed to inevitable collapse, as people with memories of the 1920s may have feared. It was not until 1966 that a recession punctured the postwar expansion. The economy recovered quickly, however, from this setback. The best of all possible worlds, namely full employment combined with near-zero inflation—another contradiction of the logic of economics—still seemed attainable.

Nonetheless, by the mid-1970s, when OPEC's quadrupling of crude oil prices thrust the West German economy into its second recession, some flaws were exposed (see Figure 26.1). Now West Germans had to face up to both rising prices and high unemployment, a nasty combination that signaled the expulsion from economic paradise. Since then, the west German economy has begun to settle into a

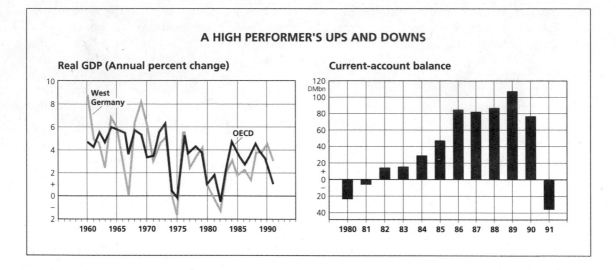

Figure 26.1 The Trading Partners of Germany, 1991. Source: Data from *Facts About Germany, 1992,* p. 237.

rhythm of moderate economic growth alternating with recessionary downturns, like the recent one in 1992–1993. Bad economic times have sharply stung some of the governments of the Federal Republic. Ludwig Erhard, the father of the social market economy, quickly fell from power as chancellor in 1966 when the economic horizon darkened during his watch. Likewise, Helmut Schmidt fell in 1982 as the West German economy suffered its deepest contraction.[5] By contrast, Helmut Kohl held on to the chancellorship through the 1992–1993 recession, though suffering a sharp drop in popularity. Kohl was extremely fortunate that 1990, the year of the unification opportunity, was by far the fattest year of the economy since he came to office in 1982. The eastern upheaval could not have come at a better moment for West Germany, as fas as the economy was concerned (see Figure 26.2).

Yet even the fat years could not mask some structural weaknesses, which recessions brutally expose. The industrial sector of the west German economy (let alone that of eastern Germany) is aging, and not very gracefully. At the same time, the service sector of the econ-omy is suffering from growing pains. Some simple numbers make this point plain. From 1950 to 1970, the industrial sector in West Germany employed most people, close to one in two. Since then, however, employment in industries has been shrinking. By 1984, 53% earned their living from a service-related job, only 41% from a job in industry. The remainder were employed in agriculture, which in 1950 still accounted for one-quarter of the workforce. The German economy has now entered the postindustrial age.

Consider a typical Rust Belt city like Essen, situated in the Ruhr Valley, Germany's industrial heartland.[6] Essen is the home of the Krupp company, Germany's steel giant and formerly a chief arms manufacturer. Belching smokestacks and mine elevators long gave Essen's skyline a distinctive, through grimy profile. Laundry hung up outdoors collected black dust before drying. Now all of Essen's coal mines are closed, monuments to an age gone by. But some have found a new purpose. The halls of one abandoned coal mine have been converted to a tennis arena. Among other things, that is also a sign that tennis has shed

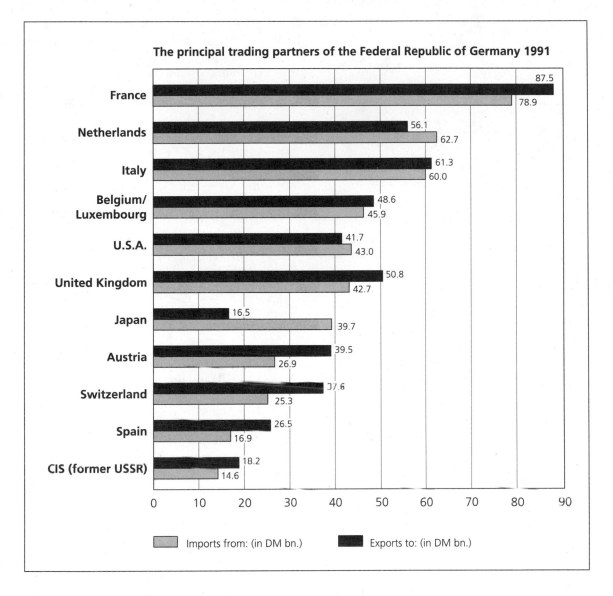

Figure 26.2 A High Performer's Ups and Downs.   Source: *The Economist,* May 23, 1992. © The Economist Newspaper, Ltd. Reprinted with permission.

its country-club image in Germany. But with the demise of the coal mines, Germany's sixth-largest city has fared poorly in the miners' sport of choice—soccer. It is long ago that Essen or any other industrial city nearby has won a soccer championship.

Declining industries like coal mining, along with shipbuilding and agriculture, are being kept on life-support systems through government subsidies, consuming roughly 6% of the gross national product. Political pressures keep the law of economic competition suspended in

Table 26.1	INDUSTRIAL LABOR COSTS PER HOUR (DM)
Germany (western)	41.96
Japan	30.00
France	27.75
U.S.	24.79
Britain	22.79

Source: Reprinted from *The Week in Germany,* May 14, 1993 published by the German Information Center, 950 Third Avenue, NY, NY 10022..

those economic domains with powerful and politically well connected interests. Perhaps the social market economy should be renamed "political" market economy. However much the industrial sector has shrunk, Germany's industrial workers rank among the world's best paid, enjoying short work weeks, long vacations, and generous fringe benefits. All of this, of course, also means high labor costs. Oddly enough, the United States is a low-cost country, by comparison to Germany. It is no surprise, then, that companies like BMW have decided to move production to the United States. But what's good for job creation in the United States is certainly not good for Germany. Long-term prospects for job growth in Europe are grim. A report by the Organization for Economic Cooperation and Development predicts that unemployment in its 19 member countries will jump to 23 million, or 12% of the work force, by 1994.

Big Wheel in the European Community

For the past 40 years, the Federal Republic has been one of the driving forces toward the economic and political unification of Europe. Besides the social market economy, growing economic integration has blessed western Germany with unrivaled prosperity. And like that economic order, the idea of European integration has long ceased to be a partisan issue and fused into political consensus in the German public. In a nutshell, European integration was an ingenious bargain that allowed West Germany to get back on its economic feet after World War II without its European neighbors fearing that they would be kicked around by an economically mighty Germany. It all began in 1950 with the Schuman Plan, named after the French foreign minister with the German name Robert Schuman. The plan envisioned a limited partnership in the coal and steel industries; the countries participating were Italy, the Netherlands, Belgium, and Luxembourg, besides France and West Germany. In 1957, the European Economic Community was formed, embracing the economies at-large of the six countries. A common market without internal tariffs and with complete mobility of labor was envisaged. With the Maastricht Treaty approved, the now twelve-member community is poised to transform itself into the European Union with a common currency.

Still, it is in the economy where the European connection is most visible for Germany. Trade with its neighbors in the European Union is the lifeblood of many industries. France ranks first among Germany's trading partners: more German exports go there than to any other country and more German imports come from France than anywhere else. The Netherlands, Belgium/Luxembourg, Italy, and the United Kingdom follow closely behind. This is truly a two-way street with roughly equal flows from Germany to Europe and the other way around. Outside the European Union, Germany's main trading partner is the United States. The German-American balance of trade, too, is fairly even, unlike the balance with another big trading country, Japan. All in all, in a typical year, close to one-quarter of Germany's gross national product derives from exports and a roughly equal proportion goes for imports. In other words, half of the German economy is trade-related.

Manufacturing continues to be a mainstay of German exports. Take state-of-the-art high-performance cars, for example. For many years, more Porsches were sold in the United States than in the country where they were built. Of all the 4.7 million cars manufactured in Germany in 1991, 2.2 million were exported. Mercedes, that symbol of automotive status, craftsmanship, engineering innovation, and elegant styling, now ranks as the top company in Germany, as far as sales are concerned, employing 375,000 people. *Made in Germany*—that British branding of goods as a stigma more than one hundred years ago has mutated into a valuable trademark. To keep up its standard of living, the Federal Republic must continue to make high-quality goods and sell them abroad. It needs innovation at home to remain competitive, and a good climate abroad for international trade to flourish, unobstructed by quotas, tariffs, sanctions, threats, or other forms of ill will. What's good for Europe is good for Germany. There is no conflict at all, unlike among some of its neighbors.

MAKERS OF
MACROECONOMIC POLICY

Whatever the Basic Law says about the chancellor determining the guidelines of policy, it would be naive to suppose that in Germany economic policy is made by a unitary actor. Instead, it is far more appropriate to see this process as a "strategic noncooperative game," that is, a "strategic game in which there are at least three fairly independent players with conflicting interests."[7] Besides the federal government under the direction of the chancellor, there is one player who is in the position of being an immovable object: the *Bundesbank,* Germany's central bank. By law and historical

experience (the hyperinflation of 1922–1923), the Bundesbank enjoys an independent status rare by international standards. It is sworn to protect the value of the Deutschmark, come recessionary hell or inflationary highwater. The Bundesbank has often stood its ground stubbornly against cries for easier money (lower interest rates, more abundant money supply). Chancellors, political parties, labor unions, and business have all at times locked horns with the Bundesbank, but have rarely forced it to budge. Not surprisingly, the Bundesbank ranks in some estimates as the "single most influential instrument of German economic policy."[8]

Outside the realm of governmental institutions, the cast of significant players in the economic-policy game includes labor unions and business associations. In Germany, these two interest groups are each organized in centralized peak associations that are capable of speaking with single and powerful voices. The *Deutsche Gewerkschaftsbund* (German Labor Federation, or DGB) encompasses unions in all branches of industry, and practically all business firms belong to the Federation of German Business (BDI). Many observers are impressed with the "organizational strength and institutional presence of both business and labor" in Germany.[9]

The typical labor union in Germany is one that encompasses a whole industry, not a particular craft. These are "industrial unions" like the ones organized in the Congress of Industrial Organization (CIO). One of them merits a special note of attention: IG Metall. The largest union in the world, the metalworkers union encompasses workers in all metal processing and manufacturing companies. Hence it combines the steelworkers and automobile workers, no matter what grade of steel or what brand of car. The threat of a strike by this union will send a paralyzing chill throughout the German economy. The IG Metall accounts for one-third of the membership included in the

German Labor Federation. Although neither the labor federation nor the affiliated unions have formal ties with any political party, the solidarity with the Social Democratic Party is no secret. Unionized workers have been the main electoral pillar of that party for more than a century.

According to a school of thought with a wide following, business and labor influence policy-making in Germany is in a "corporatist" fashion, rather than in the "pluralist" fashion common in the United States.[10] As we have seen above, the German system of vocational training has a strong corporatist flavor, with government working hand in glove with business and labor, letting them operate with quasi-political authority to implement a particular policy. But when it comes to macroeconomic policy, neither labor nor business enjoys that kind of standing. Business and labor do not set prices or wages through a form of government licensing or within the confines of wage-price guidelines. Corporatist institutions like *Concerted Action* are exceptions, not the rule. That was the name for a regular summit of labor, business, and the federal government, convened by the Grand Coalition (1966–1969). It was the brainchild of the minister of economics, Karl Schiller, and died soon after his departure in 1972.

The influence wielded by labor and business over economic policy decisions depends greatly on which parties form the federal government. With a government of the Right, as under Chancellor Kohl, business has the inside lane, whereas with a government of the Left, as under Chancellors Brandt and Schmidt, that is true for labor. Recall, for example, that almost every Social Democratic member of the Bundestag is a member of a labor union. Moreover, given the coalitional nature of most federal governments, it is wise to accord independent player status to each coalition partner. In the latter years of the Social Democrat–Free Democrat government under Chancellor

Schmidt, the sharpest line of conflict over economic policy ran right through his government. And when the major opposition party happens to control the Bundesrat (Federal Council), that party, too, has a seat at the table where the game is played. With so many players involved, the reader may wonder how the game could come to a successful end. Is it a game with a clear winner? Or does it end, as games of soccer, Germany's most popular sport, often do—in a tie?

A TURNAROUND IN MACROECONOMIC POLICY

There are few areas where science comes as close to affecting government decisions as in the realm of economic policy. The "dismal science" of economics has worked hard to hand political leaders workable prescriptions to cure ailments of the economy. Still, it is not surprising that the economic doctors disagree on what is the best cure. In a nutshell, the debate is whether government, by means of fiscal policy, can cure recessions, secure full employment, and keep prices from rising too fast. In other words, can government policy correct the failures of the market? Keynesians say "Yes"; their critics, rooted in classical economics, say "No."

In the Federal Republic, as in the United States and Britain, the debate between those two schools did not remain academic, but spilled over into the political arena. With the entry of the Social Democratic Party into the federal government in 1966, Keynesianism gained a foothold in economic policy, as exemplified by the passage of the 1967 "Law for Economic Stability and Growth." The swift recovery of the West German economy from the first postwar recession lent practical credibility to the new philosophy. But when the mid-1970s brought a combination of troublesome inflation and persistent unemployment, the belief in government fine-tuning began to wane. Bulging budget deficits and vanishing trade surpluses at the end of the 1970s doomed Keynesianism in Germany.

It is surprising, in some sense, that Keynesianism did not catch on in Germany. After all, Keynes's image of government as a benevolent actor remedying the shortcomings of the market would perfectly fit with the German image of government as the "public hand." The problem is that the major remedy calls for tinkering with public spending and taxing. In Germany, that raises strong suspicions about manipulation of public finances. The memory of getting burned by government fiddling with the currency sits too deep. It legitimizes the stalwart of monetary rectitude, the independent Bundesbank, to resist such efforts of manipulation.

Like Ronald Reagan in the United States and Margaret Thatcher in Britain, neo-conservatives in the Federal Republic called for cuts in public spending, lower taxes, deregulation, and pruning of subsidies.[11] This approach was endorsed by the Free Democratic Party, under its outspoken leader Count Otto Lambsdorff, and pitted the party against the Social Democratic Party, its coalition partner since 1969, and the labor unions. The opposition Christian alliance was prepared to join forces with the Free Democrats. The result was the "overthrow" of the Schmidt government in 1982 by means of the constructive vote of no confidence. The new government of the Christian alliance and the Free Democratic Party adopted a policy of "fiscal consolidation," the buzzword of the Kohl era, and pursued it stubbornly in the face of the deepest recession (1981–1982) since the 1930s.[12] Contrary to Keynesian dogma, the West German economy recovered, with exports booming again, and inflation subsiding. This outcome paid a handsome electoral dividend for the governing parties in the 1987 election. Still, with happier times there again, unemployment failed to decline. By way of comparison, it appears that the economic-policy turnaround in the Germany

of the 1980s, with its emphasis on fiscal rectitude, had more in common with Thatcherism than with Reaganomics.

THE EAST GERMAN ECONOMY IN TURMOIL

In some ways, the East German economy closely mirrored its West German counterpart. There was a strong emphasis on industrial production and exports. Moreover, by comparison with the other socialist countries, the German Democratic Republic was quite affluent. With Prussian determination, it seemed, East Germans made communism, or at least socialism, work. According to some accounts, the German Democratic Republic enjoyed nearly as high a living standard as enjoyed in some western countries. The enviable haul of gold medals at Olympic Games was proof that East Germany knew how to compete successfully with the West. That success was built on incentives rather than coercion, discovering talent and rewarding it handsomely. If only its rulers could have applied the lessons of athletic competition to the economy. But in economic competition with the West, the Democratic Republic had no prospect of winning any gold medals. Not even a chance to win at the trials.

Government ownership and central planning are the hallmarks of a Soviet-style economy, which the Democratic Republic adopted early on and perfected over the years, instead of pondering reform. The ruling party, with its socialist ideology, decided what was good for the economy. To be sure, jobs were guaranteed and prices fixed. Most things did not cost much, but then many goods a western consumer would take for granted were not available, or only at exorbitant prices on the black market or in stores for the *Nomenklatura*, the party elite. Bananas were an exotic rarity. There were few financial incentives for the ordinary East German workers to do their jobs well. Nor

The whole story in a dumpster: 2.4 million Trabants were on the streets of the German Democratic Republic in 1989. Hundreds of thousands of Trabi owners every year since have given up their cars for western autos.

for one company to outshine another one. No incentive to innovate, be efficient, make a profit. It was an economy designed to work without profit or competition.

Instead of the inevitable progress that was promised, this ideology delivered economic backwardness. Moreover, the socialist utopia proved to be an ecological nightmare. Take the major product of the East German automobile industry: the *Trabant*. In size, styling, and technical development, it belongs to the 1950s, save for its plastic body, which makes it unsuitable for recycling. Nonetheless, East Germans had to wait years to get their hands on a "Trabi," as the car was known affectionately. Like the Trabant, many other products of the East German economy were destined to end up in the trash compacter. Exposure to the climate of a free market is as lethal to a socialist economy as is forty-degree water to a sailor overboard. A Trabant cannot compete with a Volkswagen, let alone a BMW. In the short run, many businesses would

shut down and workers would lose their jobs. The question was how quickly the introduction of the Deutschmark and free market would revive the moribund East German economy. Would it happen much faster than expected, just like the steps of political unification?

COLD-TURKEY TREATMENT FOR THE EAST

Thus far, the answer seems to be no. The East German economy turned out to be far sicker than expected. As an executive of Deutsche Bank, West Germany's largest bank, put it, "The more we looked at the eastern part of the country, the more we realized how decrepit it really was."[13] Official statistics show that in 1991, the first calendar year after unification, industrial production in the East plummeted to a level barely one-third of what it was in 1989. That is a weight loss that no human being would be able to survive, except for morbidly obese ones. The collapse of production inevitably spelled job destruction. In April 1993, 1.1 million East Germans were counted as unemployed (14.7% of the work force), but many more worked only part-time, had taken early retirement, or were being retrained for jobs with uncertain prospects. By some estimates, almost 4 million jobs out of nearly 10 million have vanished since 1989. To characterize that calamity as a "depression" would be too mild; a more pungent term is needed. The losses of production and jobs suffered by eastern Germans in 1989–1993 dwarf the corresponding figures for Germany in 1929–1933.

The likely political fallout of such misery ought to make one shudder. Surprisingly perhaps, there is less gloom in people's outlook than the economic doom would suggest. Opinion polls show that most East Germans believe that they are better off now than before the Wall crumbled, as Table 26.2 shows. More say that their own economic situation is good rather than bad, and hope for better times ahead prevails over economic despair. How come?

It is undeniable that, aside from the free market shock, the East German economy was already ailing under the old regime. The collapse of communism in the Soviet bloc destroyed the trading network on which the German Democratic Republic depended for its relative prosperity. East Germany used to ship two-fifths of its exports to fellow socialist states. In the late 1980s, these outlets vanished. The East German public felt the resulting economic pinch months before the Wall fell. In no small measure, that economic distress fueled the political revolution that would topple it.

THE BILL FOR GERMAN REUNION

Unification brought economic freedom to the East, but it was no free lunch, as the saying goes. Neither private investors in the West nor aspiring capitalists in the East could be expected, just on their own, to turn an economic wasteland into a thriving landscape. Paradoxically, moving from a government-run economy to a market economy requires a great deal of intervention, planning, and assistance on the part of government. It began with the decision of the West German government to buy out the East German currency on very generous terms with the Deutschmark. Then, in the unification treaty, it was agreed that eastern wage levels in the style of multiyear plans should be raised to western levels. That the market could bear that parity, given the enormous gaps between eastern and western economic performance, nobody should have believed. Hence, government largesse of considerable proportion would be required. Next, a government agency was set up called *Treuhand* (the hand you can trust) to manage the privatization of thousands of state-owned enterprises, which were offi-

Table 26.2 THE ECONOMIC OUTLOOK IN EAST GERMANY, APRIL 1993 (%)

Personal Economic Situation Now	
Good	39%
Bad	13%
So-so	48%
Personal Economic Situation Next Year	
Better	24%
Worse	10%
Same	65%
Situation Now Compared to the Time Before 1990	
Better	54%
Worse	18%
Same	28%

Source: Forschungsgruppe Wahlen, *Politbarometer April 1993*; 1,060 respondents.

cially known as "people-owned." This was not a job the market was eager to take on. It seemed more designed for a social worker with a big heart and an even bigger pocketbook. An East German's trash was not a West German's treasure; it was more the other way around, and that did not help the East. Nonetheless, the Treuhand was set up to be self-financing, with additional funds coming from bonds issued by the agency. A truthful advertisement for Treuhand offerings might well read as follows:

> *For Sale: Thousands of eastern German companies, most in dilapidated condition with disputed ownership, dubious management, outmoded products, vanishing markets, heavy debts and thousands of unnecessary employees. Everything from beauty parlors to shipyards must go.*[14]

The financial costs of unity have torn a big hole in the western pocket that will not mend by itself. In 1991, the first year after unification, the federal government, along with western state governments, pumped DM 140 billion ($90 bill.) into the East. To pay for the social security checks of the retired, the jobless benefits of the previously employed, and the health care of people with jobs and without. Those billions of Deutschmark, were not a lump-sum payment, to settle matters quickly. Rather they constituted a down payment, to be followed by similar ones every year until the end of the century. At that rate, transfers to the East would consume roughly one-quarter of public spending in Germany. Without higher taxes or lower spending in the West such generosity was bound to swell the deficit and to pile up a huge mountain of debt in the future. Economic projections foresaw a rise of that debt from 42% of gross national product in 1991 to 51% by 1995.

Following Ronald Reagan's example, Chancellor Kohl had promised the East Germans a flourishing future that would not require big sacrifices from the West Germans. Gain without pain. If a government infusion of capital

was required, it would come through increased debt, not higher taxes. This policy compelled the Bundesbank, Germany's central bank, to raise interest rates, lest inflation get out of hand and devalue the Deutschmark. A more pliant central bank might have accommodated the increased demand for credit and turned on the money spigot. But the memory of the hyperinflation has tied the hands of the Bundesbank. It has resolutely resisted all complaints, mostly from outside Germany, about high German interest rates. Some have blamed the worldwide recession of the early 1990s on those high rates and painted the new Germany into a bad corner.

Debt alone nonetheless could not foot the bill for unification. But how could Kohl's government come up with a solution and not betray its election-campaign pledge? The magic trick was to propose a surcharge—a temporary sacrifice by the taxpayer. In 1991, the Bundestag and Bundesrat approved a 7.5% surcharge on income taxes, valid for one year. But that did not solve the fiscal problems of unification. As Germany, too, sank into recession amid ballooning debts and swelling unemployment rolls in 1992, the prospects looked grim. It was just as opponents to Chancellor Kohl's crash program in the year of unity had warned. As the bill grew longer and larger, they had a hard time not gloating. The magazine *Der Spiegel*—no friend of Chancellor Kohl, admittedly—pronounced unity unaffordable and Kohl's policy bankrupt. The cover of one issue (March 23, 1992) depicted Kohl as a weightlifter straining in utter futility to raise a set of weights inscribed "Deutsche Mark." The weights, if anything, grew heavier with the economic downturn afflicting Germany in 1992–1993.

In early 1993, his government put forward what it euphemistically called a "solidarity pact." It was a plan of cuts in social benefits and hikes of taxes. The major opposition party, the Social Democrats, countered the proposal with one cutting the defense budget and raising the taxes of the well-to-do. With the Social Democrats in control of the Bundesrat and the coalition parties (the Christian alliance and the Free Democrats) in control of the Bundestag, neither of those plans had much chance of being adopted. Maybe the issue would end in stalemate, or a compromise between the two plans would have to be reached. That is the price of divided government, German-style. In this case, the end game featured three independent players: the governing coalition, the Social Democratic Party, and the sixteen state governments. The main points of their agreement were:

1. renewal of the 7.5% surcharge, but not before 1995 (the year after the next federal election), and relief for low-income groups;

2. no cuts in social benefits; and

3. more sharing of the sales-tax receipts with the states.

For all intents and purposes this was an all-party and all-government decision: governing parties and opposition; federal government and state governments, if only for two and a half days on one subject, as the Social Democrat leader pronounced it. "Federalism made a great gain in Germany," lauded the *Frankfurter Rundschau*, a paper not known for kindness toward Chancellor Kohl. The *Süddeutsche Zeitung*, another liberal paper, reached for words in calling the outcome a "miracle":

> *The Bonn miracle was made possible because of a heretofore-unknown unanimity among all sixteen federal states; because of an opposition party that, finding itself faced with the tension between adaptation and refusal, ultimately decided in favor of constructive cooperation in the accomplishment of a historical task.*[15]

But perhaps this was a bill drawn up without the waiter, as a German saying goes, the waiter this time being the taxpayers in western Germany. No doubt they are being asked to pay.

Is Unity Unaffordable? *Der Spiegel,* March 23, 1992.

Have they entirely forgotten Chancellor Kohl's pledge not to raise taxes? Will they be so gullible not to think of the tax hike since it would not come due after the next election? Is voter wrath delayed, voter wrath denied? When all the major parties gang up in passing unpopular measures, betraying campaign pledges on top of it, the hour of new parties dawns.

NOTES

1. See Edwin Hartrich, *The Fourth and Richest Reich* (New York: Macmillan, 1980).

2. In the 1880s, imperial Germany under Bismarck's chancellorship pioneered national

insurance programs for workmen's compensation, sickness, and old age. Adenauer's main social policy innovation was the linking in 1957 of old-age security payments to the index of wages of the working population.

3. The classic statement is by Friedrich A. Hayek, *The Road to Serfdom* (London: Routledge and Kegan Paul, 1944).

4. See Stephen Kinzer, "Germans' Apprentice System Is Seen as Key to Long Boom," *The New York Times,* Febuary 6, 1993.

5. On the influence of the economy on the government popularity in the Federal Republic, see Christian Goergen and Helmut Norpoth, "Government Turnover and Economic Accountability," *Electoral Studies,* 10 (April 1991): 191–207.

6. See Ferdinand Protzman, "Hard Times in the Ruhr, With No Miracles in Sight," *The New York Times,* May 2, 1993.

7. See Martin Hellwig and Manfred J. M. Neumann, "Economic Policy in Germany: Was there a Turnaround?" *Economic Policy,* 2 (October 1987): 113, 199.

8. Arnold J. Heidenheimer, Hugh Heclo, and Carolyn Teich Adams, *Comparative Public Policy,* 3rd ed. (New York: St. Martin's Press, 1990), p. 158.

9. Peter J. Katzenstein, ed., *Industry and Politics in West Germany* (Ithaca: Cornell University Press, 1989), p. 349; also see Andrei S. Markovits, *The Politics of West German Trade Unions* (New York: Cambridge University Press, 1986).

10. See Philippe Schmitter and Gerhard Lehmbruch, eds., *Patterns of Corporatist Policy Making* (Beverly Hills: Sage Publications, 1982); also M. Donald Hancock, *West Germany: The Politics of Democratic Corporatism* (Chatham: Chatham House, 1989).

11. It is curious, however, that no new term comparable to "Thatcherism" or "Reaganomics" has been coined in Germany for that approach. The official term, *Wende* (turnaround), packs no ideological punch; nor does it personalize the new dogma. Some would argue that this is proof that policy really did not change much. But it may have more to do with the disinclination of the German culture to personalize economic or political doctrines, Marxism being the exception.

12. See Gerhard Fels and Hans-Peter Froehlich, "Germany and the World Economy: A German View," *Economic Policy,* 2 (April 1987): 184.

13. As quoted in Roger Cohen, "The Growing Weight of Germany's Unification," *The New York Times,* March 8, 1993.

14. Ferdinand Protzman, "Privatization in Eastern Germany Is Mired in a Collapsing Economy," *The New York Times,* March 12, 1991.

15. As quoted by *The Week in Germany,* March 19, 1993, p. 3.

REFERENCES AND SUGGESTED READINGS

Dennis, Mike. 1988. *German Democratic Republic: Politics, Economics and Society.* London: Pinter.

Erhard, Ludwig. 1962. *Deutsche Wirtschaftspolitik: Der Weg der sozialen Marktwirtschaft.* Düsseldorf: Econ.

Hancock, M. Donald, John Logue, and Bernt Schiller, eds. 1991. *Managing Modern Capitalism.* New York: Praeger (chapters by Hancock and Helm).

Hardach, Karl. 1980. *The Political Economy of Germany in the Twentieth Century.* Berkeley: University of California Press.

Huelshoff, Michael G., Andrei Markovits, and Simon Reich, eds. 1993. *From Bundesrepublik to Deutschland: German Politics after Unification.* Ann Arbor: University of Michigan Press (chapters by Allen, Baylis, and Collier).

Katzenstein, Peter. 1987. *Policy and Politics in West Germany: The Growth of a Semi-sovereign State.* Philadelphia: Temple University Press.

Smyser, William R. 1991. *The Economy of United Germany: Colossus at the Crossroads.* New York: St. Martin's Press.

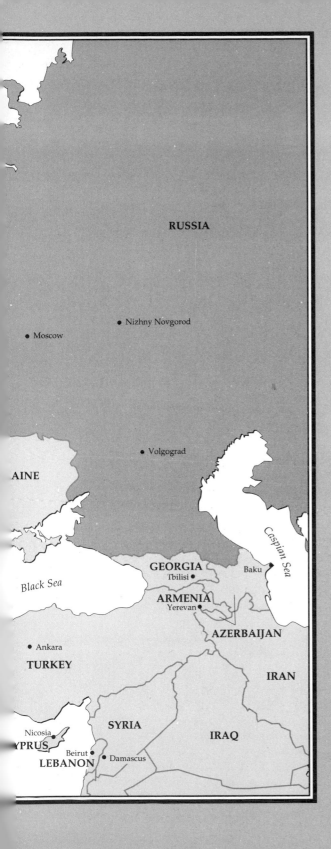

RUSSIA

• Nizhny Novgorod

• Moscow

• Volgograd

AINE

Black Sea

GEORGIA
Tbilisi •

Baku •

Caspian Sea

ARMENIA
Yerevan •

AZERBAIJAN

• Ankara

TURKEY

IRAN

Nicosia
•

SYRIA

IRAQ

YPRUS

Beirut •
LEBANON   • Damascus

V

Russia

27

The Current Situation:
Russia and the Commonwealth of Independent States

O n May 18, 1991, Sergei Krikalev, from Leningrad, blasted off toward the orbiting *Mir* space station. He left from Baikonur in the Soviet republic of Kakazhstan. Ten months later the cosmonaut returned to earth, to the very same space station but in a different country, the independent state of Kazakhstan. The man who had been general secretary of his country's only legal party, the Communist Party of the Soviet Union, was gone and so too was the party. The man who had been president of his country, the Union of Soviet Socialist Republics, was also gone, and so too was the country. And Sergei Krikalev was no longer from Leningrad; his hometown now was St. Petersburg.

On the territory that the Soviet Union once covered, fifteen sovereign countries now stand and nearly 280 million people are getting used to a new world (see Figure 27.1). Most, but not all, of these new states are members of a new "commonwealth," which has both too much in common—history, people, borders—and too little wealth. Where once a pervasive organization served the multiple roles of running the state, directing society and controlling the economy, such functions are now the prizes in a fierce political contest among hundreds of actors. Where elections were once highly structured rituals, offering a strictly limited choice of candidates and policies, people are now asked in referenda to decide the most basic questions, relating to their countries' independence, the

Figure 27.1 Successor States of the Soviet Union.

direction of economic reform, and whether their elected parliament should be dissolved. In all of the new states, structures of governance and participation are in place or being constructed while simultaneously changes are being introduced in the way the economy works—or is supposed to work. Internationally, old enemies are now friends, and formerly close comrades—while still physically close—are not always comrades.

THE COMMONWEALTH OF INDEPENDENT STATES

The Commonwealth of Independent States (CIS) is a very loose association of countries,

all of whom were once republics in the Soviet Union. Four of the former republics chose not to join the Commonwealth when it was created at the end of 1991: the three Baltic nations, Estonia, Latvia, and Lithuania—which had been independent between World Wars I and II—and Georgia, which had enjoyed a brief independence after World War I. Two others, Azerbaijan and Moldova, signed the original agreement but their parliaments did not ratify their membership. But during 1993–1994, Azerbaijan, Georgia, and Moldova did join the Commonwealth. In the first case the former Communist leader, Geidar Aliev, took power after rebels drove an elected president out and in the second, Georgian leader Edvard Shevardnadze was obliged to seek

From Commonwealth to Community?

While the Commonwealth of Independent States started off slowly, it cannot be accused of timidity in its goals. A draft treaty unveiled in mid-1993 reveals that some of the Commonwealth's leaders have in mind nothing less than a full economic community along the lines of the European Economic Community.

Explicitly modelled after the EEC's founding Treaty of Rome, the "Basic Principles" of the Commonwealth's draft treaty envision:

1. A free trade association which lowers duties, tariffs and other barriers between the members

2. A customs union which essentially eliminates all tariffs in goods between countries

3. A common market in all goods and services

4. A multi-currency system with countries' currencies fluctuating among themselves but freely tradable

5. A single currency eventually based on the strongest of the members' currencies.

While observers of the CIS might consider such aims fanciful, it is worth recalling that the European Coal and Steel Community and the founding of the European Common Market were based on such goals. Within ten years of World War II, Germany and France, which spent most of the early twentieth century fighting each other, were able to start putting them into practice.

Source: *Commersant*, June 23, 1993, p. 33.

The Commonwealth (*sodruzhestvo* in Russian) is not a replacement for the Soviet Union, nor does it have any of the significant features of a nation-state. There is no capital, no independent budget, nor any Commonwealth executive, judiciary, or legislature. Its signatories are represented by their heads of state at periodic meetings that rotate among the capitals of the member states. The members pledge to respect each other's territorial integrity and borders and to develop "equal and mutually beneficial cooperation." Beyond that, the original treaty indicates several broad areas in which ambitious cooperation is envisioned, including foreign policy, transportation and communications, and environmental protection. A "common economic space" was to be created as well as a "common military and strategic space under common military command."

While some cooperation has taken place in certain clearly defined areas, such as banking, the kind of coordination envisaged in the Commonwealth's founding documents has not occurred. In fact, in the most critical areas, economic coordination and military policy, Russia has found itself in conflict with key Commonwealth members (see Chapter 34). Attempts to utilize a common currency, the Russian ruble, have foundered (see Table 27.1) and the member states find that the paths they are following away from the command economies differ in pace and direction. The ability of a huge and potentially rich country like Russia to utilize its resources and international contacts to reform its economy is much greater than that of a new country like Uzbekistan which for nearly eighty years was only one highly specialized part of the Soviet economy. While the Commonwealth countries remain each other's main trading partners in virtually all cases, effective economic coordination has been slow in coming. Between 1991 and 1993 nearly three hundred agreements were signed among the member states, but most have remained on pa-

Russian help and Commonwealth membership after opposition and secessionist movements threatened the very existence of his country. In Moldova a new parliament was elected, dominated by parties preferring closer ties with Russia.

Table 27.1 SOVIET SUCCESSOR STATES

Country	Area (Sq. miles)	Population (Millions)	Capital	Nominal Currency*
Members of the Commonwealth of Independent States (CIS)				
Armenia	11,500	3.3	Yerevan	dram
Azerbaijan	33,400	7.1	Baku	manat
Belarus	80,200	10.2	Minsk	taler
Georgia	26,900	5.5	Tblisi	lari
Kazakhstan	1,000,000	16.9	Almaty**	tenge
Kyrgyzstan	76,000	4.0	Bishkek	som
Moldova	13,000	4.4	Chişinău	leu
Russia	6,600,000	149.0	Moscow	ruble
Tajikistan	55,200	4.4	Dushanbe	sum
Turkmenistan	488,100	3.1	Ashgabat	manat
Ukraine	233,100	51.8	Kiev	karbovanets
Uzbekistan	172,700	19.2	Tashkent	sum
Not Members of the CIS				
Estonia	17,400	1.6	Tallinn	kroon
Latvia	64,600	2.7	Riga	lat
Lithuania	65,200	3.7	Vilnius	lit

*Currencies are in various stages of introduction and in many cases are used simultaneously with government coupons and/or Russian rubles.

**In July 1994 Kazakhstan's parliament voted to move the capital to Akmola in a process to be completed by the year 2000.

per, many have not been ratified by states' parliaments, and others have been passed only with multiple and significant reservations attached by individual countries.

Military cooperation within the Commonwealth has taken the form of limited peacekeeping agreements and a collective security agreement among seven of the member states (but again not ratified in all of these). Russia at first had wanted a unified military command and even delayed establishing its own defense ministry for some months. But there was little support for military integration among the Commonwealth members. In part this reflects the strength of national feeling in countries such as Ukraine where popular support for full

independence was a key factor contributing to the breakup of the Soviet Union. Wariness of military cooperation also reflected apprehension in other new states, such as Moldova, that a Commonwealth military would simply be a Soviet military with another name. Such pressures, plus Russia's own misgivings about an integrated military, proved too great an obstacle to overcome and in June 1993 even the small Commonwealth joint military command was abolished.

Other efforts to instill life into the CIS have met with mixed reactions. In January 1993 a new charter was signed and a new interstate bank was created to facilitate trade and payments. But only seven of the members signed;

Ukraine, the most important economically after Russia, was among the new countries that declined to sign. A new attempt to force economic unity was launched in the autumn of 1993.

The weakness of the Commonwealth as a unitary actor should not be surprising. During the last years of the USSR, hostility toward both the existing Soviet system and Russian rule emerged in several republics. When these republics then became independent states, many with popularly elected leaders, their new governments were quite unwilling to give back the sovereignty they had just earned to a new supranational body. Moreover, it was immediately evident that though all fifteen former republics were now independent states, they were not all equal, in terms of size, resources, or military and economic power. Though the Soviet Union had disappeared, Russia had not.

RUSSIA

Clearly the colossus of the group, the Russian Federation represents roughly three-quarters of the area of the former Soviet Union. By itself it is still the largest country in the world, covering almost 6.6 million square miles, nearly twice the size of the United States. All of the other Commonwealth member states combined could fit inside Russia three times over. Its population of 149 million is more than half of the former USSR and contains within it some 100 different national groups—more than thirty of which number at least 100,000 people.

While they were part of the USSR, Russians made up a little more than one-half of that country's population. In Russia today, four of every five people are ethnically Russian. This still leaves some 57 million people of other nationalities, of which the largest groups are Tartars, Ukrainians, Chuvash, Bashkirs, and Belorussians. Virtually all of the world's religions are represented—and now openly practiced—in Russia, with the largest groups being Orthodox, Muslims, and Jews.

Russia took with it out of the Soviet Union the lion's share of that country's immense natural resources. These include coal, oil, natural gas, uranium, gold, and vast expanses of timber. But Russia by itself is an even more northerly country than was the Soviet Union. Virtually all of the country lies above 50 degrees north latitude, roughly that of Winnipeg, Canada. Only one-fourth of its land is suitable for agriculture. The rich "black earth" regions of Ukraine, the vast cotton fields of Uzbekistan, and the warm vegetable- and fruit-growing regions in the southern Caucasus are now part of different countries. Moreover, most of the country's exploitable natural resources lie in Siberia, where extraction and transportation—either to domestic or external markets—is not only difficult and costly but also subject to pressures and restrictions imposed by rising regional sentiment against exploitation of the country by its "center."

But Russians do not live only in Russia. Nearly 25 million Russians live in what are now independent and separate countries. Nearly 38 percent of the population of Kazakhstan and 22 percent of Ukraine is Russian. Russians make up more than one-third of the population of Latvia and nearly one-third of Estonia. The capitals of Kazakhstan and Kyrgyzstan are more than one-half Russian, and those of Tajikistan, Turkmenistan, and Uzbekistan roughly one-third Russian. Thus one of the key areas of concern and contention between Russia and her neighbors is the fate and treatment of her conationals. Historically, much of the immigration of Russians into other republics was closely tied to Moscow's plans for political control and economic development. For many in these new countries the Russian communities that remain are seen as symbols of the old system. Moreover, in most of the former republics, substantial military installations remain, along with Russian troops.

THE MOTLEY COMMONWEALTH

The remaining members of the Commonwealth display the extraordinary diversity one might expect from countries that spread from northern central Europe though Central Asia to the far east. Two, Belarus and Ukraine, are home to predominantly Slavic peoples; six have majority Muslim populations of the Sunni branch; five of these are in central Asia and of those, four (Kazakhstan, Kyrgyzstan, Turkmenistan, and Uzbekistan) have predominantly Turkic-speaking populations, whereas most of those in the fifth (Tajikistan) are ethnically Persian. The people of Azerbaijan speak a Turkish dialect as well and are Muslim but most are Shiah. Armenians trace their language and history as a people back to the time of the ancient Greeks and Romans but, like most of the other groups in the former Soviet Union, have spent precious little of that time as masters of their own fate.

These Commonwealth members do have some characteristics in common, however. All are on the geographic periphery of what had been the USSR. Thus they now share the potential for both conflict and cooperation not only with Russia, with whom they share a history as a state, but with other neighbors with whom they may share a border and a people. Azeris live in both Azerbaijan and Iran, for example, and Tajiks in Afghanistan and Tajikistan. In fact, some 65 million people of the former Soviet Union live outside the borders of what had been "their" republics.

All these states also share the legacy of Communist government, meaning decades of one-party rule, highly restricted media, state-dominated economies, and tight control from Moscow. All were part of a national economy that linked together the various resources and productive potential of what had been one country under the direction of a state-determined central plan. Production was not organized nor was trade conducted or resources utilized on the basis of regional or private decisions, or on knowledge of the market. Rather, the party leaders harnessed regional conditions to national goals. This meant a high degree of specialization, for example, producing most railroad cars in Ukraine and cotton in Uzbekistan. Breaking up what had been one highly centralized economy has left its new independent parts ill-prepared to become effective economic national or international actors.

Almost 75 percent of Uzbekistan's arable land—and 40 percent of its people—are engaged in cotton production, for example. But during the Soviet period, so little industry was sited in this republic that it has little capacity to manufacture. It is thus left as a country rich in cotton but which must import cotton shirts. Foreign trade is similarly new territory. In the former Soviet Union, Russia accounted for more than three-fourths of the country's exports. The road, rail, and communication systems of the former USSR do not neatly follow the proclamations of sovereignty that the Commonwealth members issued in 1991. Hence most have found that, like it or not, their economies and indeed their very future still depend heavily on developments in Russia.

The pace and breadth of economic reform among the states of the Commonwealth vary as well. None has embarked on as radical and rapid a path of privatizing the state economies as Russia has, and few freed prices and ended subsidies to major state industries as abruptly as Russia did in 1992. While nearly fifty thousand firms were privatized in Russia during 1992, very few were created in Ukraine or the states of Central Asia. Some, such as Kazakhstan, have welcomed foreign investment and have much to offer, including oil and natural gas; others, such as Kyrgyzstan or Tajikistan, have seen little foreign interest, due in part to their relative lack of attractive economic features, the persistence of instability, or a concern about losing newly won sovereignty to the influence of powerful external actors.

THE FUTURE OF THE COMMONWEALTH

In the eyes of some observers, the Commonwealth of Independent States was from the beginning a political fig leaf, a hastily conceived and ambiguously expressed superstructure designed to satisfy several mutually conflicting constituencies. Nationalistic Russians feared the loss of empire and worried over the fate of their conationals now living outside their homeland. Conservative leaders in Central Asia wanted more control over their own affairs but did not necessarily want to be financially independent countries. Leaders of vulnerable republics such as Moldova and Armenia desired independence but feared that as single states they would be subject to threats and attacks from more powerful neighbors. Independence-minded leaders like those of Ukraine wanted nothing less than full sovereignty and equality with the large Russian state and expected very little residual power to pass to the Commonwealth from the Soviet Union.

As it stands now, little real power has passed to the Commonwealth and only the functions explicitly agreed to it by its members have even formally been bestowed on the Commonwealth. But it is still evolving and new chal-

lenges, especially in the economic area and from further fragmentation, are forcing grudging cooperation even among suspicious new countries. The fear remains that powerful voices in the new Russia would just as soon re-create the old Soviet Union—or the old Russian empire. The new Russia is, after all, a descendant of both the Soviet Union and Tsarist Russia. It contains today elements of both these previous incarnations along with new dynamics and leaders. The result of Russia's internal struggle, the outcome of its new "time of troubles," will be a key factor in determining the fate not only of Russia and the Commonwealth, but of much of the rest of the world, including the United States.

REFERENCES AND SUGGESTED READINGS

Bremmer, Ian, and Ray Taras, eds. 1993. *Nations and Politics in the Soviet Successor States.* Cambridge, England: Cambridge University Press.

Cole, J. P. 1984. *Geography of the Soviet Union.* London: Butterworths.

Diller, Daniel C. 1993. *Russia and the Independent States,* expanded reference edition. Washington, D.C.: Congressional Quarterly.

Treadgold, Donald W. 1987. *Twentieth Century Russia.* Boulder, Colo.: Westview Press.

Twining, David T. 1992. *The New Eurasia: A Guide to the Republics of the Former Soviet Union.* Westport, Conn.: Praeger.

Wilson, Andrew, and Nina Bachkatov. 1992. *Russia and the Commonwealth A to Z.* New York: Harper-Collins.

28

Historical Antecedents

The modern state of Russia has roots in both Europe and Asia, and its territory has had conquerors from both regions. In what is now European Russia and Ukraine, various nomadic empires ruled before the birth of Christ: the Cimmerians, Scythians, Sarmatians. A brief period of Greek influence was then destroyed by the emergence of the successive power of the Goths and, from central Asia, the Huns, Avars, Khazars, and Magyars.

RUSSIA BEFORE THE BOLSHEVIK REVOLUTION

One of two European forerunners of modern Russia was the state known as Rus, which was formed around Kiev near the end of the ninth century and lasted until the mid-thirteenth century. It was during its dominion that the Slavs were converted to orthodox, or eastern, Christianity—forcibly by decree of their ruler Vladimir, at the end of the tenth century.

Kievan Rus was to disappear as an independent entity in the thirteenth century under the onslaught of the Mongols, who at the same time also conquered the area around Moscow. It was in this latter area that the core of the later Russian empire and the Soviet Union developed. The medieval state of Muscovy was able to expand its power gradually against a weakening Mongol empire and eventually, by the end of the sixteenth century, defeat and replace the power of the Khans in Europe.

But Muscovy's enemies were as numerous as the drive of its successive leaders for power was strong. Ivan IV, better known as

Ivan the Terrible, was the first to take the title of *Tsar*, possibly derived from the Roman title of *Caesar*, in 1547. But he was only one of many autocrats whose power to determine the fate of his subjects was challenged by internal rebellion or external foe, not by political institutions or culture. For the next three centuries, wars and campaigns continued against Poland, Sweden, and Lithuania in the west, the Tartars and Turks in the south, and the remains of the Mongol empire in Siberia and the far east. By the beginning of the eighteenth century, Russia was officially an empire, the title having been taken by Peter the Great in 1721. By the end of that century, with the final partition of Poland, the territorial base of the empire extended from central Europe to the Pacific.

Social, economic, and political development did not match the pace of territorial expansion, however. The power of the tsar grew and covered all key aspects of the lives of his subjects, from labor to faith. Though advisory councils and assemblies existed from time to time— even under Ivan the Terrible there was a *zemskii sobor* or landed assembly—their powers were limited and frequently changed by the ruler. The overwhelming mass of the population, which was the peasantry, had no effective representation and, under various forms of serfdom, little personal or economic freedom. Reforms could and did take place during the imperial period, with those of Peter the Great (1694–1725), Catherine II (1762–1796), Alexander I (1801–1825), and Alexander II (1855–1881) being most significant. Such reforms were important for modernizing the military, administration, and education of the empire; but they did little to increase the influence of the *narod*, or people, on government policies. Moreover, reforms could be and often were reversed—sometimes by the same autocrat who had decreed them. By the end of the nineteenth century, there had developed in the Russian empire no effective institutional structures

of the types seen in England or the United States that could counter the power of the Tsar or, just as crucial, provide a legal forum or moderate alternative for reform movements or individuals.

The Tsar sat at the center of a multinational empire. More than half the population was not Russian. National groups subject to his rule ranged from native peoples of Siberia, subdued during the empire's eastward expansion, to part or all of formerly independent countries, like Poland, which had once been empires themselves.

Economically, the empire was behind the states of western Europe at the end of the last century but was gaining fast. Coal extraction tripled between 1890 and 1905, at which time Russia was the world's fifth largest producer. At the outbreak of World War I the empire produced more steel and cotton than France and nearly as much pig iron. Though well behind the industrial powers of Germany, Great Britain, and the United States, Russia was still among the world's top five industrial powers.

But the core of the country's economy lay in agriculture. Progress in this sector was hurt by the continued economic oppression of peasants, who had been emancipated from serfdom in 1861 but who were made to pay massive compensation for the land given them. Redistributed land was usually of the poorest quality and in allotments that were too small to be economical. In addition, rapid population growth, the fastest in Europe, increased pressure on the land and in the cities. Desire was strong among the peasantry for more and better land, among the workers for better working conditions, and among various political groupings for a different, more responsive form of government.

An additional critical difference between Russia and France or Germany at this time was the absence of an industrial or commercial middle class, what historian Richard Pipes calls "the missing bourgeoisie." In Western Europe such groups were interested in stronger civil administration, political rights for people with property, and less arbitrary dictatorial rule by the king. They had been central in the struggle to reduce the power of the monarch. In Russia such a group was still tiny, owing to the economic monopoly exercised by the Tsar, the continued power of the nobility, and the fact that most of the vigorous sectors of the rapidly growing industrial economy were foreign-owned.[1]

In addition, even among people who wanted to change things in Russia, not everyone favored imitation of institutions found in western Europe. A strong strain in Russian thought during the nineteenth century was "Slavophilism," a glorification of the uniqueness of Russia and its people. Adherents to this view felt that the country should seek a return to its own values of rural, collective life and the Orthodox religion, and reject the bureaucratic states and individualism of the West. Politically, such views took the form of conservative or even reactionary political groups.

Such views were complemented by the growing strength of nationalism. As happened in western Europe during this time, nationalism tended to glorify not only the nation and its titular people, but also whatever extension of rule could be achieved through empire. Thus this period saw a more vigorous "Russification" of non-Russian peoples in the empire.

Opposing the Slavophile view were several different lines of thought, held by people considered "westernizers," or those who felt Russia could advance only by borrowing institutions and ideas from the West including, for some, socialism.

Some reform-minded groups argued that Russia could develop along the lines of the western parliamentary democracies. But the country lacked a strong force for moderate reform or any historical precedent for it. Through

the centuries, opposition to the Tsar or his policies had tended to take the form of outright rebellion, such as that of Pugachev against Catherine II in 1773–1774, conspiracy, such as that of the Decembrists against Nicholas I in 1825, or radical actions such as the terrorism of the "People's Will" group that in 1881 assassinated Tsar Alexander II.

Marxism thus came to a country which in the late nineteenth century looked quite different from that described in Marx's *Capital*. It was overwhelmingly (87 percent) rural and peasant, without a dominant bourgeoisie, a large proletariat, or the type of political system—parliamentary democracy—Marx had insisted would exist as the handmaiden of the ruling propertied class and precursor to the final, workers' revolution.

In Germany, for example, the dominant strain of Marxism at this time was social democracy. Adherents of the philosophy of "evolutionary socialism" ran for office in the *Reichstag*, developed programs for modifying the worst excesses of capitalism, and formed through parties and trade unions a representative political force for a growing working class. In Russia, faced with an unmodified autocratic system and the absence of such representative opportunities, Marxism tended toward a more radical revolutionary form. There were those such as Georgii Plekhanov, considered the father of Russian Marxism, who argued for some similar form of social democracy and for supporting in Russia the bourgeois revolution that had occurred in western Europe, only then bringing about the proletarian revolution that Marxism said would inevitably occur. But Vladimir Ilich Ulianov, born in 1870 and better known by his revolutionary name, Lenin, favored a more radical line. He argued in a booklet published in 1902, *What Is to Be Done?*, that what was needed was a small secret party of "professional revolutionaries" who would strive not for parlia-

On the morning of January 9, 1905, a procession led by the priest Georgii Gapon marched to the Winter Palace of the Tsar. During the resulting confrontation, over 1,000 people were killed. This "Bloody Sunday" ushered in the first Russian Revolution.

mentary representation or the improvement of working conditions—an approach labeled "economism"—but for the overthrow of the entire system.

Adherents of the two approaches split the Russian Social Democratic Party at its second Congress held in Brussels in 1903. Those who supported Lenin's views were declared by him to be *"bolsheviki"* or the majority, even though they had been outvoted at the congress on several key issues. Those supporting the less radical line were termed *"mensheviki,"* the minority.

There were also other groups opposed to the way the Russian autocracy was operating. There were the liberals, such as Paul Miliukov, who favored the establishment of a system of government more like that of a western parlia-

mentary democracy; anarchists, such as Mikhail Bakunin, who opposed a strong state of any kind; and there were Socialist Revolutionaries, whose program derived more from the needs of the peasantry than those of the industrial working class.

Slowly some changes did occur in the Tsarist government. In 1906 the first quasiparliamentary institution, the *Duma*, met. Though representation as well as the power of the body was severely restricted, it did represent the first institutional form by which society could possibly limit the discretion of government.

Even this limited step had been forced by revolution. In 1904, with economic grievances mounting on the side of both the peasants and the industrial workers, a disastrous

Lenin in his office in the Kremlin, 1918.

war with Japan put even more pressure on Russian society, which had to finance the war and fill the Tsar's armed forces. In St. Petersburg, which was then the capital of imperial Russia, workers marching to present their grievances to the Tsar on January 22, 1905, were attacked by palace guards. Many people were killed and "Bloody Sunday" proved a stimulus to revolution.

The attempt was ultimately unsuccessful due to the low level of organization of revolutionary forces and the fact that the Tsar's armed forces remained loyal. But the revolution of 1905 had galvanized a broad base of opposition among workers and peasants and it did force the Tsar to convene the new Duma. Though this institution remained relatively weak and grew weaker when electoral laws reduced representation of the peasantry even further—significant land reforms were undertaken by Prime Minister Peter Stolypin and the situation for industrial workers improved somewhat.

But the fundamental problems of autocratic Russia that had taken centuries to come to a head could not be solved speedily enough. Most peasants remained in desperate straits, and they as well as industrial workers still had influence over public policy only through radical action and only if the Tsar accepted it. For example, two successive Dumas were dissolved by the Tsar when they proved uncooperative.

Opposition to reforms was strong among conservative forces; and when Stolypin was assassinated in 1911 and a reputed "holy man," Grigorii Rasputin, began to have influence in the royal family because of his ability to ease the pain of the Tsar's hemophiliac son, movement toward solving Russia's difficulties stopped altogether.

The outbreak of World War I in 1914 was to prove the last straw. A peasantry eager for land and prosperity was instead conscripted to fight, and sent to do so poorly fed, clothed, equipped, trained, and led. And the numerically small but strategically located industrial workers were, in William Chamberlain's words, "sufficiently literate to grasp elementary socialist ideas, sufficiently wretched to welcome the first opportunity to pull down the temple of private property."[2] Economic and political reform was put off by the exigencies of the war, which dragged on with little hope of victory by Russia or its allies (Britain and France) against Austria-Hungary and Germany.

Revolutionary Marxists, especially Lenin, had tried to use the war as a rallying cry to get the world's proletariat to fight against their own governments instead of each other. Lenin saw the war as a battle among monopoly capitalists to divide up the world; the role of the workers was to oppose such a war and use it to bring down rather than support their governments.[3] But Lenin's call was not heeded and socialist parties throughout Europe chose to support their governments. In Russia, though, as the situation worsened, the opportunity arose for putting revolutionary words into practice.

THE BOLSHEVIKS COME TO POWER

The end of the autocracy did not come at the hands of Lenin or the Bolsheviks but as a spontaneous chain reaction begun in Petrograd (as St. Petersburg was called after 1914) as a demonstration for bread, joined by rebellious troops and ending in the abdication of the Tsar on March 15, 1917. The new provisional government, headed by Prince Georgii Lvov, was welcomed by Russia's allies and attracted the support of several nonsocialist political parties. But substantial power was also held by the *soviet* (or council) of workers' and soldiers' deputies, which was dominated by the socialist parties. The government favored and promised reform, but on the key issues troubling Russian society—an end to the war, land reform, and social welfare for workers—little movement was evident. Some of the socialist parties, such as the Mensheviks, cooperated with the new government, and in July a Socialist Revolutionary, Alexander Kerensky, became prime minister. Lenin, however, counseled against such cooperation and instead, in his famous "April theses" delivered upon his return to Russia from exile, called for continuing the revolution and handing "all power to the soviets." Indeed during the summer of 1917 a system of "dual power" developed with the provisional government exercising some authority, the workers' soviets some, and in much of the country no one exercising much authority at all.

In July another uprising occurred, this time against the provisional government, taking it and the revolutionary Marxists by surprise. Uncoordinated and lacking strong leadership, the movement was crushed by armed forces remaining loyal to the government. No sooner had this danger been defeated than a threat to the government arose from the armed forces themselves. General Lavr Kornilov, the commander-in-chief, tried to march on the capital in August and destroy the powerful Petrograd soviet. However, the government relied on parties of the Left and armed workers to defeat the coup attempt.

But the war dragged on, land reform was delayed, and the soldiers began to "vote with their feet"—they deserted their posts and the provisional government. Lenin, who had fled to Finland after the July uprising, returned to Russia in October and stunned his followers by proclaiming that the time was right to take power from the weak provisional government. The Bolsheviks were a tiny party and even among socialists they were a distinct minority except in Petrograd and Moscow, where they finally persuaded the local soviets to their views that autumn. Lenin's view on immediately taking power was supported by the Bolshevik central committee in a vote on October 10. On October 25 by the old calendar (now November 7), soldiers and sailors supporting the insurrection occupied key parts of the city, the provisional government collapsed, and, at least in Petrograd, the Bolsheviks were in power.

Having declared themselves in power, however, did not mean that Lenin and the Bolsheviks actually ruled the country. In November 1917, in the last competitive national elections the country was to see for more than seventy years, a Constituent Assembly was elected. This body, promised by the provisional government and supported by all the parties, was to determine the form and policy of the new state. But the majority of delegates were Socialist Revolutionaries; the Bolsheviks had received just under 10 million of the nearly 42 million votes cast and roughly one-fourth of the seats. When the Constituent Assembly met early the next year and refused to accept the Bolshevik program, it was dispersed by force. The new government moved to suppress opposition parties and remnants of the provisional government. Within a month after taking power it signed an armistice with Germany. In March 1918 a peace treaty was signed, ending Soviet involvement in World War I and bringing down on the new state the wrath of its former allies. British, French, American, and Japanese troops landed in northern and southern European Russia and in the Far East between 1918 and 1919. With the help of the Czech legion, a group of soldiers who had been fighting against Germany and were trapped inside Russia when the war ended, this intervention almost succeeded in "strangling the Bolshevik

baby in its cradle," as Winston Churchill put it. The Bolsheviks managed to survive, however, but soon faced a much tougher test in a vicious civil war against various groups, referred to as "Whites," who opposed the "Red" government. This civil war lasted until 1921. During this war, an additional brief war was fought in 1920 against Poland, sparked by Polish attempts to regain territory held before its dismemberment and continued by Soviet attempts to spread the revolution westward. At one point, the soldiers of the Polish state, itself a republic reborn after 1918, held Kiev. Ultimately, the success of the new Communist government against such an array of enemies can be attributed as much to the disarray and differences in political designs among its enemies (western democracies, White supporters of everything from the monarchy to peasant rebellion, and restive nationality groups) as to its own strength. Still, by the end of the civil war the Soviet government was in control of most of the old Russian empire.

POLITICS AND POLICIES BETWEEN THE WARS

In the face of its many crises, the Bolshevik approach was to try to establish virtually total control of the country's productive forces. Under what came to be known as "war communism," the government nationalized every form of production in the country and tried to exercise total state control over all citizens under what Leon Trotsky characterized as the "mobilization of labor." The state became the sole sanctioned buyer and seller of all goods. The program was a reaction to the country's extreme emergency filtered through the radical ideology of the Bolsheviks. The effect was disastrous. The historian E. H. Carr describes it:

A catastrophic decline in industrial production, due in part to the destruction of plants, in part to the disorganization of labour, in part to the cumbrous system of centralized administration represented by the glavki [chief committees that directed the economy] had been followed by a virtual breakdown of state or state-controlled distribution of commodities at fixed prices, leading to a rapid growth of illicit private trade at runaway prices and a wild currency inflation; and this in turn had prompted the refusal of the peasant, in the face of a goods famine and a worthless currency, to deliver necessary supplies of grain to the towns, so that population was progressively drained away from the industrial centres, and industrial production brought still nearer to a standstill.[4]

In 1921, after demonstrations in Petrograd and a brief rebellion among sailors in Kronstadt, a "New Economic Policy" (NEP) was declared. The new policy allowed a mixture of capitalist and socialist institutions to grow in the country. The regime retained what Lenin called "the commanding heights" of the economy: banking, foreign trade, and large industry. State control in most other areas was reversed, a market was allowed to operate again, and most important, the pressure on the country's peasantry was eased. Instead of having grain requisitioned, for example, farmers were allowed to pay a "tax in kind" after which they could sell their products on the open market. Private enterprise flourished, especially in the retail area; for example, in Moscow in 1922, 83 percent of all retail trade was private.[5]

Industry began to recover during this period—steel production increased nearly tenfold between 1921 and 1925—but investment capital was scarce, the price of industrial goods rose much faster than that of agricultural goods (the so-called scissors effect) and by most indicators the industrial development of the country was still well behind where it had been before World War I. At the same time, a political struggle was beginning among those who would succeed Lenin, who had suffered a stroke in 1922 and died in 1924. Lenin left no clear heir. But in a letter regarded as his last testament, he spoke affectionately of Nikolai Bukharin and critically about Joseph Stalin. Nevertheless, through a combination of manipulation of party personnel, political adroitness, and exploitation of the character of his opponents—Trotsky, for example, was reluctant to lead a full-scale challenge to Stalin after Lenin's death[6]—Stalin was able to outmaneuver first Trotsky and other leaders from the revolution, Grigorii Zinoviev and Lev Kamenev, and then Bukharin, to assume dominant leadership of the party by the time of the Fifteenth Party Congress in 1927. In a major ideological pronouncement, Stalin enunciated the policy of building "socialism in one country"; that is, concentrating on strengthening the one socialist country that then existed, as revolutions had by then failed throughout Europe and, in the most bloody fiasco, in China.

Economically, this policy meant pushing the country forward much more rapidly. Like Lenin before him, Stalin believed that for socialism to be possible a modern industrial economy had to be built. Unlike the policies seen during NEP, however, Stalin as well as many others in the party favored a much more rapid and state-controlled process. At the end of the 1920s, Stalin pushed the Soviet Union into what has been called a second revolution, one directed from above. Gradually at first and then abruptly, the mixed-economy policies of the New Economic Policy were replaced by more and more state control. In 1929 the first five-year plan was announced, setting extremely ambitious quotas for rapidly and broadly industrializing the country. Coal and oil production were to double in the five years, iron ore to more than triple, and campaigns were orchestrated to fulfill the plan in only four years. Millions of new workers were mobilized—employment in the state economy grew 55 percent

In December 1922 Lenin dictated a letter evaluating his potential successors. Though published in the West soon after, its existence remained a party secret until Nikita Khrushchev quoted from the letter at the Twentieth Party Congress in 1956. Of his colleagues Lenin said:

> Comrade Stalin, having become General Secretary, has concentrated an enormous power in his hands; and I am not sure that he always knows how to use that power with sufficient caution. On the other hand, Comrade Trotsky, as was proved by his struggle against the Central Committee in connection with the question of the People's Commissariat of Ways and Communications, is distinguished not only by his exceptional abilities—personally he is, to be sure, the most able man in the present Central Committee—but also by his too far-reaching self-confidence and a disposition to be too much attracted by the purely administrative side of affairs.
>
> These two qualities of the two most able leaders of the present Central Committee might, quite innocently, lead to a split; if our party does not take measures to prevent it, a split might arise unexpectedly.
>
> I will not further characterize the other members of the Central Committee as to their personal qualities. I will only remind you that the October episode of Zinoviev and Kamenev [when they voted against and publicly opposed the Bolshevik takeover] was not, of course, accidental, but that it ought as little to be used against them personally as the non-Bolshevism of Trotsky.
>
> Of the younger members of the Central Committee, I want to say a few words about Bukharin and Pyatakov. They are in my opinion, the most able forces (among the youngest) and in regard to them it is necessary to bear in mind the following: Bukharin is not only the most valuable and biggest theoretician of the party, but also

> may legitimately be considered the favorite of the whole party; but his theoretical views can only with the very greatest doubt be regarded as fully Marxist, for there is something scholastic in him (he never has learned, and I think never has fully understood, the dialectic).
>
> And then Pyatakov—a man undoubtedly distinguished in will and ability, but too much given over to administration and the administrative side of things to be relied on in a serious political question.
>
> Of course, both these remarks are made by me merely with view to the present time, or supposing that these two able and loyal workers may not find an occasion to supplement their knowledge and correct their one-sidedness.
> December 25, 1922

Ten days later Lenin added a pointed postscript about Stalin:

> Postscript: Stalin is too rude, and this fault, entirely supportable in relations among us Communists, becomes insupportable in the office of General Secretary. Therefore, I propose to the comrades to find a way to remove Stalin from that position and appoint to it another man who in all respects differs from Stalin only in superiority—namely, more patient, more loyal, more polite and more attentive to comrades, less capricious, etc. This circumstance may seem an insignificant trifle, but I think that from the point of view of preventing a split and from the point of view of the relation between Stalin and Trotsky which I discussed above, it is not a trifle, or it is such a trifle as may acquire a decisive significance.
> January 4, 1923

Source: "Lenin's Testament," *The Crimes of the Stalin Era: Special Report to the 20th Congress of the Communist Party of the Soviet Union* (New York: The New Leader, 1962). Reprinted with permission of *The Newsletter,* July 16, 1956, pp. 566–567.

between 1927 and 1932—largely from peasants driven off their land into collective farms.[7] This industrial policy, referred to as "the great turn," was matched by a complete reversal of agricultural policy. Private trading and especially better-off peasants, referred to as *kulaks*, were eliminated, and through various measures, including taxation, coercion, and widespread terror, peasants were forced to merge their land into collective farms. As in the cities, the state assumed full control of the rural economy in a breathtakingly short time. In September 1929, 7.4 percent of the land was collectivized; by December of the same year, 59.3 percent of the land had been collectivized. After a brief pause in early 1930, during which Stalin declared that those implementing the program were "dizzy with success," pressure on the peasant farmer resumed and collectivization was completed by the mid-1930s.

The economic mobilization of the country both in the cities and in the countryside was accompanied by an immense rise in the power of the state over all aspects of the society and the economy. Spheres of public and private activity not controlled by the state disappeared in a fashion not seen since before the "great reforms" of Alexander II. While the legal freeing of the serfs by that Tsar might be termed emancipation without development, this period is referred to by Moshe Lewin as "development without emancipation."[8]

Politically, the 1930s saw the rise to personal preeminence of Joseph Stalin. While the campaign to transform the country's economy and society was continuing, foes real and imagined were also eliminated by arrest, deportation, imprisonment, and execution. In 1934 Sergei Kirov, the party secretary of Leningrad and reported to be an opponent of Stalin's policies, was assassinated under circumstances that were never fully revealed. Using this as evidence of a broad conspiracy, Stalin and those supporting him launched a purge of the leadership of the party and other key institutions. Of

139 full and candidate members of the party central committee in 1934, 98 were arrested and shot by 1938, according to Nikita Khrushchev, who ought to have known. In the army, one-half the officer corps were purged, including three of five marshals, more than half of all brigade, division, corps, and army commanders, 90 percent of all generals and 80 percent of all colonels.[9] In some cases show trials were staged during which one-time political opponents were forced to confess that they had tried to undermine the system or that they were working for the country's enemies. After one such trial in 1938, Nikolai Bukharin was executed along with several other prominent "Old Bolsheviks." Leon Trotsky had long since been exiled from the country; but when he was murdered in Mexico in 1940, it was widely believed to be on Stalin's orders.

The purges and associated terror spread throughout society and reached their peak between 1936 and 1938. The exact number of people displaced, arrested, or executed may never be known, but is estimated to total nearly twenty million.[10] Their "crimes" may have been economic, for example, profiting under the NEP system; or political, being associated with one of the losing party leaders; or nonexistent, simply being the unfortunate victims of a local leader's desire to settle a score or secure the job of a purged superior. According to Stalin himself, one-half million people moved up in the party and state during this period. Whatever the national or local motives, the human misery unleashed was of staggering dimensions and transformed the Soviet Union.

Economically the accomplishments were significant. By the end of the first five-year plan, gross industrial production (as measured in 1926–1927 prices) more than doubled and national income increased by nearly 90 percent. These figures more than doubled again by the end of the second five-year plan, 1937, by which time coal production was more than three times what it had been in 1928. Oil production more than doubled, steel and pig iron output increased by a factor of four and electricity capacity by a factor of seven.[11] But the upheaval in the countryside caused by the forced collectivization and return to compulsory deliveries, as well as a lack of investment in agriculture, produced retrograde results. In resistance to collectivization, peasants slaughtered their livestock by the millions. Between 1928 and 1932, the number of horses and cattle in the country fell 42 percent, the number of pigs by more than one-half, and sheep and goats by nearly two-thirds. Grain production fell, and during 1931 and 1932 widespread famine and related diseases killed an estimated five million people.[12] Grain production did not equal 1928 levels again until 1937, and most production still had not recovered by the outbreak of World War II.

THE IMPACT OF WORLD WAR II

If the great turn, forced collectivization, and the terror of the 1930s were a homemade shock to the people of the Soviet Union, the effects of World War II were an externally generated catastrophe. As noted in Chapter 34, the Soviet Union tried to buy time by signing nonaggression pacts with its most dangerous enemies, Germany (1939) and Japan (1941). Given Hitler's ambitions and his view of the proper role in the universe for all Slavic peoples (slaves) and for Communists especially (dead), it was simply a matter of time before he got around to attacking and invading the USSR, which he did in June 1941.

During the initial period of the war that Soviet historiography referred to as "The Great Patriotic War," the Soviet Union yielded vast lands to German invasion—a territory equal to the size of France in the first six weeks. The military's retreat involved "scorching the earth" behind it so as to leave nothing of value for the approaching enemy. When in 1942 the

country was able to mount a counterattack and then an offensive against the invader, more lives were lost and land and industry suffered again. From 1941 until the middle of 1944, the Soviet Union faced Hitler's armies virtually alone in continental Europe. Though supplied by Allied lend-lease and aided eventually by the Allied landing at Normandy, France, in June 1944, the price of driving out and defeating the aggressor was immense.

During the war the political system of the Soviet Union became less ideological, more nationalistic. Citizens were asked to fight the invader for the *rodina*, the motherland, not for socialism or the revolution. Cultural repression that had accompanied the political terror of the 1930s was eased a bit as the regime sought to replace its previous war against society with as close a union as possible in order to defeat the enemy.

When the war ended, the Stalinist system of political and economic management returned. Five-year plans with high quotas, imbalance of investment favoring heavy industry at the expense of consumer goods and agriculture, and even political terror returned. Soldiers who had been in German prison camps during the war, for example, were routinely sent to labor camps, which once again became filled with those accused or suspected of disloyalty. The secret police under Lavrenty Beria resumed its role as guarantor of the political dominance of Stalin over the party and the entire society. With a country to rebuild and new Communist nations installed throughout Eastern Europe (see Chapter 37), the ideological heat was turned up again both domestically and in foreign policy. Externally, this was a period of "Cold War" with the West, as both the Soviet Union and the United States struggled to secure allies for their vision of how the postwar world should look. At home the country made a rapid recovery in the targeted industrial sectors, such as steel, oil production, and electrical energy. Production (as measured in constant prices) doubled by

Wartime Destruction of the Soviet Union

Human Cost:

20,000,000 dead,* of which:

 7,000,000 soldiers killed (4,000,000 in POW camps)

 6,000,000 died in Nazi occupied zone

 4,000,000 died in Nazi labor camps

 3,000,000 died in unoccupied zone (of war-related injuries)

1 out of every 8 Soviet citizens in 1939 died during World War II

97 percent of the males ages 17 to 20 (in 1941) died

Millions wounded, handicapped, severely weakened physically

In 1959, there were only 4 males for every 7 females ages 35–50

50 Soviet citizens died for every American who died

Physical Damage:

1,710 towns wholly or partly destroyed

70,000 villages wholly or partly destroyed

25,000,000 homeless in 1945

   50 percent of all urban living space destroyed

   75 percent of all rural living space destroyed

30 percent of national wealth destroyed

2/3 of wealth in occupied zone destroyed

 Industrial Destruction:

   31,850 industrial enterprises destroyed (formerly employed 4,000,000)

   40,000 miles of railroad track destroyed

   4,100 railroad stations destroyed

   13,000 bridges destroyed

   15,800 locomotives destroyed

   428,000 railway cars destroyed

 Agricultural Destruction:

   98,000 kolkhozi (collective farms)

   1,876 sovkhozi (state farms)

   2,890 machine-tractor stations

   137,000 tractors (= 30% of 1939 total)

   5,000,000 pieces of mechanical equipment

   7,000,000 horses (= 34% of 1939 total)

   17,000,000 cattle (= 30% of 1939 total)

   20,000,000 hogs (= 71% of 1939 total)

   27,000,000 sheep and goats (= 29% of 1939 total)

   110,000,000 poultry

In 1953, the number of horses, cattle, sheep and goats was less than that in 1928.

*Recent estimates put this figure at 27,000,000.

Source: Compiled by William Chase, Department of History, University of Pittsburgh.

1950. Once again, though, agriculture did not do as well, and in this sphere production in 1950 had not even returned to 1940 levels.[13]

CHANGE OF DIRECTION UNDER NIKITA KHRUSHCHEV

Soviet politics during the period after Stalin's death were distinguished by a shift away from what can be called a "totalitarian" phase of mass mobilization, personal dictatorship, and widespread use of terror against both political opponents and the public. Under Nikita Khrushchev politics were still dominated by the elite of the Communist Party; but new directions were attempted in both domestic and foreign policy, and battles among elites over power and policy emerged into the open.

When Stalin died in 1953, his replacement as party leader was Nikita Khrushchev, who had been party head in Ukraine, while Georgii Malenkov, another of Stalin's lieutenants, became prime minister. Malenkov began to articulate a "new course" for the Soviet Union that would include reducing the traditional emphasis on heavy industry, investing more in things the population needed— such as housing—and in agriculture, and, most important, returning to "socialist legality" by ending the use of terror. He also suggested that there could be peaceful resolution of conflicts between the Soviet Union and the West.

At first, Khrushchev opposed these notions and allied with the more orthodox members of the leadership. He held to a more hostile foreign policy position vis-à-vis the West and suggested dealing with the country's chronic agricultural problem by opening up for cultivation vast new lands in Siberia and elsewhere, the so-called virgin lands program. In April 1955 Khrushchev, with the support of the more conservative forces such as Lazar Kaganovich and Vyacheslav Molotov, succeeded in removing Malenkov from the premiership. He was replaced by Nikolai Bulganin.

But soon Khrushchev adopted many of the very policies he had previously denounced. Most significantly, he pressed the attack against the personality and policies of Stalin. In an extraordinary speech to the Twentieth Party Congress in February 1956, Khrushchev bluntly attacked Stalin for betraying the Leninist legacy, for ignoring the party, subordinating it to the will of one person, and terrorizing it with the secret police. Khrushchev named names, gave dates and statistics, and pronounced Stalin "sickly suspicious." He accused him of developing a "cult of personality," seeking self-glorification, and virtual treason in the face of the enemy. When the country needed him most, Khrushchev said, during World War II, Stalin virtually collapsed. "After the first severe disaster and defeat at the front," Khrushchev said, "Stalin thought that this was the end. . . . Even after the war began, the nervousness and hysteria which Stalin demonstrated, interfering with actual military operation, caused our Army serious damage."[14]

By enumerating Stalin's crimes, Khrushchev was not telling the party elite anything they did not know. Rather, he was declaring war on the old elite by detailing these horrors before the party and giving hope to new party cadres and the population that things would be different. For this reason, Khrushchev had to defeat more than one counterattack aimed at weakening his power, and in 1957 he removed Malenkov, Molotov and Kaganovich, whom he labeled the "antiparty group," from the party's ruling body. Replacing people wholesale at the Central Committee level and, after 1957, at the level of the *Presidium* (as the Politburo was then called) protected Khrushchev and his new policies, but he remained a vulnerable leader and ultimately aroused sufficient opposition to cause his downfall in 1964.

During his tenure as First Secretary, Khrushchev made moves aimed at reducing the dominant central control of the economy held by the government and stimulating more local control through the party and the soviets. In 1957 economic councils or *sovnarkhozi* were created throughout the country to run the economy on a regional basis instead of by the powerful ministries from the center. This reform engendered the opposition of those who enjoyed power under the ministry system, and it had the additional disadvantage of not working well for the economy either. In 1963 the effort was cut back and the number of councils reduced. After Khrushchev's departure the ministries were restored to power.

Khrushchev also favored increasing local participation both within the party and from the public. In 1962 the party was divided into industrial and agrarian branches with the aim of making the party more responsive to and involved with the economic needs of local enterprises. The machine tractor stations, which held the equipment for the collective farms and were a hallmark of the collectivization effort, were abolished in 1958, and collective farms were entitled to have their own equipment. Citizen involvement in the soviets was encouraged and Khrushchev made bold promises about "catching and overtaking" the United States in the quality of life. Though it wasn't called it at the time, Khrushchev also encouraged a limited amount of *glasnost* or voicing of problems, and allowed publication of previously banned writings. In 1962, reportedly at his personal intervention, Aleksandr Solzhenitsyn's *One Day in the Life of Ivan Denisovich*, an explicit description of life in a Stalinist labor camp, was published.

As with the *sovnarkhozi*, these moves stirred opposition: from those whose positions were threatened; from those like most of the upper echelons of the party—including Khrushchev himself—who had come to power under Stalin; and from those who feared that discussing forbidden subjects like the recent past might lead to attacks on the current system. In addition,

The Question of Responsibility

The joke is told that in 1956 when Nikita Khrushchev was giving his speech to the 20th Party Congress condemning Stalin for persecuting and executing real and imagined opponents and for the widespread use of terror, a voice from the back of the hall yelled, "Comrade Khrushchev, where were you when all of this was going on?"

Khrushchev looked up sharply, "Who said that?" he demanded

No hand was raised or person stood to acknowledge the question.

"That's where I was," said Khrushchev.

Khrushchev's foreign policy failures and embarrassments weakened his position. Despite a visit to Yugoslavia in 1955 and declaration of support for the idea of "many roads to socialism," Khrushchev was unable to woo that country back into the Soviet camp. Indeed, the next year Hungary had to be kept there forcibly. Worse than that, the leaders of the world's other major Communist country, China, began attacking what they called "revisionism" in domestic policy and Soviet moves to improve relations with the United States in the early 1960s. Their attacks soon provoked an open break, taking tiny Albania with them. In relations with the West, despite the summit with the United States, including the first visit ever by a Soviet leader to the United States in 1959, Khrushchev was unable to restrain the growth of American power. In 1961 an attempt to force the western allies out of Berlin (still occupied by the four victors in World War II) produced fruitless tension and a Soviet failure. This was followed in 1962 by an even more dangerous gambit, the placing of medium-range nuclear missiles in Cuba. In this case, the United States responded with a naval blockade of Soviet ally Cuba and a public demand that the Soviet Union remove the missiles. The world was literally taken to the brink of nuclear war, and after heated internal debate the Soviet Union agreed to remove the missiles in return for a pledge by the United States not to invade Cuba. The incident proved an international embarrassment and a domestic blow to Khrushchev.

By 1964, with the country's economy doing poorly, with policy administration in turmoil and a foreign policy going backward, Khrushchev was removed and replaced as party leader by Leonid Brezhnev and as prime minister, an office Khrushchev had assumed in 1958, by Alexei Kosygin.

The Brezhnev Era

The ensuing period of Soviet politics was generally one of increasingly conservative, even immobile, domestic policy combined with an active but not always successful foreign policy. Leonid Brezhnev, himself an associate of Khrushchev, was able to remove political rivals such as Nikolai Podgorny, who became chairman of the Presidium of the Supreme Soviet in 1965. He was eventually replaced by Brezhnev himself, who assumed what was essentially the presidency of the Soviet Union in 1977. Though Alexei Kosygin did remain prime minister until he was replaced by Nikolai Tikhonov in 1980, by the beginning of the 1970s Brezhnev was the most powerful political leader.

In contrast to the Khrushchev period, the top leadership during Brezhnev's tenure was characterized by what Brezhnev himself called "stability of cadres." For example, at Nikita Khrushchev's last party congress (1961), two-thirds of the Central Committee elected had not been full members four years before. At the time of the 1971 party congress under Brezhnev, 81 percent of the full members had held the posts five years before, and nearly 90 percent were re-elected at the next party congress (1976).[15] Changes in the Politburo—so renamed in 1966—were few and served mostly to make the top leadership older and more secure for Brezhnev. In 1973, for the first time in ten years, the head of the secret police (the KGB), Yuri Andropov, became a full Politburo member. Two other leaders who had made their careers chiefly outside the party apparatus also became full Politburo members: Foreign Minister Andrei Gromyko and Defense Minister Andrei Grechko. When Brezhnev became party leader (1964), the average age in the Politburo was 60; by the time of his death (1982) it was 67.

Broader domestic developments reflected this conservatism. The economic reforms Khrushchev had championed were undone and criticized; the ministries returned to full power and their number expanded. Reforms in prices and enterprise control that were announced in the mid-1960s were evaded, put off, and undone by the powerful bureaucracies. As Ed Hewett characterizes it, "the reform, never a terribly vibrant affair, was dead by the early 1970s."[16]

Although under Khrushchev a certain "thaw" had occurred, allowing the voicing of critical ideas and a more varied cultural scene, the policy under Brezhnev was one of relentless repression. In 1966 Soviet writers Andrei Siniavsky and Yuli Daniel were tried, convicted and sentenced to hard labor for publishing works *abroad* that were critical of the Soviet Union. Other trials and imprisonments followed and were complemented in some cases by forcing dissidents and uncompliant writers, such as Aleksandr Solzhenitsyn, to emigrate. While pursuing détente with the West and officially recognizing its obligation under its own constitution, of which a new version was published in 1977, and international treaties such as the Helsinki Accords of 1975, the Soviet regime nevertheless continued to crack down on political and human rights dissenters of all types. Groups set up to monitor Soviet adherence to international standards on human rights were smashed and their leaders sent to psychiatric hospitals or labor camps.

Without attendance to fundamental problems, the economy began to experience difficulties. The high growth rates of the 1960s and early 1970s gave way to slowing growth and stagnation. Agriculture turned in successive bad harvests and millions of tons of grain had to be imported. The living standard for the average Soviet citizen did improve but remained far behind those not only of the United States and Western Europe but of some Eastern European countries as well.

Though committed to little change at home, Leonid Brezhnev pushed an active policy of improving relations with the West, especially the United States. In this respect the Brezhnev period was a logical continuation, rather than a reversal, of the Khrushchev period. The nuclear test ban treaty of 1963 was followed by treaties banning nuclear weapons from outer space (1965), from the seabed (1970), and from being spread by the superpowers to other countries (nonproliferation, 1968). Negotiations began in 1969 for a strategic arms limitation treaty (SALT I) that was eventually signed and ratified by both sides (1972).

Despite the increased involvement of the United States in Vietnam during the 1960s and the Soviet invasion of Czechoslovakia in 1968, relations between the United States and Soviet Union improved. Summit visits were exchanged, and a treaty establishing the principles of relations between the two states was signed in 1972, in acknowledgment of the Soviet Union's status as a world power and an equal of the United States. Trade expanded in the early 1970s and in implicit response to U.S. concerns, Jewish emigration from the Soviet Union increased, reaching 35,000 in 1973.

But from the Soviet point of view, détente with the United States did not mean giving up its goal of securing more politically reliable friends worldwide. Preventing a nuclear holocaust or engaging in a mutually beneficial exchange of goods and ideas did not, in the Soviet view, mean that competition between the two systems would cease or that the USSR would stop helping revolutionary groups achieve power where they could, especially in the Third World. Soviet efforts to this effect in Africa, and their continued heavy investment in defense—especially nuclear weapons—contributed to disenchantment in the West over détente. In addition, in some areas progress was slowed or even reversed. The USSR's leaders rejected the Jackson-Vanik amendment (named after the U.S. senator and representative who sponsored it) to the 1974 trade law that explicitly linked the extension of economic benefits to the Soviet Union with its willingness to pose no barriers to free emigration. While the Soviet Union had eased emigration restrictions, as noted, they rejected the idea of letting the United States Congress annually review its behavior as a price for improved economic ties. Beyond that, continued repression of its own writers, artists, and political and religious dissenters eroded the basis of détente.

In 1979, NATO decided to install medium-range nuclear missiles in Western Europe in response to a massive buildup of such weapons in the western USSR. The presence of missiles in Europe that could hit the Kremlin in ten minutes provoked a massive—but unsuccessful—Soviet campaign directed against this decision and at stirring Western European opposition to accepting the missiles. Though negotiations on the SALT II treaty were completed and the treaty was signed in 1979 by Brezhnev and United States president Jimmy Carter, after the Soviet invasion of Afghanistan at the end of that year the president was obliged to withdraw the treaty from Senate consideration for fear it would be rejected. Détente was dead.

The last years of the Brezhnev regime saw a return to much harsher rhetoric, reminiscent of the early Cold War. The election of Ronald Reagan (1980), Soviet pressure on Poland to end the activity of the independent trade union Solidarity, and the infirmity and uncertainty evident in the Brezhnev Politburo meant that the great centerpiece of Brezhnev's international policy, détente with the United States, had been undone. Nor were there successes in Soviet relations with China, where hostility had not ceased with the death of Mao Zedong and was only increased by the Soviet invasion of Afghanistan; or with Eastern Europe, where the rise of Solidarity in Poland trumpeted profound disaffection and the economic figures throughout the whole region told bluntly of economic stagnation; or with the Middle East, where Soviet influence seemed to reach its nadir after the Israeli invasion of Lebanon in 1982 and the dispersal of the Soviet-supported Palestine Liberation Organization.

Thus in terms of domestic and international policy, the legacy of the Brezhnev regime was one of many serious problems whose solution had been put off too long. Worse, the bequest of the Brezhnev years to the country was a narrow, aging leadership that could not even attend immediately to its difficulties. When Brezhnev died in November 1982, his immediate successor, Yuri Andropov, did attempt some reforms. Campaigns were launched against corruption, which had grown to epidemic proportions under Brezhnev, and for greater labor discipline and efficiency. But at 68, Andropov's own poor health rendered him a weak leader, and his death in early 1984 ended this brief attempt to shake things up. International relations continued to deteriorate, with no ongoing negotiations with the United States on nuclear weapons. More spectacularly, the Soviet Union was condemned virtually throughout the world in September 1983 when its defense forces shot down a Korean Airlines passenger jet that had strayed over Soviet territory, killing 269 people.

Nor was Andropov's successor in any better position to revive either the Soviet economy or its international policy. Konstantin Chernenko was even older (72) than Andropov when he became general secretary in February 1984 and,

evidently, even sicker. Few policy initiatives were taken, but in early 1985 feelers were extended about beginning new negotiations on nuclear weapons once again. Chernenko was not to live to see them come to fruition, as he died in March 1985 and was replaced as general secretary by Mikhail Gorbachev.

THE PAST IN THE PRESENT

As this review indicates, some themes have persisted in Russian and Soviet history. Certainly autocratic rule, rule from the top down, has been the dominant mode. When autocracy became oppressive, the absence of moderate alternatives or effective opportunities for popular involvement in making changes was evident. Along with the violent upheavals this situation often produced, the very notion that the great mass of people have a legitimate status apart from their role as resource for the rulers to manipulate is a fairly recent one.

But the recent past has its own legacy and it may be even more detrimental to the ability of the Russian people to forge a new state, a new economy, and new relationship between government and people. Some analysts argue that decades of domination of public life and governance by the Communist Party, reinforced by pervasive restrictions on social life and economic activities, has placed an almost insurmountable barrier to democracy in the path of the current generation of Russians. It has, in this view, left a legacy of state-dependence and hostility toward government. Moreover, Soviet communism adopted a hostile posture toward most of the national communities of the country. Now, reactions against this may take the form of highly particularist nationalisms and scapegoating as people seek new communities to identify with and make up for their lack of participation in deciding their own fates. At best, reactions against omnipresent government and recurrent "mobilizations" could yield political apathy and passivity. Ironically, of course, both reactions could open the way for new threats to the very democracy some Russians are trying to create.

If the proposition suggesting decline in faith in government and growth in skepticism articulated in Chapter 2 is right for western Europe, it may be doubly so in Russia. Here the country's quite recent and very brief exposure to the mechanisms of democratic government has coincided with sharp economic decline, a degree of differentiation between rich and poor unknown since Tsarist days, and, for most people, a high degree of personal insecurity. Under such conditions and with such a legacy, the appeal of those who offer "order" instead of democracy and "empire" instead of commonwealth may prove irresistible.

At the same time, it is not unheard of for states to emerge from recent periods of even severe dictatorship to create working democracies, even under extremely difficult economic circumstances. Both Germany and Japan did so after World War II. The new democracies of Eastern Europe for the most part have created functioning and sometimes remarkably effective tools of governance in the very brief time they have had since the fall of Communist rule.

And despite its history of autocracy, Russia has had no lack of those willing to envision—and fight for—greater democracy. In the depths of the bureaucratic party dictatorship of Leonid Brezhnev, Andrei Sakharov, a "Hero of the Soviet Union" and a person with much to lose, articulated striking demands for personal liberty and a new and different Soviet state. Others, less well known than Sakharov, were ready to take risks and push for democratic change, even when it seemed that nothing would change.

But Russia has changed, and not just recently. It should be clear that even before the current upheavals, neither Russia nor the Soviet Union was an immobile, unchanging society with a fixed and immutable government. Just in this century alone this country has gone from a largely peasant, rural-based empire, through revolution and civil war to forced urbanization, industrialization, and collectivization of agriculture, two world wars, two recoveries, emergence into a position as world superpower, and, most recently, disintegration altogether.

Persisting throughout Russian history has been a certain kind of change—that is, one directed "from the top" by the rulers. Mikhail Gorbachev was not the first leader to try to make the system work better. Changes widespread enough to call them revolutions were instituted by Peter the Great, Alexander II, by the first Bolshevik leaders, and by Stalin. And both contemporary and earlier history show numerous examples of the "top" wanting subsequently to stop the changes once started, or even reverse them. Often the consequences of the changes begun—for example, by broadening the education of the population or by ending serfdom—proved unexpected or dangerous. Just as often they proved irreversible. That same dynamic occurred when changes were initiated by Mikhail Gorbachev. At the end of his period of reform, both he and the system he headed had disappeared.

Notes

1. Roger Muntig, *The Economic Development of the USSR* (New York: St. Martin's Press, 1982), p. 34; Richard Pipes, *Russia under the Old Regime* (New York: Charles Scribner's Sons, 1974), pp. 191–198.

2. William H. Chamberlain, *The Russian Revolution*, 2 vols. (New York: Grosset & Dunlap, 1965), vol. 1, p. 275.

3. Vladimir Ilich Lenin, *Imperialism: The Highest Stage of Capitalism* (New York: International Press, 1939) (originally published 1917).

4. E. H. Carr, *The Bolshevik Revolution*, 3 vols. (London: Penguin Books, 1970), vol. 2, pp. 271–272.

5. Muntig, p. 49.

6 Leonard Schapiro, *The Communist Party of the Soviet Union* (New York: Vintage Books, 1971), pp. 302–306.

7. Mikhail Heller and Aleksandr M. Nekrich, *Utopia in Power: The History of the Soviet Union from 1917 to the Present* (New York: Summit Books, 1986), pp. 225–226.

8. Moshe Lewin, *The Making of the Soviet System: Essays in the Social History of Interwar Russia* (New York: Pantheon Books, 1985), p. 273.

9. Schapiro, p. 424.

10. See the discussion in Robert Conquest, *The Great Terror: A Reassessment* (New York: Oxford University Press, 1990), pp. 485–486. One of the most prominent critical historians during the Soviet period, Roy Medvedev, estimates that for the entire Stalin era, between labor camps, forced collectivization, famine, and executions, some 20 million people died. *New York Times,* February 4, 1989, pp. 1, 4.

11. Muntig, p. 93.

12. Heller and Nekrich, pp. 237–242.

13. Muntig, p. 126.

14. Nikita S. Khrushchev, "The Crimes of the Stalin Era," in *The Crimes of the Stalin Era: Special Report to the 20th Congress of the Communist Party of the Soviet Union* (New York: The New Leader, 1962), p. 540.

15. Jerry F. Hough and Mark Fainsod, *How the Soviet Union Is Governed* (Cambridge, Mass.: Harvard University Press, 1979), pp. 232, 262.

16. Ed A. Hewett, *Reforming the Soviet Economy* (Washington, D.C.: The Brookings Institution, 1988), p. 238.

REFERENCES AND SUGGESTED READINGS

Carr, E. H. 1966. *The Bolshevik Revolution,* 3 vols. London: Penguin Books.

———. 1970. *Socialism in One Country,* vol. 1. London: Penguin Books.

Cohen, Stephen F. 1973. *Bukharin and the Bolshevik Revolution.* New York: Knopf.

Conquest, Robert. 1990. *The Great Terror: A Reassessment.* New York: Oxford University Press.

Dmytryshyn, Basil. 1977. *A History of Russia.* Englewood Cliffs, N.J.: Prentice-Hall.

Getty, J. Arch. 1985. *Origins of the Great Purges: The Soviet Communist Party Reconsidered, 1933–1938.* New York: Cambridge University Press.

Goldhurst, Richard. 1978. *The Midnight War: The American Intervention in Russia.* New York: McGraw-Hill.

Haimson, Leopold H. 1966. *The Russian Marxists and the Origins of Bolshevism.* Boston: Beacon Press.

Hosking, Geoffrey. 1993. *The First Socialist Society: A History of the Soviet Union from Within,* second enlarged ed. Cambridge, Mass.: Harvard University Press.

Lenin, V. I. 1939. *Imperialism the Highest Stage of Capitalism.* New York: International Publishers (originally published 1917).

———. 1971. *State and Revolution.* New York: International Publishers (originally published 1917).

———. 1943. *What Is to Be Done?* New York: International Publishers (originally published 1902).

McCauley, Martin, ed. 1987. *Khrushchev and Khrushchevism.* Bloomington: Indiana University Press.

Medvedev, Roy A. 1989. *Let History Judge: The Origins and Consequences of Stalinism,* revised and expanded edition. New York: Columbia University Press.

Schapiro, Leonard. 1987. *The Origins of Communist Autocracy.* Cambridge, Mass.: Harvard University Press.

Solzhenitsyn, Aleksandr. 1974 and 1985. *The Gulag Archipelago,* 2 vols. New York: Harper & Row.

Tucker, Robert C. 1973. *Stalin as Revolutionary, 1879–1929.* New York: W. W. Norton.

———. 1992. *Stalin in Power: The Revolution from Above.* New York: W. W. Norton.

———. 1972. *The Marx-Engels Reader.* New York: W. W. Norton.

> *Comrades, we are feeling even more sharply at the moment how powerful and monolithic the ranks of the Communists are, how united and unified our Soviet people are. At the recent elections the Soviet people again expressed unanimous support for the course of our party and state. This support inspires us and places commitments on us.*
>
> MIKHAIL GORVACHEV, speaking to the Central Committee of the Communist Party of the Soviet Union, on the day of his election as General Secretary, March 11, 1985
>
> *Dear compatriots, fellow citizens: As a result of the newly formed situation, creation of the Commonwealth of Independent States, I cease my activities in the post of USSR president.*
>
> MIKHAIL GORBACHEV, announcing his resignation to the nation, December 25, 1991

29

Mikhail Gorbachev and the End of the Soviet Union

ikhail Gorbachev became General Secretary of the Communist Party of the Soviet Union in March 1985. Within three years, a significant but still limited restructuring of the Communist Party's political and economic control of society was underway. Within five years, virtually all of the international regions once dominated by the USSR had broken away. After one more year, the country Gorbachev led as party leader and president was gone. These events surprised and stunned the world's leaders, most of all those of the Soviet Union itself. But unlike many other such changes in history, they were not the result of an external enemy's attacks, nor of a cataclysmic war and catastrophe such as had heralded change in the last days of Tsarist Russia.

The end of Soviet communism was the unplanned result of planned change. It occurred because the most powerful leader of the country recognized the need for change and the weakness of the current system but not its precarious fragility. Mikhail Gorbachev realized that fundamental changes were needed in the Soviet Union and said so. More than that, he was willing to start the country on the road toward giving the public more effective involvement in public affairs and economic management. In pushing change forward, however, there remained a tension, evident in Gorbachev himself and the policies he championed, between the need for change and the need for control. While Mikhail Gorbachev was bolder in support of change than any other postwar Soviet leader, he was also vigorous in trying to draw greater power to himself and in trying to limit and control the impact of the very changes he was creating. In the end neither he nor any of the country's other leaders foresaw the powerful combination of forces that would end their rule altogether. Among these forces were long-simmering demands of national groups within the Soviet Union to control their own fate; the speed with which a diverse range of political groups would coalesce to push back the limits of one-party rule; the brittleness of Communist Party rule in Eastern Europe and its rapid disappearance; and, conversely, the fear of and hostility toward reform on the part of longtime party leaders. In the end it was their attempt to cut short the reform process that proved the catalyst for the collapse of the system they were trying to save.

THE NEED FOR REFORM

By the mid-1980s the evidence was clear that the Soviet economy was slowing down and, in some instances, stagnating. Growth rates, which had averaged more than 4 percent between 1960 and 1975, declined to just over 2 percent between 1976 and 1985. Critical areas of the economy were not performing. Oil production, overall energy production, and other indicators of achievement—for example, industrial growth and agricultural production—lagged to below half of what they had been in the 1960s and 1970s.

Qualitatively the economy was also soft. Labor productivity, a measure of how much one worker produces, was roughly half the level of the United States. Investment in new machines and equipment, which had grown at more than 10 percent per year during 1960–1965, grew at less than 5 percent annually during 1981–1985.[1] Consequently, some 35 to 40 percent of Soviet industrial equipment was between fifteen and twenty years old, and repair of aging plants and equipment absorbed the efforts of 6 million workers and cost 35 billion rubles per year.[2] At one point Soviet Prime Minister Nikolai Ryzhkov said that less than 30 percent of the Soviet Union's manufactured goods could meet world standards.

In the workplace, growing absenteeism, apathy, lack of ambition, and lost work due to abuse of alcohol weakened production. With the consumer goods sector continually starved by the emphasis on heavy industry, workers found little to buy with their wages, which they received regardless of how well or how often they worked. By 1987, 13 percent of Soviet enterprises were operating at a loss, according to official Soviet estimates.

While the Soviet Union was relatively self-sufficient as an economy, it was isolated from many of the advances seen in more dynamic economies. Technological innovation especially proceeded only slowly. Enterprise managers had no incentive and little opportunity to buy or adopt the latest technology for their production. Everything that came from a Soviet factory was purchased by the state at fixed prices and losses were made up by the state. International markets were few and those were mostly in other socialist countries where "demand" was assured by state control. Hence, there was little need to worry about competition or meeting world standards.

But the Soviet Union did need to buy some things from the rest of the world—for example, grain. Since the currency of the USSR, the ruble, was not convertible (that is, it did not have a market-generated value in relation to other currencies of the world), the Soviet Union had to earn hard currency, such as dollars, to be able to buy what it needed on the world markets. As harvests were especially poor in the later Brezhnev years and continually failed to keep pace with demand, Soviet agricultural purchases began to take more and more of the country's precious hard currency earnings. In 1981 Soviet grain and agricultural purchases cost more than $11 billion and represented more than 40 percent of all dollar imports. More significantly, this sum was nearly half of what the country earned in hard currency through its exports.[3] Then, at the beginning of the 1980s, the major item the Soviet Union could sell to the West, oil, began to bring lower prices on the world market, even as it was costing more to extract it from places like Siberia and the Arctic regions.

Thus at the national level the Soviet economy was in need of major repairs. The country's ability to satisfy its own needs—that is, to keep its industrial base growing and improving and therefore to feed its own population—was weakening with each passing year.

Moreover, the impact of a weakening economy on the daily life of Soviet citizens was becoming clear. After the passing of Stalinism and the crises of the 1930s and the war years, the Soviet population had, at long last, begun to enjoy a degree of personal security, an end to mass arrests and totalitarian terror, and some economic progress. In return for satisfying those basic human needs, the Soviet rulers enjoyed a degree of public political acquiescence and a low likelihood of the kind of social upheaval seen in Hungary or Poland. Living standards improved, access to apartments and appliances expanded, food supply became more assured and varied, and educational and employment opportunities grew. Overall, per capita private consumption—a measure of how much of what the country produces is consumed by individuals—grew between 1953 and 1970 by an average of 4.1

percent annually (in comparison, the figure for the United States during this period was 2.2 percent).[4]

However, with the onset of economic difficulties in the late seventies and early eighties, the regime's ability to keep its end of the bargain eroded. The continued emphasis on heavy industry and neglect of investment in agriculture or consumer goods meant that beyond basic needs, the economy could not keep the standard of living growing. The rate of annual growth of per capita private consumption fell to 2.6 percent between 1970 and 1981 and was less than 2 percent in the last part of the 1970s. The standard of living for the average Soviet worker remained far behind that of a counterpart in the West, as it always had been (see Table 29.1), but it also lagged behind the standard achieved in other Communist countries. In 1981, for example, Soviet consumers ate less meat and more grain and potatoes than their comrades in Eastern Europe. Consumers in Hungary, Poland, East Germany, and Czechoslovakia had more home appliances and many more private cars than people in the Soviet Union. Urbanization of the country put increased pressure on an already inadequate housing stock and educational system. Health care provision proved inadequate. The infant mortality rate increased. For the first time since World War II, a modern industrial country showed a *decline* in life expectancy. The gaps in the standard of living caused by stagnating and uneven growth were exacerbated by the politics of the Brezhnev regime, which tolerated corruption and privilege for members of the elite and those connected with them.

Thus Mikhail Gorbachev and the Communist Party faced a problem that was both national and individual, both economic and political. Gorbachev and those who supported him recognized this and began, slowly at first, to try to reform—and in this way save—the Soviet system.

Table 29.1 COMPARING COSTS IN THE MID-EIGHTIES

How many minutes (unless otherwise noted) of work time it takes an average industrial worker in Washington and Moscow to purchase various goods and services.

	Wash-ington	Moscow		Wash-ington	Moscow
One loaf of rye bread	18	11	A bar of soap	3	17
One chicken	18	189	Bus fare for two miles	7	3
One grapefruit	6	112	Baby sitter per hour	44	279
One liter of milk	4	20	First class postage stamp	2	3
One liter of red wine	37	257	Men's haircut	62	34
One head of cabbage	7	7	A pair of jeans	4 (hours)	56 (hours)
Three ounces of tea	10	36	A pair of men's shoes	6 (hours)	37 (hours)
Car wash	40	139	Washing machine	46 (hours)	177 (hours)

Note: Study conducted in October 1986.

Source: *New York Times,* June 28, 1987; Radio Free Europe/Radio Liberty.

FIRST STEPS

Politically, Gorbachev and his supporters took a major step by publicly identifying the problems affecting the economy and labeling them for what they were. This in itself represented a significant change in a political system in which leaders had only spoken of success. At the Twenty-seventh Party Congress in 1986, Gorbachev said:

The situation today is such that we cannot limit ourselves to partial improvements. A radical reform is needed. Its meaning consists in truly subordinating the whole of our production to the requirements of society, to the satisfaction of people's needs, in orienting management towards raising efficiency and quality, accelerating scientific and technological progress, promoting a greater interest of people in the results of their work, initiative and socialist enterprise in every link of the national economy, and, above all, in the work collectives.

In this speech and several others, Gorbachev went on to outline specific problems that needed to be addressed, such as producing not simply more of something but better things more efficiently, improving the fit between scientific research and the needs of the economy, improving planning, finance, the system of prices and supply, and strengthening basic Soviet enterprises against "the petty tutelage" of ministries and departments.

The willingness to address frankly the system's problems was part of a policy of *glasnost* or "voicing" of real issues. Newspapers and journals as well as radio and television began to feature discussions, exchanges, even call-in shows on all sorts of previously restricted subjects, such as the war in Afghanistan, or previously missing subjects like crime, drug addiction, and AIDS. Relaxation of strictures in cultural areas brought back to society the contributions of poets and writers such as Vladimir Vysotsky and Boris Pasternak, whose work had been banned in the Soviet Union, and

Mikhail Gorbachev

His actions and their intended and unintended consequences brought the Soviet era to an end, precipitated the dissolution of his country and a radical shift in the global power structure that had existed for forty-five years. Where did such a person come from? Was he a revolutionary and visionary from the start? His career path offers little evidence to support such a view. Instead it stands out for its very ordinariness, except for the speed with which he rose through the ranks of the party.

Mikhail Gorbachev was the first of a new generation of post–World War II Soviet leaders. Born in Privolnoye of the Stavropol region of the Russian Federation, he was only ten when World War II came to the USSR. He worked on a collective farm and graduated from secondary school with a good enough performance to enter the law faculty of prestigious Moscow State University in 1950. He joined the party in 1952, too late in the Stalin era to bear responsibility for, or to build his career on, the excesses of the purges. Gorbachev received his law degree in 1955—making him the first leader of the party since Lenin with higher education. His professional career was based entirely on organizational work within the party. After working in the Komsomol (Communist youth league) at Moscow State, he returned to the Stavropol region in 1955 and worked in the agitation and propaganda department there. He rose quickly to become Komsomol first secretary of the region in 1958.

Gorbachev moved to the party apparatus in 1962 and there moved up just as fast: from head of the party organizational department in 1962 to first secretary for the city of Stavropol in 1966, to first secretary of the entire region in 1970, at the age of only 39. Along the way, Gorbachev devoted special energy to agricultural issues and by correspondence received an additional degree in agronomics from the Stavropol Agricultural Institution in 1967.

By the time he was 40, Gorbachev was a full member of the Communist Party central committee and in 1978 was appointed a Central Committee secretary with special responsibility for agriculture. Though agricultural difficulties continued and even grew worse, Gorbachev was neither blamed nor demoted. In fact he sped up to the Politburo, spending only one year as a candidate (or nonvoting) member before becoming a full member in 1980. At 50, Gorbachev was twenty years younger than the average Politburo member. In the Andropov and Chernenko interregnum, Gorbachev's responsibilities grew and eventually included the economy, foreign affairs, ideology, and party cadres. In essence during this period of infirm Soviet leadership, it appears that Gorbachev was a shadow general secretary. In 1985, within twenty-four hours of the death of Konstantin Chernenko, he formally assumed the top position.

In 1988 Gorbachev was elected chairman of the Supreme Soviet under the old system and then to the same, but much stronger, post by the new Congress of People's Deputies in 1989. In 1990 a new presidency was created for him with stronger powers that were further enhanced that year and the next.

The attempted coup of August 19, 1991, undid Gorbachev, not least because the attempt to seize power was made by people he himself had appointed. After the coup, Gorbachev resigned his post as general secretary of the Communist Party and, at the end of the year, with the Soviet Union itself declared out of existence, the presidency.

Sources: *Congressional Quarterly, The Soviet Union* (Washington, D.C.: *Congressional Quarterly, Inc.,* 1986); Christian Schmidt-Hauer, *Gorbachev: The Path to Power* (Topsfield, Mass.: Salem House, 1986).

even those of Aleksandr Solzhenitsyn, exiled under Brezhnev, as well as new writings, plays, and films with critical themes.

With regard to economic reform, glasnost facilitated criticism of poor performance and identification by Gorbachev of those who

WHAT? JUST COMRADE GORBACHEV
WALKING HIS DOG,
"GLASNOST"

DANZIGER
The Christian Science Monitor

might try to block reform to protect their own prerogatives. One of the aims of glasnost was to alert people who were responsible for the performance of the economy that their shortcomings, simply doing what had always been done, or blocking or undermining needed reforms would become public knowledge. But glasnost served a broader political purpose as well. For the average citizen who was aware of the system's failings, even if these were not acknowledged by the leadership, such discussions validated what they already knew. It was a step toward closing the gap between the regime and the public and between regime pronouncements and real life.

Moreover, glasnost was part of an attempt to recruit a key sector of society, the *intelligentsia*, or well-educated, highly trained people. Ur-

banization and rapid modernization of the Soviet Union, especially since World War II, created a new generation of urban professionals desirous of greater freedom as well as better living conditions.[5] Gorbachev recognized that the talents and ideas of such people were crucial to the improvement of the country's situation. This meant that a more open political environment was needed, one in which people knew that if they spoke out, criticizing poor performance or specific policies, they would not be labeled "dissidents" or, worse, suffer the fate of Andrei Sakharov, one of the fathers of Soviet nuclear science. He had been exiled to Gorky in 1980 for criticizing Soviet policy and supporting human rights activists. The release of Sakharov from exile in 1987 and the more tolerant treatment of dissidents after that were part of glasnost and were important signals to the intelligentsia that Gorbachev wanted their contribution.

At the elite level, Gorbachev moved to ensure his own political power by removing opponents. These included those who might have been more conservative, such as Politburo member and party chief of Leningrad, Grigorii Romanov, and those who seemed to want to go too far too fast, such as the candidate (nonvoting) Politburo member and party leader of Moscow, Boris Yeltsin. In the changing of the guard, Gorbachev was aided by nature (the death of several key holdovers) and circumstance (the unimpeded flight into Moscow in 1987 of a small private plane piloted by a young West German, which provoked a housecleaning in the defense ministry). In the Politburo, in the Central Committee, in the central government, and throughout the republics, a political purge took place, beginning in 1985, and accelerating after a Central Committee plenum in January 1987. By the beginning of 1988, virtually the entire Politburo had been replaced or removed (leaving the Politburo at twelve members) and the Secretariat had been expanded from four to fourteen members and filled with Gorbachev appointees. Gorbachev appointed his own prime minister, KGB head and foreign minister Andrei Gromyko, who had held this last post for twenty-eight years, became president of the Presidium of the Supreme Soviet for a short time, and then was replaced as president by Gorbachev himself and removed from the Politburo. In Gorbachev's first three years as party leader, eleven of thirteen deputy chairmen of the Council of Ministers and three-quarters of the council itself were replaced. Six of fourteen republican party chiefs were replaced, as well as roughly half of all secretaries (including first secretaries) of *oblast,* city and district party committees.[6]

But Gorbachev knew that economic reform was running into opposition lower down. Hence, a key aspect of Mikhail Gorbachev's plans for reform involved infusing the system of elected soviets, or councils, with greater power and responsibility. These ranged from local and provincial bodies to the two-chambered Supreme Soviet at the national level. In his speech to a party plenum in February 1988, he said it was necessary

> *to take a better look at how the Soviets are formed. This means upgrading our election system so that the process of forming the bodies of power makes for active involvement of the people and for a careful selection of persons capable of ensuring the soviets' activities with respect to the goals of perestroika.*

Accordingly, the Communist Party of the Soviet Union, at a special national party conference called for the purpose in June 1988, approved plans to reform the Soviet state government. In December the first part of the plan was approved by the Supreme Soviet. The new "supreme organ of USSR state power" was the Congress of People's Deputies. This body was elected in March and April 1989 in the first multicandidate, secret-ballot elections since 1918. There were 2,250 people's deputies elected, one-third of whom came from districts of equal size and one-third from national units (union republics, autonomous republics, autonomous oblasts, and autonomous *okrugs*). The remaining third were not elected publicly but reserved for local party organizations, trade unions, and veterans and youth groups.

Despite the restricted nature of these first elections (there were still no political parties other than the Communist Party) the party received a rude shock when many of its key regional officials—including the first secretaries of Riga, Minsk, Kiev, Kishiniev, and Alma Ata, and the first *and* second secretaries in Leningrad—all lost. Many party candidates lost in districts even where they ran unopposed, because they did not get the required majority

General Secretary Mikhail Gorbachev presides over the nineteenth All-Union CPSU Conference in June 1988.

of "for" votes. (People could vote both "for" and "against" candidates.) Overall, many outspoken supporters of glasnost and *perestroika* (economic restructuring), including former dissidents such as historian Roy Medvedev and physicist Andrei Sakharov, won seats to the Congress. Notwithstanding the electoral success of many reformers, the Congress of People's Deputies still contained 86 percent party members. This Congress then elected a two-chambered Supreme Soviet to act as the country's legislature. This new body of 542 members excluded many of the country's most prominent exponents of radical reform.

Gorbachev himself was elected chairman of the Supreme Soviet, a previously largely symbolic post that was strengthened to include more presidential powers. Gorbachev gained the power to initiate legislation, and to nominate the prime minister and other key posi-

tions. This marked the beginning of a period of continual strengthening, at least formally, of executive power in the Soviet Union. Gorbachev saw this as necessary to secure the needed reforms and to ensure that such reforms were not blocked either by the new legislature or by the institution that still held the key to power in the USSR, the Communist Party.

Gorbachev moved even further in this direction during 1990 and 1991. He persuaded the Congress of People's Deputies to create a new, stronger presidency and to elect him to it. This new presidency had the power to propose and veto legislation, to appoint key people and to call for national referenda on key issues. The president could also decree states of emergency and even overturn governmental decisions.[7] These powers were further expanded in September 1990 when Gorbachev was granted temporary emergency powers, including the power to issue decrees with the force of law, the power to declare presidential rule and even to dissolve elected bodies if he saw fit. Other changes continued to be introduced that made Gorbachev look more and more like an American president and, more importantly, shifted the basis of his power from the Communist Party to state bodies. He acquired a cabinet (replacing the Council of Ministers), a vice president, and several new councils that reported to him, not the legislature. Initiative and formal power increasingly passed to Gorbachev and the presidency as party conservatives, bureaucrats, and economic mangers became increasingly nervous about the country's economic and political situation.

THE RISE OF NATIONS

Mikhail Gorbachev and the people who supported him had at least a rough idea of what they thought was necessary to reform and revitalize the Soviet Union's ailing economy. And they were bold enough to link those changes to reforms in the political system, which they saw as necessary to achieve perestroika. But neither Gorbachev nor apparently anyone else recognized the degree to which something needed to be done to ameliorate grievances harbored by many of the country's more than one hundred constituent nationalities. Nor did they appreciate in advance the degree to which glasnost and the changes in the political system would weaken the power of the ruling party and allow those grievances to take political form.

Nationality issues were in part economic. Poor regions felt exploited and abandoned as the disparity between rich and poor regions were not overcome. In daily life contrasts were sharp. Between 1971 and 1986, 43 percent more new housing units were built in Russia than in the non-Russian republics. In 1986 infant mortality was 60 percent higher outside Russia; the number of medical personnel 19 percent lower.[8]

Regional Disparity in the 1980s: Richer European USSR, Poorer Central Asia

One consequence of the location of most heavy industry and technologically advanced production in the European parts of the former USSR was a higher standard of living for the inhabitants there. In the resource-rich but industry-poor sections of the country, chiefly Central Asia, opportunities for better paying, highly skilled jobs were fewer. Educational opportunities were also typically better in European parts of the country.

Republic	Earned Income for All Workers*	Enrollment in Higher Education**
	(Figures for 1986)	
Estonia	221	122
RSFSR	207.8	100
Latvia	201.4	109
Lithuania	194.7	117
Turkmeniya	193.1	NA
Kazakhstan	192.7	92
Armenia	184.5	89
Belorussia	180.5	84
Ukraine	179	86
Georgia	170.6	119
Kirgiziya	166.4	86
Uzbekistan	165.9	69
Tajikistan	162	65
Moldavia	161.8	52
Azerbaijan	161.7	NA

*Average per capita monthly income in rubles.

**Ratio of titular nationality to Russians attending schools of higher education.

Source: From David Lane, *Soviet Society under Perestroika*, pp. 107–200. Copyright © 1990, 1992. Reprinted by permission of the publisher, Routledge.

At the same time, resource-rich areas began to try to assert their power vis-à-vis the dominant "center." But anticenter feeling was also anti-Russian, as years of centralized control had been accompanied by Russification and, in many places, a large immigration of Russians into non-Russian regions. This was especially true in the Baltic States. The number of Russians in Estonia, for example, nearly doubled between 1959 and 1989. In Kazakhstan, Russians and Ukrainians together outnumbered Kazakhs. Some opposition to Moscow was also stimulated by resistance to perestroika and political reform, because local leaders feared it would endanger their positions. In Alma Ata removal of the leader of the party and rebublic, a Kazakh, and his replacement by someone more favorable toward perestroika , but a Russian, led to public demonstrations and rioting in 1986.

Glasnost allowed grievances of all sorts to become public, and political reform, including the prospect of elections, allowed groups to form around national issues to press for change. "Popular Front" movements became very strong in the Baltics, Armenia, and Ukraine, and acted as vehicles for republican and national assertion. But perhaps the chief beneficiary of the diluting of the power of the Communist Party of the Soviet Union was the largest unit of the USSR, Russia.

Though the Soviet Union was usually seen by outsiders as coterminous with "Russia" and its language and leaders were usually Russian, the Russian republic did not in fact hold a special position of privilege in the Soviet Union's structure. On the contrary, the Russian republic, itself a federation of many subunits, lacked the internal prerogatives and institutions that other republics had. Moscow made decisions for it as well as for the country as a whole. Most importantly, until 1990 there was not even a separate Russian Communist Party. But as republican and national movements began to grow elsewhere, the idea of guarding Russian interests began to be very popular. In 1990 the Russian Congress of People's Deputies, like

that of the USSR, was elected. It in turn elected a smaller Supreme Soviet and Boris Yeltsin was elected the chairman of the body. But unlike the USSR elections, those for the Russian Congress had not guaranteed a proportion of the seats for the Communist Party or other organizations. Yeltsin firmly allied himself with people who supported Russia's sovereignty within the Soviet Union and used the new parliament to challenge Gorbachev. Yeltsin's backers included both reform Communists, like himself, who wanted perestroika and political reform to move faster, and more conservative Russian nationalists who felt that Russia needed a stronger position within the USSR.

Over the next year Yeltsin articulated a public stance that combined assertion of the need for greater political and economic democracy with fierce protection of Russian—as opposed to Soviet—prerogatives. In outlining his plan for a new Russian constitution, he blasted the central government, calling it "the cruel exploiter, the miserly benefactor, and the favorite who does not think about the future. . . . We must put an end," Yeltsin said, "to the injustice of these relations. Today it is not the center but Russia which must think about which functions to transfer to the center and which to keep for itself." Yeltsin argued that all of Russia's resources should be "used exclusively in the interests of Russia." By the same token, he argued strongly for political pluralism, a multiparty parliametary system, and protection of "all forms of ownership" (meaning both private and state), a position not yet embraced by Gorbachev.[9]

Meanwhile, republican leaderships in many other parts of the country grew bolder, spurred by events elsewhere and by fears that changes could be reversed. By the end of 1989 all of the East European states had thrown off Communist one-party rule (see Chapter 37) and multiparty and presidential elections were due in most. Meanwhile, many who favored such democratic practices in the Soviet Union were fearful that Mikhail Gorbachev would push reform only so far, but ultimately resist fundamental changes. These fears seemed confirmed in late 1990 and early 1991. In September 1990, Gorbachev rejected the so-called Shatalin plan that called for a 500-day "shock therapy" program for economic change. Then several reform-minded members of Gorbachev's team, including Stanislav Shatalin, a member of the Presidential Council for whom the economic plan was named, and Interior Minister Vadim Bakhatin left the cabinet. Most dramatically, in December Foreign Minister Edvard Shevardnadze resigned in front of the Congress of People's Deputies, warning that "dictatorship is coming."

Challenges came from republics in varied forms. In Russia, Boris Yeltsin moved to increase the spheres of responsibility for the government of Russia, at the expense of the Soviet Union. Russia declared itself "sovereign" in June 1990, meaning that it could decide which laws of the Soviet Union applied on its territory. Key functions like internal security moved to Russian rather than Soviet control. In June 1991, Yeltsin was elected president of Russia by direct popular vote, something that neither Mikhail Gorbachev nor any previous ruler of Russia could claim. In the election Yeltsin soundly defeated former Prime Minister of the USSR Nikolay Ryhzkov, making the vote a rejection of Gorbachev personally, as well as of the old Soviet Union.

Interethnic violence flared in Azerbaijan, Georgia, Tajikistan, and Uzbekistan and Soviet troops were rushed in. In Lithuania, the republic's Communist Party ended both Moscow's power over it and its own formal monopoly of political power. A new nationalist parliament was elected in February 1990, and almost immediately declared full independence from the Soviet Union. It was the first republic to mount such a direct challenge. Latvia soon followed but declared a "transition period" during which it would continue to implement Soviet law.

These actions provoked pressure from Moscow. A brief oil blockade of Lithuania was instituted in early 1990 and in January 1991 Soviet security forces attacked and occupied key buildings in Vilnius, the capital of Lithuania, and Riga, the capital of Latvia. This use of force, backed by rump Communist parties still loyal to Moscow and local "national salvation committees" resulted in nineteen deaths and many more wounded. Far from suppressing national opposition, such crackdowns stimulated it. In the long run they proved disastrous for Mikhail Gorbachev. Advocates of greater rights for republics and nationalities saw him as willing to sanction the use of force to keep the Soviet empire intact, while Gorbachev's conservative opponents saw the action as too little, too late. By the middle of the year no less than ten of the country's fifteen republics had declared some form of sovereignty. Efforts to formulate a new union treaty at the end of 1990 and beginning of 1991 proved unsuccessful despite the fact that in succeeding drafts more and more powers were ceded to the republics. Finally, in June 1991 agreement was reached among nine republics that would have made them virtually sovereign states. The three Baltic States and three others—Georgia, Armenia, and Moldova—refused to participate. But within a short time, the question of a new Soviet Union proved moot as a desperate attempt to save the union wound up killing it.

THE AUGUST COUP

At 6 o'clock on the morning of August 19, 1991, Moscow residents were startled by the news that a "State Committee for the State of Emergency" had relieved Mikhail Gorbachev of his duties "owing to the state of his health." Pointing to the "all-round crisis of political, ethnic and civil confrontation, chaos, and anarchy" that they said was threatening the country, this group tried to seize governing power and preserve the old order. Headed by Gorbachev's own hand-picked vice president, Gennady Yenaev, the State Committee included the head of the KGB; the country's prime minister, who had tried and failed to get the Supreme Soviet to vote him into power two months before; the defense minister; the interior minister; and three others. The State Committee immediately moved to suspend all activities and regional governing authorities that it considered dangerous, banned all demonstrations and strikes, and tried to re-establish control of the media.

The coup was supported by the Soviet Cabinet of Ministers—which had also been appointed by Gorbachev—and by key leaders of the Communist Party. Tanks were put on the streets of Moscow, more units moved toward that city and Leningrad, and in the Baltics, ports were blockaded. Mikhail Gorbachev, at a dacha in the Crimea, had been confronted the night before by representatives of the coup leaders, who demanded that he hand over his powers and renounce the upcoming union treaty. When he refused he was placed under house arrest. But Boris Yeltsin, who had only returned to the city the day before, was not arrested. In addition, key military leaders, like the chief of the air force, Yevgeny Shaposhnikov, and many regional commanders elsewhere in the country did not support the coup. Political leaders in the Baltic states, in Moldova, Ukraine, and Kazakhstan denounced the action.

People spilled into the streets in Moscow and challenged the uncertain troops in front of the Russian parliament building, known as the White House. There Boris Yeltsin stood atop a tank and condemned the coup. Soon after, tanks of the Taman Division of the army turned their turrets from the White House and faced outward, toward whoever might have been

When Boris Yeltsin made his dramatic speech on top of a tank in front of the Russian parliament building less than six hours into the attempted coup d'état, he threw down the gauntlet to those who had tried to seize power and galvanized public support against the small group of military and Communist leaders. No microphones were present, but an eyewitness recalled Yeltsin's words:

Citizens of Russia . . . the legally elected President of the country was removed from power . . . we are dealing with a rightist, reactionary, anti-constitutional coup . . . Accordingly we proclaim all decisions and instructions of this committee to be unlawful . . . We appeal to citizens of Russia to give fitting rebuff to the putschists and demand a return of the country to normal constituional development.

Others, less well known, rose to the challenge as well. Konstantin Kobets, the defense minister of Russia, climbed on the same tank and was defiant:

Soldiers and officers, I am the defense minister of Russia. Not a hand will be raised against the people or the duly elected president of Russia.

Source: Reported by Oleg Kalugin, major general of the KGB, in Stuart Loory and Ann Imse, *Seven Days That Shook the World* (Atlanta, Ga.: Turner Publishing, Inc., 1991), p. 90.

planning an attack against the building. The Russian government continued to operate inside the White House and apart from one feeble attempt to push through the barricades, military action was absent. By August 20 some fifty thousand people were protecting the Russian government, troop movements toward the capital stopped and troops in Moscow mingled with, more than intimidated, the people in the streets. The next day troops were withdrawn from Moscow and Gorbachev was released from house arrest. He returned to

Moscow, under escort from a Russian government delegation.

The attempt to forcibly remove the Soviet president had been unleashed by those who feared the loss of their power, those who sought to salvage the position of the Communist Party, the KGB and the armed forces. They also feared that the very end of the Soviet Union was at hand, with the government ready to disperse its power to previously subordinate republics. The attempt to take power in this way was an extraordinary occurrence for the Soviet Union. Not since the civil war had ended in the nineteen-twenties, despite all the upheaval and tragedies that the country had endured—some brought on by the leadership itself—had there ever been such an attempt. Its failure was due to the plotters' own ineptitude; to the willingness of its opponents, especially in Leningrad and Moscow, to challenge the coup in the streets; to the unwillingness of key actors, especially in the military, to support the coup; and to the keen recognition of Boris Yeltsin that by seizing the moment to resist the coup he could not only thwart it but take over the mantle of national leadership from a severely weakened Mikhail Gorbachev. When he climbed onto that tank on August 19, 1991, Boris Yeltsin climbed over the man who had unleashed the reform process to take for himself the leadership of the new Russia.

THE END OF THE SOVIET UNION

Though Mikhail Gorbachev survived the coup meant to unseat him, politically he was mortally wounded by the attempt. For one thing he had personally appointed the people who led the coup, including Interior Minister Boriss Pugo, Defense Minister Dmitri Yazov, Prime Minister Valentin Pavlov, and his own vice president. For another, the coup was made by people defending the position and prerogatives of the Communist Party of the Soviet Un-

ion, an organization of which Gorbachev was still General Secretary. Though he promptly resigned after the coup, Gorbachev did not condemn the party and refused to outlaw it from the Soviet Union. Though he had, by his own account, been steadfast in refusing to cooperate with the coup makers, it was Boris Yeltsin who had confronted the troops in the streets and whose presence in Moscow had galvanized opposition in the early hours of the attempt to seize the state. Moreover, Yeltsin had already resigned from the party more than a year before, had banned its activities from workplaces in Russia, and, after the coup attempt, suspended the Russian party altogether, an act which, not incidentally, rendered Gorbachev's refusal to do so superfluous.

Throughout the fall, the entire Soviet government apparatus and soon Gorbachev himself became superfluous. The August coup sparked full declarations of independence from Estonia and Latvia, followed soon by Ukraine and eight other republics. Unlike the earlier attempt by Lithuania, the central government was this time in no position to block such actions, and diplomatic recognition of the Baltic States soon followed. The Congress of People's Deputies of the USSR did approve the loose union treaty negotiated earlier and an economic union was announced in October, but without the key resources of the Ukraine. On December 1, the people of Ukraine voted overwhelmingly for complete independence and Russia recognized them the next day.

With plummeting influence and little territorial domain, the powers of the Soviet central government were taken over by Russia. In response to the attempted coup, Boris Yeltsin had taken military powers and control of all enterprises in Russia. To this was added control of KGB activities and the Soviet central bank. Appointment of people favorable to reform was forced upon Gorbachev and by the end of November, the Russian government had in most respects replaced that of the Soviet Union.

The last chapter was written the next month. On December 8 the presidents of Russia, Ukraine, and Belarus—representing four-fifths of the territory of the Soviet Union— declared the USSR dead. They signed an agreement to form a Commonwealth of Independent States, then reformulated the agreement twice more to create an organization consisting (at the time) of eleven members. Russia took over the Soviet foreign ministry, the KGB, and all Soviet embassies. Internationally, it was accorded the status of successor state to the Soviet Union and thus assumed its seat as a permanent member of the United Nations Security Council.

On December 25, 1991, roughly six and one-half years after he had assumed leadership of the country, Mikhail Sergeevich Gorbachev resigned as president of the Union of Soviet Socialist Republics and the next day its own parliament voted itself and the country out of existence. At 7:38 P.M. the flag of the Soviet Union was lowered over the Kremlin. Twelve minutes later it was replaced by that of Russia.

NOTES

1. U.S. Congress Joint Economic Committee, *Gorbachev's Economic Plans* (Washington, D.C.: U.S. Government Printing Office, 1987), vol. 1, p. 151.
2. Timothy Colton, *The Dilemma of Reform in the Soviet Union,* revised and expanded ed. (New York: Council on Foreign Relations, 1986), p. 40.
3. Joan P. Zoeter, "U.S.S.R. Hard Currency Trade and Payments," in U. S. Congress, *Soviet Economy in the 1980's: Problems and Prospects,* part 2 (Washington, D.C.: U.S. Government Printing Office, 1982), pp. 501, 502.
4. Gertrude Schroeder, "Soviet Living Standards in Comparative Perspective," in *Quality of Life in the Soviet Union,* ed. Horst Herlemann (Boulder, Colo.: Westview Press, 1987), p. 21.
5. Moshe Lewin, *The Gorbachev Phenomenon* (Berkeley: University of California Press, 1988).
6. Jerry F. Hough, "Gorbachev Consolidating Power," *Problems of Communism,* 36 (1987): 34; Thane Gustafson and Dawn Mann, "Gorbachev's Next Gamble," *Problems of Communism,* 36 (1987): 10.
7. Brenda Horrigan and Theodore Karasik, "The Rise of Presidential Power Under Gorbachev," in Eugene Huskey, ed., *Executive Power and Soviet Politics: The Rise and Decline of the Soviet State* (Armonk, N.Y.: M. E. Sharpe, 1992), pp. 107–108.
8. Nadia Diuk and Adrian Karatnycky, *New Nations Rising* (New York: John Wiley & Sons, 1993), pp. 47–48.
9. "Speech to the Russian Federation Congress of People's Deputies," May 22, 1990, reprinted in Alexander Dallin and Gail W. Lapidus, eds., *The Soviet System in Crisis* (Boulder, Colo.: Westview Press, 1991), pp. 334–337.

REFERENCES AND SUGGESTED READINGS

Balzer, Harley D., ed. 1991. *Five Years That Shook the World: Gorbachev's Unfinished Revolution.* Boulder, Colo.: Westview Press.

Goldman, Marshall I. 1992. *What Went Wrong with Perestroika.* New York: W. W. Norton.

Lane, David. 1992. *Soviet Society under Perestroika.* London: Routledge.

Sakwa, Richard. 1990. *Gorbachev and His Reforms.* New York: Prentice-Hall.

Smith, Hedrick. 1990. *The New Russians.* New York: Random House.

Wieczynski, Joseph L., ed. 1993. *The Gorbachev Encyclopedia: Gorbachev: The Man and His Times.* Salt Lake City: Charles Schlacks, Jr.

A totalitarian system leaves behind it a minefield built into both the country's social structure and the individual pyschology of its citizens. And mines explode each time the system faces the danger of being dismantled and the country sees the prospect of genuine renewal.

ANATOLY SOBCHAK, Mayor of St. Petersburg

30

Political Culture:
A Society in Flux

*I*n any complex modern society it is risky to try to offer a summary assessment of "the" political culture. If we define political culture as the attitudes and behavior of individuals directed toward their political institutions, most countries will show evidence of many such orientations, as can be seen in the discussions of France in this volume, for example.

In the case of Russia, the picture of political culture is likely to be even more complex because the institutions and the very state itself, to which such orientations are directed, are undergoing fundamental change. What exists at present is a mixture of old and new. The country has an elected president and more than two dozen political parties with the word *Democratic* in their name. A parliament was first elected in 1990, when Russia was part of the USSR and under a system that did not allow for competing parties. Only in late 1993 did multiparty elections for a new parliament occur, and then under conditions established by decree of the president. The overwhelming majority of representatives in the 1990 body were Communist Party members, as was the president for nearly thirty years. For its first two years, the new Russia functioned on the basis of a constitution written for a different entity—a republic of the Soviet Union—by a Communist Party whose "leading role" was guaranteed. Since the death of Leonid Brezhnev in 1982, Russian society has seen aging conservative leaders replaced by younger vigorous Communist reformers; the institution of perestroika and glasnost; the establishment, then rapid suppression, of the Russian Communist Party; the end of one-party rule and the simultaneous emergence of both political pluralism and Russian nationalism. Russia's democratic institutions are very young and the rules of the political game are not well established. For months, for example, several competing draft constitutions were put before Russian society, but even the method of choosing was not clear or broadly accepted. Russian society is caught up in the process of forging fundamentally new directions in *both* the political and economic systems. It should not be surprising, then, that the evidence suggests a political culture in some turmoil.

Current indicators suggest that Russian society is quite undecided about democracy and its post-Communist partner, economic reform. It is struggling with questions relating to what the new mechanisms of government should be and what values, if any, of the most recent system, that is, communism, should be preserved. And Russia existed before communism, of course, so many argue that the country's future can be found in its *pre*-Communist past. In a modern replay of the nineteenth-century debate between "westernizers" and Slavophiles, some suggest the new Russia will not—or should not—ape western styles in its politics but should find its own way.

Russian political culture today is less a coherent value system with different strands than a public arena in which many values compete for dominance. That competition has roots in the recent Soviet past, in the pre-Communist period, in the period of reform unleashed by Gorbachev, and the most recent time of revolutionary upheaval that was the unintended consequence of perestroika and glasnost. The impact of these clashing values must be considered as we assess the chances of contemporary Russia achieving democratic rule.

THE LEGACY: RUSSIAN AND SOVIET

Autocratic rule is a persistent feature of the history of the Russian empire, of the medieval states of Muscovy and Kievan Rus that preceded it, and of the period of Mongol domination that lasted three centuries. This does not mean there are no instances of limitations on the personal rule of the leader or even of limited participation by certain groups of the governed. The *zemskii sobor* (Landed Assembly) of the sixteenth and seventeenth centuries, the *boiarski duma*, and other executive councils established under Peter the Great and Catherine II often wielded enormous influence. The Tsar himself was chosen by election, not dynasty, until the eighteenth century. But especially after Peter the Great, the representativeness and power of such assemblies and councils—including that of the first broadly elected Duma established after the Russian revolution of 1905—were a product of regime design rather than popular will. Neither the groups that held power, which before the revolution usually went with property, nor the ruler himself were effectively limited by these weak institutions. When the last Tsar of Russia (Nicholas II) was faced with a more troublesome Duma than he liked, he dissolved it. The electoral law was changed and a more manageable assembly elected.

Administration of the state and use of its resources was the privilege of the few, whose position was assured by property, lineage, and loyalty to the personal power of the Tsar. The "sacredness of the state" was to be protected against those at home who might want to reform or even overthrow it. Finally, both the state and the empire were to be guarded against encroachments from abroad and supported in its expansion, even if it stretched resources beyond capacity.[1]

Russian history has few examples of institutions that afforded the opportunity on a regular basis for public influencing of the policy process. Instead it has numerous instances of state-directed campaigns aimed at increasing the public's contribution to, rather than determination of, state goals. And in the absence of a regularized legitimate vehicle for public input into policies affecting them, the history of the country has included numerous instances of public insurrections, violence against the government—some four thousand officials were killed by revolutionaries in 1906–1907 alone—and revolution. While such a history does not of course predetermine that a population is forever locked into a choice between subordination and revolution, it does mean that as a part of contemporary political culture, people cannot harken back to earlier periods of broad popular influence. Such periods do not exist.

By the same token, a strong theme in Russian history is the struggle for reform either by autocratic leaders or groups aiming to curb their power. From the Decembrists of 1825 through socialists and liberals at the turn of the century to dissidents who challenged Communist rule, there have been those who felt that Russia should build a democratic structure and mechanisms allowing for greater popular rights and control of arbitrary government.[2] Paul Miliukov, for example, leader of the liberal Kadet Party at the end of the Tsar's dynasty, outlined one Russian future:

> *Russia wants a political representation, and guaranties of what are called the fundamental rights of individuality; i.e., freedom of belief and of speech, the right of association and of public meetings, liberty of the press, a strict regime of law, and the free course of justice . . .*[3]

But another challenger to the old system, the leader of the Bolshevik faction of the Russian Social Democratic Party, saw it somewhat differently:

> *The state is a special organisation of force; it is the organisation of violence for the suppression of some class. What class must the proletariat sup-*

press? Naturally, the exploiting class only, i.e., the bourgeoisie. . . . Democracy for an insignificant minority, democracy for the rich—that is the democracy of capitalist society. . . . Only in Communist society, when the resistance of the capitalists has been completely broken, when the capitalists have disappeared, when there are no classes . . . only then "the state ceases to exist," and "it becomes possible to speak of freedom."[4]

Instead of either individual liberty or democracy, the system that replaced the Tsarist autocracy wound up outdoing its predecessor in exercising political, economic and social control. Wielding the state in line with its own vision, the Communist Party that was Lenin's "vanguard" of the revolution sought to reshape peoples' views of the world and to put in place a distinctly Soviet political culture. The goal of Soviet society was determined to be the construction of socialism. This was deemed completed under Nikita Khrushchev and "mature" or "developed" under Leonid Brezhnev. In such a society, Soviet theorists explained, there still exist different classes, such as workers, peasants and intelligentsia. But all accept the working class's interests as their own and support the Communist Party as the interpreter of those interests and the guide to further development. In political terms, and in policy pronouncements, this meant that other interests that might have challenged those of the workers (as interpreted by the party) were restricted. This included interests based on religion or on private control of property. It also meant that the interests of state took precedence over the desires of individuals.

Thus the Soviet constitution, after proclaiming that its citizens enjoyed "in full the social, economic, political and personal rights and freedoms" including freedom of the press, speech, assembly and conscience, pointed out that "enjoyment by citizens of their rights and freedoms must not be to the detriment of the interests of society or the state, or infringe the rights of other citizens." Individual liberty, including both political and economic liberty, was thus circumscribed.

At the same time, this view of the political preeminence of the working class was accompanied by endless assertions of the steady material progress made under communism. At every party congress, the advancements made by Soviet workers were chronicled; their gains in standard of living, health care and housing adumbrated. At the Twenty-fourth Party Congress (1971), for example, Leonid Brezhnev reported:

> In the past five years, real income per capita increased by 33%, as against the 30% envisaged in the Directives of the 23rd Party Congress and the 19% in the preceding five-year period. . . . As you know, comrades, in this five-year plan the minimum wage of workers and office employees was increased to 60 rubles a month. The average wage of workers and office employees for the country as a whole increased by 26%. The incomes of collective farmers from the communal sector increased by 42%. Guaranteed pay has been introduced, the pension age has been lowered, and the payment of sickness and disability allowances has been established for collective farm members. . .[5]

Mikhail Gorbachev amended the official view to suggest that a diversity of economic interests was possible under socialism, to include even different forms of property ownership. Gorbachev also offered the obligatory statistics on progress. But unlike his predecessors he publicly acknowledged difficulties, including a stagnating economy, a lack of citizen involvement, and a party-state that was retarding, not encouraging, advancement. To ensure the full achievement and promise of socialism, Gorbachev argued, a broad democratization of the state and party were necessary. This view formed the ideological basis of the reforms he initiated (see Chapters 29 and 33). Moreover, it marked a public recognition among the Communist Party leadership of what society already knew: the system wasn't working.

During the period in which Gorbachev became politically active, Soviet society had been transformed from a chiefly rural and agricultural one beset by internal and external crises, to a chiefly urban, industrial society with a better-educated and more secure public. As a result, expectations of a better life and consequent demands on the regime grew. As Gail Lapidus writes, "a significant shift in values was taking place in the Brezhnev era: growing pessimism about the Soviet future, increasing disillusionment with official values, and an accompanying decline in civic morale."[6]

Under conditions of glasnost, but also of economic difficulty, Soviet polls documented a very low level of popular satisfaction with living standards. Soviet sociologists in their own studies of workers' attitudes found that it was not enough to provide high wages and to praise the "social value" of labor. Increasingly, workers' satisfaction with their own jobs and their attitudes toward work in general were found to be a function of work conditions, such as the location of the job and the amount of stress associated with it, and of long-standing and family attitudes that the regime's incessant glorification of labor had not succeeded in erasing. One Soviet study of students' attitudes toward work, for example, found that on a scale of ten, workers' occupations (as opposed to those of professionals) rated less than a five. One of the most influential Soviet sociologists, Tatiana Zaslavskaia, wrote in 1984:

> A low level of labor and production discipline, indifferent attitudes toward the work being done, low quality of work, social inertia, low importance of work as a means of self-realization, strongly pronounced consumer orientations, and low level of morality are traits common to many workers, which have been shaped during recent five-year plans.[7]

Soviet studies reported increasing difficulties in finding people to take managerial positions in factories, and economic statistics showed falling worker productivity. Overcoming this evident erosion of faith was the aim of at least one aspect of the economic reform under Mikhail Gorbachev, referred to as activating the "human factor."

Disappointment in the regime's performance eventually produced disillusionment with its view of society and of the political system itself. Gorbachev recognized this when he argued that broadening of political participation was necessary; he was eager to bring back into the system people who had been alienated from it. And alienated they were. In 1990 the New Soviet Citizen Survey revealed that in Russia itself only just over one-quarter of the people felt that they could trust their leaders "always or most of the time." More than half said they could trust them "only some of the time" and more than 13 percent said "never."[8] Surveys further revealed that it was not just the current leaders whom people distrusted. In 1989, two years *before* the attempted coup, only 22 percent of the people surveyed showed high confidence in the Communist Party; but even that was higher than confidence in local *soviets*, trade unions, or the Council of Ministers.[9] The 1990 survey found that more than 46 percent gave the ruling Communist Party a negative rating and more than half felt the country should have multiple parties. Even among the party itself a loss of confidence was evident. As one party veteran put it,

> I grew up a full-blooded Stalinist like millions of Soviet people who were also fooled by our ideology. I was an active Komsomol member—a Communist organization for teenagers—and the Communist ideology was life for me. I did not propagate ideology. I advocated an honest way of life and fought against injustice. It did not occur to me to criticize the party leadership. I believed that Sakharov and dissidents were anti-Soviet men because that is what our media said. I never read what they wrote because I thought they had betrayed their country. Now I understand that they were much wiser than I.[10]

Letters to the editors of papers had long been an outlet for complaints, even before the age of *glasnost*. During that time, even expressions of loss of faith in the ruling party became possible. The following letter, published in the paper *Sobsednik* in August 1990, made the point.

> *I'm thirty-four, a non-Party member, have a higher education, and all my conscious life have been forced to approve or keep silent. But I'm not blind, I'm not deaf. Doing like they all do— that's the slogan of my existence, so as to be left in peace, to be left alone. Yet there's a limit to everything. Only the blind can't see what we have come to. Where is great Russia, where oh where? For all of seventy-three years the Party has bamboozled the people, the Party has brought the economy to rack and ruin, and has finally driven out the man in whom I believed. All right, M. S. Gorbachev makes mistakes; all right, he wears two hats, but you can hardly put him on a par with comrades Polozkov and Ligachev!*
>
> *As for socialism, it hasn't justified itself in its soviet form. And here I find myself in agreement with delegates to the First Coal Miners' Congress.*
>
> *There's no faith left in the CPSU [Communist Party]—it's had its last chance. If a split does occur, I'd like to see myself in a party headed by comrade Sobchak. . . . Only my belief in Gorbachev brought me to write this letter. I hate to think what would have happened to me ten years ago. Brr-rr-rr. There's no way back.*
>
> O. Khodosevich
> Ordzhonikidze, Northern Caucasus

Source: From *Dear Comrade Editor: Readers' Letters to the Soviet Press Under Perestroika* translated and edited by Jim Riordan and Sue Bridger, 1992, pp. 37–38. Copyright © 1992. Used by permission of Indiana University Press.

Between January 1990 and July 1991, more than four million party members quit the party. Thus after seventy years of Communist rule, in the face of weakening economic performance, years of deferred improvements and dramatic changes taking place in Communist states in East Europe, a growing number of people were coming to reject the only system they or their parents had ever known.

There had always been those who rejected Soviet Communist rule. *Dissidenti* had been part of the scene virtually since the beginning of Soviet rule. Opposition to the policies of Lenin had been voiced by his own comrades; Stalin had purged thousands who had opposed his views; and during the Brezhnev era many who considered themselves socialist, such as historian Roy Medvedev, challenged the regime or its policies. Other brave and some highly public dissidents were willing to challenge the Communist system in its entirety. Aleksandr Solzhenitsyn called Marxism–Leninism "a grim jest of the twentieth century" and

blasted the "myth" of eternal progress. For his opposition and for openly writing about the system's tyranny, he was exiled from the country in 1974. (He did not return until 1994.) Others, such as physicist Andrei Sakharov, based their challenge on the assertion of fundamental human rights that they asserted were being repressed in the Soviet Union. For his views Sakharov, too, suffered exile, in the city of Gorky (now Nizhni Novgorod) from 1980 to 1987. Throughout the Brezhnev period a small corps of human rights advocates, religious activists, and national groups also tried to bring the system's failures to light.[11]

But despite these repressions, at the end of the 1980s there apparently was general acceptance in society of the view that something was wrong with the system and that it could not be

Not So Fast, Comrade

As Mikhail Gorbachev and his supporters frequently pointed out, there were many opponents to his policies, especially that of glasnost or voicing of previously unspoken issues. In March 1988 a long letter was published in *Sovetskaya Rossiya* complaining about the "excesses" of the new situation, especially as it related to education and the country's past. The writer, a teacher from Leningrad named Nina Adreyeva, was particularly exercised about the treatment of Stalin:

> I have been reading and rereading sensational articles. For example, what can young people gain—disorientation apart—from revelations about "the counterrevolution in the USSR in the late twenties and early thirties," or about Stalin's "guilt" for the advent in power of fascism and Hitler in Germany? Or the public "reckoning" of the number of "Stalinists" in various generations and social groups?
>
> The industrialization, collectivization, and cultural revolution which brought our country to the ranks of great world powers are being forc-

> ibly squeezed into the "personality cult" formula. All this is being questioned. Matters have gone so far that persistent demands for "repentance" are being made of "Stalinists" (and this category can be taken to include anyone you like).
>
> It is the champions of "left-wing liberal socialism" who shape the tendency toward falsifying the history of socialism. They try to make us believe that the country's past was nothing but mistakes and crimes, keeping silent about the greatest achievements of the past and the present.

The letter was reportedly personally embellished by conservative opponents of Gorbachev and praised by Yegor Ligachev, a member of the Politburo. It was taken as an attack on the whole Gorbachev approach, and after some delay, supporters of reform rallied to defend perestroika and glasnost. In the autumn of 1988, Ligachev's responsibilities in the secretariat were reduced.

Source: *Sovetskaya Rossiya*, March 13, 1988, p. 3 (Foreign Broadcast Information Service, Soviet Union, Daily Report, March 16, 1988, pp. 49, 50, 52).

fixed with one more leadership change at the top. This view was especially prevalent among better-educated, urban dwellers, young people, and those who held technical or professional jobs, and especially among those who rated the government's overall economic performance poorly.[12] Not everyone agreed, of course, and faith in the Communist Party and even a desire to return to old ways before Gorbachev's perestroika were still held by many. Soviet surveys showed great concern about the growing inequality in the system, which a departure from socialism would only exacerbate. A survey in 1989 found that only 30 percent of the people surveyed agreed with the need to change the whole "administrative–command" economic system and only 14 percent with the idea that "only private property and market economy can lead the country out of the dead end."[13] In sum, what had emerged by 1991 was what one Russian observer called "split consciousness": people still supporting the abstract socialism of official political culture, but in practice supporting measures, such as multiparty elections, to change it fundamentally.

THE NATIONAL QUESTION: THE UNEXPECTED CHALLENGE

Official political culture under communism touted the notion that socialist society, based on the interests of workers, would overcome divisions based on nationality. Narrow assertions of national rights or dominance would be replaced by a new consciousness. The Soviet constitution said a "new people—the Soviet people"—had come into being on the basis of "legal and factual equality of all nations." The official view was that a drawing together (*sblizhenie*) of different nationalities was occurring, replacing ethnic antagonisms but allowing for the preservation of national culture and heritages.

Under the Soviet system, most of the country's major national groups could point to their "own" republics in which the Communist Party leader was a member of their ethnic group. Between 1954 and 1976 more than 86 percent of forty-four different republican party first secretaries were non-Russians. In 1990 the first secretaries of all republics were members of that republic's titular nationality.[14] But despite a certain amount of autonomy and "nativization," real governing power lay with Moscow, often represented in the region by a Russian second secretary of the party. Especially as the country became more industrialized and centralized under Stalin, "Russification" through migration of Russians into all territories became common. The Russian language was mandatory not only in schools but for career advancement. Still, Russification was not entirely successful. Soviet studies showed that as of the 1970s, apart from Byelorussia and Ukraine, an average of just 39 percent of local people knew Russian. Conversely, outside of these two republics, only 12 percent of Russians knew the local language.

More dramatically, as glasnost in the 1980s allowed greater expression of grievances of all sorts, indications surfaced that the political culture in fact included a great deal of internationality hostility. In February 1988 an estimated 1 million Armenians marched through the capital of that republic demanding that a predominantly Armenian part of the neighboring Azerbaijan Republic, called Nargono-Karabakh, be joined with the Armenian Republic. In the aftermath of some demonstrations inside the disputed region, and in Azerbaijan and Armenia, riots occurred in which scores of people were killed and thousands fled their homes in both directions. Order was restored in these regions only when Soviet troops were put on the streets. At the beginning of 1990 violence between Azerbaijanis and Armenians escalated into virtual civil war. Thousands of Soviet interior ministry and army troops were again sent to the region. Between 1988 and 1990 it is estimated that more than six hundred people died in interethnic violence in this region as well as in Georgia, Uzbekistan, Kazakhstan, and Tajikistan.

In many parts of the country, long-suppressed grievances against central Russian rule surfaced. National movements or popular fronts took advantage of the new freer atmosphere to challenge the local Communist Party. Such groups were especially strong in the Baltic republics, in Moldova, Armenia, Azerbaijan, and in Ukraine. The particulars varied but the crux of the challenge was that for most nationalities, sblizhenie in fact meant suppression; that local areas were seen as natural resource reserves to be exploited and abused by the center; and that instead of genuine power, the regions were governed by well-connected local "mafias" that served the interest of the centers. Belatedly recognizing the "national question," the Communist Party of the Soviet Union tried to respond in the old way, with a special Central Committee plenum held in September 1989 devoted to the issue. But it was too late for such methods. The elections in 1990 of national popular fronts armed with a long list of demands for Moscow demonstrated clearly how deep the split was between the official political culture and the popular culture on this issue.

Today in Russia the issue of nationality has not disappeared. As we saw in Chapter 27, Russia remains a multiethnic country and in many ways it faces the same demands from smaller nationalities that the USSR faced. The twenty-one republics of Russia are all based on a particular nationality, but in only eight is that group the most numerous and in only five are they the majority (see Table 31.1). Resentments against Russian immigration, combined with strong desire for local political and economic autonomy, have led to a range of challenges to the Russian government. Two republics, Chechenya and Tartarstan, declared

independence altogether from the Russian federation and subnational units ranging from republic to oblast have pushed for greater control of their destinies.

At the same time Russian nationalism takes the form of strong sentiments among many political figures that Russian interests at home and internationally can and should be served more effectively, that the territorial integrity of the country must be preserved and Russians living outside the country's new borders—an estimated 25 million of them—need to be protected.[15] One of the predominant themes of the political culture of the Communist period—especially during and after World War II—is that of national patriotism. Books, films, speeches, and national policies reflected as profound a commitment to the Soviet Union as a country as to its political-economic ideology. Often such views became indistinguishable from Russian nationalism and provided support for Russian dominance of the other nationalities living in the Soviet Union. As one observer put it, "although Lenin thought of himself as a sworn enemy of great-Russian chauvinism, Russian nationalism nevertheless became a determining element of the Soviet system."[16]

Therefore, it should not be surprising that sentiments of national pride and assertiveness, concern for conationals and for the fate of what is left of the *rodina* (motherland) should play a prominent role in contemporary Russian politics. Especially at a time of great uncertainty, change and loss of national and international status, nationalist sentiments of both a positive, nation-building type and an exclusivist, aggressive type, are to be found.[17] Several political parties brandishing extreme nationalist platforms have also developed. The sentiments and fearful scenarios cast up by Aleksandr Rutskoi—at the time vice president of the country—are illustrative:

Let me remind you that more than 130 nations and nationalities now live on Russia's territory.

So, as a result of the activity of some of our "intellectual giants" and the fathers of Russian "democracy" we might in fact get more than 100 "banana republics." But that would suit those who openly say that this is Russia's historical destiny. . . . One gets the impression that now nothing can stop the "flood of Presidents" and that the breakup of the once united Army could be followed by the formation of not only republic armies but also province, city and perhaps even village armies. And then we might run up against a "flood of iron" that would leave the Russian land bloody and in ruins . . .[18]

In the December 1993 parliamentary elections, the misnamed Liberal Democratic Party (LDP) led by an outspoken newcomer to politics, Vladimir Zhirinovsky, put forth extreme nationalist positions appealing to the sense of humiliation and loss suffered by the Russian people. Calling for the restoration of the Russian empire (including Alaska), full employment, and an end to defense plant conversions, and promising to "raise Russia from her knees," Zhirinovsky's party won the largest percentage of votes cast (22.8 percent) for any single party. Combined with delegates elected individually, the Liberal Democratic Party emerged as the second largest party in the lower house of parliament. Nor was this group alone in pushing the nationalist line. The third largest party in parliament is now none other than the former Communist Party (renamed the Communist Party of the Russian Federation), which also espoused a nationalist agenda.

Prospects for Democracy: An Emerging Civic Culture

For Russia, as for the rest of the former Soviet republics, a key new question involves the country's openness to democratic practice. After centuries of autocratic rule and decades of one-party domination, is there anything identi-

fiable as a democratic political culture in the country? Is resurgent nationalism compatible with democratic governance? Assessment of the level of support for democracy is now possible to an extent in Russia because previous restrictions on the use and publication of public opinion surveys have fallen away. Surveys on virtually all aspects of life are being done in Russia. The 1990 New Citizen Survey mentioned previously was undertaken specifically to assess the fertility of Russian ground for democracy, based on theoretical and survey work in political science. It draws especially on the work of Robert Dahl, which indicated the presence of key values as building blocs of democracy. Specifically, the survey explored where Russians fall on six key values:

1. political tolerance;

2. evaluation of liberty;

3. rights consciousness;

4. support for dissent and opposition;

5. support for an independent media; and

6. support for competitive elections.[19]

The survey found that intolerance was relatively high in Russia; that is, that most people believed that groups whom they identified as "most disliked" should not be allowed to make speeches, hold public rallies, or run for office—or they should be banned. For the largest group of people surveyed, neo-Nazis were the most disliked group, but other disliked groups included Stalinists and, for some, nationalists. A majority of people surveyed were also willing to suffer restrictions on liberty rather than tolerate extremist and possibly disruptive views. For example, in the survey only one-quarter of the people questioned disagreed with the statement that "it is better to live in a orderly society than to allow people so much freedom that they can become disruptive."

Such a question seems to tap into another element of Russian political culture with roots in the past. Some observers see a pattern of a historic preference for a strong leader, even one like Stalin. Writing during the Brezhnev period, reporter Hedrick Smith quoted one Soviet worker:

> The intelligentsia may dream of democracy but the huge mass of people dream of Stalin—his strong power. They are not reactionary but they are being mistreated by their petty bosses, who cheat and exploit them, suppress them. They want a strong boss to "put shoes on" the petty bosses. They know that under Stalin [economic] conditions were not as good, but the state farm directors and other officials were not robbing them under Stalin, were not mocking them. There was a check on local authorities.[20]

Does such a longing exist today? A survey done just before the December 1993 elections revealed support for the idea of a strong leader and nearly a third of the people polled specifically supported a return to pre-1985 (Gorbachev) days.[21] The latter result fits reasonably well with the strong showing of the new Russian Communist Party and its ally, the Agrarian Party, which openly call for a return to the Communist period.

This would seem to suggest relatively poor prospects for democracy in Russia. Moreover, surveys repeatedly show low and falling confidence in both the current holders of power and the new institutions of political democracy. Most broadly, when asked in another survey, "What is democracy?" 47 percent of those asked were either unable or refused to reply.[22]

Yet in many democratic countries levels of tolerance and knowledge are not markedly higher than in Russia. And when asked specific questions regarding the assertion of individual rights, such as freedom of speech, safety, cultural autonomy, equality before the law, right to work and hold property, Russians overwhelmingly believe that such rights should always be protected. In the New Citizen Survey, Russians were also found to support on balance the right to dissent, an independent (that is, nonstate)

media, and multiparty competitive elections. Finally, the December 1993 elections, despite the strong showing of nationalists and Communists, did show some continued support for the direction of political and economic reforms. Though reform-oriented groups were fragmented, their votes together account for roughly 30 percent of the party-list votes in the lower house.

Thus the picture is somewhat mixed. Surveys show that support for democratic values is not uniform in Russian society and is found more frequently among people who are younger, male and better educated. It often takes particular circumstances to really test a population's willingness to struggle to create a democratic system. In Russia such a circumstance occurred in August 1991, when antidemocratic forces tried to abort the broad changes that were occurring. At that moment thousands of Russians showed more than an abstract willingness to have democracy and risked their lives actually to protect its beginnings. But many others did not do so or even supported the coup. Public opposition to the state of emergency was confined largely to the cities—Moscow, St. Petersburg, Kishiniev—confirming surveys that suggested that the urban population is more eager for reform and more supportive of democracy.[23]

The December 1993 elections gave further evidence of a strong urban-rural split in the country, with smaller towns and rural areas generally favoring Liberal Democratic, Communist and Agrarian candidates and voting against the reform policies of the Yeltsin government. In part, this is a specific manifestation of the "declinist" thesis: the areas of Russia which have not gained by the policies of the new form of government, which see themselves as hurt by the need to compete economically and by the coming breakup of the collective farms, do not yet see the gains from the Yeltsin reforms and have rejected the government that brought them. One Russian daily newspaper characterized this disparity as a

Revenge of the *Rodina:* Taking *Glasnost* Seriously

One of the earliest and most vigorous challenges to the dominant Soviet political culture was mounted by writers who took the opportunity afforded by glasnost to denounce the effects of mindless, state-run industrialization on the countryside and its people. Drawing on the venerable tradition of village prose, or literature that focused on the rugged but simple and presumably purer life of the Russian village, such writers frankly and directly criticized the process by which the Soviet state had despoiled the system of human values along with the air, land, and water of the motherland (*rodina*) itself in its unrestrained effort to build socialist society.

Probably the most famous of these writers is Valentin Rasputin, a native of Siberia who wrote both novels and essays decrying the mindless destruction of Siberia and the traditional life tied at least as much to the past as to the "bright future." In his famous novella, "The Fire," he broods about what the needs of modern industry have done to the land and its people:

And the town stood naked, defiantly exposed, repulsive, and nondescript. Rarely did a birch tree or a mountain ash in some flower garden warm the heart and gladden the eye. Back in the old villages where they'd come from, people couldn't have imagined life without some greenery under their windows; here those same people didn't even have flower gardens on display.

And the whole street howled and looked through their windows without interruption. And once again none of the town ordinances about planting trees and gardens got any results. Or to put it more precisely, when you're cutting down thousands of hectares of taiga every year, when you're opening up huge expanses right and left, it's pointless to try to take cover from the penetrating winds and the penetrating view behind a bird-cherry bush. This is the way we live . . .

Two words: timber industry—the State procurement of wood for commercial purposes. This explained much of the sloppiness and disorder in the town's layout. Cutting timber is not like planting crops, when the same tasks and the same worries are repeated season after season and no matter how long you live, you'll never finish tilling the soil. Once timber has been clear-cut, it takes decades and decades to grow back. With today's technology they can clear-cut a forest in a matter of years. And then what? Then pack up and move on. Leaving behind your little houses, cowsheds, and bathhouses, leaving behind the graves of your fathers and mothers and years of your own life, get onto the caterpillars and into the lumber trucks and go where the forest still stands. And start all over again.

Source: Valentin Rasputin, "The Fire" in *Siberia on Fire, Stories and Essays by Valentin Rasputin* (De Kalb, Ill.: Northern Illinois University Press, 1989), p. 110. Translated by Gerald Mikkelson and Margaret Winchell. Reprinted by permission of Northern Illinois University Press.

"clear delimitation of the country into 'liberal market-oriented' regions (mainly around the capital) on the one hand, and conservative-communist and national-opposition territories with a greater or smaller influence of the communists, on the other."[24]

But here the declinist thesis will only take us so far. For another aspect of political culture that these elections—and others in East Europe—revealed is what might be termed the "revenge of the countryside." The rural areas of Russia, as in much of East Europe, suffered the most from Communist experimentation and transformation. It has always been the fate of the countryside to carry out the policies, and some would say political whims, of the cities. In the nineteenth century it was the abolishing of serfdom, in the twentieth, collectivization;

and now, privatization. In part, the reformers' losses outside the major cities in December 1993—a vote that repeated a poor performance in the April referendum—was the voice of the countryside saying "enough." When Vladimir Zhirinovsky railed against "the new clan of bureaucrats . . . growing and spreading" it had a distinct appeal in the smaller towns and villages of Russia.

The transformation of the country has sorely tested the Russian people's commitment to both reform and democracy. When asked in the April 1993 referendum if they retained confidence in Boris Yeltsin, 58.7 percent said they did. Moreover when asked if they supported continued economic reform, which has caused great hardship for many, 53 percent said they did. And nearly two-thirds of all eligible voters participated in that referendum.

The vote in December, however, showed the effects of continued turmoil and decline. Though Boris Yeltsin was not running personally, the policies he championed were certainly the main issue. As noted, the parties supporting continued reform gained just under 30 percent of the party vote and, in combination with seats gained in single-member districts, gained roughly one-third of the seats in the new parliament. By any calculation this is a drop from the April support of Yeltsin's referendum. The draft constitution supported by the president (see Chapter 31) did pass in the referendum, receiving 58.4 percent support. But the number of people eligible who actually voted in the parliamentary elections was the lowest of any of the elections since those of 1989 (54.8 percent). In seventeen regions, too few people voted for the constitutional referendum to be valid.[25]

SUPPORT FOR MARKET REFORMS

The question of Russian views of democracy and its political character cannot be separated from an assessment of Russian views of changes in the economy. Though begun with modest goals by Mikhail Gorbachev in 1985, the pace of reform accelerated after 1987 to include putting more of the economy on a footing of self-financing (*khosrachet*). While strictly speaking only individual private enterprise was legal until the end of the USSR, cooperatives—associations of individuals—sprang up quickly and began to act like private companies. Russia moved more quickly than the country as a whole, legalizing private property, for example, in 1990. After the breakup of the Soviet Union, the Russian government began in earnest to dismantle the state-run economy. It was doing so at the same time that democratic practices such as open elections and multiple parties also began to play a role. Thus economic reform and reform of the political system have gone hand in hand, and surveys have indicated that there tends to be a relationship between one's socioeconomic status and support for or opposition to economic reform. Given the significance of this question, it is worth considering where the Russian people seem to come out on key questions involved in restructuring their economy.

After World War II, the Russian people had enjoyed relative economic stability and steady improvement in their situation for roughly three decades. Jobs were guaranteed, accompanied by all the social services the state provided such as health insurance, vacations, free education, and housing and staples at low, relatively unchanging prices. Prices for utilities had not changed since the end of World War II; rents were the same as they had been in the twenties, and food prices were controlled and held down. As late as 1989, price increases were held to 2 to 3 percent per year.[26]

Changing the economic system meant freeing prices; allowing private enterprise to operate meant allowing prices charged for goods and services to rise to a level that covered costs plus something officially discouraged for years: profit. Not surprisingly, the Russian people worried about prices, which jumped more than 20 percent per month in 1991. In September of that year, a survey undertaken in European Russia found that 81 percent of the people questioned agreed with the statement that "price increases must be stopped." Interestingly enough, however, that number dropped to 67 percent by October of the next year, despite the continued price increases.[27] This suggests that the necessity for increases had found a degree of acceptance among Russians and that the resulting increases in supply allowed by higher prices had compensated for the higher prices in the minds of some.

Apart from the specific pain of such changes, what about the principles of socialism? How deeply has the official ideology of the collective good penetrated Russian political consciousness? Repeated surveys have shown strong commitment on the part of Russians to relative equality in society. If any one aspect of socialist political culture appears to have been internalized by the Soviet public it was support for the idea of general equality and opposition to great variations in personal wealth. In late 1992 a survey carried out in European Russia found that nearly two-thirds of the people polled preferred a system that promoted greater security for society as a whole to one that guaranteed greater liberty for the individual.[28] But capitalist economics is inherently unequal; in such a system some people will succeed when others will not. Here too the evidence indicates that as reforms are introduced, Russians have become less hostile to the idea and practice of inequality. A survey in April 1991 found that 56 percent of the people agreed with the notion that differences in income should be minimized; by September, 48 percent agreed and by May 1992, 42 percent. But the idea that the state should provide certain guarantees of personal welfare remains strong in Russia and has support even from those who favor the country's movement toward a market economy.[29]

What about private enterprise? If there is a building bloc of a market economy, it is private initiative and entrepreneurship aided—or at

least not opposed—by a powerful state. Such a situation has never existed for the mass public in Russia but became possible when private entrepreneurship and ownership of the land became possible. It was facilitated further by a program begun in Russia in 1992 to take out of the hands of the state the enterprises it ran, which until 1991 were most of them. For more than sixty years private enterprise was equivalent to illegal enterprise, to buying and selling on the "black market" goods either stolen or somehow secured from the socialist economic sector. Such activities were tolerated under the old regime—or even encouraged by high-level corruption—because they provided goods and services in quantities and quality that the state economy could not. Thus, for example, before private agriculture was legalized, peasants' small "household plots" still provided 60 percent of the Soviet Union's fruit, 28 percent of its meat, and 23 percent of its milk—all while accounting for less than 2 percent of the country's land. But private trading was always part of the underground economy and carried the official stigma of corruption and personal profit. And such trade excluded people who were not lucky enough to possess the right connections or enough money to be active in such an economy. How then has Russian society reacted to a reform process that has in several ways encouraged the growth of legal private economic activity? At best, Russian attitudes can be characterized as ambivalent. In surveys done in 1989 and 1990 among urban dwellers, only 45 percent believed that cooperatives should be developed.[30] In another survey, more than 50 percent of Russians expressed negative attitudes toward workers in cooperatives.[31] Once again concerns about these enterprises had to do with an increase in crime, the fear that that they would not fulfill consumer demands, and concern over inequality of incomes.

But once again, as reforms moved forward opposition declined. While only 31 percent had supported private enterprise in November 1989, 44 percent did so in December 1990. Over time, people in Russia have come to support the idea of hiring others to work in enterprises and to express a desire to be owners themselves.[32] And though surveys showed substantial skepticism about government plans to sell off its enterprises, the sales were very successful. By the middle of 1993 more than seventy thousand state enterprises had been sold and some 150,000 private businesses were operating in Russia.

But how far can the apparent elasticity of views on reform go? By the middle of 1993, nearly 1 million Russians were unemployed officially (unofficial figures are five times that), 5 percent of all workers were on unpaid leave, and the real income of all workers was below what it had been in 1985. Will Russian society—which has known only full employment—ever accept the idea that some people will have to be unemployed? A survey in October 1992 showed that two-thirds of Russians felt that reforms should not lead to unemployment. All governments watch their unemployment figures and economic indicators with extreme care. The richest Russians now make eleven times what the poorest Russians make. As American president George Bush learned in 1992, if unemployment goes up and production goes down, if people do not begin relatively quickly to see improvement in their lives, the political opposition has a powerful weapon with which to attack them. The December 1993 elections showed that this is no less true of the Russian government. In virtually its infancy, this government faces not just the challenge of reelection but the task of trying to create both a new and more open government and an economic system that offers more than promises of a bright future.

Notes

1. See the discussion in Frederick C. Barghoorn and Thomas F. Remington, *Politics in the USSR* (Boston: Little, Brown, 1986), pp. 1–18.
2. S. Frederick Starr, "A Usable Past," in Alexander Dallin and Gail Lapidus, eds., *The Soviet System in Crisis* (Boulder, Colo.: Westview Press, 1991), pp. 11–15.
3. Paul Milyoukov, *Russia and Its Crisis* (Chicago: The University of Chicago Press, 1905), p. 563.
4. V. I. Lenin, *State and Revolution* (New York: International Publishers, 1917), pp. 22, 72, 73 (italics in original).
5. "Brezhnev: Central Committee Report," in *Current Soviet Policies, VI, The Documenary Record of the 24th Congress of the Communist Party of the Soviet Union* (Columbus: American Association for the Advancement of Slavic Studies, 1973), p. 16.
6. Gail W. Lapidus, "State and Society: Toward the Emergence of Civil Society in the Soviet Union," in Alexander Dallin and Gail W. Lapidus, eds., *The Soviet System in Crisis* (Boulder, Colo.: Westview Press, 1991), p. 135.
7. Cited in Vladimir Shlapentokh, "Evolution in the Soviet Sociology of Work: From Ideology to Pragmatism," *The Carl Beck Papers in Russian and East European Studies*, no. 404 (Pittsburgh, Pa.: University of Pittsburgh, Center for Russian and East European Studies, 1985), p. 65.
8. Arthur H. Miller, "In Search of Regime Legitimacy," in Arthur H. Miller, William M. Reisinger, and Vicki L. Hesli, eds., *Public Opinion and Regime Change: The New Politics of Post-Soviet Societies* (Boulder, Colo.: Westview Press, 1993), p. 100. The New Soviet Citizen Survey was conducted by the University of Iowa during May–June 1990, and is described in the *Appendix, Idem.*
9. Nikolai P. Popov, "Political Views of the Russian People," *International Journal of Public Opinion Research*, 4, No. 4 (Winter 1992), pp. 328–330.
10. "Anatoly," described as "The Last Communist" by Lois Fisher, *Survival in Russia: Chaos and Hope in Everyday Life* (Boulder, Colo.: Westview Press, 1993), p. 150.
11. See Irina Kirk, *Profiles in Russian Resistance* (New York: Quadrangle, 1975), and Peter Reddaway, *Uncensored Russia: Protest and Dissent in the Soviet Union* (New York: American Heritage Press, 1972).
12. Miller, "In Search of Regime Legitimacy."
13. Popov, "Political Views," pp. 331–332.
14. Zvi Gitelman, "Nations, Republics and Commonwealth," in Stephen White, Alex Pravda, and Zvi Gitelman, eds., *Developments in Soviet*

and Post-Soviet Politics (Durham: Duke University Press, 1992), p. 138.

15. This figure is based on the 1989 census and is presumed to be somewhat lower now due to migration from the independent republics since that time. In mid-1993 the Federal Migration Service estimated that 200,000 people had immigrated to Russia, *The New York Times*, June 2, 1993, p. A4.

16. "What Is 'Soviet'—What Is 'Russian'? A Conversation with Adam B. Ulam," in G. R. Urban, ed., *End of Empire: The Demise of the Soviet Union* (Washington, D.C.: American University Press, 1993), p. 159.

17. Walter Laqueur, "Russian Nationalism," *Foreign Affairs*, 71, No. 5 (Winter, 1992/93), pp. 103–116.

18. *Pravda*, January 30, 1992, pp. 1, 3.

19. James L. Gibson and Raymond M. Duch, "Emerging Democratic Values in Soviet Political Culture," in Miller, Reisinger, and Hesli, *Public Opinion and Regime Change*, pp. 69–94.

20. Hedrick Smith, *The Russians* (New York: Ballantine Books, 1976), p. 327.

21. Amy Corning, "Public Opinion and the Russian Parliamentary Elections," *RFE/RL Research Report*, 2, No. 48 (December 3, 1993), pp. 21–22.

22. *Moscow News*, January 26–February 2, 1992, p. 7.

23. Gibson and Duch, "Emerging Democratic Values."

24. *Segodnya*, December 21, 1993 (Russia/CIS Intelligence Report, 26 December 1993).

25. Vera Tolz, "Russia's Parliamentary Elections: What Happened and Why," *RFE/RL Research Report*, 3, No. 2 (January 14, 1994), p. 3.

26. *PlanEcon Report*, VIII, Nos. 4, 5, 6, February 12, 1992, p. 30.

27. Mary Cline, "Attitudes toward Economic Reform in Russia," *RFE/RL Research Report*, 2, No. 22, May 28, 1993, p. 44.

28. Amy Corning, "How Russians View Yeltsin and Rutskoi," *RFE/RL Research Report*, 2, No. 12, March 19, 1993, p. 58.

29. Corning, "Public Opinion," p. 20.

30. S. Shpil'ko, "The Attitude of the Population Toward Privatization of Property," *Problems of Economics*, 34, No. 7 (November 1991): 28–29.

31. William M. Riesinger and Alexander I. Nikitin, "Public Opinion and the Emergence of a Multi-Party System," in Miller, Reisinger, and Hesli, *Public Opinion and Regime Change*, pp. 181–183.

32. Shpil'ko, "The Attitude of the Population."

REFERENCES AND SUGGESTED READINGS

Diuk, Nadia, and Adrian Karatnycky. 1993. *New Nations Rising*. New York: John Wiley & Sons.

Fisher, Lois. 1993. *Survival in Russia: Chaos and Hope in Everyday Life*. Boulder, Colo.: Westview Press.

Friedberg, Maurice, and Heyward Isham, eds. 1987. *Soviet Society under Gorbachev*. Armonk, N.Y.: M. E. Sharpe, Inc.

Gorbachev, M. S. 1986. *Speeches and Writings*. New York: Pergamon Press.

Lane, David, ed. 1992. *Russia in Flux: The Political and Social Consequences of Reform*. Hants, England: Edward Elgar.

Tucker, Robert C. 1987. *Political Culture and Leadership in Soviet Russia*. New York: W. W. Norton.

Ulam, Adam B. 1993. "What Is 'Soviet'—What Is 'Russian'?" in G. R. Urban, ed. *End of Empire: The Demise of the Soviet Union*. Washington, D.C.: American University Press, pp. 155–177.

31

National and Subnational Government

For more than 60 years the country known as the Soviet Union was ruled by the Communist Party in accordance with its activist philosophy of the role of government in modern society. It had come to power with an ideology that invoked large-scale change as its goal. Its aim was nothing short of the total transformation of the economic and political structure of Tsarist Russia. The practices in support of that ideology were modified over the years as a revolutionary party became a governing party and as its commitment to far-reaching transformation waned. But certain key features of Communist Party rule remained salient until roughly midway through the Gorbachev period. The disappearance of these features accounts for some of the great uncertainty gripping Russia in its current "time of troubles."

Key aspects of the legacy of Communist Party rule are:

◆ Central control: With the end of the civil war and the New Economic Policy and the emergence into political dominance of Joseph Stalin, the Soviet Union increasingly began to be ruled from the political center— that is, Moscow. The introduction of central planning, the forced industrialization and collectivization of the 1930s, and the political purges reinforced a venerable Russian tradition of direction from the "center." Local and regional leaders retained a measure of autonomy in some sectors, but the system of *nomenklatura*, or appointment to key positions from party-approved lists, assured that such leaders and their actions were subject to control by the party's highest ranks. The main direction of the country's developments, the use of its resources, and the nature of political friends and enemies were determined by the people in these ranks and carried out in the provinces.

◆ Communist Party dominance of lawmaking: After 1918 the Communist Party of the Soviet Union (CPSU) was the only legitimate political party in the country. As the workers' "vanguard," it represented their interests. Measures decided on by the party were then dutifully enacted into law by the formal organs of the government: the legislature and executive. Until 1989, the Supreme Soviet had been both the national legislature and the highest state body—at least in theory. This *soviet*, or council, represented the people of the Soviet Union in decision making. Like the United States Congress, it had two chambers, a Soviet of Nationalities and a Soviet of Unions.

The Soviet of Nationalities represented the country's constituent regions and therefore many of its nationalities. Different subnational units, depending on their level in the hierarchy, sent different numbers of deputies. The Soviet of Unions represented Soviet citizens on the basis of elections in single-member electoral districts of equal size. In the old parliament each chamber had 750 members, with candidates for seats chosen by the local party. The voter in most cases was relieved of the burden of choice, having the option only to approve or strike out the name of a candidate. Choice was not critical, however, since this parliamentary body was more symbolic than powerful. It met only twice a year for two or three days and virtually always unanimously supported party policy.

◆ Leadership control of the party: The fact that the Soviet Union had one party until 1990 does not mean there was no politics. Political battles over control of state policy and resources took place within the one sanctioned party. Leadership control was not total; even under Stalin there were debates and challenges of various sorts.[1] Succession battles were often fierce precisely because whoever won would wield enormous power, including the ability to replace key personnel throughout the country, to direct the use of natural and human resources stretching over one-seventh of the earth's surface, and to formulate and seek to implement his vision of the socialist future.

◆ Socialist parameters of governance: The Soviet Union was defined as a socialist country of workers and peasants, in which the state controlled the means of production and established the method and form of economic activity. Though some particulars varied around the country, neither national nor local governments could breach these key tenets of government. The role and very existence of independent political units, parties, or local councils, as well as individual rights and prerogatives, were set in a national constitution that had gone forty years, from 1937 to 1977, without significant revision. When it was changed, the new "Brezhnev constitution" strengthened the dominance of the party and tightened ideological control.

It is fair to say that with the disappearance of the Communist Party, indeed of the USSR itself, these key structures of Soviet governance disappeared. Central control, one-party control of lawmaking, leadership control of that party, and the socialist parameters of government are not today key features of national or subnational government in Russia. Instead, a new form of government is being created at all levels. Though a new constitution has been agreed on and a new national legislature and presidency in place, the struggle to define both the policies and prerogatives of those in office is continuing. Keeping in mind the length of time it has taken for British, French, and American democracy to find its way should help us have some perspective on the turbulent process now underway in Russia. Nor can we be certain that the success of the Russian "work-in-progress" is assured.

THE GORBACHEV TRANSITION

The current state of flux did not simply emerge out of the sudden collapse of Soviet communism. Reform and dismantling of that system began, as might be expected, at the top. Mikhail Gorbachev recognized early in his tenure as general secretary that the kind of economic transformation he envisioned had to be accompanied by political change. In particular, the changes he urged and instituted involved increasing popular impact on policymaking; increasing local autonomy vis-à-vis the center; strengthening the national legislature in relation to the party; and, somewhat paradoxically, strengthening the executive in relation to both the party and the legislature.

As noted, Gorbachev unleashed the policy of glasnost and an end to repression of dissidents. He encouraged individuals to do what they had previously had little power to do: make their voices heard in the creation, not just the implementation, of state policies. The elections set up as part of the reform of the role of the national legislature meant that for the first time the actions of the Communist Party would be subject to public approval. The Soviet legislature elected in 1989, though not the product of true multiparty elections, still represented the first assertion of elective and legislative power against the long-dominant power of the party. As one observer noted: "The mere fact that a parliament existed began to marginalise the party, its Central Committee, and even more so its apparatus."[2] The presence of this alternative source of power was backed by key reform elements within the party and especially by Gorbachev himself, whose own power was increased, first as chairman of the Supreme Soviet, then as president.

But Gorbachev's challenge to his own party was not the only one unleashed by reforms. In accordance with the drive to strengthen the power of local soviets, constitutional amendments passed in 1989 and 1990 opened up the nomination and election process to these bodies and at least formally strengthened them at the expense of local executives, who were inevitably the party leaders.[3]

At the same time, in several republics national groups began to challenge the center. Nationalist "popular fronts" won elections in the Baltic republics, Moldova and Armenia. In all of these republics, and in Russia, the aim of such movements was to take power away from the central government. Boris Yeltsin's election as chairman of the Russian Supreme Soviet in 1990, that legislature's declaration of sovereignty, and then Yeltsin's direct election as president in 1991 hastened the collapse of the CPSU and the system of governance of the Soviet Union. By the end of the Soviet Union, the Russian Republic was already acting much as a nation unto itself and was well poised to take over the crumbling power from the old "center." But no sooner had that happened than the new Russian "center" became embroiled in a struggle to define a post-Communist and post-Soviet Russian form of national and subnational government.

GROWTH AND STRUGGLES IN THE RUSSIAN GOVERNMENT

At the end of 1991 the Russian state replaced the Soviet state in both form and name. The main features of this new state were in some ways quite similar to those they replaced and in some ways similar to those seen in other countries treated in this book. There is a president who is the head of state, a prime minister and government with direct responsibility for the country's domestic and foreign policies, and a two-tiered legislature. But in each case important differences exist between these institutions and those seen elsewhere. Probably more importantly, the nature of the power of these institutions and their very existence have been challenged and changed in the very short period of their existence.

The Russian Parliament

In 1990 elections were held for a Congress of Peoples' Deputies of the Russian Soviet Federated Socialist Republic, and 1,068 deputies were elected. Like the elections for the USSR's Congress in 1989, opposition political parties were not formally recognized. Eighty-six percent of the people elected to the Congress were Communist Party members. But in this election seats were not reserved for the Communist Party or for any other organization, and informal groups were very active in promoting their candidates. The largest of these were Democratic Russia, a reform-oriented coalition that pushed hard for Russian sovereignty and a multiparty system. They supported Boris Yeltsin. Opposing them were the Communists of Russia who opposed Yeltsin and favored retention of the dominance of the Communist Party. While neither group gained a majority in the elections, Democratic Russia was able to hold together a coalition and lead sharp attacks on the outgoing Russian and Soviet government.

This Congress elected a smaller (252-member) Supreme Soviet to act as the sitting parliament. This parliament was itself divided into two chambers, a Council of the Republic and a Council of Nationalities, each with 126 members. While these bodies were supposed to formulate the laws that would change Russia, in fact their work was overshadowed by the Congress, which had the legal right to modify the power relations among the bodies in the government. The Congress continually redefined this relationship; for example, first it gave the Russian president (Yeltsin) extraordinary powers and then challenged acts taken under those powers, stripped him of those powers, impeached him, and finally defied him.

The parliament, like its predecessor, elected a presidium, an executive body that organizes and coordinates the work of both the Congress and the Supreme Soviet. It wielded enormous influence in its ability either to facilitate or to hinder the passage of programs through the legislature. As the struggle between the president and the two legislative bodies heated up in 1992 and 1993, the presidium became the base of operation from which Supreme Soviet chairman Ruslan Khasbulatov challenged Boris Yeltsin, much as Yeltsin had challenged Mikhail Gorbachev in 1990 and 1991.

The Russian Presidency

The Russian presidency did not exist until 1991. Previous to that, the Russian Supreme Soviet had elected a chairman, whose office, like that of the USSR Supreme Soviet, was largely ceremonial. But as Russia asserted itself against the Gorbachev government, this office took on importance as a symbol of Russian sovereignty. In 1990 Boris Yeltsin was elected chairman in a narrow victory over the sitting Russian prime minister, Alexander Vlasov. He proceeded to use this office to the fullest measure. Though not formally empowered to do so, he was able to dictate who would be in the new Russian government (the Council of Ministers) and who would be its chairman (the prime minister). And as Jonathan Harris writes, "with a combination of bullying and cajolery managed to subordinate it [the government] to the decisions of the Supreme Soviet."[4]

As with Gorbachev himself, Boris Yeltsin wanted both to reform the country's existing system—especially the way the economy worked—and gain for himself the power to ensure that those reforms would go forward. Thus when Gorbachev pulled back from radical economic reform in the fall of 1990 and seemed to line himself up with those eager to

Boris Yeltsin: A Zigzag to the Top

The path of Boris Yeltsin's life does not unmistakably suggest a person who would precipitate the disintegration of the entire political and economic system in which he grew up—or that he would be the architect of a new system to replace it. His most enduring characteristics appear to be a strong streak of individualism, a desire to investigate—and, if necessary—change things himself, personal courage, and an impatience with the often slow workings of large organizations. Like many other officials in the Communist system, he benefited from the party's control of society and the economy and from powerful patrons. But unlike most such officials, he showed himself willing to challenge his patrons and collaborators both publicly and privately—which accounts for the ups and downs in his career.

Boris Yeltsin did not even join the Communist Party until 1961, when he was already 30 years old. Born in a village in the Sverdlovsk region, Yeltsin graduated from the Urals Polytechnical Institute in 1955. A specialist in construction, he learned his trade from the bottom up, signing on at first as an apprentice laborer, not the typical beginning for a graduate engineer.

His first party work involved supervising construction for the provincial party, which he eventually came to direct in 1975 as party secretary for construction and industry. The next year, when the provincial party leader moved to Moscow, Yeltsin became first secretary of the Sverdlovsk party. By his own admission, the provincial party boss was "a god, a Tsar" yet Yeltsin displayed a degree of openness—going on television to answer questions, and riding public transportation—and independence of mind. He showed no interest in following a career path through Moscow.

But in 1985 he came to Moscow to become head of construction for the Central Committee and became a party secretary that year—the same year that Mikhail Gorbachev became general secretary. His career takeoff continued under Gorbachev's patronage when he replaced the Brezhnev-era leader of the Moscow party and was elected a candidate (nonvoting) member of the Politburo in February 1986. His style in Moscow was much as it had been in Sverdlovsk. He purged corrupt officials from the Brezhnev days, railed against special party privileges, appeared unannounced in public—sometimes standing in line for provisions—and kept pushing the national party to move further and faster on reform.

It was that impatience and aggressiveness that brought him into conflict with both party conservatives, such as Yegor Ligachev, and Gorbachev himself. In a speech in October 1987, Yeltsin attacked the slow pace of perestroika and Gorbachev for not repudiating the conservatives. Under tremendous pressure from the party leadership, Yeltsin resigned from the Politburo and after that from the Moscow party leadership. He spent the next two years working in the State Committee for construction.

The creation of elected state bodies in both the Soviet Union and Russia gave Boris Yeltsin the opportunity to reenter public politics. In 1989 he won a seat in the Congress of People's Deputies of the USSR as a delegate from Moscow, where his visibility and attacks on corruption made him popular. He was a cofounder of the Interregional Group of Deputies and continued to press vigorously for faster and broader reform. But it was in the Russian Republic that he was able to regain substantial power, winning election to the Congress there and then the chairmanship of the Supreme Soviet in 1990. Challenging Gorbachev and the central government from that base, Yeltsin was elected president directly in 1991, defeating a Gorbachev ally and former prime minister, Nikolai Ryzhkov, in June of that year. Two months later, he faced down the "Emergency Committee" that had tried forcibly to halt and reverse the pace of change in the Soviet Union. By the end of that year he was president of a newly independent Russian Federation.

Sources: John Morrison, *Boris Yeltsin: From Bolshevik to Democrat* (New York: Penguin, 1991); Joel C. Moses, "Yeltsin, Boris Nikolaevich," in Joseph L. Wieczynski, ed., *The Gorbachev Encyclopedia* (Salt Lake City: Charles Schlacks, Jr. Pub., 1993), pp. 406–415.

preserve the old system, Yeltsin moved to push Russia to the forefront and to gain for himself a stronger presidency.

In the spring of 1991 a nationwide referendum was held in the Soviet Union on the country's future. In Russia a question was added asking people if they wanted an elected presidency. Seventy percent answered "Yes" and the Russian Congress of People's Deputies agreed to the holding of direct presidential elections. In June 1991 Boris Yeltsin won that election with nearly 60 percent of the vote. While the powers of the office were strengthened somewhat prior to the election, it was Yeltsin's public stand during the August coup attempt and his relentless assertion of Russian national interests after it that made him, by the end of the year, the dominant political figure in the country. So much so that in November he was granted emergency powers by the Russian Congress of People's Deputies to enact needed economic reform by decree, to reorganize the government ministry system, and simultaneously to hold the post of prime minister.

Given the turbulence the country was undergoing in its search for both a new political and new economic system, it would have been remarkable if a purely presidential system had emerged smoothly. In fact, faced with the sharp decline in the standard of living brought on by the freeing of prices at the beginning of 1992 and by a desire to retain some control over governing the country, the Congress of People's Deputies began increasingly to line up against Yeltsin's actions and the people he appointed to implement them. At the same time, many democrats were worried that the accretion of power to Yeltsin could produce a presidential dictatorship instead of democracy. Indeed Yeltsin had taken several peremptory actions at the end of 1991 that showed his willingness to use power. He appointed presidential envoys (*predstaviteli*) to the country's republics and regions to ensure implementation of his directives. He persuaded the Con-

gress to put off local elections and allow him to appoint heads of regional administration. He did reorganize and streamline the Council of Ministers and make himself prime minister. In November he banned the Communist Party throughout the country, a move that some saw as undemocratic.

Attacks on both the power and policies of the Russian president produced a steady decline in the president's power and growth of that of the Congress and Supreme Soviet. In February 1992 Yeltsin was obliged to yield the prime ministership, appointing Yegor Gaidar to push the economic reform. But that government soon suffered so many attacks that it too tried to resign. Though the president refused to accept this resignation, by mid-1992 the Congress and Supreme Soviet had both become sounding boards for dissatisfaction with the pace and pain of economic reform and presidential prerogative. By the end of the year the Gaidar government was gone and soon thereafter President Yeltsin's emergency powers were as well.

In response to the shifting momentum of governing power toward a conservative and fractious Congress, President Yeltsin tried to declare a period of "special rule" in March 1993. Describing the Congress as "a dress rehearsal for revenge by members of the former Party *nomenklatura*," Yeltsin said it was "impossible to govern the country and its economy, especially in a time of crisis, through votes and rejoinders at the microphone, through endless gabfests in parliament and meeting after meeting. This is anarchy; it is a direct path to chaos, to the death of Russia." With this decree, the president announced that a referendum would be held as a vote of confidence in him, to confirm a new constitution, and elections which would be held to a new Russian parliament. He also declared that a list of most urgent economic measures was being drawn up that would be implemented in order to "stabilize the situation." All actions that were counter to the president's decrees were declared to have "no legal force."[5] The president was counting on his demonstrated electoral popularity to provide him with legitimacy and to steamroll the Congress, but almost immediately this action was declared unconstitutional by the Constitutional Court. A move was mounted in the Congress to impeach Yeltsin but he narrowly survived.

The president has also tried to counter the power of the legislature by creating a large and potentially powerful presidential apparatus. At the beginning of 1992 the number of government ministries and state committees was reduced from 46 to 23. At the same time the number of state secretaries, counselors, and agencies attached to the president grew. By mid-1993, there were eleven presidential counselors, each with a specific area of responsibility—for example, defense and security, "families, mothers and children," and environment and health. Thus the Russian president, like the American, has a cabinet, but as in the French system, there is also a government responsible to the Congress. President Yeltsin has found this parallel arrangement useful in keeping supporters close to him. When the Congress forced the resignation of Gennady Burbulis as first deputy prime minister in 1992, for example, he became a presidential counselor. There is also a large presidential office of administration that grew from a tiny group to more than one thousand in less than a year.[6] Finally, there are also no fewer than sixteen different commissions, committees, and councils that are part of the executive branch. The most important of these is the Security Council, which has a sizable staff of its own, is a key actor in foreign policy coordination, and whose head serves as a close adviser to the president. The president has also used this method to draw directly into his circle representatives of the country's republics and regions by adding them to the Security Council when necessary, and appointing them as members of the Council of Heads of Republics of the Federation.[7]

Before the new constitution was adopted, the position of the Russian president was weakened by the role of his own vice president. Created at Yeltsin's request, this office had only vaguely defined powers and, except for waiting to succeed the president, the officeholder had little to do except what the president assigned him. In this case the person holding the office was Aleksandr Rutskoi, a retired air force major general and veteran of the war in Afghanistan who had thrown his support to Yeltsin during a crucial test of strength with orthodox Communists in the spring of 1991. But during his term in office Rutskoi became an increasingly outspoken critic of Yeltsin, allied with his foes in the Congress and even campaigned against him in the April 1993 referendum. After that Yeltsin relieved Rutskoi of his duties and in September suspended him on charges of corruption. The next month Rutskoi led a violent challenge to Yeltsin, which eventually led to his arrest. The constitution adopted in December 1993 does not provide for a vice president.

This points to a key feature of the still-being-created Russian system: the weakness of political parties. Since these are new in Russia and have not had the benefit of electoral campaigns to weld them into effective action groups, they tend to be weak, vaguely defined groups that form, splinter, and re-form very quickly. Hence unlike the British system, for example, the head of the government cannot call his or her own party in line based on party discipline. And unlike the American case, the president cannot count on a core group of longtime party leaders to help him forge and pass programs. In Russia the former vice president led his own political party and criticized the actions of his own running mate.

Lacking a strong political base in the legislature, President Yeltsin has made good use of a more direct democratic device: the referendum.

Challenged by the legislature over both his program and his own powers, Yeltsin repeatedly called for national referenda in which people would be asked directly whether they had faith in him or the Congress and whether they supported continued economic reform. The results (see box on page 518) proved generally supportive for the president but not decisive. More to the point, such a device cannot be used as an effective tool for making specific policies. Hence during 1993, both President Yeltsin and leaders of the Congress drew up plans for a new system that would clarify—and increase—their respective powers. Once again a referendum was used to determine the outcome and once again President Yeltsin got what he wanted: a new constitution with a much stronger presidency.

DUELING CONSTITUTIONS

One of the reasons for this continuing state of flux is that after its independence, Russia was operating under a charter written for a republic that was part of another country. The Russian constitution was drafted in 1978, when Leonid Brezhnev was still in power, and was amended more than three hundred times after that. As new offices were created and fundamental changes contemplated (such as the status of private property), the old constitution was recognized to be inadequate.

In response, both President Yeltsin and the Russian parliament drew up constitutions that they insisted should be adopted as the law of the land. The Yeltsin draft was formulated by a constitutional assembly. This body, called together in the summer of 1993, involved some 750 delegates, but had no claim to the right to draft a new constitution. The Congress of People's Deputies on the other hand could point to the fact that under the law creating it, only the Congress could change the Constitution. President Yeltsin countered that the mandate given him in the April 1993 referendum and the fact

that the Congress was elected before there was an independent state of Russia gave his assembly the right to draft the constitution.

The two constitutions were quite similar in many respects. Both envisioned a Russian president, directly elected, a two-chambered national legislature and a constitutional court. But the two documents provided for key powers to lie in different places. Under the constitution drafted by President Yeltsin's commission, the president needed approval only for his choice of prime minister and then only from the lower house of parliament, called the State Duma. The rest of the government—the deputy ministers and heads of key agencies—would not need legislative approval. The upper chamber, called the Federation Council, would approve the judges of the Constitutional Court and the State Duma would approve the director of the Central Bank (Article 83).[8] In contrast, the parliamentary commission's draft provided for the whole government—the prime minister, the deputies, and heads of all key ministries—to be approved by the parliament and by both houses at that. Both houses would also have the right to approve the constitutional judges, and the parliament could both appoint and relieve the head of the Central Bank (Article 86).[9]

The Yeltsin constitution allowed the president to dissolve parliament under certain conditions and call referenda (Articles 84 and 85). The parliamentary draft did not provide for presidential dissolution, allowed only the legislative branch the right to call referenda, and limited the range of issues for those. It also allowed for a government to fall without entailing new elections, something that does not typically happen in western parliamentary systems (Articles 86, 90, 98). In the Yeltsin draft, the president could force new elections if the government lost a vote of no confidence (Article 116). There was no vice president foreseen in the Yeltsin draft, while the Parliament stipulated that one would be elected directly, along with the president (Articles 92, 96). It was also

Yeltsin's supporters as well as his attackers were in evidence during the battle with parliament in the autumn of 1993. The sign reads: "The president must win!"

casier in the system proposed by the parliamentary commission to override a presidential veto of legislation and to impeach the president (Articles 89 and 95).

As of mid-1993, not only were these two versions of the constitutional future vying with each other, but it was not clear or established how either would be adopted, since neither the president nor the legislature seemed inclined to accept the other's draft.

The Showdown

The standoff between the Russian president and the parliament reached a climax in October 1993. All through the summer, the parliament moved to slow the pace and even reverse the direction of economic reform (see Chapter 33). In the midst of delicate negotiations between Russia and Ukraine over the status of the Black

Sea fleet (see Chapter 34) and a continuing controversy over the status of the territory of Crimea, the parliament declared the fleet's home base, Sevastopol, to be Russian territory. New restrictions on foreign banks were passed and in a stunning move, the Central Bank, which reported to parliament, declared all pre-1993 currency invalid. This last move caused widespread fear as citizens rushed to convert old notes under the limited terms allowed by this action.

President Yeltsin moved to ease the impact of this last action soon after, in order to maintain some confidence in the country's currency. But the overall aim of the parliament's moves was unmistakable. In fact, most Yeltsin supporters had begun boycotting the parliament in early summer. Many of the parliament's measures undoing economic reform were passed only after it lowered its requirement for a quorum from two-thirds to a simple majority. Finally, on

Burning of the Russian White House, October 1993.

It is my duty as president to acknowledge that the present legislative corps has forfeited the right to be at the major levers of state power. The security of Russia and its peoples is of higher value than formal compliance with the contradictory norms created by a legislative power that has finally discredited itself. The time has come for the most serious decisions.[10]

But the parliament refused to be dispersed. Instead, armed with a Constitutional Court ruling declaring Yeltsin's actions unconstitutional, the legislature impeached and removed Yeltsin and elected his vice president, Aleksandr Rutskoi, to the presidency. For nearly two weeks a paralyzing showdown held Moscow and all the country transfixed. Supporters came to the "White House," the Russian Parliament building, and at one point negotiations carried on under the auspices of the Orthodox Church seemed to suggest a resolution of the crisis.

A resolution did come—but through violence, not negotiations. On the morning of October 3, supporters of the rump parliament marched to the White House and then attacked the nearby office of the mayor of Moscow and the site of the country's main radio and television stations. As he had in August 1991, Yeltsin rose to the challenge. The next day a ferocious attack by tanks and airborne troops was launched on the house of parliament itself. In the battle of one branch of government against another, 144 people were killed, almost 900 were wounded, and the country's legislative assembly building was wrecked. The chairman of the parliament, Ruslan Khasbulatov, and the one-time vice president Rutskoi were arrested. Parliament was not only dissolved, it was destroyed.

In this way the contitutional Gordian knot was cut. In the aftermath of the crushing of parliament, President Yeltsin declared that new elections would be held two months later for a new parliament. And on the same day, voters would be asked to approve or disapprove a new constitution. Their approval moreover

September 21, despite the fact that he had no clear constitutional right to do so, Boris Yeltsin declared the parliament suspended. Arguing that the parliament "has been seized by a group of persons who have turned it into the headquarters of the irreconcilable opposition," Yeltsin appealed to a higher duty:

Hiding behind the backs of deputies, feeding like a parasite on collective irresponsibility and secret ballots, it has been nudging Russia toward an abyss. To fail to notice this, to tolerate it and do nothing is no longer possible.

would be considered valid if 50 percent of all eligible voters voted and more than 50 percent of those voting approved it.

That document was unveiled in mid-November and provided for the strong presidency envisioned earlier by Boris Yeltsin. In the referendum in December the new constitution was approved by a vote of 58.4 percent in favor, 41.6 percent opposed.[11]

Under the new constitution, the holder of the office of president is the country's head of state and has authority to "define the basic domestic and foreign policy guidelines of the country" (Article 80). Presidents have extensive decree power (Article 90) and even the power to invalidate acts of lower bodies of government if they contravene the country's constitution or, in the case of the appointed ministers, the presidents' own decrees. As Yeltsin had wanted, the new constitution gives the lower house of parliament (the State Duma) the right to vote only on his choice for prime minister (Article 83); the

other ministers are appointed and dismissed by Yeltsin himself (see Figure 31.1).

As with the American president, the Russian president is the commander-in-chief of the armed forces and appoints a security council. But he also has the explicit constitutional right to "supervise the conduct of the foreign policy" of the country and the right to institute martial law as well as states of emergency.

The New Parliament

The new legislative body elected in December 1993 was that described in the Yeltsin draft constitution of the previous summer. Called the Federal Assembly, it consists of an upper chamber, called the Federation Council, with two representatives from each of the country's eighty-eight regions and republics, plus Moscow and St. Petersburg. The lower house, the State Duma, elects 450 members, some in sin-

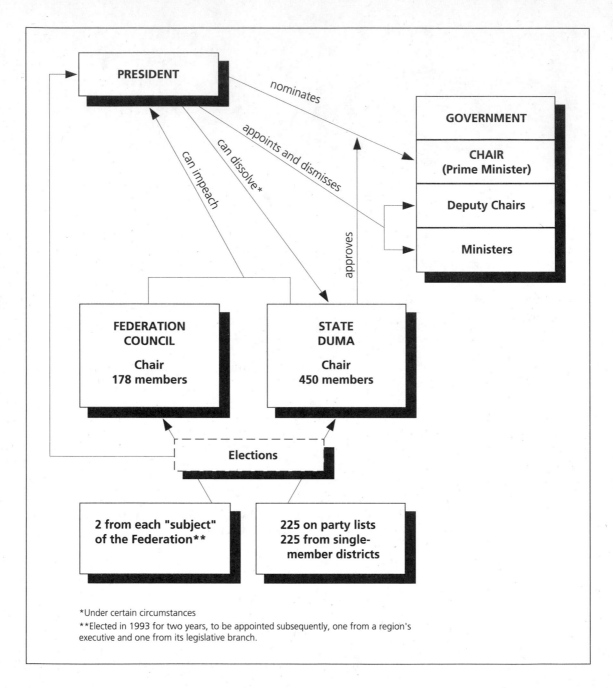

Figure 31.1 The New Russian Political System.

gle-member districts—that is, where the largest vote-getter wins, and some apportioned by party lists.

Under the new constitution, the parliament finds itself in a much weaker position than the Congress of Deputies did, especially because during the period of the Congress of Deputies, definitive answers to key questions of power were not available. Hence the Congress was able to deny, for example, that the president could dissolve them or call new elections. Under the new constitution, the president can dissolve the State Duma and call for new elections if that body rejects his choice for prime minister three times. While this may seem unlikely, this power does allow the president to present a "take it or face new elections" choice to the lower house. In addition, if the State Duma votes a resolution of no confidence in the government twice within three months, the president has the option of nevertheless keeping the government and forcing the State Duma to stand for new elections. Beyond that, the prime minister can force new elections by asking for a vote of no confidence (Article 117). These provisions mean that the Parliament cannot simply keep voting against government measures without themselves facing the prospect of new elections. In this respect the new constitution is closer to the British system. Such changes from the Congress period represent a gain in power for the president.[12]

Members of the State Duma are elected for four years and have the responsibility for passing all federal laws. The other chamber, the Federation Council, has the obligation to pass on laws only if they deal with budget, taxes, finance, international treaties, or borders of the federation. In an unusual provision, the State Duma can actually override a negative decision on a law by the Federation Council by passing it by a two-thirds majority. While in the United States, for example, most laws need passage in both the House of Representatives and the Senate to be enacted, in Russia one house can override the other. As in the American case, both

houses need to pass laws by a two-thirds majority to override a presidential veto.

In several other respects the presidency is stronger now than in the Congress period. Now it is much more difficult to impeach a president. Such an action requires two separate court rulings, a two-thirds vote to put forth charges by the State Duma, and another two-thirds for impeachment by the Federation Council (Article 93). The new president has the right to call a referendum under certain circumstances, something Boris Yeltsin has shown himself eager to do; and it is quite difficult to change or even amend the constitution. Finally, the members of the Federation Council, although elected in 1993, are to serve for only two years, with subsequent members to be appointed. By whom and with what degree of presidential influence is yet to be determined.

THE CONSTITUTIONAL COURT

After the collapse of Communist Party power, the country had for the first time a judicial body that could review measures taken by those acting in the name of the state, and could and did declare them valid or not according to the country's constitution. Established by the Congress of Peoples' Deputies in October 1991, the Constitutional Court of the Russian Federation had fifteen members who were nominated by political parties or groups and elected by the Congress. Despite their charge to be nonpartisan and to eschew political questions, the nature of their nomination and election, and the kinds of questions that came to them, ensured that they and their declarations would not be above the political process. As of mid-1993, only thirteen seats on the court had been filled, and the court was itself as much a part of the upheaval in Russian government as were the other branches.

From the beginning, the court was not shy about its rulings. Within weeks of its formation and in its first rulings, the court held that Boris

Yeltsin could not ban the Communist Party completely for its support of the failed coup of August 1991. Only its ruling bodies could be proscribed, said the court. The court canceled the president's proposed merger of the country's Ministry of Interior with the successor to the KGB, the Ministry of Security. It ruled soon after that Yeltsin could not ban another group, the National Salvation Front, despite its extreme nationalist views. In direct interventions into the ongoing political struggle, the court held in March 1993 that President Yeltsin could not declare "special rule" in the country and, as noted above, judged his dissolution of the parliament in September 1993 to be both unconstitutional and grounds for impeachment. After his victory over parliament the next month, President Yeltsin forced the resignation of the court's chairman, Valery Zorkin, and then suspended the court altogether.

The new constitution provides for an independent judiciary, which is considered a basic building bloc of a democratic system. There are in fact three high courts in the new Russia. The Constitutional Court with nineteen judges has supreme authority on constitutional issues, those affecting the power of the federation and its subordinate bodies, jurisdictional disputes, and whether acts of the president and legislature are constitutional. The Supreme Court rules on civil, criminal, and administrative cases and a Supreme Arbitration Court rules on economic disputes (Articles 125–128). The president appoints the members of these courts, with the approval of the Federation Council, and appoints all other federal judges without such approval being required.

SUBNATIONAL GOVERNMENT

Like the USSR before it, Russia is an amalgamation of various nationalities. The most numerous of these gained increased autonomy over local affairs through changes underway even before the Soviet Union disappeared. In 1990

Russia contained within it sixteen autonomous republics, each named for a non-Russian nationality indigenous to the area. That year their formal designation was changed to simply "republics." The next year four more republics were created by redesignating existing autonomous *oblasts* [regions]. In 1992 one of the republics, Checheno-Ingushestia, split into two, yielding a total of twenty-one republics. (See Table 31.1.)

These republics do not cover the full extent of Russia; in fact they account for only some 29 percent of the country's territory and 15 percent of its population (see Figure 31.2).[13] But they and their status hold the key to the integrity of the new Russian state. Because each of them represents a national group, they are potential vehicles for such groups to challenge Russian dominance of the country, just as national groups did to the Soviet Union in 1990 and 1991. In only a handful of them does the titular nationality have a majority, but the possibility of internationality conflict, such as between the Chechen and Ingush, or conflict with Russians living there, poses a potential threat to the country's progress. Moreover, some of these republics object to their very presence in Russia. Tartarstan, a land of nearly 4 million people in the heart of central Russia, and Chechnya in the north Caucasus have both declared their independence.

After the collapse of the Soviet Union, the republics gained both formal and real governing authority. In part this has been the result of attempts by President Yeltsin to enlist regional and republican leaders to his side in the struggle to rule Russia. In part, gains have come because Russia has simply been unable to exercise governing authority. When Chechnya declared itself independent in 1991, Yeltsin declared an emergency and sent troops. But the parliament annulled this action and the troops were withdrawn.

In 1992 a federation treaty was signed by all republics except Chechnya and Tartarstan. The treaty stipulated that "complete state power"

Table 31.1   RUSSIA'S REPUBLICS: POPULATION IN ABSOLUTE FIGURES AND SHARE OF TITULAR NATIONALITY AND RUSSIANS IN PERCENTAGES (1989 census figures)

Adygeya	432,000	Karelia	790,000
Adygei	22.1	Karelians	10.0
Russians	68.0	Russians	73.6
Altai	191,000	Khakassia	567,000
Altai	31.0	Khakass	11.1
Russians	60.4	Russians	79.5
Bashkortostan	3,943,000	Komi	1,251,000
Bashkirs	21.9	Komi	23.3
Russians	39.3	Russians	57.7
Tatars	28.4	Marii-El	749,000
Buryatia	1,038,000	Mari	43.3
Buryats	24.0	Russians	47.5
Russians	69.9	Mordovia	964,000
Checheno-Ingushetia*	1,270,000	Mordvins	32.5
Chechen	57.8	Russians	60.8
Ingush	12.9	North Ossetia	632,000
Russians	23.1	Ossetians	53.0
Chuvashia	1,338,000	Russians	29.9
Chuvash	67.8	Sakha (Yakutia)	1,094,000
Russians	26.7	Yakuts	33.4
Dagestan	1,802,000	Russians	50.3
Dagestanis	80.2	Tatarstan	3,642,000
Russians	9.2	Tatars	48.5
Kabardino-Balkaria	754,000	Russians	43.3
Kabardians	48.2	Tuva	309,000
Balkars	9.4	Tuvins	64.3
Russians	31.9	Russians	32.0
Kalmykia	323,000	Udmurtia	1,606,000
Kalmyks	45.4	Udmurts	30.9
Russians	37.7	Russians	58.9
Karachaevo-Cherkessia	415,000		
Karachai	31.2		
Cherkess	9.7		
Russians	42.4		

*Note: There are no separate data for Chechnya and Ingushetia, since Checheno-Ingushetia was officially separated into two republics only in 1992.

Source: From "Russia's Republics: A Threat to Its Territorial Integrity?," by Ann Sheehy, *RFE/RL Research Report,* Vol. 2, No. 20, May 14, 1993, p. 38. Used by permission.

resides in the "sovereign republics" except for those areas specifically allocated to the competence of the federal government. Republics were designated as "independent participants in international and foreign economic connections." But the treaty went further. It also made

Figure 31.2 Map of Russia's Republics. Source: From Ann Sheehy, "Russia's Republics: A Threat to Its Territorial Integrity?" *RFE/RL Research Report,* Vol. 2, No. 20, May 14, 1993, p. 35. Used by permission.

regions other than republics virtually their equal. *Krais* (territories), oblasts (regions) and the cities of Moscow and St. Petersburg, as well as autonomous oblasts and autonomous okrugs (districts), were granted similar status as "independent" actors and were granted the right to draw up their own basic charters, similar to the republics' constitutions. All of these subunits were granted increased power over critical questions such as disposition of natural resources, taxation, local self-administration, and civic rights and freedoms.[14]

But the implementation of the treaty awaited adoption of a new constitution and the deliberations over that document included fierce debates over the status of the republics and other regions in Russia. Regional leaders wanted to retain for themselves maximum power to control resources within their areas and to protect the cultural autonomy of the people in their areas. Opponents of strong republics argued that such an arrangement would severely weaken the ability of the central government to implement economic and political reform and to govern the country as a coherent entity.

In his battle with parliament, Boris Yeltsin turned for support to the country's regions, appealing to their leaders over the heads of the deputies to the Congress. In an attempt to insure their support for his vision of the future,

Yeltsin structured the constitutional assembly he called in a way that insured satisfaction of regional wishes. Fearing that regions which were not full republics would be shortchanged in the new structure, some areas, including President Yeltsin's own home region of Sverdlovsk, declared themselves to be full republics.

As a result of such pressures, the draft constitution that emerged in the summer of 1993 was very favorable to subnational government at the expense of the center. First, the full Federal Treaty was incorporated as part of the draft constitution—something that had not been included in the first drafts of the document or in the parliament's draft constitution. Second, the Yeltsin draft referred to all subunits of the country—no less than eighty-eight of them—as "subjects," in an effort to avoid invidious dis-

tinctions between republics and other regions. Finally, the proposed arrangement granted somewhat more power to the legislature's upper house, the Federation Council, in which each "subject," no matter how small, was to have two representatives.

While that election provision was retained in the new constitution adopted in December 1993, the increased status of the regions and republics was not. After the defeat of the parliament, Boris Yeltsin took action against many regions that had sided with that body. He fired some regional executives, transferred functions from local soviets to presidential appointees, and urged local councils to disband themselves. Finally, he disbanded the councils himself. The new constitution reflects Yeltsin's ire at the lack of regional support. The autono-

Siberia: The Next Country?

By itself it would be the second-largest country in the world. Traveling by train it takes seven days to cross. A lake in its midsection (Baikal) is bigger than Massachusetts and Connecticut combined and contains one-fifth of all the Earth's fresh water. Its very name conjures up images of cold, desolation, and exile. But Siberia is in fact a vibrant—and vital—part of today's Russia. It is home to more than 32 million people and has four cities with a population of more than 1 million. Representing three-fourths of Russia's landmass, the region is the source of more than 70 percent of the country's oil—the Tyumen province alone produces more oil than any country except Saudi Arabia and the United States. It produces nearly 90 percent of Russia's gas, 60 percent of its coal, and virtually all of its rich store of diamonds.

Within the Russian Federation, Siberia has no political-legal structure of its own; nor did it in Soviet times. Administratively, there are four republics and nine "autonomous areas" encompassing the

coal and oil fields of western Siberia, a vast flat central region ("eastern Siberia"), and a far eastern region rich in gold and diamonds and boasting a 5,600-mile coastline. The far eastern Sakha Republic is the largest governmental unit of the region and, like many others, has been trying to wrest maximum control over the extraction and sale of these resources.

In 1990 an association known as the Siberian Agreement was formed in the western and central regions to press the central government for more investment in and more control over the method by which its resources are exploited. The Agreement has survived the breakup of the Soviet Union and from time to time some of its members have threatened secession. Others tend to argue instead for a greater appreciation, and accompanying support, for the development of the region. As Vitaly Mukha, chairman of the Council of the Siberian Agreement, put it: "We are all aware that Siberia must unite to help itself and to offer its shoulder to Russia, as so often in the past."

mous status previously accorded the "subjects" was not part of the new constitution. And whereas the Federation Treaty had explicitly vested "all state power" to the subunits, except those powers designated to the federal government, the new constitution reverses the equation: all powers not exercised by the federal government nor in joint jurisdiction reside with the local authorities (Article 73).[15]

This change of status is reflected in the new constitution's treatment of republican prerogatives on natural resources. While both earlier drafts and the new constitution provide for joint control and management of such resources, the Federation Treaty had said: "The land, minerals, water, flora, and fauna will belong (or be owned) by the people living on the territory of the corresponding republics." The new constitution does not include this provision.

Local government had also gained increased autonomy due both to central government struggles and changes in government. Elections for local councils were held in Russia in 1990. In Moscow, Leningrad (as it was at the time) and other big cities, reform groups took control of local parliaments, elected reform-minded executives, and some moved faster than the central government in implementing market reforms. For example, in one district of Moscow, Nikolai Travkin, the head of the Democratic Party of Russia, succeeded in pushing economic competition and privatization ahead through a series of progressive and innovative measures. Local taxes were kept low to encourage entrepreneurs and certificates of private title were issued for property in the name of the district council, to be replaced when national laws on private property were adopted.[16] However in many other regions, the residual power of local bosses, a fear of change, and the collapse of and confusion in state power have held back the progress of economic, if not political change.

The new constitution provides only a few fairly vague descriptions of local government and, as indicated in Chapter 30, political distinctions among various areas can be substantial. While it is clear that the current president is dissatisfied with the support for change he has won at the local level, it is not at all clear whether the national government is yet in a position to reimpose its will in all the country's towns and villages.

NOTES

1. See the discussion in J. Arch Getty, *Origins of the Great Purges: The Soviet Communist Party Reconsidered, 1933–1938* (Cambridge: Cambridge University Press, 1985); and Jonathan Harris, "The Origins of the Conflict Between Malenkov and Zhdanov: 1939–1941," *Slavic Review,* 35, No. 2 (June 1976), pp. 287–303.

2. Richard Sakwa, *Gorbachev and His Reforms, 1985–1990* (New York: Prentice-Hall, 1990), p. 148.

3. Jeffrey W. Hahn, "State Institutions in Transition," in Stephen White, Alex Pravda, and Zvi Gitelman, eds., *Developments in Soviet and Post-Soviet Politics* (Durham: Duke University Press, 1992), pp. 104–105.

4. Jonathan Harris, "President and Parliament in the Russian Federation," unpublished manuscript (University of Pittsburgh, 1994), p. 12.

5. *Rossiiskiye vesti,* March 23, 1991 (*Current Digest of the Post-Soviet Press,* April 21, 1993, pp. 1–2).

6. Eugene Huskey, "The Rebirth of the Russian State," in Eugene Huskey, ed., *Executive Power and Soviet Politics* (Armonk, N.Y.: M. E. Sharpe, 1992), p. 256.

7. The role of the Security Council in foreign policy is described in Peter J. Stavrakis, "Government Bureaucracies: Transition or Disintegration?" *RFE/RL Research Report,* 2, No. 20, May 14, 1993, pp. 26–33. The exact membership of the Security Council has changed repeatedly, but at the beginning of 1994 it included the foreign minister, defense minister, directors of the foreign and federal intelligence services, ministers

of interior, justice, nationalities affairs, and civil defense.

8. *Izvestia*, July 16, 1993, p. 4.

9. *Rossiyskaya Gazeta,* May 8, 1993 (*Summary of World Broadcasts,* "Special Supplement," SU/1690, May 17, 1993, pp. C1/18).

10. Address by President Boris Yeltsin to the nation in Moscow, Ostankino Television First Channel, September 21, 1993 (FBIS, 22 September 1993, p. 2).

11. *Rossiyskaya Gazeta,* December 25, 1993 (FBIS, 27 December 1993), p. 2.

12. The power to dissolve is limited in that the State Duma cannot be dissolved in its first year, nor when it has brought charges against the president, or during times of martial law or state of emergency (Article 109).

13. Ann Sheehy, "Russia's Republics: A Threat to Its Territorial Integrity?" in *RFE/RL Research Report,* 2, No. 20, May 14, 1993.

14. Tass, March 14, 1992 (*Foreign Broadcast Information Service,* March 16, 1992, pp. 67–68) "*Dogo-vor . . .*" [Agreement . . .] *Izvestia,* July 16, 1993, pp. 3, 5–6.

15. In addition, in 1994 separate treaties delineating powers were signed between the central government and the republics of Bashkortostan and Tartarstan.

16. See Philip Hanson, *Local Power and Market Reform in the Former Soviet Union* (Munich and Washington, D.C.: RFE/RL Research Institute, 1993), p. 33.

REFERENCES AND SUGGESTED READINGS

D'Encause, Hélene Carrère. 1993. *The End of the Soviet Empire.* New York: HarperCollins.

Huskey, Eugene. 1992. *Executive Power and Soviet Politics: The Rise and Decline of the Soviet State.* Armonk, N.Y.: M. E. Sharpe.

McAuley, Mary. 1992. *Soviet Politics 1917–1991.* New York: Oxford University Press.

Tolz, Vera. "Drafting the New Russian Constitution," *RFE/RL Research Report,* 2, No. 29, July 16, 1993, pp. 1–12.

32

Parties and Elections in the New Russia

urrently Russia appears to have a system not unlike that operating in western Europe. There is a parliament, prime minister and government, as in Britain, and multiple political parties striving for power and to have their policies implemented, as in Italy. As in France, there is also a president elected directly by the voters and thus not dependent on a parliamentary majority.

But the French and British can trace the roots of their systems to parliamentary revolutions that are more than two hundred years old and most of western Europe has had successfully functioning parliamentary systems for decades. The people of Russia have been working on theirs since 1990. It was only that year that the monopoly of the Communist Party of the Soviet Union on political activity was removed, open competitive elections could be held for a new Russian parliament, and the possibility emerged for there to be publicly active political parties.

Though it has been brief, this period has seen parliamentary and competitive politics take place at a time when fundamental changes in the very nature of the state are also taking place. Russia ceased to be a republic of one country and became its own state. The government's monopoly on economic activity has been broken and struggles over the form of the Russian government itself and its guiding constitution have dominated politics. Elections and parties have played a central role in this. They have been part not simply of the continued functioning of a system of competitive politics, but its very creation.

THE COMMUNIST PARTY UNDER SOVIET COMMUNISM

From the end of the civil war, the Communist Party of the Soviet Union (CPSU) was the only legal political organization. This monopoly was justified on ideological grounds, since the party was created as the guardian of the interests of the working class. It alone was the purveyor and interpreter of the guidance provided by Marxism-Leninism on building socialism and communism. Other political parties, by this definition, represented interests hostile to those of socialism. The Communist Party did not submit its revolutionary mandate to a popular vote and hence, unlike ruling parties in the West, did not fear being voted out of office. Members of the Supreme Soviet, the parliament of the USSR, were approved by or usually were members of the CPSU.

As the sole legitimate political actor, the party in the Soviet Union pronounced the official interpretation of the country's past and present, and defined what the society should look like in the future. In 1961 the party program adopted under Nikita Khrushchev declared that, with the building of socialism complete, the country was now constructing communism. The current state structure was not a dictatorship of the proletariat, which carried with it the need for repression, but an "all peo-

ple's state" in which greater public involvement was encouraged.[1] Under Leonid Brezhnev this view was modified somewhat to hold that the Soviet Union was in a state of "mature" or developed socialism, and the attainment of full communism was by omission put off again to the uncertain future. The third party program, adopted in 1986 under Mikhail Gorbachev's guidance, accepted this premise but linked the achievement of full communism more directly to the need to improve the country's economic performance. The reform begun by Mikhail Gorbachev was not designed to change the Soviet Union overnight into a western-style parliamentary democracy. Rather, it aimed at improving the functioning of socialism, which Gorbachev believed in to the end of his political career, and at ensuring, not preventing, the achievement of full communism. To do this, Gorbachev pushed for a redefinition of the party's role in Soviet society and urged the party to draw on its own past for fruitful ideas that might help Soviet society prosper.

The country's past, like its future, was written and rewritten by the party, not always for the sake of historical accuracy but to serve a current political purpose. For example, for nearly fifty years after his execution under Stalin, Nikolai Bukharin and the ideas he propagated about allowing more individual and private enterprise under socialism were anathema to the Soviet party leadership. But in 1987 Mikhail Gorbachev spoke favorably of the man and his ideas, and in 1988 Bukharin was formally "rehabilitated" by a party commission. By rehabilitating Bukharin and placing his policies in a more favorable light, the party leadership was indicating that such ideas could and should be considered as a way of dealing with current problems. Similarly, drawing attention to the period of the New Economic Policy in the 1920s, Gorbachev pushed for a redetermination of the role of private enterprise. A Central Committee plenum in 1987 gave greater latitude to this form of economic activity and paved the way for legislation to be enacted allowing for business cooperatives and even individual private business.

Though such actions indicated a change in course, the fundamental method of governance in the Soviet Union remained the same: a single legitimate party made a determination of the country's proper course and, soon after, an obedient government put it into law. Public input was minimal and challenges from other parties nonexistent.

Political competition did exist in the Soviet political system. Struggles took place *within* the party itself and most critically at its highest echelons. The party tried to eliminate such competition at its Tenth Congress in 1921 by banning factions, and under Stalin, opponents were arrested, sometimes tried, and usually put into prison camps. Still, as the historical review indicates, differences over policy, combined with personal desires for power, ensured that political struggles among party leaders continued, even when it was less subject to public input and less visible to the outside world than in the West. In 1990, in response to the changes and reforms pushed forward by Mikhail Gorbachev and the revolutionary changes that swept Eastern Europe, a formal faction of the party was organized. Called the Democratic Platform, this group declared itself in favor of rapid, thorough democratization of the Communist Party. It also advocated making the party one of several competing for political influence, rather than the only one through constitutional monopoly. This change was in fact made that year.

If the party's political base was more narrow than parliamentary parties in the West, its role and responsibilities were much broader. To use T. H. Rigby's term, the Soviet Union was a "mono-organizational" society, one in which all of the country's social, economic and political activities were subject to the directives of the dominant organization, the Communist Party.[2]

Because it was acting in the name of the workers, peasants and intelligentsia, and because its goal was to create an effective, productive, prosperous socialist society, it was the party that had both immediate and ultimate responsibility for how the economy was running. This responsibility ran from the very top of the party, where members of the secretariat had responsibility for certain sectors of the economy, down through regional first secretaries who oversaw developments in their own oblasts or krais, to party leaders in the factories and enterprises. In the United States, if a large automobile factory in, say, central Michigan is performing poorly, the local Democratic Party leader does not have to answer to the president. In the Soviet Union, however, one of the local party secretary's key functions was to ensure the productive functioning of the economic units in his area. His or her career advancement could depend on such performance. As noted above, the party also established the acceptable range of individual and collective behavior, both political and economic.

The party also defined the nature of the country's relationship with the outside world. In this, the party leadership was attentive to ideological concerns, in particular the desire to support movements and states that espouse some adherence to socialist principles. But, like ruling parties elsewhere, it also served what it saw as the needs of the Soviet state—that is, the desire to create a nonthreatening, physically secure, politically supportive, and economically beneficial external environment. The general secretary of the party, the most internationally visible and politically powerful individual, usually tried to reshape this relationship in accordance with his view of Soviet foreign policy. Mikhail Gorbachev, for example, clearly tried to imbue Soviet foreign policy with "new thinking" (*novoe myshlenie*), including an effort to reduce international tensions in order to make domestic economic restructuring possible (see Chapter 34).

In foreign policy, domestic governance and control of the economy and the restriction of political competition to the top usually meant that a party general secretary did not have to worry about public reaction to the party's actions. Instead he had to satisfy his most immediate and powerful constituency: the other members of the highest party organs.

But the party did want to *mobilize* society, not for votes as in a competitive system but to get people to make their contributions, to work productively, and to play their supporting role in fulfilling the tasks set for them. Under Stalin the method of choice was terror; suppressing real or imagined opponents of the system through arrest, imprisonment, and execution, and frightening everybody else into passivity. With Khrushchev, widespread use of this type of terror ceased and briefly during his time and later under Gorbachev, the party began to encourage a greater degree of public participation and involvement, especially by the most highly trained and well-educated members of society. This was seen as a way of mobilizing the talents and skills of the intelligentsia into the tasks of running a modern complex economy and counteracting the tendency to ossification noted in the introduction to this volume.

Because of its control of both the government and the economy, the party was able to offer attractive rewards for political activism and economic achievement. People gained career advancement, access to scarce goods, travel within and beyond the borders of the Soviet Union, the possibility of influence with higher authorities, and some authority of their own, all through the party. In the Soviet system, the spheres of a person's life—for example, one's job, political activity, education, family life, or recreation—areas that might in another society be kept separate from each other, were spheres in which the party played a direct or indirect role and that were shaped to support the goals of socialist society. That power, plus the absence of an effective alternative, attracted some

20 million people to membership in the Communist Party as of 1989, an estimated 200,000 of them being full-time, paid party workers, or *apparatchiki*.

The party was organized hierarchically (see Figure 32.1) with its highest body, in principle, being a national party congress. Between congresses, which were usually held every five years, the party's authority rested with its Central Committee. This group, which varied in size, included virtually all of the key political, economic and military elites of the Soviet Union from the national down to the regional level, as well as the leaders of party-sponsored organizations, such as trade unions and youth and cultural organizations.

But even the Central Committee proved too cumbersome for continuous decision making for a large and complex state. Its full sessions or plenums were usually held twice a year and were important largely for marking key personnel or ideological changes. A session in 1988, for example, brought Mikhail Gorbachev several of the most important changes at the top of the party. That top is represented by the party's Politburo (called the Presidium between 1952 and 1966) and included the most important leadership positions of the country. In 1989 the Soviet Union's prime minister, president, foreign minister, and head of state security (KGB) were full members of the Politburo while the first deputy prime minister, defense minister, and the premier of Russia were candidate (or nonvoting) members. This interlocking membership ensured Communist Party control over the key levers of government and the economy.

The other critical body atop the Soviet system was the Secretariat. A body of varying size, it grew from 6 at the time of the death of Leonid Brezhnev to 14 under Gorbachev and was formally subordinate to the Central Committee. As the statutory and organizational arm of the party, the Secretariat, through its control of the Central Committee's various commissions,

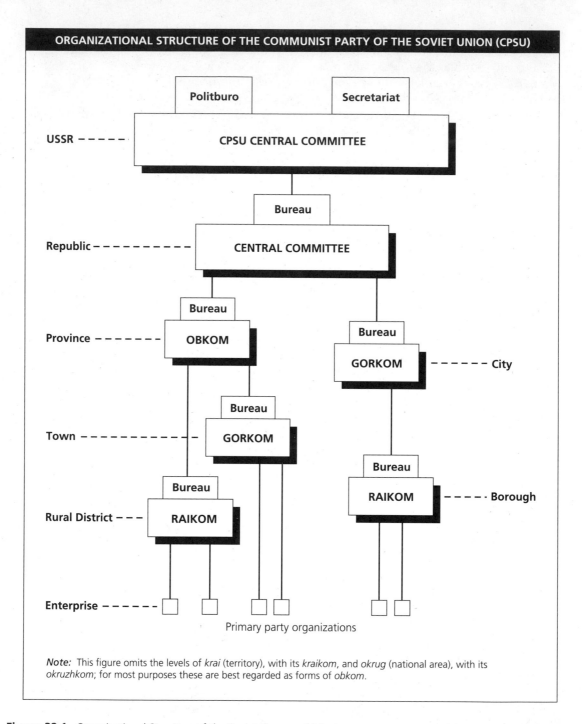

Figure 32.1 Organizational Structure of the Soviet Communist Party. Source: Adapted from Ronald J. Hill and Peter Frank, *The Soviet Communist Party*. This figure omits the levels of *krai* (territory), with its *kraikom,* and *okrug* (national area), with its *okruzhkom*; for most purposes these are best regarded as forms of *obkom*.

had responsibility in key policy areas such as personnel, agriculture, and social and economic policy. It was the direct link to the vast central party *apparat* and Gorbachev was careful to appoint his supporters to this body.

From Lenin to Gorbachev the leader of the party was the most powerful figure in the country. Lenin was officially party chairman but Stalin utilized the staff office known as general secretary to facilitate his rise to power. He then retained that position formally for more than thirty years. From 1953 to 1966, the party leader was known as first secretary, reflecting somewhat lesser power. Soviet leaders after Stalin gained and held party power by creating supporting coalitions whose fate and views were close to those of the leader. Leonid Brezhnev regained the title of general secretary in 1966 but did not achieve the near-absolute power held by Stalin.

After Mikhail Gorbachev gained the position in 1985, he set about changing both the size and composition of key party bodies in order to insure a base for the controversial actions he felt were necessary. In his first three years as general secretary, Gorbachev replaced all but two full Politburo members, all candidate members of that body, and all but one member of the Secretariat.

After 1988, well aware of the hostility toward change held by the party apparatus, Gorbachev began to move the base of his power away from the party toward the government, and especially toward a new presidency that was created for him. As glasnost spread, as new types of economic enterprise grew, and especially as challenges grew to central authority, Gorbachev relied less and less on the dwindling authority of the Communist Party and more on his role as national chief executive. With the elections of 1989 and especially the end of the party's monopoly role in 1990, the privileged position of the party as definer and defender of the nation's course ended. It was in an attempt to regain that role that Communist Party leaders launched their abortive seizure of the government in August 1991. This move precipitated Mikhail Gorbachev's resignation as general secretary of the party, the banning of the party's activities for a time, and ultimately the breakup of the USSR.

ELECTIONS OLD AND NEW

There were elections in the Soviet system, but they served a very different purpose from that in competitive party systems. Elections essentially were held to ratify and support the political choices made by the Communist Party. Elections outside the party, such as for the Supreme Soviet or local councils, usually had a single slate of candidates, determined by the local or national Communist Party. The public's choice was to support this candidate or either abstain or somehow indicate a rejection of the candidate (usually not a wise course of action). Thus, election returns typically showed near unanimity in support of the candidate. Within the party, genuine elections, for positions in the hierarchy were rare, as posts were typically filled on orders from above. The actual process of "staffing" elections and thus the posts they filled, was part of a system known as *nomenklatura*. This refers to the party's practice of naming people for lower posts in the party itself, in all government agencies, in the economy, and in fact in all key institutions of government. The privilege of nomenklatura embodied the party's authority and was the vehicle of its penetration of both political and what might in other systems be considered nonpolitical areas of life in the Soviet Union. It is estimated that some 2 million managerial and influential posts inside and outside the party were filled through the nomenklatura system.[3]

Reforms enacted in 1988, however, expanded the use of real elections within the party. The party's last congress, the twenty-eighth, in 1990, included elections for positions in the Central Committee and Politburo. More sig-

The Russian people shocked the ruling party with their votes in the 1989 elections.

nificantly, 1989 saw the first multicandidate elections to the new Congress of People's Deputies. For the first time the real action was taking place outside the party, in the battle to fill new institutions that were taking increasing responsibility for the country's affairs.

A New Ball Game: The 1989 Elections in the USSR

The measures enacted at the end of 1988 provided for competitive elections to the new Congress of People's Deputies but not for competing parties. At this point there was still one legal party, the CPSU, and through control of local nomination procedures, the party was generally able to see to it that "approved' candidates were nominated. But not always. In Moscow, Boris Yeltsin, former party boss of the city who had been removed from this position and the Politburo in 1988, secured nomination. Andrei Sakharov was originally left off a list of

one hundred nominees allocated to scientific organizations, but he was then included after a public outcry.

The elections, as noted in Chapter 29, provided a rude shock to the ruling party despite its ability to clear nominees. Party leaders lost in several big cities and in some cases even where they ran unopposed—due to their failure to win at least 50 percent of the votes cast. But it was the process itself that had an even deeper impact. All across the country, people participated in meetings to nominate and question potential nominees. One study estimates that more than six thousand candidates were discussed for the fifteen hundred seats publicly contestable in the new Congress.[4] Some meetings to nominate candidates were dutiful, as the crowds accepted local party nominees; some were raucous, as nominations "from the floor" came in; and some were dramatic. In Leningrad an elderly man challenged the local party apparatus to include a young candidate nominated by a nonparty organization. After

The CPSU's Fall from the Heights

From its beginnings as a faction of the Russian Social Democratic Workers' Party, the Soviet Communist Party achieved power unexpectedly and against the odds in 1917. The party then banned all others, survived civil war, internal purges and strife, and brutal invasion as it penetrated all geographic areas and political and economic arenas of Soviet society.

The Soviet constitution of 1936 listed the party as one of many social organizations but it was described as "the vanguard of the working people" and the "leading core" of all organizations. The new constitution of 1977 enshrined the party as "the leading guiding force of Soviet society and the nucleus of its political system and of state and social organization." No organizations not sanctioned by the party were tolerated.

However in 1990, under pressure from Mikhail Gorbachev and over the objections of party conservatives, the Central Committee voted to recommend that the party's "leading role" clause be dropped from the constitution. The party, Gorbachev argued, should compete democratically for its influence which he felt sure it would retain. In March the Congress of People's Deputies made this change and the party became one of many others competing for policies and positions.

While the party's membership had reached 20 million by 1989, defections multiplied as the party seemed unable to cope with either the country's chronic economic problems or the demands of many groups and nations for more democracy. The party fell to some 17 million by 1991 and after the coup attempt of 1991 was briefly banned. Supporters formed several succcessor parties. One of these, the Communist Party of the Russian Federation, claimed 600,000 members in the spring of 1993 and was itself briefly suspended after the events of October of that year. But it was allowed to resume activity and in the December election received just over 12 percent of the votes on party lists. The CPSU's property holdings, which were vast, in line with its pervasive role in society, and estimated to be worth some 4 billion rubles, were nationalized in the wake of the August coup attempt.

---

an impassioned speech, the man collapsed and died. Soon after, the young candidate was nominated and elected.[5]

Because of the dominance of the party, the reservation of one-third of the seats for election by organizations, and the control of the nomination process, the Congress that emerged was hardly a modern version of the 1789 French National Assembly. In fact, the Congress had more members of the Communist Party in it than did the old Supreme Soviet. But it also contained many well-known and outspoken reformers who now had a very public and legally created platform from which to do something people had only done at their peril until then: challenge the Soviet government. Even the limited openness of the nomination process, the ability for average people to meet and discuss issues with candidates—and then to vote against them or for other candidates—proved electrifying. In nearly two-thirds of the open election districts across the country, people could choose from two candidates, in 150 others they could choose from three or more.[6] Nationwide, 89 percent of the eligible voters went to the polls. The election genie was out of the bottle.

Republican Elections in 1990

While the 1989 elections had staffed the new national bodies, similar elections were held in the fifteen republics of the USSR in 1990. The disappearance of the Soviet Union the next year was due in no small measure to the pressure exerted on the central government of Mikhail Gorbachev by these new popularly elected parliamentary bodies.

In many of these republican elections, genuine contests emerged, even though multiparty systems were not formalized. In the absence of parties, large and popular informal groups came together to challenge the role of the Communist Party. In several republics, popular fronts mobilized around national themes to challenge not only the Communist Party but Russian rule. These groups won overwhelming victories in the Baltics States, in Armenia, Georgia and Moldova. New majorities quickly transformed the parliaments into platforms from which to launch attacks on central authority. In Lithuania the victorious Sajudis popular front dominated parliament—Communists won only 7 seats out of 90—and within two weeks the legislature declared the country's independence from Moscow.

In Russia, groups formed around the question of the pace and direction of political and economic reform. The Interregional Group of Deputies included those most eager to end the dominance of the Communist Party and rallied behind Boris Yeltsin. The Communist Party itself spawned a reform group, known as the Democratic Platform, which envisioned transforming the party into a west European-style social democratic party. Elections for the Russian parliament were held for all 1,068 seats on a geographic basis; no seats were "reserved" for the party or anyone else. Still, 86 percent of those elected to the Russian Congress of People's Deputies were Communist Party members. But the majority favored pushing change forward quickly and, especially as the Gorbachev government turned away from reform and cracked down in the Baltic States, asserted a stronger role for Russia within the Soviet Union. A group that later became known as Democratic Russia was formed in 1990. It threw its weight behind Boris Yeltsin, securing his election as chairman of the Russian Supreme Soviet. A Bloc of Centrist Forces came together that favored a more conservative approach and a group known as Interfront sought to protect the position and rights of Russians living outside Russia. There were also orthodox Communists who opposed the direction of "Russia and reform" favored by Yeltsin.

Both before and after the dissolution of the Soviet Union in 1991, such groups formed the core of what would become political parties. There are currently hundreds of parties, but their identity, membership and principles are hardly fixed. Across the country they range from supporters of western-style parliamentary democracy to proponents of Russian dominance, to social democrats, to Soviet-style Communists. Parties have formed, split and re-formed with dizzying speed. By mid-1993, for example, there were no less than seven different Communist parties. Nor are labels a good guide. The Liberal Democratic Party, for example, is hardly liberal. Its leader, Vladimir Zhirinovsky, campaigned for the presidency in 1991 on a platform of nationalism and restoration of the Russian empire. Despite the failure of the August coup, Zhirinovsky suggested what he would do if he gained power: "A new State committee for the State of Emergency will be created. I will immediately declare a state of emergency, shut down all the newspapers and disband all parties."[7] As Zhirinovsky has declared his intention to run in the next presidential election in 1996, and as the new presidency has extensive decree powers (see Chapter 31) such views may be of more than historical interest.

Without the galvanizing effect of regular national elections to pull them together, parties so far have tended to have little impact on the political process. They tend to represent supporters of charismatic individuals who offer particular solutions to Russia's difficulties. In a replay of nineteenth-century struggles between westernizers and Slavophiles, many political views polarize around the issue of whether Russia should follow western models or should try to find "its own way."

Those supporting President Yeltsin have typically expressed preference for "joining world civilization." For example, Nikolai Fyodorov, the minister of justice under Yelstin, describes the Yeltsin team:

> These are people who were not simply picked according to some considerations of loyalty and devotion; they are people who combine professional qualities with the political conviction that it is necessary to accelerate the implementation of reforms in the direction of the standards of world civilization—liberal economics, a genuine market economy and a civil society.[8]

Yeltsin's foreign minister sees Russia's situation the same way:

> We are not surrounded by states exhausted by war or on the verge of fighting. Around us is a civilized international community that has learned to place the interests of the individual above all else and is open to contact and cooperation. . . .
>
> We have declared our commitment to democracy, the supremacy of the individual, human rights and a free market. And we have done this not to indulge the West, but above all for our own sake.[9]

But people opposed to Yeltsin are bitter about what they see as the destruction of Russian society through a policy of supine worship of "the myth of the 'civilized, prosperous West'" and the denial of the unique characteristics of Russian history. As one such view puts it:

> It is Russia that for centuries has been developing a different model of humanism, an alternative to the one that is based on "universal human values" and "human rights" in their present-day, ultraliberal, Western sense. And for Russia the development of Western ultraliberalism at home means nothing short of suicide. . . . The basic principles of the reforms we propose stem from

> Russia's distinctive culture and history and need to unite East and West, tradition and progress in the reform process.[10]

The country's willingness to accommodate western concerns is a particular target of such criticism. The chair of the Subcommittee on International Security and Intelligence of the Russian parliament, 1990–1993 version, was direct:

> For people of a Westernizing turn of mind—and the current [Foreign] Minister is such a person—there is a danger of losing touch with one's native soil. When they come to power, Westernizers should stop being Westernizers.[11]

In post-Communist Russia, parties tend to be creations of individual political personalities, acting as vehicles for their advancement, rather than effective organizations in their own right. As one Russian observer noted, "The role of parties in working out the ideological and practical aspects of government policy has been minimal. They have not produced a single one of the well-known serious programs for societal and economic transformation. . . . Nor do party channels have any practical significance in the interaction of various state institutions, either horizontally or vertically."[12]

During the period of the Russian Congress, the impact of parties or groups lay mostly in their effectiveness in forming or participating in a parliamentary bloc or faction. These factions came together as a coalition either to support or to block the various changes that the Russian government had proposed. Such parliamentary political groups were not related to their own national party program or political base the way parliamentary parties are in the West. Rather groups tended to be made up of members of various parties who came together on the basis of their attitude on four basic issues:

1. the nature, pace and speed of democratic reform, in particular constitutional change;

Table 32.1 FACTIONS IN THE CONGRESS OF PEOPLE'S DEPUTIES (1993)

Faction	Number of Deputies	Orientation to Reform
Accord for Progress	53	Strongly Support
The Agrarian Union	130	Strongly Opposed
Communists of Russia	80	Strongly Opposed
Democratic Russia	49	Strongly Support
Fatherland	51	Strongly Opposed
Free Russia	56	Divided
Homeland	52	Divided
Industrial Union	52	Opposed
Left Center/Cooperation	61	Support
Radical Democrats	50	Strongly Support
Rising Generation/New Policy	53	Opposed
Russia	55	Strongly Opposed
Sovereignty and Equality	49	Opposed
Workers' Union	51	Opposed

Source: Pavel Gutionov, "Who's Who in the Russian Parliament," *Grazhdanin Rossii,* February 1993 [*The Current Digest of the Post-Soviet Press,* Vol. XLV, No. 8, March 24, 1993], p. 1, except for number for Communists of Russia Faction, taken from Vera Tolz, Wendy Slater, and Alexander Rahr, "Profiles of the Main Political Blocs," *RFE/RL Research Bulletin,* 2, No. 20, May 14, 1993, p. 19.

2. the nature and pace of reform of the economy, in particular the privatization of state firms and freeing of prices and wages;

3. the proper role of the federal Russian government and the constituent regions and republics; and

4. their view of Boris Yeltsin.

Table 32.1 indicates the main factions in the 1990–1993 Russian parliament and the orientation toward reform they generally displayed in the parliament.

Elections for the New Parliament

After the rump Congress of People's Deputies was dissolved and those left in parliament physically removed in October 1993, President Yeltsin banned many parties and groups that had opposed him. This proscription was directed against parties of the extreme left, such as the Russian Communist Workers' Party and a group known as Working Moscow, as well as nationalist parties like the National Salvation Front which Yeltsin had tried to ban in 1991. But soon most such groups were allowed to resume activities, and a total of ninety-one parties were allowed to try to gather signatures to compete in the December elections.

Nearly two dozen parties succeeded in gaining the 100,000 signatures needed to field candidates in the election. Their views spanned the spectrum on issues of reform, democracy, nationalism and, most importantly, Boris Yeltsin himself.

The elections themselves proved a rude shock to people pushing Russia on the road to reform (see Table 32.2). As noted in Chapter 30, reform-oriented parties won enough seats to hold on to roughly one-third of the current State Duma. But more than half of those seats were won in single-member districts, not by securing a strong vote for reform groups. The leading reform group, Russia's Choice, won the majority of its seats in individual districts and came in second, behind the Liberal Democratic Party, on party preference lists. Viewing the new parliament in terms of party attitude toward reform, we see a body almost evenly divided. This gives smaller groups, as well

as independents, power to bargain their support in return for support for projects or views they hold.

But in fact the situation in the Russian parliament is much more fluid than formal election returns or seats would suggest. Because of the weakness of parties, the importance of personal ties and charisma, and not least the rapidly changing political and economic situation, factions and groups form and reform almost issue by issue, with a stable politi-

Table 32.2 THE NEW RUSSIAN PARLIAMENT

In December 1993, elections were held for a new Russian Federal Assembly. One-half of the members of the 450-member lower house, the State Duma, were elected on the basis of voters' preference for a group or party. In order to earn seats this way, a party had to gain more than 5 percent of the vote. The other half of the seats were determined by individual winners in each district. In the upper house, the Federation Council, two representatives were elected from each of eighty-eight republics and regions of the federation plus Moscow and St. Petersburg. The results and general orientation of the groups in the two houses are listed below.

	State Duma		
Parties	Total Seats	Obtained on Party Lists	Obtained in Single-Member Districts
Pro-reform			
Russia's Choice	96	40	56
Yabloko	70	59	11
Party of Unity and Concord	27	18	9
Russian Movement for Democratic Reform	8	0	8
Centrist			
Women of Russia	25	21	4
Democratic Party of Russia	21	14	7
Civic Union	18	0	18
Communist or affiliated			
Communist Party of the Russian Federation	65	32	33
Agrarian Party	47	21	26
Nationalist			
Liberal Democratic Party	96	40	56
Others			
Independents	30	—	30
Dignity and Charity	3	0	3
Russia's Future	1	0	1

Table 32.2 (continued)

Council of the Federation

Political Affiliation	Approximate* Number of Seats
Proreform democrats	48
Russia's Choice	40
Yavlinsky-Boldyrev-Lukin bloc	3
Party of Russian Unity and Concord	4
Russian Movement for Democratic Reforms	1
Moderate reformers	23[†]
Centrist opposition to the government	36[‡]
The communist and social opposition	20
Communist Party of the Russian Federation	15
Agrarian Party	3
Socialist Workers' Party	1
Labor Party	1
Extreme nationalists	2
Cossacks' movement in Kuban	1
Russian National Council	1

*The numbers can only be approximate, as most candidates failed to identify their party affiliation, so their political sympathies can be judged only from speeches and other secondary information.

[†]Many are close to Prime Minister Viktor Chernomyrdin.

[‡]Many of them are close to the Civic Union.

Sources: Vera Tolz, "Russia's Parliamentary Elections: What Happened and Why," *RFE/RL Research Report,* 3, No. 2, January 14, 1994, p. 3; Vera Tolz, "Russia's New Parliament and Yeltsin: Cooperation Prospects," *RFE/RL Research Report,* 3, No. 5, February 4, 1994, p. 5.

cal landscape not yet in sight. For example, despite the presence of substantial support for Boris Yeltsin in the parliament, the State Duma voted 253 to 67 to amnesty those who were accused of trying to overthrow the Soviet government in August 1991 and those, including former vice president Aleksander Rutskoi—who challenged Boris Yeltsin in 1993. Such a vote suggests that in the current environment, political labels do not adhere very well. It may also indicate that people supporting reform are nevertheless taking heed of what they see as the lessons of the December 1993 vote for na-

tionalists and Communists. (In the amnesty vote, nearly 30 percent of the representatives did not vote.)

Other Elections: Local Councils and Referenda

The Soviet Union in 1990 also saw elections for local parliaments, governing its thousands of cities and districts. As with the election in the Russian federation as a whole, the rules of these elections did not guarantee seats for the party.

In several major cities, including Moscow and St. Petersburg, outspoken reformers won dominant positions in the local parliament and the office of mayor. In general more rural areas and smaller cities tended to return more conservative leaders, including the local Communist Party leaders, to office.

But the new conditions of government in Russia means that all local leaders, whether radical reformers or conservatives, found themselves with new power. Elected local leaders have been accorded some of this power constitutionally. But they have gained more in the past few years through the collapse of central order, the dismantling of the state-dominated economy, and the disintegration of the Communist Party. Some regions have embraced this new freedom with a vengeance, developing local authorities and enacting their own laws on the economy without waiting for the national legislature to act. An example of this was the actions of the local council in Moscow, mentioned in Chapter 31. In Kalmykia, in southwestern Russia, the local leaders adopted their own commercial code and moved to set up their republic as a tax-free zone in an effort to attract western investment and circumvent political difficulties in Moscow. Others have taken advantage of the new freedom to try to increase local revenues by applying "export" taxes to goods sent out of their region.[13] This adds up to yet another fundamental change for the people of Russia: the replacement of a once highly centralized state with a vast variety of local authorities. And each of these authorities, facing the prospect of elections, can only ignore their constituents' needs at their peril.

Elections themselves have also been used as part of the reform. Both Mikhail Gorbachev and Boris Yeltsin have used the technique of the nationwide referenda to try to leap over recalcitrant conservatives and push reform forward. In March 1991, in a desperate attempt to hold the fissiparous Soviet Union together,

Gorbachev sponsored a referendum asking people: "Do you consider it necessary to preserve the Union of Soviet Socialist Republics as a renewed federation of equal sovereign republics, in which the rights and freedoms of people of any nationality will be fully guaranteed?" The response: three-fourths of those who voted said "Yes." Gorbachev's attempt to hold the union together on this basis—embodied in a proposed union treaty—was cut short by the coup attempt of August 1991. But even had the coup not occurred, it was clear that some republics wanted nothing short of independence, not "renewed federation." The three Baltic States, plus Armenia, Georgia and Moldova, did not hold the referendum at all and some republics added questions and earned results stressing their independence.

In Russia the referendum opportunity was used to ask people if they wanted a directly elected president. When they said "Yes" with a 70 percent majority, the republic's Congress of Peoples' Deputies duly created such an office. The same month, a referendum in Georgia backed independence overwhelmingly as one in Lithuania in February had done, and as one in November in Ukraine would do.

The most controversial and significant referendum, before the constitutional vote, occurred in Russia in April 1993. After struggling with an increasingly contentious and conservative Congress of People's Deputies, Boris Yeltsin proposed that a referendum be held in which the Russian people would be asked directly whether they trusted him or the Congress to enact reform. The Congress had initially granted Yeltsin emergency powers but became uneasy over the course of 1992 as the pain of economic reform grew. Many opposed the sudden freeing of prices, resented his young, western-oriented government team, and feared the rapid growth of presidential power. A political battle at the end of 1992 seemed to produce a compromise: the resignation of Yeltsin's acting prime minister, Yegor Gaidar, but the retention by Yeltsin of power to rule by decree. When that deal fell apart, Yeltsin proposed that a referendum be held on the form of government itself, that is, whether Russia should be a presidential republic, and whether a constituent assembly should adopt a new constitution. But though the Congress agreed to the idea of a referendum, this deal, too, fell apart over the proposed wording of the questions.

It took both sides going to the very brink of crisis to achieve an agreement on the referendum. When Congress moved to strip Yeltsin of the rest of his governing powers at the beginning of 1993, the president announced that he was imposing a "special regime" on the country, by which he would rule by decree and hold the referendum he wanted on a constitution. The Constitutional Court invalidated the special regime immediately and the Congress tried to formally impeach Yeltsin. This move narrowly failed but a compromise on a referendum was worked out.

Four questions were asked of the Russian people [see page 516]. The question on social policy (number 2) was added by the Congress in an attempt to tap public discontent and force the end of economic reform, of the Yeltsin presidency, or both. Yeltsin insisted on asking people for a vote of confidence (number 1) and if they wanted new elections for the Congress (number 4). The Congress agreed, but in return added the question on early elections for Yeltsin (number 3).

The results were a modest success for Boris Yeltsin. Nearly two-thirds of the eligible voters turned out. A majority expressed support for Yeltsin and his policies, despite the difficulties. Just under one-third of all eligible voters wanted new presidential elections, while more than 40 percent wanted new parliamentary elections. Yeltsin was buoyed by the results.

The citizens of Russia have displayed their best qualities in the referendum. They have turned out to be wiser than they were thought to be by

On April 25, 1993, after months of legal and political battling, a referendum was held across most of Russia asking the country's citizens four direct questions:

1. Do you have confidence in the Russian President Boris Yeltsin?

Number of people voting	68.86 million
Percent of eligible voters voting	64.2
Percent of *voters* who voted "yes"	58.7

2. Do you approve of the social policy pursued by the Russian president and the government of the Russian Federation since 1992?

Number of people voting	68.76 million
Percent of eligible voters voting	64.1
Percent of *voters* who said "yes"	53.0

3. Do you think it is necessary to hold early elections of the president of the Russian Federation?

Number of people voting	68.76 million
Percent of eligible voters voting	74.1
Percent of *eligible voters* who said "yes"	31.7

4. Do you think it is necessary to hold early elections of people's deputies of the Russian Federation?

Number of people voting	68.8 million
Percent of eligible voters voting	64.1
Percent of *eligible voters* who said "yes"	43.1

The Congress of People's Deputies had resisted Boris Yeltsin's calls for a referendum and agreed in March 1993 only after inserting the questions on early presidential elections and, more significantly, the requirement that at least 50 percent of all *eligible voters* approve before any actions could be taken. Yeltsin appealed to the Constitutional Court which ruled that this stricture applied only to questions 3 and 4, both of which called for a specific action. As these measures did not achieve this almost impossible standard, no elections were held.

Sources: ITAR-TASS, May 5, 1993 (*Foreign Broadcast Information Service*, May 5, 1993, p. 27); Commission on Security and Cooperation in Europe, *Report on the April 25, 1993 Referendum in Russia* (Washington, D.C.: Commission on Security and Cooperation in Europe, 1993).

many deputies at the congress and by opposi-
tion leaders. People have realized and have
sensed the main thing: Russia can embark on
the road of resurgence only through reforms, no
matter how hard they may be. There is no other
way.[14]

He took the opportunity to relieve his vice president, Aleksandr Rutskoi, who had challenged him openly on reform, of his duties and insisted that he now had the mandate to call an assembly to draft a new constitution.

The Congress on the other hand was not forced into new parliamentary elections. Moreover, despite the president's clear claim to a vote of confidence, this vote had no legal consequences and did not change the fact that according to the existing—if often amended—constitution, only the Congress could write a new constitution. Nevertheless, sensing the political momentum turning his way, Boris Yeltsin did call together a constitutional assembly in the summer of 1993 and, as seen in Chapter 31, did get a constitutional draft to his liking.

The referendum was used once again in December 1993 to secure approval for a slightly revised draft constitution offered by the president. Fresh from his defeat of parliament, Yeltsin asked for a simple "Yes" or "No" vote on his draft, which, as noted in Chapter 31, provided for a strong presidency. Moreover, Yeltsin was able to dictate the terms of the referendum—since after October there was neither a parliament nor a constitutional court to challenge him—and he decreed that it would be approved if a simple majority of those voting said "Yes." In the vote, just over 58 percent of the voters approved of the new constitution. Somewhat troubling was the nearly 42 percent who voted against the constitution, revealing a degree of polarization of Russian voters. Moreover, just over half (54 percent) of all eligible voters took part in the vote, down considerably from the two-thirds turnout of April 1993. In the vote itself, then, the constitution was actu-

ally approved by less than one-third of all eligible voters.[15]

While sobering, especially in the current volatile context, the parliamentary elections and the adoption of a new constitution, even if by less than overwhelming vote, provides at least the basic framework for the ferocious political competition that is continuing in Russia. The parliamentary vote provided an electoral outlet both for those opposed to and those in favor of government policy—something not to be taken for granted in Russia. The constitutional vote also removed at least some fundamental issues from contention—issues that had brought the country to violence in October 1993. And when, as noted above, the new Parliament used its constitutional prerogative to pardon his political opponents, the president accepted it, even though he strongly opposed the action. It was a small but important step toward the rule of law.

In the new Russia, elections—if not political parties—have provided new opportunities for the Russian people to become involved in the process of governance. They have had the opportunity for the first time to choose directly the people who are dealing with the fundamental questions they face and to indicate their support for the direction of policy in general terms. Elections have been used to evaluate both form (of government) and reform (of the economy). But parliamentary elections and especially referenda are only general and often cumbersome methods for handling the enormous and complex tasks of creating both a democracy and new economy at once. And since in this process some are certain to suffer even as others gain, the elections in Russia, as these results show, are often as much a judgment by the voters on how the process is working for them as it is on the more profound questions of democracy and market economy. As the journal *Commersant* put it, ". . . the crowd is not concerned with who is breaking the Constitution . . . but who is a threat to their lives, property and well-being."[16]

Notes

1. Jerry F. Hough and Merle Fainsod, *How the Soviet Union Is Governed* (Cambridge: Harvard University Press, 1979), p. 226–227.

2. T. H. Rigby, "Politics in the Mono-Organizational Society," in *Authoritarian Politics in Communist Europe,* ed. Andrew C. Janos (Berkeley, Calif.: Institute of International Studies, 1976).

3. T. H. Rigby and Bohdan Harasymiw, eds., *Leadership Selection and Patron-Client Relations in the USSR and Yugoslavia* (London: George Allen & Unwin, 1983), p. 3.

4. Jeffrey Hahn, "State Institutions in Transition," in *Developments in Soviet and Post-Soviet Politics,* eds. Stephen White, Alex Pravda, and Zvi Gitelman (Durham: Duke University Press, 1992), p. 94.

5. Mary McAuley, *Soviet Politics 1917–1991* (New York: Oxford University Press, 1992), p. 97.

6. Hahn, "State Institutions," p. 95.

7. *Izvestia,* September 4, 1991 [*Current Digest of the Soviet Press,* XLIII, No. 36 (1991), p. 35].

8. *Rossiiskiye vesti,* No. 26, November 1991, p. 11 [*Current Digest,* XLII, No. 46 (1991), p. 7].

9. *Izvestia,* January 2, 1992 [*Current Digest,* XLIV, No. 1 (1992), p. 22].

10. *Nash sovremennik,* No. 7, July 1992 [*Current Digest,* XLIV, No. 40 (1992), p. 13].

11. Quoted in *Komsomolskaya pravda,* September 3, 1992 [*Current Digest,* XLIV, No. 35 (1992), p. 13].

12. Vyacheslav Nikonov, "On the Near Approaches to Power—Thoughts on Russian 'Party Building,'" *Nezavisimaya Gazeta,* August 7, 1992 [*Current Digest of the Soviet and Post-Soviet Press,* Vol. XLIV, No. 33 (1992), p. 17].

13. Philip Hanson, *Local Power and Market Reform in the Former Soviet Union* (Munich: RFE/RL Research Institute, 1993), p. 19.

14. *TV Rossiya,* May 6, 1993 [Federal News Service, May 6, 1993].

15. Confidence in that number was weakened by subsequent charges of electoral manipulation.

16. Maxim Sokolov, "Coup d'Etat or Constitutional Reform?" *Commersant,* September 29, 1993, p. 6.

References and Suggested Readings

Bielasiak, Jack. 1982. "Party Leadership and Mass Participation in Developed Socialism." In *Developed Socialism in the Soviet Bloc,* ed. Jim Seroka and Maurice D. Simon. Boulder, Colo.: Westview Press, pp. 121–154.

Hahn, Jeffrey W. 1991. "Local Politics and Political Power in Russia: The Case of Yaroslavl," *Soviet Economy,* 7, No. 4, pp. 322–341.

Laird, Roy D. 1986. *The Politburo: Demographic Trends, Gorbachev, and the Future.* Boulder, Colo.: Westview Press.

Pribylovskii, Vladimir. 1992. *Dictionary of Political Parties and Organizations in Russia.* Washington, D.C.: Center for Strategic and International Studies.

33

Policy Case I:
Economic Restructuring

he *Krasny Proletary* (Red Proletariat) factory is typical. It once worked for the Soviet Ministry of Defense producing computer-driven lathes to be used in the nuclear industry. It employed six thousand people and had one customer, the Soviet government. Under perestroika it was cut loose, state orders dropped and the firm was kept in "business" by government subsidies producing lathes no one needed. Now it is being privatized and more than three-fourths of the company's workers are now owners. A business consultant has been hired, new products developed, and people have been laid off. Now forty-five hundred people work at the factory, which still makes lathes, but also bricks, and it recently sold more than $1 million worth of goods at a Chicago trade fair.[1]

As the Russian people deal with the loss of nearly one-quarter of their former country, as they are presented greatly varying and often rapidly changing alternatives for a new system of government, they are also dealing with a fundamental change in the economic dynamics of their lives. The state-dominated, centrally planned system that Mikhail Gorbachev inherited in 1985 was not fundamentally altered by the time of his resignation six years later. But several key features of that system had been undermined deliberately by the Gorbachev reformers as they strove to improve the system. Then, despite or perhaps because of the changes, the decline of the economy accelerated. Finally, the social and political upheaval unleashed by the political reform throughout the country contributed to bringing the country into full-blown economic crisis just as the August coup provoked its dissolution.

Thus the current leaders and people of Russia face a task even more daunting than that of Gorbachev: not "reforming" the inefficient, poorly operating (but at least still functioning) economy, but fashioning a new national, integrated, responsive and productive economy out of the pieces and practices of what was left to them in the collapse of the USSR.

THE COLLAPSE OF THE SOVIET ECONOMY

At the time of the August coup attempt, virtually all key indicators of the Soviet economy were down and dropping. Industrial production in 1991 was down by more than 6 percent; gross national product by 12 percent; labor productivity by 12 percent; all in comparison to already poor results in 1990. Investment by the central government fell more than 10 percent and could not be made up by funds generated by enterprises themselves. That meant that new equipment, even if available, could not be purchased, old equipment could not be repaired, and much equipment remained idle as orders were not filled by suppliers. With less investment, fewer projects were begun and fewer were finished. In 1990 only two-fifths of the projects considered "high priority" were finished.

Life for the average consumer became even more difficult. The amount of goods available in shops fell dramatically as production slowdowns reduced already poor supplies of consumer goods. Lines grew longer for the fewer goods making their way to the state stores and prices rose on newly tolerated private and still illegal "black" markets. Price increases were spurred by partial decontrol at the wholesale level, and even substantial gains

in nominal incomes could not assist people in acquiring goods which were not available, a phenomenon economists refer to as "repressed inflation." Retail price inflation was officially reported at 14 percent for 1990 and 100 percent for 1991. In real terms the Soviet consumer's lot, already difficult, was becoming even more so.

With less to buy at the store, people saved their money in banks or simply kept it at home. It was estimated that in 1989 the country had a "ruble overhang" (unspent money) great enough to buy everything available in the country twice over.[2] In a country with a market economy, money flows to banks and investments driven by the need to earn a return. In the Soviet system, there was no market for this capital, no mechanism for private profit, and the government controlled the direction of investments. Hence this surplus money did not drive other parts of the economy, and since people had little to gain from earning more, incentives for producing and initiative were undermined. During these last years of perestroika it was much better to have goods like winter boots or parts for a television set, which had a clear value and use, than money, which did not. Hence people were inclined to buy even what they did not need to hold for later trading. This "household hoarding," which nine out of ten Soviet citizens practiced, only further contributed to the goods shortage.[3]

Though designed to try to improve the system, the policies of perestroika in some ways contributed to weakening it fatally. A highly centralized economy such as that of the Soviet Union relied on the control and dominance of its "leading organization"—that is, the Communist Party. But as noted earlier, Gorbachev's reforms worked precisely to undercut party control. Gorbachev felt the party had become stagnant, bureaucratic and unable to serve the country. Encouraging local initiatives, including competitive elections and strengthening local parliaments, undercut the authority of the party at the local level, while Gorbachev's moves to increase the power of the national legislature and presidency hurt the party at the national level. Thus the power of the regional party first secretary, who in the past had been speaking on behalf of a dominant central authority, was eroded. Newly important local governments for the first time had to worry about their constituents' reactions to a deteriorating situation. Many localities began instituting local coupons and other rationing systems that restricted purchase of goods in short supply to people who lived in their cities or regions.

At the same time, the growth of national and republican power centers willing and able to challenge the center also affected the national economy. As production slipped and groups began to raise grievances against the center, provision of supplies according to quotas set by the center declined. Republican leaders were under strong pressure to keep resources at home, to barter them directly with other republics, or to sell them to other countries for goods needed in their regions. In late 1991, for example, Ukraine banned the sale to Russia of all of its goods. This hurt the Russian food supply, and in retaliation Russia stopped shipping fuel, which grounded aircraft in Ukraine.[4] Contributions to the federal budget also fell as republics, led by Russia, withheld their contributions to pressure the central government. In mid-1991, for example, the Soviet central government had received roughly half of what it was supposed to get from the republics.

As internal trade declined, production fell and republics withheld their contributions, the central government faced a crisis not unknown in the West: a burgeoning budget deficit, too little revenue for too many tasks. From 14 billion rubles, or less than 2 percent of the country's gross domestic product (GDP) in 1985, the deficit jumped to R52 billion or 6.3 percent of GDP in 1987, more than R80 billion (8.8 percent of GDP) in 1989, and more than R150 billion

(9.0 percent of GDP) by the end of 1991.[5] The Soviet government, as others elsewhere have done, responded by simply printing more money, which literally papered over the deficit, but at the same time gave a strong boost to inflation.

Russia was also deeply in debt abroad. The production and sale of key commodities that earned hard currency like coal and oil was either flat or dropping. Exports of oil to the West were down in 1990 and 1991. This put economic planners in a serious bind. To avoid a huge trade imbalance (more imports than exports), the country had to cut imports; but to do that meant giving up the very things the economy needed to improve, such as high-quality manufactured goods, information and communications technology, and critical modern equipment. And the country still needed to buy grain. Moreover, as part of perestroika, foreign trade was no longer controlled from the top; instead, many ministries and enterprises acquired the right to trade on their own. And with Soviet citizens, who were now voters, angry and suffering, more consumer goods had to be bought from abroad. To finance needed imports, Soviet debt increased; borrowing from the West nearly doubled in two years (1987–1989). By the time the USSR was dissolved, the country owed the world some $80 billion in hard currency, with $7 billion owed for 1991 alone.

There were some flickering bright spots on the economic horizon. The number of people working in the cooperative and private sector grew rapidly under the Gorbachev reforms to the point that more than 10 million people or 6 percent of the work force was no longer working for the state by mid-1991. The devolution of economic responsibility to enterprises paralleled the devolution of some political responsibility to local government. Unfortunately, the need to operate profitably on the business side meant that for the first time in Soviet history, real unemployment appeared in the country.

This was estimated officially at two million jobless in 1991 or roughly 1.5 percent of the work force, quite low by western standards. But in a country where the right to work was enshrined in the constitution, where unemployment was virtually unknown and the mechanisms for dealing with it nonexistent, the social alarm caused by even relatively little unemployment was substantial.

FIXING THE ECONOMY: BURDENS OF THE PAST AND PRESENT

Why is the task of creating a smooth-running productive economy in Russia so difficult? Why is a country so rich in natural resources, with a large, well-educated population, a rich heritage of ideas, and a long list of historic achievements having such a hard time? Part of the answer lies in the fact that the change that is taking place is so fundamental; the challenge involves not simply making a weak economy run a little better, but creating—on a vast scale and almost from scratch—a new economy. Finally, the very principles on which this new economy is supposed to work have not been legally and publicly functioning in the country for generations.

Some aspects of economic reform must deal with things that are not reformable or at least less susceptible to reform. The country's vast size, for example, presents daunting problems of communication, transportation and labor mobility. Russia's great store of natural riches lie overwhelmingly in Siberia, far from the industrial heartland of European Russia. The country's infrastructure, the blood and sinew of the economy, is poorly developed, old and deteriorating. In the beginning of the 1980s, there were fewer telephones in the USSR than in France or West Germany, countries with roughly one-fifth the Soviet Union's population; a fraction of the number of cars, trucks and

Specialization with a Vengeance

One of the legacies of the Soviet Union is that various republics—including Russia—must try to restructure their economies as integrated wholes after decades of being a part of a larger economy. In the Soviet system central control reinforced tendencies for certain products to be produced in one part of the country and distributed throughout rather than have many suppliers or producers. One analyst described the situation in 1991.

A plant in Armenia is the only source of a part that is needed in every power station in all the republics. The world's largest polyester factory, in Byelorussia, produces 90 percent of Soviet output. A plant in Moldavia makes 99 percent of die-casting machines. Single plants in Russia produce most of the automobiles (58 percent), trolleys (97 percent), polypropylene (71 percent), sewing machines (100 percent), printing ink (90 percent), combine harvesters (71 percent), oil drilling rigs (two plants produce 100 percent), and all of most grades of boilers and turbines needed by power plants. Factories in the Ukraine build the vast majority of coal hoists (82 percent), coking equipment (78 percent), corn harvesters (100 percent), forklifts (86 percent), diesel locomotives (96 percent). A plant in Uzbekistan produces 75 percent of cellulose acetate, an important artificial fiber used in rayon, film, and automobiles.

Source: Tim Snyder, "Antitrust for USSR," *Christian Science Monitor,* October 2, 1991. Used by permission of the author.

buses; and fewer paved roads in the whole country than there are in Texas.

Such problems are especially critical for the energy sector, where the natural resources are now more remote from the industrial plants that use them. In the agricultural sphere, the poor performance of Russia is made somewhat more understandable when one realizes that though the country is nearly twice the size of the United States, it actually has less high-quality growing land. The climate, soil conditions and water supply in most Russian territory are not naturally conducive to productive agriculture.

The country's population also represents a problem. As the economy is more labor intensive than those in the West, more labor is required for each job. As long as the population, and hence the labor force, is growing and new workers can be found, this is not a problem. But the growth in Russian population has been slowing for years. The rate of natural increase in the population (births minus deaths) fell from 5 percent per year in 1981 to less than 1 percent by 1991. In 1992, for the first time since World War II, there were more deaths than births, a trend that accelerated in 1993. Moreover it is an aging population. The number of pensioners grew nearly fivefold between 1960 and 1970 and exceeded 40 million, or nearly 15 percent of the population of the USSR, by the mid-1980s. Finally, years of heavy investment in industrial development and inadequate protection of the country's air, water and soil, and human population have left a legacy of ecological hazards and human illness that will require immense investment to overcome.

Many of the present problems of the economy are the direct result of the way it had been set up to operate under communism. Since the time of the Bolshevik revolution, the determination of economic policy for the country was a tightly held monopoly of the Communist Party leadership. Though at different times the party leadership allowed more or less freedom for decisions at lower levels, fundamental economic power, for example, over allocation of resources and responsibility for their use, remained a prerogative of the very top of the political structure. This meant that an astonishing number of specific and concrete economic decisions, as well as the determination of central policy direction, were made at the top of the political system. In a study of Politburo

agendas, Ed Hewett found that this body, the top layer of decision making in the USSR, would typically

> ... *hear reports and issue decrees relating to the Yamburg natural gas pipeline, the preparation of livestock for winter, the development of the television industry, changes in selected retail prices, and the rational use of the various bus fleets in the USSR. The development of a particular town, the state of shoe production, and the use of a Soviet-developed technology in assembly lines, techniques for stock-breeding, the management of the Chernobyl disaster, and the fall harvest are additional, fairly random samples of what Politburo members discuss and make the subject of decrees.*[6]

Of course the Politburo did not work out every detail of the economy. But such central direction spawned an immense bureaucracy that decided not only on the production and distribution of millions of products but also on the resources necessary for the millions of other materials needed to produce those. In this situation, no market gave signals as to what the economy needed, competition did not correct for poor choices, and prices were set administratively not by real cost considerations. Often decisions as to where to put investment and what to produce reflected the results of political battles more than the economy's real needs. This gave the Soviet economy in Charles Lindbloom's words, "strong thumbs and no fingers." A factory manager operating in this kind of economy has no incentive to improve a product or even to try to sell more of it than the year before. It was only necessary to fulfill the state-set quotas. Indeed, if a Soviet manager wanted to produce more of a product by introducing new technology or offering workers higher wages, such decisions would usually not be his or hers to make.

Finally, the Soviet economy also gave rise to duplication of economic effort within sectors. Because enterprises and ministries were answerable essentially only to those above

With the blossoming of glasnost, the breadth and depth of environmental deterioration and disasters in the USSR became more subject to public discussion. River, sea, and air pollution and misuse of land and other natural resources have shown to be major problems.

them—they did not have to compete for real customers—there was a strong incentive for ministries and enterprises to control all aspects of whatever it was they produced. Thus, instead of buying from a supplier the electronic components or raw materials that go into making, say, a truck, the Soviet ministry of automotive industry would produce its own components and materials. More than that, because production was the key to success, factory managers and ministries would try hard to attract workers and keep them satisfied by making sure they received the things they needed most. Hence consumer goods, housing, and even food were typically produced or provided through enterprises and ministries that normally would have nothing to do with those

sectors. Control of resources was the name of the game and since the government made up any "losses" and enterprises could not go bankrupt, there was no pressure to reduce costs.

In the Soviet period, these difficulties were compounded by an ideological favoritism toward heavy industry, as opposed to consumer goods. This emphasis was partly derived from Marxism, which stresses industrial development, and was reinforced by a Soviet desire to become and remain a world industrial power. For the Soviet economy this meant that building new plants and equipment for heavy industry had first claim on the investment budget, while funds for agriculture, transportation or consumer goods received smaller pieces of the pie. In 1980, for example, of more than 1.7

"We treated the land without mercy"*

The drive for industrialization in the Soviet Union combined with the lack of opportunity for public lobbying and dissemination of information produce a nightmare of disastrous effects on the country.

◆ Three-fourths of all surface water in the country is polluted; one-half of the water is not drinkable; one-quarter is not treated at all.

◆ Thirty percent of all food and 40 percent of all baby food is contaminated.

◆ One half of the arable land is in fact not usable because it is waterlogged or completely swamped.

◆ Fifteen percent of the urban population breathes clean air; one-third of the country's population breathes air with concentrations of toxic substances ten times higher than allowable concentrations.

◆ An estimated 50 billion tons of waste has accumulated in Russia, with 44.5 billion tons being added each year. More than 250 million acres of the country are buried under waste.

Such a vast array of damage, plus an overburdened and poorly supported health care system, take a terrible toll on the human ecology:

◆ In 1990, less than one-half of all draft-age men in the Soviet Union were fit for duty; between 1991 and 1992 the number of people discharged from the service for health reasons increased by 30 percent.

◆ In 1992, 14 percent of Russian children were in good health; 15 to 20 percent of preschool children suffered from chronic diseases; 10 percent of all children are anemic.

◆ Russian women die during pregnancy and childbirth at a rate ten times higher than in the West.

◆ The life expectancy for a man in the Soviet Union in 1964 was 66.1 years; the life expectancy for a man in Russia in 1993 is 60. A man of 50 at the time Mikhail Gorbachev became general secretary could not expect to live as long as one who turned 50 on the eve of World War II.

◆ In 1992 there were four cases of diphtheria in the United States; that same year there were two thousand in the city of Moscow alone.

◆ One-fourth of all currently operating hospitals in Russia were built before 1940; 42 percent have no hot water supply; 12 percent have no water supply at all.

*Nikolai Vorontsov, chairman of the State Committee for the Protection of Nature, Soviet Union, in 1989; quoted in Feshbach and Friendly, *Ecocide*, p. 49.

Sources: *Nezavisimaya Gazeta*, October 7, 1992 [*The Current Digest of the Soviet Press*, November 11, 1992]; Murray Feshbach and Alfred Friendly, Jr. *Ecocide in the USSR* (New York: Basic Books, 1992); *The New York Times*, October 4, 1992, p. 5.

---

billion rubles of investment, two-thirds went into "productive" capital, and of that, fully one-half went to industry—especially machine building, metals, fuels, and power—and only 20 percent into agriculture.[7] In addition, the country's immense military needs and establishment made a constant claim on some 20 percent of the country's productive capacity. Changing such an emphasis in the economy thus ran up against both ideology and politics.

As Mikhail Gorbachev recognized, introducing any form of independent decision making at the factory or local level meant taking power away from the Communist Party and the national government.

Moreover, any economic reform that introduced uncertainty—for example, the possibility of being fired—was likely to provoke concern and opposition from workers who feared for their livelihood. And workers *as con-*

sumers were used to low prices for their goods. When Mikhail Gorbachev became general secretary, rents had not changed in the country since 1928, utility prices since 1946, and state-regulated food prices were as they had been 20 to 30 years before. These low prices helped avoid the kind of upheaval seen in Poland in the 1970s and 1980s and gave the Soviet worker a sense of economic security that was uncommon in the West. Housing costs for the average Soviet family, for example, took only 6 percent of the family budget. But such prices did not reflect real costs and government subsidies made up the difference, taking roughly one-fifth of the state budget. On the other hand, to raise prices, especially in the era of glasnost and broadening political freedom, risked strikes and demonstrations and further damage to the economy. Hence, price reforms were consistently put off.

The Beginnings of Reform under Gorbachev

Gorbachev pushed the party to begin taking actions on the economy. These actions amounted to the most far-reaching attempts since the New Economic Policy to change the way the system operated. In 1987, a law was passed making some 60 percent of the economy "self-financing." That is, enterprises were supposed to be able to find their own suppliers, determine wage levels in accordance with employee performance, and raise their own financing. Put into effect at the beginning of 1988 and modified over the next two years, the new system did weaken central control. But ministries remained responsible for the overall performance of enterprises in their sectors and state orders still accounted for roughly 90 percent of industrial production. Most enterprise profits were still appropriated by the ministries. As a spur to efficient performance, a specifically capitalist device was introduced. In 1987 the first enterprise, a construction firm in

Leningrad, went bankrupt and two thousand workers were switched to other jobs. In an attempt to improve the quality of output, a new ministry, *Gospriomka*, was set up to inspect the output of many factories. But putting this policy into practice involved rejecting some production, and workers' salaries, which were tied to production norms, fell. As one worker explained, "The number of buses coming off the conveyor belt decreased. Instead of 33–34 a day we were making 20–25 so we were not getting our bonuses any longer. I used to make an extra 100 rubles. Everybody lost at least 60–70 rubles."[8] This situation, combined with dwindling supplies of most goods, sparked worker dissatisfaction and strikes spread. In 1989 some 7 million workdays were lost to the economy; the number reached 10 million in 1990.

Also in 1987 the government moved to make legal the operation of individual private enterprise in most services (for example, taxis). Individuals were allowed to run small shops and restaurants but could not employ anyone outside their own families. Other new policies encouraged the development of cooperatives that could hire employees and operate in various sectors of the economy. In a very short time the number of cooperatives expanded rapidly. By 1989 there were already an estimated 100,000 operating in the country.

But such moves provoked substantial opposition. Workers feared for their jobs and many people equated private business with illegal business, which it had been for decades. The possibility that some could get rich or obtain income privately, along with the feared loss of control on the part of the Communist Party, produced many restrictions on and criticisms of the activities of the cooperatives and private businesses. Gorbachev was constantly obliged to fight against the desire to retain the status quo. During a Central Committee plenum in 1988, he complained about this tendency:

No sooner do people in pay-your-own-way collectives get pay raises through better final results, than protests and irritated voices come to be heard, complaining that those people are allegedly earning too much.

Under socialism, however, the question can only be whether the wages have been earned or not, rather than whether they are high or low.

In December 1988, the Council of Ministers announced new restrictions on the business activities of cooperatives and the next year a bill in the Supreme Soviet to outlaw cooperatives was only narrowly defeated. What emerged was, in Marshall Goldman's words, "halfhearted toleration of cooperatives and private trade."

In the agricultural sector, reform was similarly hemmed in. New policies removed restrictions on the sale of output from small private plots and allowed collective farms to sell the surplus—whatever was not required to be sold to the state—on the open market.[9] A law introduced in 1988 allowed peasants to lease land, but ownership rights were restricted. In 1990, ownership was allowed but again restrictions made operating a private farm uneconomical. Farmers could not sell their land, meaning that raising capital for equipment and seed was still problematical. Even more crucial, farmers could not employ anyone to work the land. The number of private farms did grow, but with little recent history of large-scale private agriculture, few government incentives such as loans, or a clear legal position for private ownership, the dismantling of the country's large collective farm proceeded only slowly. One observer of a collective farm in central Russia captured the individual perspective:

For decades, people here have learned that personal gain was wrong, even criminal. Until two years ago, anybody who picked for himself the potatoes left in the field by the clumsy harvester could go to prison. Sometimes whole fields of potatoes were left to rot in the soil. Now everybody can pick all they want, but old fears die hard.[10]

Other changes were aimed at opening the Soviet economy to the outside world. Recognizing the need for better access to foreign trade and technology, Gorbachev attacked the state monopoly on foreign trade by extending to enterprises and cooperatives the right to engage in their own foreign trade, to deal with their foreign suppliers and customers directly, and to buy and sell the foreign currency they would need to do business. Other new laws allowed direct foreign investment in the Soviet Union for the first time, and scores of foreign businesses making everything from plastics to pizza began joint ventures. Within a short time, the laws and practices were modified further to encourage investment—for example, by allowing majority ownership by western partners.

The attempt by Mikhail Gorbachev and the people he recruited to alter the Soviet economy radically met with opposition at every level. Politically conservative Communist Party leaders, such as Yigor Ligachev, worried about the effect of these changes on the role of the party. Entrenched institutions, accustomed to running things from the top down, recognized the danger to their positions and prerogatives inherent in Gorbachev's reforms. People appointed throughout the country to run the economy saw their own role eroded as greater autonomy was given to individuals and enterprises. Ideologically orthodox Communists throughout the party opposed the growth of private enterprise and the possible reappearance of *kulaks*, rich peasants, in the countryside.

Moreover years of certain practices of a planned, structured economy left their mark on people's psyches. In the Soviet system, money and prices played what economists call a "passive role" in the allocation of goods. With consumer goods scarce, for example, and resources politically allocated, one's place in the state structure was more important than money income in determining how one lived. High party officials lived better than low party officials, who lived better than nonparty people or workers in a firm. As rigid as this may seem to outsiders, the capitalist system's inequalities may seem even more daunting to those who have lived most of their lives in such an economy. The potential disappearance of much of the predictability and security of the state-run economy left many Russians frightened that they would wind up much worse off.

Nor did changing the economy take place in isolation. Instead it was happening against the background of broad political changes that gave interested parties, such as workers and collective farmers, a voice, a chance to register their fears and complaints. Concomitantly, the resurgent power of regions and nations challenged the central power on other issues. What often emerged, then, were compromise measures, steps that weakened central control but put nothing effective in its place. For example, without either central command or what economists call "market clearing prices," suppliers found little incentive to increase or even maintain output; hence supplies contracted even further. With little to buy, neither workers nor farmers were attracted by promises of higher wages or greater gains under privatization. And with regions increasingly asserting themselves, national distribution began to collapse. Price increases, authorized or not, began to pervade the economy.

In the end, Mikhail Gorbachev was faced with the choice of proceeding with a more rapid, more radical economic plan, offered to him by his advisers in 1990, or moving more slowly in an attempt to avoid drastic political consequences. He chose the latter but the consequences came anyway.

CHANGING SAILS IN A STORM: ECONOMIC REFORM IN RUSSIA

Boris Yeltsin declared himself in favor of rapid political and economic reform before the breakup of the Soviet Union. Indeed one of the reasons for his clash with Mikhail Gorbachev and his dismissal as a candidate member of the Politburo was that he wanted to move faster than the Communist Party leadership did. As president of the Russian republic, he secured passage of legislation that moved faster in several key economic areas than did the Soviet Union as a whole. Private property was legalized, enterprises were allowed to exchange rubles for hard currency, and Yeltsin banned political activity (which essentially meant the Communist Party) from in the workplace. While Gorbachev rejected the radical economic plan put forth by Stanislav Shatalin at the end of 1990, Russia—and especially Boris Yeltsin—embraced it. In addition, as noted earlier, Yeltsin pushed hard for Russia to take control of its resources away from the central government.

Thus when Russia became an independent country, Yeltsin had already laid the groundwork for moving quickly. Conservatives and orthodox Communists had been discredited by the coup attempt. Yeltsin was at the height of his prestige, having defied those who tried to overthrow the government, and then abruptly elbowed aside Mikhail Gorbachev and his Soviet government.

The first economic measures taken after the breakup of the USSR were designed to do what Gorbachev had so long avoided: free prices. On January 1, 1992, prices were freed on most goods and services; prices were increased for key commodities like fuel, although not freed entirely. A program was announced to cut the budget deficit, mostly by cutting subsidies and defense spending and utilizing a profit tax and a new "value-added tax" (on the increased value a product gains as it moves through the manufacturing process). The Yeltsin government pledged itself to making sure that those least well off would be protected by providing compensation to pensioners and increasing the minimum wage.

An ambitious program was announced to privatize the Russian economy; that is, take the state out of the business of running most industry, services, and retail and wholesale trade, and putting these in the hands of private companies and individuals. A system was set up whereby all citizens of the country were given privatization vouchers—funds that could be used to buy the stock of companies. Auctions were then held in which shares were sold in companies of all sizes, from small shops to giant firms like ZIL, which makes cars and refrigerators and employs more than a hundred thousand people.[11] By the middle of 1993 more than seventy thousand firms had moved into private hands (see Figure 33.1), and more than one in every seven workers was employed in the private sector. The significance of this achievement is clear when we recall that private enterprise was not even legal until 1987 and as late as 1991 less than 3 percent of the work force in the Soviet Union was privately employed. Almost one-half of more than fourteen thousand large state companies have also been privatized. In addition, nearly 150,000 new private firms were established and, with prices freed and a new decree allowing lifelong leaseholding of land, the number of people willing to try private farming also grew. By mid-1993 there were six times as many private farms as the year before. Ironically, capitalism is producing what more than seventy years of the workers' revolution had failed to produce: the Russian people are gaining ownership of the means of production.

But the cost of this wrenching shift is high. By mid-1993 official figures put unemployment at 1 million while unofficial estimates were much higher. As companies slimmed payrolls to try to achieve profitability and the economy lost central direction, production declined. Cuts in investment and military spending and fragmentation of supply systems produced an overall drop in output of 30 percent in 1992. Prices, freed from restraints, grew at more than 2,000 percent. While wages and income also grew, the average person could not keep up. As Figure 33.2 shows, real wages by mid-1993 were not only nearly 40 percent lower than they had been in 1990, but they were lower than they had been in 1985! While some in the new

As economic circumstances grew more difficult many people in Russia sold household goods or resold purchased items in an attempt to earn money.

Russia have done extremely well, many others find that what bought a meal two years ago now buys only bread. The government itself declared in January 1993 that more than one-third of the country's population was living below the poverty level.

Many enterprises have stayed in business by cutting back the pay of workers still employed. As many as 45 percent of those employed in

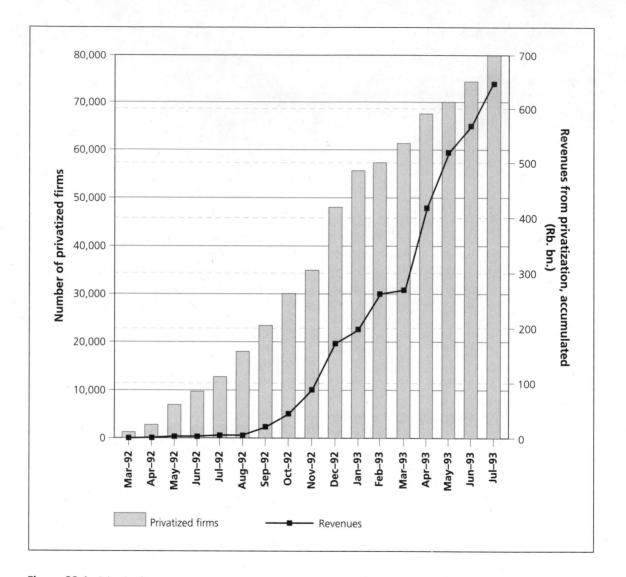

Figure 33.1   Privatization.   Source: *Russian Economic Trends,* September 29, 1993, p. 8.

mid-1993 were actually working on short time or on temporary layoff.[12] Firms also borrowed from the state and from each other. Interenterprise debt reached 500 billion rubles by mid-1993. Freed from an oppressive state but without common practices or well-developed business law, much business activity fell into the hands of organized criminals or—what was worse in the minds of some—back into the hands of the nomenklatura who had been running it all along. Enterprise managers employed by the state and administrators in the ministries remained in the best position to evaluate and take control of newly "privat-

MiGs Я Us?

Fly a *MiG-29* at Mach 2.5 In Moscow*

MIGS *etc.*, in conjunction with the Russian aerospace industry, has a limited number of high-performance military flight packages available for immediate booking. Flights on MiG-29, MiG-31, Su-27, and L-39 jets are offered.

You need not be a pilot. Accompanied by a top Russian test pilot, you will take the controls of a legendary supersonic fighter with a flight plan you help design.

Flight packages from $6,000.

*No, really

MIGS *etc.*, Inc.
800 MIGS ETC {USA]
813 923-0607
813 923-8815 fax

The Ultimate in Defense Conversion. In an attempt to earn hard currency, some branches of the Russian military began marketing their own particular products and services. "Flight packages" promoted in this ad ranged from flying a jet at 2.5 times the speed of sound to a top-of-the-line aerial combat package that ends in a mock dogfight. The cost: $45,000.

Source: *The New York Times*, October 18, 1993, p. A7.

ized" businesses, leaving many ordinary citizens to wonder if anything had changed.[13]

In part because of these problems and in part because the changes are both dramatic and fundamental, the question of economic reconstruction has become central to the Russian political scene. It is part of a titanic battle that is being fought out over questions of economic restructuring, but it is just as much a battle over who will run the new Russian state.

Critics of Boris Yeltsin's approach charge that he is wrecking the country's economy in a

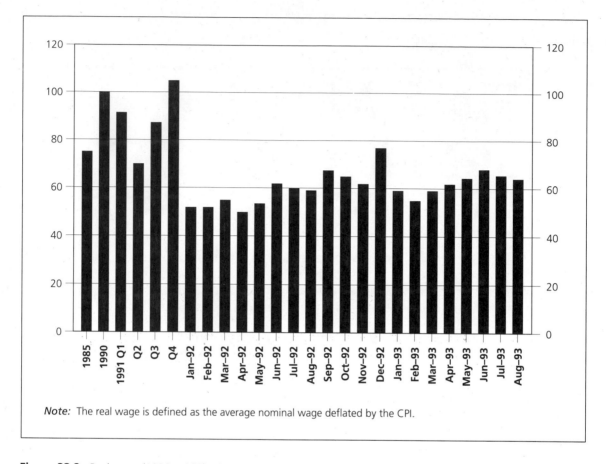

Note: The real wage is defined as the average nominal wage deflated by the CPI.

Figure 33.2   Real wage (1900 = 100).   Source: *Russian Economic Trends,* September 29, 1993, p. 6.

unrestrained rush to privatize. They argue that by moving so fast he has dismantled the old economic system before a new one exists to take its place. Critics in the Congress of People's Deputies and in the new Parliament have railed against the growing unemployment and raging inflation that price reform stimulated. Aleksandr Rutskoi, at the time President Yeltsin's own vice president, accused the government of "economic genocide" against the people of Russia.

Privatization also strikes directly at the power of the old nomenklatura, the Communist and Communist-appointed managers of the economy. Enterprises that are sold belong to new owners—who in about half the cases are the workers in the enterprise. Those who have run them for years fear for their jobs and their ability to control the country's recourses. Such concerns lead people who were powerful under the old system to support a slower pace of privatization, the retention of central direction for a time, and the reimposition of price controls—even as they position themselves to take advantage where they can of changes in ownership. In the Congress of People's Deputies, a major bloc—the Civic Union—formed to challenge the president. It included influential people from various economic sectors, represented by the Union of Industrialists, the leader of an opposition political party (the Democratic Party), and then vice president Rutskoi. At the end of 1992 this group, with the support of the Congress, was able to force one of its own, Viktor Chernomyrdin, on Boris Yeltsin as his prime minister.

With central governing power greatly diluted, local sovereignties, including regions and cities, are adopting their own approach to privatization. While some of these have been more vigorous than the national program, many local elites, eager to retain control of resources, prevent the implementation of a national program.[14]

A second issue of increasing importance is that of foreign involvement in the economy. The Yeltsin government has made it clear that it cannot achieve this transformation of the economy without massive support from the West. Russia began to receive aid in the form of credits and direct grants and loan forgiveness in 1991 and 1992. This has come from rich western countries represented by the Group of 24, from individual countries like Germany, from the European Community, and from global financial organizations, such as the International Monetary Fund and the World Bank. But the price, especially of aid from the IMF, is that Russia get its financial house in order: deficits must be cut, privatization must move forward, and the government must allow prices to reflect real costs, including the cost of borrowing money. Such conditions apply not only to transition loans like the $4 billion promised to Russia by the IMF itself, but also to much larger aid packages offered by western countries and to deals on rescheduling the country's foreign debt. For example, much of the $24 billion in aid promised in 1992 and a debt rescheduling agreement for $30 billion of the country's debt were tied to IMF conditions. Economic prescriptions from western organizations strike at the heart of national, central control of the

Objections to privatizing the Russian economy are evident in this cartoon from *Pravda* (April 10, 1993) where the figure of Boris Yeltsin is placed in contrast to the heroic figures of Soviet labor. Two of the signs held by the people read: "I buy vouchers [privatization certificates]." The figure just below Yeltsin is Foreign Minister Andrei Kozyrev whose sign reads "I am selling the motherland." To his right a sinister figure holds the sign "I sell everything and everyone." To his right is the figure of Mikhail Gorbachev whose sign reads "I [will] change the Canaries for Foros." This is a reference to the Canary Islands, a favorite vacation destination of the newly rich, and to the Crimean dacha where Gorbachev was briefly detained during the 1991 coup attempt.

economy. For example, the Russian Central Bank repeatedly responded to pleas from sink-

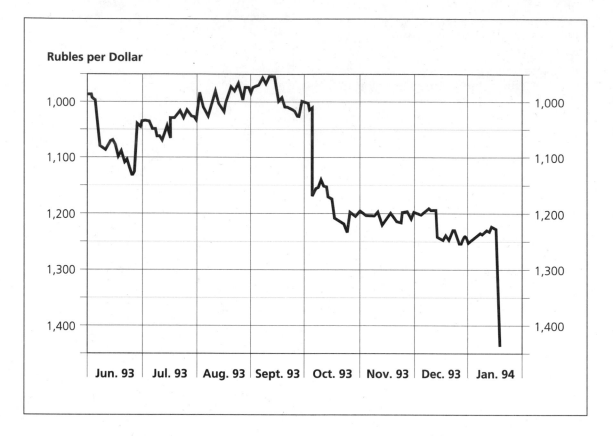

Figure 33.3 The Ruble's Fall Against the Dollar. Source: From *Financial Times*, January 18, 1994, p. 2. Used by permission.

ing enterprises with huge supplies of credits. This keeps weak enterprises afloat and spurs inflation; it makes a balanced budget difficult to achieve and lowers confidence in overall reform. Such problems are often reflected in the falling value of the national currency, which has certainly happened in Russia (see Figure 33.3).

The previous parliament argued that such practices were necessary to keep business functioning and hold down unemployment. The reformers argued that doing so only prolonged the practices of the old system. Firms do not have to worry about losing money because the state covers their losses. Reformers point out that this makes it hard for Russia to attract

international backers and impossible to satisfy the conditions necessary to secure western loans. But many key political figures reject this argument, saying that Russia should be run by and for Russians, not the International Monetary Fund or its backers. In January 1993, the Union of Industrialists harshly rejected what they called a "distorted model replica of a stereotype understanding of the American economy," which they said was being forced on the country by "ideologists of the market reforms."[15] In addition, critics point out, western "aid" often amounts to very little real transfer of resources. Of the $24 billion mentioned above, only about $1 billion had actually been disbursed more than one year later.[16]

There are also many unreformed Communists who reject the whole idea of moving the economy into private hands. They still cling to the socialist vision and to models of central control. In the previous parliament they acted in concert with nationalists and those opposed to rapid reform to challenge the Yeltsin government. In mid-1992 the government had to reimpose some price and currency controls and delay the beginning of privatization. New appointments diluted the reform elements of the government and put the former head of the Soviet Central Bank in charge of the Russian Central Bank. He promptly began issuing credits to enterprises—more than 1 trillion rubles' worth in two months—to help them keep afloat. At the end of that year, parliament forced the president to dismiss his prime minister, Yegor Gaidar, who had championed rapid reform, and to replace him with a more conservative head of the government, Viktor Chernomydrin, who had spent most of his career directing the state gas monopoly. And as we saw in Chapter 31, the Congress also challenged the power of the president himself to run the country. They took away his decree power and throughout the summer of 1993 tried to slow the pace of privatization and exert their own control over the federal budget, in ways that contravened IMF lending guidelines.

For his part, the president argued that the results of the April 1993 referendum—which supported both his economic policies and him personally—gave him the right to move ahead. He labeled the increasingly recalcitrant Parliament as "irreconcilable opponents" of reform and, as described in Chapter 31, first dissolved and then physically dispersed the parliamentary opposition in October 1993.

ONCE MORE INTO THE BREACH

In the aftermath of the defeat of parliament, Boris Yeltsin used his new position virtually

The potentially vast Russian market has been a draw to companies marketing everything from candy to computers.

alone atop the Russian political system to resume economic change. He brought back into government the reformist he had lost in December 1992, Yegor Gaidar. Prices were freed on some staple commodities, including bread, and decrees were issued removing restrictions on the sale of private land and smoothing the way for farmers to receive land from collective farms. Steps were taken to limit government

extension of credits, though the head of the Central Bank remained in place.

But the challenge from the old parliament and the elections to the new one demonstrated the power of those who want to slow, halt or reverse the dramatic changes in the Russian economic system. In recognition of this power, President Yeltsin did not remove his conservative prime minister, Chernomydrin, or prevent from competing in the December elections several parties and blocs that oppose either the direction or speed of economic change, or both. Before the elections, some steps were taken to restrict foreign investment in the country's vital energy sector, foreign banks not already operating in the country were banned from serving Russian customers until 1996, and new subsidies to the country's agricultural sector were approved. After the elections, virtually all the vigorous reformers, including once again Yegor Gaidar, left the government.

These moves call to mind Mikhail Gorbachev's retreat from reform in 1990–1991, but in one sense, such moves indicate that Russian democracy is doing what it is supposed to do: translate public preference into public policy. The evident slowing or redirection of reform is born of political compromise and balancing, in much the same way policy is created in the West. If Boris Yeltsin is responding to the political challenge thrown up by the elections and the parliament, isn't that what a democratic leader should do? If he ignored it, perhaps reform would move faster, but could we say that Russia had moved very far from its age-old method of reform from the top? As much from the formulation and execution of economic policy as from the policy itself we will learn about prospects for democracy in Russia.

NOTES

1. *New York Times,* June 13, 1993, p. 5.
2. Figures in Gertrude E. Schroeder, "The Soviet Economy on a Treadmill of Perestroika: Gorbachev's First Five Years," in Alexander Dallin and Gail W. Lapidus, eds., *The Soviet System*

in Crisis (Boulder, Colo.: Westview Press, 1991), p. 381.

3. Central Intelligence Agency and Defense Intelligence Agency, "Beyond Perestroyka: The Soviet Economy in Crisis," in Dallin and Lapidus, *The Soviet System in Crisis,* p. 403.

4. *Christian Science Monitor,* September 30, 1991, p. 3.

5. Donald W. Green, "The Soviet Economy Through Nine Months of 1991," *PlanEcon Report,* VII, Nos. 43–44, p. 2.

6. Ed A. Hewett, *Reforming the Soviet Economy* (Washington, D.C.: The Brookings Institution, 1988), p. 164.

7. Robert Leggett, "Soviet Investment Policy in the 11th Five-Year Plan," in U.S. Congress, *Soviet Economy in the 1980's: Problems and Prospects,* part 1 (Washington, D.C.: U.S. Government Printing Office, 1982), p. 131.

8. *Financial Times,* October 16, 1987, p. 3.

9. Richard Sakwa, *Gorbachev and His Reforms: 1985–1990* (New York: Prentice-Hall, 1990), pp. 287–288.

10. *New York Times,* November 17, 1991, p. 6.

11. For a description of the voucher process see Bozidar Djelic and Natalia Tsukanova, "Voucher Auctions: A Crucial Step Toward Privatization," *RFE/RL Research Report,* 2, No. 30, July 23, 1993, pp. 10–18.

12. RFE/RL, *Daily Report,* August 9, 1993.

13. See the bitter essay by Yuri N. Afanasyev, "Russian Reform Is Dead," *Foreign Affairs,* 73, No. 2 (March/April 1994), pp. 21–26.

14. See Philip Hanson, *Local Power and Market Reform in the Former Soviet Union* (Munich: RFE/RL Research Institute, 1993).

15. *Nezavisamaya Gazeta,* January 21, 1993 (Federal News Service, January 21, 1993).

16. Interview with Dimitri Simes, *Moscow News,* No. 28, July 9, 1993, p. 6.

REFERENCES AND SUGGESTED READINGS

Campbell, Robert W. 1991. *The Socialist Economies in Transition.* Bloomington: Indiana University Press.

———. 1992. *The Failure of Soviet Economic Planning.* Bloomington: Indiana University Press.

Frydman, Roman, Andrzej Rapaczynski, and John S. Earle et al. 1993. *The Privatization Process in Russia, Ukraine and the Baltic States.* London: Central European University Press.

Kaufman, Richard F., and John P. Hardt, eds. (for the Joint Economic Committee, Congress of the United States), 1993. *The Former Soviet Union in Transition.* Armonk, N.Y.: M. E. Sharpe.

Kornai, Janos. 1992. *The Socialist System: The Political Economy of Communism.* Princeton: Princeton University Press.

Poznanski, Kazimierz Z. 1992. *Constructing Capitalism: The Reemergence of Civil Society and Liberal Economy in the Post-Communist World.* Boulder, Colo.: Westview Press.

34

Policy Case II:
A New Russia in a New World: Managing International Relations

*D*espite the urgency of the domestic tasks it faces, Russia cannot make the world go away while it attends to them. Unlike the nineteenth-century American republic, Russia does not have the luxury of expansive oceans and few neighbors, which would allow it to concentrate on rebuilding its political and economic systems. Instead, the country finds itself surrounded by many new states that used to be part of the same state. Some of its new neighbors have nuclear weapons and in many, unstable and dangerous conflicts are occurring. Now, millions of Russians reside in foreign countries without ever having moved and, like other states in similar situations, Russia considers itself responsible for their situation.

But farther out, the game has changed too. With the disappearance of the USSR, the bipolar standoff that characterized international politics since World War II also disappeared. The ideological, geopolitical, economic and military competition between the United States and the Soviet Union has been replaced by a new sort of relationship, but one with unclear dimensions. The United States has a large stake in helping Russia achieve economic and political stability. But with a country this size, even American support and advice can only be of limited assistance. And while the Communist ideology no longer dominates in Russia, potential and real conflicts based on differing national views of the world remain. Russia has not disappeared as a state, and its leaders—and those who aspire to be its leaders—have not abandoned the idea of trying to influence the world in ways that make it a better place for Russia.

Finally, the Russia that is trying to manage its relationship with the changed and changing outside world must now do so in a different way. No longer a dictatorship of one elite group, the Russian government must formulate its foreign policy amid the competition and struggle of a noisy, and occasionally bloody, internal political process. The new parliament, like the old, does not consider foreign affairs to be beyond its competence. The president and his ministers must face challenges to their policies both publicly and within the halls of government. Nor do the media obediently follow one international line, as they did during the Communist days. All of Russia's international activities are subject, at least potentially, to the scrutiny of political competitors, elected representatives, and, for the first time, public opinion.

THE HISTORICAL LEGACY

The modern history of Russia from the time of the emergence of the medieval state of Muscovy from Mongol domination (the fourteenth century) until the Soviet period was one of continual struggle to gain governing control over its own territory and to expand the definition of what "its own territory" meant. During the sixteenth and seventeenth centuries, while the growing country suffered many grievous defeats and intrusions at the hands of more powerful European neighbors in the west, and the Ottoman Empire in the south, Moscow's rule did expand into Central Asia and the Far East. By the end of the eighteenth century, with the weakening of both the Polish commonwealth and the Turkish empire, Russia was able to reverse its fortunes, gain territory and influ-

ence, and become the largest and most populous country in Europe.

Wars and rebellions in the Russian empire continued, however, and after the defeat of Napoleon's invading forces in 1812, the nineteenth and early twentieth centuries were not times of foreign policy successes. As the Ottoman Empire decayed in the Balkans and new states were emerging, Russia showed a keen interest in spreading its own influence into this region, in the Black Sea and over the narrow straits separating this body from the Mediterranean Sea. But Russian interests in the region were repeatedly blocked by a combination of Austria-Hungary, Prussia and, especially, Great Britain. Defeat in the Crimean War (1856) at the hands of a European coalition led by England was followed by embarrassment at the Congress of Berlin in 1878. After securing major gains in a war against Turkey in 1877–1878—including Romanian independence, occupation of a large Bulgaria, and substantial Russian influence elsewhere in the Balkans—Russia was obliged to give back many of these gains and acquiesce to continued British predominance in the Turkish straits and the Black Sea. The empire was simply not strong enough to challenge the major European powers. Its other rival for influence in the Balkans, the Austro-Hungarian Empire, was handed administration of Bosnia-Herzogovina at the 1878 conference, a territory which it annexed in 1908—again over futile Russian objections.

Russia's most spectacular humiliation of the period was its defeat by Japan in the Russo-Japanese war of 1904–1905. In the space of ten months, both the Russian Pacific and Atlantic fleets were destroyed, and major Japanese gains in the Far East were ensured. The costs and results of fighting this war contributed to the domestic upheaval of the 1905 revolution. Similarly, the strain on the empire and its ineffectiveness in World War I contributed directly to the final collapse of the autocracy and to the emergence of the Soviet Union.

Though the Bolshevik regime's goals were different—promoting world revolution, for example—it was no more successful in foreign relations than its predecessor had been. Forced to sue for peace to prevent further German advance (the Treaty of Brest-Litovsk of 1918), the new socialist republic surrendered the share of Poland it had held since the eighteenth century, along with substantial portions of territory in Ukraine and Byelorussia. The Baltic republics of Latvia, Estonia, and Lithuania became independent, and in the south, Bessarabia (which had gone back and forth in the nineteenth century) was lost to Romania.

Between 1918 and 1920 the regime did succeed in holding off a combined intervention by the United States, Britain, and France in European Russia and (along with Japan) in the Far East; and in 1920, in the brief Polish war, Russian armies did save Kiev and drive back Polish forces until a treaty established the eastern boundary with that reborn state. But despite the expansion of Bolshevik control into most of the old empire and the establishment in 1919 of the Comintern, or Communist International, revolutions failed to take and hold power elsewhere. Thus Soviet interwar diplomacy followed dual, and in fact contradictory, tracks. On the one hand, to protect the Soviet state and try to gain for it what benefits could be derived from international involvement, the government signed agreements and established relations with countries such as Great Britain and even its former enemy, Germany. On the other hand, through the instrument of the Comintern, the Communist Party of the Soviet Union supported the world revolution its leaders expected and hoped would come, even in states with whom it was officially conducting friendly relations.

By the end of the 1920s, though, with failures of revolutions in Germany, Hungary, Finland, and especially China (where Communists were massacred in 1927), the promise of world revolution had faded. At the same time, the self-absorption and upheaval that accompanied rapid industrialization and collectivization kept the USSR as weak as it had always been in affecting affairs outside its borders.

In 1938 this weakness was made starkly clear in its own front yard. Faced with growing German power and the successful moves of Adolf Hitler in reoccupying the Rhineland, rebuilding and equipping his army and forcing union with Austria, the leaders of Great Britain and France met with Hitler in Munich in September. There they agreed to the German demand to hand over from the new state of Czechoslovakia—created after World War I—the extreme western and mostly German part of Czechoslovakia known as the Sudetenland. Agreeing to this demand crippled Czechoslovakia, and was soon followed by its total absorption by Germany. For the Soviet Union, the Munich agreement had broad and frightening implications. The acquiescence of the West in the dismemberment of Czechoslovakia proved to Moscow that the western capitalist powers would do nothing to restrain Hitler as long as he moved toward the East, that the western powers could not be trusted, and that their long-standing hostility toward the Bolsheviks, evident in the intervention in the civil war, still prevailed. From the Soviets' point of view, territories on their own border had been handed over to a mortal enemy, and they had been powerless to prevent it.

Faced with such a situation and fearing the rising power of *both* Germany and Japan, which was already engaged in a full-scale war in China, the Soviet Union moved to avoid or put off its most dreaded nightmare, war on both western and eastern fronts. Nonaggression pacts were signed with Germany in 1939 and Japan in 1941. The former, known as the Molotov-Ribbentrop Pact after the respective foreign ministers, also contained secret protocols by which Germany agreed to allow the Soviet Union to occupy nearly one-third of what was then Polish territory, as well as Finland, Estonia

Glasnost and Foreign Policy

Under Mikhail Gorbachev past foreign as well as domestic policies came in for scrutiny and fuller disclosure. In August 1988, as nationalism began to take on wider expression in the Baltics, the secret protocols signed between the Soviet Union and Germany in August 1939, which had never before been published or even officially acknowledged in the Soviet Union, were published by an Estonian newspaper. Though brief and phrased in bland diplomatic language, they signified the loss of independence of the Baltic States—until regained in 1991. Other territorial changes came at the expense of Poland, whose borders remain those fixed by these protocols, and Romania, which lost territory that today makes up the bulk of the independent state of Moldova.

The text of the protocol reads as follows:

On the occasion of the signing the nonaggression treaty between the German State and the Union of the Soviet Socialist Republics, the undersigned, fully authorized representatives of both sides, have discussed, in strictly confidential talks, the delineation of their respective spheres of influence in Eastern Europe.

These negotiations lead to the following result:

1. *In case of a territorial and political reorganization of the area belonging to the Baltic States (Finland, Estonia, Latvia and Lithuania), the northern border of Lithuania will also make the boundary between the German and the USSR spheres of influence. In this connection, both sides will recognize the interests of Lithuania in the region of Vilnius.*

2. *In case of a territorial and political reorganization in the area belonging to the state of Poland, the approximate boundary between the German and the USSR spheres of influence will run along the line of the Narew, Vistula and San rivers.*

   The question of whether or not preserving an independent Poland will serve the interests of both sides, and what should be the boundaries of that state, can finally be settled only in the course of future political development.

   In any case, both governments will settle this question by way of an amicable agreement.

3. *In southeastern Europe, the Soviet side asserts its interests in Bessarabia. The German side declares a complete lack of political interest in that region.*

4. *Both sides will keep this document in strict secrecy.*

Source: *Rahua Haal* (Tallinn), August 10, 1988 (FBIS, September 16, 1988, p. 69).

---

and Latvia, and to retake Bessarabia from Romania. Except for Finland, which fought Soviet armies to a standstill during the Winter War of 1939–1940, all these territories, as well as Lithuania and additional territory in northeastern Romania (northern Bukovina), were occupied by the Soviet Union in 1940.

None of this prevented invasion by Germany, which began in 1941 and was not halted until later that year in Moscow and in 1942 in Stalingrad (now Volgograd). It was only Germany's defeat and dismemberment and the occupation by the Soviet Union of most of Eastern Europe that gave the country for the first time the power to set things up in this region the way it preferred. For the USSR the lessons of the late Tsarist period and the interwar period were clear: the West could not be trusted except on a temporary basis as necessary; only the Soviet Union's own involvement could ensure that dangers would not develop in regions that were considered vital to national security; military power was the ultimate guarantor of that involvement and in all cases must be kept at a level sufficient to ensure the defeat of the country's attackers and adversaries.

SOVIET FOREIGN POLICY AFTER WORLD WAR II

After World War II, achieving these goals proved easier in some respects but more complicated, expensive and dangerous in others. Old enemies, such as Germany and Japan, were defeated, occupied, and, in the case of Germany, divided. Soviet troops were in occupation from Berlin to Asia, and even former western adversaries such as Britain and France were economically and militarily exhausted. Moreover, within five years after the end of the world war, the number of states that were Communist and allied with the Soviet Union grew to ten and included half of Europe as well as the world's most populous state, China. The Soviet Union was now a superpower, and its major adversary was now the world's other superpower, the United States.

Thus foreign policy management for the Soviet Union after World War II became an attempt to achieve persisting goals under new circumstances. The old ideal of unchallengeable protection against foreign invasion, especially from Germany, remained prominent and was ensured through the existence of a substantial conventional armed force both inside the USSR itself and in Eastern Europe. To this was added the need for alliance management, as the Soviet Union tried to ensure conformity and support from the new Communist states in Eastern Europe and China. But beyond this historical legacy, protection after World War II meant insuring that the only state really capable of doing great harm to the USSR or its new

international situation, the United States, be prevented from doing so.

Alliance management proved difficult from the first. Differences as to how socialism was to be applied in Eastern Europe combined with old-fashioned nationalism and internal Soviet politics to create upheavals in Hungary, Poland, and Czechoslovakia. Yugoslavia and Albania, each for its own reasons and at different times, broke with the Soviet Union altogether. Others such as Poland and Romania began in the 1960s to pursue external policies that were in significant ways quite at variance with those of the Soviet Union. The Soviets used various means to try to keep the "socialist commonwealth" in line, including bilateral diplomacy, military pressure and force, and the mechanism of multilateral alliances, the Council for Mutual Economic Assistance (1949) and the Warsaw Pact (1955).

The most significant loss to the new Soviet international position was the break with China in the early 1960s. The roots of the dispute extend back to the prewar period when the Soviet party, then the only ruling Communist Party, seemed not to appreciate the differences between its situation and that of the Chinese, and gave often inappropriate advice to its Chinese comrades (such as to cooperate with the non-Communist Kuomintang in a rebellion in 1927—which ended in a massacre of Chinese Communists). Soviet support for the Chinese Communists fighting for control after World War II was decidedly restrained, evidently to forestall western fears and involvement. At the end of World War II, the Soviets even signed a treaty with the then ruling non-Communist government of China under Chiang Kai-shek, while continuing to help the Communist forces militarily in Manchuria. After the Chinese Communists' victory in 1949 and throughout the 1950s, the two states did cooperate extensively. But differences appeared, especially over foreign policy and specifically over how to deal with the United

States. When domestic reform under Nikita Khrushchev was combined in the early 1960s with a more conciliatory approach toward the United States and some progress on arms control, the regime of party leader Mao Zedong unleashed a torrent of criticism of Soviet policies, accused Moscow of "revisionism," capitulating to the United States, and not supporting the rule of the Chinese Communist Party. What became known as "the Sino-Soviet split" burst into view.

The two Communist giants contested with each other—sometimes violently—over issues both domestic and international. For the Soviet Union, this meant that in addition to a powerful global adversary in the form of the United States, it faced a vigorous and often very active opponent in China. While much weaker militarily, the Chinese challenged the Soviet influence in various parts of the world, including Africa and especially Asia. Ideologically, the Chinese break sundered Soviet claims of being the leading Communist Party and the spiritual center of communism. In the 1960s and early 1970s, the Chinese accused the Soviet leadership of abandoning the revolution at home and of joining with the United States in a division of the world between two "hegemonies," that of imperialism (United States) and "social-imperialism" (the Soviet Union).

In the late 1970s and the 1980s, as the Chinese themselves modified their views and practices—encouraging private enterprise and engaging in a wide variety of international diplomatic and economic ties—the ideological aspects of the Sino-Soviet conflict receded. But the traditional aspects of interstate conflict remained. The Chinese opposed the extension of Soviet influence into Asia and especially the substantial Soviet military buildup in Southeast Asia, following the American withdrawal from the area. They countered Soviet support for the Vietnamese invasion and occupation of Cambodia, begun in 1978, by sending arms of their own to Khmer Rouge guerrillas fighting

there. The Soviets' own invasion of Afghanistan in 1979 presented a further obstacle to any improvement in Soviet-Chinese relations. Finally, the presence of some 1 million Soviet troops along their common 4,500-mile border and inside the Soviet-allied People's Republic of Mongolia was seen as a military threat to China. The exact specifications of much of the border are in dispute, and occasional armed clashes occurred.

Relations with the United States

The only genuine military threat to the Soviet Union, however, and its major global competitor was the United States. Policy toward this country was the centerpiece of Soviet foreign policy. In managing this complex and dangerous relationship, Soviet aims were to:

1. ensure the physical security of the USSR;

2. attach to itself as many political and military allies as possible while ensuring that the United States did not wean away any of its existing allies;

3. erode U.S. and, later, Chinese influence wherever possible; and

4. secure from the global economy the wherewithal to allow the Soviet economy to function as effectively as possible, while ensuring that the ideological and structural bases of socialism were not threatened.

Despite the intensity of this adversarial relationship and notwithstanding their verbal commitment to world revolution, Soviet leaders since Khrushchev did realize that nuclear war could utterly destroy their state and all of its gains. To protect the Soviet Union and to assert its own pretensions to global power, Moscow strove to match or exceed the American nuclear arsenal. The United States exploded a nuclear device in 1945; the Soviet Union did so in 1949; the United States exploded a hydrogen bomb in 1950, the USSR in 1953. Both the United States and the Soviet Union developed new and more sophisticated ways of depositing these bombs on each other, including intercontinental ballistic missiles, multiple warhead missiles, and missiles launched from land, submarines, and aircraft. While the United States held clear nuclear superiority through the 1960s, by the end of the 1970s the two sides had what was described as "rough parity" in nuclear forces. The Soviets had a nuclear force based on a larger number of land-based intercontinental ballistic missiles and sea-launched ballistic missiles, while the U.S. force had more missiles with multiple warheads and more long-range bombers. After reaching a high point in 1962 tensions over mutual nuclear buildups eased a bit during the 1960s. Treaties were signed on a limited test ban (1963), against placing nuclear weapons in space (1965), and on preventing the spread of such weapons (Nonproliferation Treaty, 1968).

The Long Peace—with Moments of Terror

While the growing power and size of the U.S. and Soviet nuclear forces added a balance of terror to the complex superpower relationship, direct military conflict between the United States and the Soviet Union did not occur. In fact, the incidence of international warfare in general was less after World War II than it had been before the bipolar postwar world was created, leading some to refer to this period as "the long peace."

However, the world was taken to the brink of nuclear war in October 1962, when the Soviet Union, at that time led by Nikita Khrushchev, placed nuclear-capable medium-range missiles, accompanied by forty-two thousand support troops, on the island of Cuba, ninety miles off the shore of the United States. When this secret action was revealed by spy planes, the United States publicly demanded the removal of these missiles and assurances that they would not be reintroduced in Cuba. From the Soviet point of view such an action was a necessary defense of Communist ally Fidel Castro, who had thwarted a small invasion force of anti-Communist émigrés in 1961. It also allowed for a relatively cheap and rapid way to even the balance of nuclear forces which at that time favored the United States.

For nearly two weeks a face-to-face showdown held, with the United States considering and planning an invasion of Cuba and establishing a naval blockade around the island. Both the United States and the Soviet Union worked to avoid a direct clash while the blockade was in force. At one point some Soviet ships heading for Cuba stopped and others returned home, prompting U.S. Secretary of State Dean Rusk to declare that in this eyeball-to-eyeball confrontation, "the other fellow just blinked." But work on the missiles in Cuba continued along with tense negotiations.

In trying to defuse the crisis, the American administration was faced with two sets of demands from Moscow:

1. that the U.S. pledge not to invade Cuba and

2. that it remove its own medium-range missiles from bases in Turkey.

Using both public and private channels of communication, U.S. president John Kennedy and Nikita Khrushchev worked out an agreement by which the Soviet Union would dismantle and withdraw the missiles and the United States would issue the pledge on Cuba. At the same time Kennedy secretly assured the Soviets that U.S. missiles in Turkey would be withdrawn. Indeed Kennedy had already ordered their removal more than a year before the crisis, seeing them as a dangerous provocation. On October 28, 1962, the world's first nuclear crisis ended.

Negotiations on limiting nuclear weapons began in 1969 and did produce a very limited Strategic Arms Limitation Treaty (SALT I) in 1972. The treaty put a cap on land- and sea-based missiles and left out bombers and qualitative improvements, such as adding more warheads to a missile. The second treaty on strategic weapons, SALT II, took nearly seven years to negotiate. Signed in 1979, this treaty did affect weapons with multiple warheads and bombers, but still only limited, rather than cut, the size of each side's arsenal.

By the end of the 1970s, however, the U.S.-Soviet détente that had spawned the negotiations had badly eroded because of conflicts over trade, the deployment in Europe of intermediate-range nuclear missiles, and Soviet involvement in Africa and especially Afghanistan. SALT II thus stood little chance of being ratified by the U.S. Congress when President Jimmy Carter withdrew it from consideration after the Soviet invasion of Afghanistan in December 1979. Though each side pledged to uphold the terms of the treaty if the other did, the "new cold war" in the early 1980s found the United States and the Soviet Union no longer willing or able to engage in fruitful arms control negotiations. Amid angry rhetoric, events multiplied that poisoned the negotiating atmosphere:

♦ Between 1980 and 1981 the Soviet Union exerted military and political pressure on Poland to crush *Solidarity*, the region's only independent trade union;

♦ in 1983 the United States invaded Grenada to oust a Marxist regime there;

♦ the Israeli invasion of Lebanon in 1982 brought Israel and Soviet ally Syria into direct conflict, and U.S. marines to Lebanon;

♦ NATO determination to proceed with installation of its own medium-range missiles in Europe to counter a huge Soviet preponderance in that area prompted Moscow to break off negotiations

on intermediate-range missiles in 1983—at the time, the only negotiations going on; and

♦ finally, in late 1983 the low point was reached when Soviet air defense forces shot down a Korean civilian airliner that had strayed over Soviet territory in the Far East, killing all 269 people on board, including a U.S. Representative.

Tools of Soviet Foreign Policy

Soviet attempts to create a world in which there were more states favorable to it and fewer friendly toward its adversaries utilized a combination of international diplomacy and action—including military action if necessary. Of the means of international power available to the Soviet Union, the military method often proved attractive, perhaps because of the relative weakness of its other options. In 1956, for example, the Soviet Union invaded Hungary to prevent changes and the possible overthrow of the Communist regime in that country. In 1968 the USSR and all of its allies except Romania invaded Czechoslovakia to put an end to reforms there which, though started by the Czechoslovak Communist Party, would have profoundly altered the form of that regime and possibly others in the region. In 1979, after failing in every other way to create and secure an effective regime in Afghanistan on its southern border, the USSR invaded that country also; but it found that in this case the military option did not succeed, and Soviet troops began to withdraw in 1988. In none of those cases was the foreign policy of the target state the major issue; but in all cases the leadership in the Kremlin feared that Soviet political interests would suffer a setback, in that a less controllable government might take over, which could lead to a weaker military position and, at the least, a gain for adversaries of the USSR.

On this basis the Soviet Union also supported or created allies by providing the wherewithal for them to use force on their own. This was done successfully in Angola where, in 1975, revolutionary groups supported by the Soviet Union and Cuba became the government. This approach was less successful in the Middle East, where military force alone proved insufficient to bring Soviet allies victory over their adversary, Israel. In the Middle East and elsewhere, the Soviet Union, like the United States, took an *instrumental* view of regional conflicts. That is, it saw them in terms of how they would affect the overall struggle for influence between itself and its adversaries, the United States and China. While ideological concerns were not absent, sides were often chosen by the Soviet Union, as they were by the United States, on the basis of "whatever he's for, I'm against."

During this period of intense U.S.–Soviet competition, support of allies occasionally put Moscow in the position of supporting military actions and risking conflict with the United States. When that happened and Soviet allies faced defeat, as with Syrian forces in Lebanon in 1982, the USSR usually chose to forgo the danger of all-out support for its allies. But in the 1973 Yom Kippur War, a confrontation with the United States did occur when Israel surrounded an Egyptian army and was in a position to annihilate it. The Soviet Union put some troops in southern Ukraine on alert and threatened Israel. In response, the United States put its forces on full military alert worldwide. Israel responded to both American and Soviet pressure and did not destroy the surrounded Egyptian army. While such confrontations were rare, conflicts of this type were a constant source of tension and obliged the USSR, in its view, to create and sustain an expensive capacity to project its military power and political influence around the world.

At the same time, because of the inadequacies of the Soviet economy, leaders of the country had to insure at least a modicum of workable relations with the West. This was because of the country's need to secure what it could not produce itself in sufficient quality or quantity; in particular, high technology and manufactured goods, as well as food. For most of the Cold War period, the Soviet Union had no choice but to try to buy much of these commodities from the West. To pay for these goods the USSR needed to sell its own commodities, chiefly oil and natural gas. But being dependent on selling these meant the country earned less when the price of oil fell, as it did in the beginning of the 1980s. By Soviet estimates, for example, the falling price of oil cost the Soviet Union $66 billion between 1985 and 1988.

Pursuing its own economic health also conflicted with the goal of keeping its friends and allies happy. The Soviet Union sold oil and natural gas, as well as other raw materials, to the Eastern European countries—at special "friendship" prices. During the 1970s these were below world prices. Though the prices did rise, these states for the most part did not pay in convertible currencies such as dollars, which could be used to buy things on the international market, but paid in their own commodities. Thus the Soviet Union incurred a substantial *opportunity cost* because it could not sell this part of its oil and gas to the West for usable currency. Moreover, since many of the manufactured goods it bought from the Eastern European states were overpriced and of poor quality, the Soviet Union in effect subsidized these economies. One analysis suggests this subsidy cost Moscow more than $87 billion between 1960 and 1980.[1]

The inadequacies of its own economy often weakened Soviet diplomacy. For example, while the Soviet Union proved quite capable of assisting favored revolutionary groups into power, such as in Angola and Mozambique, its ability to assist the new regimes often proved quite limited. Nor was the Soviet Union a major actor in the world economy. It was not a member of the International Monetary Fund or the General Agreement on Tariffs and Trade (GATT). As noted in Chapter 33, part of the economic reform introduced between 1986 and

1988 was designed to increase Soviet contacts through foreign trade and by allowing joint ventures with capitalist partners.

The Soviet approach to the task of trying to mix cooperation and competition with its adversaries involved continuing to support groups and states favored by Moscow while at the same time trying to achieve economic gains and arms control treaties. The West, and particularly the United States, was not always willing to make such a distinction. Hence a worsening of U.S.-Soviet political relations usually was accompanied by an economic "cold war" as well. After the invasion of Afghanistan, President Carter imposed an embargo on trading several classes of goods with the Soviet Union, including grain, and after the crackdown on the independent trade union Solidarity in Poland, the United States placed economic sanctions not only on Poland, but also on the Soviet Union, and encouraged the western allies to do the same.

THE FOREIGN POLICY APPROACH OF MIKHAIL GORBACHEV

The foreign policy of Mikhail Gorbachev demonstrated the most explicit linking of domestic economic needs and Soviet international behavior. His approach to securing physical and political security was to try to resolve as expeditiously as possible the most dangerous issues and to try to reduce international tensions that might derail economic restructuring. Just as perestroika and glasnost characterized Soviet domestic change under Gorbachev, foreign policy was revised and reoriented under the broad rubric of "new thinking." Dusting off some long-standing Soviet international policies and combining them with startling revisions of long-held orthodoxies, Gorbachev and his foreign policy team moved the USSR toward a posture of cooperation and accommodation with its rivals. Gorbachev argued that in the

current age "universal values" took precedence over those promoted by a single class or ideology. As Khrushchev had, Gorbachev explained that the Leninist idea of inexorable conflict between competing social systems no longer applied. But going further, Gorbachev said different states and systems should not just coexist, but cooperate within an international order buttressed by strong institutions. Thus, several initiatives were offered to strengthen global organizations like the United Nations.[2]

Related to this was the notion that Soviet foreign policy should be informed by and should act upon national interests, including domestic economic interests, as much or even more than broad notions of international class struggle. This "de-ideologizing" of Soviet policy was designed to allow the Soviet Union to effect compromises with adversaries where common interests could be identified and, perhaps more importantly, to allow it to extricate itself from conflicts in far-flung places where vital Soviet interests were few.

The Soviet leadership also argued that the instrumental use of force by nations to achieve their ends should be reevaluated, that the possibility of nuclear destruction of all humanity was now too great to tolerate either the practice of war or the arms race that supported it. In this realm the doctrine of "reasonable sufficiency" underscored Soviet desire to achieve sharp cuts in nuclear and conventional arms.[3]

The specific steps taken on international questions indicated that Gorbachev had more than theoretical reorientation in mind. Many of the most contentious issues which were poisoning relations with the United States were ameliorated. Soviet troops were withdrawn from Afghanistan between 1988 and 1989. The release of most human rights activists from prison and an easing of political and cultural repression at home contributed as well. The number of Jews allowed to leave the country, which had hovered near 1,000 in the mid-1980s, exceeded 8,000 in 1987, was nearly 19,000 in

1988, and surpassed 71,000 in 1989. In the critical area of arms control, Gorbachev made far-reaching and comprehensive proposals for cutting strategic arms. At a summit meeting with President Ronald Reagan in Reykjavik, Iceland, in 1986, Gorbachev offered a 40 percent cut in nuclear warheads, to take place within five years. These proposed cuts were rejected by the United States because they included restrictions on development of the Strategic Defense Initiative (the so-called Star Wars scheme to try to build a defensive system against nuclear attack). But a treaty on intermediate-range nuclear weapons was signed in 1987, made possible by repeated Soviet acceptance of U.S. terms, including the elimination of all Soviet weapons of this type while the British and French retained theirs; the elimination of short-range weapons and of intermediate-range weapons in Asia where the United States had none; and for the first time, the acceptance of on-site inspection of weapons plants inside the USSR itself. In 1988 at the United Nations, Gorbachev announced a unilateral cut of 10 percent in Soviet conventional forces as well as varying cuts in numbers of tanks, planes and artillery.

Overtures were also made toward China, including a withdrawal of forces from the Far East, the withdrawal of Soviet forces from Afghanistan, the acceptance of the Chinese position on one key border dispute, and a visit to Beijing by Gorbachev himself in 1989, the first trip to China by a Soviet leader in thirty years. The result was a return to full party and state relations between the two Communist adversaries. Attention was also devoted—less successfully—to improving relations with Japan, which was one of the first places visited by Edvard Shevardnadze, the Soviet foreign minister, and the non-Communist nations of Southeast Asia. In the Middle East, the Soviet Union re-established relations with Israel (broken since 1967) and initiated ties with several conservative Arab states with which the country had not had previous official relations.

The aim of all of this movement was to try to make the world somewhat less dangerous for the Soviet Union, and to provide for Gorbachev the stability and normalcy in international ties that would allow economic restructuring to progress. As Gorbachev himself put it,

Before my people, before you and before the world, I state with full responsibility that our international policy is more than ever determined by domestic policy, by our interest in concentrating on constructive endeavors to improve our country.[4]

Perhaps the most significant foreign policy step of Mikhail Gorbachev involved something he did *not* do. During the momentous turbulence of 1989 in East Europe (see Chapter 37) he did not step in, as Soviet leaders had typically done before him, to stop the movement toward democracy and change. It was one thing to encourage reform and openness in the region, but in 1989 the question was unmistakably raised: what exactly were the limits of change? In 1968 Leonid Brezhnev had defined the limits clearly in Czechoslovakia: ". . . your country lies on territory where the Soviet soldier trod in the Second World War. We bought that territory at the cost of enormous sacrifices, and we shall never leave it. The borders of that area are our borders as well."[5] With Communist regimes crumbling rapidly, what would Moscow do in 1989 to protect those borders? By not intervening to stop the changes—indeed by explicitly tolerating the appointment of a non-Communist prime minister in Poland—Gorbachev took a huge step toward creating the post-Cold War world.

But the commitment of the Soviet leadership to this world was tested further, as the two parts of Germany moved quickly toward unification. Long opposed to unification, Moscow fought briefly to try to attach conditions to its agreement, such as a stipulation that a unified Germany could not be part of NATO. By mid-1990, however, the Soviet Union gave its blessing to the new Germany and watched East Germany disappear, less than one year after Gorbachev had visited that country to celebrate its 40th anniversary.[6] Soon after, at a meeting of European heads of state that formulated the new Charter for Europe ending the Cold War, Gorbachev summed up the Soviet contribution:

Our country, while remaining great, has changed and will never be what it was before. We have opened up to the world, and the world has opened up to us in return. This has predetermined a radical turnaround in the main area of international relations—toward a fundamentally different way in which states perceive one another.[7]

At that same summit, Gorbachev acknowledged that "the breakthrough in USSR-US relations was the key thing." Within that realm the question of arms control was most difficult. Here too enormous progress was made in the final years of the Gorbachev regime. Be-

gun in 1982, interrupted in 1983, and begun again in 1985, negotiations on a new Strategic Arms Reduction Treaty (START) had proven more difficult even than those of SALT. In part this was because the stated goal was to cut nuclear forces—not simply limit them—by as much as 50 percent. Finally, in July 1991 a treaty was signed providing for cuts in all types of "strategic nuclear delivery vehicles"— for example, land- and sea-based missiles and bombers; warheads; and missile size (throw-weight).[8] During the fall, U.S. president George Bush and Soviet president Gorbachev outdid each other with proposals and unilateral actions aimed at removing or eliminating nuclear weapons of various types. In January 1992, an even more ambitious treaty was signed by President Bush and Boris Yeltsin. START-2 envisages reducing the number of American and Russian warheads to less than 30 percent of the number each held in 1990.[9] By the time the Soviet Union was declared out of business, several real steps had been taken toward doing the same to the superpower nuclear arms race. A feature of international politics for

Table 34.1 STRATEGIC NUCLEAR FORCES, PAST AND PROJECTED (IN NUMBER OF WARHEADS)

	1990	START I	START II
Total warheads			
United States	12,646	8,556	3,500
Soviet Union	11,021	6,163	3,000
Total warheads on land-based missiles			
United States	2,450	1,400	500
Russia	6,612	3,153	504
Total warheads on multiple-warhead, land-based missiles			
United States	2,000	1,100	0
Russia	5,958	2,460	0

Source: From *Congressional Quarterly*, January 2, 1993, p. 34. Copyright © 1993. Used by permission.

From left to right, U.S. President Bill Clinton, British Prime Minister John Major, Russian President Boris Yeltsin, and German Chancellor Helmut Kohl.

four decades—the relentless growth and matching of nuclear arsenals by the superpowers—was reversed.

FOREIGN POLICY UNDER BORIS YELTSIN: NEW CHALLENGES

Boris Yeltsin continued to make offers of drastic cuts in arms, as Mikhail Gorbachev had, but the Russian leader found that questions of nuclear arms—as well as many other critical international issues—looked somewhat different from what his predecessors had seen. Perhaps even more important, the Yeltsin team found that it had to make and execute foreign policy in a domestic political and economic environment completely different from that in which Mikhail Gorbachev had operated.

For Russia now the task of providing physical, political and economic security has taken on new dimensions, because of the changed international environment. This can be seen in each of three basic realms of Russian policy.

Relations with the CIS

In the new Russian parlance, relations with the "near abroad" [*blizhnee zarubezhe*] means Moscow's dealings with the new states that emerged from the collapse of the Soviet Union. In part this is a question of what kind of organizational arrangement might be constructed among the former Soviet republics. As seen in Chapter 27, this has been difficult to determine, much less put into practice. Because of its size and the dominance of its resources, Russia has consistently pushed for a greater say in the economic interactions of the region—pushing for a ruble zone, for example, and the creation of an interstate bank. While the latter has been accomplished, the former has certainly not.

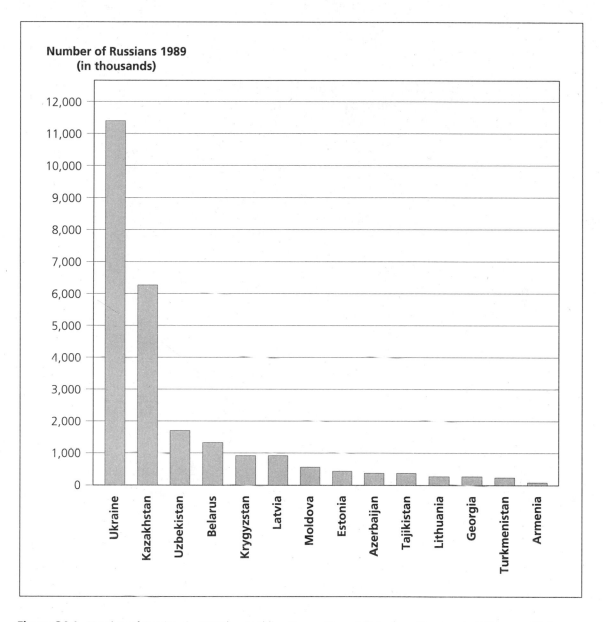

Figure 34.1   Number of Russians in 1989 by republic.   Source: Figure 1 ("Number of Russians in 1989 by republic"). Harris, Chauncy D. (1993). The New Russian Minorities: A Statistical Overview. *Post-Soviet Geography,* 34 (1), p. 3. Used by permission of V. H. Winston & Son, Inc.

Even more explosive is the issue of some 25 million Russians now living as minorities in the new states (see Figure 34.1). From its earliest days, the Yeltsin government indicated it would review very carefully the performance of the new states on the question of how they treat their Russian minorities. Are they given equal rights? Are they discriminated against politically or economically? No Russian government, except perhaps an authoritarian one that can ignore the voices and votes of its population, can be seen to be indifferent to the fate of its conationals living in the new Commonwealth states.

From the standpoint of many of the new states, however, these populations represent a colonialist legacy and should at the least be required to meet language and residence requirements and renounce other citizenships before being accepted. Nor do these states accept the idea that the Russians in their countries can be accorded special status or, most especially, that the Russian government has a right to intervene on their behalf.

The case of Estonia, formerly the smallest of the Soviet republics, is a good example. Upon achieving independence, the new state promptly passed a law declaring that only people who had resided in Estonia when it was an independent country before World War II, or their descendants, were automatically citizens of the country. Others, including the country's substantial Russian minority (30 percent), could apply to become citizens after a two-year waiting period, after learning Estonian and passing a language test, and upon taking a loyalty oath. The Russian minority in Estonia is largely a result of a substantial immigration encouraged by the Soviet government, which annexed the country in 1940. (In 1937 the country's population was just over 8 percent Russian.) Hence the Estonian government takes the position that this group should now apply to become Estonian citizens, if they choose, in accordance with procedures used for immigrants in other countries.

But many Russians have lived their whole lives in Estonia and feel that since they chose to stay after 1991 they should be citizens just as Estonians are. They charge that they are being discriminated against on the basis of their eth-

nicity. The Russian government agrees. Boris Yeltsin, Foreign Minister Andrei Kozyrev, and numerous other Russian officials have repeatedly complained to the Estonian government and through international organizations about the Estonian government's actions.

In some cases the Russian government has used or tolerated the use of military pressure to press its point. The withdrawal of Russian troops from Estonia (as well as Latvia) has from time to time been held up and accompanied by warnings to these governments to insure the rights of its minorities—that is, Russians. In Moldova the Russian fourteenth army has openly interceded on behalf of a secessionist movement based just east of the Dniester River. While acting to prevent full-scale civil war, the Russian army has also prevented full integration into the country of the region, which has a substantial Ukrainian and Russian minority.

Russian forces have also been involved in civil wars in Georgia and Tajikistan, and in 1993 began patrolling the borders of Turkmenistan on behalf of that government. The continued role of Russian troops in these countries, combined with steady pressure on Azerbaijan and Georgia to join the Commonwealth, recalls in the minds of some either the Russian or Soviet imperial past. But failure to act, especially where Russian communities are involved, would open the Yeltsin—or any other—government to charges of passivity in the face of threats to the country's borders and conationals.

Potentially the most dangerous of conflicts within the CIS involves the two largest countries, Russia and Ukraine. When the latter departed the Soviet Union, it did so with 176 long-range nuclear missiles still on its soil, carrying more than 1,600 warheads, plus an estimated 3,000 tactical nuclear weapons and some long-range nuclear-capable bombers. While Ukraine, along with Belarus and Kazakhstan, which inherited smaller forces, pledged to become nonnuclear states, there has been some

The New Nuclear Powers

After the breakup of the Soviet Union in 1991, powerful remnants of its nuclear force wound up on the territory of three newly independent countries. Though all pledged to become nonnuclear, the expense, risk and complexities of eliminating such weapons has proven a political challenge. By the beginning of 1994, all three states had signed agreements or had actually begun to take steps to remove these weapons—as well as thousands of smaller tactical nuclear weapons—from their soil.

CIS member	Long-range missiles	War-heads (missiles only)	Long-range bombers
Ukraine	176	1240	42
Kazakhstan	104	1040	40
Belarus	80	80	—

Source: From *The Military Balance 1992–1993*, pp. 233–235. Copyright © 1992. Used by permission of the International Institute of Strategic Studies.

delay in implementing this. For one thing it is costly and dangerous to destroy nuclear weapons. Russia and Ukraine have both been offered funds to help accomplish this.

But the real issue is political. Should Ukraine, a country of 53 million people with a nearly one thousand-mile border with another country that ruled it for hundreds of years, give up its only real deterrent to future attack? Many Ukrainian leaders say they should not, or should do so only under certainly clear and strict conditions, most important of which is a guarantee of their security. But the Russian government has not been prepared to offer public assurances to Ukraine's satisfaction. Moreover, Moscow contends that it owns the nuclear weapons by virtue of its role as the successor to the USSR and wants to be sure it does not face a new nuclear threat to its south. The United States finds itself drawn into the dispute because of its concern about preventing the spread of nuclear weapons and its desire to avoid possible conflict between these two powerful neighbors. Both Russia and the United States have stated that the entire START treaty implementation process cannot begin until all parties with nuclear weapons, including the three former Soviet republics, ratify the treaty. Under steady pressure from both Moscow and Washington, Ukraine did ratify the treaty in February 1994, and the president of Ukraine agreed to the dismantling of the country's nuclear force.

Not surprisingly, this issue cannot be isolated from other key issues between the two countries. One of these involves the dispensation of the more than 300-ship Black Sea fleet (see box). Related to that is the question of the status of the Crimean region of Ukraine, ceded to Ukraine by Russia in 1954 but with a Russian majority. In the 1991 referendum on independence in Ukraine, the Crimean region voted against it; in 1992 the local parliament voted for Crimean independence. In 1994 the region elected a Russian nationalist as president. A third issue is Ukraine's substantial debt to Russia, from which the country must buy the bulk of its fuel. With its own economy in ruins and very little reform begun, Ukraine has been unable to pay for the fuel it must have. By the middle of 1993 Ukraine reportedly owed Russia some $2.5 billion.

All three of these issues involve real assets: territory, arms, money. But almost as important, to both Russia and Ukraine, are the symbols involved. For Russia, adjusting to its status as the largest among newly sovereign equals represents a difficult transition. After all, the assets in question—and indeed the country in which they sit—used to all belong to the Soviet Union. For Ukraine, as for the other Commonwealth members, newly won sovereignty is

The Black Sea Fleet

As a major military power, the Soviet Union developed navies that operated from its east, west and south coasts, including the Black Sea. Though limited in usefulness because of the ability of an adversary to choke exit from the Black Sea, the fleet there nevertheless contained more than 40 major warships and 18 submarines at the time of the breakup of the USSR. The fleet also includes some seventy thousand personnel, both Russian and Ukrainian, but a majority of the officers are Russian.

After the collapse of the Soviet Union, both Ukraine and Russia lay claim to the entire fleet. Several sets of negotiations, both bilateral and through the Commonwealth of Independent States, eventually produced agreements in principle to divide the fleet. In June 1993, Russia also agreed to financial support for the city of Sevastopol, the home of the fleet, and other areas where there were bases.

But in September Presidents Yeltsin and Leonid Kravchuk of Ukraine made a new deal under which the entire fleet would go to Russia in return for Russia allocating the cost of the Ukrainian half toward that country's debt for oil and gas. While this appeared to ease both the fleet problem as well as the debt issue between the countries, Ukraine's ability to consummate the deal remains very much in doubt. That is because Ukraine, like Russia, now has to make foreign policy in a more open and democratic manner and many Ukrainian leaders, especially those in the military, are not sure they like the idea of selling the country's fleet to pay its debt.

Sources: *Financial Times*, October 11, 1993, 12; John Lepingwell, "The Black Sea Fleet Agreement: Progress or Empty Promises?" *RFE/RL Research Bulletin*, 2, No. 28 (July 9, 1993), pp. 48–55.

targeted against the United States) or support a heavily armed modern navy, its leaders are committed to making every effort to guard the territory of the country against all contingencies. As all of the CIS members, including Russia, share a similar concern, finding the optimum method for achieving their security is a complex and challenging task.

Relations with Central Asia and the Far East

Dealing with the Commonwealth states means also dealing with several new states in Central Asia, which, as noted in Chapter 27, have mostly Muslim majorities. Thus how Moscow deals with these new states is part of a larger question of how Russia relates to the Islamic world as a whole. Russian influence in the region, while still predominant and based on these states' military and economic dependence on Moscow, now has distinct competition from Islamic states of both the secular type like Turkey and the messianic type like Iran. The revival of Islam in this region and the opening of contacts and trade with what had been relatively isolated regions presents both an opportunity and a threat to Russia. In some parts of the former Soviet Union—as in the Balkans—state conflicts have enlisted and exploited confessional differences to deepen hostility and broaden bloodshed. No government of Russia, which still embraces a range of diverse communities, can be indifferent to the appearance of nationalistic or messianic movements in this part of the world. By the same token, the Russian government has to be careful to avoid falling back on its predecessor's patterns of imperial and cultural domination in this region—if for no other reason than to avoid provoking just the kind of negative development it seeks to avoid.

Outside the CIS, the two key actors for Russia are China and Japan. In the former case, the sharp ideological exchanges that previously

equally precious and not to be surrendered lightly. Even if Ukraine could not really launch a nuclear strike against Russia (its missiles are characterized relations have disappeared, despite the fact that China continues to hold to Communist Party dominance as a form of governance. Avoiding conflictual relations is central to the security of each of the two giant states; Russia remains an Asian as well as a European power. Economic change in both countries and diminished political hostility have allowed trade ($6 billion in 1992) and diplomatic contacts to grow.

Russian relations with Japan are one of the areas in which the enormous changes inside the USSR have produced little movement or change in the basic relationship. Russia sees Japan as a potentially rich source of investment and provider of the manufacturing know-how and technology it very much needs. But Japan has been most reluctant either to aid in the Russian economic recovery or to invest in its future. In part this is due to a hesitance Japan has shown elsewhere in the former Communist world and a desire to focus its efforts on profitable activities in other parts of the world. In the Russian case, improved political and economic relations have also been hampered by the persistent issue of continued Soviet—now Russian—occupation of four small islands north of Hokkaido, the main Japanese island. Held since the end of World War II, these islands, part of the Kurile Island chain, represent a stumbling block to improved relations. In 1992 and 1993, two trips by President Boris Yeltsin had to be postponed, though a third did occur and evoked a Russian pledge to remove remaining Russian troops on the islands.

The end of the Cold War meant a new era in U.S.-Russian political and military relations.

Relations with the United States and the West

Russia's relationship with the United States has altered fundamentally. As the earlier review indicates, for virtually all of the postwar period these two countries have been bitter adversaries whose political and military struggle led them to spend billions of dollars and thousands of lives to counter each other's influence. Political and, where possible, economic power was used to gain advantage for one side and to disadvantage the other. Other states, even large powerful states like China, were most often viewed in terms of their potential value in this bipolar struggle. For the two protagonists, their only real opponent—at least the only one with the power to badly hurt them—was the other.

For Boris Yeltsin now, the likelihood of nuclear war with the United States or even war by proxy such as was seen in Korea or Vietnam, is remote. Each side has been eager to reduce the tension, the cost, and the arms involved in the nuclear competition. Along with the agreements mentioned, both sides have agreed to retarget their remaining nuclear missiles away from each other. The West in general and the United States in particular is now seen as a prominent partner in the Russian attempt to remake its political and economic system. The United States has made it clear that it strongly supports the direction of reforms undertaken by the Yeltsin government. After Yeltsin routed an obstructionist parliament by force in October 1993, U.S. president Bill Clinton said:

> The United States continues to stand firm in its support of President Yeltsin because he is Russia's democratically elected leader. We very much regret the loss of life in Moscow, but it is clear that the opposition forces started the conflict and that President Yeltsin had no other alternative than to try to restore order. It appears as of this moment that that has been done. I have as of this moment absolutely no reason to doubt the personal commitment that Boris Yeltsin made to let the Russian people decide their own future, to secure a new Constitution with democratic values and democratic processes, to have a new legislative branch elected with democratic elections, and to subject himself, yet again, to a democratic vote of the people. That is all that we can ask.[10]

The Yeltsin foreign policy team also makes clear that it needs western assistance and has not been shy about asking for it or complaining about its absence. Between 1992 and 1993, more than $50 billion in aid was promised by the world's industrialized democracies and multilateral lending institutions. But by the time of elections for the new parliament, less than one-half of that had actually been delivered. Much of the rest was in the form of credits to buy merchandise in the West or loans with strict conditions attached. While the size of Russian needs are immense, the relatively low level of both western aid and investment leaves many Russians questioning the sincerity of the new partner.

The skepticism of some goes beyond the particulars of aid. As noted in Chapter 33 many feel that Russia should not be so eager for western aid, especially since it often comes with severe strictures on Russian government economic policy. International Monetary Fund requirements, as noted in Chapter 33, typically mandate an end to price controls, interest rates that involve real costs, and rapid privatization. All of these can add up to serious losses for many ordinary people and feelings of loss of hard-won independence or even humiliation in the face of external demands. Many influential Russians argue that Russia needs a different kind of plan, one more suited to its unique situation and needs. Taking the case further, many see the West and especially the United States as trying to exercise imperial domination over Russia, as trying to win through economic diplomacy what it could not accomplish during the Cold War. In his battle with Boris Yeltsin, for example, the chairman of the Supreme Soviet, Ruslan Khasbulatov, charged that Russia was being treated as a colonial possession of the United States.[11]

Thus for the Russian government, management of relations with the West is now a qualitatively different policy problem than it was during the Cold War. The previous superpower relationship was one in which national goals were fairly clear and the challenge was to achieve them against the efforts of a committed and powerful adversary. Now the West is a partner but one whose commitment and abilities are uncertain. Even more problematic, Russia's goals themselves are less easy to define and more subject to intense and often public dispute. It is this latter aspect that constitutes the greatest change in managing foreign relations in the new Russia.

THE CHALLENGE OF DEMOCRATIC FOREIGN POLICY

Foreign policy typically falls within the purview of chief executives of countries. This was certainly true in the days of the Soviet Union when the general secretary of the Communist Party, whether or not he was head of state, was able to put his stamp on the foreign policy of the country. In general, Soviet leaders worried very little about either legislative or public support for foreign policy. Even under Gorbachev the extension of power to the newly elected soviets and the creation of the new Congress of People's Deputies did little to weaken his ability to initiate or accomplish foreign policy acts. As the power of the party weakened, Gorbachev's own power increased via the presidency. In the foreign policy realm, this was further strengthened by the creation of a Security Council that included the prime minister, foreign and defense ministers, and head of state security, among others, and the weakening of the Defense Council, which had been powerful under his predecessors.[12]

Nevertheless the new Congress and Supreme Soviet did begin to exercise influence on foreign policy issues by introducing genuine testimony and debate on issues and by providing a platform for the expression of varying points of view on foreign policy issues. In addition, the expansion of media freedom meant that foreign policy issues, as with all others, could and did become subject for commentary of both the supportive and critical type, the latter being the new form. During the ratification process for the first START treaty, for example, a commentator in *Sovetskaya Rossia* wrote of the proposed treaty: "I can't shake the feeling that the treaty is not to our advantage."[13] Such sentiments would never have been published in earlier days.

Boris Yeltsin, like chief executives the world over, has tried to retain foreign policy control as close to himself and his office as possible. In the new constitution the president is the head of state, commander-in-chief of the armed forces, and has the right to appoint his own Security Council. The president holds sole responsibility for developing the basic posture of foreign policy and for supervising its execution. Boris Yeltsin has asserted forcefully his own views as to what principles should guide Russian foreign policy.[14] He has also sponsored the promulgation of a new, revamped defense policy, which stresses mobile forces, local conflicts, peacekeeping roles and development of military technology.[15] As president, he has tried to insure that the machinery of foreign policy creation and execution stay within his reach. In this respect key actors have been the foreign ministry and certain state secretaries who report directly to Yeltsin and are not subject to parliamentary approval. In addition, Yeltsin also created a Security Council, under whose auspices a Foreign Policy Commission was given extensive power for coordinating foreign policy actions.[16]

Still, it should not be surprising that in the new Russia the parliament has begun to assert itself in foreign policy. On many issues, such as arms control, relations with Ukraine and other Commonwealth countries, and the status of the islands off Japan, deputies in the parliament made their views known either in debate, by passing declarations on their own, or when asked for approval of some action.

During the summer of 1993, for example, when the Russian government was involved in delicate negotiations over the status of the Black Sea fleet, but when Boris Yeltsin was himself involved in negotiations with the parliament over the pace of reform and his own powers, the Supreme Soviet voted to declare Sevastopol, the home of the fleet, "Russian territory." The new parliament elected in December 1993, containing as it does a substantial number of representatives of groups opposed to the president, is equally likely to try to assert itself on foreign policy issues. While more common in the West, legislative involvement in foreign policy in Russia represents a new dimension of foreign policy management that previous leaders of the country did not have to worry about.

Less commonly tolerated in the West is the open assertion or action by the armed forces in support of its own views on national foreign policy. Since the end of the Soviet Union, the Yeltsin government has found that the armed forces have acted almost unilaterally in Moldova and the Baltics and often made clear their own preference for certain kinds of foreign policy actions. After the army came to President Yeltsin's rescue in October 1993, it became more likely that any Russian leader will have to insure the continued support of the armed forces by, among other things, being attentive to their defense and foreign policy concerns.

And neither Boris Yeltsin nor any other leader can count on a compliant yes-press when they propose or take international action. More likely, the government, as with governments in the West, will find itself with hostile as well as supportive commentary on both specific issues such as arms control measures, as well as on the nature of the overall relations with key actors, such as the United States.

Finally, the most fundamental change of all in Russia, the fact that the government, president, and legislature must now be elected and re-elected, means that for the first time the leaders must answer for their policies, domestic and foreign. Even if such issues are submerged from time to time in legislative debate or media attention to the rigors of daily life, it is unlikely that the questions of Russia's role in the world will escape the attention of potential office-holders. After the December 1993 elections and the gains of nationalist candidates, the Yeltsin government began to demonstrate a new assertiveness on key international issues, ranging from opposition to East European membership in NATO, to support for the Ser-

bian government in the war in Yugoslavia, to protecting the rights of Russians in the "near abroad." As in domestic policy, the government of the new Russia must answer for its foreign policy as well.

Notes

1. Michael Marrese and Jan Vanous, *Soviet Subsidization of Trade with Eastern Europe* (Berkeley, Calif.: Institute of International Studies, 1983), p. 3.
2. Steven Kull, *Burying Lenin: The Revolution in Soviet Ideology and Foreign Policy* (Boulder, Colo.: Westview Press, 1992).
3. R. Craig Nation, *Black Earth, Red Star: A History of Soviet Security Policy, 1917–1991* (Ithaca and London: Cornell University Press, 1992), pp. 285–298.
4. *New York Times*, February 17, 1987, p. 1.
5. Brezhnev's statement to the Czechoslovak Politburo after the Soviet invasion of 1968; quoted in Zdenek Mlynar, *Nightfrost in Prague* (New York: Karz, 1980), p. 240.
6. F. Stephen Larrabee, "Moscow and German Unification," *The Harriman Institute Forum*, 5, No. 5 (May 1992).
7. "Speech by M. S. Gorbachev," *Pravda*, November 20, 1990 (*Current Digest of the Soviet Press*, XLII, No. 47, December 26, 1990, p. 1).
8. *US Department of State Dispatch*, August 19, 1991, pp. 619–622.
9. *New York Times*, January 4, 1993, pp. A1, 6.
10. William J. Clinton, "Remarks to the AFL-CIO Convention in San Francisco, California," October 4, 1993, *Compilation of Presidential Documents*, 29, No. 40 (October 11, 1993), p. 1982.
11. Cited in Allison Stanger, "Remembrance of Things Past: Russian Foreign Policy from Coup to Coup," paper presented at annual meeting of American Association for the Advancement of Slavic Studies, Honolulu, Hawaii, November 19–22, 1993.
12. Brenda Horrigan and Theodore Karasik, "The Rise of Presidential Power under Gorbachev," in Eugene Huskey, ed., *Executive Power and Soviet Politics* (Armonk, N.Y.: M. E. Sharpe, 1992), pp. 115–116.

13. A. Silantyev, "Security or the Logic of Linkage?," *Sovetskaya Rossia*, August 10, 1991, in *Russian Foreign Policy Today: the Soviet legacy and post-Soviet beginnings*, Gordon Livermore, comp. and ed. (Columbus, Ohio: *Current Digest*, 1992), p. 98.

14. Jeff Checkel, "Russian Foreign Policy: Back to the Future?," *RFE/RL Research Bulletin*, 1, No. 41 (October 16, 1992), pp. 15–29.

15. *Krasnaya Zvezda*, November 3, 1993, pp. 1, 3.

16. See the discussion in Checkel, "Russian Foreign Policy."

REFERENCES AND SUGGESTED READINGS

Arbatov, Alexei G. 1993. "Russia's Foreign Policy Alternatives," *International Security*, 18, No. 2 (Fall), pp. 5–43.

Bialer, Seweryn. 1986. *The Soviet Paradox*. New York: Vintage Books.

Hough, Jerry. 1988. *Russia and the West: Gorbachev and the Politics of Reform*. New York: Simon and Schuster.

Kennan, George. 1961. *Russia and the West under Lenin and Stalin*. Boston: Little, Brown.

Lynch, Allen. 1992. *The Cold War Is Over—Again*. Boulder, Colo.: Westview Press.

Porter, Bruce D. 1994. "A Country Instead of a Cause: Russian Foreign Policy in the Post-Soviet Era," in Steven L. Spiegel and David J. Pervin, eds., *At Issue: Politics in the World Arena*. New York: St. Martin's Press, pp. 118–135.

Ulam, Adam B. 1968. *Expansion and Coexistence: The History of Soviet Foreign Policy, 1917–1967*. New York: Praeger.

Zagoria, Donald. 1962. *The Sino-Soviet Conflict, 1956–1961*. Princeton: Princeton University Press.

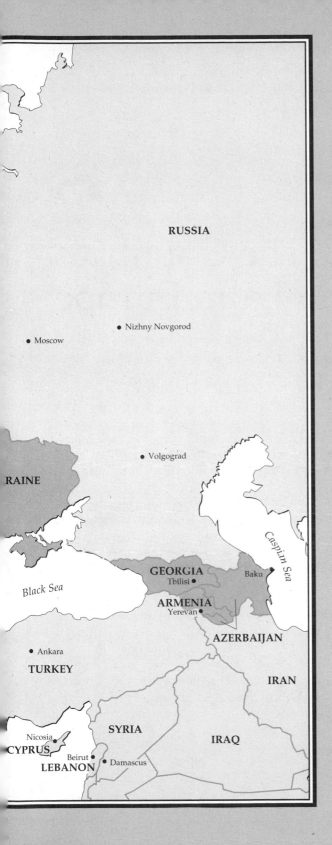

VI

*L*atin Europe, Scandinavia, and Eastern Europe

35

The Countries
of Latin Europe

t is traditional to group the countries of Southern
Europe together: Italy, Spain, and Portugal, with France on the
borderline.[1] Such a classification is both helpful and misleading. It
is helpful because, as we shall see, there are many similarities
among the politics of these countries. It is misleading because there
are many differences among them as well. Broadly, France, Italy,
Spain, and Portugal share many similarities of language and
culture, but differ considerably in their economies and political
institutions. Economically, Portugal and southern Italy have significantly lower levels of economic development. Spain has been
growing rapidly in the last two decades and northern Italy has
been so dynamic as to make Italy the third largest economy in
Western Europe, surpassing Britain by some measures (although
British economists dispute this). Politically, Spain and Portugal
have relatively fledgling democracies, whereas Italy for a long time
had not moved beyond the politics of fragile coalitions reminiscent
of the French Third and Fourth republics until it changed dramatically in the spring of 1994.

POLITICAL DEVELOPMENT

Spain

As might be expected, the countries of Southern Europe have had
varied pasts. There is some controversy among historians as to

whether Spain experienced feudalism in the same way as the rest of Europe. Part of this depends on one's definition of the concept. However, if one means by *feudalism* a historic form of social organization governed by hierarchical classes—including royalty, aristocracy and peasantry—where each group enjoys historically defined rights and obligations, and where the market economy was extremely limited, then it is reasonable to consider Spain as having experienced feudalism. Spain developed an absolutist monarchy much like that of France. In fact it was the first great absolutist monarchy in Europe, growing out of the kingdoms of Castille and Aragon, which were united by the marriage of Ferdinand and Isabella in 1469.[2]

Spain's early success as a mercantilist empire, however, impeded its evolution. Wealth from the Americas disinclined the king to encourage the development of commerce within Spain. The growth of commercial classes interested in modernizing the Spanish political system simply did not occur in sufficient strength to influence authority structures before the intrusion of Napoleon in 1808. Moreover, the agricultural policies of absolutism created large, inefficient estates (latifundia) in the south, while protecting sheepherding to the detriment of the small holdings in the north. The Inquisition led to the expulsion of Moors and Jews in 1492, leaving the country with a decimated financial sector. To the extent that entrepreneurial activity occurred at all, it was largely on the periphery, especially in the Catalan and Basque regions (north and northeast of Madrid). Eventually, industrialization, such as it was, would become associated with regionalism.[3] All in all, the legacy of absolutism and the regimes that followed it in the nineteenth century would be a stagnant economy and an underdeveloped political system.

Change, although hardly improvement, came with Napoleon's imposition of his brother Joseph on the Spanish throne in 1808. Shaky from the beginning, Joseph Napoleon's regime became the target of traditional Spanish elites and the few Spanish liberals who could assemble in the *Cortes* (parliament) of Cadiz between 1810 and 1812. The revolt against Napoleonic domination was successful by 1812, but it ushered in a period of instability that would characterize the entire century.[4] According to one author, "Between 1815 and 1875 Spain experienced six different constitutions, one royal charter, 35 *pronunciamientos*, or coups (eleven of these successful), one republic, two periods of military regency, and two protracted civil wars!"[5] The end of the century saw the re-establishment of authoritarian royal rule under Alfonso XII whose son, Alfonso XIII was overthrown by the general Primo de Rivera in 1923. The latter was a figure not unlike Italy's Benito Mussolini, but he lacked the Italians' mass base of support.

The authoritarian rule of Primo de Rivera was undermined by the Depression. In 1931 the Second Republic was declared. In the words of one political scientist:

> The Second Republic was Spain's first genuinely democratic regime, but it was plagued by the misfortune of being born within the context of the volatile and highly mobilized society of post–World War I Spain. It tried to graft parliamentary democracy onto a society experiencing rapid social change, but still characterized by elitism, class division, and semifeudal agrarian conditions. The result was a chaotic and fragmented party system, polarized from the start.[6]

The problems of the Depression confounded the difficulties of forming a stable governing coalition. The electoral system exaggerated the results of minute shifts in votes, and the policies of Spain shifted dramatically with the rise and fall of governments.[7] This climate of instability and frustration encouraged the military to revolt against the left-wing Popular Front government of 1936. Jumping off from North Africa, General Francisco Franco led the major portion of the army and sympathizers of the traditional Right into an attack on the Spanish

Republic. Even with the aid of Adolf Hitler, Benito Mussolini, and most of the regular Spanish army, it took Franco until 1939 to subdue the Loyalist defenders of parliamentary democracy and to ensconce his authoritarian regime. Originally established with the trappings of fascism—a single party; corporatist interest organization; repression of unions; and a consequent low-wage, procapitalist economy—the Franquist regime gradually reverted to traditional authoritarianism, although fascists remained, to some extent, influential in the bureaucracy.[8] Franco was supported by the historic bloc of conservative landowners, clerics, and business people who had backed previous dictatorships; but he did not seek to mobilize the masses, as Hitler and Mussolini had done, so much as to depoliticize public life. The later stages of Franquism were characterized by a regime of technocrats, many of whom were associated with the Catholic lay organization *Opus Dei.* The latter, by initiating economic modernization, to some extent facilitated the transition to democracy after Franco's death in 1975.

Spain was able to negotiate a smooth transition to democratic government thanks to the political skills of King Juan Carlos I, Franco's designated successor, and Adolfo Suarez, the king's prime minister. The latter ably included both Franquist and opposition figures in reorganizing the *Cortes* as a constituent assembly. A new constitution was adopted with the participation of all groups of Spanish society, legitimating the new institutions as a product of broad consensus. The democratic constitution was approved by 87.8 percent of the vote December 6, 1978.[9]

Portugal

Portugal, though much smaller, followed a path of political development similar to that of Spain, of which it had formerly been a part.

Traditionally, Portugal dates its independence to the year 1140 and except for an interregnum from 1580 to 1640, when the kingdom fell under Spanish Hapsburg rule, it has remained (at least nominally) independent ever since.[10] Like France and Spain, Portugal also experienced a period of absolutism dating from the sixteenth century reconquests of territory from Moorish and Castillian occupiers. While political authority remained highly centralized throughout Portugal's history, regionalism never developed along the lines of that within its Iberian neighbor.

Portugal's integration into the world economy, like Spain's, inhibited economic development, but for different reasons. Whereas Spanish mercantilist success diverted attention from developing a dynamic bourgeoisie at home, Portugal's dependent trade relationship with Britain had a similar effect. According to one author, "The Anglo-Portuguese relationship which emerged from this economic arrangement was one of strong dependence by Portugal on England, although it reinforced the [royal] Braganza House and the landed interests, and thus the aristocracy and church."[11] The incoming wealth from the Portuguese empire, like Spain's, disguised the fundamental weakness in the metropole's domestic economy for some time.

A weak bourgeoisie in a society dominated by an agricultural elite proved a formula for authoritarian rule into the dawn of the twentieth century.[12] The First or "Democratic" Republic inaugurated in 1910 probably had more in common with the brief French Second Republic and Napoleon III's Second Empire than with the truly democratic French Third or Spanish Second Republic. Elections were manipulated; politicians were motivated by a spirit of *enrichissez-vous;* and the short-lived parliamentary regime was unsurprisingly dotted with military coups. The Democratic Republic ended when quasifascist elements in the Lisbon Barracks, influenced by Primo de Rivera in

Spain, seized power in 1926. Military incompetence gradually made them dependent on their civilian minister of finance, Antonio de Oliveira Salazar.[13] The latter gradually created a regime extraodinarily similar to the one Franco would establish in Spain.

Like the Franquist regime, Salazar's *Estado Novo* (New State) was a personalistic dictatorship with the outward trappings of fascism. The system was corporatist and clerical, justified by reference to Pope Leo XIII's *bulla*, "Rerum Novarum," which envisioned a society of hierarchically organized nonconflictual interest groups. Like Spain, only a National Movement, rather than political parties, was permitted to link citizen and state. In fact, like Franco, but unlike Mussolini and Hitler, Salazar had no interest in mobilizing the citizenry.

Salazar became incapacitated by a stroke in 1968 and died two years later, succeeded by Marcelo Caetano, a Salazar *apparatchik.* Caetano was less adept at manipulating the enormous bureaucracy devised by his predecessor, but his ultimate undoing proved to be his mishandling of the uprisings in Portugal's African colonies. Guerrilla activity had begun as early as 1961 in Angola, Mozambique, and Guinea-Bissau. By the early 1970s, no end was in sight and disaffection grew with the prosecution of colonial wars that seemed only to claim scarce national resources and many of the nation's youth. It was the armed forces that eventually revolted in 1974. For the first time in Portuguese history, the army intervened from the Left.

While the stolid General Antonio Spinola as titular head of the regime gave the Portuguese revolution conservative credentials, the leftist orientation of the junior officers who masterminded the coup soon brought the country to the brink of radical social change. The officers were divided, however, and a countercoup on November 25, 1975, by Colonel Antonio Romalho Eanes halted the leftward movement of

the revolution and established political institutions well within the mainstream of West European democracy.[14]

Italy

Unlike the other countries of Latin Europe, Italy never experienced a period of absolutism. The early development of merchant capitalism in the city-states of the north undercut the landed aristocracy whose support was necessary for full-blown absolutism.[15] Instead, lacking a unifying force, Italy remained divided into a number of petty principalities. In the south the Kingdom of the Two Sicilies, an outpost of Spanish Bourbon rule, preserved a feudal system based on latifundia. The middle of the peninsula harbored the repressively administered Papal States. The north was composed of smaller principalities dominated by Austria in the northeast and Piedmont in the northwest, as the previously free city-states of the Renaissance fell to external domination.

In many ways the political history of Italy parallels that of Germany: a divided, economically backward set of principalities with a weak bourgeoisie and a conservative, landed aristocracy. Liberal republicans failed in the abortive nationalist revolutions of 1848 in Italy just as in Germany. Whereas Germany was united under Otto von Bismarck and the Prussian Junkers, so Italy gradually became consolidated under the conservative regime of Victor Emmanuel II, king of Piedmont. The middle classes' nationalist aspirations took the form of the *Risorgimento* (national resurgence) whose heroic reperesentative was Giuseppe Garibaldi, an enterprising general who captured the south from the Spanish Bourbons. Garibaldi and his followers were outmaneuvered by Victor Emmanuel's prime minister, Camillo Benso di Cavour, and this heterogeneous group eventually accommodated the conservative, but constitutional, *Piemontese* monarchy. Partially by conquest, partially by diplomacy, Italy was gradually united by 1870.

Italy, like the other countries of Latin Europe, was a late developer. Especially in the north, economic growth was a rapid and alienating process. The rise of radical trade unions and left-wing political activists, responding to the stresses of industrialization, provoked anxiety in the urban middle classes and suspicion among the very large peasantry. This proved to be fertile ground to nourish fear of democracy, liberalism, and socialism. The solution to these fears for many was a former socialist journalist named Benito Mussolini. A demagogue of considerable skill and few principles, Mussolini saw his opportunity to attract a constituency on the far right, quickly abandoning his earlier ideas. He and thousands of followers, uniformed in black shirts, marched on Rome in October 1922. Frightened conservative politicians threw their support to the Fascist Party which, after manipulating elections in 1924, acquired a large majority in the parliament. By 1925 the country was ruled by dictatorship.[16]

Like the Iberian regimes, Mussolini's Italy was loosely based on the fascist ideas of turn-of-the-century Europe. Interest groups were organized along corporatist lines, a concordat was reached with the Catholic Church. Democracy was scorned, elitism and hierarchy praised, and the regime was guarded by the repressive apparatus of the state. Unlike the Iberian countries, but like Nazi Germany, popular support was mobilized around an expansionist foreign policy and the alleged virtues of war.

The imperial aims of the fascist regime proved to be its undoing. The very term "fascist" was taken from the *fasci* (rods surrounding an axe) that formed the symbol of power in Ancient Rome. Mussolini aimed at conquering a new empire, essentially in Africa, to recapture lost glory and to divert attention from domestic political conflict. The latter, according to fascist theory, did not exist, for the nation was idealized as a smoothly functioning, integrated whole in much the same way that Pope Leo XIII's "Rerum Novarum" envisioned a society composed of nonconflictual interests. But denying conflict did not dispel it, and Mussolini's imperial drive led him into an alliance with the other fascist powers and ultimately into defeat. Not only was Mussolini defeated by the Allies in 1943, but his regime was undone from within by Italian partisans (many of them Communists) who never shared the fascist vision of an organic nation captained by a dictatorial state.

A new, democratic constitution was completed by 1947. Italy gained a strong parliament that looked very much like that of the French Fourth Republic, or indeed, the parliament of Spain established thirty years later. What is important to recognize is that democratic institutions were established by indigenous groups with wide popular support.

. . . I sometimes find it difficult to communicate directly the value and certain aspect of our Constitution. And this is because there are, around our Constitution, certain intangibles that have to be explained in historical terms, and for that reason you have to go back to the beginning of democratic Italy, which is very recent . . . [Y]ou have the problem of having [Americans] understand that we, the old country, Italy of so many centuries of civilization is the recent, new, young democratic country, and . . . young America, has the oldest democratic constitution in the world. . . . [America] is the old country of freedom and liberty and individual rights, and ours is the country in which individual rights, freedom, liberty and the values of democracy were discovered recently . . .

Source: Prof. Furio Colombo, President of Fiat, USA, Inc. Quoted in "The Fortieth Anniversary of the Italian Constitution," From *Italian Journal*, 2, No. 4 (1988). Copyright © 1988. Used by permission.

CULTURE

Certainly the most evident similarity among the countries of Latin Europe is linguistic. As the name implies, the citizens of France, Spain, Italy, and Portugal all speak languages based on Latin. To some extent similarities of language bespeak a common culture. Similar words often mean similar visions and concepts, similar ways of viewing the world. One should not, however, push this too far. Significant populations of France have historically spoken Celtic (*Breton*) or Germanic (*Alsacien*) languages (see Chapter 13). France and Spain both have significant Basque-speaking populations, a language totally unrelated to Latin. Even within Italy, diverse dialects are often mutually incomprehensible and "standard" Italian is viewed by many of the country's citizens as an artificial invention, an imposed vehicular language. By contrast, English and German both have many Latin borrowings, while neither Britain nor the Federal Republic of Germany has ever been considered a Latin country. Linguistic similarities do, however, bear witness to at least some elements of a common history.

Another similarity, politically much more important, has been the role of Catholicism in all four countries. The vast majority of the citizens of Latin Europe are, at least nominally, Catholic. In all of these countries the historic role of the Church has been similar. As in France, the Church has tended to be associated with political conservatism in Italy, Spain, and Portugal. In all four countries the Church historically allied with oligarchies resistant to the forces of change. This took on especially tragic proportions in Spain when the cleavage between Left and Right ultimately led to a long and bloody civil war (1936–1939) with conservative clerics lining up clearly with the "Nationalist" forces of General Francisco Franco in his rebellion against the short-lived Spanish Second Republic.

In fact, the clerical-versus-secular conflict that motivated so much of French politics during the Third Republic was mirrored equally in Italy and Spain (and in a somewhat more constrained way in Portugal where secular forces were weaker). The political result, however, was different in the four countries. In France the issue seethed continually, but more or less nonviolently, until it gradually faded. In Spain the church–state issue was part and parcel of a hecatomb that no one wished to repeat after Franco died in 1975. Church influence became formalized in Italy. The nineteenth-century statesman Cavour argued that Italy should have "A free church, a free state," but a clear separation of church and state was not to be. Mussolini signed a concordat with the Holy See in 1929 (not unlike Napoleon's in 1802 or Spain's during Franco) and the persistence of a powerful Christian Democratic Party after 1945 preserved the influence of the Church in such issues as education, divorce, and abortion. While the Church was also associated with political conservatism in Portugal, the left-wing revolution in 1974 that brought democracy to that country also brought secular government.

These countries, owing to their delayed economic development, have all had very significant peasantries whose views of central authority have been similar. Peasants have traditionally been suspicious of the forces of modernization, especially as they came from the city. Even when not aggravated by the existence of ethnic minorities who felt threatened by the national culture based in the capital, peasant resistance to the demands of the modern secular state have provided the raw materials for reactionary movements. It is not an accident that France, Spain, Portugal, and Italy have all had conservative, authoritarian experiences.

Hitler himself recognized the peasantry as a pillar of his own fascist revolution:

Our revolution would not have been possible at all if a certain part of the nation had not lived on

Portuguese Political Culture

One of the salient features of Portuguese society—and one which does not differentiate it in kind from any other south European society—is the prevalence of networks of kinship and patronage. Lengthy and complicated laws and regulations may be constantly drawn up, promulgated and revised to settle the rules by which society is to operate, but in practice every Portuguese knows that such rules are there to be bent or circumvented as one's own needs dictate and in so far as means can be found to achieve this. For historical reasons, including the political instability of the last two centuries, it can be said that no concept of objective legitimacy of law or government has ever taken root in Portugal. It is assumed that those who make law or government do so to further their own interests rather than those of society as a whole, and therefore the taking of countermeasures in self-defence is a natural and legitimate activity. From time to time there is a breakdown of the governmental system, a change of political regime and new laws result, but these changes do not usually make much impact on the substructure of social relationships.

Source: Richard Robinson, *Contemporary Portugal* (London: George Allen and Unwin, 1979), pp. 22–23.

---

the land. If we review the revolution soberly we must admit that it would not have been possible to accomplish this revolution from the cities. In the urban communities we could not have reached a position which gave to our policies the weight of legality.[17]

ECONOMIC ANTAGONISMS

Related to the religious cleavage, class cleavages in the Latin countries of Europe have been roughly similar. Just as in France, issues of secularization reinforced class antagonisms. People siding with the Church tended to be the bourgeoisie or peasantry, while anticlerical sentiment ran highest among the working classes and urban intellectuals. Landless agricultural workers in all four countries tended also to be anticlerical and left wing. Proportionately, this group has been especially important in Portugal, particularly in the Alentejo region.

Like France, the coincidence of class and religious cleavage separating the same groups meant that levels of trust between these groups would be especially low. This lack of "overlapping memberships," as in France, meant that the conditions for democratic stability would not be auspiciously present. In Spain social cleavages were so deep as to erupt in civil war (1936–1939), which in turn provided the Franco regime (1939–1975) with an excuse to suppress democracy entirely. Even without civil war, when feuding segments of society were represented in democratic parliaments, the result was often political immobilism, which invited dictatorial coups. Italy, Spain, and Portugal all experienced long periods of authoritarian rule because democratic forces were divided and weak.

Corporatism

One solution operated by the conservative governments of Latin Europe to the problems of class antagonisms was corporatism. The ideology of corporatism preached a vision of society as an organic whole with each group making a specific contribution, and benefiting from its particular place in a rigid hierarchy.

Rather than projecting a society of self-interested individuals whose free interactions would maximize prosperity—that is, the liberal ethos of the United States and Britain—corporatism preached value by identification with a hierarchy. Groups were perceived as not inherently in conflict, but rather, naturally in harmony, provided each stayed in its place. This ideology of group interaction made all of the

Corporatism in the Ibero-Latin Tradition

If modern political analysis in the Northern European and Anglo-American tradition was to lead to the glorification of the accomplished fact and of political pragmatism, to materialism and the success theory, was also derived principally from the experiences of these nations, then Iberic-Latin culture can surely claim as its basis a moral idealism, a philosophical certainty, a sense of continuity, and a unified organic-corporate conception of the state and society. This conception derives from Roman law (one can still profitably read Seneca for an understanding of the Iberic-Latin tradition), Catholic thought (Augustine, Aquinas), and traditional legal precepts (the *fueros* or group charters of medieval times, the law of the *Siete Partidas* of Alfonso the Wise). In comprehending the Iberic-Latin systems, one must think in terms of a hierarchically and vertically segmented structure of class and caste stratifications, of social rank orders, functional corporations, estates, juridical groupings and *intereses*—all fairly well defined in law and in terms of their respective stations in life—a rigid yet adaptable scheme whose component parts are tied to and derive legitimacy from the authority of the central state or its leader.

Source: *World Politics*, 25, No. 2 (January 1973). Vol. 19. Reprinted by permission of the Johns Hopkins University Press, Baltimore/London.

societies of Latin Europe susceptible to fascist demagogues who preached inherent hierarchies and organic nationalism.

Radical Politics

If the countries of Northern Europe have largely been able to develop a kind of consensual politics where the fear of revolution hardly menaced any of the political bargaining, the same cannot be said for Southern Europe.

The deep class antagonisms and religious conflict polarized Left and Right. Alienated workers turned to radical parties in all of Latin Europe. While Italy and Spain had strong anarchist traditions, the emphasis of Communists on strong organization, well adapted to clandestinity, made them the most durable opponents to the fascist regimes of Southern Europe. (But only in Italy did the Communists remain influential after fascism was defeated.)

As in France, the radicalized workers' movements were partially the product of late industrialization. Firms in all of these countries were relatively small and, therefore, less likely to be unionized. Thus, Left political parties developed without the support of a more pragmatic trade union movement. Because unions were small and too weak to support long strikes, labor strategy turned to short strikes, meant to be symbolic and to underline *political* demands rather than economic ones.

Fear of a radical Left drove the peasant and middle classes into the arms of the Right. Since the latter were more numerous, conservative government has tended to be the norm in Southern Europe, at least until the 1980s.

Dirigisme and Politically Oriented Interest Groups

Late development has also reinforced the tendency for a significant state role in the economies of Latin Europe. This leads us to the familiar phenomenon of *dirigisme,* a French word meaning "state economic interventionism." The lack of entrepreneurs and the small size of firms in these countries meant that the role for amassing large sums of capital necessary for industrialization fell to the state. As the first and second propositions in Chapter 2 predicted, this began to change in the 1980s, as economic liberalization made inroads into most European countries. Nevertheless, a long history of state intervention has marked the political and economic terrain of all the countries of the region, and long-held habits are not overturned easily.

This history of *dirigisme* reinforced the political orientations of interest groups. It was necessary to influence the state to achieve one's economic goals and this often meant aligning with political parties. For labor, competing trade union organizations developed in Spain, Italy, and Portugal. In Italy, the CGIL labor confederation aligned primarily with the Communists, the CISL with the Christian Democrats and the UIL with the center-left parties. In Portugal, the CGTP aligned with the Communists, the UGT with the Socialists. In Spain, the UGT and *Commissiones Obreros* reflected the political positions of Socialists and Communists respectively. There were, of course, no independent trade unions permitted during the periods of fascist rule.

Business groups have consistently been in an easier position in Southern Europe. Long periods of conservative government were conducive to their general interests, but over long government protection made businesses stodgy and uncompetitive. Here, Italy is a notable contrast, where, in the north especially, businesses are highly competitive. Uncompetitiveness of Spanish and Portuguese businesses led to especially high unemployment as these countries entered the Common Market in 1986.

The Spanish economy has grown rapidly ever since its entry into the European Union, but while profits rose rapidly, unemployment continued at over 18 percent. This failure of the majority of Spaniards to share in the new wealth led to a general strike in December 1988. As our third proposition of Chapter 2 predicted, groups began to change orientations and alliances. This was especially marked in the growing tensions between the nominally socialist government and the UGT trade unions.

Regional Disparities

All of the countries of Western Europe are troubled by regional disparities, but these are especially severe in Southern Europe. Italy perhaps offers the greatest problem in strictly economic terms. The north of Italy is a fabulous success story. Per capita income is among the highest in the world and by some estimates Italy is the third largest economy in Europe, after Germany and France, and ahead of Britain.[18] This performance is all the more impressive when one considers the backwardness of the *Mezzogiorno*, the half of the country south of Rome. It is a tragic fact that southern Italy has more in common with the Third World than with Western Europe. While economically the backward *Mezzogiorno* provided the north (and much of Europe) with a reservoir of cheap labor, politically this largely rural area served to keep the Christian Democrats (and after 1994 the neofascists) in power.

Regional disparities had a different impact in Spain. The culturally distinct areas of Catalonia

---

A Matter of Rank

. . . the Italian economy has caught up with, and possibly surpassed, Britain's. That appears to be true both in terms of sheer size, as measured by the Gross Domestic Product yardstick, as well as per-capita income. Some economists and politicians, in Italy and Britain alike, have been quick to point out that exchange rate distortions may be responsible for Italy's promotion to fifth place among the world's industrial democracies, and Britain's demotion to sixth. There is no denying, however, that over the last few years the country that used to be dubbed "Europe's sick man" and "NATO's soft underbelly" has undergone momentous changes.

Source: "Special Report: Italy" advertising supplement to the *Washington Post*, March 25, 1987.

---

and the Basque country have traditionally been suspicious of Madrid. The democratic government that succeeded Franco in 1975 devolved considerable autonomy onto the local governments of these regions to placate separatist sentiments and rising terrorism on the part of the Basque ETA.[19] Whereas Italy's south had never industrialized, the Basque and Catalan regions of Spain were among the most developed in the country. Since the 1970s, however, it is precisely the industries in these regions that are in decline and the diminishing prosperity aggravated traditional tensions.

The Alentejo region of southeastern Portugal, a region of latifundia, was the area of the country most sympathetic to communism. Initially, the radical Left government that replaced the conservative dictatorship in 1974 divided the area into collective farms. After 1975, as the radical Left was defeated in Lisbon, the parliament retracted the reforms and lands were returned to their former owners.

POLITICAL STRUCTURES AND PARTIES

All the governments of Southern Europe are essentially parliamentary in character. That is, there is a fusion of executive and legislative power, where the prime minister and his cabinet must enjoy the confidence of the parliament. The president of Italy and king of Spain hold positions that are essentially ceremonial, although they may exert some influence in whom they pick as candidates to form a government. Usually, however, they merely ratify the decisions of party leaders. Portugal, after 1975, chose to create a presidency somewhat closer to the French model, although weaker than that of France. The president of Portugal enjoys greater flexibility, especially in foreign affairs, than does the head of state of Italy or Spain. In 1982, however, the power of the presidency was somewhat weakened in Portugal,

but the country still has a stronger head of state than the other countries of Southern Europe.

There are, however, significant differences in the nature of parliamentary politics in these countries. Portugal, Spain, and France have all known stable majority parties for significant periods, whereas Italy has not had a majority party under its present constitution. For most of the postwar period, Italian politics resembled France during the Third and Fourth republics. Coalitions were fragile and governments rarely lasted a year. The persistence of a large Italian Communist Party commanding a consistent 30 percent of the vote limited the room for maneuver of the non-Communist parties and led to the *de facto* dominance of the Christian Democratic Party for more than four decades, until the electoral system changed.

Like Fourth Republic France as well, unstable Italian coalitions in parliament were complemented by a stable pool of elites from which cabinet ministers were drawn, consistently representing the five major non-Communist parties.[20] Italy also has a powerful, clientelistic bureaucracy. This *clientela* meant that interest groups penetrated and dominated various agencies. Bureaucratic careers were determined by patronage, while ministries were controlled by different parties.[21] This pattern even filtered down to the large nationalized industries, though sometimes the pattern reversed: Enrico Mattei, the longtime entrepreneurial president of ENI, the state-owned oil company, used financial contributions from his company to play one party off against another.[22]

When the Cold War came to an end in 1989, it brought a sea change to Italian politics. Fear of communism disappeared, and with it the hold of the Christian Democrats and their allies on Italian politics. A series of corruption scandals grew to a crescendo by 1993 and gradually compromised almost every major politician in the Christian Democratic and Socialist parties. A small group of reformist politicians put to the voters a major referendum in April 1993 in which the electoral system for the Senate was changed, 75 percent of which would be elected by a first-past-the-post single ballot (see Chapter 13). The chamber of deputies then agreed to restructure the lower house elections in a similar fashion. This electoral change, which was also extended to local government, meant that small parties, especially those in the center of the political spectrum, would probably disappear, and that stable majority governments would probably become commonplace.[23] The municipal elections that followed in the referendum, in November 1993, showed that support for the Christian Democratic and other centrist parties had collapsed. Remaining on the Italian landscape were the former Communists, now called the Party of the Democratic Left (with a new social democratic philosophy), the neo-fascist Italian Social Movement, and a new populist party with strength in the northern cities, the Northern League.

The success of the former Communists in the 1993 municipal elections struck fear into the hearts of the conservatives. The Christian Democratic Party, despite rechristening itself the Popular Party of Italy (its pre–World War II name), was too deeply compromised in the corruption scandals to draw a large vote, as were its coalition partners: the Socialists, Liberals, and Republicans. Seeking to mobilize the traditional conservative constituency, media magnate Silvio Berlusconi declared himself the right wing's bulwark against a Left victory. In a matter of months he used his vast wealth and business organization and the stable of media stars in his employ to create *Forza Italia* ("Go Italy!") as a vehicle for his political ambitions. Recognizing that the new electoral system required that he form an alliance with other parties, Berlusconi joined the Northern League and the neo-fascists (renamed National Alliance) to contest the March 1994 elections. The results of the elections were impressive, if disquieting. Berlusconi's coalition, the Freedom Alliance with 42.9 percent of the votes cast, captured an absolute majority in the Chamber of Deputies, defeating the Left's Progressive Alliance, and the rump Christian Democrats' centrist Pact for Italy. The Right's 366 of the 630 seats were obtained thanks to the new electoral law that meant individual districts could be won by a mere plurality, rather than a majority. They also achieved a qualified majority in the Senate (that is, they had a plurality of senators, whereas even the opposing coalitions combined could not outvote them).

The new electoral system meant that the configuration of Italian politics had permanently changed. Instead of a plethora of parties, the parliament had a majority government (see Figure 35.1). However, at the time this chapter was being written (May 1994), it was not clear that the members of the majority could agree on enough to govern. With Berlusconi's Forza Italia preaching free market policies, while the fascists preached state intervention, and the Northern League emphasized policies that helped the north to the detriment of the fascist base of support in the south, it was hard to see what policies would emerge from this marriage of electoral convenience.

Politics are even harder to judge in Portugal and Spain, which have known democracy only since the 1970s. The Portuguese parliament was especially unstable, reflecting the deep problems of that benighted land and the lack of consensus on how to approach them. In 1987, the country for the first time elected a majority of center-right Social Democrats to manage their entrance into what was then the European Community. The policies advocated by this relatively conservative party, including significant reductions in the public sector, represent a dramatic shift from the political ideas of the 1974 revolution. The effect of this new majority remains to be seen.

After the death of dictator Francisco Franco in 1975, Spain cautiously adopted democratic government under the leadership of King Juan Carlos. Unlike Portugal, where the army pushed the country to the Left, Juan Carlos had to navigate between an influential army on the

Supporters of Italy's right-wing National Alliance gave the traditional fascist salute and chanted slogans reminiscent of the days of Mussolini after election returns showed sizable gains for the alliance.

far right and separatists on the far left. The failure of an abortive coup in May 1981, however, indicate that the Spanish army, most of whose units remained loyal, is no longer as deeply conservative as it was under Franco.

A relatively conservative socialist party, the Partito Socialista Obrero Español (PSOE), dominated Spanish politics throughout the 1980s, after gaining the majority for the first time in 1982. (The party received a plurality in the legislative elections of 1993, but had to seek the support of small parties to its right in order to govern.) The party was, in fact, so conservative that its associated labor confederation, the UGT, disavowed the alliance, and in fact called a general strike against the government. As our first two propositions in Chapter 2 suggested, the Italian Socialists, the Portuguese Social Democrats, and the PSOE have pushed for a rollback of the state. Unlike the French situation, there was simply much more of the state to roll back in Spain and Portugal, largely because both countries have only recently emerged from fascist-style state-directed economies. However, it is not so much that the public sectors were larger, but rather, years of fascist bureaucracy had made them much less dynamic than in France.

THE ROLE OF THE EUROPEAN UNION

France and northern Italy are perhaps most starkly different from their Iberic neighbors in their levels of economic development. While France and Italy are among the seven richest

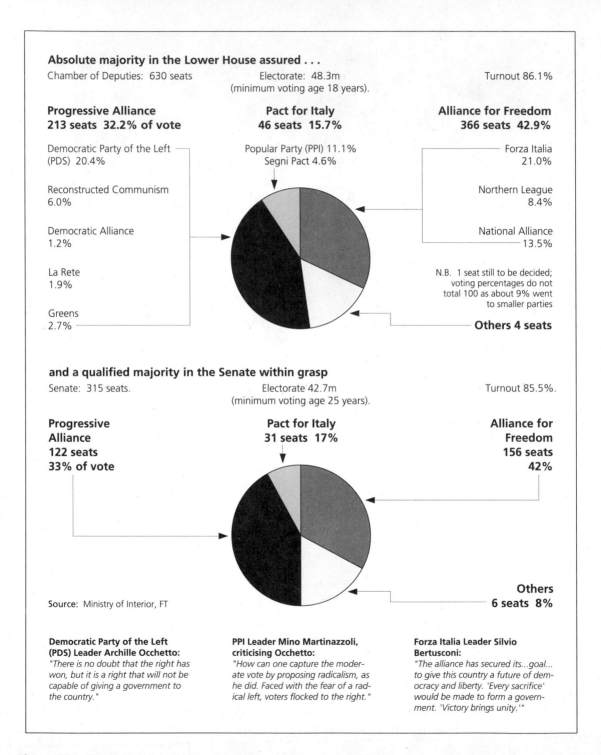

Absolute majority in the Lower House assured . . .

Chamber of Deputies: 630 seats

Electorate: 48.3m
(minimum voting age 18 years).

Turnout 86.1%

Progressive Alliance
213 seats 32.2% of vote

Pact for Italy
46 seats 15.7%

Alliance for Freedom
366 seats 42.9%

Democratic Party of the Left
(PDS) 20.4%

Reconstructed Communism
6.0%

Democratic Alliance
1.2%

La Rete
1.9%

Greens
2.7%

Popular Party (PPI) 11.1%
Segni Pact 4.6%

Forza Italia
21.0%

Northern League
8.4%

National Alliance
13.5%

N.B. 1 seat still to be decided;
voting percentages do not
total 100 as about 9% went
to smaller parties

Others 4 seats

and a qualified majority in the Senate within grasp

Senate: 315 seats.

Electorate 42.7m
(minimum voting age 25 years).

Turnout 85.5%.

**Progressive
Alliance
122 seats
33% of vote**

**Pact for Italy
31 seats 17%**

**Alliance for
Freedom
156 seats
42%**

**Others
6 seats 8%**

Source: Ministry of Interior, FT

**Democratic Party of the Left
(PDS) Leader Archille Occhetto:**
*"There is no doubt that the right has
won, but it is a right that will not be
capable of giving a government to
the country."*

**PPI Leader Mino Martinazzoli,
criticising Occhetto:**
*"How can one capture the moder-
ate vote by proposing radicalism, as
he did. Faced with the fear of a radical left, voters flocked to the right."*

**Forza Italia Leader Silvio
Bertusconi:**
*"The alliance has secured its...goal...
to give this country a future of democracy and liberty. 'Every sacrifice'
would be made to form a government. 'Victory brings unity.'"*

Figure 35.1 The Right Romps Home. Source: *Financial Times*, March 30, 1994, p. 2. Used by permission.

countries in the capitalist world, Spain and Portugal lag far behind. Portugal is especially underdeveloped and industrially weak. Spain, considerably more developed than Portugal, is, nevertheless, industrially backward, with over a quarter of its population still involved with agriculture.

Both countries (along with Greece) saw the solution to their underdevelopment in the European Union. Europe would offer tremendous new markets for their agricultural produce and the cheap labor would be attractive to European industries that could then sell Spanish and Portuguese assembled goods to the rest of the Union without worrying about tariffs. The Spanish economy did especially well for these reasons. However, entry into the European Monetary System, combined with a dismantling of credit controls, has led to very high interest rates in Spain. This has made it very difficult for Spanish manufacturers to borrow money to modernize, so that the future impact of the European Union may not bode well for uncompetitive Spanish industry.[24]

From the European perspective the new members were an additional burden. Not only would the agricultural production of the new members compete with the farmers of France and Italy, but the huge subsidies paid by what was then the Union through the Common Agricultural Policy would become a monumental burden on the industrial producers of Europe.

While this burden increased the number of European advocates for an overhaul of agricultural policy, it also led many others in the developed part of the Union to propose *l'Europe à deux vitesses* (Europe with two speeds): a different set of rules and subsidies for Spain, Portugal, and Greece.

Moreover, the somber example of southern Italy stood as a caution to the advantages of economic integration. Clearly, there are disadvantages as well. Economic integration with the highly industrialized parts of Europe meant "infant industries" in the south could not be protected from the efficient competition of the north. Free movement of capital might just as easily mean capital flight *from* as well as *to* Spain and Portugal. Indeed, the high interest rates that both economies experienced in the early 1990s were a direct result of trying to encourage capital *not* to go abroad. This benefited the local banks, but hurt industry.

CONCLUSION: LATIN EUROPE IN COMPARATIVE PERSPECTIVE

This all-too-brief survey of Latin Europe offers us an additional perspective from which to view the nature of comparative politics. Most importantly, the quick overview of these countries underlines the need for caution when we try to suggest explanations for the development of Europe's political and economic institutions. If, as Max Weber suggested in his *Protestant Ethic and the Spirit of Capitalism,* culture explains the level of economic development,[25] then a look at Latin Europe weakens the argument. The cultures of these countries are quite similar, while their levels of economic development are vastly different.

Politically, however, the intense segmentation characterizing the cultures of these countries is instructive. The deeply divided and frequently unstable parliaments and party systems of Latin Europe are in many ways explained by their divisive cultures. Parliaments that represent the people represent their divisions as well.

Yet, the respective experiences of Spain, Portugal, and France demonstrate that these divisions are not insurmountable. Moreover, the case of Italy suggests that the divisions need not be overcome: prosperity can be achieved *without* solving the problems of cultural conflict.

Finally, these countries illustrate the great variety of political arrangements produced by cultures and circumstances that are broadly similar. Similarities at one level yield differences at another. By studying the mechanisms that produce the convergences and divergences in political systems, we learn something more about the nature of politics in general. It is not only a study that is enriching, but in a disquieting world, the comprehension of politics is a requisite for survival.

NOTES

1. Greece is often grouped with these countries as a "Mediterranean democracy." While Greece shares many characteristics with Latin Europe, some cultural and historical dissimilarities, as well as economy of space, have led us to omit discussion of this country, although it is part of Southern Europe. For linguistic reasons, of course, Greece is not "Latin." For a discussion of the notion "Mediterranean democracy," see Arend Lijphart, Thomas C. Bruneau, P. Nikiforos Diamandouros, and Richard Gunther, "A Mediterranean Model of Democracy? The Southern European Democracies in Comparative Perspective," *West European Politics*, 11, No. 1 (January 1988), 7–25.

2. Perry Anderson, *Lineages of the Absolutist State* (London: Verso, 1979), chap. 3.

3. This argument relies heavily on Donald Share, *The Making of Spanish Democracy* (New York: Praeger, 1986), chap. 1.

4. Pierre Vilar, *Histoire de l'Espagne* (Paris: Presses Universitaires de France, 1947), p. 50; Share, p. 8.

5. Share, p. 8.

6. Share, pp. 12–13.

7. Richard Gunther, Giacomo Sani, and Goldie Shabad, *Spain After Franco* (Berkeley and Los Angeles: University of California Press, 1988), pp. 17–20.

8. Sofia A. Perez, *State, Banks, and Central Bankers: The Politics of Spanish Financial Regulation in Comparative Perspective*, Ph.D. dissertation, The George Washington University, 1993, chapter II.

9. On the transition to democracy, see Gunther, Sani, and Shabad, pp. 34–36; Share, pp. 198–217; and Kenneth Maxwell, "Spain and Portugal: A Comparative Perspective," in Stanley G. Payne, ed., *The Politics of Democratic Spain* (Chicago: Chicago Council on Foreign Relations, 1986), pp.

10. 256–273. On the constitutional referendum, see Dimitri-Georges Lavroff, *Le Régime Politique Espagnol* (Paris: Presses Universitaire de France, 1985), p. 6.

10. For a brief introduction to the history of Portugal, see Richard Robinson, *Contemporary Portugal* (London: George Allen and Unwin, 1979), chap. 1; and Thomas C. Bruneau, *Politics and Nationhood: Post-Revolutionary Portugal* (New York: Praeger, 1984), chap. 1.

11. S. Sideri, *Trade and Power: Informal Colonialism in Anglo-Portuguese Relations* (Rotterdam: Rotterdam University Press, 1970), p. 5, quoted in Bruneau, p. 14.

12. See especially Barrington Moore, Jr., *Social Origins of Dictatorship and Democracy* (Boston: Beacon Press, 1966), p. 418.

13. For a detailed look at this period, see Robinson, chap. 2.

14. For a conservative appraisal of this period, see Maxwell, pp. 256 ff.

15. Perry Anderson, *Lineages*, pp. 143–172.

16. This account draws heavily on Stephen Hellman, "Italy" in Mark Kesselman and Joel Krieger, et al., *European Politics in Transition* (Lexington, Mass.: D. C. Heath, 1987), pp. 320–343.

17. Quoted in Alexander Gerschenkron, *Bread and Democracy in Germany* (Berkeley and Los Angeles: University of California Press, 1943), p. 3.

18. The Italians called their bypassing of Britain as *il sorpasso*.

19. *Euskadi ta Askatasuna*, an ultra-nationalist group seeking total independence for the Basque region. For an analysis of Spanish separatist movements, see Goldie Shabad, "After Autonomy: The Dynamics of Regionalism in Spain," in Stanley G. Payne, ed., *The Politics of Democratic Spain* (Chicago: The Chicago Council on Foreign Relations, 1986), pp. 111–180.

20. Christian Democrats, Socialists, Social Democrats, Liberals, and Republicans.

21. Joseph La Palombara, *Interest Groups in Italian Politics* (Princeton: Princeton University Press, 1964), chaps. 8, 9.

22. Paul Frankel, *Mattei, Oil and Power Politics* (New York: Praeger, 1966).

23. Robert Graham, "An Experiment in Voting," *Financial Times*, Survey, June 30, 1993, p. II.

24. For a detailed examination of this issue, see Perez, *State, Banks, and Central Bankers.*
25. Max Weber, *The Protestant Ethic and the Spirit of Capitalism* (New York: Charles Scribner's Sons, 1958), first published in 1904–1905.

REFERENCES AND SUGGESTED READINGS

Gunther, Richard, Giacomo Sani, and Goldie Shabad. 1988. *Spain After Franco.* Berkeley: University of California Press.

Haycraft, John. 1985. *Italian Labyrinth.* Harmondsworth: Penguin.

Kayman, Martin. 1987. *Revolution and Counter-Revolution in Portugal.* London: Merlin Press.

Kurth, James, and James Petras, with Diarmid Maguire and Ronald Chilcote. 1993. *Mediterranean Paradoxes: The Politics and Social Structure of Southern Europe.* Providence: Berg.

Lange, Peter, and Sidney Tarrow, eds. 1980. *Italy in Transition: Conflict and Consensus.* London: Frank Cass.

La Palombara, Joseph. 1987. *Politics Italian Style.* New Haven: Yale University Press.

Payne, Stanley G., ed. 1986. *The Politics of Democratic Spain.* Chicago: The Chicago Council on Foreign Relations.

Putnam, Robert D., with Robert Leonardi and Rafaella Nanetta. 1993. *Making Democracy Work: Civic Traditions in Modern Italy.* Princeton: Princeton University Press.

Robinson, Richard. 1979. *Contemporary Portugal.* London: George Allen and Unwin.

Share, Donald. 1986. *The Making of Spanish Democracy.* New York: Praeger.

36

Scandinavia

Political events in Scandinavian countries rarely make headlines in the American press. A country like Norway probably received more coverage during the 1994 Winter Olympics in Lillehammer than it has since gaining independence in 1905. For the most part, the Scandinavian countries remain in a dead spot of American awareness. Their domestic politics lacks drama, and in world politics those countries have long ago relinquished any ambition of playing a main role. The number of people living in Sweden, Norway, and Denmark combined barely approximates one-third of Britain's population. In short, Scandinavia is neither a big wheel, nor a squeaky one in need of oil. So why bother with its politics?

THE POLITICS OF CIVILITY

In a world of politics that often approximates Hobbes's account of the state of nature as "war of all against all," Scandinavia presents a welcome contrast. The Scandinavian countries entered the modern age of industrialization and mass democracy without political revolution, terror, civil war, authoritarian backlash, threats of coups, fascist uprisings or other kinds of violence. The last two hundred years witnessed a steady textbook progression from undisputed monarchical rule to a political order premised on the principles of liberty, equality, and community. It all has the ring of a Hans Christian Andersen fairy tale.

How did the Scandinavian countries manage to engineer such a smooth passage through the turbulence of modernization? What made them adapt so successfully to conditions that elsewhere proved so upsetting and perilous for the ideal of democratic government?

The Wealth-and-Welfare State

To many observers, modern Scandinavia is synonymous with "welfare state." Economic adversity, illness, or other misfortunes of life have lost their sting with the provision of "womb-to-tomb" services by the government. The Scandinavian countries typically top the list of public sector spending in the western world. In the 1980s, the share of government spending as a percentage of the gross domestic product reached a staggering 57 percent in Sweden,[1] with Denmark's share being quite similar and Norway's not far below. Such an extensive reach of government may strike many as socialism. But at the same time, the Scandinavian countries have achieved fabulous prosperity, with standards of living at a par with that enjoyed by Americans and ahead of most other Europeans. The fact is that the "wealth-and-welfare" states of Scandinavia have done little to impede the workings of a free market economy. Businesses are run by business, not government bureaucrats. In other words, the goose that lays the golden eggs has not been slain.

So long as communism posed an alternative, albeit a threatening one, to capitalism, the Scandinavian countries were often considered proof that a "middle way" was possible. They seemed to be achieving extensive equality in the economic and social standing of citizens without infringing on their political liberties. It was a model of economic and social progress without curbs on the exercise of democracy. The model worked because of historic compromises forged at criticial junctures of economic and social development between agrarian and urban interests, or between business and labor.

Social Democracy

Politically speaking, Scandinavia has proved uniquely hospitable to a phenomenon virtually unknown in the United States under that name, though quite familiar in Germany: *social democracy*. More than just the name of a political party, this refers to a political configuration that arose from the working class with strong ties to labor unions and a breath of Marxist ideology. In Sweden, a party called the Social Democratic Labor Party governed for more than 50 of the past 60 years; in Norway and Denmark, equivalent parties did so for most of those years, too. No other countries have experienced social democratic government for such extended periods.

The dominant role of social democratic parties thus is another feature that sets Scandinavian politics apart from the rest of the world. How did these parties manage to come to power so early and hold on to it so long in Scandinavia? How did they handle their socialist impulses of wanting to overthrow capitalism and bourgeois rule? Has the enjoyment of their lengthy stay in power robbed them of any socialist zeal? How have they dealt with

---

Scandinavia Spells Social Democracy

Social democracy offers to the world one of the most durable and successful labor movements ever, and Scandinavian social democracy stands out as the international model.

Source: Gösta Esping-Andersen, *Politics Against Markets: The Social Democratic Road to Power* (Princeton: Princeton University Press, 1985), p. 312.

Table 36.1 VITAL STATISTICS ON SCANDINAVIA

	Denmark	Norway	Sweden
Population (mill.)	5.1	4.3	8.6
Area (1,000 square miles)	17	125	174
Religion (Lutheran)	90%	94%	95%
GDP/capita	$15,200	$17,400	$16,200
Real Economic Growth (1989–1992 average	2.0%	2.1%	0.4%
Inflation (1989–1992 average)	2.8%	4.9%	8.3%
Unemployment	2.8%	4.9%	1.4%

Source: *The World Almanac 1993* (New York: St. Martin's Press, 1992); OECD.

some of the troubling issues that have recently driven left-wing parties from power in many western democracies?

Geographic Isolation

Among many advantages enjoyed by Scandinavia, geography is certainly one (see Figure 36.1). For all practical purposes, Norway and Sweden form an island—an island, moreover, whose climate and mountainous terrain combine to deter invasions by other powers. Except for the Germans in World War II, no foreign power has occupied any of the Scandinavian countries in 1,000 years, if not longer. Sweden has not been at war with anyone since the days of Napoleon.

The outside world has not intruded much in the domestic development of Scandinavia, which in turn has stayed aloof from the rest of Europe for long stretches of history. The Scandinavian countries were fortunate enough to stay out of World War I, which brought down a tsar in Russia, an emperor in Austria–Hungary and a kaiser in Germany, with far-reaching consequences for the political regimes of each of those three countries.

Unicultural Societies

Left to and by themselves, the Scandinavian countries have each emerged as highly homogeneous societies with a firm sense of national identity. Ethnically, all but perhaps a small percent of the population of Sweden is of Swedish stock; and the same goes for the Norwegians in Norway and nearly the same for the Danes in Denmark. As for religion, nearly all belong to the (Lutheran) Protestant Church of their respective countries (see Table 36.1). And with regard to language, only Norway is less than perfectly uniform, with *Riksmal*, a Danish version of Norwegian, being challenged by *Nynorsk*, a more indigenous one.

Even with that complication, one is hard pressed to find countries in the world with a lower potential for ethnic strife, religious turmoil, or linguistic disputes than Scandinavia. Much of what makes politics dramatic but also violent is simply missing there. Scandinavia has been spared the traumatic and often bloody clashes arising in the process of nation-building.

Nonetheless, it would not be difficult to imagine a more violent course. What if, for example, one of the three countries had seriously attempted to forge a Greater Scandinavia? And what if that power had tried to impose its religion and language on the others? While at one time or another, the Danes and later the Swedes may have harbored pan-Scandinavian ambitions, neither of them sought to achieve that goal with "blood and iron" during the past century and a half. As compatible as the three were with each other, they wound up as separate states in the twentieth century, feeling secure and content with their modest role in world politics.

Royal Democracies

It is no accident that each of the three Scandinavian countries remains a monarchy. They are among the few nations left with an established crown. The Scandinavian "royal democracies," like Britain, are living proof that monarchy and democracy are by no means mutually exclusive political principles. Democracy requires neither a republican form of state nor a revolution. The kings and queens of Scandinavia, of course, do not rule anymore. They make no policy, but serve in the most unpretentious way as ceremonial heads of state. It was not easy picking Norway's King Harald out of the crowd during the Lillehammer Winter Olympics. Most important, the Scandinavian monarchs are a symbolic thread connecting their countries' present with a past of nearly one thousand years. They are living proof that once-dominant forces in politics and society were able to make peace with newly aspiring forces within existing traditions.

No doubt, not all traditions have survived, and power has shifted, but the old rulers were not deprived of life or liberty, and many of the old institutions stayed in place. To American observers, the Scandinavian countries appear to be both very traditional and very modern, the oldest monarchies run by the most entrenched socialist parties.

FROM ARISTOCRATIC MONARCHY TO ROYAL DEMOCRACY

Nation-Building

Of the three Scandinavian countries, it is Denmark, the smallest, that can look back at the longest tradition as an independent country. It boasts the oldest kingdom in Europe, dating back to A.D. 900, if not earlier. Moreover, the same dynasty has occupied the Danish throne for more than five hundred years by now. At times, Denmark played aggressive power politics, invading and occupying parts of England, Norway, Sweden, and Germany, as well as overseas territories. As late as 1864, Denmark

Figure 36.1 The Countries of Scandinavia.

tangled with a Prussia bent on unifying Germany; it lost that tussle and a province called Schleswig. Even by the time of World War I, Denmark's reach extended as far as the Caribbean islands. It was during that war that the United States acquired its Virgin Islands (St. Thomas and St. John) from Denmark. In any event, whatever wars Denmark fought, it managed to do so on the territory of other countries. Except for the German occupation in World War II, the Danes have not been conquered by foreign powers.

At the same time, Denmark has not shied from conquering its Scandinavian neighbors. It is curious to note that Sweden established—better perhaps, reestablished—its national independence in a fight against Denmark in the 1520s. The leading figure of that struggle for independence was Gustav Vasa, Sweden's

"founding father" and first king (1523–1560). Clearly, not all politics in Scandinavia happened peacefully and by mutual accommodation, but one has to go back nearly four hundred years to find instances of violent clashes.

Norway also gained its modern-day national independence from a fellow Scandinavian country—actually, from two. For centuries, going back to 1380, Norway was under Danish influence, which almost succeeded in extinguishing any Norwegian sense of national identity. With the redrawing of Europe's political map in the wake of the Napoleonic Wars in 1814, the Danes were deprived of their centuries-long control over Norway. That, however, did not mean full independence for Norway. Instead, Norway was handed to Sweden, so as to compensate the latter for its loss of Finland to Russia.

Norway did not look kindly on its new Scandinavian ruler and tried to resist this new imposition in a brief "war" that ended with an amicable compromise: near political autonomy for Norway, but with recognition of the Swedish monarch as supreme ruler of what was called the "union" between Sweden and Norway. Even though Swedish rule, unlike the Danish rule before, was benign and did not greatly impinge on Norway's domestic political life, nationalistic fervor grew in Norway and full independence was demanded. Without bloodshed, Norway finally obtained it in 1905 from a Sweden resisting the temptation to maintain the union by force. The prospect of a civil war was averted.

Of the three Scandinavian countries, Norway could have been perhaps the one to experience violent upheavals, driven by resentment against its fellow Scandinavians. Only in Norway did the process of nation-building even remotely resemble the kind of struggle that many other nations underwent, notably Germany in the period from 1848 to 1871. Still, the last two hundred years have not witnessed in

Norweigan fans at the Men's Downhill Race at the 1994 Winter Olympics in Lillehammer, Norway.

Norway a traumatic struggle that cost the lives of thousands of people in a civil war or in battle with the armies of other countries.

Constitution-Building

Modern democratic government arrived in the Nordic countries without revolution or much domestic strife. And it did not cost them the monarchy. Traditional institutions redefined their roles through reform and managed to survive. The dominant forces made enough concessions at the right time to forestall violent changes. This is especially true for Sweden, a country with a vigorous parliamentary tradition that dates back, some say, as far as the 1350s. Most agree that the *Riksdag* was firmly established as the Swedish parliament by the time of the rule of King Gustav Vasa.

The Swedish Parliament ca. 1750

The distribution of power within the Riksdag can be partly gauged from the numbers in the different Estates. About 300 nobles, representing approximately 1,000 families, usually attended the Riksdag sessions. The clergy numbered 75, including all the bishops, with the archbishop presiding ex officio. Some 100 members represented the burghers. The peasantry (or rather the freeholders and crown tenants only) numbered around 150 who were usually selected by district on the basis of indirect elections. Obviously, the nobles enjoyed disproportionate influence through sheer numbers; if needed they could mobilize close to 1,000 members. Moreover, by virtue of their control of high administrative offices, the nobles could lay special claims to representing the Establishment.

Source: Kurt Samuelsson, *From Great Power to Welfare State: 300 Years of Swedish Social Development* (London: Allen & Unwin, 1968), p. 118.

The Organic Law of 1617 spelled out the powers of the four estates that made up the Riksdag. These estates were the nobility, the clergy, the burghers, and the peasants. Note the unusual fact that the peasantry is recognized as a separate estate. It was a tribute to the considerable economic importance of this group and bore historical witness to its leading role in the fight for Swedish independence from Denmark. At the beginning of the seventeenth century, the Riksdag was securely institutionalized in the Swedish monarchy. Its existence was not a matter of royal grace but of laws rooted in tradition. The Swedish king was no absolute monarch, but one who learned to deal with the representatives of the four estates in the Riksdag. In fact, the king was supposed to govern through a council that was responsible to the Riksdag. The members of the council, in turn, were subject to dismissal by the Riksdag.

In Sweden's Age of Liberty (1720–1772), the ideas of the Enlightenment spread among the educated. Economic change in the preindustrial era created a growing class of wealthy merchants, shippers, and manufacturers. The Riksdag, as constituted along estate lines, afforded them insufficient influence. Pressure for reform coalesced in a group called the Caps, whose antagonists were called the Hats. In the best spirit of the Enlightenment, the Caps opposed any form of privilege and favored equal rights, free elections, parliamentary rule, and economic *laissez-faire*.

Against the backdrop of growing pressure for political reform, as well as a war with Russia, King Gustav III (1771–1792) struck a curious deal with the Riksdag. On one hand, he asserted the principle of royal absolutism in matters of war and peace. But on the other hand, he went against his traditional ally, the nobility, in meeting the demands for reform by strengthening the position of the burgher estate and the peasantry. By taking the side of the newly aspiring forces, the king ensured the continuity of the monarchy in Sweden.

In the aftermath of the French Revolution of 1789, yet without a revolution of its own, Sweden formally adopted a "constitution" in 1809. Until the mid-1970s, when it was to adopt a new constitution, Sweden enjoyed the distinction of having the oldest constitution in Europe. The 1809 document defined a monarch with strong executive powers checked by an independent judiciary and legislature. It also provided for an *ombudsman,* an investigator of citizen complaints about official misconduct.

Without the revolutionary turmoil afflicting most European countries in 1848, Sweden proceeded with its course of political reform. The demands by the growing middle class for more political influence led to a sweeping parliamentary reform in 1866. The four-estate institution gave way to a bicameral legislature, but the name *Riksdag* remained. The upper chamber was to be indirectly elected, thus ensuring the continued influence of the nobility, while the lower house was to be elected by the "people." Property and income requirements were set such that approximately 25 percent of adult males were eligible to vote at the time.

The elections resulted in a lower house dominated by rural and agricultural interests—that is, well-to-do farmers without noble title. Still, urban and commercial interests had a voice, too, in this body. On the other hand, Sweden's vast majority then, the less-well-off agrarian population, lacked both the vote and parliamentary representatives, as did the growing industrial working class. All in all, the pace of political change in nineteenth-century Sweden must be considered slow and deliberate. It was certainly too slow for ardent advocates of democracy, though always too fast for the nobility. More important, it was apparently just right to avoid inciting one side to revolution and the other to reactionary backlash.

On Toward Mass Participation

It was not until 1909 that mass democracy, in the sense of the right to vote, arrived in Sweden, at least for adult males; women were granted suffrage in 1918. Technically, executive power still lay largely in the hands of the king, who chose the prime minister. However, the choices made by the newly enfranchised electorate at the polls soon rendered this a hollow prerogative. Any attempt to exercise that prerogative in a manner contrary to the dominant sentiments of the lower house would most likely provoke a political crisis that might jeopardize the monarchy. By appointing a prime minister enjoying the support of Liberals and Social Democrats in 1917, the king tacitly recognized the principle of parliamentary responsibility of the government. Without much upheaval or a formal amendment to the constitution, Sweden had become a parliamentary monarchy as well as a mass democracy.

Although getting a later start, the other two Scandinavian countries, if anything, moved more briskly toward modern democracy. Despite its semicolonial status, Norway adopted a far more progressive constitution in 1814 than what Sweden chose in 1809. Sweden allowed Norway to retain its constitution at the price of recognizing the Swedish monarch as the supreme ruler of the union, which Norway did until 1905. Denmark meanwhile installed a two-house parliament with the adoption of the 1849 constitution. The right to vote was vastly expanded in 1901, ushering in the parliamentary system and ending conservative rule.

If you can't beat them, let them join you. The ease with which the three Scandinavian countries transformed themselves from feudal monarchies in the seventeenth century to mass democracies in the twentieth century is truly remarkable. This was not simply a matter of naturelike evolution, but a matter of conscious choices of political actors. Elites, that is, groups with political power, now and then have to decide whether to share some of their power with groups demanding a say in government, or a larger share than heretofore accorded them. If the elites refuse, they have to be prepared to defend their power with oppressive means, if necessary. In doing so, they provoke possible revolution and risk losing their power altogether. In the three Scandinavian countries, the behavior of the haves demonstrated an unusual ability and willingness to make concessions to have-nots without surrendering power altogether. Over the past two hundred years the institutions of the monarchy have proved adaptable enough to accommodate the demands for reform before the revolutionary storms could gather force.

The inherent pluralism of the four-estate order, with the monarch as the supreme broker, must be credited in large part with that success. It created a political framework in which no single group could expect to dominate the political process. There was simply no homogeneous elite that wielded all the power. Even in the estate of the nobility there was an element of pluralism, owing to the considerable stratification of titles. Three hundred years before the advent of party competition and the ascent of the mass public, politics in Scandinavia was a process of competition that was accepted by the privileged few who were allowed into the game.

In such an established pattern of orderly competition for power, some parts of the elite, in an effort to strengthen their own sides, will try to enlist additional support from outside, and those outside, strong enough to voice demands, will look toward some on the inside to do their bidding and facilitate their inclusion. What is important to realize is that such a process lends itself to change by adaptation. Once competition was regularized on the inside, the circle of participants could be widened without abandoning the old system.

COLLECTIVE ACTION IN A COMMUNAL SOCIETY

The account of Scandinavian politics thus far may have a familiar ring, echoing familiar accounts of British politics. There, too, we find evidence of piecemeal and peaceful adaptation to new economic circumstances and political demands under the umbrella of a monarchy prepared to facilitate change. Yet, as we come to the main actors of democratic politics we are forced to take note of startling differences in their roles and relationships.

Poor but Free

One of the distinctive characteristics of Scandinavia has been the role of an independent peasantry. In Sweden especially, the nobility typically did not own the vast amount of arable land, but instead saw its main role in administration and the military. The peasants on the land typically were not serfs. They were not subject to the jurisdiction of a local lord, tilling his land and having no political voice. In Sweden, royal policy encouraged the ownership of land by freeholding peasants, often to the chagrin of the nobility that would have liked to claim such lands. It was not unusual for the Swedish king to enlist the peasantry as his ally against the nobility.

During the seventeenth century, through what became known as the Great Reductions, the peasants gained possession of half of all arable land. Many plots, to be sure, were not especially efficient economically, but owning your own land meant representation in one of the four estates of the Riksdag. Thus a large part of the Swedish population had a political voice and was able to select leaders that could play the political game with king, nobility, and the other estates. Viewed this way, the politics of that era may not seem to be such a far cry from contemporary politics.

With the political reforms of the late eighteenth and nineteenth centuries, agrarian influence reached its peak. The directly elected houses of parliament typically witnessed the dominance of independent farmers, not of urban-commercial interests. Meanwhile the nobility, with its entrenched position in the administration, held on to control of the upper house. This did not change until the reforms of the early twentieth century that recognized belatedly the consequences of industrialization.

Late but Not Little

Industrialization in Scandinavia arrived later than it did in Britain, France, or Germany; not any sooner, actually, than in Russia. Agriculture still employed over 70 percent of the Swedish population by 1870. Sweden did not really begin to industrialize in earnest until after 1880. But then it did so at a furious pace. By 1910 less than half the people earned a living from the land. Meanwhile the population also grew rapidly, as did agricultural productivity, one of the side effects of industrialization being the rationalization of agricultural production.

A heavy flow of emigration helped alleviate some of the resulting hardship. From 1860 to 1910, nearly 1 million Swedes settled in the United States, at times as many as half the natural increase of the population and far more than the number that migrated from the countryside to towns. For Norway the figures are similar. It was a case of "flesh and blood in America" rather than "skin and bones at home."

Many of the goods produced by the rapidly churning industrial machine in Sweden went for exports, from paper and wood products to steel ingots. Industrialization fed on two plentiful natural resources in Sweden, trees and iron, which also proved helpful for the building of railroads. Given the wide geographical dispersal of the key natural resources, industrialization in Sweden did not lead to a heavy concentration of the working class in urban ghettos. Most industrial enterprises were of modest size and situated in small communities.

Like many new things, industrialization holds out a promise and a curse. It promises an escape from the poverty and confinement of village life but it also deprives people of a sense of security nourished nearly undisturbed in village communities for many centuries. Although village life was by no means idyllic and bountiful, it endured on the strength of a communal spirit bolstered by a common religion. Industrialization turned the countries of Scandinavia into affluent societies, but it somehow did not destroy the communal spirit. That spirit still thrives in the urban societies that the Scandinavian countries have become, although religion has little to do with it anymore.

The Organized Society

To an astonishing degree, citizens of the Scandinavian countries are organized in groups. The classic economic interests—farmers, business, and labor—have long-standing organizations that leave few members uncovered. In Sweden, over 90 percent of blue-collar workers belong to a labor union, the highest percentage in western democracies; Denmark and Norway lag somewhat behind that level, but still exceed Britain, France, and Germany as well as the United States (see Figure 36.2). Blue-collar workers belong to unions within the labor federation called the *Landsorganisationen* (LO), founded at the end of the nineteenth century.

In recent years, unionization has also caught up with the growing white-collar ranks in the

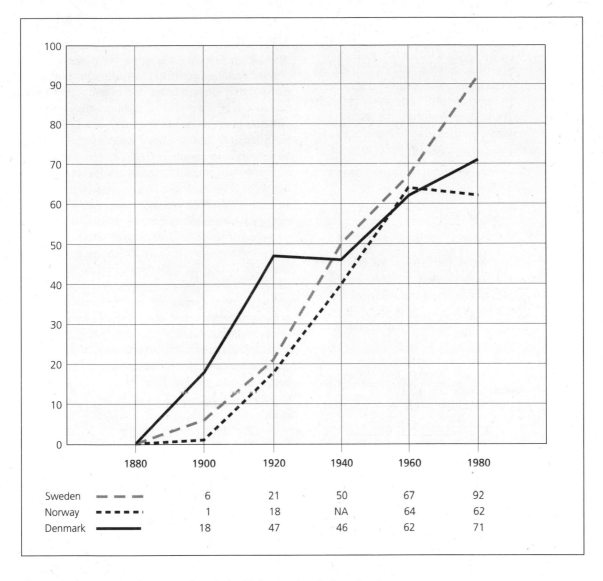

		1880	1900	1920	1940	1960	1980
Sweden	– – –		6	21	50	67	92
Norway	•••••		1	18	NA	64	62
Denmark	——		18	47	46	62	71

Figure 36.2 Growth of Unionization of Blue-Collar Workers in Scandinavia. Source: Esping-Andersen, *Politics Against Markets*, p. 64.

work force, though largely outside the LO orbit. In Sweden, again the most advanced case, over 70 percent of white-collar workers belong to a union, most of whom are affiliated with the TCO federation (Central Organization of Salaried Employees).

The key class-related groups maintain close ties to political parties, their patrons in the political arena. The tie between the LO and the Social Democrats is institutionalized in Sweden by means of "collective affiliation" of a union with the party. In plain English, that means the union members are all members of the party as well. However, unlike in Britain, the union leaders cannot influence party politics through a bloc vote of their respective membership. Farmers' associations maintain a close though less formalized rapport with agrarian parties; and business associations, with conservative parties. There is no pretense of any of those groups' being independent of party politics.

Settling Class Warfare Swedish-style

Even in Scandinavia, the arrival of labor organizations was not greeted warmly by business. Industrial relations until the mid-1930s were known more for strikes and lockouts than for the social peace one now associates with these countries. To forestall government regulation of business-labor relations, in the 1930s the leaders of the labor unions and the Swedish Employers' Federation arranged to meet in the Baltic resort of Saltsjöbaden. It took them nearly two years to reach the famous Saltsjöbaden Agreements in 1938, as the rest of Europe braced for war with Germany and Italy.

That deal deserves to be noted not only for the rules it laid down for collective bargaining and for the far-reaching effect on industrial unrest, but also for the ability of social adversaries to transform a relationship of distrust and animosity into one of trust and compromise.The Saltsjöbaden Agreements laid the foundation for a system of collective bargaining between business and labor that had two noteworthy features: (1) it was centralized and (2) it did not envision government interference. Both sides guaranteed that their respective rank and files would abide by deals reached at the top. They also agreed on provisions regarding layoffs and rehirings. Many observers believe that the Saltsjöbaden Agreements ushered in an age of unprecedented labor peace in Sweden.

The Spirit of Saltsjöbaden

We had our first meeting in the SAF [Swedish Employers' Federation] offices in Stockholm, but soon realized that we had to be able to get away from everyday political and labor disputes, telephone calls and the rest. . . . We settled on the Grand Hotel in Saltsjöbaden because it was close enough to be able to send people in to get material and yet far enough so we would spend our leisure time our there . . . It was absolutely necessary to create an atmosphere that was free from politics and ideology, a business-minded atmosphere that concentrated on practical and reasonable solutions. . . . We grew together out there. Of course, there were one or two on both sides who had difficulty adapting themselves. I remember at the beginning one of our men came up to me. He felt ill at ease and worried to see that his colleagues had apparently dropped titles with the labor delegates and were calling them by their first names. After he got over this initial uncertainty he fitted in just fine.

Source: Gustaf Soderlund, president of SAF in the 1930s, as quoted in Frederic Fleisher, *The New Sweden: The Challenge of a Disciplined Democracy* (New York: McKay, 1967) pp. 80–81.

MANY PARTIES ARE CALLED . . .

Although their political development seems to have much in common with Britain, the Scandinavian countries have spawned party systems more like the ones of France and Germany of an earlier era. In Denmark, the array of parties is downright bewildering, and the names of many parties are more confusing than enlightening to outsiders. Yet the Scandinavian countries have not been known for the paralysis and instability of government typically associated with multiparty systems. This raises some intriguing questions about the conditions of political stability. But before engaging in that discussion let us sketch the background of the Scandinavian party systems.

Electoral System

No doubt, the use of proportional representation as an electoral system has something to do with party diversity. Unlike Britain or the United States, none of the Scandinavian countries uses the first-past-the-post system of electing one representative per district. Instead, when universal and equal voting rights were granted in the early twentieth century, those countries all adopted some method of allocating seats in parliament to the political parties in proportion to the votes cast for them.

It may come as a surprise that it was the established forces who pressed for the proportional method, not the newly aspiring forces demanding political rights. The adoption of proportional representation in conjunction with mass voting thus marks another one of the historical compromises of Scandinavian politics. It calmed the fears of the ruling forces of being swept aside in the new era of mass participation, while guaranteeing the forces on the outside a share of parliamentary representation commensurate with their popular strength.

The party system that took shape in the aftermath of that compromise some eighty years ago has survived remarkably well to this day. Some names have changed, to be sure, and so have ideological positions as well as electoral constituencies, but the parties have preserved much of their original identities. What is more, in none of the three Scandinavian countries has a new party succeeded in becoming the dominant one. Proportional representation has proved to be a good preservative of the party system of the early 1900s. It has allowed those parties to adapt deftly to new issues.

Main Cleavages of Party Conflict

However much the rules of the electoral system may either magnify or compress political divisions, those rules nevertheless do not create them. What prompts the creation of parties are

The Center-Periphery Cleavage in Norway

The provinces resented the dominance of the capital. The awakening rural communities resisted the influence of an alien and foreign-oriented urban culture. The peasantry found it more and more difficult to accept the standards set by the officials and the patrician establishment; the urban language, the *riksmal*, so remote from the inherited dialects of the countryside, the rationalist Lutheranism of the State Church, the foreign manners, the tolerant morals, and the convivial drinking prevalent in the open urban society. . . . Mobilization did not lead to cultural integration; instead it produced a widespread breakdown in human communication and generated a number of "counter-cultures" essentially hostile to the established standards and models of the original elite.

Source: Stein Rokkan, "Norway: Numerical Democracy and Corporate Pluralism," in Robert Dahl, ed., *Political Opposition in Western Democracies* (New Haven and London: Yale University Press, 1966), pp. 76–77.

social divisions (*cleavages*, as they are commonly called by European electoral scholars) that upset or excite significant groups of people. Parties are products of the dominant cleavages when people get the right to vote and leaders forge organizational machines to mobilize the newly eligible populace. Political parties position themselves in such a way as to capitalize on support for one side of a particular conflict.

Scandinavian political parties are often placed at the intersection of two dimensions of conflict. One of them seems distinctively Scandinavian: the center-periphery cleavage, pitting the peasantry in the countryside against the political elite in the nation's capital city. It is rooted in the struggle between the peasant estate and the nobility, with echoes from the battles between the dominant forces of the two houses of the nineteenth-century parliament.

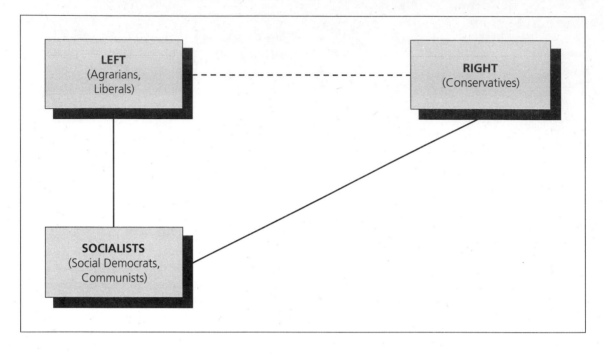

Figure 36.3 The Triangle of Party Competition.

The two political groupings, *protoparties* as they may be called, arising out of that conflict adopted the labels Right and Left. While partly economic, their conflict went to the heart of cultural concerns, including even religion and language in Norway.

Cutting across this center-periphery axis is the social class dimension, pitting working class against middle class. This cleavage realigned the party system in the wake of the suffrage extensions in the early twentieth century. It gave rise to Social Democratic parties in all three Scandinavian countries, and rearranged the existing parties. To emphasize the essential feature of the new party system (in a way that oversimplifies the complex partisan changes), let us view it as a triangular competition, as depicted in Figure 36.3.

Industrialization and the rise of a powerful Social Democratic Party did little to close the gap between the Right and Left of yesterday. Far from it. The adoption of proportional rep-

resentation did not help fuse some erstwhile adversaries and create a single "bourgeois" (nonsocialist) counterweight to the emerging Social Democrats. Instead, the largely agrarian Left underwent several splits, too complicated to relate in detail here. Suffice it to say that the Scandinavian party systems typically comprise the following political parties, using generic labels: Conservatives, Agrarians, Liberals, Social Democrats, and Left-Socialists. Some newcomers in recent years include tax-revolt Progress parties, religiously oriented Christian parties, and, most recently, the antiforeigner New Democracy Party in Sweden.

The Parties

Among the Scandinavian countries, Sweden is the one with the most compact party system. We will use it here as an example to delineate the basic divisions of party conflict and the identities of the parties. It is simplest to view Sweden's party politics as a battle between a socialist bloc and a bourgeois bloc, with the Left Party (formerly the Communists) and the Social Democrats forming the one bloc and the Agrarians, Liberals, and Conservatives the other. Note, however, that this is more a shortcut to simplify a complex world than an indication of party behavior in practice. Old rivalries and distinctive clienteles keep the "bourgeois" parties at arm's length from one another.

The Conservatives. Known since 1969 as the Moderates (and in Norway literally as the "Right"), the Conservatives have their roots in the nobility of the preindustrial society. They were the ones who controlled the upper house of parliament in the second half of the nineteenth century as well as the country's administration. Their main historical adversary was the peasantry, which then gained control over the lower house of parliament. Officially the Conservative Party was founded in 1904. Formed in defense of an essentially aristocratic monarchy, the party nevertheless accepted political reform such as universal suffrage, and has survived remarkably well in the age of democracy.

It subsequently became the adopted party of the entrepreneurial middle class and today is identified primarily as the party of business and free enterprise. This is more remarkable than it may seem, for the old Conservatives, through their dominance of the state bureaucracy and army, were quite favorable to state intervention. Indeed, the party is at present "conservative" in the sense of the word familiar to American ears. And that goes for its Danish and Norwegian counterparts as well. The Conservative leaders of the 1980s were ideological cousins of Margaret Thatcher and Ronald Reagan.

The Liberals. Currently known as the People's Party in Sweden, the Liberals derive from what was known as the Left in the nineteenth cen-

tury. Organizationally, the party took shape during the struggle for parliamentary rule and suffrage extension late in the nineteenth century. It was officially founded in 1902. The key adversary of the Liberals then was the conservative elite, which was resisting such change and organized its political party two years later. But with the big issue of the constitutional order long settled, that animosity is barely a historical reminiscence.

Both are now parties of the better-off middle class, with the Liberals perhaps more prone to proposals for social reform. While sometimes favorable toward Social Democratic policies, the Liberals can be counted on to raise their voice to defend individual rights and to challenge sweeping state intervention in the economy. In that regard, they are not primarily "liberal" in the American sense of the term. Of all the parties, the Liberals lack a clear interest group connection and a distinctive electoral profile. In Denmark, the party actually comes in two versions, one of which better fits the mold of the agrarian parties in Norway and Sweden.

The Agrarians. Now officially known as the Center, this party has deep roots in the Left. It goes back to the representatives of the independent peasantry that constituted the fourth estate of the old Swedish parliament and controlled the lower house of the bicameral parliament of 1866. Back then its main adversary was the establishment dominated by the nobility. This antagonism was rooted in the "center-periphery" cleavage, an urban-rural division with overtones of cultural chasms that have never been entirely overcome. It has proved most troublesome for Norway, where some resentment over the long domination by Denmark and later Sweden still lingers.

Formally founded in 1921 through a merger of existing parties with agrarian appeals, the Farmers' Party, as it was then known, could count on a firm group foundation in the electorate. This has allowed the party to survive

An Uncompromising Center Party

No government post is so important to me that I will hedge on my conviction in this matter. . . .I will not take part in a government that starts one more reactor.

Source: Thorbjorn Fälldin, Swedish Center Party; quoted in Hugh Heclo and Henrik Madsen, *Policy and Politics in Swedish Principled Pragmatism* (Philadelphia: Temple University Press, 1987), p. 42.

but not exactly to thrive. Its natural base, after all, has been shrinking inexorably; fewer than one in ten now live off the land. What has helped the party remain a considerable force and even attract the political spotlight is its espousal of new issues such as the environment and decentralization. In particular, this party took a determined stand on an issue alarming western publics in the 1970s: nuclear power. Under the leadership of Thorbjorn Fälldin, the Swedish Center Party embarked on a crusade against an energy source viewed by others as the panacea for a Sweden overly dependent on foreign oil.

True to its roots as the party of the simple life in the periphery and of protest against heavy-handed bureaucrats and sophisticated technocrats in the capital, the party went to the Swedish voters with an absolute "No" on this issue. More than any other existing party, the Center was uniquely positioned to take advantage of the "greening" of politics, given the party's concern for ecology and its aversion to large-scale technology. In the 1970s, the Center improved its electoral showing to the point that, together with the other two nonsocialist parties, it finally ousted the ruling Social Democrats in 1976. However helpful the nuclear issue may have been for displacing the Socialists, it proved too fissionable for the "bourgeois" coalition, which soon afterward exploded. Swedish politics entered into an era of middling government trying to muddle through.

The Social Democrats. In Sweden, as in the other Scandinavian countries and almost everywhere else (except in the United States), industrialization spawned viable socialist parties. Moreover, the message of Karl Marx fell on receptive ears, and the model of a working-class party established in Germany, called the Social Democratic Party, was eagerly embraced in Scandinavia. At its founding in 1889, the Swedish Social Democratic Labor Party vowed to end the exploitation and misery of the proletariat under capitalism and to create a socialist society.

However revolutionary that sounded, the party at that time lacked the key prerequisite of a political party: voters. The party's mission was addressed to a population that was almost entirely shut out of politics, given the restrictions on the Right to vote in force then. That might actually have been a blessing in disguise for the newly formed Socialist Party. Why? Because it meant that none of the existing parties made serious attempts to woo the working class. That clientele remained to be tapped.

The Socialist Party thus pressed for universal voting rights, a goal that was also endorsed by the Liberals, who were attempting to displace the conservative elite. A general strike by an increasingly well-unionized working class raised the stakes of the suffrage struggle and hinted at threats of revolution. With the gates for male electoral participation fully opened in 1909, it did not take the Socialist Party ten years to win the largest share of votes in elections. That put the party in a position, with help from the Liberals, effectively to institute parliamentary rule and by 1918 extend voting rights to women.

There can be little doubt that the extension of suffrage so close on the heels of rapid industrialization gave the young Socialist Party—which was actually older than the nonsocialist parties—maximum advantage in rallying what it considered its natural constituency. The other parties proved neither willing nor able to compete effectively for this vast new electoral resource. For the rest of the twentieth century they would pay the price for this lack of will or ability. True, they had managed to survive the entry of the working class into the political arena, but they would have to sit on the sidelines for the most part from now on.

Like the Democrats in the United States, Sweden's Social Democrats happened not to be in power at the time of the Great Depression of the late 1920s. They were thus in the fortunate position to take advantage of the ruling parties' misfortune. In 1932, 30 percent of the labor force was out of work in Sweden. The election that year put the Social Democrats in office, just as it did the Democrats in the United States. In Sweden this was the beginning of more than fifty years of Social Democratic rule. In the United States, it was the beginning of an almost equally long control of the U.S. Congress by the Democrats.

Sweden's Social Democrats thus have had plenty of opportunity to put their ideological stamp on policy. In appraising that record, it is as important to note what they did not do, as well as what they did. They did not nationalize private industry, introduce state planning of the economy, or precipitate a political or social revolution. True, their control of parliament was tenuous, often requiring support from others. But even when the party held a solid majority, it did not attempt to usher in a brave new socialist world overnight.

Instead the party concentrated on achieving full employment while striving for an ever more perfect welfare state. These were the ingredients of Social Democratic success at the polls. More than anything else, the party engineered Sweden's recovery from the hardships of the Depression. Since that time, social democracy has spelled "prosperity" in Scandinavia.

This is not a party inspired by socialist dogmas and sounding the call of class warfare, but a party of pragmatic reform with a Scandinavian twist. Its longtime leader and prime minister (1932–1946), Per Hansson, identified the party's mission with the vision of a "people's home," to provide the individual in today's society with the same sense of security and belonging that an (ideal) family does for its members. However appealing this vision may be, it entails a commitment to government intervention that at every step may look innocuous but that reaches far and deep when allowed to accumulate unchallenged for more than half a century.

Whatever the appeal of its ideals, the Social Democratic Party has ensured better than any of its rivals that it can win where it counts most in a democracy: at the polls. Thanks to the collective affiliation of unions with the Social Democrats, this party can rely on roughly 1 million members, almost one of every five Swedish voters. At election time, thousands of officeholders in the labor unions and government bureaucracy provide active help. A score of party newspapers sound the party message, while numerous private associations affiliated with the party disseminate it among their members. To be sure, not every

Social Democratic Therapy

In the Social Democratic vision, politics is a kind of therapeutic exercise. Its mission is the slow, careful eradication of disease and the establishment of a regimen of good health in society. It is always to be done with the patient's consent, but also with the recognition that some unpleasant medicine and restrictions may need to be accepted because they are good for people.

Source: Hugh Heclo and Henrik Madsen, *Policy and Politics in Sweden: Principled Pragmatism* (Philadelphia: Temple University Press, 1987), p. 27.

member is an active one; in fact, many resent their union's collective affiliation with the party, but it provides the Social Democratic Party with a core constituency unmatched by any of its competitors.

The Left Party. A significant force to the left of the Social Democrats in Sweden is a party that used to be known as the Communist Party, but since the early 1990s calls itself simply the Left Party. A legacy of the 1917 Bolshevik Revolution in Russia, the Swedish Communist Party long accepted the Soviet Union as a model for Sweden. In the late 1960s, however, the party began to sound more independent, joining the chorus of the New Left that swelled among student radicals and activists of new social movements. Now the voice of educated discontent, the party has shed much of its blue-collar image. In so doing, the Swedish Communists avoided the fate of their counterparts in the other Scandinavian countries. In Norway and Denmark, left-wing socialist parties captured much of the new left ideology. As a result, they relegated the Communist parties in their respective countries to insignificance. That, however, came as little relief to the Social Democrats, who found it no easier to accommodate the left socialists than the Communists before.

The Voters' Choices

Scandinavians are avid voters. In Sweden, which again leads the field, voting turnout hovers above the 90 percent mark. Like so many other things, the turnout curve shows a steady upswing since the 1920s. With present rates in the upper and lower 80 percent range respectively, Denmark and Norway are not far behind Sweden. This high level of electoral mobilization, one suspects, is not so much a matter of excitement with the candidates and issues of the specific campaigns as a matter of so many individuals belonging to social groups with a political and partisan flavor. It is evidence of successful collective action, especially among social strata that otherwise would be much less inclined to go to the polls.

In all three Scandinavian countries the respective Social Democratic parties (called the Labor Party in Norway) capture the lion's share of electoral mobilization. In election after election, they gain more votes than any other single party. That has been the "law" of electoral politics in Scandinavia for more than fifty years, although the law has come under increasing challenge in the past twenty-five years. The story of Scandinavian voting since then has been the erosion of Social Democratic strength. The party finds itself squeezed between more radical parties on its left and centrist and revitalized conservative parties on its right.

Especially in Denmark, something has been "rotten" with the party's electoral performance. Here the Social Democrats have lost much ground in fierce competition with left-wing rivals. Those prickly thorns in their left side have stung the Social Democrats especially painfully over foreign policy issues such as Denmark's NATO membership. The issue of NATO membership has also cut into the support of the party's counterpart in Norway. Not being a member of this Alliance, Sweden has been spared the fallout from that issue.

In Denmark and Norway, the debate on joining the European Community further scrambled the party system in the 1970s. Opposition to such a move grew so strong in Norway that a referendum was called, resulting in Norway's withdrawal from the Community. In Denmark, moreover, disenchantment with the cost of the welfare state led to the formation of an antitax party under Mogens Glistrup (the share of that party is included under the Conservative column in Table 36.2). Sweden, in turn, experienced a sharp rise of support for the (agrarian) Center Party in the 1970s over such issues as nuclear power. For a number of rea-

Table 36.2 VOTER SUPPORT FOR FOUR PARTIES (BLOCS) IN SELECTED ELECTIONS IN SWEDEN, DENMARK, AND NORWAY (PERCENT)

	Left Wing	Social Democratic	Liberal/ Center	Conservative
Sweden				
1948	6%	46%	35%	12%
1960	4	48	31	16
1973	5	44	36	14
1985	5	45	27	21
1991	5	38	24	22
Denmark				
1947	7%	40%	39%	12%
1960	7	42	29	21
1973	11	26	38	25
1984	15	32	25	27
1990	8	37	27	22
Norway				
1949	6%	46%	30%	18%
1961	5	47	28	20
1973	11	35	30	22
1985	5	41	18	34
1993	8	37	29	23

Source: Ole Borre, "Critical Electoral Change in Scandinavia," in Russell J. Dalton, Scott C. Flanagan, and Paul Allen Beck (eds.), *Electoral Change in Advanced Industrial Democracies* (Princeton: Princeton University Press, 1984), pp. 333, 363; *Der Fischer Weltalmanach '87* (Frankfurt: Fischer Verlag); *Keesings Record of World Events*.

sons, some quite diverse, the 1970s offered gloomy prospects for the future of social democracy in Scandinavia.

The performance of the economy did little to help. While less affected than many other western countries, Scandinavia also experienced economic setbacks during the worldwide recessions of the mid-1970s and early 1980s. Economic growth slowed, while inflation and unemployment both rose. As in Britain and the United States, conservative parties scored significant electoral gains with their promises of new recipes for dealing with economic stagnation and decline. Their gains in

Scandinavia, however, seem to have come largely at the expense of Center-Liberal parties, as Social Democratic parties have recovered some ground.

The Fraying of Class Ties

One of the remarkable features of change in the parties' electoral foundations is the blurring of the class division. The Social Democratic parties used to have the nearly undivided attention of the working class. A vote for this kind of party was a reflex of class identification, unimpeded by concerns about either the personalities at the head of the parties or political issues. By the same token, the nonsocialist parties together enjoyed a monopoly over the middle class, however fiercely they fought with each other over different chunks of that class.

Until 1960, over 70 percent of the working class typically voted Social Democratic, compared to less than 20 percent of the middle class (including white-collar employees). That 50-point gap in class voting has shrunk in half by now. For the Social Democrats that is partly good news, partly bad. The bad news for the party is the loss of support in the working class, which is also shrinking in size. The good news for the party is the gain in the middle class, especially among the growing ranks of white-collar voters. The Swedish Social Democrats show the most favorable balance sheet, while their Danish cousins have done least well in this type of transaction.

For the party system the loosening of the old class alignment spells increasing volatility. The parties cannot count anymore on their hard core, their strongholds, to deliver comfortable returns regardless of the particular circumstances of each election. This gives more leverage to short-term forces connected with new issues and leading personalities. Furthermore, evaluations of party performance in critical areas like the economy, social security, and foreign policy are not likely to be reflexes conditioned by a voter's party identification. The electoral verdict no longer carries the clear group message it did before.

Still, it is important to emphasize that the old alignments have not been obliterated, nor are they close to extinction. Except perhaps for the Popular Socialists in Denmark, no new party has caught on with large segments of the electorate, however spectacular its early showing (for example, the antitax Progress parties in Denmark and later in Norway, or Sweden's anti-immigrant New Democracy Party in

1991). While much has changed, the Social Democrats are still the single largest party in all three of the Scandinavian countries; and the nonsocialist parties have not "realigned" into a cohesive alternative to them. They are as jealously distinctive as ever, mired in divisions as old as great-grandparents. What is perhaps most astonishing is the parties' instinct for adaptation and survival, for making comebacks after setbacks.

... But Only One Party Is Chosen to Govern

In constitutional terms, politics in the Scandinavian countries is guided by the rules of the parliamentary system. The government is headed by a prime minister, who is responsible to parliament. In the three countries considered here, parliament today consists of only one chamber, Sweden being the last to abolish its upper house in the 1970s. For all practical purposes, a prime minister can stay in power until and unless a parliamentary majority expressly registers its lack of support by way of a no-confidence vote. In case of a vacancy in the prime minister's office, it has been typically the right of the monarch (the speaker of parliament in Sweden nowadays) to ask a promising candidate to form a government and then to appoint him or her. As always in such situations, practical considerations make it advisable to pick a candidate with a good chance of commanding enough support in parliament, lest the appointee immediately be ousted by parliament.

At the same time, the choice of a prime minister is not necessarily a foregone conclusion. The reason is that in Scandinavian elections each party typically receives a share of seats in parliament proportional to its share of the votes cast in elections. This kind of electoral system does not easily reward a single party with a

Table 36.3 THE GOVERNING PARTIES IN SCANDINAVIAN GOVERNMENTS

Year	Sweden				Norway				Denmark			
	L	S	C/L	K	L	S	C/L	K	L	S	C/L	K
1946		x				x					x	
•		x				x					x	
•		x				x				x		
•		x				x				x		
1950		x				x				x		
•		x	x			x					x	x
•		x	x			x					x	x
•		x	x			x					x	x
•		x	x			x				x		
1955		x	x			x				x		
•		x	x			x				x		
•		x	x			x				x	x	
•		x				x				x	x	
•		x				x				x	x	
1960		x				x				x	x	
•		x				x				x	x	
•		x				x				x	x	
•		x				x				x	x	
•		x				x				x	x	
1965		x				x				x		
•		x					x	x		x		
•		x					x	x		x		
•		x					x	x			x	x
•		x					x	x			x	x
1970		x					x	x			x	x
•		x				x					x	x
•		x				x				x		
•		x					x			x		
•		x				x					x	
1975		x				x					x	
•		x				x				x		
•			x	x		x				x		
•			x	x		x				x		
•			x			x				x	x	

Table 36.3 Continued

Year	Sweden				Norway				Denmark			
	L	S	C/L	K	L	S	C/L	K	L	S	C/L	K
1980			x	x		x				x		
•			x			x				x		
•			x					x		x		
•		x					x	x			x	x
•		x					x	x			x	x
1985		x					x	x			x	x
•		x				x					x	x
•		x				x					x	x
•		x				x					x	x
•		x				x					x	x
1990		x					x	x			x	x
•		x				x					x	x
•			x	x		x					x	x
•			x	x		x				x	x	

Key: L = Left-wing parties, S = Social Democrats, C/L = Center/Liberals, K = Conservatives.

Source: Alastair Thomas, "Denmark: Coalitions and Minority Governments," in Eric Browne and John Dreijmanis (eds.), *Government Coalitions in Western Democracies* (New York: Longman, 1982), p. 118; *Keesings Contemporary Archives; Keesings Record of World Events*.

majority of seats for winning the most votes. When no single party emerges from elections with a seat majority, which would give that party an indisputable claim to govern, such a majority must be found by agreements among several parties. This can take the form of explicit coalitions, with each participating party getting control of some ministries and a say in cabinet deliberations. Or else it can be done in a more informal way, by letting one party form the government, even though it lacks a majority, while other parties pledge support without claiming portfolios or a say in cabinet deliberations.

For more than sixty years now, the Social Democrats have won a plurality of votes in Scandinavian elections, but not typically a majority of seats. Only in Norway have they enjoyed a lengthy stretch of majority control. Yet even without firm parliamentary majorities, the Social Democratic parties have managed to control the government for most of the last sixty years (see Table 36.3). The Danish Social Democrats came to power in 1929 with support from (radical) Liberals, while their Swedish cousins did so in 1932 with help from the Agrarians. Both renewed their respective connections occasionally in the 1950s and 1960s. And even when not in formal coalition agreements with those allies, social democracy in both countries could count on their tacit support—or at least, on the assurance that

There is no other country in which women play such a large and highly visible role in both national politics and government as Norway, where the prime minister and the leaders of the opposition parties are women. Prime Minister Gro Harlem Brundtland meets with U.S. President Bill Clinton in Washington, D.C., 1993.

they would not join the opposition on a no-confidence motion. So long as that was the case, the notion of a "bourgeois" coalition remained a fiction.

Norway

It was only in Norway that under the solitary, though long, rule of the Social Democrats (called the Labor Party) the nonsocialist parties found common ground in their poor and brutish life out of power. In 1965, they won the election and a majority of seats in the *Storting*, the Norwegian Parliament. They proceeded to form a government that endured until the next election, but soon afterward split in the middle of the parliamentary term, less from the ham-

mer blows of the out-of-power Social Democrats than from the corrosive effect of internal bickering.

Since the historic turnover of power in 1965, Social Democrats have traded places with nonsocialist governments several more times in Norway. But elections rarely precipitated those trades. More often, issues arising with special vehemence, like the debate over membership in the European Community in the early 1970s, and again in the late 1980s, wreaked havoc on the parties in the middle of their term in government. One thing was sure: no gilded age of "bourgeois" rule would supplant the iron age of social democracy. While no longer fiction, bourgeois coalitions were quite fragile and fissionable. The political pendulum had begun to swing frequently but uneasily.

Poul Schlüter, who became Denmark's first Conservative prime minister in 80 years, with Uffe Ellemann-Jensen of the Liberal Party, his longtime foreign minister. In Norway, the Conservatives captured the prime minister's office in 1989, and in Sweden in 1991.

coming capitalism and pro-western orientation in foreign policy) precluded a formal coalition. Yet at the same time these left-wing socialists would shrink from lending a hand to attempts by the class enemies to oust the Social Democrats from power. Rather a Social Democratic government that they can harass and hold to the fire than a nonsocialist government that they cannot blackmail.

Perhaps the most striking feature of parliamentary politics in Norway is the high degree of female participation and influence. The current prime minister is a woman, Gro Harlem Brundtland, who belongs to the Labor Party. Like Margaret Thatcher, a contemporary though partisan adversary, she is a three-term prime minister (1981, 1986–1989, and 1990–). Dr. Brundtland, a Harvard-trained physician, is not a lone figure of inspiration for Norwegian women. Nearly four of ten representatives in the Norwegian Parliament are female. What is more, the leaders of two major nonsocialist parties are women. Hence, should the Labor Party fall from power, the next prime minister of Norway would most likely be a woman as well, Anne Inger Lahnstein of the Center Party or Kaci Kullman Five of the Conservatives.

Sweden

In Sweden, the seemingly perennial rule of the Social Democrats has by now come to a halt twice. The 1976 election gave the combination of Center, Liberals, and Conservatives a majority of seats. Like their counterparts in Norway a decade earlier, they proceeded to form a government, with the prime minister coming from the Center Party. And just as in Norway, the coalition soon disintegrated, first over the inability of the participants to come to grips with the nuclear power issue, and then over how to deal with the economic crisis of the early 1980s.

When the Social Democrats returned to power they typically formed a minority government. Their margin of security came from a party on the left sideline. The Left Socialists would not formally join the Social Democrats in government, but neither would they add their weight to the "bourgeois" opposition. Their dissatisfaction with the moderate tone of social democracy (lack of radicalism in over-

The spectacle of the indecisive and incompetent nonsocialist alternative boosted the public stock of the out-of-power Social Democrats to an extent well beyond what they could have devised themselves. "We told you so," was all they had to say. The memory of the Social Democrats rescuing Sweden from the scourge of the Depression in the 1930s contrasted sharply with the economic deterioration under the present-day "bourgeois" government. And so, in the 1982 election the Social Democrats beat their three-party replacement. They returned to power as a minority government with the tacit help of the Left Party.

But in an age of affluence, economic discontent and misgivings over an ever-expanding public sector drove the Social Democrats from power, again, in the 1991 election. The new prime minister, Carl Bildt of the Conservatives (now known as the Moderates), promised "more freedom of choice and opportunities" to a country where taxes account for close to 60 percent of the gross domestic product, the highest in the western world.

Denmark

The task of government formation has proved more formidable in Denmark than in Sweden or Norway. Governments in Copenhagen change hands more frequently and stay in office less long than their counterparts in Oslo and Stockholm. Still, the Social Democrats managed to form governments for most of the time until 1982. Often, however, they did so as a single party without a majority. In the early 1960s their hold on government weakened as gains by left-wing socialists eroded electoral support for the Social Democrats.

The rise of left-wing socialists poses a strategic dilemma for the Social Democrats. If they try to accommodate this new Left, they risk the loss of the old Left—that is, the (radical) Liberals—on whose support they have come to rely.

Conservative Renewal in Denmark

[Conservative Prime Minister Poul] Schlüter has said that Karl Marx is dead. I know that. He died in 1883. But what Schlüter is presenting is Adam Smith's philosophy of the free market packed in cellophane and presented with charm.

Anker Jorgensen, Social Democrat and former prime minister of Denmark (quoted in *The New York Times*, September 7, 1987).

Unlike their counterparts in Norway and Sweden, the Danish Social Democrats lost so much electoral ground in the 1970s that even tacit support from the left-wing socialists no longer provided them with a majority, nor would support from the (radical) Liberals. Liberal support, in any event, was not forthcoming as long as the Social Democrats continued their courtship of the left-wing socialists. The prospects for Social Democratic rule in Denmark appeared gloomy indeed.

For more than a decade (1982–1993), a Conservative held the prime minister's office, Poul Schlüter, the first one of that party to do so in Denmark in 80 years. His own party joined with three liberal-centrist parties to form what has been dubbed the "four-leaf clover coalition." Nevertheless the coalition required outside help from supportive parties in parliament who declined to join the government formally. The Schlüter government has confronted serious challenges to its attempts to trim the sprawling welfare state and inject more free enterprise into the economy, and over Denmark's commitment to the European Union.

After several coalition reshuffles and with a changing cast of outside supporters, the Schlüter government has become the longest-serving nonsocialist government in Scandinavia to date. Its record may go to prove that in Denmark "coalition government" is no contradiction in terms. In Norway and Sweden that has yet to be shown. There the Social Democrats have retained enough strength to claim control of government with just a little help from "friends" in parliament; and their non-socialist adversaries have proved unable to bury old rivalries or keep new ones from wreaking havoc on their joint attempts at governing.

We can conclude by saying that government by party coalitions is not congenitally a part of Scandinavian politics. That is a disdain shared with British political culture, even though the lack of a (parliamentary) two-party system makes that luxury hard to afford. At the same time, Scandinavians are not clamoring for rule by a majority party, either. They appear to have an extremely high tolerance for minority governments. To be governed by a party without majority control of parliament is a striking feature of Scandinavian politics. Few people seem to mind this condition. It does not provoke loud demands for constitutional reform to make it easier for a party or a coalition to attain a majortiy. But perhaps the issue of majority government is a moot point, since parliament and the parties are, as some claim, a sideshow anyway in Scandinavia.

Harpsund Democracy

It is a widely heard refrain of political commentary that parliaments in western democracies have lost influence and that even governments no longer control policymaking. Instead, key interest groups—business, labor, and farmers—are said to have gained a foothold in important domains of policy.

In Sweden they call this kind of government *Harpsund democracy.* Harpsund is a retreat for the prime minister, where top-level meetings with leaders of interest groups take place away from the capital. Political scientists refer to it as "corporatism" or "neocorporatism," meaning that government policy is effectively made out-

Corporatist Politics

The crucial decisions on economic policy are rarely taken in the parties or in Parliament: the central area is the bargaining table where the government authorities meet directly with the trade union leaders, the representatives of the farmers, the smallholders, and the fishermen, and the delegates of the Employers' Association. These yearly rounds of negotiations have in fact come to mean more in the lives of rank-and-file citizens than the formal elections. In these processes of intensive interaction, the parliamentary notions of one member, one vote and majority rule make little sense.

Source: Rokkan, "Norway: Numerical Democracy and Corporate Pluralism," p. 107.

side the formal channels through bargaining with the leaders of powerful interest organizations. To put it bluntly, the parties, the members of parliament, and even the cabinet are presented with *faits accomplis.* They find themselves reduced to rubber stamps.

No doubt, the key economic interests are well organized in the Scandinavian countries, firmly connected with political parties and deeply entrenched in the process of policymaking. Scandinavia puts much stock (and faith) in the consultation of interests affected by a prospective policy. "Commissions of inquiry" are an everyday feature of political life. Before embarking on a major new policy initiative, the government assembles a commission from representatives of interested parties (including also political parties), civil servants, experts, and so on. The commission's report then goes to government agencies as well as interest groups for *remiss,* that is, comments. Only after digesting this multicourse diet of suggestions will the government decide whether to proceed at all and what kind of legislation to propose to parliament.

The Downside of Corporatist Politics

There are many ways in which structured consultation sanctions and rigidifies approved behavior. Conflict becomes channeled in predictable forms. Political aspirations for reform become merged with issues of technical detail. Those recognized as having a stake in an issue are offered a sense of due process in the making of policies.

Source: Heclo and Madsen, *Policy and Politics in Sweden,* p. 15.

Some observers, however, suspect that this politics of patience may conceal more than it reveals. The form is consultation, to be sure, but the spirit may not always be compromise.

POLICYMAKING: THE WAGE EARNER FUND

As a case of Scandinavian policymaking, let us examine an issue that stirred much political heat in Sweden in the 1970s. It concerns a proposal that one side touted as the coming of economic democracy whereas the opposition condemned it as the end of economic freedom. The proposal, which originated with the Swedish labor federation in the 1960s, envisioned the creation of investment funds fed by company profits but controlled by workers. In this way, so the justification went, workers would gain influence over the decision making of private business. The plan would redress what many considered a grossly uneven distribution of economic power in Swedish society, notwithstanding a half century of welfare state expansion.

The *Meidner Report,* which was drafted by the leading economist of the labor federation, Rudolf Meidner, spelled out the details of the plan in 1975 and prodded the partisan allies of labor, the Social Democrats, to take up the cause and put it into policy. The Meidner plan quickly aroused the ire of the Swedish business confederation, which denounced it as creeping socialism and a power grab by labor. Not only the Conservatives, but also the Liberals and the Center, echoed those objections. The gauntlet had been tossed for full-fledged class-party warfare, except that the Social Democrats did not immediately assume their role as the partisan advocate of labor's plan. The party leadership instead took evasive action. It neither endorsed nor rejected the plan. The party leader at the time, Olaf Palme, emphasized the complexity of the issue and pointed out that the unions as a whole had not fully resolved the matter.

The Swedish Social Democrats were obviously caught in a quandary: endorse the plan and jeopardize the carefully fostered image of a moderate party comfortable with capitalism; or reject the plan and affront your key clientele, your historic ally. It was a classic dilemma between policy and politics. While policy dictated taking the unions' side, politics dictated the opposite. Their defeat in the 1976 election took the Social Democrats off the hook as far as immediate policy action was concerned. In the meantime, a government commission on wage earner funds proceeded with its work. But its attempts to compromise the opposing positions of business and labor failed to win the support of both groups. While profit sharing, in principle, proved acceptable to business, labor refused to accept any form of individual ownership of the fund. Yet business, in turn, would have none of the collective ownership of the fund. At heart, collective, not individual, control of business profits was the key to labor's demand, just as much as it was the key to business's opposition. The commission, headed by a series of chairmen, was unable to paper over, let alone resolve, that profound disagreement. What it finally produced in 1981 was a mass of data but no

The Wage Earner Fund Debate: Pros and Cons

PRO: THE UNIONS

Power over people and production belongs to the owners of capital. With wage earner funds the labor movement can repeal this injustice. If we do not deprive capital owners of their ownership, we can never fundamentally alter society and carry through economic democracy.

Wage earner funds should be owned and administered collectively. An individually based profit sharing system would not involve anything like increased worker influence.

Through investment decisions of high-profit firms, a large and essential part of social development is determined. These decisions should be democratized.

Source: Labor unions' newspaper *Fack* (reprinted in Heclo and Madsen, p. 298).

CON: THE EMPLOYERS

The wage earner funds only serve the purpose of transferring the power and the ownership of commercial and industrial life to the union organization.

Wage earner funds lead to fund socialism: In the long run, all large companies in the country will have one and the same owner: the union organizations.

The market economy is abolished and is replaced by a "union planned economy."

Sweden's economy has been built through free enterprise and private ownership. That foundation would be destroyed if wage earner funds are introduced. The alternative to wage earner funds is a preserved market economy and dispersed ownership.

Source: Statement of Swedish Employers' Federation (reprinted in Heclo and Madsen, p. 304).

policy recommendation of any use to the political antagonists.

In the interim, however, one gap closed, though not through the efforts of the commission. By late 1981, the Social Democrats found a modus vivendi with the labor federation on their cherished plan. The party endorsed the principle of collective ownership but did not cede to the unions clear-cut control over the funds to be established. By that time too, the Social Democrats no longer had as much to fear in electoral terms. The government formed by three nonsocialist parties in 1976 had done more to self-destruct than to accumulate a glowing record for reelection in 1982. Popular attention then focused more heavily on the negatives of the governing parties than on the proposals of the out-of-power Social Democrats.

Back in power after the 1982 election, the Social Democrats proceeded to turn the plan into policy with a minimum of fanfare, playing down any implication that it would radically transform Sweden's mixed economy or enhance worker control over the economy. Instead, the emphasis was placed on increasing the supply of venture capital. The three nonsocialist parties pledged to dismantle any such plan once they returned to power. The business federation, in turn, refused even to participate in the formalities of consultation.

While the legislation that ultimately established the wage earner funds did not fulfill the original dreams of the labor movement, the way in which it was passed left little doubt that it was not by consultation or compromise. Instead, it was adopted through the superior power of one party, which was little restrained by its adversaries. That party, perhaps with some reluctance, accepted the demands of its key clientele and ultimately delivered a policy acceptable to it. It was the display of a party able to control its own ranks (while enjoying the benign neutrality of the Communists) and in no need or mood to accommodate its partisan opposition on the right. And just as surely did the Conservatives and their allies pledge to dismantle the fund once they returned to office.

Beyond the Middle Way

In early 1986, the Swedish prime minister, walking home after watching a movie in downtown Stockholm, was assassinated. In any country, the assassination of a political leader is a shocking event, but for Sweden it was nearly incomprehensible. Had not political violence, like smallpox, been eradicated in that country? With fewer than one hundred homicides a year, compared to more than 1,500 in New York City, which has roughly the same population, Sweden is not accustomed to daily stories of murder and mayhem.

Palme's death at the hands of an assassin nonetheless was a brutal reminder that paradise was still postponed in Scandinavia. Politics in that region had long won acclaim for solving the problems of modern life, but the last two decades have raised serious doubts as to whether that record could be sustained. Palme himself, and the Swedish Social Democrats with him, were ousted from power in 1976, although they regained it six years later; and his counterparts in Oslo and Copenhagen experienced similar political turbulence in office. In Denmark, in particular, new parties with agendas challenging the Social Democrats from left, right, and center rendered Hamlet's kingdom virtually ungovernable in the 1970s.

The Middle Way—that was supposedly the recipe of the Scandinavian success story. In a nutshell, the middle way referred to key partnerships and compromises, among political parties, among interest groups, between such groups and government, between rival doc-

The Middle Way

The socialist-agrarian partnership [of the 1930s] was the solid foundation on which the reforms of future years were based. . . . The political partnership between the socialists and the farmers was paralleled by an economic partnership between labor and industry, underwritten by the pact of Saltsjöbaden. . . . Here was a mutual recognition of the accepted roles of the two principals in the economic process, each motivated by a sense of well-being of a country dependent on sales abroad to live. . . . So long as the international competitiveness of industry, privately owned up to 90 or 95 percent, continued to increase, with prosperity thereby sustained, the growing scope of welfarism could be supported through taxation that tended to keep pace with welfare benefits. A highly disciplined and comprehensive labor movement . . . was an important element in the stability of the country.

Source: Marquis W. Childs, *Sweden: The Middle Way on Trial* (New Haven and London: Yale University Press, 1980), pp. 18–19.

trines like free enterprise and communal values, and between individuals making money and a government caring for people.

But the prosperity sustaining the ever-expanding welfare state could not be taken for granted in the rough climate of international competition; nor did the welfare state, for all its accomplishments in making life secure, abolish economic inequality. A sputtering economy revived public interest in nonsocialist alternatives fashionable among conservatives, who felt emboldened by the examples of Margaret Thatcher and Ronald Reagan. On the other hand, the persistence of economic inequality fueled demands for "economic democracy," fashionable on the left. While one side demanded tax cuts for individuals and program cuts by government, the other demanded more say by workers collectively over the profits and decisions of private companies.

The Social Democrats, the longtime navigators of the middle way, now felt they were being pulled in opposite directions. To secure enough support to govern they began relying on the parties on their left instead of the agrarian/liberal parties on their right. Meanwhile, proposals for such radical policies as wage earner funds gravely strained the partnership between business and labor. What is more, the numerically strong, but for years politically feeble, gathering of nonsocialist parties grew bolder in its challenge of social democracy.

As a result, politics in Scandinavia has discovered the principle of government turnover, with power now changing hands frequently in a party system polarized between a struggling, though still formidable Social Democratic Party on the left and an assortment of Centrist/Liberal and Conservative parties bent on reining in welfare state expansion on the right. A keener sense of political competition does not spell the end of stability for Scandinavian countries. Past accounts have probably erred in underestimating the extent of partisan polarization in that region. The future will have to prove whether the fabled "middle way" remains a practical model or winds up as no man's land separating political adversaries.

NOTE

1. See Steven Prokesch, "Discontent in Egalitarian Sweden Threatens Socialists in Vote Today," *The New York Times*, Sept. 15, 1991. By way of comparison, the U.S. share was barely 30 percent, with the average percentage of industrialized nations in 1990 being 39.

REFERENCES AND SUGGESTED READINGS

Boje, Thomas P., and Sven E. Olsson Hort, eds. 1993. *Scandinavia in a New Europe*. Oslo: Scandinavian University Press.

Castles, Francis G. 1978. *The Social Democratic Image of Society*. London: Routledge & Kegan Paul.

Damgaard, Erik, and Jerrold Rusk. May 1976. "Cleavage Structures and Representational Linkages: A Longitudinal Analysis of Danish Legislative Behavior." *American Journal of Political Science*, 20: 179–206.

Flanagan, Robert, et al., eds. 1983. *Unionism, Economic Stabilization, and Incomes Policies*. Washington, D.C. Chs. 4, 6, and 8.

Hancock, M. Donald, John Logue, and Bernd Schiller, eds. 1991. *Managing Modern Capitalism: Industrial Renewal and Workplace Democracy in the United States and Western Europe*. New York: Praeger.

Katzenstein, Peter. 1985. *Small States in World Markets*. Ithaca, N.Y.: Cornell University Press.

Korpi, Walter. 1983. *The Democratic Class Struggle*. London: Routledge & Kegan Paul.

Paldam, Martin. 1990. "The Development of the Rich Welfare State of Denmark." In Magnus Blomström and Patricio Meller, eds., *Diverging Paths: A Century of Scandinavian and Latin American Economic Development*. Baltimore: Johns Hopkins University Press.

Petersson, Olof. 1991. "Democracy and Power in Sweden," *Scandinavian Political Studies* 14 (1991): 173-191.

Strom, Kaare. 1990. *Minority Government and Majority Rule*. New York: Cambridge University Press.

37

The New Eastern Europe

After World War II the term *Eastern Europe* became a form of political shorthand, referring to the part of Europe that was governed by Communist parties. But during the roughly forty years of Communist control and dominance by the Soviet Union, the region's eight states showed significant variation in the form of socialism they each sought to implement, the nature of the regimes' relationship with their societies, and the type of foreign relations they pursued. Now, with one-party regimes overthrown in all of these states, with open competitive political systems operating in most of them, and with national boundaries changed in some, the region's diversity is more evident than ever.

For one thing, instead of eight states there are now twelve. Two multiethnic ones, Yugoslavia and Czechoslovakia, have fragmented into multiple states, the former in a process accompanied by war and terrible bloodshed, the latter peacefully. Another state, the German Democratic Republic, has disappeared altogether, merging with its larger, powerful cousin, the Federal Republic of Germany, within one year of the collapse of the Berlin Wall.

All of the East European states have new political systems and have held both national parliamentary and local elections. Presidents in the region have been elected either directly or by parliaments. Most have moved to dismantle the state-dominated economic systems they inherited from the Communist past, though progress on this score is very uneven. Only recently has economic growth returned to the region—and then only in a few places (see Table 37.1).

Table 37.1 CENTRAL AND EAST EUROPE: BASIC DATA

	Area (Sq. Mi.)	Popul. (Thousands)[1]	GDP Per Capita 1992 (dollars)
Albania	11,097	3,300	470
Bulgaria	44,365	8,473	815
Czech Republic	30,441	10,302	2,550
Hungary	35,900	10,335	3,446
Poland	120,700	38,309	1,895
Romania	91,699	22,760	610
Slovakia	19,049	5,300	1,820

[1]Dates for censuses vary.
[2]For Hungary and Slovakia, figure is for 1992; for others, 1993.
[3]Figure for Albania is for 1992.

Though the people of the region have changed governments and to some extent economic systems, they cannot change their location on the planet. Wedged between a revolutionary and somewhat volatile Russia and a powerful and prosperous Germany and the rest of Western Europe, the region continues to be profoundly influenced by developments in these two areas. As the history of this century demonstrates, what happens in these "lands between"[1] is likely also to have a significant impact on the lives of its neighbors.

RECENT HISTORY

Central and Southeastern Europe has in modern times usually been the chessboard of the great empires, with its peoples and their aspirations as pawns. It was not until the collapse of the three European empires at the beginning of the century that independence could be achieved, if only briefly. Virtually all of the East European states began this century as part of one or even two of the empires that dominated Europe: the Ottoman, Hapsburg (Austro-Hun-garian), and Russian. Poland, an empire once itself, had disappeared from the map of Europe at the end of the eighteenth century, divided among its neighbors Prussia, Austria, and Russia. A Polish rump state created after the defeat of Napoleon in 1815 was dominated by Russia and virtually totally absorbed into the Russian Empire after an insurrection in 1830–1831. It did not re-emerge as an independent country until the collapse of the Russian autocracy at the end of World War I.

Central Europe was dominated until this century by the Austro-Hungarian Empire, which stretched from Cracow and Prague in the north to Dubrovnik on the Adriatic Sea. Parts of present-day Poland, Hungary, Romania, Slovenia, Croatia, Serbia, and Bosnia, as well as the Czech Republic and Slovakia, were all once under the control of the dual monarchy, ruled from either Vienna or Budapest. For Hungary the situation created after World War I meant the loss of virtually all of its share of the empire and adjustment from a role as ruler of some 20 million people to a land of less than 8 million, with more than 3 million Hungarians left outside its new borders. To its north came a brand-new

ΔGDP 1993 (%)	Private Share of GDP (%)[2]	Unemployment, 1993 (% of work force)	Inflation, 1993 (Annual %)
8.0	NA	40.0[3]	120.0[3]
–3.5	10	16.3	50.4
.0	50	3.5	16.8
1.0	40	12.2	19.2
5.0	50	15.7	32.4
1.0	30	9.6	150.0
–6.5	20	14.2	22.8

Sources: *The Economist,* March 13, 1993; William Coplin and Michael O'Leary, eds., *East Europe & the Republics* (Syracuse, N.Y.: Political Risk Services, 1993); *PlanEcon Report,* Vol. IX, Nos. 49–50–51–52 (February 10, 1994); *RFE/RL Research Report,* Vol. 3, No. 1 (January 7, 1994).

state formed by merging the Czech lands of Bohemia and Moravia with Slovakia through a pact signed in Pittsburgh, Pennsylvania, in May 1918.

Also new on the twentieth-century map of Europe was Yugoslavia, an amalgamation of territories and peoples liberated from both the Hapsburg and Ottoman empires. To the Balkan state of Serbia, which had gained independence from Turkey in 1878, were added Croatia, Bosnia-Herzogovina, and Slovenia in the west, and Vojvodina in the north, all from the defeated Austro-Hungarian Empire; and parts of Macedonia to the south and east, at the expense of Bulgaria. Thus was created a country of some 11 million people, of more than a dozen nationalities, 47 percent Eastern Orthodox (chiefly Serbs, Montenegrins, and Macedonians), 40 percent Roman Catholic (chiefly Croats and Slovenes), 11 percent Muslim (chiefly Albanians and Bosnians).[2]

Romania too had been independent before World War I, having profited from the Russian defeat of Turkey in 1877. But the prewar state that embraced Moldavia and Wallachia more than doubled in size at the end of World War I

by adding to its territory Transylvania, at the expense of Hungary; Dobrudja from Bulgaria, also a loser in World War I; and taking Bessarabia from the weak new Soviet state. For Bulgaria, such losses were only the latest in a string of humiliations dating back to 1878, when the country's victory over the Ottoman Empire on the battlefield was reversed by the major powers at the Congress of Berlin.

The boundaries and status of this region's states had always been drawn for the advantage and convenience of controlling and usually opposing empires. Nothing illustrates this so much as the creation of Albania, the smallest of the East European states, on the shores of the Adriatic Sea. When in 1878 Albanian nationalists petitioned the powers at the Congress of Berlin to establish a national state for them within the defeated Turkish empire, they were rebuffed. Otto von Bismarck, the German chancellor and the inspiration behind the Congress, remarked, "There is no such thing as the Albanian nationality." But thirty-five years later, when the independent state of Serbia had profited from a new Balkan war against Turkey, the great powers feared that a powerful Serbian

The Old Bridge in the Bosnian city of Mostar was damaged by fighting and finally destroyed by Croatian gunners in November 1993. Standing since 1566, the bridge was once one of the most graceful examples of Ottoman architecture.

state would emerge. Hence they now assented to the creation of Albania to block Serbia's access to the sea.

After World War I, the redivision of Eastern Europe into seven different—and some completely new—states left virtually all of them with disputes with their neighbors. Two of the states, Hungary and Bulgaria, emerged from the war with significant losses in territory and prestige and a powerful predisposition toward changing the consequences of that war. On the other hand, the winners in the new situation—Czechoslovakia, Romania, Yugoslavia, and Poland—were concerned with keeping the status quo or improving it, if the opportunity arose. Most of these states were fearful of Germany, the biggest loser of all in World War I, and in some cases, such as in Poland and Romania, there was also the danger of possible territorial conflicts with the Soviet Union. Po-

land had in fact fought a brief but inconclusive war with the Soviet Union in 1920–1921, at one point laying siege to the Ukrainian capital of Kiev. In all the new states except Czechoslovakia, there was profound concern about the revolutionary goals and tactics of the new Communist USSR.

Economically, interwar Eastern Europe depended heavily on agriculture, with only Czechoslovakia and some parts of Poland having significant industrial resources. In most cases, but especially in the Balkans, the agriculture was still of a primitive and unproductive kind. For example, in Yugoslavia the average wheat yield was under 2,500 pounds per acre; in Denmark the average exceeded 8,000 pounds.[3] At the same time the number of nominally free but poor and indebted peasants eager for loans was substantial. In Eastern Europe nearly 60 percent of the population depended

Figure 37.1 East Europe.

on agriculture, while in the West the figure was 24 percent.

Nor was the region a fertile ground for the emergence of democratic institutions. Limited advisory councils or parliaments had operated in parts of the Austro-Hungarian Empire during the nineteenth century, and before its partition Poland had employed a representative system that was the most advanced of its time. But for the most part, the leadership of these new states, with uncertain international security and in difficult economic straits, had little experience with or inclination toward the process or mechanics of parliamentary democracy. Most slid quickly into military or other forms of dictatorship.

In Hungary, a postwar liberal government was overthrown in 1919 by the first Communist revolution outside the Soviet Union, led by Béla Kun. The regime, a curious mixture of radical socialism and nationalism directed against its neighbors, was itself undone before the year was out with the help of the victorious Allies, including troops from Romania. A conservative antidemocratic regime under Admiral Miklós Horthy led eventually to a full-scale dictatorship under Gyula Gömbös and, later, alliance with Adolf Hitler, who promised to undo the consequences of World War I. Similarly, the radically propeasant rule of Alexander Stambolisky in Bulgaria was ended in 1923 by a military coup; the new military regime, with the support of King Boris, also pursued a nationalist line and lined itself up with resurgent Germany.

In Poland the parliamentary experiment lasted a bit longer, but proved weak and ineffective in governing the country. The extremely popular Józef Pilsudski, who had led the Polish armies against the Soviet Union, took power in 1926 and at his death in 1935 passed on virtually total control to a military dictatorship known as the "regime of the colonels." Both Romania and Yugoslavia had similarly unrewarding experiences with representative legislatures that proved unable to resolve ethnic disputes, deal with the serious economic situation, especially the needs of the peasantry, or prevent the manipulation of the system by rival groups aspiring to power. In these two cases the monarchy, which had been preserved with constitutional limitations, violated these limitations and took full power by the end of the 1920s.

Only in Czechoslovakia was the process of representative democracy made effective. A two-chambered parliament based on universal suffrage and proportional representation gave expression and the opportunity to participate to a variety of political parties and national groups. In addition some effective economic measures were taken to help new landowners prosper. But Czechoslovakia, like the rest of Eastern Europe, was undone by its precarious situation, caught between disgruntled neighbors such as Hungary and even Poland, which made claims on the border city of Cieszyn (also known as Teschen), and Germany, which claimed the western part of the country, known as the Sudetenland. That pressure, in addition to the economic collapse that struck the entire industrial world at the beginning of the 1930s, hardly made for a stable governing environment.

The growth of protectionism against imports and the accompanying worldwide economic collapse devastated the already weak economies in Eastern Europe, cutting off trade possibilities and throwing millions out of work. In Czechoslovakia there had been fewer than 90,000 people unemployed in 1929; by 1932 that figure was more than 900,000. The Depression fueled the growth of militant nationalism, militarism and *fascism,* a movement to strengthen the powers of the state. This was especially true in Germany, where Adolf Hitler's Nazi Party dominated the elections of 1933, allowing him to become chancellor. Hitler was determined to change the map of Europe, to restore what he saw as Germany's rightful place, and establish a "thousand-year reign" of Aryan rule over what he considered lesser peoples, including Slavs. After coming to power he was able to challenge the divided and apprehensive allies of Britain and France by rearming his country, reoccupying the Rhineland (1938) and forcing union with Austria (1938). Then, at a meeting in Munich in September 1938, Britain and France agreed to hand the Sudetenland from Czechoslovakia to Germany. Representatives of the Czechoslovak government, though present in Munich, were not even consulted or made party to the dismemberment of their country. With the loss of 30 percent of its population, one-third of its territory, and 40 percent of its national income, "the country ceased to be economically or strategically viable."[4] Within six months it was totally absorbed by Germany; Slovakia, the country's eastern part, was set up as a puppet state. When Hitler, in August 1939, pressed claims on Poland and they were refused, the invasion of that country produced declarations of war from Great Britain and France and, in short order, World War II.

The war brought destruction and occupation to most of Eastern Europe, but no country suffered as did Poland. Already having been struck a mortal blow by its division between the Soviet Union and Germany in their 1939 Nonaggression Pact, it was quickly occupied by Hitler. Over the next five and a half years until its liberation, more than 6 million Poles were to die—more than one of every six people—including more than 3 million Jews, virtually annihilating what had been Europe's most numerous Jewish population. Other Eastern European countries either accommodated to Hitler's growing power, as did Hungary and Bulgaria, or were attacked and occupied, as was Yugoslavia in 1941. In some cases old scores were settled. With Hitler's blessing, Hungary took back Transylvania from Romania, and in Yugoslavia the fascist puppet state of Croatia unleashed attacks against Serbs, Jews, and Romanies (Gypsies) on its territory. Romania was able to keep Germany at arm's length by virtue of the vigor of its own fascist movement and its eagerness to cooperate in joining the German attack on the Soviet Union in 1941.

It was that attack that ultimately led to Hitler's defeat. But this did not occur for four more years, after the monumental battle of Stalingrad (now Volgograd) in which more than 200,000 German soldiers were killed and nearly 100,000 captured, and after the German armies were driven out of Eastern (and Western) Europe. In the East, except in Albania and Yugoslavia, the key military force was Soviet troops, usually aided by domestic antifascist groups. In one case, that of East Germany, the boundaries of what was to become a completely new state were set by the final battle lines.

The dominating presence of Soviet troops throughout the region meant that they would be the ultimate force in determining the postwar political situation in this area. At Teheran in November 1943, Winston Churchill and Franklin Roosevelt agreed to Soviet demands to retain the eastern third of Poland, and all three leaders agreed to throw their support in Yugoslavia behind the communist forces led by Broz Tito. "By the end of 1944," writes historian John Lukacs, "no power existed in East Europe that could effectively resist the Russian conquerors."[5] Churchill had already informally proposed to Joseph Stalin a division of the region in which the Soviet Union would have predominant influence (Churchill suggested 80–20 percent) in Bulgaria, Romania and Hungary and the British would retain power in Greece. Yugoslavia was to be divided "50–50." At a meeting in Moscow in 1944 Churchill wrote these numbers on a slip of paper and slid it across the table to Stalin, who indicated his approval by making a check in the bottom right-hand corner. This so-called "percentages agreement" was yet another division of the region by outside powers, and it also reflected the new reality of Soviet power. The agreements at Yalta in February 1945 essentially ratified this situation while extracting from the USSR pledges that free elections would be held in the Eastern European countries.

After the war such pledges were given short shrift, as in the Soviet view the key to its own security lay in establishing friendly, compliant socialist governments on its borders, something it had never had before. As Communist parties gained full control in the region and suspicion and hostility replaced wartime cooperation between East and West, the entire region became trapped behind what Churchill would call in 1947 an "iron curtain." Though the details differed in each country, the process and the end result were the same: coalition government was replaced by Communist-led or all-Communist rule; opposition parties and political activity were banned; and by 1948, with the end of multiparty rule in Czechoslovakia, the new empire in Eastern Europe, this time a socialist Soviet-dominated one, was established.

THE REGION UNDER THE COMMUNISTS

The leaders of the Communist parties in Eastern Europe became the effective rulers of these various states soon after the end of World War II. While all were bent on transforming their societies, the dilemma each faced was finding policies that would serve their countries' political, economic, and social needs while also meeting their obligations to the dominant power in the region, the Soviet Union. In some cases the decision as to how to proceed was made for them; Soviet power simply dictated what would be done in their respective states; a leader's choice was to comply or be removed. In other cases, public demand or the leaders' own desire for greater autonomy put them into

potential or real conflict with the Soviet Union. Sometimes, when Soviet concerns were not addressed sufficiently, full-scale military intervention occurred.

For the first five years after Communist rule was fully established, the Eastern European states followed plans for economic development not unlike those that had characterized the Soviet Union during the "great turn" (see Chapter 28). Investment was poured into heavy industry, and collectivization of agriculture was instituted. The result was tremendous social upheaval as societies were virtually transformed. A "new proletariat" was created as peasants, deprived of private ownership of the land, joined the urban industrial labor force. Nearly half a million people made this transition in both Bulgaria and Yugoslavia, more than three-quarters of a million in Hungary and Romania, and almost 2 million in Poland.[6]

Apart from the defection of Yugoslavia, the first significant variation in political and economic behavior did not occur until after the death of Joseph Stalin in 1953. While the leadership in the Soviet Union embarked in fits and starts on a new direction in economic policy and replaced the cult of personality with collective leadership, some of the states in Eastern Europe followed suit and some did not. For example, new leaders emerged in Bulgaria, Hungary, and Poland, but not in East Germany or Czechoslovakia; and in Romania the party leader at the time, Gheorghe Gheorghiu-Dej, used the de-Stalinization process to weaken his opposition and consolidate his own position.

ECONOMIC AND POLITICAL DIFFICULTIES: POLAND AND CZECHOSLOVAKIA

The wave of change set off by de-Stalinization in the Soviet Union in the mid-fifties had consequences in East Europe. In both Poland and

Yugoslavia: The First Heretic

When Soviet troops entered Yugoslavia in 1944 to assist in driving out the German invaders, they found that, unlike in Romania or Hungary, a strong, functioning and popular Communist movement, led by Josip Broz Tito, was already in existence. Almost immediately the question of who would determine the country's future, the Communists in Moscow or those in Belgrade, became inflamed into a conflict. Yugoslavs objected to Stalin's attempt to restructure the country's government and army along Soviet lines, to what they saw as exploitation of the country's resources and Soviet unwillingness to support full-scale industrialization in the country. In addition, old-fashioned nationalism was not muted by common socialist inclinations. Tito publicly rejected any kind of great power agreement (such as "50–50") on the country's fate; there was resentment of Russian cultural arrogance—Vladimir Dedijier, a Yugoslav journalist and biographer of Tito, reports that in the first few years after the war the Yugoslavs published more than 1,800 Soviet books while "they published two of ours"—and at lack of Soviet support for Yugoslavia's dispute with Italy over Trieste or for the creation of a "Balkan federation," with Yugoslavia at the head.

After the foundation of the *Cominform* (the acronym for Communist Information Bureau) in 1947, the conflict became internationalized, with the Soviet Union and its Eastern European allies combining to try to pressure Yugoslavia to get in line. Yugoslavia was thrown out of the Cominform, all the Eastern European states cut economic ties with the country, and a massive propaganda campaign was unleashed against Tito and the leaders of the Yugoslav party. But the Soviet regime overestimated its power—Stalin said, "I will shake my little finger and Tito will fall"—and underestimated the cohesiveness of the Yugoslav party, forged in a guerrilla war against the Germans. Despite the economic boycott and increased military tension on its borders and almost complete political isolation, Yugoslavia did not return to the fold. In the early 1950s the country began to explore the possibility of relations with the West, expanded economic ties with the United States and Western Europe, and began to create its own form of socialism, known as workers' self-management. In the 1960s Yugoslavia became one of the founding members of the nonaligned movement.

Sources: George W. Hoffman and Fred W. Neal, *Yugoslavia and the New Communism* (New York: Twentieth Century Fund, 1962). Alvin Rubinstein, *Yugoslavia and the Nonaligned World* (Princeton, N.J.: Princeton University Press, 1970); Robert L. Wolf, *The Balkans in Our Time*, rev. ed. (New York: W. W. Norton and Co., 1974).

Hungary popular anti-Stalinist leaders reemerged into prominence. In Poland, waves of workers' strikes, plus intellectual ferment and deep-seated opposition to collectivization, led the party to turn to Władysław Gomułka, who had been purged from the party as a "nationalist" in 1949. After 1956 some reforms were instituted in Poland; collectivization was ended, pressure was eased on the Catholic Church, and workers' councils were established in the factories. But soon Gomułka began to strengthen his political power and to undo many of the social and economic changes he had promised. Though collectivization was not tried again, the private agricultural sector languished under a combination of neglect and restrictions. By the late 1960s the failure to reform the economy alienated workers eager for some return from the country's development; moreover, economic growth itself was slowing down. Food was costing more to produce than it could be sold for because prices were kept low to forestall worker unrest. Thus subsidies consumed increasing amounts of the state budget. Just before Christmas 1970, the government announced immediate and substantial price increases. Worker demonstrations broke out; in Gdansk the party headquarters was attacked, and when the Soviet Union turned down a request for military assistance, Gomulka himself was replaced.

The new leader, Edward Gierek, faced the same dilemma as had his predecessors: how to get the economy to function more productively while keeping within the bounds of socialism and not taking any actions, such as decentralization, that would threaten the position of the party or the interests of the Soviet Union. In an attempt to solve its problem, the Polish party followed what became known as the "Gierek strategy." The country began to vigorously import western technology, licenses, and sometimes whole factories to try to improve productive capacity rapidly. As Poland's own exports to the West—chiefly coal but also food—were insufficient to pay for all these imports, the government began to borrow. In the mid-1970s, western governments were eager to build economic ties to strengthen East-West détente, and banks had billions in oil revenue deposits that they were eager to lend. From the Polish point of view, the plan was to use the new industrial capacity the country would build to expand exports to the West and thus pay for new machinery and the loans.

But there was another need driving the desire for new technology, one derived both from the Polish experience of 1956 and 1970 and the experience of Czechoslovakia in 1968. In that country economic stagnation in the early 1960s and long-delayed political reform—including the continuation of the Stalinist leadership of Antonín Novotný—finally produced a political and social movement for change. In January 1968, Novotný was removed, and the Czechoslovak party under Alexander Dubček began easing control of the press and other media, rehabilitated former political prisoners, and issued an action program calling for full-scale economic and political reform. As discussion became more vigorous and independent political activity more a possibility, strong pressure to clamp down came from the Soviet Union and other Eastern European states, including Poland. But domestic social pressure on the Prague government was also strong: to move further and faster, to allow non-Communist political activity, full and open discussion of all questions, and a stronger voice for the country's Slovak minority (19 percent of the population). The leadership of the Czechoslovak party was caught between what it saw as changes necessary to improve the governance of the country and Soviet desire to prevent what its leaders described as "counterrevolution."

When the Soviet Union became convinced that reforms were not going to be reversed and that an upcoming extraordinary (that is, scheduled before the usual five-year interval) party congress would install reform-minded cadres throughout the party, a decision was made to intervene with force. On August 21, 1968, troops from the Soviet Union and all allied countries except Romania crossed the borders of this fraternal ally and quickly occupied the country.

Though reforms were systematically undone in Czechoslovakia, and party leaders who had instituted political and economic change were removed, the regime there and others throughout Eastern Europe realized that stable rule increasingly depended on the ability to provide economic satisfaction, in the form of more and better housing, automobiles, consumer goods and foodstuffs. Thus in most of the Eastern European states, attempts were made to improve the economic situation of the population while holding off political reform. This so-called social contract held throughout the 1970s, or as long as the relatively weak economies of those states could manage it.

In Poland, therefore, an additional component of the Gierek strategy was to produce more consumer goods to satisfy the population and avoid the trauma of what had happened in Czechoslovakia in 1968 and what had already occurred in Poland in 1956 and 1970. For a while, the strategy worked; the situation for Poland's consumers improved. But the Polish economic system proved unable to absorb the new technology fully, and western imports of machines and licenses led to more western imports of spare parts and new equipment. Though exports grew, they were not enough to cover the growing import bill or the cost of interest and debt repayment. And loans spent on equipment that produced consumer goods for the politically important domestic market brought in no hard currency at all for loan repayment.

External events contributed to the difficulties. In the mid- and late 1970s, most of the Eastern European states, but especially those like Poland that were heavily involved with the western international economy, were hit indirectly by the effect of the quadrupling of oil prices. Most of the region—including Yugoslavia—bought its oil from the Soviet Union. But oil price hikes produced recessions in the major western economies, like the United States and those of Western Europe, leading them to lower their imports from Eastern Europe. With expected sales thus not being realized, Poland and several other Eastern European countries like Romania, Hungary, and Bulgaria, needed to borrow even more. In 1976 Poland's net debt was $11.3 billion. By 1980 this figure had grown to $23.5 billion. Romania owed more than $9 billion, and Hungary, with less than one-half Romania's population, nearly $8 billion. By the beginning of the 1980s most of the Eastern European economies were in trouble.

It was in Poland once again that tight economic straits precipitated political crisis. An attempt in 1976 to raise prices had spawned worker riots, attacks on party headquarters, and government retreat on the economic issue. Unlike in 1970, the party leadership was not

changed; but neither were economic reforms implemented. By 1980 the situation was desperate. The Polish economy showed a negative growth rate in 1979, debt payments were absorbing virtually all export earnings, and food subsidies alone were taking 20 percent of the state budget. The Polish people were no longer looking forward to a steadily improving situation, but they were no better informed as to the true seriousness of the situation and no more able to determine public policy than they had been before. When in the summer of 1980 price increases were once again announced, the result at first seemed the same: worker strikes, wage increases, government promises, talk of reform. But this time the Polish workers recognized the need for a more thoroughgoing transformation. With the assistance of groups such as the Committee for the Defense of Workers (KOR), they articulated demands for broader change, chiefly through formation of the first nongovernmental labor union, which became known as Solidarity.

From September 1980 until December 1981 the dilemma of all Communist parties in Eastern Europe was starkly illustrated in Poland: at home the party was faced with clear demands for change, including a major role in government for the workers, in whose name the state was supposed to be ruling. But the party did not want to relinquish its own monopoly of political power and it had to assure the Soviet Union that its interests in the region were being protected. In the Gdansk Agreements of August 1980, Solidarity was grudgingly legalized. But over the next year the party leadership fought the union on each specific aspect of reform, such as the demand for a farmers' union and the workers' demand to put an end to Saturday work and for greater control over the key decisions regarding the country's economy. Though Solidarity recognized "the leading role of the Polish United Workers Party" (the Communist Party) and pledged adherence to Poland's existing "system of international alliances," Soviet pressure on Warsaw to crack down was intense and over the next sixteen months included massive troop movements and maneuvers, personal letters from Leonid Brezhnev, and several high-level visits. Ultimately the Polish party saved its nominal rule by declaring martial law on December 13, 1981. At that time the military, headed by Wojciech Jaruzelski, who was also party leader, took power. Military rule was suspended at the end of 1982 and formally ended the next year but Jaruzelski remained president until 1990.

Different Approaches: Hungary and Romania

In contrast to Poland, the situation in Hungary in 1956 moved beyond the control of the party leadership. Here too a popular leader, oriented toward the country's special needs, had come to power after the death of Stalin. Imre Nagy pushed the party toward putting more investment into consumer goods, ending the drive for collectivization, providing higher pay and lower quotas in industry, and tolerating broader intellectual freedom. During much of his attempt to dismantle Stalinism, Nagy had Soviet support. But opposition to these actions within the party leadership in Hungary and uncertain signals from the Soviet Union as Moscow grappled with its own de-Stalinization weakened his control. By late 1956 popular demand for change outdistanced whatever reformers in the party leadership wanted to do and thoroughly alarmed conservatives. Soviet troops, stationed in the country under the terms of the Warsaw Pact, were invited to restore control. When pitched battles broke out and overthrow of the Communist system seemed imminent, a full-scale invasion was mounted and Imre Nagy was arrested and executed.

While the new party leadership of János Kádár completely reestablished control, by the beginning of the 1960s a political accommodation with the population was signaled by Kádár's statement that "he who is not against us is with us." In 1968 the leadership began wide-ranging economic reforms that reduced the authority of the central plan, allowed enterprises a greater degree of autonomy, and introduced some market mechanisms. Though reform slowed a bit in the mid-1970s, it regained momentum soon after. The government adopted a policy of providing more information about the country's situation so that when difficult decisions needed to be taken the public was not shocked and alienated. When in the late 1970s and early 1980s adjustment to changing and difficult international circumstances required some austerity, the Hungarian regime was able to avoid the upheaval and challenges that occurred so often in Poland.

In contrast to the Hungarian path of reform, the Romanian party determined that it would continue to strive for rapid broad industrial development. It did this even when the Stalinist period of Soviet domination of the region ended and even though its own base of natural resources, including raw materials and good land, made it more suited to a role as provider of primary products. But rejecting the role it had played before the war as the "gas station and breadbasket" of Europe, the regimes of Gheorghe Gheorghiu-Dej and, after 1965, of Nicolae Ceauşescu began pursuing a broad range of contacts with western countries to secure what it could not get in the East: machines and equipment to expand its manufacturing and technology base. In support of this policy, which was at variance with official Soviet aims of a high degree of specialization within the region, Romania followed a foreign policy often quite different from that of Moscow. In 1967 it established full diplomatic relations with West Germany without waiting for its allies. On the grounds that each party had the right to utilize policies most appropriate to its own situation, Bucharest condemned the invasion of Czechslovakia and maintained good relations with China even after that country and the Soviet Union split the world Ccommunist movement in the mid-1960s. This independent foreign policy earned Ceaușescu's regime the support of the United States and other western countries, and domestically it appealed to Romanian nationalism. It was not, however, accompanied by domestic reform. The economy remained totally controlled by the state and by the central planning apparatus. A nascent free trade union movement and occasional worker demonstrations, as well as the activities of the few dissidents who spoke out, were crushed.

THE END OF COMMUNIST DOMINANCE IN EASTERN EUROPE

The ascension to power in Moscow of Mikhail Gorbachev and his push for glasnost and perestroika in the social, political, and economic systems of the USSR had profound repercussions for Eastern Europe. Reform in the dominant state in the region made change easier in the smaller states by giving reform leaders and ordinary people alike the hope that Soviet pressure, which had stifled change so often before, would not do so this time.

In Poland, suppressing Solidarity with military rule had not solved the country's economic problems. The effects of years of neglecting agriculture and of blocking real economic reform came home to roost. Net national product fell by almost one fourth between 1980 and 1982 and barely returned to 1978 levels by the mid-1980s. The need for economic reform and a degree of political openness were finally recognized by the party after widespread strikes in 1988. In early 1989 the Communist government accepted the participation of Solidarity, once again legalized, in competitive elections and a new two-chambered legislature. The elections then proved disastrous for the Communist Party, which managed to hold on only

to the seats that it was allocated by law. Unable to form a working government, the party yielded control for the first time since World War II and a leading Solidarity adviser and its newspaper editor, Tadeusz Mazowiecki, became prime minister.

Though its situation was the most dramatic, Poland was not alone. Unbalanced overinvestment and the growing debt burden, in addition to the lack of ability to respond quickly to changing international conditions, left most of the other Eastern European states with similar difficulties. Average growth rate for the Eastern European "six" for 1980 to 1985 was a meager 1.1 percent; for 1985 to 1990 it was negative. In Hungary, where previous reform already provided for some opportunity for private economic behavior, the Communist Party tried to retain political control by changing its leadership in the spring of 1988 and again in 1989. Neither move satisfied the public's growing desire for political pluralism and the Hungarian party was also forced to sanction independent political activity and open elections. In the fall of 1989 the once-dominant Hungarian Socialist Workers Party dissolved itself, changed its name (to the Hungarian Socialist Party), and found itself struggling for popularity and votes.

These changes in Poland and Hungary had a significant impact on the people and governments of the neighboring states. As people in the rest of the region learned of the democratic changes in Poland and Hungary through now-freer media in these countries and greater access to western media in their own, pressure began to build. In May 1989 Hungary announced that it would open the border between itself and neighboring Austria, in places tearing down what had figuratively been an iron curtain between East and West. The possibility of leaving this way attracted thousands of East German citizens, for decades penned up in their state by a regime fearful of losing its population. In September the Budapest government suspended an agreement with East Germany under which it was obliged to prevent the exit of East German citizens without valid visas. By November some 45,000 people had taken this route to the West; back in East Germany itself, public pressure grew to enact democratic reforms. For the first time since 1953 thousands of East German citizens took to the streets—nearly 100,000 people marched in Leipzig—demanding change. In October Soviet General Secretary Mikhail Gorbachev had visited East Germany to help celebrate the state's 40th anniversary. He gave indirect but unmistakable public backing to people who were calling for change, urging the East German party to cooperate with "all forces in society." On October 18 longtime party leader Erich Honecker resigned, but his successor, Egon Krenz, lasted only long enough to remove one of the most hated symbols of the division of East and West: the Berlin Wall. On the night of November 9, 1989, all East German borders were opened—including the Wall, and within weeks, more than 5 million East Germans visited the West. But this was not enough—or perhaps it was too much, since many East Germans were now stunned to find out just how far behind their western cousins they were. At the beginning of December Krenz was replaced by Gregor Gysi, a lawyer best known for his defense of political dissidents. But here too the party was forced to yield its political monopoly: independent political activity was allowed, roundtable talks with opposition leaders were held, elections were promised, and the party's legally enshrined "leading role" was abandoned.

Now surrounded by countries in which reform was riding high, the Czechoslovak party found its days of dominance numbered. Huge demonstrations and workers' strikes increased pressure on the regime to get in line with its neighbors. On the night of November 17, 1989, the government tried force, unleashing police on student demonstrators in Prague. The effect of this brutal action was the opposite of that

intended as it brought even more people to political action. Within a week the Communist Party leadership had resigned, with Karl Urbanek replacing Miloš Jakeš as party secretary general. But with the party in disarray and on the defensive over its handling of the demonstrations—not to speak of its twenty-year commitment to conservatism—the leadership was obliged to change once again. At the end of December Ladislav Adamec, who had been prime minister from October 1988 until December 1989, became leader of the party.

But by this point such changes were almost irrelevant. With dizzying speed the party in Czechoslovakia, as in Hungary, had moved from the center and top of a political stage it once controlled, to the wings, as parties and groups of all political persuasions began to take action. In Czechoslovakia, as in East Germany and Hungary, elections were scheduled, the leading role of the party was dropped, and, as in Poland, a new government was formed with Communists, for the first time since 1948, in the minority. To complete the political circle, Alexander Dubček, the man who had led the party into the reforms of the "Prague Spring" in 1968 was elected chairman of the Federal Assembly. Gustav Husák, who had directed the "normalization" of Czechoslovakia after 1968, resigned as president. Václav Havel, a renowned playwright and dissident leader for more than twenty years, who had begun the year in prison for taking part in public protests and whose works were banned in Czechoslovakia, became president.

What happened in Czechoslovakia has been termed "The Velvet Revolution" because of the relative lack of violence. Not so in Romania. As the nature of Communist rule in this country had been so different, so too was its transition, which came upon the country suddenly and violently in the week before Christmas 1989. As often happens in revolutions, the immediate catalyst was a seemingly isolated event, the attempt by the government of Nicolae

Ceauşescu to evict an outspoken Hungarian priest, Laszlo Toekes, from his home in Timişoara on December 15. Protest had been rare in Romania under Ceauşescu, but this time a small crowd gathered to try to protect their pastor. They were soon joined by many others and a now-large demonstration moved to the center of town. It was the regime's response to this demonstration that was to start its downfall. On the personal orders of Ceauşescu, heavily armed security forces opened fire on the crowd, even on those who had put their children ahead of them thinking they would be safe. Hundreds were killed in this and further actions by the hated *securitate* (secret police). Confident of his absolute power, Nicolae Ceauşescu called for a demonstration in Bucharest on December 21. This was to be one of the old type, orchestrated and carefully staged to show support for the government. The result was a revolution. Instead of showering Ceauşescu with cheers, some in the crowd, mostly students, began to boo and jeer. The party and state leader was rattled and, when the crowd could not be controlled, abruptly left off speaking. Emboldened, masses of people filled the streets of Bucharest demanding the downfall of Ceauşescu. With breathtaking speed their wish was granted. At noon on December 22 Mircea Dinescu, a dissident poet and target of various attacks by the Ceauşescu regime, spoke to the nation on Radio Bucharest: "Please remain calm. There are moments in which God has turned his face toward Romania. . . . The army is with us! The Dictator has fled!"[7] That day a group calling itself the National Salvation Front declared itself the new government in Romania.

But more tragic events were still to occur, as the security forces loyal to Ceauşescu sought to quell the uprising in blood. Fierce battles raged in Bucharest in particular, especially for control of the radio and TV stations in the capital. In general the army sided with the revolution but this mostly conscript, poorly equipped and trained force was severely pressed. They were joined by groups of students and others ready to die to save the new government. On Monday, Christmas day, the National Salvation Front announced that Nicolae Ceauşescu and his wife, Elena, captured the day after they fled, had been executed after a summary trial. The trial and their dead bodies were immediately shown on Romanian television. The level of violence dropped, possibly because the security forces were now deprived of the possibility of restoring their leader. By year's end, the country had a new government headed by Prime Minister Petre Roman, a 43-year-old engineer and professor of hydraulics. The National Salvation Front was expanded to nearly 150 people with members ranging from students and civil rights activists to former high Communist Party officials such as Ion Iliescu, the president of the Front.

Not even Bulgaria, in general the most quiescent of the East European states, could escape the sweep of change in the region. At the beginning of November independent groups used the opportunity of an all-European conference on ecology in Sofia to acquire public support for their demands for change. Demonstrations grew and the response of the regime of Todor Zhivkov, anxious to avoid international criticism, wavered. On November 17 Zhivkov resigned as party and state leader and was replaced by Petar Mladenov, the country's foreign minister for the last eighteen years. Soon after, as in the other states, roundtable talks began, elections were pledged, and the party's monopoly of power ended.

EAST EUROPE SINCE THE REVOLUTIONS OF 1989: DEMOCRACY AND FRAGMENTATION

In most of the region national parliamentary elections were held in 1990. As might be expected, the results varied, though the electoral process everywhere proved a stimulant to the return of genuine public politics. In Czechoslovakia and Hungary center-right coalitions emerged, led by the forces that had come together to topple communism: the Civic Forum–Public Against Violence alliance in the former and the Hungarian Democratic Forum in the latter. But in East Germany parties with close ties to their counterparts in West Germany pushed aside the New Forum and other groups that had forced the Communist government's downfall. The vote there showed overwhelming support for rapid unification with the West.

The results were quite different in the Balkans. In Romanian elections in May 1990, a reconstituted National Salvation Front won two-thirds of the seats in the national legislature. The Front's leader, Ion Iliescu, once a close associate of Communist dictator Nicolae Ceauşescu, was elected president with 85 percent of the vote. Reborn parties from before the war and newly energized opposition groups proved too weak and too unorganized to challenge the Front so soon after the revolution. In Bulgaria the political landscape took yet another form. Elections there gave the renamed Communist Party, now called the Bulgarian Socialist Party, a slim majority—but they were unable to form a government or launch a reform program. By the end of the year a nonparty prime minister was installed as head of a caretaker government until new elections could be called.

In Poland, where roundtable talks had first produced the cascade of falling Communist governments, a new legislature was not elected until October 1991, though Lech Wałesa, the leader of Solidarity labor union, did replace Wojciech Jaruzelski as president in direct elections in 1990. Unlike the "roundtable parliament," the new body gave representations to the entire range of political forces. More than one hundred parties and groups had contested the elections and no fewer than 29 held seats in the legislature. No one party had more than 14 percent of the seats in the lower house of parliament. Coalitions proved fractious and unstable, and relations with President Wałesa were often tense and unproductive.

In Yugoslavia, elections fragmented the country in another way. In virtually all of its constituent republics, parties presenting nationalist programs were victorious. Moreover, within some of Yugoslavia's republics, referenda—sanctioned and otherwise—demonstrated strong sentiments for adjusting the country's political system in ways that were not mutually compatible.

Tiny Albania, isolated after breaks with virtually all of its former comrades, was not able to escape the impact of the changes all around it. Pressure built on the regime of Ramiz Alia to begin economic reform. During 1990 some private farming was allowed and broadening of civil and political rights for the country's population—including the holding of open elections—soon followed. In 1991 the now reform-minded Communist Party won a majority in parliamentary elections and Alia was elected president by the parliament. But the next year, Albania's desperate economic situation and the slow pace of reform contributed to a victory by the opposition Democratic Party and the election of the country's first non-Communist president, Sali Berisha.

Most of the East European states began a process of reform or restructuring of their economies even as they were creating democratic political systems. First out of the chute was Poland, which ended price controls, government subsidies, and trade restrictions and made its currency convertible on January 1, 1990. Private business was encouraged. But unemployment appeared and grew; and for those employed, real wages dropped 20 percent in one year. Still the currency's value remained relatively stable, aided by forgiveness of roughly half of Poland's hard currency debt to other governments and the establishment of a hard currency fund to back up the newly convertible *złoty*. More goods appeared in the market and prices stabilized. Poland attracted more than $1 billion in foreign investment and despite a slowdown in the overall pace of reform, economic growth returned in 1992.

The other Central European states have been equally successful in attracting foreign investment—a total of $11 billion by the end of 1993—and the private sector of their economies has been steadily growing. Both the Czech Republic and Hungary have ended the decline in economic growth and reined in previously high rates of inflation (see Table 37.1).

But the social costs have been high. Virtually throughout the region unemployment has climbed steadily, reaching levels of 10 percent to 15 percent of the work force. This is not only twice as high as we are used to in the United States; it is shocking in a region where, under the Communists, unemployment was unknown. Similarly, even "moderate" inflation of 15 percent to 20 percent a year is difficult in economies in which prices had hardly changed in years. Raising wages alone is usually insufficient to assuage popular fears about runaway prices. In any case, real wages in most of the region are still well below what they were before the changes of 1989.

Changing to a market-based economy also means that some people and some sectors of the economy do better than others. Western investment, for example, has tended to flow to more competitive, efficient, and productive sectors, leaving behind more wasteful industries and their workers. Economic competition has created a degree of economic and social stratification we are accustomed to in the United States, but which is difficult for many people in East Europe to accept. For example, a survey in Hungary in 1991 found that nearly three-fifths of the people interviewed supported the idea of using taxes to impose a maximum income on people.[8]

Overall economic success has been slower in coming in the southern parts of the region. Romania, Bulgaria, and Albania—not to mention war-torn Serbia, Croatia, and Bosnia—have not received as much western attention either in the form of investment, aid, or debt forgiveness. Nor have the governments there been inclined to push privatization or other forms of reform as vigorously as have their northern neighbors.

RECENT ELECTIONS: THE END OF TRANSITION GOVERNMENTS

The slow pace and uneven distribution of economic progress has eroded the political base of support for many of the political groups that had helped create the new Eastern Europe. In line with a trend noted throughout this volume, electorates have made newly democratic governments pay for the pain of the economic transition.

This has been true, ironically, even where that transition has showed clear signs of success. In Poland the impact of free market competition on small Polish farms, continuing high unemployment, and the political fracturing of the Solidarity-based coalition opened the door for a return to power of parties on the Left. In elections in September 1993, the Democratic Left Alliance and their allies, the Polish Peasant Party, gained 36 percent of the vote and two-thirds of the seats in the lower house of parliament (the *Sejm*) and 73 of 100 seats in the Polish Senate. A new government was formed with Waldemar Pawlak, leader of the Peasant Party, as premier.

Once again developments in Poland proved a harbinger of political developments elsewhere. In Hungary in May 1994, the ruling coalition led by the Hungarian Democratic Forum was routed in the elections and the Hungarian Socialist Party, made up of reform

After the Cold War, Still Out in the Cold

After the revolutionary changes of 1989, the states of East Europe moved quickly to end their enforced alliance with the Soviet Union. The Warsaw Pact, established in 1955 in response to German entrance into NATO, and the Council for Mutual Economic Assistance, an economic grouping that failed to promote integration, were both abolished. Leaders throughout the region expressed the desire to join West European organizations based on market economies, such as the European Community (now the European Union), and those based on political pluralism and protection of citizens' rights, such as the Council of Europe. In addition, cut adrift in a dangerous world, many of the East European states expressed interest in joining the North Atlantic Treaty Organization, with its forceful assertion to potential aggressors that an attack on one member is considered to be an attack on all fourteen, including the United States.

Five years after the sweeping changes in the region, all are members of the Council of Europe and submit to its monitoring of their practices on civil and political rights. None, however, is a member of either the European Union or NATO. The European economic organization instead extended associate membership to the new democracies, most of which dramatically shifted their trade from east to west after 1989. But trade barriers on key exports, such as steel, textiles, and agricultural products, remain. As one observer put it ruefully, "Experts still fly in to improve Polish cherries, while Western duties kill Polish cherry exports."

Nor has NATO been eager to extend its mantle eastward. Instead, at the beginning of 1994 a U.S. plan for a "Partnership for Peace" was offered to all the East European states, Russia, and the other states of the former Soviet Union. The plan offers support for cooperation and joint exercises but, in the event of "a direct threat" to the security of the East European states, only a promise to consult. East European leaders grumbled, some pointed nervously to a possible resurgence of nationalism in Russia, but all signed on.

---

communists from the pre-1989 era, won more than half of the seats in the new parliament.

There were indications elsewhere in the region that support for thorough economic and political change had peaked. In Romania, local elections in February 1992 showed surprising support for opposition parties that wanted to move more quickly than the ruling National Salvation Front. The Front itself split in March of that year, with former Prime Minister Petre Roman setting up his own party. But the opposition coalition, led by the Democratic Convention, did not do well enough in national elections in the fall of 1992 to unseat the ruling party, which renamed itself the Party of Social Democracy. President Iliescu's party retained control of the government with the help of several nationalistic and reborn Communist groupings in the parliament. Iliescu himself was re-elected president on a campaign that "adroitly exploited anxieties triggered by the transition to a market economy."[9]

In Bulgaria, the non-Communist government of the Union of Democratic Forces lasted less than one year and was replaced by a "government of experts" supported by a coalition of the Bulgarian Socialist Party—the former Communist Party—and a party based on the country's Turkish minority, the Movement for Rights and Freedoms.

Nor could the political alliance that had guided Czechoslovakia toward democracy

How one observer characterized the NATO Partnership for Peace program. Source: *Christian Science Monitor*, February 2, 1994, p. 23.

hold together. In mid-1992, a coalition led by a staunch advocate of market reform, Václav Klaus, emerged as the strongest group in the Czech Republic. In Slovakia, a nationalist party that favored a more moderate pace of economic change, the Movement for Democratic Slovakia (MDS), outdistanced its rivals. Economic change had been more wrenching in Slovakia, which represented 38 percent of the territory of Czechoslovakia but which hosted a large proportion of huge state-run enterprises, including arms manufacturers. When trade with the Soviet Union and its successors collapsed and the central government tried to restrict arms sales abroad, Slovakia felt the pinch. Unemployment was several times higher in Slovakia than in the Czech Republic, the region was not seeing the level of western investments that Prague and the western part

of the country had, and there was the feeling among some leaders that the moment was right for Slovaks to create their own state, a pledge that MDS leader Vladimir Meciar offered the voters.

In negotiations between Klaus and Meciar after the elections, it was apparent that Czechoslovakia would in fact split up, despite the fact that public opinion polls in both Slovak and the Czech lands indicated preference for the continuation of the country in some form. But with Meciar preferring only a weak confederation and Klaus a strong central government, finding a common method of governance—much less a method for economic reform—proved impossible. By agreement of the two sides, the country of Czechoslovakia ceased to exist on December 31, 1992, and two states, the Czech Republic and Slovakia, emerged.

THE WARS OF YUGOSLAV SUCCESSION

Yugoslavia had always been unique in the postwar Communist world. Having broken first with Stalin and his plans for the region to become virtually an economic and political adjunct of the Soviet Union, party leader Josip Broz Tito oversaw the creation of a distinctive, yet still Communist state. State power was administered through several ethnically based republics, reflecting the country's major population groups. In 1974 a complicated constitution enshrined virtual sovereignty in the republics of Serbia, Croatia, Slovenia, Macedonia, Montenegro, and Bosnia-Herzegovina, and gave almost identical power to two autonomous provinces within Serbia: Vojvodina, which had a Serb majority but large Hungarian minority, and Kosovo, which was overwhelmingly Albanian.

With substantial power devolved to the republics, significant though uneven economic progress, and a fiercely nonaligned foreign policy, Yugoslavia displayed a degree of governmental innovation and independence not found in states closely tied to the Soviet alliance system. The economy was socialist but directed through a complicated system of workers' self-management. Yugoslavia had extensive trade ties with both East and West, maintained open borders and a noncollectivized peasantry. The League of Communists of Yugoslavia, Tito himself, and a clear desire on the part of both superpowers to avoid a confrontation over the country all served as guarantees of the state's territorial and political integrity.

With the onset of severe economic difficulties in the 1980s, the death of Tito, the explosion of democratic demands in the rest of Eastern Europe, and finally the end of the Cold War, the opportunity for alternative political forces to take the stage emerged. Communist governance was discredited by the country's failing economy—gross national product per capita fell by an average of 2 percent per year after 1985—its constitutionally protected political monopoly, and what many saw as an attempt to forcibly impose "Yugoslavism" on separate nationalities. Many Serbs felt that under Tito they had been kept purposely weak, with internal boundaries that left more than 2 million of them outside their republic. Serbia was the only republic to be fragmented with two autonomous provinces and many Serbs felt excluded from and discriminated against in Kosovo, an area considered the birthplace of the Serbian nation.

But other national groups feared a Serbian ascendancy. Recalling the interwar period, leaders of less numerous nationalities worried that a post-Communist Yugoslavia would be dominated by Serbs. Such fears were not assuaged when Serbian party leader Slobodan Milosevic engineered the removal of party leaders in Montenegro, Vojvodina, and Kosovo in 1988, and then rammed through changes in the Serbian constitution which effectively eliminated the powers of the two provinces.

Slovenia and Croatia, the country's two most prosperous republics, resented what they saw as a drain on their resources by less-developed parts of the country. Slovenia had long seen itself as the loser in the federal arrangement and wanted the new Yugoslavia to allow for less, not more, control from the center. They viewed Serbian moves in Kosovo in particular as pointing in the latter direction. At the end of 1989 they prepared the way for open competitive elections and at the same time altered the republican constitution to have it declare Slovenia "sovereign and independent." The republic asserted its right to approve the use of federal armed forces on its territory. Such moves promoted a bitter war of words between Slovenia and Serbian leaders and a brief battle of economic boycotts at the beginning of 1990.

nationalism, Franjo Tudjman, won the presidency and his party, the Croatian Democratic Union, took control of the parliament. In Bosnia, election returns mirrored national lines, with a Muslim party winning a plurality, followed by Serbian and Croatian parties.

Other ballots were used to back up republican leaders in an ever fiercer battle to secure their political power. Serbian leader Milosevic used a referendum in 1990 to underpin his rewriting of the Serbian constitution and eliminate the legislature of Kosovo completely. Kosovar Albanians responded with their own vote showing nearly unanimous support for sovereignty. Slovene leaders got overwhelming support for proposed independence in a vote at the end of December 1990. When negotiations in 1991 on a new kind of Yugoslav state proved fruitless, the newly elected Slovene legislature declared it would soon secede. In the spring of that year Serbia moved to block the rotation to the federal presidency—which had worked smoothly for more than a decade after Tito's death—when a Croatian leader was next in line.

Slovenia succession did take place in June 1991 and produced only a brief armed clash. But the exit of Croatia, announced at the same time, proved much more bloody. Serbia objected to the new state taking with it a 600,000-person Serbian minority. Many in this group felt threatened by measures taken by the new Croatian government, such as the creation of an all-Croatian police force and the use by the new government of symbols used by the Croatian facsists during wartime. In the Krajina region, where roughly half of Croatia's Serbs lived, a referendum in 1990—declared illegal by the Croatian government—showed nearly unanimous support for autonomy of the region. In February 1991, the region declared its independence from the newly independent Croatia and its desire to join Serbia. Incendiary rhetoric and media on all sides and numerous armed incidents led to full-scale war in

Figure 37.2 The former Yugoslav republics.

That year elections took place in all the republics of Yugoslavia, and parties espousing nationalist platforms won virtually throughout the country. Sometimes former Communists retained power along with their party, as happened in Serbia. In Slovenia a former Communist, Milan Kucan, was elected president but the non-Communist opposition, grouped in a coalition called DEMOS (Democratic Opposition of Slovenia) won the legislature. In Croatia a former Communist once imprisoned for his

1991. Fighting raged for six months, led to six thousand deaths, an estimated one million homeless and the brutal destruction of what had been beautiful and multiethnic cities. In January 1992, a cease-fire was arranged and later United Nations forces were interposed between Serbs and Croats. Croatia achieved independence and recognition, but roughly one-third of its claimed territory is effectively occupied by Serbia.

Despite the steady buildup of tension and even the outbreak of hostilities, fighting had not occurred in Bosnia-Herzegovina as late as 1992. Virtually a mini-Yugoslavia, this region had a population, according to the 1991 census, that was roughly 34 percent Serb, 17 percent Croat, and 43 percent Muslim. The last was more a national than religious distinction, established to provide a national basis for the constituent republic of Bosnia. Eager to avoid a repeat of the Croatian events, the European Community urged that a referendum be held in Bosnia to ascertain sentiment for independence. As in Croatia, Serbs feared becoming a minority in the new state and boycotted the referendum, which showed a 99 percent vote for independence.

Soon after, urged on and armed by nationalists in Serbia, Bosnian Serbs began to occupy parts of the country and attack the weaker multiethnic Bosnian government. The country's capital, Sarajevo, was surrounded by Serb forces and subjected to a cutoff of vital supplies and power and almost daily bombardment. After a brief alliance with the Bosnian government, Croats too began to seize parts of the new country and engage in their own fierce battles with their former allies. In many parts of the country "ethnic cleansing" was practiced to drive members of the other group from the territory. Within a very short time, Serbs came to occupy 70 percent of the territory of the new state. Condemned by the international community as an aggressor against the independent and recognized state of Bosnia, the rump state of Yugoslavia—meaning Serbia and Montenegro—has been subject to economic, diplomatic, and military sanctions since 1992, though the impact has been blunted by evasion and smuggling. In 1994, for the first time, NATO forces undertook air attacks against Serbian forces in support of the United Nations demands for free access to some besieged cities in Bosnia.

The war in Bosnia has raged without effective action by the international community or any individual outside power. More than 200,000 people have died and another 2 million people—roughly half the population of the country—have been displaced. In January 1993 a European Community report accused Serb forces of widespread use of rape of Muslim women as part of a campaign to terrorize local populations. In May the United Nations established a War Crimes Tribunal to gather evidence of atrocities of which all sides have been accused. Numerous peace plans and cease-fires have been proposed and some even agreed to, but without producing a durable peace on the ground. At the beginning of 1994, the Bosnian government and the Croats in Bosnia announced the formation of a federation designed to share governance in the parts of Bosnia they control.

THE FUTURE OF EAST EUROPE

Many observers view the tragic and bloody implosion of Yugoslavia as a harbinger for the rest of the region. As Table 37.2 indicates, few states in the new East Europe are ethnically homogeneous and, as was true during the period between the two world wars, political boundaries do not neatly reflect historical or cultural communities. Suppressed and discredited for years by Communist Party dictatorships, nationalist sentiments may re-emerge in such uncompromising and murderous form as to destroy the fragile institutions of democracy. Especially in times of economic stress,

Table 37.2 MINORITIES IN EASTERN EUROPE

Country	Number	% of Population	Country	Number	% of Population
Albania			*Montenegro*		
Greeks	58,758	1.85	Muslims	89,932	14.62
Bosnia-Herzegovina			Serbs	57,176	9.29
Muslims	1,902,954	43.60	Albanians	40,880	6.64
Serbs	1,370,476	31.40	*Poland*		
Croats	755,071	17.30	Ukrainians-Ruthenians	315,000	0.81
Bulgaria			Belarusans	200,000	0.52
Turks	822,253	9.70	*Romania*		
Romanies (Gypsies)	287,732	3.40	Hungarians	1,620,199	7.12
Pomaks	65,546	0.77	Romanies (Gypsies)	409,723	1.80
Croatia			Germans	119,436	0.52
Serbs	581,663	12.16	*Serbia*		
Muslims	43,469	0.91	Albanians	1,727,541	16.70
Czech Republic			Montenegrins	520,508	5.03
Moravians	1,359,432	13.20	Hungarians	345,376	3.34
Slovaks	308,962	3.00	Muslims	327,390	3.16
Hungary			Romanies (Gypsies)	137,265	1.33
Romanies (Gypsies)	404,461	3.90	Croats	115,463	1.12
Germans	175,000	1.69	*Slovakia*		
Slovaks	110,000	1.06	Hungarians	566,741	10.76
Macedonia			Romanies (Gypsies)	80,627	1.53
Albanians	427,313	21.01	Czechs	53,422	1.01
Turks	97,416	4.79	Ukrainians-Ruthenians	30,784	0.58
Romanies (Gypsies)	55,575	2.73	*Slovenia*		
Serbs	44,159	2.17	Croats	54,212	2.76
			Serbs	47,911	2.44
			Muslims	26,842	1.37

All figures are based on official censuses and estimates.
Source: Janusz Bugajski, "The Fate of Minorities in Eastern Europe," *Journal of Democracy,* Vol. 4, No. 4 (October 1993), p. 90.

power-hungry politicians will not shrink from trying to exploit differences to advance their political futures (a process not unknown outside of East Europe).

But might not there be another future for East Europe, one where national or regional expression can take a positive form and contribute to both the cultural diversity and democracy of the states of the regions? If fragmentation oc-

curs, might it not be in the form it took in Czechoslovakia rather than Yugoslavia?

The answer to this question will depend in part on the vigor of those new institutions and the commitment of these countries' leaders and populations to the values underlying them. Democratic formation of public policy is often slow, cumbersome and the product of compromise in which no one group is totally satisfied but many are mostly satisfied. After years of economic and political deprivation, will the populations of East Europe and dissatisfied groups within larger populations have the patience to wait for such solutions and the forbearance to accept less than perfect solutions? This is not, in itself, a different question than might be asked of the people of France, Great Britain, or the United States. But for the people of East Europe, as for those of Russia, struggling for answers within systems that are still being invented presents an extraordinary challenge.

Notes

1. A. W. Palmer, *The Lands Between: A History of East-Central Europe since the Congress of Vienna* (London: Macmillan Co., 1970).
2. Joseph Rothschild, *East Central Europe Between the Two World Wars* (Seattle: University of Washington Press, 1974), p. 202.
3. F. B. Singleton, *Background to Eastern Europe* (London: Pergamon Press, 1965), p. 60.
4. Rothschild, p. 132.
5. John Lukacs, *A New History of the Cold War* (New York: Doubleday and Co., 1966), p. 47.
6. Zbigniew Brzezinski, *The Soviet Bloc: Unity and Conflict,* rev. and enlarged ed. (Cambridge: Harvard University Press, 1971), p. 102.
7. Radio Bucharest, December 22, 1989.
8. Gyorgy Gcepeli, Tamas Kolosi, Maria Nemenyi, and Antal Orkeny, "Our Futureless Values: The Forms of Justice and Injustice Perception in Hungary in 1991," *Social Research,* 60, No. 4 (Winter 1993), p. 876.
9. Michael Shafir and Dan Ionescu, "Romania: Political Change and Economic Malaise," *RFE/RL Research Report,* 2, No. 11 (January 1993), p. 110.

References and Suggested Readings

Brown, J. F. 1988. *Eastern Europe and Communist Rule.* Durham, N.C.: Duke University Press.

———. 1991. *Surge to Freedom: The End of Communist Rule in Eastern Europe.* Durham, N.C.: Duke University Press.

Gati, Charles. 1990. *The Bloc That Failed.* Bloomington: Indiana University Press.

Glenny, Misha. 1992. *The Fall of Yugoslavia.* New York: Penguin Books.

"1989: A Year of Upheaval," *Report on Eastern Europe,* No. 1. 1990.

Rothschild, Joseph. 1993. *Return to Diversity: A Political History of East Central Europe Since World War II.* New York: Oxford University Press.

Rusinow, Dennison. 1987. *The Yugoslav Experiment, 1948–1974.* Berkeley: University of California Press.

Skilling, H. Gordon. 1976. *Czechoslovakia's Interrupted Revolution.* Princeton, N.J.: Princeton University Press.

Stokes, Gale. 1991. *From Stalinism to Pluralism: A Documentary History of Eastern Europe Since 1945.* New York: Oxford University Press.

———. 1993. *The Walls Came Tumbling Down: The Collapse of Communism in Eastern Europe.* New York: Oxford University Press.

White, Stephen, Judy Batt, and Paul G. Lewis, eds. 1993. *Developments in East European Politics.* Durham, N.C.: Duke University Press.

Credits (continued from p. iv)

Name Index